NEW ZEALAND ATLAS

NEW ZEALAND
ATLAS
EDITED BY IAN WARDS

A. R. SHEARER GOVERNMENT PRINTER WELLINGTON 1976

First Published March 1976
Reprinted 1976

The text is printed in 10/12 Plantin monophoto
Type for all cartography is Times New Roman, Concord and Univers
The title page is set in Perpetua
Display lines and captions are set in Univers
Photo-offset printing was used throughout
The paper is Mellotex Smooth, High White
Twin Wire Cartridge, 105 gsm
The standard binding cloth is New Zealand Buckram
and the blocking is in gold foil
The book was printed and bound in the
Government Printing Office, Wellington, New Zealand.

ISBN   0 477 01000 8

FOREWORD

By I. F. Stirling, Surveyor-General

It has been my privilege since 1973 to have been Chairman of the Atlas Committee that has guided this volume through the various stages of preparation and printing. The idea for a revised edition of *A Descriptive Atlas of New Zealand,* edited by the late Dr A. H. McLintock, began to take shape in February 1970 when Mr R. P. Gough, Surveyor-General at the time, convened the first meeting of this Committee.

Atlas Committee members have included Mr A. E. Shearer, Government Printer, Mr E. C. Keating, Deputy Government Printer, Mr D. A. Kerr, Department of Internal Affairs, Professor D. W. McKenzie, representing the New Zealand Geographical Society, Mr I. McL. Wards, the Editor, Mr G. F. Jeune, the Cartographer and Mr D. G. Francis, Department of Lands and Survey, who also acted as Secretary. It was a committee of experts, each predominant in his own field and I am certain that the Atlas could not have eventuated as it is without their sound guidance. It is also fitting to record the enthusiasm and standard brought to the project by the many authors, cartographers, photographers, printers and others. The standard of this atlas illustrates the calibre of their efforts. Above all, I must pay tribute to the Editor, Ian Wards. Although many share the credit, his perseverance and untiring effort in the search for perfection must identify him always with this publication.

The *New Zealand Atlas* as you now see it is, with minor exceptions, an entirely new work. It aims to explain New Zealand, its history, its shape and substance, its people and its economy in a series of articles, maps and photographs. It relates these in an authoritative way to our physical situation. I am confident that a wide range of people in New Zealand and overseas will share my proud belief that this has been well accomplished.

I. F. Stirling

SURVEYOR-GENERAL

31 August 1975
DEPARTMENT OF LANDS AND SURVEY.

ATLAS COMMITTEE

INTRODUCTION

Cartography as an art, as a science, as a working tool of adventurous men, as an essential component of a scholar's library—cartography in all these guises has for centuries had a prominent place in the creative thinking of man. A modern atlas is a cartographic compendium on the one hand, a flowering of the printer's skill on the other. For these reasons, and in response to fresh challenges as work progressed, I feel particularly fortunate, as editor, to have had the privilege of combining and focussing the diverse skills that have gone into the making of this atlas.

The aim has been an even balance between cartographic exposition, textual explanation and photographic illustration, each complementary to the other. For instance, many of the maps show that in New Zealand there is an intimate relationship between land and water: few of the photographs are without water, in the form of rivers, lakes or sea. Maps, texts and photographs reveal geological youth and deep dissection. The illustration of the drowned valleys of the Marlborough Sounds could not more exactly mirror the cartographer's description. Similarly, the thematic maps both complement and enhance the texts which they support.

There has not been room for everything. The intention has been to create an inventory of New Zealand the land, New Zealanders the people, and factors such as climate and industry influencing both. So that a strong theme in harmony with the cartography could be developed, illustrations are mainly concerned with the great variety of landforms. There is a tremendous residue of untouched material, cultural, historical, industrial and social.

In presentation, the goal has been clarity and a high regard to the unifying and enhancing quality of a discriminating use of colour. Typographically, there was a certain initial handicap in an early policy decision, on grounds of economy, to use as much as possible of the Times Roman type associated with the section maps of *A Descriptive Atlas of New Zealand*. This rendered out of the question an entirely new approach, but many innovations have proved possible. The lay-out was strictly conditioned by the position of the guarded sections and the placing of all maps with relevant texts.

Only two maps, the first two in the section 'New Zealand in the World', are repeated from *A Descriptive Atlas of New Zealand*. All the rest of the material, cartographic and textual, is specially prepared for this atlas. Nevertheless, I acknowledge most warmly my debt to my immediate predecessor, the late A. H. McLintock, who was the pioneer in this field.

ACKNOWLEDGEMENTS

Perhaps in the nature of things, no list of acknowledgements could be either complete or adequate, and I can only express my great regret should any individual be overlooked. The length of the list, incomplete though it may be, is an indication of the monumental nature of the project and of the broadly based, highly expert assistance devoted to its completion.

In the planning stage I was indebted to an interdepartmental planning committee convened to generally discuss atlas requirements. Most members submitted written suggestions. With the editor as chairman, members were: A. G. Bagnall, Chief Librarian, Alexander Turnbull Library; M. L. Cameron (or substitute P. R. Stephens), Director, Farm Advisory Division, Ministry of Agriculture and Fisheries; G. L. Easterbrook-Smith (or substitute J. G. Watkinson), Deputy Secretary, Department of Industries and Commerce; Sir Robert Falla, Chairman, Nature Conservation Council; C. W. Franks, Assistant Secretary for Marine; Dr J. F. Gabites, Director, New Zealand Meteorological Service; E. A. Harris, Deputy Government Statistician; J. M. McEwen, Secretary for Maori and Island Affairs; R. G. Norman, Deputy Commissioner of Works; Dr E. I. Robertson, Assistant Director-General, Department of Scientific and Industrial Research; G. H. S. Sadler, Chief Cartographer, Department of Lands and Survey; H. J. Wakelin, Senior Investigating Officer, Mines Department; W. J. Wendelken, Assistant Director Forest Management, New Zealand Forest Service; D. H. Winchester, Geography Department, Victoria University of Wellington; D. G. Francis, Superintendent of Draughting Services, Department of Lands and Survey, who also acted as Secretary.

Also in this stage, I must express my warm appreciation of the work of David Connell, Overseer, Bindery, Government Printing Office, who discovered and perfected a method by which the principal maps and illustrations could be bound on guards, efficiently and mechanically. The whole presentation was materially and beneficially affected by this major achievement.

Again, whilst planning, I benefited greatly from conversations, jointly, with John Drawbridge and Janet Paul on a range of colours for the section maps and, separately, with Janet Paul on typography. These enlivening conversations were seminal in effect. John Drawbridge later designed the cover, giving the most graphically sympathetic atlas cover I have ever seen anywhere. Keith Burns of the Photo-Litho Branch, Government Printing Office, made the blocks for this design.

There were thirty-one authors and each of these competed with the limitations of restricted space to achieve the general purpose of the Atlas—succint, authoritative, up-to-date essays. I am proud of the opportunity of working with them. When the article on soils was first discussed, I had the advantage of the interest of Dr M. Fieldes, who died before his first draft was completed. The eventual author, M. L. Leamy, who acknowledges his debt to Dr Fieldes as joint author, re-worked the whole article and himself made a remarkable and original contribution. I am also grateful to the late Dr R. W. Willett, for his general support and his early interest in the article on the Antarctic.

MAPS

It was my great good fortune to be associated with Graham Jeune, Assistant Chief Cartographer of the Department of Lands and Survey, during the production of the Atlas. I could not have wished for a more constructive, happier relationship. No editor could have had a more supportive colleague, one so valuable in criticism, so reliable in performance.

All the maps were prepared in the Cartographic Branch of the Department of Lands and Survey, under G. H. S. Sadler, Chief Cartographer. To Mr Jeune was delegated the major cartographic involvement in the Atlas, and assisting him with supervision was B. K. Bradley, to whom I am much indebted for careful work and original ideas. Mr L. P. Lee, a most distinguished computer, was responsible for the projection planning of 'New Zealand in the World' and the highly original 'New Zealand in the Pacific', together with 'The South-West Pacific'. Two maps only, 'The World from New Zealand' and 'New Zealand in the World', both drawn by E. M. Jones, although freshly presented, are reproduced from *A Descriptive Atlas of New Zealand*.

The production of the maps was the work of the following: New Zealand (pp 2–3), **B. K. Bradley, H. E. Macfarlane;** Sectional Maps 1–6 (pp 6–7, 10–11, 14–15, 18–19, 22–23, 26–27), **W. Fryer, D. M. Toole, M. L. Phillips, G. D. Aitken, H. E. Macfarlane;** Islands of New Zealand (p 4), Urban Areas – Greymouth, Timaru, Invercargill & Bluff (p 40), **L. R. Bamford;** Urban Areas – Auckland (pp 30–31), Wellington & Hutt (pp 34–35), Napier & Hastings, Gisborne, Rotorua (p 38), New Zealand in the Pacific (pp 46–47), Population (pp 64–65), Seismicity (p 78), Magnetic and Gravity Fields (p 79), Forests (pp 104–107), Fishing (p 153), Mineral Resources (p 157), Energy Resources (p 161),

The South-West Pacific (pp 196–197), **D. M. Toole;** Urban Areas – Christchurch (p 32), Dunedin (p 33), Tauranga, Wanganui, Whangarei (p 36), Discovery (p 50), Land Use (pp 142–143), **W. Fryer;** Urban Areas – New Plymouth, Hamilton, Palmerston North, Masterton (p 37), Nelson, Ashburton, Oamaru, Blenheim (p 39), Patterns of Settlement (p 56), **P. N. French;** Administrative Divisions (pp 67–69), **H. E. Macfarlane, W. Fryer, M. L. Phillips;** Landforms (pp 74–75), **J. Petro;** The Sea Floor (p 81), **H. E. Macfarlane;** Climate (pp 83, 85, 87, 88, 89), Antarctica (pp 184–185), **G. J. Dyer;** Geology (pp 96–97), **L. R. Bamford, D. M. Toole;** Fauna (pp 120–121), **D. J. Pimblott, W. Fryer;** Soils (pp 138–139), Land Classification (pp 140–141), Transport & Communication (pp 176–177), **D. J. Pimblott;** Manufacturing (pp 170–171), **R. P. Pickering;** Pacific Islands (pp 193–195), **W. Fryer, M. L. Phillips;** Tourist Resources (pp 202–203), **D. W. Lawrence.** Other cartographers associated with the production of the maps were **C. R. Solomon** (Map Editor), **R. C. Child** and **R. N. E. Duncan.** Diagrams in the text were prepared by **D. M. Toole, R. P. Pickering, W. Fryer** and **D. J. Pimblott.** The relief shading drawings were the work of **D. W. Lawrence,** and the Gazetteer of **W. Fryer** and **D. J. Pimblott.**

PHOTOGRAPHS

During the selection of the photographs, a task of gargantuan proportions, my *alter ego* was John Johns of the Forest Service. He completely identified himself with the requirements of the Atlas, and his advice was invaluable. Piet van Asch, Managing Director of New Zealand Aerial Mapping, and many of that unique company, particularly Don Trask, Frank Peach and Cyril Whitaker, gave much assistance and general support, far beyond even the generous limits set by the Department of Lands and Survey, within whose contract the work was done. Piet van Asch consistently supplied warm encouragement and thoughtful advice. Sometimes, John Johns and Piet van Asch worked together, an irresistible pair. On the technical side, John Johns gave much assistance, as did also New Zealand Aerial Mapping, and K & J Bigwood who competed with urgent transparency requirements. Ken Bigwood was resourceful and expert. In this area, I am also grateful to C. J. Reid of Kodak NZ Ltd for the provision of chemicals in short supply.

The photographs of areas of the South Island taken by Earth Resources Technology Satellite, United States, were made available by Dr Peter Ellis of the Physical Laboratory, Department of Scientific and Industrial Research. I am grateful to him and to his colleagues for their assistance in all to do with these photographs. The flora photographs on page 112 were made available through the generosity of Professor John Salmon, who supplied a sufficient number for this selection to be made. Ralph Wheeler worked out the long caption for the Antarctic photographs, five of which were selected from the collection of the Antarctic Division of the Department of Scientific and Industrial Research.

So many others helped with the illustrations. My initial concept had been to include a much wider range, covering many more aspects of man's use of the land, industry, technology and so on. My final decision, to concentrate on landforms, meant that literally hundreds of excellent photographs were not required. Here let me emphasise my debt to all those who so willingly co-operated, in particular to V. C. Browne of Christchurch, to Allan D. Warren of Rotorua and to the Royal New Zealand Air Force for the photograph of the Wellington Fault. Bruce Clark, of National Publicity Studios, and his team met every request made.

A photograph sub-committee had been formed, consisting of Professor D. W. McKenzie, Dr A. T. Johns, Mr Ian Beaumgart, Mr van Asch and Mr D. G. Francis. Its invaluable work lay in defining areas and subjects for inclusion in a photographic survey of landforms, and, with the addition of John Johns and M. L. Leamy, in the provision of the expanded captions given with the list of illustrations.

PRINTING

During the printing of the Atlas, I have greatly appreciated the thoughtful consideration shown to me by the Government Printer, A. R. Shearer. His Deputy, E. C. Keating, was invariably positive and extremely helpful. The printing itself was carried out under the supervision of M. C. Macrae, a very experienced printer. A large printing team was involved and I am sure that I may be excused if in thanking those with whom I had personal, often daily, association, I appear to overlook those who worked quietly in less obvious places. I most sincerely appreciate the efforts and skill of all who put their craftsmanship at the service of this project.

At Douglas Street, where all material is prepared and brought to plate stage, B. A. Paterson, Superintendent of the Photo-Litho Branch, supported the project with skill and understanding; S. M. J. Tobin, Technical Instructor, was responsible for much of the camera work and for the excellence of the reproduction of the illustrations. With him were David Pycroft, Lawrence Bailey, Stephen Magyar and Richard Maclachlan. Ian Telfer did most of the film contacting and processing for the cartography. Mr G. E. Ritchie, Overseer, Photo Composing Section, Keith Findlay, Monokeyboard operator, who set all the text, and compositors W. P. Herlihy and F. M. Betts, worked consistently throughout the complete project. I learned to respect the judgment of both Michael Tobin and Gary Ritchie and greatly enjoyed working with them.

At the Printing Branch, Kemp Street, H. Thomson, Superintendent, gave me every assistance. Mr J. R. Hill, Overseer, was watchful and helpful. For most of the printing of the Section Maps, B. M. Swanerton was foreman in charge of the job. He was followed by D. W. Aldridge, who in addition took under his competent wing a new, additional four-colour machine. The offset machinists were J. D. Grogan, C. A. Wilkinson and R. A. Barden. I came to rely implicitly on the skill of these printers and for much of the job was in the careful hands of Don Aldridge and C. A. Wilkinson. I thank them all.

At the Printing Office at Mulgrave Street, A. Harris, Assistant Government Printer, gave the whole project much support. Many others should be acknowledged, amongst them Brian Bridgeman, Bob Lines, and John Fletcher who was of great help during the early period of test printing. Paul Abbott and Frank Levick, together with the bindery team, did much meticulously accurate work.

GENERAL

Others, from many different areas, in no special order, who have greatly assisted are Professor John McCreary, for providing the age-sex diagram; C. E. Nixon, T. G. Shadwell and J. H. G. Milne for assistance with the Energy article and map; K. Gorbey, who provided most of the information on early Maori settlement; W. R. Dale, who helped with the land utilisation maps; G. D. L. White, New Zealand Ambassador in Washington, who accelerated the despatch of urgently needed liquid concentrate developer; W. Parris of Morrison Inks and Machinery Ltd., who gave me much useful information about printers' inks; Peter Morrison of the Wildlife Service for his invaluable compilation material for the fauna maps and P. Barton, Map Librarian, Alexander Turnbull Library, for his assistance.

In my own office, I am indebted to my assistant, Penelope Wheeler, who not only checked proofs, compiled the index, checked the gazetteer and performed a multitude of editorial chores, but also maintained an efficient 'homebase'.

For all this visible support, and for so much that is evident only in the finished result, I am sincerely grateful. To the Atlas Committee, particularly to its present and longest-term chairman, Ian Stirling, my debt is incalculable.

I. McL. Wards

Historical Publications Branch
Department of Internal Affairs
Wellington
31 August 1975

CONTENTS

TEXTS   *page*

NOTES ON THE SECTIONAL MAP AREAS *(with maps)*

    North Auckland 5
    South Auckland, Gisborne 9
    Taranaki, Hawke's Bay, Wellington 13
    Nelson, Marlborough 17
    Westland, Canterbury 21
    Southland, Otago 25
        R. G. Lister, BA(Lond), Professor of Geography, in association with R. P. Hargreaves, MA(NZ and Wis), PhD(Otago),
        Geography Department, University of Otago

NEW ZEALAND IN THE WORLD *(with map)* 44
        F. L. W. Wood, CMG, BA(Sydney), MA(Oxon), emeritus Professor of History, Victoria University of Wellington

DISCOVERY *(with map)* 51
        Janet Davidson, MA, E. Earle Vaile Archaeologist, Auckland Institute and Museum

PATTERNS OF SETTLEMENT *(with map)* 53
        Raewyn Dalziel, BA, PhD, Lecturer in History, University of Auckland

GOVERNMENT 57
        Mary Boyd, MA, Reader in History, Victoria University of Wellington

POPULATION *(with maps)* 60
        Miriam G. Vosburgh, MA, PhD, Assistant Professor of Sociology, Villanova University, Pennsylvania, USA

ADMINISTRATIVE DIVISIONS *(with maps)* 66
        R. J. Lowe, MA, Investigating Officer, Town and Country Planning Division, Ministry of Works and Development

LANDFORMS AND RESOURCES *(with maps)* 71
        D. W. McKenzie, MSc, emeritus Professor of Geography, Victoria University of Wellington

GRAVITY, MAGNETISM & SEISMICITY *(with maps)* 76
        G. A. Eiby, MSc, FRAS, FRASNZ, Seismological Observatory, Geophysics Division, and W. I. Reilly, BA, BSc, DSc, AOSM,
        Superintendent, Geophysical Survey, Department of Scientific and Industrial Research

THE SEA FLOOR *(with map)* 80
        D. J. Cullen, BSc, PhD, Scientist, New Zealand Oceanographic Institute, Department of Scientific and Industrial Research

CLIMATE *(with maps)* 82
        A. I. Tomlinson, MSc, Dip Stats, Climatologist, New Zealand Meteorological Service

GEOLOGY *(with maps)* 90
        R. P. Suggate, MA, DSc, Director, New Zealand Geological Survey, and Patricia M. Riddolls, BSc, Geologist, New Zealand
        Geological Survey, Department of Scientific and Industrial Research

FORESTRY *(with maps)* 98
        W. J. Wendelken, BSc, BForSc, Assistant Commissioner, Commission for the Environment

FLORA *(with photographs)* 108
        E. J. Godley, MSc, PhD(Cantab), FRSNZ, FLS, Director, Botany Division, Department of Scientific and Industrial Research

FAUNA *(with maps)* 114
        R. A. Falla, KBE, CMG, MA, DSc, FRSNZ, Chairman, Nature Conservation Council

SOIL *(with maps)* 122
        M. L. Leamy, MSc, Chief Pedologist, and M. Fieides, DSc, formerly Director, Soil Bureau, Department of Scientific and Industrial
        Research

FARMING 144
        P. R. Stephens, MA, Senior Agricultural Economist, Ministry of Agriculture and Fisheries

FISHING *(with map)* 151
        V. T. Hinds, BSc, Fisheries Management Division, Ministry of Agriculture and Fisheries

MINERAL RESOURCES *(with map)* 154
        B. N. Thompson, MSc, Geologist, New Zealand Geological Survey, Department of Scientific and Industrial Research

ENERGY RESOURCES *(with map)* 158
        Alison D. Allen, BA, Research Officer, Legislative Department

CONTENTS

MANUFACTURING AND INDUSTRY *(with maps)* 162
    G. R. Sanderson, MA, *Executive Officer, Industrial Development Division, Department of Trade and Industry*

TRANSPORT AND COMMUNICATIONS *(with maps)* 172
    R. J. Polaschek, BA, MCom, DPA, ACA, FCIT, *Secretary for Transport*

TRADE AND COMMERCE 178
    J. C. Mosley, MA, PhD, *Department of Trade and Industry*

ANTARCTICA 186
    Trevor Hatherton, OBE, DSc, PhD, DIC, FRSNZ, *Director, Geophysics Division, Department of Scientific and Industrial Research*

THE PACIFIC NEIGHBOURHOOD *(with maps)* 190
    Barrie K. Macdonald, BA, PhD, *Lecturer in History, Massey University*

TOURISM *(with map)* 200
    J. S. McBean, MA, *Assistant Director, Development and Research Division, Tourist and Publicity Department*

MAPS

NEW ZEALAND TOPOGRAPHICAL 2–3
    This map, and the thematic base maps, are on the Lambert conformal (or orthomorphic) conic projection with two standard parallels, the meridians being straight lines, the parallels arcs of concentric circles. The standard parallels have been selected at latitudes 37° and 45°, the scale variation reading a maximum of +0.40 per cent near North Cape. The scale at any point is independent of direction; between the standard parallels it is a little smaller, and outside them a little greater, than the nominal scale of the map. For most purposes the scale can be regarded as constant.

ISLANDS OF NEW ZEALAND, in the Pacific 4
    For compilation notes, *see under* 'Pacific Islands'

SECTION MAPS
    North Auckland 6–7
    South Auckland, Gisborne 10–11
    Taranaki, Hawke's Bay, Wellington 14–15
    Nelson, Marlborough 18–19
    Westland, Canterbury 22–23
    Southland, Otago 26–27
    These maps are on the Lambert conformal (or orthomorphic) conic projection with two standard parallels, the meridians being straight lines, the parallels arcs of concentric circles. The standard parallels have been selected at latitudes $36\frac{1}{2}°$ and $45\frac{1}{2}°$. The scale at any point is independent of direction; between the standard parallels it is a little smaller, and outside the standard parallels a little greater, than the nominal scale of the map, giving a range of scale variation of ± 0.35 per cent over the land area. For most purposes the scale can be regarded as constant.

URBAN AREAS
    Auckland 30–31
    Christchurch 32
    Dunedin 33
    Wellington 34–35
    Tauranga, Wanganui, Whangarei 36
    New Plymouth, Hamilton, Palmerston North, Masterton 37
    Gisborne, Napier, Rotorua, Hastings 38
    Nelson, Blenheim, Ashburton, Oamaru 39
    Greymouth, Invercargill, Timaru, Bluff 40
    These maps are compiled from the most recent New Zealand Map Service, Series 1, and are at a scale of 1:125 000. The relief shading was drawn by D. W. Lawrence. The Reference notes and symbols are shown at *page 29.*

THE WORLD FROM NEW ZEALAND 41
    This map, freshly presented, is repeated from *A Descriptive Atlas of New Zealand*, 1959. 'This map is drawn on an oblique equidistant azimuthal projection centred on Wellington. This resulted in every great circle through Wellington becoming 'unrolled' into a straight line in the projection plane, with its correct length and its correct initial direction preserved. The antipodes of Wellington, a point in Spain, therefore becomes the external circular boundary of the map. The scale is correct along every straight line (great circle) through Wellington; but when a direction is transverse to any such straight line the scale increases with increasing distance from the centre of the map, slowly within the central hemisphere and more rapidly in the outer hemisphere. This results in very great distortion of shape near the margins of the map.
    'Azimuths and distances from the centre are correctly represented and can be measured with the scales provided. The azimuth, reckoned eastward from north, of any point from Wellington is obtained by drawing a straight line from Wellington to that point and producing it to the external circular scale. For example, the azimuth to New York is 66° 20′; the distance, measured on the linear scale below the map, is 8,950 miles.'

NEW ZEALAND IN THE WORLD 42–43
    These maps, with different colours, are repeated from *A Descriptive Atlas of New Zealand*, 1959. 'These two maps are drawn on oblique Hammer projection. . . . Designed primarily to show transport routes from New Zealand to Europe, they have been arranged to feature the sea route westward through Suez . . . and the sea route eastward through Panama. . . . In each case the sphere is represented within an ellipse whose major and minor axes are in the ratio 1.75:1. The major axis is a great circle which crosses the equator at the centre of the map and crosses the parallels of 40° latitude at a longitude interval of 80° from the centre. Thus [on p 42] the major axis crosses the equator at longitude 75° E, and passes through the points, 40° N, 5° W, and 40° S, 155° E. [On p 43] the major axis crosses the equator at longitude 90° W, and passes through the points, 40° S, 170° W, and 40° N, 10° W.
    'The area scale is constant over the whole extent of the maps. As the linear scale at any point is dependent on direction, these maps are not readily adapted to the measurement of distances.'

NEW ZEALAND IN THE PACIFIC 46–47
    This map shows the entire Pacific coastline, including the Antarctic and the entrances from the Arctic, Indian and Atlantic oceans. The

area can be contained within an approximate ellipse, with a centre at 10° S latitude and 165° W longitude and with a minor axis inclined at about 17½° to the meridian of the origin. Mr L. P. Lee found that a conformal projection of this area could be devised from a transformation of the stereographic, as already demonstrated by O. M. Miller. The scale coefficient ranges from 0.721 at the centre to 1.279 at the boundary, considerably less than in any projection so far used for the Pacific. Air routes are those being used in July 1973 to the principal airports of the main island groups and all countries bordering the Pacific. Major routes to Europe and the Middle East are also shown. Generally, the shortest route with the least number of stops has been shown.

DISCOVERY 50
The base map is a modern outline from the New Zealand Map Service, Series 1. The information of the early Polynesian settlement of the Pacific and their voyage path to New Zealand was supplied by the author based on her reading of most recent sources. The voyage path of **Abel Janszoon Tasman** was plotted by Graham Jeune, assisted by information from Commander G. B. W. Johnson, Wellington Harbour Board, and Commander I. S. Morro, Hydrographer RNZN, from the following sources:
Tasman, Abel Janszoon, Journal of his discovery of Van Diemen's land and New Zealand in 1642 . . . photo-lithographic facsimilies of the original manuscript in the Colonial Archives at the Hague with an English translation and facsimiles of original maps to which are added life and labours of Abel Janszoon Tasman by J. E. Heeres and observations made with the compass on Tasman's voyage by W. van Bemmelen, Amsterdam, 1898, *Abel Janszoon Tasman & the Discovery of New Zealand,* Department of Internal Affairs, Wellington, MCMXLII; *The voyages of Abel Janszoon Tasman,* Andrew Sharp, Oxford [1968]; photostat of F. J. Visscher's chart from the Huydecoper MS in the Mitchell Library, Sydney (Turnbull Library Map Collection); photostat from Tasman's chart, State Archives, The Hague (Turnbull Library Map Collection).
The voyage path of **James Cook** is compiled from:
'A chart of Newzeland . . . by Lieutt. J. Cook . . .' Reproduced from the original chart in the British Museum, The Friends of the Turnbull Library, 1969; *The Journals of Captain James Cook on His Voyages of Discovery: The Voyage of the Endeavour 1768–1771,* Vol. 1, with folio of charts, edited by J. C. Beaglehole; the point of entry into New Zealand waters, 6/7 Oct 1769, and the voyage path to the south-west of the South Island, were amended from information by Commander G. B. W. Johnson.
The voyage path of **De Surville** was compiled from:
'Plan de la Baye de Lauriston . . . 1769' and 'Carte de la Nouvelle Zelande . . . 1769', both photocopies from MSS in the Bibliothèque Nationale, Paris (Turnbull Library Map Collection).
Place names and spelling;
The place names and chart information of Tasman's voyage (green) have been translated.
The places named by Cook (red) are a selection of places from Cook's chart of his first voyage.
The Maori place names (brown), from material supplied by the author, have been given modern spellings/translations for ease of identification.

PATTERNS OF SETTLEMENT 56
The base map is from the New Zealand Map Service, Series 1. The main areas of Maori settlement are shown from information supplied by K. Gorbey, Director of the Waikato Art Museum, and with particular reference to the South Island and the Taupo area by D. R. Simmons of the Auckland Institute and Museum, collated by the editor. The special settlements are shown from information supplied by the editor and the more recent immigration from information from the Department of Statistics.

POPULATION 60
Age and Sex Structure, *diagram*
Prepared by Professor J. McCreary, Sociology Department, Victoria University of Wellington.
Population 64–65
Prepared from information supplied by the Department of Statistics on a base map from the New Zealand Map Service, Series 1. The area of any one screened (light red) circle is centred on and proportional to the population it represents, and is completely independent of any other screened circle and/or solid (dark red) symbols that fall within it. All population within gazetted Urban Statistical Divisions has been shown as urban, which will account for the apparent lack of rural population around larger cities.
Some of the cities and boroughs in the Auckland vicinity have been grouped within four main areas represented by individual screened circles:

Northshore	Auckland West	Auckland Central	Auckland South
Takapuna (city)	Henderson (borough)	Auckland City	Papatoetoe (city)
Devonport (borough)	Glen Eden (borough)	Newmarket (borough)	Otahuhu (borough)
Northcote (borough)	New Lynn (borough)	Mt Albert ,,	
Birkenhead (borough)		Mt Eden ,,	
		Mt Roskill ,,	
		One Tree Hill ,,	
		Onehunga ,,	
		Ellerslie ,,	
		Mt Wellington ,,	

Other screened circles in the vicinity of Auckland are centred on:
East Coast Bays (borough)   Te Atatu (county subdivision)   Titirangi (county town)   Manukau (city)
Glenfield (county town)   Kelston (county town)   Howick (borough)   Papakura (borough)
Groupings in the Wellington vicinity are:
Wellington (city)   Upper Hutt (city)   Tawa (borough)   Wainuiomata (county borough)
Lower Hutt (city)   Porirua (city)   Petone (borough)   Heretaunga-Pinehaven (county town)
Groupings in the Christchurch vicinity are:
Christchurch (city)   Riccarton (borough)   Hornby (county borough)
Waimairi (county)   Sockburn (county borough)
Groupings in the Dunedin vicinity are:
Dunedin (city)   St Kilda (borough)   Green Island (borough)

ADMINISTRATIVE DIVISIONS
Local Authorities, Statistical Areas, Education & Land Districts 67
Health and Works Districts 68
Water and Electricity Districts 69
Unless the date is shown on the face of the map, the information on local authorities and statistical areas is dated to November 1974; on Education Board boundaries and electricity distribution to February 1973. All boundaries are as shown in the *Atlas of New Zealand Regional Statistics,* Town and Country Planning Branch, Ministry of Works, Wellington 1968, with later amendments by the relevant authority to the date shown.

LANDFORMS IN RELIEF 74–75
This map was drawn by J. Petro, then Cartographic Branch, Department of Lands and Survey, in 1963–64 on a base from the New Zealand Map Service, Series 1. It was subsequently revised by the Cartographic Branch.

SEISMICITY, MAGNETIC AND GRAVITY FIELDS
Seismograph Stations, 1972; Deep Earthquakes, 1964–65; Shallow Earthquakes, 1961–65; Historic Earthquakes 78
Cross Section of the Main Seismic Region; the Magnetic Field in 1975; the Gravity Field 79
From information supplied by the Geophysics Division, Department of Scientific and Industrial Research.

THE SEA FLOOR 81
This map is based on Lawrence, P., 1967: New Zealand Region; Bathymetry, 1 : 6 000 000, N.Z. Oceanogr. Inst. Chart, Miscellaneous Series, 15.

CONTENTS

CLIMATE
Weather Map with associated Satellite Cloud Picture; Climate Districts 83
Average Annual Rainfall; Days of Rainfall; Annual Variation of Rainfall 85
Mean Annual Temperature; Wind Flow Characteristics; Annual Variation of Temperature 87
Average Annual Duration of Bright Sunshine; Average Number of Days per year with a maximum Temperature of ±5°C or greater; Average Number of Screen Frosts per year; Monthly Accumulated Sunshine Hours; Average Daily Incoming Radiation; Fluctuation of Average Temperature 88
The Variability of Average Rainfall; Average Annual Water Deficit; Highest Rainfall for One Day; Heating Degree Days; Average Annual Number of Days on which Thunder is heard; Damaging Hailstorms 89
These maps are all based on material supplied by the Meteorological Service.

GEOLOGY
The New Zealand Coastline throughout the Cenozoic Era, *diagram*, after C. A. Fleming 90
Geology 96–97
Compilation material is based on 'Geological Map of New Zealand, 1:1 000 000, 1952'.

FORESTS
Vegetation *circa* 1840 104–105
This map is based on information from *National Forest Survey of New Zealand, 1955*, Vol 1, *The Indigenous Forest Resources of New Zealand*, by S. E. Masters, J. G. Holloway and P. J. McKelvey, Wellington 1957.
Contemporary Forest Cover 106–107
This map is compiled from: F.S. Mapping Series No 1, updated by Forest Service Conservencies and by the Forest Research Institute; F.S. Mapping Series No 12, 2nd Edition, June 1973; F.S. Mapping Series No 15, 1st Edition, 1974.

FAUNA 120–121
This map is compiled from information supplied by P. Morrison, Wildlife Service, Department of Internal Affairs.

SOILS, LAND CLASSIFICATION AND USE
Land Classification and Land Use, *photographs and diagrams*
Reefton and vicinity 136
Satellite photograph of area of North and Central Otago, using, for *diagram*, key on *p 141* 137
Soils 138–139
The base map is from the New Zealand Map Service, Series 1, and the information is based on figs. 3.1.1 and 3.1.2, in *Soils of New Zealand*, Vol 1, Wellington 1968, and from material collated by M. L. Leamy from soil surveys by officers of the Soil Bureau, Department of Scientific and Industrial Research. The reference table is the conception of D. J. Pimblott and B. K. Bradley, Cartographic Branch, Department of Lands and Survey.
Land Classification 140–141
The information on this map was supplied by the author, M. L. Leamy, Chief Pedologist, Soil Bureau, Department of Scientific and Industrial Research. The reference table is by D. J. Pimblott and B. K. Bradley.
Land Use 142–143
The information on this map was supplied by M. L. Leamy, W. R. Dale, Department of Scientific and Industrial Research, and D. G. Jeffery, Department of Lands and Survey.

FISHING 153
This map is based on information from *New Zealand Fisheries*, compiled by J. G. Watkinson and R. Smith, Wellington 1972; *Fisheries Research Publication No. 219*, undated; information Dr G. Eggleston, Ministry of Agriculture and Fisheries.

MINERAL RESOURCES
Extensive Aggregate and Mineral Deposits 157
Localised Metallic and Non-Metallic Minerals 157
These maps are based on information supplied by B. N. Thompson, Geological Survey, Department of Scientific and Industrial Research, to 31/12/73; information from Mines Department.

ENERGY RESOURCES 161
This map is compiled from information supplied by C. E. Nixon, Electricity Department; T. G. Shadwell, Maui Pipeline Project; Ministry of Works; *World Energy Conference, Development of Energy in New Zealand*, Wairakei, 1972.

MANUFACTURING
Historical Summary, 1900–01 to 1971–72, *diagram* 162
Size of Establishments according to number of persons engaged, 1971–72, *diagram* 165
Manufacturing 170–171
The diagrams and maps are based on information supplied by the Department of Trade and Industry and the Department of Statistics.

TRANSPORT & COMMUNICATIONS 176–177
For the sake of clarity, the air routes on this map are diagrammatic, not actual. The map is based on information from the Ministry of Transport, the Ministry of Works and Development, the Post and Telegraph Department, New Zealand Railways, the New Zealand Broadcasting Council, Air New Zealand, the National Airways Corporation, Mt Cook Airlines, Air North and Safe Air.

ANTARCTICA
Ross Dependency 184
McMurdo Sound - Scott Base areas 185
These maps are based on NZMS 135, Ross Sea Regions, 2nd Ed, January 1970. They are on a stereographic projection centred on the South Pole, the parallels being represented by circles and the meridians by their radii. The scale, which is independent of direction, is constant along any one parallel, but increases outwards from the Pole.

PACIFIC ISLANDS
Fiji, Western Samoa 193
Tonga, Cook Islands 194
Niue, Tokelau Islands 195
These maps were drawn from information supplied by the Cartographic Branch, Department of Lands and Survey; Ministry of Foreign Affairs; J. B. McEwen, and Professor Bruce Biggs, Department of Anthropology, University of Auckland.

THE SOUTH-WEST PACIFIC 195–197
This map was compiled by the Cartographic Branch, Department of Lands and Survey. Bathymetric information was supplied by the Oceanographic Institute, Department of Scientific and Industrial Research; information on nomenclature by the Ministry of Foreign Affairs, the Ministry of Defence and the Department of Maori and Island Affairs; Professor Bruce Biggs and J. B. McEwen supplied information on contemporary spellings.

The map is on a Lambert conformal (or orthomorphic) conic projection with two standard parallels, these being at $0°$ and $45°$ S. The meridians are straight lines and the parallels arcs of concentric circles.

The scale at any point is independent of direction; between the standard parallels it is a little smaller, and outside the standard parallels a little greater than the nominal scale of the map.

The variation from the nominal scale of 1 : 25 000 000 ranges from -8 per cent at latitude $22°$ $30'$ S to $+11$ per cent at latitude $12°$ N and $55°$ S.

TOURIST RESOURCES 202–203
This map was designed in the Cartographic Branch, Department of Lands and Survey. For a base, a cardboard model was made by L. P. Lee, which was then photographed by National Publicity Studios (who also prepared the sea vignette). The drawing was then done by D. W. Lawrence from a selected perspective. Type sizes reflect tourist density.

ILLUSTRATIONS

End Paper: RAKAIA RIVER TERRACES   *Lloyd Homer, Geological Survey*

The outwash plain was built by alpine debris and is dissected by a braided river, with headwaters in the main massif. The terraces are formed throughout phases of warm and cold climate by the processes of plain building and periodic spreading and cutting with consequent terrace structuring.

Frontispiece: MOUNT COOK   *NZ Aerial Mapping*

Called Aorangi, the Cloud Piercer, by the Maori, the three peaks of New Zealand's highest mountain are, in this view from the south, Southern, *left*, Mid and Northern.

CAPE REINGA   *Robin Smith Photography Ltd*

p 8   The site of a lighthouse marking the sea lane between the north of New Zealand and Three Kings Islands. It is the traditional departure point for spirits of the Maori leaving for the other world.

THE TAUPO VOLCANIC ZONE UNDER SNOW   *National Publicity Studios*

p 12   Linking the regions to the north and south is the great Taupo Volcanic Zone. Seen under winter snow from above Mt Ruapehu, the active cone of Ngauruhoe almost obscures the several craters of Tongariro. The western cliffs of Lake Taupo lie beyond.

AT TOMOANA   *NZ Aerial Mapping*

p 16   Rich Hawke's Bay farmland extends from the site of an Agricultural and Pastoral Society Show, an annual event in most rural districts to display new farming methods, products and a way of life.

WELLINGTON CITY   *J. H. Johns*

p 20   The capital, with its wharves verging the deep water of a drowned depression, its commercial and political centre partly on reclaimed land, and its residential suburbs now mainly beyond the encircling Green Belt.

THE AVOCA VALLEY   *J. H. Johns, NZ Forest Service*

p 24   100 kilometres to the north-west of Christchurch, it shows typical Canterbury high country, with the boulders of a braided river bounded by tussock grassland of the foothills of the Southern Alps.

THE EGLINTON VALLEY   *NZ Aerial Mapping/J. H. Johns*

p 28   Broadly glaciated and now under beech forest, the valley lies between the Earl and Livingstone mountains. It is part of Fiordland National Park and provides the land route between Lake Te Anau and Milford Sound.

LANDFORMS   *NZ Aerial Mapping/J. H. Johns*

p 70   The deep and extremely fine dissection of the ridges of the southern Richardson mountains in Central Otago. The tussock-clad ridges contrast with beech forest on the shady, southern aspect.

A SELECTION OF SPECIES OF NEW ZEALAND FLORA   *J. T. Salmon*

p 112   1. Tree Daisy, *Senecio laxifolius* 2. Wild Spaniard, *Aciphylla horrida* 3. Kakaramu, *Coprosma robusta* 4. Maori Onion, *Bulbinella hookeri* 5. Haast's Buttercup, *Ranunculus haastii* 6. Chatham Island Forget-me-not, *Myostidium hortensia* 7. *Dracophyllum fiordense* 8. Flax, *Phormium tenax* 9. *Celmisia traversii* 10. Manuka, *Leptospermum scoparium* 11. Toetoe, *Cortaderia fulvida* 12. Kohekohe, *Dysoxylum spectabile* 13. Cabbage Tree, *Cordyline banksii* 14. Wheki Fern, *Dicksonia fibrosa* 15. Lacebark, *Hoheria populnea* 16. Celery Pine or Tanekaha, *Phyllocladus trichomanoides* 17. Taupata, *Coprosma repens* 18. Orchid, *Thelymitra longifolia.*

p 113   Lancewood, *Pseudopanax crassifolius*   *J. H. Johns*
           Mount Cook Lily, *Ranunculus lyallii* }   *J. H. Johns, NZ Forest Service.*
           Southern Rata, *Metrosideros umbellata* }

SPECIMENS OF NEW ZEALAND FAUNA

p 117   Tuatara, *Sphenodon punctatus*   *J. H. Johns*
           An adult male, with unbroken tail, may grow to between 550–600 mm. Its weight could reach 1000 g.

p 118   Snail, *Paryphanta lignaria annectens* Powell   *J. H. Johns, NZ Forest Service*
           Kakapo, *Strigops habroptilus*   D. V. Merton ⎫
           New Zealand Sea Lion (female), *Otaria hookeri*   A. Wright   ⎬ *Wild Life Service*
           Takahe, *Notornis mantelli*   C. R. Veitch ⎭

p 119   Kea, *Nestor notabilis* }   *J. H. Johns, NZ Forest Service*
           Katipo, *Latrodectus katipo* }
           Stephens Island frog, *Leiopelma Hamiltoni*   *J. H. Johns*

SOIL TYPES, FOUR EXAMPLES   *Quentin Christie, Soil Bureau, DSIR*
pp 134–135

REEFTON AND VICINITY   *Lloyd Homer, Geological Survey*
p 136   To demonstrate soil classification and land use.

AN AREA OF NORTH AND CENTRAL OTAGO   *National Aeronautics and Space Administration (US)*
p 137   To show soil zones and land forms.

CAPE MARIA VAN DIEMEN   *K. & J. Bigwood*
p 205

ABEL TASMAN NATIONAL PARK, TOTARANUI   *R. L. Kay*
p 205

CITRUS FRUIT ORCHARDS, KERIKERI   *NZ Aerial Mapping/J. H. Johns*
pp 206–207 This area of intensive fruit farming results from a combination of factors, chief of which are soil, climate and retirement needs.

NINETY MILE BEACH   *Robin Smith Photography Ltd.*
p 208

MARSDEN POINT OIL REFINERY   *NZ Aerial Mapping/J. H. Johns*
p 208

ILLUSTRATIONS

AUCKLAND   *NZ Aerial Mapping/J. H. Johns*

p 209   The self-contained suburban house sections, so clear in the foreground, are largely responsible for the engulfing sprawl over the Auckland isthmus.

PUKEKOHE MARKET GARDENS AND TOWNSHIP   *NZ Aerial Mapping/J. H. Johns*

pp 210–211   Unchecked housing development could threaten the use of the rich volcanic soil for market gardens.

RICH WAIKATO FARM LAND   *NZ Aerial Mapping/J. H. Johns*

p 212   Exotic trees form boundary hedges and shelter belts for the concentrated dairy farms on this volcanic soil.

ESK VALLEY VINEYARDS   *NZ Aerial Mapping/J. H. Johns*

p 212

MATURE KAURI, WAIPOUA STATE FOREST   *NZ Aerial Mapping/J. H. Johns*

p 213

KAINGAROA STATE FOREST AND VILLAGE   *J. H. Johns, NZ Forest Service*

pp 214–215   Vast exotic forest has been established on previously undeveloped pumice lands in the central North Island.

LOGS FOR EXPORT, PORT MAUNGANUI   *J. H. Johns, NZ Forest Service*

p 216   In Tauranga harbour, this port at Mt Maunganui is the major outlet for timber and its products from the whole of the central North Island.

MAJOR HILL-COUNTRY EROSION, TARNDALE SLIP, MANGATU   *NZ Aerial Mapping/J. H. Johns*

p 217   A major example of the possible effect of forest removal from unstable land. Indiscriminate clearing of the natural forest cover has produced devastating erosion.

THE POVERTY BAY PLAIN   *NZ Aerial Mapping/J. H. Johns*

pp 218–219   Looking across the Waipaoa River to Young Nicks Head. Sweetcorn is the major crop on the rich, alluvial soil of this coastal plain south of Gisborne.

SHEEP AND CATTLE COUNTRY, OKAWA   *NZ Aerial Mapping/J. H. Johns*

p 220   In this Hawke's Bay hill country, differing shades of green at the fence lines show techniques of grassland farming.

LAKE TUTIRA AND SURROUNDING FARM LAND   *NZ Aerial Mapping/J. H. Johns*

p 221   After accelerated erosion, the ridges in the middle distance are responding to aerial topdressing.

THE TUTAEKURI RIVER, HAWKE'S BAY   *NZ Aerial Mapping/J. H. Johns*

pp 222–223   Entrenched meanders cross the surrounding plain of the Dartmoor district. The Kaweka Range in the background provides the headwaters of the river.

THE COASTLINE AT TONGAPORUTU, NORTH TARANAKI BIGHT   *R. L. Kay*

p 224   The horizontal strata of the tertiary cover rock, a contrast to the more common twisted greywacke, are shown in steep cliffs facing the Tasman Sea.

THE LADY KNOX GEYSER, WAIOTAPU   *A. D. Warren*

p 225

THE WAIRAKEI THERMAL VALLEY   *NZ Aerial Mapping/J. H. Johns*

p 225   Geothermal steam provides electric power for the national grid.

LOOKING OVER THE CRATERS OF MT TONGARIRO   *NZ Aerial Mapping/J. H. Johns*

pp 226–227   to the cone of Mt Ngauruhoe and the snowclad peaks of Mt Ruapehu.

THE TERRACES OF TURAKIRAE HEAD   *Lloyd Homer, Geological Survey*

p 228   The coastal bench shows the stranded ridges of successive uplifts of coast, each ridge being marked by a line of sand. The ridge at the foot of the cliff, *middle right*, is about 4900 years old, while the three seaward ridges were formed, successively, about 3100, 515 and 120 years ago. The last was caused by the 1855 Wairarapa earthquake. In the middle distance are raised and tilted terraces of earlier shore lines. The whole series is a tectonic calendar of coastal uplift.

MT EGMONT AND THE ENCIRCLING NATIONAL PARK   *NZ Aerial Mapping*

p 229   This vertical photograph shows the circular spread of lava from a central volcanic vent. The defined outer circle, which has a six-mile radius from the central cone, distinguishes the forest of the National Park from the surrounding farmland.

FANTHAMS PEAK, *left*, AND THE SUMMIT OF MT EGMONT   *NZ Aerial Mapping/J. H. Johns*

p 229

THE TARANAKI PLAINS   *NZ Aerial Mapping/J. H. Johns*

pp 230–231   Looking over the coast to the town of Hawera and Mt Egmont.

THE WELLINGTON FAULT LINE   *E. R. Schroder, RNZAF*

p 232   along the western side of the harbour and the Hutt Valley. This remarkable photograph, taken by the RNZAF from 30 000 feet, shows the active fault running through the centre. The north-south ridges to the south-east are drowned to form the Wellington Harbour, the primary reason for the location of the city. The depression of the Hutt Valley and the Trentham basin lies to the north-east, with the Wairarapa and the Manawatu plains beyond, far right and left.

THE DROWNED VALLEYS OF THE MARLBOROUGH SOUNDS   *J. H. Johns, Lands and Survey*

p 233   This drowned valley system contrasts with the faulted system of the north-east side of Cook Strait. The intricate drowned ridges are not markedly cliffed by wave erosion. The photograph looks seawards down Pelorus Sound.

A WEST COAST STAND OF KAHIKATEA OR WHITE PINE   *J. H. Johns, NZ Forest Service*

pp 234–235   Dense forests of white pine, the tallest indigenous species, formerly flourished on fertile alluvial soils in both North and South Islands. Its timber, entirely free from smell, was ideal for butter boxes and churns. Stands are now reduced to fragmented remnants threatened by farm development.

NELSON CITY AND PORT   *Lloyd Homer, Geological Survey*

p 236   beyond the reclamation and mudflats between the foothills and Boulder Bank.

THE PUNAKAIKI ROCKS   *V. C. Browne*

p 236   skirted by the coastal highway between Westport and Greymouth.

LIMESTONE CAVES AT PATURAU, NORTH-WEST NELSON   *Lloyd Homer, Geological Survey*

p 237

THE SOUTHERN ALPS   *J. H. Johns, NZ Forest Service*

pp 238–239   between Mt Elie de Beaumont, *left*, and Mt Cook, the highest peak on the right, lie beyond Westland podocarp forest. The view is from Okarito Trig.

THE KARAMEA RIVER VALLEY   *NZ Aerial Mapping/J. H. Johns*

p 240

RIVER TERRACES AND FOOTHILLS FLANK THE CLUTHA RIVER   *NZ Aerial Mapping/J. H. Johns*

p 241

THE CANTERBURY PLAINS   *NZ Aerial Mapping*

pp 242–243   spread to the sea from the Southern Alps. The accordant summit level on the skyline marks the uplifted block of the axial ranges of the Southern Alps. Vast quantities of debris have been deposited as confluent fans by the major rivers of the Canterbury plains, such as the Waimakariri river shown on the right of the photograph. The smaller Hawkins River on the left, a tributary of the Selwyn, occupies an inter-fan depression.

THE WAIKAKAHO VALLEY (*incorrectly captioned* ONAMALUTU VALLEY)   *Lloyd Homer, Geological Survey*

p 244   nestles in the foothills beyond the Wairau river. The pattern of finely textured dissection is characteristic of large tracts of greywacke hill country throughout New Zealand. Indigenous forest covers the far ridges, while in the middle distance cleared and grassed ridges are reverting to secondary growth on the shaded slopes. There are exotic trees and improved pastures on the valley floor.

CHRISTCHURCH   *V. C. Browne*

p 245   The international airport at Harewood is in the foreground, with the business district beyond Hagley Park in the centre. Sumner lies to the top left, with Lyttelton Harbour beyond the Port Hills at the top right.

DUNEDIN   *NZ Aerial Mapping/J. H. Johns*

p 245   The city lies at the head of Otago Harbour with Macandrew Bay in the foreground and Ravensbourne middle right.

MT COOK, *left*, AND MT TASMAN   *NZ Aerial Mapping*

pp 246–247   with the Ball, Hochstetter and Tasman glaciers. Ascents of Mt Cook often begin after a climb up the Haast ridge to the right of the Hochstetter Icefall, which drops from the Grand Plateau at the foot of Mt Tasman. Climbers then cross the Plateau, skirt Mt Tasman to climb first the Linda glacier between the two massifs and finally the high Northern Peak.

BENMORE, THE EARTH DAM AND POWER STATION   *NZ Aerial Mapping/J. H. Johns*

p 248   with the great stretch of artificial lake.

THE UPPER TAIERI RIVER   *NZ Aerial Mapping/J. H. Johns*

p 249   flows through tussock grassland. The range and basin topography of Central Otago is illustrated by the block of the Rock and Pillar Range, *right*, and the down-faulted Styx basin.

THE OBELISK ON THE OLD MAN RANGE, OTAGO   *NZ Aerial Mapping/J. H. Johns*

pp 250–251   Subalpine vegetation and stark schist tors characterise the higher ranges of Central Otago.

THE ALPINE FAULT AND THE WEST COAST
BETWEEN JACKSON HEAD AND THE GREY RIVER   *National Aeronautics and Space Administration (US)*

p 252   This photograph was taken from an Earth Resources Technology Satellite at a height of about 500 miles. The colours are false and show contrast only. The darker brown areas indicate podocarp forest on ridge slopes, while the lighter red areas show pasture, farm land or perhaps freshly planted exotic forest. The dark areas of inland water, for example Lake Brunner, show clear water, and contrast with the light green of the moraine of the upper arm of Lake Tekapo and other shingle or sediment saturated water. Similarly, the green of the river beds indicates the shingle areas of a braided river rather than water, shown as a dark thread. Light brown areas near Tekapo show dried out tussock or other grassland pasture. The large areas of white are cloud, but areas of snow on the tops also show white. In the sea, the light green along the shoreline shows shingle and sediment, and the dark area, clear sea water.

MILFORD SOUND   *NZ Aerial Mapping/J. H. Johns*

p 253   The valley lies between the Wick, *left*, and Darran mountains. Mitre Peak is on the left of the Sound. In the foreground is the Gulliver River which leads through to the Cleddeau, along which the highway continues to Milford. It is an area of classic land-forms resulting from valley glaciation.

THE LAMMERLAWS   *NZ Aerial Mapping/J. H. Johns*

pp 254–255   This subalpine, tussock-covered Otago upland shows a dissection pattern caused by small streams cutting into an uplifted landscape.

SIX ANTARCTIC VIEWS   First five: *Antarctic Division DSIR*
                                                                                                 last: *R. H. Wheeler*

p 256   The south fork of the upper Wright Valley; the summit camp, Mt Erebus Expedition 1967–68; descending the traverse on Axel Heiberg Glacier; Emperor penguins, Cape Crozier; the Wright Valley; Victoria Glacier, Upper Victoria Valley.
               These pictures are of the more diverse, western side of the Ross Dependency. Those on the left of the page and on the bottom right are scenes from the eastern flank of the Trans-Antarctic Mountains that 'obstruct' the ice cap. The upper and centre right photographs are of Ross Island, some 60 kilometres from the mainland coast.
               The Axel Heiberg glacier is tiny compared with the Byrd, Nimrod or Beardmore glaciers. The flat, featureless Ross Ice Shelf is seen as the horizon in the top right of this picture. In the photograph to the right, the Ross Ice Shelf again appears, this time in its distal section at Cape Crozier at the eastern extremity of Ross Island. Adult Emperor penguins of the local colony are escorting their maturing chicks at the foot of a block calved from the 'Barrier', the terminal cliff of the Shelf and the birth place of the characteristic flat-topped Antarctic icebergs.
               The ice-free landscapes, *top and bottom left and bottom right*, are exceptional features of Antarctica, with a climate and situation that do not sustain ice-filled valleys. These Dry Valleys are not merely scenic and accessible but are prized geological 'windows' in the almost unbroken shroud of the ice of the continent. Both the Wright Valley photographs show rare and scientifically informative exposures of rock, here consisting of alternate layers of warm-coloured tan sandstone and contrasting black dolerite which long ago was injected horizontally whilst molten between the sandstone strata. In this unvegetated oasis, the tan provides visual relief to the surrounding eternity of the whites and blues of sky, ice and snow. In the blue of the middle distance of the upper Wright Valley can be detected both the rock contrast and the consequent benching (hill, *middle left*). The floor of the valley in both Wright Valley photographs is littered with morainal debris, largely resistant dolerite, which is often wind sculptured by sand abrasion and bears a lustrous polish. The photograph, *bottom right*, of another Dry Valley, the Upper Victoria, shows a stagnant glacier in the upper reaches and a now empty main valley beyond is occupied by a proglacial lake, ponded by overdeeping by ice and recessional moraine. This 'lake' is solid ice, but some, as in the Wright Valley, are still liquid due to a high degree of salinity and are a subject of much scientific speculation. The stationary Upper Victoria glacier, like many other retreating or stationary tributary glaciers of the Dry Valleys, is spectacularly cliff-sided from radiation melting caused by reflection of the sun from the bare rock valley sides. The three New Zealanders are passing through *penitentes*, melt sculptured litter from huge slabs of ice that have 'calved' from the glacier's lateral wall. The lamination, *top right*, in the top of the glacier is the ice of a 'perched' tributary glacier which joined the main glacier some four kilometres further up the valley.
               The photograph, *top right*, of Mt Erebus, higher than Mt Cook by thirty metres, shows another unusual feature of Antarctica—its only active volcano. In this photograph, the slopes of Erebus are unusually heavily clad in snow, and the normal contrast of black volcanic rock and snow slopes is masked. The almost constant, gentle, white plume of smoke and ash is also temporarily absent. The photograph shows the life style of the New Zealand field parties in Antarctica. Here is the traditional double-skinned pyramid tent of Scott's day still in use, albeit now of more durable synthetic materials. Sleds too are still used but are pulled by a motor toboggan, the mechanical if less reliable substitute for the husky dog. These toboggan tracks make a contrast to the dog-sled trails in the foreground of the Axel Heiberg photograph of only a few years earlier.

GAZETTEERS

New Zealand   258
Beyond New Zealand   279

INDEX   287

REFERENCE

Communications

Railway	——————
Railway Tunnels	
State Highway	——————
Other Road	——————
Road Tunnel	
Track	- - - - - - -
International Airport	✈
Major Aerodrome	⌖
Aerodrome	±

Hydrography

Rivers	——————
Braided River	
Canal	——————
Hydro-electric Tunnel	——————
Saltwater Lagoon	
Lake, Freshwater Lagoon	- - - - - -
Tidal Area	
Rocky Coast	
Sandy Coast	
Saltpans	
Bathymetric Contours	
Swamp	
Icefields & Glaciers	

Populated Places

Over 40 000	WELLINGTON
20 000–40 000	TAKAPUNA
7000–20 000	MASTERTON
2500–7000	Kaiapoi
250–2500	Tuakau ○
25–250	Waima ○

Other Features

Dam	
Saddle, Pass	)(
Cliff, Escarpment	
Dunes	
Spot Elevation (in metres)	· 503
Contours	

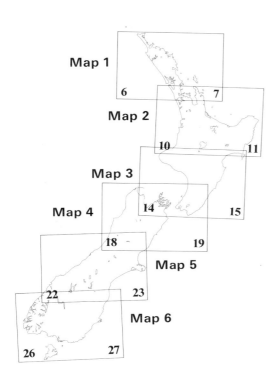

Map 1
6   7
Map 2
10   11
Map 3
14   15
Map 4
18   19
Map 5
22   23
Map 6
26   27

INDEX TO SECTIONAL MAPS

Sectional Map 1 pages 6–7   North Auckland

Sectional Map 2 pages 10–11   South Auckland, Gisborne

Sectional Map 3 pages 14–15   Taranaki, Hawke's Bay, Wellington

Sectional Map 4 pages 18–19   Nelson, Marlborough

Sectional Map 5 pages 22–23   Westland, Canterbury

Sectional Map 6 pages 26–27   Southland, Otago

COMPILATION NOTES

THE NEW ZEALAND TOPOGRAPHICAL MAP on pages 2–3 is at a scale of 1 : 3 750 000 and was compiled from Sectional map information. THE SECTIONAL MAPS cover the whole of New Zealand in detail at a scale of 1 : 1 000 000. Some unavoidable overlapping is due to the attempt to include on the one sheet areas of administrative unity or influence.

THE SOURCES include the revised black sheets of *A Descriptive Atlas of New Zealand, 1959*. New line drawings were prepared on transparent foils from the 1 : 500 000 published map series and from photographically reduced prints of the 1 : 63 360 topographical map series for areas of later survey. Extensive areas of South Island high country and the main ranges of the North Island have now been mapped from aerial photographs and this information is included. Bathymetric data was supplied by the New Zealand Oceanographic Institute, Department of Scientific and Industrial Research.

THE GRADING of populated places is based on information listed in 'New Zealand Census 1971' and includes cities, boroughs, towns and localities. The status of these is shown in the Gazetteer.

THE SPELLING of place names has followed the rulings of the New Zealand Geographic Board.

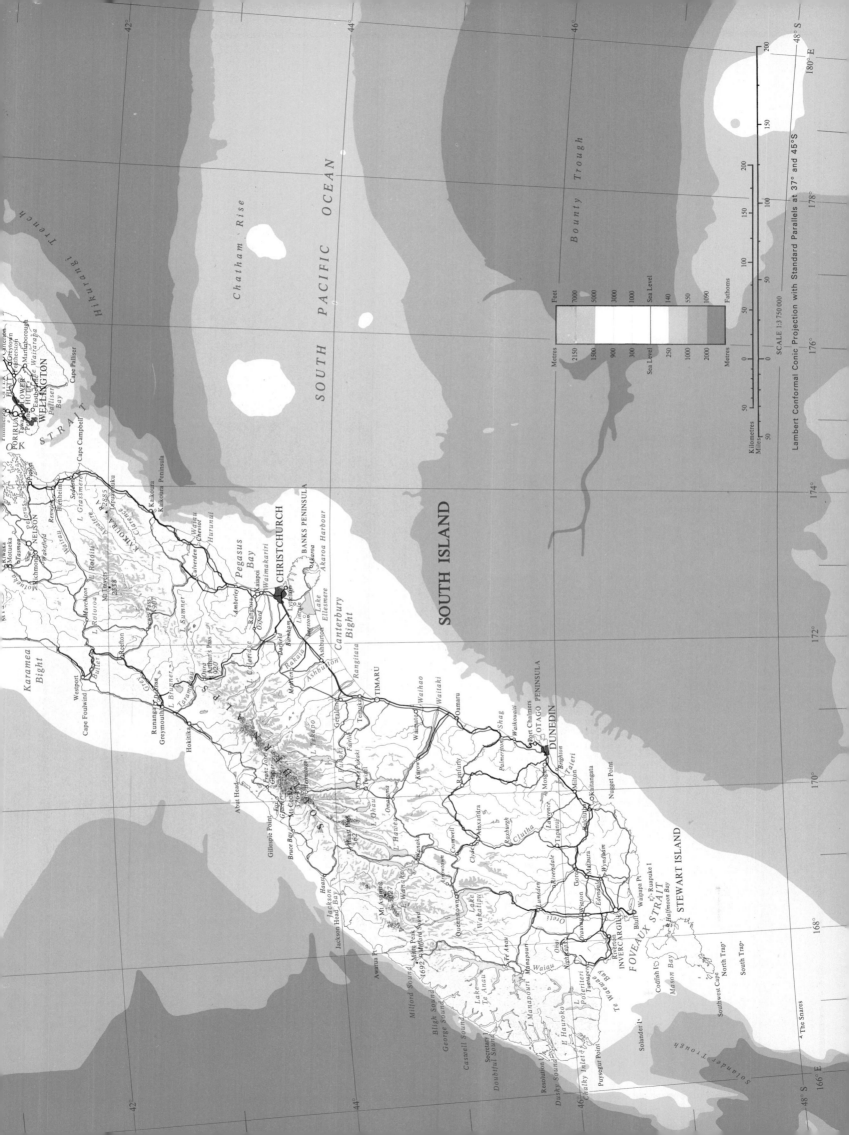

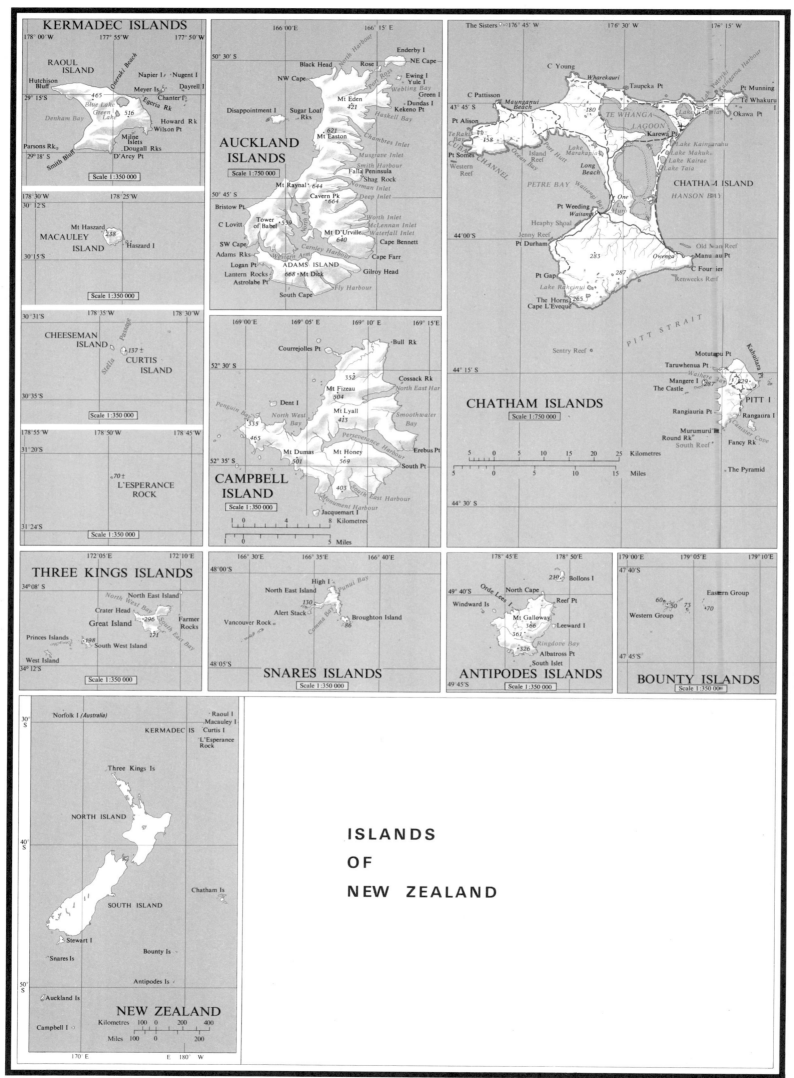

KERMADEC ISLANDS

178° 00'W · 177° 55'W · 177° 50'W

RAOUL ISLAND

Hutchison Bluff
Oneraki Beach
465
Blue Lake
Green Lake
516
Denham Bay
29° 15'S
Napier I · Nugent I
Meyer Is
Chanter I
Egeria Rk
Howard Rk
Wilson Pt
Milne Islets
Dougall Rks
Parsons Rk
29° 18'S
Smith Bluff
D'Arcy Pt

Scale 1:350 000

178° 30'W · 178° 25'W

30° 12'S
Mt Hazard
238
Haszard I

MACAULEY ISLAND

30° 15'S

Scale 1:350 000

30° 31'S · 178° 35'W · 178° 30'W

CHEESEMAN ISLAND

Stella Passage
137 ±

CURTIS ISLAND

30° 35'S

Scale 1:350 000

178° 55'W · 178° 50'W · 178° 45'W

31° 20'S

70 ±

L'ESPERANCE ROCK

31° 24'S

Scale 1:350 000

166° 00'E · 166° 15'E

50° 30'S

Enderby I
NE Cape
Black Head
Rose I
NW Cape
Port Ross
Ewing I
Yule I
Green I
Dundas I
Webling Bay
Kekeno Pt
Haskell Bay
Mt Eden
421
Disappointment I
Sugar Loaf Rks
621
Mt Easton
Chambres Inlet

AUCKLAND ISLANDS

Scale 1:750 000

Musgrave Inlet
Smith Harbour
Falla Peninsula
Shag Rock
Norman Inlet
50° 45'S
Mt Raynal 644
Cavern Pk 664
Deep Inlet
Bristow Pt
C Lovitt
Worth Inlet
Tower of Babel 538
McLennan Inlet
Waterfall Inlet
SW Cape
Mt D'Urville 640
Cape Bennett
Adams Rks
Western Arm
Carnley Harbour
Cape Farr
Logan Pt
Lantern Rocks
ADAMS ISLAND
668 · Mt Dick
Gilroy Head
Astrolabe Pt
South Cape
Fly Harbour

169° 00'E · 169° 05'E · 169° 10'E · 169° 15'E

Courrejolles Pt
Bull Rk
52° 30'S
352
Cossack Rk
Mt Fizeau 504
North East Har
Dent I
Mt Lyall 413
Smoothwater Bay
North West Bay
335
Perseverance Harbour
465
Erebus Pt
Mt Dumas 501
Mt Honey 569
South Pt
52° 35'S

CAMPBELL ISLAND

Scale 1:350 000

403
South East Harbour
Monument Harbour
Jacquemart I

0 ___ 4 ___ 8 Kilometres
0 ___ 5 Miles

The Sisters · 176° 45'W · 176° 30'W · 176° 15'W

C Young
Wharekauri
Taupeka Pt
Pt Munning
Te Whakuru
C Pattisson
Maunganui Beach
180
Lake Te Rangatira
Kaingaroa Harbour
43° 45'S
Pt Alison
TE WHANGA LAGOON
Karewa Pt
Okawa Pt
Te Raki
158
Lake Kaingaroa
Pt Somes
CUBA CHANNEL
Island Reef
Ocean Bay
Lake Makuku
Western Reef
Long Beach
Lake Kairae
Lake Taia
PETRE BAY
Waitangi Bay
CHATHAM ISLAND
HANSON BAY
44° 00'S
Pt Weeding
Waitangi
One Huri
Heaphy Shoal
Jenny Reef
283
Pt Durham
Old Nan Reef
Owenga
Manu au Pt
287
C Fournier
Pt Gap
Renwecks Reef
Lake Rakeinui
The Horns 265
Cape L'Eveque

CHATHAM ISLANDS

Scale 1:750 000

Sentry Reef

PITT STRAIT

44° 15'S

Motutapu Pt
Taruwhenua Pt
Mangere I
287
The Castle
229
Waihere
Rangiauria Pt
PITT I
Rangaura I
Murumuru
Round Rk
Fancy Rk
South Reef
44° 30'S

The Pyramid

5 0 5 10 15 20 25 Kilometres
5 0 5 10 15 Miles

172° 05'E · 172° 10'E

THREE KINGS ISLANDS

34° 08'S
North West Bay
North East Island
Crater Head
Great Island
296
Farmer Rocks
151
Princes Islands
198
South West Island
South East Bay
West Island
34° 12'S

Scale 1:350 000

166° 30'E · 166° 35'E · 166° 40'E

48° 00'S
High I
Punui Bay
North East Island
130
Alert Stack
Broughton Island
Vancouver Rock
86
Coimna Bay

SNARES ISLANDS

48° 05'S

Scale 1:350 000

178° 45'E · 178° 50'E

210
Bollons I
Orde Lees I
North Cape
49° 40'S
Windward Is
Reef Pt
Mt Galloway 366
Leeward I
361
Ringdove Bay
326
Albatross Pt
South Islet

ANTIPODES ISLANDS

49° 45'S

Scale 1:350 000

179° 00'E · 179° 05'E · 179° 10'E

47° 40'S
60
50 73
Eastern Group
70
Western Group

BOUNTY ISLANDS

47° 45'S

Scale 1:350 00

30° S

Norfolk I (Australia)
Raoul I
Macauley I
KERMADEC IS
Curtis I
L'Esperance Rock

Three Kings Is

NORTH ISLAND

40° S

Chatham Is

SOUTH ISLAND

Stewart I

Bounty Is

Snares Is

Antipodes Is

50° S

Auckland Is

NEW ZEALAND

Campbell I

Kilometres 100 0 200 400
Miles 100 0 200

170° E · E 180° W

ISLANDS

OF

NEW ZEALAND

NORTH AUCKLAND

R. G. Lister

Northland is a long, narrow, north-west oriented peninsula with no point more than thirty kilometres from the coast. It consists of generally rolling hill country with some steep hills and limited areas of flats. The eastern coastline is deeply indented, while the west coast has long sandy beaches broken only by a few bar harbours, notably the Kaipara and Hokianga. Only in Northland are mangroves a significant feature of New Zealand's tidal rivers and harbour margins, and in a few places these have been reclaimed and converted to farm land.

Numerous off-shore islands are typical of the east coast, and many perform a significant role as sanctuaries for rare native fauna. Along the west coast, sand encroachment on to farm land has caused problems, but this has been brought under control with the planting of marram grass, lupin and, more recently, conifers. Although Northland has adequate rainfall and numerous rivers, the area suffers from extremes: in some years drought seriously cuts back dairying production, whilst in others flooding causes serious problems to both farms and communications.

Northland can justly claim to be the 'cradle of New Zealand', for this was the site of some of the earliest trading, and of the first missionary contacts, between Maori and European. In 1814, Anglican missionaries established the first mission station in New Zealand at the Bay of Islands, and over the next three decades vigorously pursued, both here and at other stations, the ideal of 'civilising' as well as Christianising the Maori. In the pre-1840 era the Bay of Islands was the major port in New Zealand, frequented by whalers and traders of many nations. At Waitangi the Treaty signified New Zealand's entry into the British Empire. After 1840 the focus of political attention shifted away and Northland became the scene for exploitation, first of the superb kauri timber and then of its gum. Large areas of land were laid waste. Other more permanent forms of economic development, however, were slow to emerge.

Among its settlers were several organised colonising groups, and today the names of families living in the Waipu district give evidence of their Highland origin (via Nova Scotia), whilst to the south round Puhoi, German names reveal the origin of the first local settlers. Scattered through Northland are the descendants of Dalmatian gumdiggers who have turned to other pursuits and, particularly in the Henderson district, have made a significant contribution to the development of the successful New Zealand wine industry.

The Maori population forms a vigorous element in Northland, and is particularly concentrated in the more northern counties. As is the trend elsewhere, there is a marked movement of the younger Maoris from the rural districts to the towns, especially to Auckland.

For decades isolation was the major problem faced by the communities of Northland, and the area became popularly known as the 'roadless north'. Until the late 1930s much of the freight and many of the passengers to Auckland were carried on small coastal vessels or scows, although the completion of the North Auckland trunk railway in the mid-1920s had marked the beginning of change. Roads, however, were rarely upgraded until after the Second World War.

Despite the earliest European farming at mission stations in the 1820s and 1830s, farm development did not flourish until recently, because of isolation, leached soils, large areas of Maori land and the small size of many holdings. Today, thanks to government land development, the use of fertilisers and trace elements, together with improved transport, dairying and cattle grazing are important amongst both European and Maori farmers. Sheep farming remains less so. Northland enjoys an almost semi-tropical climate which has encouraged the growth of citrus and other fruits such as tamarillos, feijoas and kiwifruit. Citrus orcharding has been particularly developed in the Kerikeri district.

Whangarei provides the regional focus for most of Northland although the proximity of Auckland has always tended to overshadow it. Since the early 1960s Whangarei has boomed as a manufacturing centre, particularly with the construction of sheet glassworks, meat export works and a fertiliser works, while New Zealand's only oil refinery is situated at Marsden Point at the entrance of Whangarei Harbour. The refinery, which came 'on stream' in 1964, made Whangarei New Zealand's major port in terms of tonnage handled.

A warm climate, numerous sandy bays, sheltered water and proximity to Auckland have meant that tourism and recreational activities are of growing significance throughout Northland. The Bay of Islands attracts visitors both from within New Zealand and from overseas, offering not only historical sites such as the Waitangi Treaty House, but also deep sea fishing and scenic beauty. On the west coast the Waipoua State Forest includes the last remaining large groves of kauri. The growth of Auckland City has increased the demand for recreational areas, particularly in the southern counties of Northland, and a number of coastal reserves have been purchased by the Regional Authority. The Hauraki Maritime Park is the most recent of the national parks, and it embraces islands and several peninsulas in the gulf.

The Coromandel Peninsula exhibits many similarities to Northland, with its hill relief, indented coastlines, historical associations with the kauri timber and gum trades, and comparatively slow economic development. Today, population is sparse, with farming limited to small coastal pockets. Its recreational functions, however, are of growing importance, especially around the beautiful coastline.

The entire coastline of Northland and Coromandel is under pressure from Aucklanders seeking beach recreation, sailing and water sports. Holiday accommodation, second homes or weekend baches mushroomed during the prosperous years of the sixties, and they show every sign of continuing to increase during the seventies.

The demand for land by individuals and by developers is unprecedented in New Zealand and legislative measures to direct or control it locally in the counties, or through national administration, have seriously lagged. Sailing and holidaying in the Gulf is a cherished right of a high proportion of Aucklanders, but it has also become a threat, appreciated not only by the conservationists, to the environmental quality of the very scenes that people, in almost overwhelming numbers, are seeking to enjoy under conditions not yet adequately geared to meet the situation.

Map labels

Top margin coordinates: 172°E · M · 30' · N · 173°E · P · 30' · Q · 174°E

Cape Reinga
Hooper Point
Tom Bowling Bay
Surville Cliffs
North Cape
Spirits Bay
Sandy Bay
·309
Motuopao I
·311
Cape Maria van Diemen
Te Hapua
Ohao Point
Parengarenga Harbour
Scott Point
Paua

Motupia I

Te Kao
Great Exhibition Bay
Lake Wahakari
The Bluff

Ngataki
Grenville Pt
Moturoa Is
Cape Karikari
Waihopo
Houhora
Rangaunu Bay
Karikari Peninsula
Pukenui
·237
Houhora Harbour
Karikari Bay
Knuckle Point

Motutangi
Lake Waikaramu
Tokerau Beach
Berghan Point
Lake Waiparera
Doubtless Bay
Karaui Point
Stephenson
Cavalli Is
Waiharara
Rangaunu Oha Harbour
Coopers Beach
Mangonui
Akatere
Whangaroa Bay
Flat I
Motukawanui I
Paparore
Lake Ohia
Taipa
Oruaiti
·377
Waimu
Wainui
Step I
Waipapakauri
Kaingaroa
Parapara
Totara North
Matanguru
Matauri Bay
Sweetwater
Awanui
Oturu
Perja
Oruru
Kenana
Kaeo
Whangaroa
Oioroa
Takou Bay
Kaitaia
Fairburn
Peria
Kaikoa
Omaunu
Waiare
Rocky Poi
Mangatete
Fern Flat
Pupuka
Pureru
Panakareao
Victoria Valley
Ti
Cap
Tauroa Point
Ahipara Bay
Pukepoto
Puigoere
Kapiro
Omaunu
Waiare
Purerua
Ahipara
Mangapa
Kerikeri
Kerikeri Inlet
Russ
Te Rore
Mangamuka
Wapapa
Waitangi
Diggers Valley
Omahuta
Puketi
Whangae
Takahue
751
Mangamuka Bridge
Haruru
Paketona
Paihi
Manukau
Broadwood
Umawera
Waihou Valley
Iruna
Oromahoe
Opu
Awaroa
Pukekohe
Maraehana
Okaihau
Waimate North
Te Korio
Pakaraka
Ngawha
Kawakaw
Herekino Har
Papoioa
Horeke
Ngawha Springs
Whangape
Te Huahua
Kohukohu
Otiria
Waiomio
Pawarenga
Matakaraka
Pekaraka
Pokapu
Rap
Panguru
Motuti
Motukiore
Rawene
Kaikohe
Ngawha
Whangape Har
Mitimiti
Te Iringa
Ohaeawai
Taikirau
Punakitere Valley
Tautoro
Opahi
Rangi Point
Whirinaki
Omanaia
Ngahuhi
Matawaia
Huker
Waima
Otaua
Opononi
·776
Matarua
·626
Omapere
Waiotemarama
Kaikou
Hokianga Harbour
Waimamaku
Wekaweka
Awarua
Alpiwai
Otakaira
Waimamaku
Nukutawhiti
Purua
Ruatangata
Waipoua Forest
Tutamoe
·695
Waimatenui
Kaihu
Opouteke
Pakotai
Toroiti
Maunganui Bluff
·770
Wharekohe
Whatiji
Kaihu
Fouto
Pekerekaurau
Parakao
Tangiteroria
Kaiara
Maungakaramea
Omamari
Aroca
·627
Kirikopuni
Pukehuia
Tangowahine
Omana
Baylys Beach
Dargaville
Windy Hill
Rehutai
Mount Wesley
Turiwiri
Okaihu
Kaiwaka
Te Koperu
Aoroa
Mititai
Tatarariki
Rehia
North Head

TASMAN SEA

Scale / legend

Metres	Feet
600	2000
300	1000
150	500
Sea Level	Sea Level
250	140
1000	550
Metres	Fathoms

Kilometres 10 5 0 10 20 30 40 50

Miles 10 5 0 10 20 30 40 50

Bottom margin coordinates: 172°E · M · 30' · N · 173°E · P · 30' · Q · 174°E

1

30′

2

S O U T H   P A C I F I C   O C E A N

Cape Brett
362

3

Ngaiotonga   Home Point

Whangaruru North
Cape Home
Whangaruru Harbour

na Bay
461
Rimariki I
Taukawau Point

Poor Knights Is

30′

hipuhi
Kaimamaku
Opuawhanga   Whananaki
Motutara Point
Sandy Bay

Marua
Matapouri
Matapouri

Hikurangi
Kaiatea
Tutukaka
Tutukaka Head

Kauri
Kamo Springs
Kiripaka
Glenbervie
Hikurangi
Kareora
*Ngunguru
Bay*

WHANGAREI
Taiharuru Head

Onerahi
Tamaterau
Taiharuru

Portland
Parua Bay

4

One Tree Point
Takahiwai
Parikura
McLeod Bay
Ocean Beach
Marsden Point
491
Bream Head
Springfield
Lady Alice I

Ruakaka
PARRY CHANNEL
Marotiri Is

Waipu
North
Kiri
Bream Bay
Hen and Chickens

Burgess I

Mokohinau Is

Taranga I
427
Fanal I

36°S

puha
Branch
Waipu Cove
Bream Tail

Mareretu
Langs
Beach
Bream Tail

Waireia
Brynderwyn
Moleswortu
430
Mangawhai Heads

hemo
rau
Thickerstelle
Tara

Maungaturoto
Kaiwaka
Mangawhai

Aiguilles I

Miners Head

Katherine Bay
Maunganui Pt

CRADDOCK CHANNEL

Matakohe
Te Kakao
Pt
Te Arai Pt
Te Arai

Ngatamahine Point

*Port
Abercrombie*
Okiwi
Rakitu I

Topuni
Tomarata
Pakiri
Little Barrier I   722

Kaikoura I
Port Fitzroy
621
Whakatautuna Point
Mt Hobson

Batiy
Oruawharo
Te Hana
Wellsford
Whangaripo
Leigh
Cape Rodney

Albert
Wayby
Whangateau
Ti Point
Point Wells
JELLICOE CHANNEL

Pig Is
GREAT BARRIER ISLAND

Wellsline
Hoteo
North
Wayby
Big Omaha
Omaha Flat
Omaha Bay

Horn Rock

TaPora
Dome
Valley
Makakana

Claris

Kaipara
Flats
Streamlan
Sandspit
Takatu
Tokatu Point

Blind Bay
Tryphena

Shag Point
Tryphena Hbr

Head
Woodcocks
358
Glori
Ahuroa
Pohuehue
*Martins
Bay*
182
Mahurangi

Cape Barrier

COLVILLE CHANNEL

Komokoriki
Araparera
Kakanui
Tahekeroa
Puhoi
Kawau I

Channel I
Square Top I

Cuvier I

ly Beach
Makarau
Waiteitei
Waitoki
Waiwera
Hatfields Beach

HAURAKI GULF

Cape Colville
Port Jackson

Harbour
Kaukapakapa
Kanohi
Waimu
Silverdale
Orewa
Red
Beach

Moehau
892
Port Charles
Te Anaputa Point

Motuora I

*Waikawau
Bay*

Mercury Is

Parkhurst
Te Pua
Helensville
Waitoki
Whangaparaoa
Manly
Arkles Bay
Tiritiri Matangi I
*Whangaparaoa
Peninsula*

Colville Bay
Colville

Great Mercury I
247
Red Mercury I
Kawitihu I
Korapuki I

Loch Norrie
Coatesville
Dairy Flat
Redvale

**EAST
COAST
BAYS**

Motukawao
Group

Kennedys Bay
Tokarahu Point

Olrangi
Ararimu
Albany
The Noises

Papaaroha

Kopuetuaki Bay
Whangapoua
Kuaotuna

Whataipa
Woodhill
Hewitt
Riverhead
Paremoremo
Greenhithe
Rakino I
**WAIHEKE
ISLAND**
Thumb Pt
Motuoruhi I
Oamaru
Bay
Long Bay
Retanga
Ohena I

Waimauku
Kumeu
Whenuapai
Motutapu I
Onetangi
Palm Beach
Motuihe I
Waimate I
Coromandel

Mercury Bay

Taupaki
Hobsonville
Rangitoto I
Otetanga
Surfdale
Pakatoa I
Whanganui I
Coromandel
Coromandel Hbr
Whitianga
Ferry
Landing
Mahurangi I
COROMANDEL

Waitakere
Massey
AUCKLAND
Motuihe
Omiha
Rotoroa I
Rangipukea I
Kouma
Cooks
Bay
Hahei

Swanson
Henderson
Bucklands
Beach
Beachlands
Maraetai
Connells
Bay 9
Ahimia
Castle I

Piha
Titirangi
Laingholm
Mangere
Bridge
Maraetai
HOWICK
Diders
Beach
Ponui I
Kereta
Kaimarama
PENINSULA

Bethells
482
Paran
Huia
PAKURANGA
OTAHUHU
Pakihi I
Whenuakite

Karekare
Cornwallis
PAPATOETOE
Brookby
Kawakawa
Bay
Orere Point
Waikawau
Teroglen

MANGERE
Manukau Harbour
Ness
Valley
Clevedon
Matingarahi
Camels Back
819
The Aldermen Is

MANUREWA
Takanini
FIRTH
Tapu
Shoe I

Muriwai Beach
Manukau
Heads
Grahams
Beach
Weymouth
PAPAKURA
688
30′
Waiomu
Te Puru
*OF
THAMES*
Tairua
837
Slipper I

5

30′

6

37°S

Cape Reinga is the site of a lighthouse marking the sea lane between the north of New Zealand and Three Kings Islands. It is the traditional departure point for spirits of the Maori leaving for the other world.

SOUTH AUCKLAND, GISBORNE

Across this widest part of the North Island people have developed a great variety of environments, from the north-west third of the map where there is the densest area of population in New Zealand, to one of the country's most inaccessible and empty regions in the Urewera and the Raukumara Range in the north-east.

The close network of roads extending northward from a line between Te Kuiti and Rotorua demonstrates the fact that here live almost a third of New Zealand's population. Before the days of European settlement, the Maori found the local resources suited his way of life, and abundant field evidence shows that the Maori population was concentrated here probably more than in any other region of the country. This area has continued to attract the lion's share of growth since the Second World War.

Auckland serves in many ways as the focus of New Zealand economic life. Occupying the narrow isthmus between Northland and the Waikato country, the city has its principal harbour off the Hauraki Gulf, although the shallow Manukau Harbour on the southern side is still used by a few coastal vessels. The metropolitan area extends northwards outside the shores of Waitemata Harbour for almost fifty kilometres along the attractive bays and headlands of the east coast. To the south, a typically open urban landscape extends for a similar distance. Aucklanders enjoy unrivalled opportunities for sailing, provided by the sheltered waters among the beautiful islands of the Gulf, well protected by the Coromandel Peninsula on its eastern side.

The Waikato, which rivals the Clutha as New Zealand's longest river, rises in numerous tributaries that drain first into Lake Taupo, which covers 600 square kilometres at an elevation of about 350 metres. The river descends rapidly from Taupo to the plain around Cambridge 300 metres lower and eighty kilometres to the north. Along almost the entire distance electric power is generated through the turbines of nine power stations. The alluvial lowlands below Cambridge have been unevenly filled so that lakes and marshes with peaty swamps abound alongside the lower course of the river.

European settlement in the Waikato basin was comparatively late because of the Maori Wars. From about 1880 forests were cleared, marshes drained, and dairy farms established. Today, sheep are seen as often as dairy cows, and beef cattle are also numerous. Pockets of bush survive in the hills but are now so restricted that there is public concern over any proposal to reduce them further.

Hamilton, New Zealand's largest inland city, is the focus of a prosperous rural community reaching back to Rotorua in the east and to the coast in the west.

The western fringe from the Waikato mouth southward to Taranaki presents rugged and difficult farming country. There is coal in the hills, as there is also on the plain around Huntly, but hydro-electric energy and imported oil have tended to reduce the importance of the small mining townships. Raglan and Kawhia harbours attracted very early mission settlements, but they are too shallow for modern shipping and remain little changed by progress. Limestone at Waitomo has been carved by underground river action into superb caves, with a well-known glow-worm display.

South of Te Kuiti the land still bears the stamp of pioneering, for the King Country has been cleared and made productive only during the present century. Numerous small towns serve as local centres for the farming communities and provide some local industrial employment.

West of the Taupo country, some of the largest remaining stands of indigenous forest protect the watersheds. Both here in the King Country and on the Kaimai Range, further to the north, native timbers are still being milled under licence.

Since the Second World War, new techniques have finally enabled the pumice country to be successfully farmed and the most recent agricultural settlement areas in New Zealand were developed from the western slopes above Lake Taupo, reaching towards Rotorua.

Taupo has grown during recent years as a recreation centre and the Rotorua district has long been one of the country's principal attractions for overseas tourists, with its remarkable hot springs, geysers and Maori culture. Geothermal steam has been harnessed at Wairakei, near Taupo, to provide 220 000 kilowatts of electricity for the national grid.

Numerous lakes and volcanic hills dot the plateau around Rotorua, all the result of volcanic action. At about the turn of the century it was decided to plant pines extensively, since cattle and sheep would not thrive on the pumice soils. Today, perhaps the largest man-made forest in the world is established here, covering more than 400 000 hectares of former scrub and tussock landscape. Two of New Zealand's newest and most impressively large industrial plants now produce pulp and paper at Kinleith in the west and Kawerau in the east. There are, too, successful farms where stock raising is made possible by the application of absent trace elements to the soil.

To the east of the Kaimai Range, the Bay of Plenty stretches along a narrow lowland strip from Waihi Beach eastward to Opotiki. This is predominantly dairy country and the green pastures extend to the lower ridges of the volcanic ash country to the south. Citrus fruit orchards and small hedged enclosures give a local character to the landscape around Tauranga, now one of New Zealand's leading ports as a result of expanding timber exports. White Island, fifty kilometres off-shore, is an active volcano which frequently carries a plume of steam.

To the east of the volcanic plateau, on the ranges that represent the main divide of the North Island, there are substantial areas under native bush. In the Urewera ranges most of the forest is in a national park, while on much of the steep hill country between Lake Waikaremoana and East Cape it has now been designated protection forest. Here are some of the most eroded hillsides in New Zealand and the river beds of the Waipaoa River system reveal the immense quantities of shingle and silt which have been transported down from the hills to the restricted lowlands during the period of clearing and settling of the last century. The New Zealand Forest Service is now undertaking re-afforestation in order to conserve both the hillsides and the good farming country of the lower slopes and valleys.

The fringe around the whole East Cape peninsula between Opotiki and Gisborne includes numerous small settlements that have a strong Maori component. Sandy bays alternate with striking headlands. Pohutukawa trees bloom along the cliffs around Christmas time, and early mission churches may be seen beside the local Maori meeting houses.

Gisborne has grown as the centre of the East Cape country. The Poverty Bay flats are not extensive but are intensively farmed, notably for maize. They have one of the sunniest climates in New Zealand.

Between Hawke's Bay and East Cape the country is divided mostly into large sheep stations. The first European settlers did not need to clear bush as the east coast hills were immediately available as grazing country, being covered with bracken, coarse grass or light scrub.

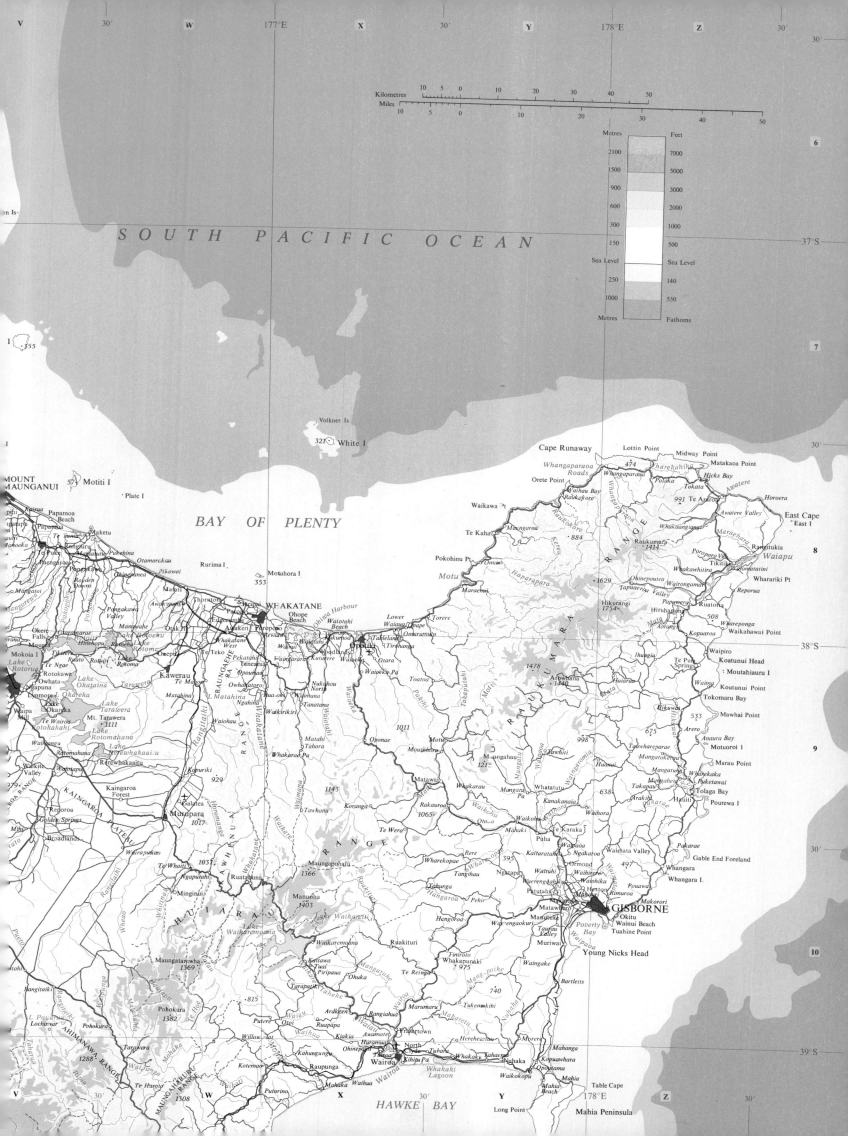

Linking the regions to the north and south is the great Taupo Volcanic Zone. Seen under winter snow from above Mt Ruapehu, the active cone of Ngauruhoe almost obscures the several craters of Tongariro. The western cliffs of Lake Taupo lie beyond.

TARANAKI, HAWKE'S BAY, WELLINGTON

The main mountain axis of the North Island tends to dominate this map from the Tararua and Ruahine ranges in the south, to the broad complex of the Kaimanawas and Kaweka Range towards the north. East of Palmerston North the main divide is at its lowest and the Manawatu River has managed to maintain its course through the ranges from east to west throughout the recent geological period of uplift. All other streams flow either east or west from the axial ranges to form plains of shingle, silt and sand along the coasts.

Higher than these main ranges, however, are the striking volcanic mountains which form two clusters. One consists of snow-capped cones rising from the tussock and scrub of the pumice plateau on the west of the main divide. Ruapehu rises above 3000 metres with the striking active cone of Ngauruhoe (2500 m) nearby and the fragmented dormant Tongariro crater complex a little further to the north.

The second cluster, Egmont, 130 kilometres further west, rises majestically from encircling forest to form the western bulge of the North Island map, the coast swinging in an arc twenty-five kilometres from its crater peak (2750 m). Egmont is, in fact, the most prominent cone of a small cluster, as there is an older, worn down cone to the north, represented by the ridges extending towards New Plymouth. A small subsidiary cone, Fanthams Peak, clings to the southern flank of Egmont.

Wellington, on the shores of Port Nicholson, was selected by the New Zealand Company on account of its superb, sheltered harbour. As the capital city since 1865, Wellington has been developed on a difficult site. Its government buildings and nearby commercial core stand largely upon reclaimed land while its residential areas scramble upwards on the steep sides of the surrounding ridges. It has expanded northward along the available valleys to produce a metropolitan area now incorporating numerous outlying settlements. The expansion of manufacturing in the Hutt Valley has caused such growth that population there now rivals that of Wellington City, while its dormitory areas are closely linked with the functions of the capital. Along the adjacent west coast, the main railway north has provided a life-line for a string of commuter suburbs over a distance of more than fifty kilometres. Between suburbs the hills have been largely stripped of forest and today there are steep pastures providing a rural backdrop to the suburban Wellington scene. In the higher, eastern ranges of the Rimutakas and Tararuas extensive bush remains and provides seemingly remote recreational areas for the hill-climber and the tramper from near-by cities.

Palmerston North was a town that developed much later, from its beginnings as a small clearing in the bush in the 1880s. Once the railway came through from Wellington, the town expanded rapidly. It has flourished with the growth of agricultural output from the Manawatu lowland and the nearby low hill country and it is one of New Zealand's very few inland cities. The Manawatu lowland has a balance of dairy cows, beef cattle and sheep. Palmerston North, as the chief market centre, has prospered as a commercial focus for a growing industrial sector.

The Manawatu area today represents the product of the dramatic transformation from bush country to pasture land that took place in much of the western North Island after the 1880s. In the early years, dairy cows wintered in the bush, farms were extended a little each season, new pastures being sown among the stumps in the ashes of the bush fires. Such a pattern of small farms was well established by the First World War when the rural proportion of New Zealand's population was at its maximum.

Wanganui developed around its small coastal port, just upstream from the mouth of the Wanganui River, as the outlet of its hilly hinterland. The valley is one of several steep drainage basins that descend from the central plateau to the Taranaki Bight. Rapid felling of the forests on the soft mudstones and sandstones of the inland Taranaki hill country left these areas subject to serious soil erosion. On many steep slopes secondary growth of the native bush has now helped to restore stability, and aerial topdressing has produced far more productive grazing country than seemed possible a generation ago.

All around Mt Egmont the green, lush landscape of Taranaki supports one of New Zealand's chief concentrations of dairy cows. Thorn hedges divide the small paddocks; bush-clad valleys intersect the farms where numerous fast-flowing streams radiate from Mt Egmont. Dairy factories were built from the 1880s every few kilometres and each served as the focus of a small rural township. Since 1960 there has been a strong trend towards amalgamation of the local dairy companies into larger, more efficient units.

Today new elements have appeared—gas found at Kapuni in the midst of the paddocks and piped to Auckland and Wellington markets. When Maui gas arrives on shore from the massive field discovered off the coast there will be scope for great new developments.

Between Egmont and Ruapehu lies a tangled mass of part-forested ranges. Roads follow most of the valleys to reach remote hill sheep stations, where output has been boosted since the 1950s by technological advances involving the use of landrovers and aircraft.

In the central North Island around Waiouru are found the North Island's largest expanses of tussock. This area is the main training ground for the New Zealand armed forces and the Desert Road leads directly north from Waiouru towards Taupo and Hamilton across open landscape on a pumice plateau at an elevation of more than 1000 metres. The plateau, or 'desert', is little dissected by the headwaters that develop such deep ravines nearer the coast.

Napier began as a port town on a rocky bluff. In 1931 one of New Zealand's most spectacular earthquakes raised the coast some three metres to produce dry land. Where previously lagoons had existed, suburbs and a factory estate now spread across the new land.

Less than twenty kilometres to the south of Napier, Hastings is virtually a twin town. It is surrounded by the fine, silty Heretaunga lowland where the first major soil survey to be undertaken in this country was carried out in the mid-1930s. Subsequently, scientific skills and vigorous management have combined to give this small lowland unrivalled productivity in fruit and vegetables.

The east coast has a number of striking headlands. Cape Kidnappers is famed for its gannet colony and is the first of a succession of rocky bluffs that extends south to Cook Strait. Roads and close settlements follow the broad inland valley south of Hastings through Dannevirke to Masterton in the Wairarapa. No continuous lowland adjoins the east coast. This broad inland valley is bounded by pronounced fault lines that are perhaps most clearly seen at the foot of the Rimutakas in the south and again beside the Hutt Valley, extending straight through Wellington to be clearly recognised again beyond Cook Strait in the Wairau Valley. These fault scarps offer vivid reminders of New Zealand's recent and continuing geological changes.

At Tomoana, rich Hawke's Bay farmland extends from the site of an Agricultural and Pastoral Society Show, an annual event in most rural districts to display new farming methods, products and a way of life.

NELSON, MARLBOROUGH

South of Tasman Bay to Kaikoura successive ranges and intervening fault-line valleys reach the coast, vividly indicating that the mountain axis of the Southern Alps and the alpine fault bounding it to the west have here fanned out into a series of well-marked structural units.

The Seaward Kaikoura Range rises abruptly behind Kaikoura to almost 3000 metres, within a few kilometres of the sea. Inland, the trench of the Clarence River separates it from the Inland Kaikoura Range where Tapuaenuku exceeds 3000 metres. The Awatere River is then succeeded by the Raglan Range and the Wairau River, while the Richmond Range descends eastwards into the sea leaving only its crest lines above the waters of the Marlborough Sounds.

This series of near-parallel faults continues to the north of Cook Strait where there are alternating ranges and fault valleys in the Wellington area and the Wairarapa. Wellington's reputation as a windy city is the result of the funnelling effect of its situation between the two series of ranges.

To the north of the Buller River and west of Tasman Bay are irregular mountains with rivers flowing outward on all sides. This ancient geological block ranks with Fiordland as one of the oldest blocks in New Zealand. There is evidence on their margins of direct geological matching, but they are on opposite sides of the great Alpine Fault and today some 500 kilometres apart. The valleys of the Tasman block reveal numerous scars from recent major jolts of the Alpine Fault, with slips and ponding of small lakes.

The contrast in landscape from east to west across the northern South Island also reflects sharply different local climates. East of the main divide there are semi-arid conditions and the valleys of inland Marlborough are among New Zealand's driest pockets. There is heavy rainfall on all the western ranges beyond the Spenser Mountains, and forests of mixed bush extend almost to the crests of the ranges.

These physical differences have been reflected in settlement and land use. Several phases of New Zealand's critical early development of local resources took place in the Cook Strait area. Whaling was based on the Sounds and the first New Zealand Company settlements were at Wellington and Nelson. After their introduction to the Wairarapa and eastern Tararuas sheep were brought to the Wairau Plains in the late 1840s. The Marlborough valleys then served as the spring-board for building up the flocks of Canterbury and Otago in the next decade.

The tussock country of inland Marlborough proved unable to withstand the heavy grazing demands made towards the end of the nineteenth century. Perhaps the most extreme example of soil erosion in New Zealand developed on the Molesworth Station in the upper Awatere Valley, where finally the government was left to take over the derelict property in the 1930s. The past twenty-five years, however, have proved that with long-term plans and scientific management even the worst examples of deterioration can be remedied. Since the Second World War the Molesworth property has been rehabilitated and has been able to show an economic return on the whole re-development programme.

On the West Coast other resources were exploited. Gold miners in the 1860s provided the first wave of settlement. Coal mining followed on both flanks of the Paparoa Range and further north, from Westport along the coast and in the adjacent hills. Gold as a viable industry barely survives today, though one dredge still operates successfully. During the 1960s coal production also declined. As a result the West Coast ranks as a depressed region although recent government policy provides fresh impetus through regional development assistance.

The bush has been an important source of West Coast wealth for more than a century, having been exploited largely through numerous small sawmilling companies. In 1972 the New Zealand Forest Service announced plans for large scale sustained management of the beech forest, based on the middle Grey Valley, so introducing a new era in forest development under State management. Plans involve more than half a million acres of managed native beech forest, including an element of planting of exotic pines, during the next few decades.

Forestry has long been an important asset in Nelson also, where the Golden Downs pine plantations are yielding their harvest. The products are exported through Nelson.

The bays along the north coast, with their northerly aspect, high sunshine hours and facilities for yachting and water sports, have attracted resort development. From Collingwood to the Sounds, camping grounds, motels, and holiday homes have multiplied during the last two decades. The Abel Tasman National Park has preserved the attractions of the glorious coastline north of Riwaka, while the Nelson Lakes National Park, established around lakes Rotoiti and Rotoroa, offers ski-ing, boating, and tramping. Nelson City continues to grow with the expansion of its function both as a popular holiday resort and as a retirement centre.

Around Tasman Bay a number of mineral resources have been developed, though never on such a scale as that on the West Coast. In the Dun Mountain behind Nelson a remarkable range of minerals is found, though apparently not in economic quantities. Limestone products come from the Takaka hills and cement is produced and distributed from Golden Bay. In recent years uranium was discovered in the upper Buller valley and gas has been found in Cook Strait to the north of Golden Bay.

The closely settled parts of the northern South Island make up a very small proportion of the total area. The main concentration of people is found around Tasman Bay where fruit, tobacco and hop growing are distinctive features of the landscape, each product supplying New Zealand demands, with apples providing a significant export market.

In most years the highest record of sunshine in New Zealand is found in the lower Wairau plains round Blenheim. Irrigation on the limited available fertile area of the lower terraces encourages excellent crops of cereals, grass seed and lucerne, with grapes a recent addition.

Agriculture is also part of the West Coast economy. Despite the high rainfall, there is also a good sunshine record and in the Grey Valley and several smaller pockets to the south of Greymouth cattle and sheep are successfully raised.

Since the earliest days the critical barrier of Cook Strait has been an important feature of New Zealand life, in terms of communications, culture and politics. Some would add inter-island rivalry to the list. Today the Cook Strait road and rail ferries run between Picton and Wellington several times a day, providing a vital link for passengers and goods. Air freight is handled through Woodbourne near Blenheim and Rongotai in Wellington City, playing an increasingly important part in the handling of goods passing between the two islands. Submarine power cables have been laid across the Strait from Cloudy Bay to the Wellington area in order to convey South Island power to North Island markets.

Wellington City, the capital, with its wharves verging the deep water of a drowned depression, its commercial and political centre partly on reclaimed land, and its residential suburbs now mainly beyond the encircling Green Belt.

WESTLAND, CANTERBURY

This 'waist' of the South Island shows the most pronounced contrasts from east to west, from the largest plain in New Zealand to the highest mountains, from low to high rainfall, from a close network of communications to areas where few or no tracks exist, from intensively used agricultural land to areas where natural vegetation of tussock or bush is dominant.

The dissected hill country of volcanic Banks Peninsula with its drowned valleys is relatively sparsely populated, in sharp distinction to the neighbouring Canterbury plains. The earliest European settlement at Akaroa was made by the French in 1840, and indications of its French origin are consciously encouraged in the town. For many years significant as a dairying area, the Peninsula now runs livestock for lamb, wool and beef.

Host city for the 1974 Commonwealth Games, Christchurch is the South Island's largest city, second only to Auckland as a metropolitan centre. Founded in 1850 by the Anglican Canterbury Association, the city retains more than any other urban centre evidence of its English origins, with its Square dominated by the Cathedral, its tree-lined, gently flowing River Avon, and its attractive parks and gardens. Christchurch is also a major manufacturing centre, producing carpets, machinery, textiles, leather goods, fertiliser, clothing and footwear. A planned satellite city near Christchurch will further enhance the city's pre-eminence in the South Island.

The close network of straight roads on the map adequately reveals the extent of the Canterbury plains. The land rises imperceptibly inland to about 400 metres before merging into downlands and the foothills of the main mountain chain to the north and west. The agricultural landscape of the plains is interrupted by major rivers from the main divide, the Waimakariri, Rakaia and Rangitata, which have highly variable flows—and by lesser rivers from the foothills, such as the Ashley, Selwyn and Ashburton. The major rivers have broad beds with braided channels, which, though liable to flood, are occupied for much of the year by only a few small streams of water. The low rainfall experienced on the plains (often less than 750 mm), together with the porous nature of the soils, has made irrigation essential in many areas for farming to be carried on in any intensive form.

This is New Zealand's major grain-growing area, with fat-lamb raising the essential basis of the farm economy. Originally tussock-covered and first used for carrying sheep for wool production alone, the conversion of the natural grassland into pastures of English grasses with their higher carrying capacity began during the bonanza wheat-growing decade of the 1870s, but received its major boost with the introduction of refrigeration in 1882. This opened up a new market overseas for New Zealand meat. For almost a century 'Canterbury Lamb' has been regarded as among New Zealand's finest. Here and there more specialised farming is undertaken, as for example the recent expansion in the Timaru area of vegetable production for quick freezing.

In the higher country bordering the plains, settlement is sparse, and open dun-coloured tussock slopes replace paddocks of English grasses except in those parts of the valleys where the sheep are brought down to winter. Finding that burning the tussock each spring resulted in fresh growth which was more palatable to their flocks, early runholders used fire without realising that it was also causing permanent depletion of the vegetation cover. For almost a century from the 1860s rabbits caused further damage, with the result that on steeper, unstable slopes the ground became badly eroded. Today large areas of scree bear witness to man's misuse of the land, and only slowly are conservation practices repairing some of the damage.

The glacially excavated lakes of Tekapo, Pukaki, Ohau, Hawea and Wanaka all offer tourist attractions, as well as providing water storage for hydro-electric stations built on the lower reaches of the rivers which drain them. Twizel is a new town built in the Mackenzie Basin to service the upper Waitaki hydro-electric power stations, utilising the water resources from lakes Ohau, Tekapo and Pukaki.

The Southern Alps act as a major barrier, both physical and cultural, between the West Coast and Canterbury, with the one railway link containing steep grades and an eight kilometre tunnel at Otira limiting the amount of bulky goods that can be transported. The Arthur's Pass road, reaching more than 1000 metres above sea level, is used primarily by tourists, most commercial vehicles following the better Lewis Pass road to the north. To the south the Alps are traversed by the easier Haast Pass route, opened in 1966, and this provides a superb round trip for tourists, through Canterbury, Otago and the West Coast.

The Alps offer major attractions for tourists and winter sports enthusiasts from throughout New Zealand, as well as from overseas. Seventeen peaks exceed 3000 metres, with Mt Cook reaching 3764 metres. Glaciers, particularly at Mt Cook and on the western flanks, add to the interest of the area and on the West Coast are unique in that they terminate close to dense evergreen bush, although for several decades their terminal faces have been slowly retreating.

Confined between the Alps and the Tasman Sea, the West Coast lowlands are never more than fifty kilometres wide. Much of their area remains clothed in native vegetation, primarily rain forest. The coast offers no harbours except river mouths, and the only viable port, Greymouth, is often closed for short periods by inclement weather.

The West Coast owes its initial wave of settlement to the discovery of gold in 1864. Miners flocked here from the older fields of Otago as well as from elsewhere in New Zealand and from Australia. As the gold was worked out other extractive industries were developed, particularly the mining of coal and the cutting of timber. This reliance on natural resources brought population and wealth, but subsequently proved to be too narrow a base for economic stability. With the decline in reserves, coupled with a lessening of demand for the products, an outward movement of population became chronic as employment opportunities lessened for the Coast's young people. Agriculture has not hitherto been of great significance, hindered as it has been by poor soils (pakihi), a wet climate and poor transport. Emphasis is now being placed on scientifically based farming as offering the best prospects for the future. Manufacturing and forest management are also receiving close attention.

The West Coast has a life-style of its own, and the Coasters are renowned for their hospitality, for their rugged independence and for their awareness of their past. Whereas Canterbury had a strong English and Anglican past, the West Coast had a significant influx of Irish Roman Catholics, and even today this cultural heritage is but one further factor which is evident in the difference between east and west in this part of New Zealand.

The Avoca valley, 100 kilometres to the north-west of Christchurch, shows typical Canterbury high country, with the boulders of a braided river bounded by tussock grassland of the foothills of the Southern Alps.

SOUTHLAND, OTAGO

This widest part of the South Island illustrates New Zealand's characteristically broad range of physical landscapes and types of development within remarkably small distances.

In the west, Fiordland is remote, mountainous and still for the most part inaccessible and unpopulated; forest-clad fiords, with an annual rainfall of more than 6000 millimetres, line the coast. Less than 150 kilometres to the east, the valleys of Central Otago regularly record more than 2000 annual sunshine hours, receive a rainfall of less than 250 millimetres, and produce trees only where European man has planted them during the last 100 years.

The Southland plain presents a prosperous, pastoral landscape of intensive sheep and cattle farming. Stewart Island has a natural charm and sense of detachment from the pace of modern life, while Dunedin's urban area presents a metropolitan city landscape, with its business and manufacturing facilities, and its nationally important medical school within its University.

Each of these different environments has presented problems and sometimes major difficulties. Their challenge has been met since the earliest days of European settlement.

After James Cook had welcomed the shelter of Dusky Sound as a refuge from the storms of the ocean, and reported on the coastal resources of the south, sealers and whalers set up a series of stations on off-shore islands or in the lee of promontories around the coast, often in complete isolation and in the face of harsh living conditions. Modern fishermen continue to reap a profitable harvest from the sea, though on a different basis, despite difficult conditions, especially off Fiordland, where for almost half the days of each month it is too rough for them to take their boats to sea.

Dunedin was first selected for the Scottish Presbyterian Church settlement because of its safe anchorage, its timber resources and the potential of the district for farm settlement. Southland, on the other hand, was regarded initially as a bleak and swampy plain, scarcely conducive to human settlement. Gold miners, working in the valleys of the Clutha and its tributaries in Central Otago, had to contend with very severe winter conditions—the nearest approach to a continental climate that New Zealand can show. During the following years road and railway builders found southern New Zealand difficult country to work in, because of its ranges, gorges, lakes and swamps.

Each environment has, however, been developed to yield an economic output that supports a prosperous community.

Dunedin gained its impetus a century ago from the wealth of the Otago gold rush. Despite slow growth in recent decades it continues to act as a commercial and manufacturing centre, with some encouragement from the regional development policies of government.

Scenic beauty has become widely appreciated and, as a result, southern New Zealand's tourist industry has reached important national proportions. Scenic areas have been designated from the Otago Peninsula on the east coast to the largest of New Zealand's national parks—Fiordland—in the west. At all times of the year Central Otago's sunshine hours are high and its resort facilities for winter and summer sports are increasingly popular with New Zealanders and with international tourists.

Early explorers reported enthusiastically on the scenic splendour of lakes Wakatipu, Wanaka and Te Anau, and a century later Queenstown on Lake Wakatipu has emerged as the premier tourist centre of New Zealand. The southern lakes have established an international reputation for their great beauty.

Milford Sound has an outstanding tourist hotel, attracting visitors to see the grandeur of the fiord, approaching it through mountain valleys and through the Homer Tunnel beneath the main divide. The fiords also offer shelter to crayfish boats working a difficult but lucrative trade, principally for markets in the United States.

Southland's farming skills, supported by government land development programmes, have provided the basis for an expansion of sheep and cattle numbers every year since 1950. Farming continues to achieve more intensive levels on the plains, through drainage and scientific management policies. State subdivision of large sheep stations in northern Southland has been bringing in sown pastures on a large scale for farm settlement schemes, so that output has risen strikingly, and Invercargill has grown and prospered as the servicing centre for the region.

The south provides New Zealand's largest resource area of water power, in the Waitaki and Clutha rivers and the southern lakes. The Waitaki will be fully harnessed from the Mackenzie Basin to the sea during the next decade.

The Roxburgh power station was built on the middle Clutha in the early 1950s as the first of a proposed series of Clutha stations that are to follow the Waitaki schemes in a programme for the 1980s.

Lake Manapouri, linked with Lake Te Anau as a storage facility, is the largest single power station in the country, harnessed for the Bluff aluminium smelter where Australian bauxite is processed by New Zealand hydro power for the world market.

Widespread public concern during the 1960s over the fate of Lake Manapouri served to focus national attention on issues embracing overseas commercial interests and electricity priorities in relation to national parks policies. A long controversy led to the emergence of a strong and deeply rooted respect for environmental quality, both in the community and in government circles.

When gold sluicing declined towards the close of the nineteenth century, the need for irrigation for agricultural purposes enabled many of the water-races to continue in use. The valleys of Central Otago then became distinctive among all high country valleys of New Zealand for their comparatively close settlement and intensive fruit production. Apricots and peaches are the best-known products, though a variety of other fruits is also grown.

Alexandra has expanded as the focus for commerce, government services and many tourist attractions in Central Otago. Several irrigation storage dams were built during the depression years of the 1930s to augment available water supplies around Alexandra and Roxburgh. New policies are enabling further expansion of irrigation facilities to be achieved, in the lower Waitaki basin in particular.

The valleys of Central Otago are, however, far exceeded in area by the extensive stretches of hill country between them. These schist hills under tussock grass show greatly improved vegetation cover since the virtual elimination of rabbits in the 1950s. The hills serve as collecting grounds for water needed in increasing quantities for hydro-electricity production, town supplies, and irrigation. Although increased returns from stock on higher pastures have been a feature of recent years, the value of mountain tussock country for water catchment purposes is now perhaps equally as important as its potential for increased stock carrying capacity.

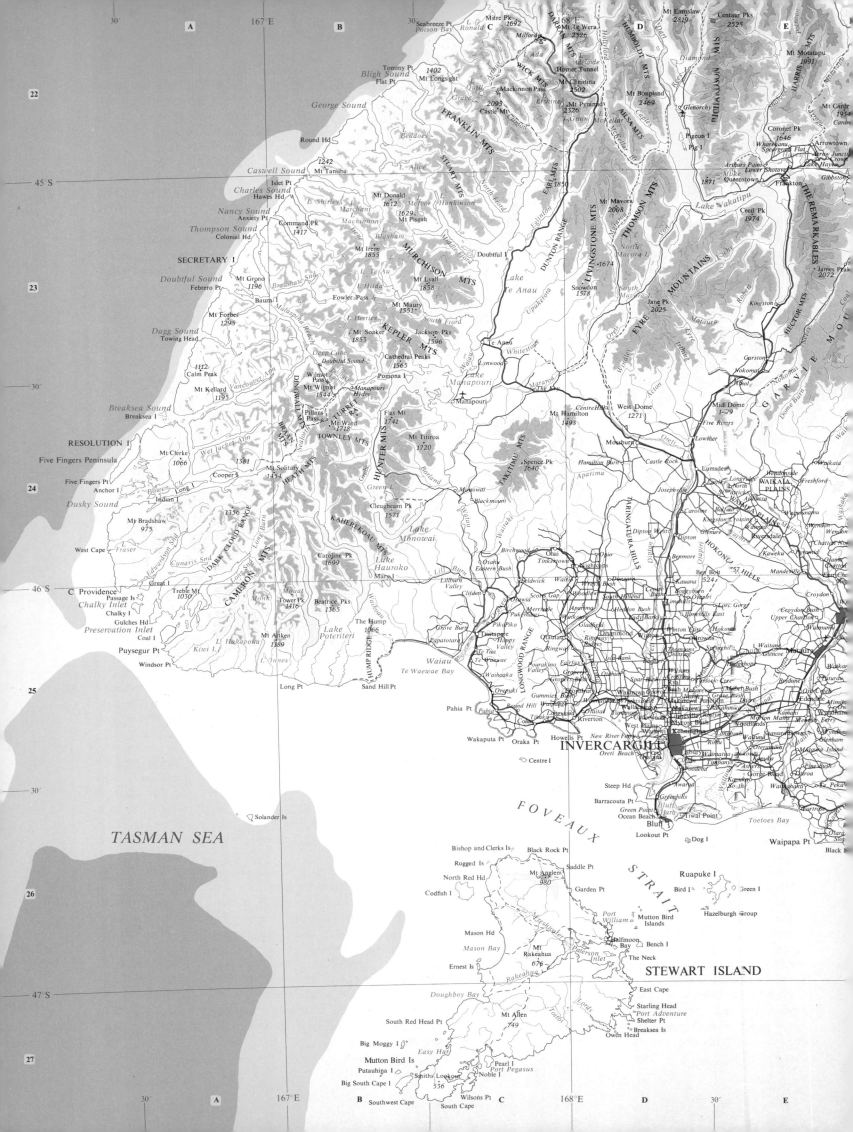

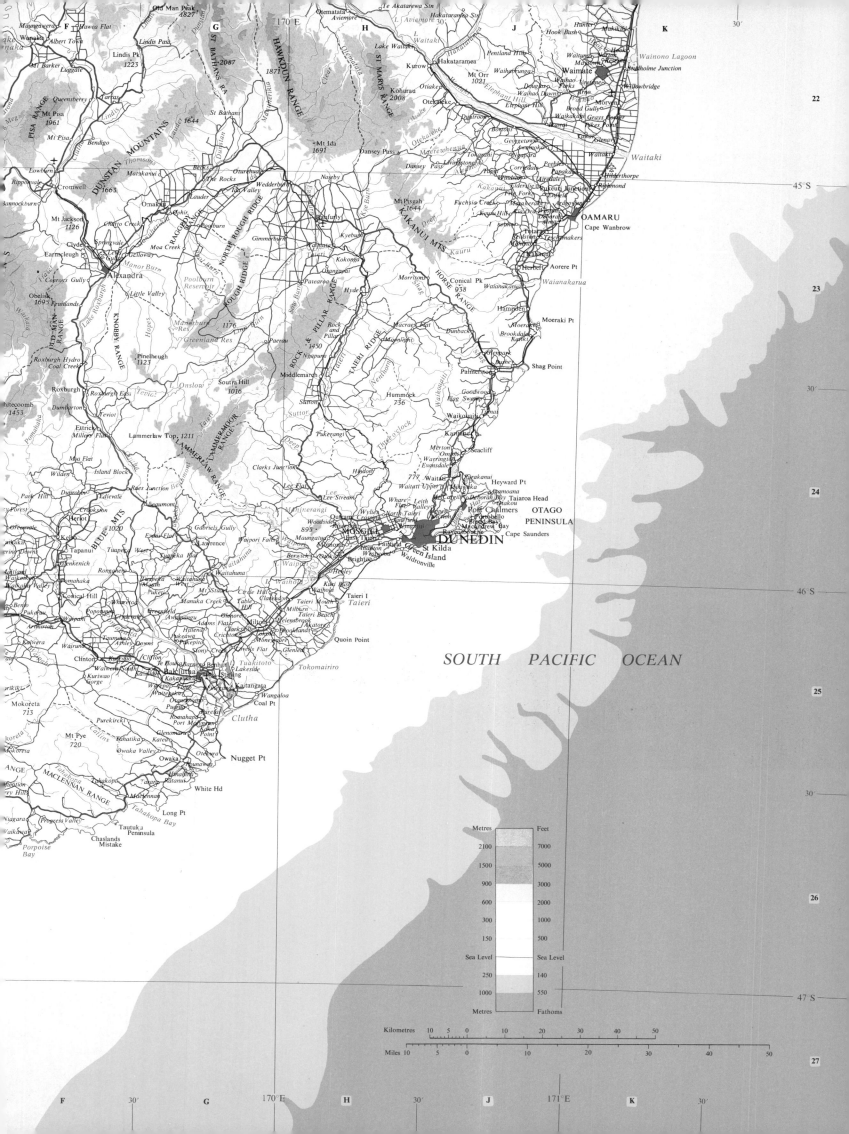

The Eglinton valley, broadly glaciated and now under beech forest, lies between the Earl and Livingstone mountains. It is part of Fiordland National Park and provides the land route between Lake Te Anau and Milford Sound.

URBAN AREAS

Auckland	pages 30–31
Christchurch	page 32
Dunedin	page 33
Wellington & Hutt	pages 34–35
Tauranga, Wanganui, Whangarei	page 36
New Plymouth, Hamilton, Palmerston North, Masterton	page 37
Napier & Hastings, Gisborne, Rotorua	page 38
Nelson, Ashburton, Oamaru, Blenheim	page 39
Greymouth, Timaru, Invercargill & Bluff	page 40

REFERENCE

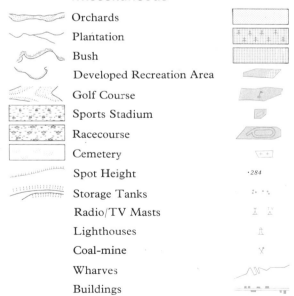

Communications

Railway	
Railway Station	
Motorway	
State Highway	
Main Road	
Other Roads and Streets	
Track	
Aerodrome	
Ferry Route	

Populated Areas

Large Towns	MOSGIEL
Boroughs	*Hornby*
Suburbs	*Burnside*
Towns or Localities	*Kaikoura*
Main Commercial Areas	
Built-up Areas	

Hydrography

Main River	
Other watercourses	
Rocky Coastline	
Sandy Coastline	
Tidal Flats	
Swamp	
Mangrove Swamp	
Dunes	
Cliffs or Escarpment	
Stopbanks	

Miscellaneous

Orchards	
Plantation	
Bush	
Developed Recreation Area	
Golf Course	
Sports Stadium	
Racecourse	
Cemetery	
Spot Height	·284
Storage Tanks	
Radio/TV Masts	
Lighthouses	
Coal-mine	
Wharves	
Buildings	

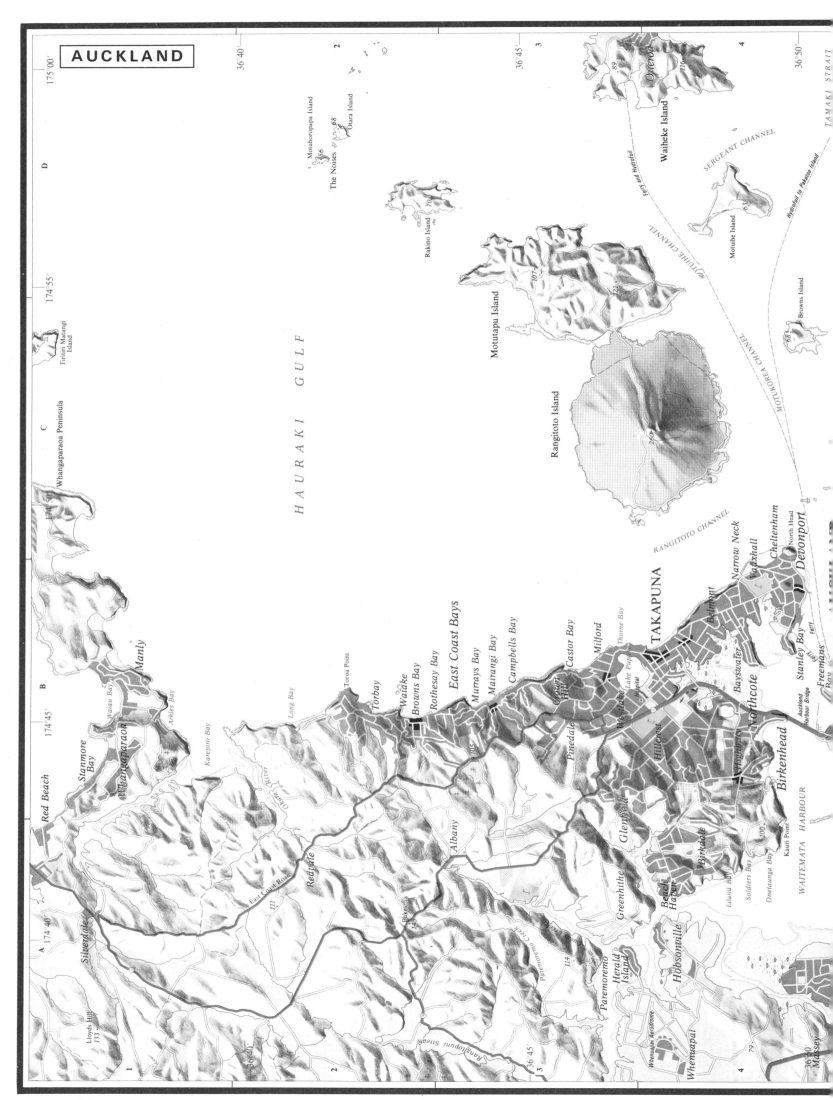

AUCKLAND

175°00'

36°40'

174°55'

174°50'

174°45'

174°40'

36°45'

36°50'

36°50'

TAMAKI STRAIT

Oneroa

89

116

Waiheke Island

SERGEANT CHANNEL

ferry and Hydrofoil

Hydrofoil to Pakatoa Island

Motuihe Island

63

MOTUIHE CHANNEL

MOTUKOREA CHANNEL

Browns Island

68

The Noises

Motuhoropapa Island

56

Otara Island

68

Rakino Island

70

107

121

Motutapu Island

Rangitoto Island

260

Tiritiri Matangi Island

Whangaparaoa Peninsula

HAURAKI GULF

RANGITOTO CHANNEL

North Head

Cheltenham

Devonport

Vauxhall

Narrow Neck

Stanley Bay

Belmont

Freemans Bay

Bayswater

Northcote

TAKAPUNA

Thorne Bay

Milford

Castor Bay

Crown Hill

Westlake

Lake Pupuke

Hospital

Hauraki

Campbells Bay

Mairangi Bay

Murrays Bay

Hillcrest

Auckland Harbour Bridge

Birkenhead

East Coast Bays

Rothesay Bay

Browns Bay

Waiake

Torbay

Toroa Point

Highbury

Kauri Point

WAITEMATA HARBOUR

Birkdale

Glenfield

Beach Haven

Pinedale

105

Long Bay

Karepiro Bay

Greenhithe

Soldiers Bay

Onetaunga Bay

Herald Island

Paremoremo

Hobsonville

Whenuapai

79

Whenuapai Aerodrome

Lucas Creek

Albany

Okura River

East Coast Road

Redvale

111

Pibberton

115

114

Paremoremo Creek

Rangitopuni Stream

36°40'

36°45'

36°50'

MASSEY

Silverdale

Lloyds Hill

133

Red Beach

Stanmore Bay

Manly

Whangaparaoa

Waiau Bay

Arkles Bay

A

B

C

D

1

2

3

4

30

Scale 1 : 125 000

Elevations in Metres

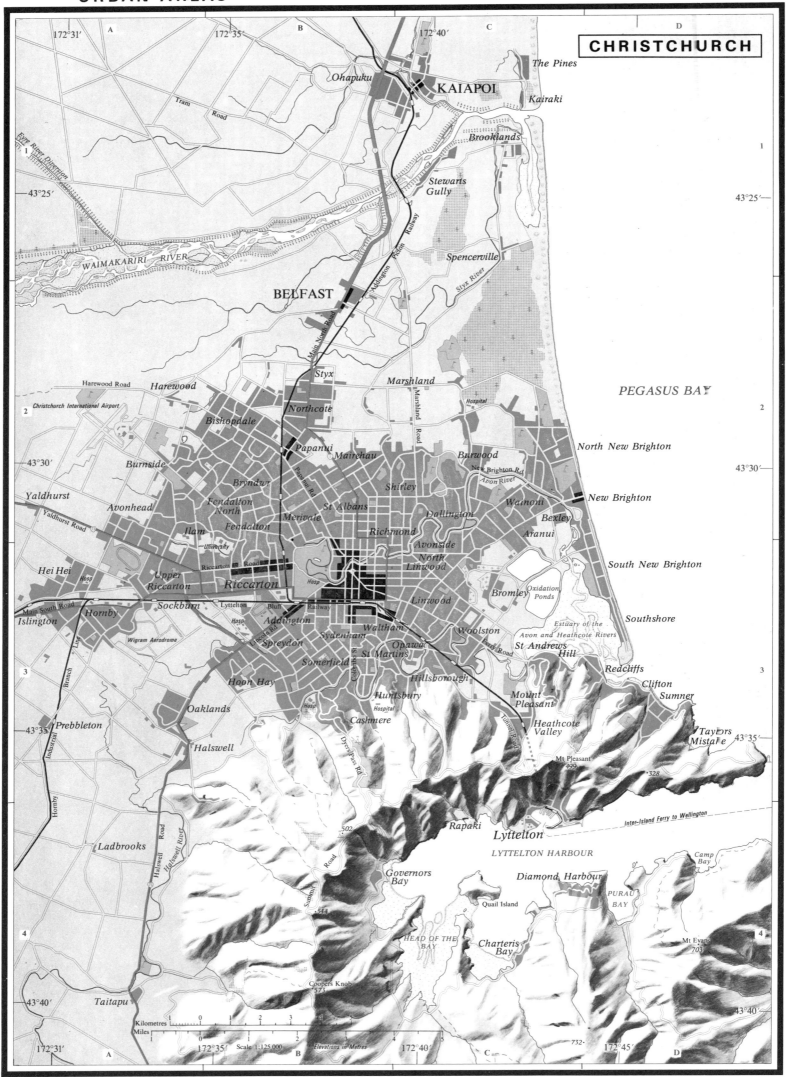

CHRISTCHURCH

172°31'   172°35   172°40'

The Pines

Ohapuku   KAIAPOI   Kairaki

Brooklands

Stewarts Gully

43°25'

Spencerville

WAIMAKARIRI RIVER

BELFAST

PEGASUS BAY

Styx   Marshland

Harewood Road   Harewood   Hospital

Christchurch International Airport   Northcote   2

Bishopdale   Papanui   Mairehau   Burwood   North New Brighton

Burnside   North New Brighton Rd   New Brighton   43°30'

Bryndwr   Shirley   Avon River

Yaldhurst   Fendalton North   St Albans   Dallington   Wainoni   New Brighton

Avonhead   Merivale   Bexley

Yaldhurst Road   Ilam   Fendalton   Richmond   Aranui   South New Brighton

University   Avonside

Hei Hei   Hosp   Upper Riccarton   Riccarton Road   North Linwood

Riccarton   Hosp   Bromley   Oxidation Ponds   Southshore

Sockburn   Lyttelton   Railway   Linwood   Estuary of the Avon and Heathcote Rivers

Islington   Hosp   Bluff   Railway   Addington   Waltham   Woolston   St Andrews Hill

Main South Road   Hornby   Hosp   Lincoln Rd   Sydenham   Opawa   Redcliffs

Wigram Aerodrome   Spreydon   St Martins   Hillsborough   Clifton   Sumner

Hoon Hay   Somerfield   Mount Pleasant

Oaklands   Huntsbury   Heathcote Valley   Taylors Mistake   43°35'

Prebbleton   Cashmere   Mt Pleasant 499   328

Halswell

Rapaki   Inter-Island Ferry to Wellington

502   Lyttelton

Ladbrooks   LYTTELTON HARBOUR

Governors Bay   Diamond Harbour   Camp Bay

544   PURAU BAY

Quail Island   HEAD OF THE BAY   Charteris Bay   Mt Evans 703

Taitapu   Coopers Knob 573   732

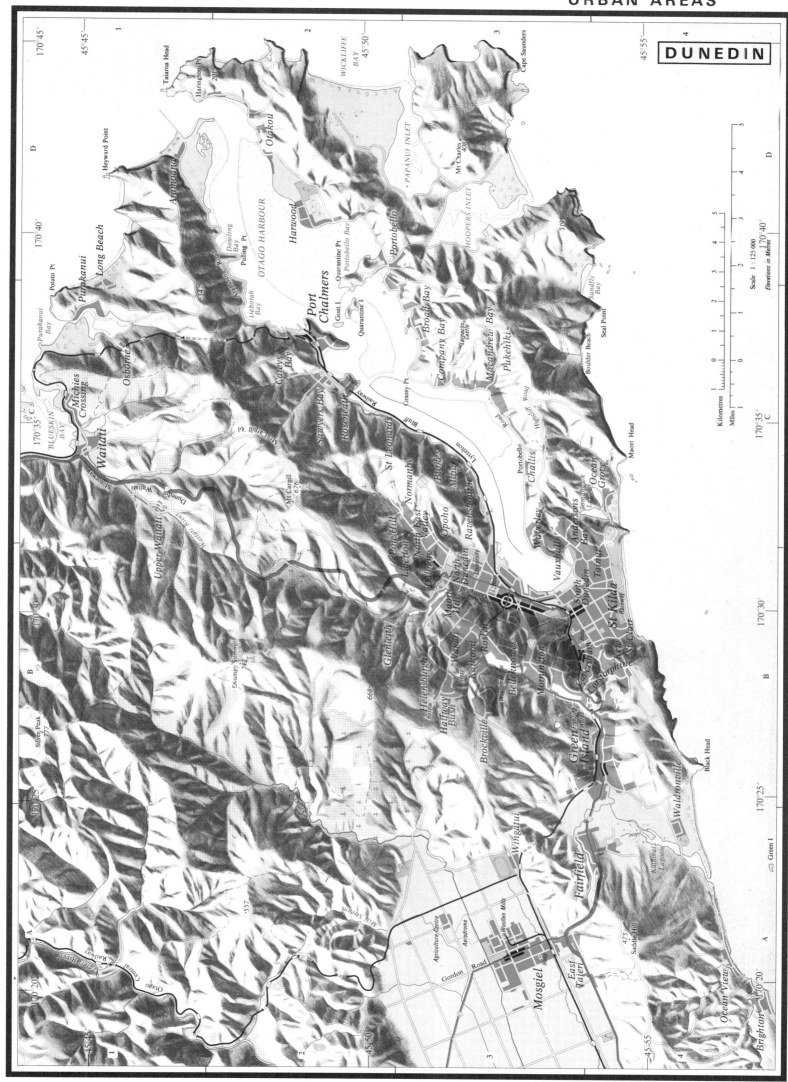

DUNEDIN

Scale 1 : 125 000

Elevations in Metres

WELLINGTON AND HUTT

Scale 1:152 000

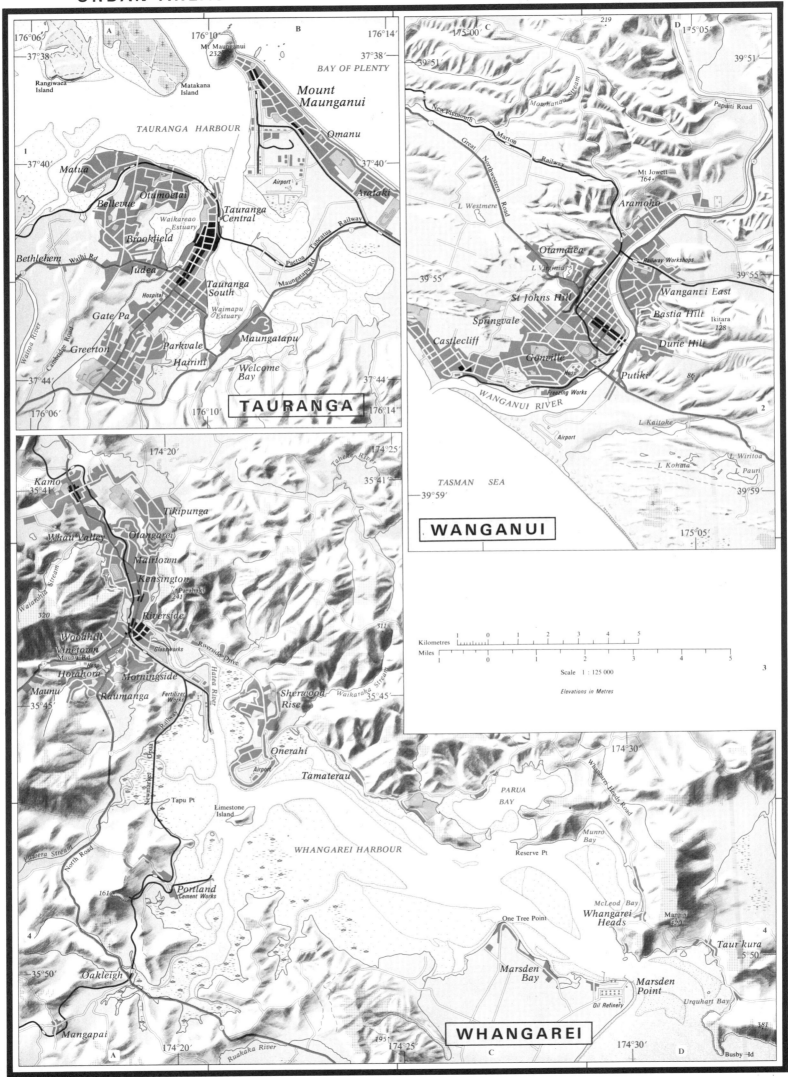

TAURANGA

WANGANUI

WHANGAREI

Kilometres | Miles

Scale 1 : 125 000

Elevations in Metres

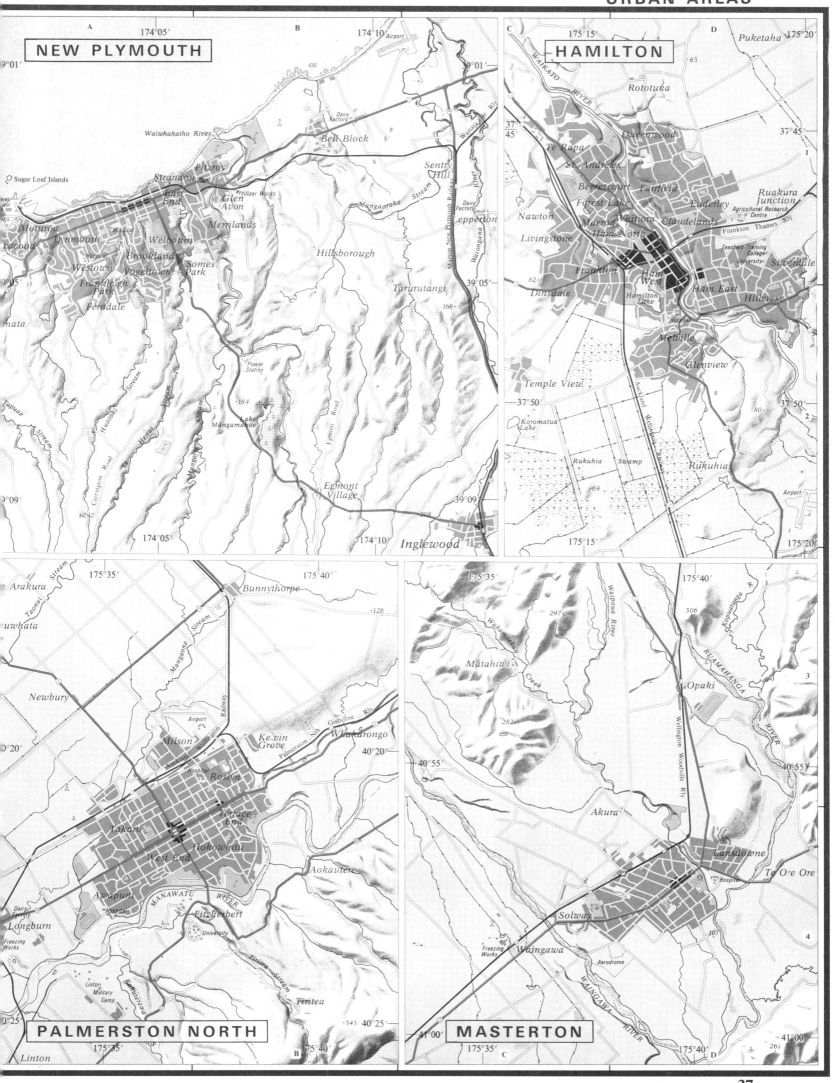

NEW PLYMOUTH

PALMERSTON NORTH

HAMILTON

MASTERTON

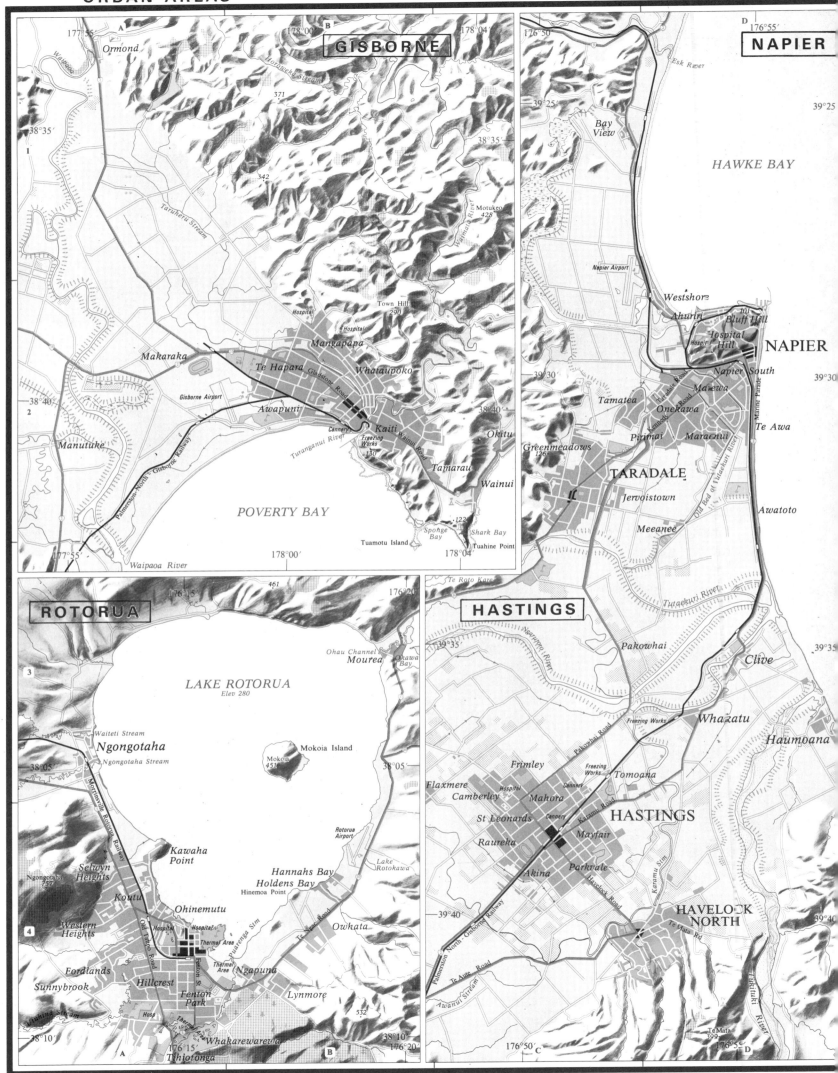

GISBORNE

Ormond

Horoiweka Stream

371

342

Taruheru Stream

Town Hill
290

Hospital

Motukeo
428

Waimata River

Hospital

Mangapapa

Makaraka

Te Hapara

Whataupoko

Gladstone Road

Gisborne Airport

Awapuni

Manutuke

Turanganui River

Cannery

Kaiti

Wainui Road

Freezing
Works
130

Okitu

Tamarau

Wainui

Palmerston-North - Gisborne Railway

POVERTY BAY

Sponge
Bay

122

Shark Bay

Tuamotu Island

Tuahine Point

Waipaoa River

177°55′   178°00′   178°04′

38°35′
38°40′

NAPIER

176°55′

Esk River

Bay
View

HAWKE BAY

Napier Airport

Westshore

Ahuriri

101
Bluff Hill

Hospt

Hospital
Hill

NAPIER

Napier South

Kennedy Road

Marewa

Tamatea

Onekawa

Te Awa

Taradale Road

Greenmeadows
1265

Pirimai

Maraenui

TARADALE

Jervoistown

Old Bed of Tutaekuri River

Meeanee

Awatoto

39°25′
39°30′

ROTORUA

461

176°15′   176°20′

Ohau Channel

Mourea

Okawa
Bay

LAKE ROTORUA
Elev 280

Mokoia Island

Waiteti Stream

Ngongotaha

Ngongotaha Stream

Mokoia
451

Morrinsville - Rotorua Railway

Ngongotaha
757

Selwyn
Heights

Kawaha
Point

Hannahs Bay
Holdens Bay
Hinemoa Point

Lake
Rotokawa

Rotorua
Airport

Koutu

Ohinemutu

Owhata

Western
Heights

Hospital

Hospital

Thermal
Area

Te Ngae Road

Puarenga Stm

Fordlands

Sunnybrook

Old Taupo Road

Hillcrest

Fenton St

Hosp

Fenton
Park

Thermal
Area

Ngapuna

Lynmore

Utuhina Stream

Thermal Area

Whakarewarewa

Tihiofonga

38°05′
38°10′

176°15′   176°20′

HASTINGS

Te Roto Kare

Tutaekuri River

Pakowhai

Ngaruroro River

Clive

Freezing Works

Whakatu

Pakowhai Road

Haumoana

Frimley

Flaxmere

Camberley

Freezing
Works

Hospital

Cannery

Mahora

Tomoana

St Leonards

Cannery

HASTINGS

Raureka

Mayfair

Karamu Road

Akina

Parkvale

Havelock Road

Karamu Stm

**HAVELOCK
NORTH**

Palmerston North - Gisborne Railway

Te Aute Road

Awanui Stream

Te Mata Rd

Te Mata
399

Tukituki River

39°35′
39°40′

176°50′   176°55′

38

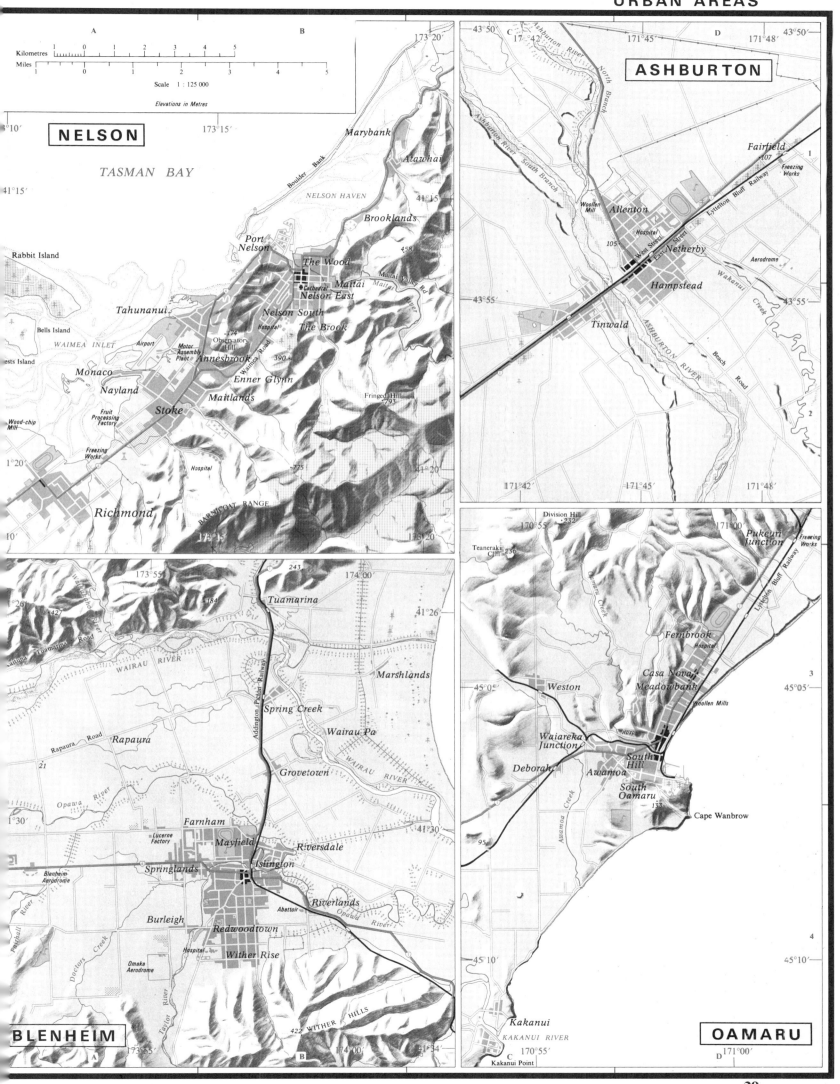

NELSON

TASMAN BAY

Kilometres
Miles
Scale 1 : 125 000
Elevations in Metres

A   B

173°20'

Marybank
Atawhai

NELSON HAVEN

41°15'

Brooklands

Rabbit Island

Port
Nelson

458

The Wood

Maitai

Tahunanui

Cathedral
Nelson East

Maitai Valley Rd

Nelson South
The Brook

WAIMEA INLET

Bells Island

Hospital

Airport
Motor
Assembly
Plant

-174
Observatory
Hill

Maitlands Road

390

ests Island

Wood-chip
Mill

Monaco

Nayland

Annesbrook

Enner Glynn

Fringed Hill
-793

Fruit
Processing
Factory

Maitlands

Stoke

Freezing
Works

1°20'

Hospital

-775

41°20'

Richmond

BARNICOAT RANGE

10'

173°15'

173°20'

ASHBURTON

C   17°42   171°45'   D   43°50'

43°50'

Ashburton River
North Branch

Ashburton River South Branch

Fairfield
107

Freezing
Works

1

Woollen
Mill

Allenton

Lyttelton Bluff Railway

Hospital
105

West Street

East Street

Netherby

Aerodrome

43°55'

43°55'

Hampstead

Wakanui
Creek

Tinwald

ASHBURTON RIVER

Beach
Road

2

171°42'   171°45'   171°48'

173°55'

243

174°00'

27

184

Tuamarina

41°26'

1°26'

427

Waitohi Road

Tuamarina Road

Marshlands

WAIRAU RIVER

Addington Picton Railway

Spring Creek

Wairau Pa

Rapaura Road

Rapaura

WAIRAU RIVER

21

Grovetown

Opawa River

Farnham

1°30'

Lucerne
Factory

Mayfield

Riversdale

41°30'

Springlands

Islington

Opaula River

Blenheim
Aerodrome

Burleigh

Abattoir

Riverlands

Redwoodtown

Doctors Creek

Hospital

Wither Rise

Omaka
Aerodrome

Taylor River

WITHER HILLS

422

BLENHEIM

A   173°55'   174°00'   41°34'

Division Hill
-232

170°55'

171°00'

Pukeuri
Junction

Freezing
Works

Teanerake
Cliff -236

Oamaru Creek

Lyttelton Bluff Railway

Fernbrook

Hospital

3

45°05'

Weston

Casa Nova
Meadowbank

45°05'

Woollen Mills

Waiareka
Junction

Hosp

Deborah

Awamoa

South
Hill

Awamoa Creek

South
Oamaru

-133

Cape Wanbrow

95

45°10'

45°10'

Kakanui

KAKANUI RIVER

OAMARU

Kakanui Point

C   170°55'   D   171°00'

4

39

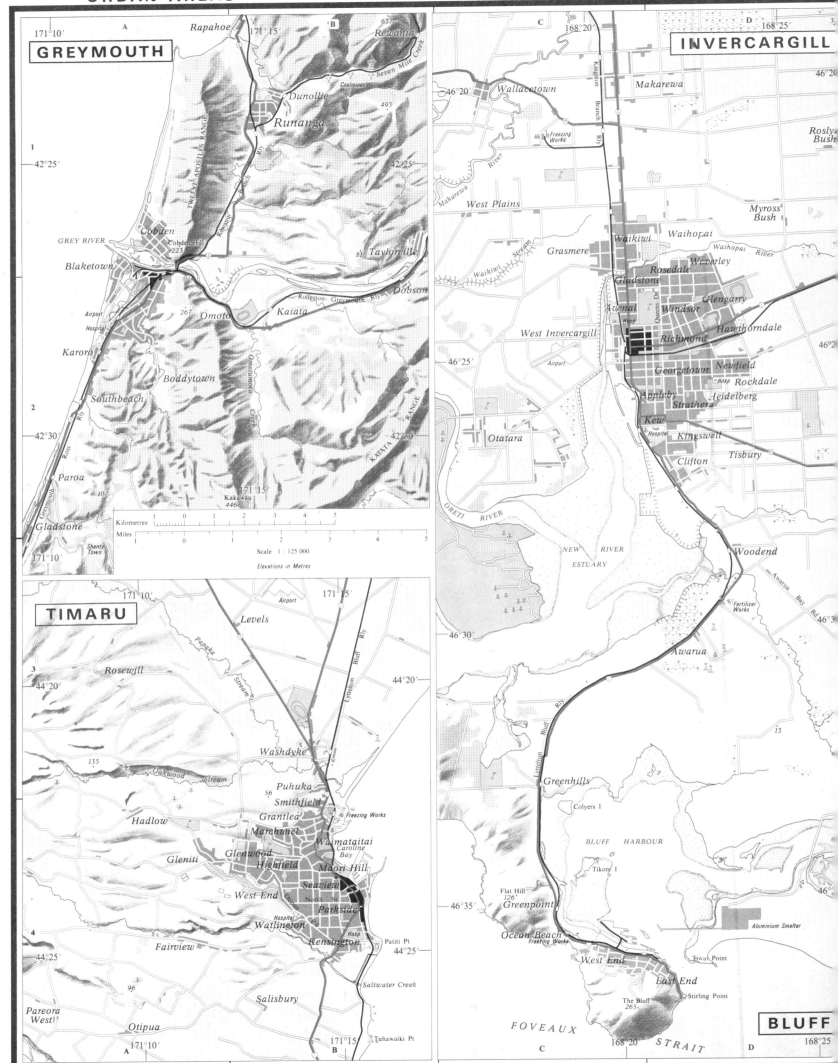

GREYMOUTH

Rapahoe
171°15'
Rewanui
637
Seven Mile Creek
Coalmines
Dunollie
493
Runanga
171°10'
A
B
42°25'
42°25'
81
Taylorville
TWELVE APOSTLES RANGE
GREY RIVER
Cobden
Cobden Hill
223
Blaketown
Rolleston
Greymouth
Dobson
Rly
267
Omoto
Kaiata
Airport
Hospital
Karoro
Omotumotu Creek
Boddytown
Southbeach
42°30'
42°30'
Ross Rly
Greymouth
KATATA RANGE
Paroa
107
171°15'
Kakawau
446
Gladstone
Shanty Town

Kilometres 1 0 1 2 3 4 5
Miles 1 0 1 2 3 4 5
Scale 1 : 125 000
Elevations in Metres

TIMARU

171°10'
Airport
171°15'
Levels
Rosewill
Papaka Stream
Lyttelton Bluff Rly
3
44°20'
44°20'
135
Washdyke
Oakwood Stream
Puhuka
56
Smithfield
Freezing Works
Hadlow
Grantlea
Marchwiel
Waimataitai
Caroline Bay
Gleniti
Glenwood
Highfield
Maori Hill
West End
Seaview
Oreti
North St
Parkside
Hospital
Watlington
Hosp
Kensington
Patiti Pt
4
Fairview
44°25'
44°25'
96
Saltwater Creek
Pareora West
Salisbury
Otipua
171°10'
171°15'
Tuhawaiki Pt
A
B

INVERCARGILL

168°20'
168°25'
Kingston Branch Rly
Makarewa
46°20'
46°20'
Wallacetown
Rosly Bush
Freezing Works
River
Makarewa River
West Plains
Myross Bush
Waikiwi
Waihopai
C
D
Waikiwi Stream
Grasmere
Waihopai River
Waverley
Rosedale
Gladstone
Glengarry
Arterial
Windsor
Hosp
Queens Dr
Hawthorndale
West Invercargill
Richmond
46°2
46°25'
Airport
Georgetown
Newfield
Hosp
Rockdale
Appleby
Heidelberg
Otatara
Strathern
Kew
Hospital
Kingswell
Clifton
Tisbury
ORETI RIVER
NEW RIVER
ESTUARY
Woodend
46°30'
Awarua Bay Rd
46°3
Fertilizer Works
Awarua
13
Lyttelton Bluff Rly
Greenhills
Colyers I
BLUFF HARBOUR
Tikore I
46°35'
Flat Hill
126
Greenpoint
Ewan Point
Ocean Beach
Freezing Works
West End
Stirling Point
East End
The Bluff
265
Aluminium Smelter
FOVEAUX
STRAIT
168°20'
168°25'
C
D

BLUFF

Great circle azimuths (or bearings) and distances from Wellington to all parts of the World.

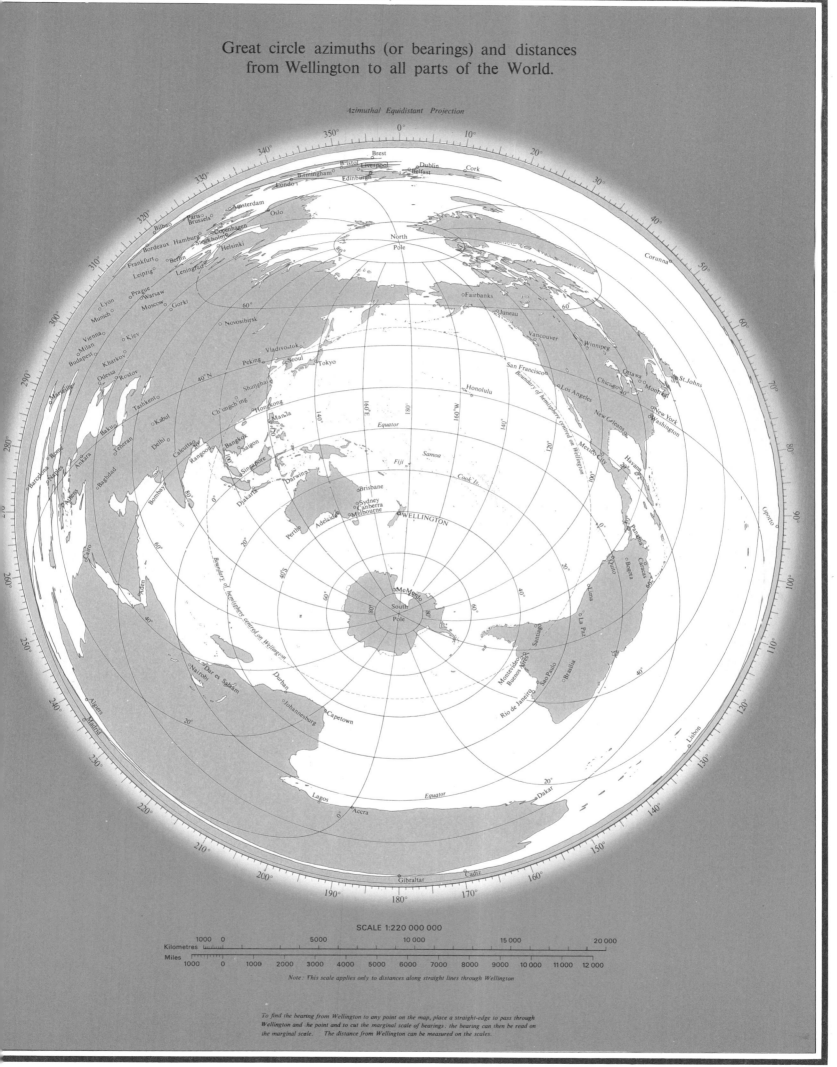

Azimuthal Equidistant Projection

SCALE 1:220 000 000

Note: This scale applies only to distances along straight lines through Wellington

To find the bearing from Wellington to any point on the map, place a straight-edge to pass through Wellington and the point and to cut the marginal scale of bearings: the bearing can then be read on the marginal scale. The distance from Wellington can be measured on the scales.

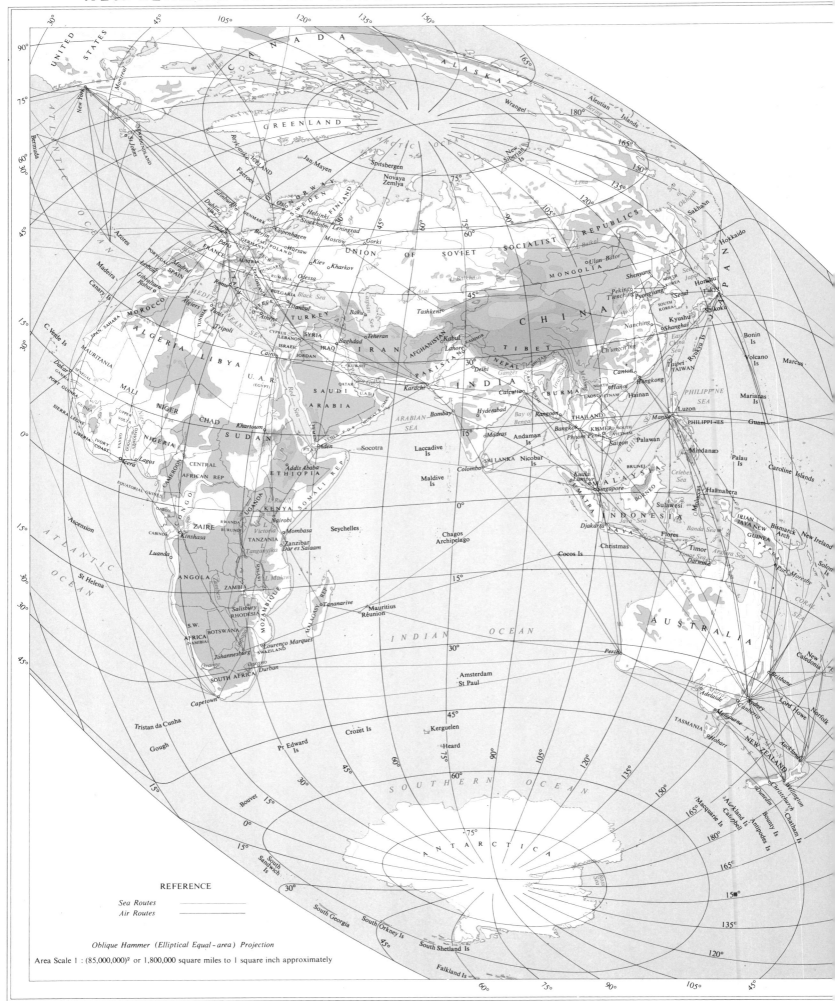

REFERENCE

Sea Routes ——————
Air Routes ——————

Oblique Hammer (Elliptical Equal-area) Projection

Area Scale 1 : (85,000,000)² or 1,800,000 square miles to 1 square inch approximately

NEW ZEALAND IN THE WORLD

F. L. W. Wood

The New Zealand community has been moulded by the cultural traditions imported by immigrants and by the pressures on her peoples of their physical environment. Of those pressures the most persistent has been that of isolation: the vast distances separating New Zealand from the outside world, and the geographical barriers to internal travel which for many years divided the young colony into a series of isolated settlements, only loosely linked together. Accordingly, the propensity of small groups of people both to cling to their past and to develop their own habits of thought and conduct has been a major factor in New Zealand history.

There is a difference here between the main waves of immigrants. The Maori, who were left in undisturbed possession until the late eighteenth century, were cut off from their island kinsmen for centuries and only in the post-second-world-war world has a new wave of immigration from the Pacific islands added to the native-born Polynesian community. The pakeha on the other hand always kept lively connections with their traditional homelands, both by personal travel and by techniques of culture contact unavailable to the pre-European Maori. With them accordingly the tension between nostalgia for the old and the impulse to build anew was often acute.

When European trade and Christian missions broke into the Polynesian world a situation was created similar to that experienced in previous contacts between Europeans and native peoples, and yet significantly different. The differences arose both from the nature of the Maori community and from recent developments in England.

During their centuries of isolation the Maori had developed an uncommonly tough, resilient and stable society. They lacked, it is true, some of the early achievements of European technology: the wheel, for example, the plough, and the use of metals, and of clay for pottery; but they had successfully adapted their Polynesian inheritance to the New Zealand environment. Much was, from the European viewpoint, barbarous, but the Maori had, as compared with most 'native' peoples, the wit to recognise the superiority of their invader's technology, the ability to adapt and use it, and the strength to resist wholesale subjugation. Moreover, this strength was not only that of military prowess; it concerned also their own ethos. When the white man's world failed them, they retained the power to discriminate, to reject (sometimes wildly), or to forge lively combinations of the old and the new.

To confront this exceptionally intelligent and responsive native people were officials and settlers amongst whom the cruder motives for Imperial expansion were not lacking, but who were deeply influenced by new currents of British thought. Their government was pushed into action by a combination of factors that ranged from international attitudes towards territorial acquisition in the Pacific, to the actions of traders and missionaries who were unofficially making New Zealand an economic extension of New South Wales. It wished to proceed not only legally but honourably. Hence the Treaty of Waitangi.

Humanitarianism spoke powerfully in contemporary England even within the Establishment, and radicalism was attacking the axiom of human inequality. There was enough of such thinking in the intellectual—and moral—atmosphere of Britain and early New Zealand to give the Maori people a status unusual for a colonial society. Blunders and disasters lay ahead—years of warfare, bitterness and devastation—inflicting fewer casualties perhaps than epidemic disease and the musket wars that preceded the pacification of the tribes and their conversion to Christianity, but preparing the way for such consequences of colonisation as land confiscation, wholesale land-purchase and European political domination. For decades there were indications that the Maori people might, after all, not survive. Nevertheless, on the pakeha side the element of idealism and the obligations of the Treaty of Waitangi were never quite lost; the broad tradition of British humanitarianism helped to preserve it, and Maori competence in peace and war commanded respect. Moreover there were Maori leaders who never admitted defeat or the loss of cultural identity. The King and Kotahitanga movements thought in terms of local self-government and administration of remaining lands, and by the turn of the century the Young Maori Party was working for the advancement of its people in association with, and not separated from, the pakeha—but holding fast to Maoritanga.

New Zealand, therefore, was from the first in some sense a bi-racial society, in which the cultural traditions of two races played a part. There existed foundations on which the principle of racial equality could be built.

Admittedly, the framework was European, or, more precisely, British. Other immigrant groups—Scandinavians and Dalmatians, German, Dutch and Chinese prominent amongst them—made their individual contributions, but leadership was mainly in British hands, and British law and institutions, literature, and economics predominated. Leading colonists were men of education, many of them by English standards radical. Wider opportunities for land-owning and self-betterment ensured that the rigid English class structure should become eroded, that privileges, whether of wealth or status, should be challenged, that governors and governments should behave in a way that would have been unbelievably liberal in England. The trappings of British middle-class culture remained, but a rough and ready egalitarianism became characteristic of colonial life, and pressed hard on government policy-making. The poor man, as everywhere, often suffered bitterly, but had his say and his opportunities to an extent unknown in the older world.

In short, in early New Zealand the strength of the Maori people, aided by the humanitarian views of many pakeha, gave a lead towards healthy race relations, and the tinge of radicalism, imported but flourishing in the colonial atmosphere, gave a hint of welfare politics. Thus very tentatively appeared tendencies which were to be consolidated in the developing community. They represented a modification of the continuing, broad, dominant stream of British cultural influences; and they influenced New Zealand's social and economic policies, its attitude towards its Pacific neighbourhood, and its policies in international affairs.

Before New Zealand could have policies worth analysing, it needed a viable economic base: this was provided by the exploitation of natural resources, and in particular by wool, by gold, by the technology which made possible major exports of frozen meat and dairy produce, and more recently by forest products and manufacturing. It also needed more people: they came, principally from Britain and Australia, partly through government aid, and partly through the prospects offered to enterprising men to improve their lot. And it needed some sense of cohesion, some framework of institutions and sentiment to knit together its isolated settlements. The geographical obstacles to cohesion were gradually removed by roads and railways, by coastal steamers and aeroplanes.

The political framework matured with the transition from Crown colony rule to an elaborate system of self-government by provincial councils topped by the General Assembly, and ultimately with the abolition of the provinces and a central government consequently reigning supreme. Finally, a sense of New Zealand nationality slowly emerged from the confusion of crude colonial self-assertion jostling with an uncritical reverence for the 'Mother Country'.

This evolution by no means extinguished New Zealand's historic regional differences; in the 1970s the palpable differences between the main centres are a lively inheritance from the past, and they have been accentuated, not created, by such modern trends as the drift of population from the South Island to the North, and the concentration of the newer industries round the burgeoning metropolis of Auckland. The central government, however powerful it may be legally, must take careful account of a multiplicity of local institutions and local loyalties. Nevertheless, since the 1870s that government has grown in strength, and has clearly had the main responsibility for dealing with national issues and policies of development, as for example: with race relations; with education; with external affairs, including trade and defence; with the great economic depressions of the 1880s and early 1930s, and the consequent clamour that something should be done to find a remedy for poverty and insecurity.

In dealing with such matters, New Zealand governments acted along the lines of British political tradition, modified by colonial and more particularly by New Zealand experience. All could agree that the economy's mainspring remained private enterprise; but the state recognised the need from time to time (and increasingly) to control it, to stimulate it, even to guide a change in its direction.

Faced by the poor man's suffering in depression times, the Liberal Government of the 1890s launched an ambitious programme of labour legislation, closer settlement and social welfare; and, aided by world economic recovery and the new technique of refrigeration, much was achieved. In particular, the development of a small-man's industry, dairy farming, helped the legislators to break up some big pastoral estates, and introduced a new and influential type of farmer to balance the sheep-men. Tiny old-age pensions marked a small step—bitterly resisted—towards social security, and the arbitration system aimed, with some success, to encourage the growth of trade unions and promote industrial harmony. Something was done, especially after the emergence of the Young Maori Party, to encourage Maori health work and to slow down the pace of Maori land purchase—though no government help was given to Maori land development before Sir Apirana Ngata became Minister of Native Affairs in 1928.

It was a commonsense, humanitarian kind of programme, backed not by social theory but by the scale of values which, despite local variety, had come to permeate the New Zealand community. And this same pattern was followed, more spectacularly, by New Zealand's first Labour Government, which won power in 1935, as the world was recovering from the great between-wars depression. Guaranteed prices offered the farmer—in particular the small dairy farmer—security from slumps originating overseas. Public works were vigorously reactivated and the unemployed absorbed in government-financed enterprise. Encouragement of local industry attempted to broaden the basis of New Zealand's economy—there was some little success here, soon to be eclipsed by achievements during World War II and the subsequent expansion. Above all, the great Social Security Act of 1938 codified and improved the various schemes of pensions and other social welfare benefits, available in principle to all needy New Zealanders, of whatever race or social class. Political leaders (mainly British by birth and New Zealand by adoption) recognised their responsibility to treat Maori and pakeha alike. The Maori, regarded in law as equal citizens, were encouraged to achieve equality of opportunity.

The broad programme, resisted like that of the 1890s by the still substantial conservative minority, was no innovation, but essentially the further development of accepted New Zealand welfare policies. Even before the great days of 'King Dick' Seddon, realistic conservatives like Harry Atkinson recognised the necessity, in a colonial community, for the state to lead effectively in this direction. The Labour Government's programme was not too different from the thinking of its immediate predecessors, and was promptly accepted, in practice if not in principle, by its opponents and successors as the necessary basis of social policy.

Wartime experience and post-war reconstruction increased the powers of the state, and strengthened the community's conviction that the state's duty was to promote social welfare. There remained rich and poor in New Zealand but by overseas standards the gap between them was small, living standards were high, and the element of averagely well-to-do was unusually numerous. Egalitarianism as a social ideal (applicable of course to both races), unformulated but pervasive, marked an increasing deviation within the British—and Polynesian—traditions. No politician, and few businessmen, would dare to challenge it. The worth of the individual man, his right and capacity to frame his own life, meeting practical problems with persistent ingenuity; his right to share fully in governing the community of which he was a member, and to expect that community's strength and wealth to help, if not to guide, his free self-development—such thoughts became the unwritten axioms of twentieth century New Zealand life.

When, in New Zealand's external affairs, it was necessary to frame policies, the same basic traditions prevailed. For very many years the British connection was the overriding, simplifying factor. It was a relationship between a tiny, vulnerable, but self-assertive community and an overwhelmingly strong Mother Country, sympathetic, but in economic matters businesslike. As the New Zealand economy developed, it was geared closely into the British system: Britain was the source of capital for development, a major supplier of manufactured goods, the principal (sometimes virtually the only) market for its produce. This was an arrangement of mutual advantage, but involving colonial dependence—New Zealand's economic growth was moulded as well as aided by Britain's need for cheap food and raw materials; a situation threatened but not seriously disturbed till Britain entered the European Economic Community.

So far as politics were concerned, New Zealanders were intensely loyal—always willing, it is said, to fight overseas in any British war—but they assumed that as of right they had the privileges of British subjects and that their community lived under the protection of British world power. They were conscious of New Zealand's insignificant size but not backward in pressing their views at Imperial

45

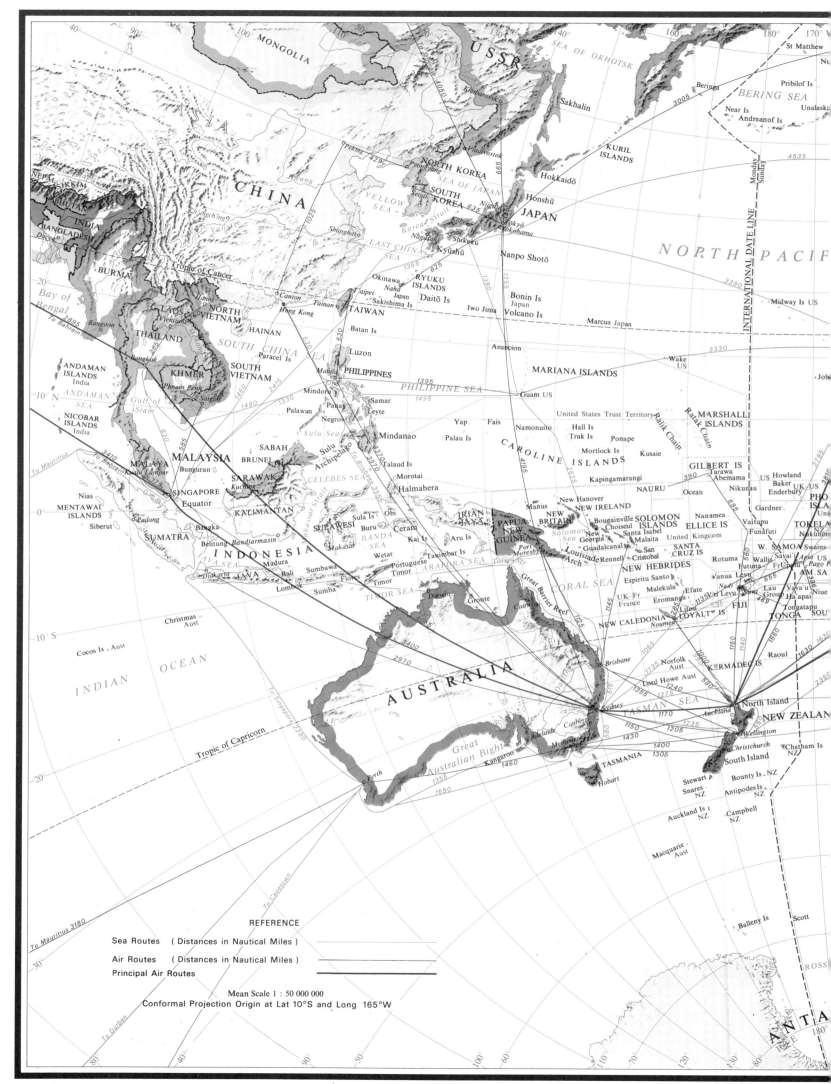

REFERENCE

Sea Routes   (Distances in Nautical Miles) _____

Air Routes   (Distances in Nautical Miles) _____
Principal Air Routes   _____

Mean Scale 1 : 50 000 000
Conformal Projection Origin at Lat 10°S and Long 165°W

46

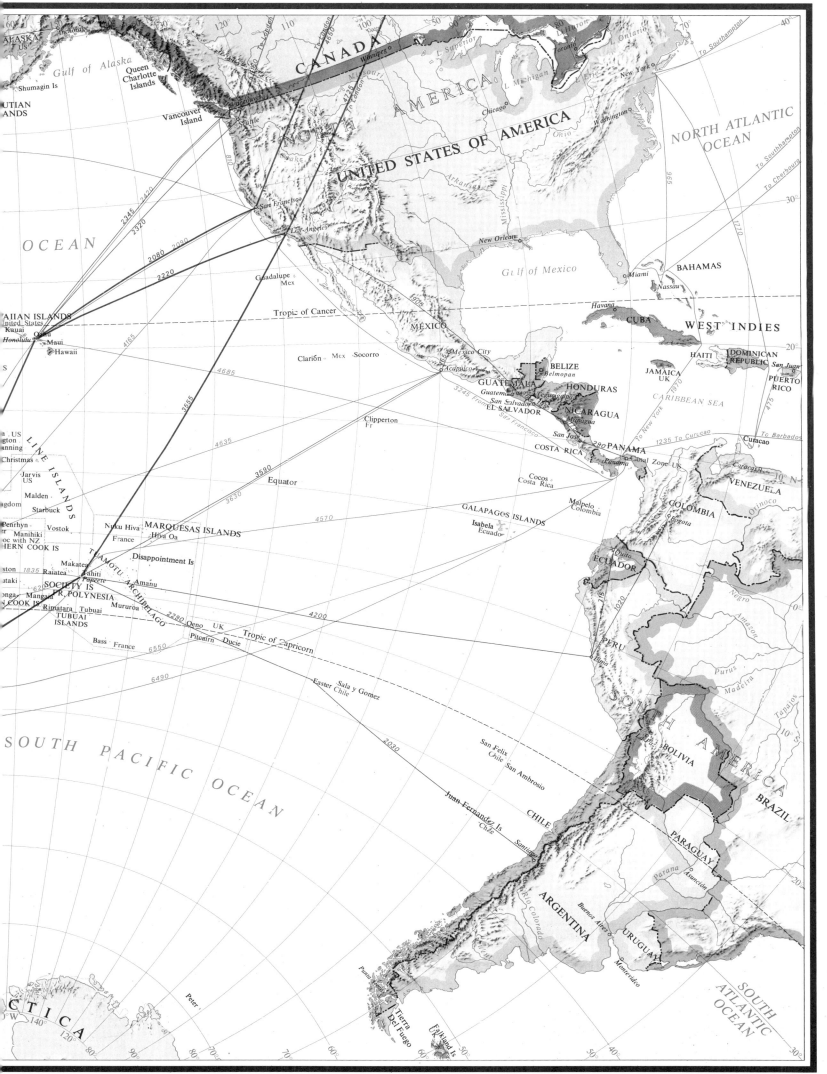

Headquarters in London when New Zealand's interests were involved—for instance in trade, or when threatened by foreign expansion in the Pacific. But for New Zealand, foreign policy consisted in putting discreet pressure on the United Kingdom. In the face of the outside world, New Zealand was slow to claim any place other than that of a small, co-operative element in the Empire. However, its slowly developing nationalism here followed the same path as that in fellow Dominions, towards an awareness of interests and attitudes for which each must be its own advocate, not only in Imperial consultations, but in the wider sphere of international affairs.

This realisation sharpened between the wars, especially after the election of the Labour Government at the end of 1935. It was a period of dissolving certainties. It was becoming apparent that the British market for New Zealand produce was not unlimited, and in international politics the rise of Fascism and Nazism cast a lurid shadow: would there after all be peace in our time, and would democracy and prosperity necessarily prevail? What stand would the great kindred power of the United States take should war break out in Europe—or in the Pacific; and in a crisis involving the Empire, what would be the attitude of Japan, our ally in 1914?

In face of these uncertainties, New Zealand's response was two-fold. Primarily, if it came to fighting it looked to Britain; in the end, British victory, wherever won, would be its only guarantee of survival, and its wartime effort must be applied to promote that victory. However, loyalty to Britain was co-existent with a long-term strategy with which British statesmen did not always agree, but which was in line with New Zealand's own domestic traditions, fortified in this instance by the internationalist principles of the New Zealand (and British) Labour movements. The impulse towards democracy and egalitarianism, sensitivity for the interests of the underdog, social welfare as a solvent for tensions, the enforcement of law (as based on moral principle) if conciliation should fail—in the thinking of a small power, such principles dictated support for the League of Nations, for the International Labour Office, and in particular for collective security. Here, even in the 1930s, there seemed to be marked out the most hopeful path by which the peace and progress achieved over the years in individual civilised countries might one day be attained in the community of nations.

For a foreign policy thus conceived, New Zealand could not rely on consistent support from any great power, not even Britain. On such issues as the Spanish Civil War, the reform of the League in 1936, and the Japanese attack on China, it stood on principle with increasing moral fervour, and if necessary alone, asserting its right of nationhood. When the Second World War actually broke out, New Zealand by its own deliberate decision joined Britain as promptly as in 1914: Britain was still the protector, age-old loyalties were overwhelmingly strong, and the final decision to resist Hitler was in line with principles steadfastly advocated. However, in the planning of the war effort New Zealand combined willing co-operation with its great military allies—Britain and (later on) America—with firm insistence on its own independence in policy decisions.

This independence was exercised both in the control of its armed forces and in dealing with the political problems of the wartime situation: relations with Russia for example, with America, with Japan—and more particularly the planning of the peacemaking and reconstruction. In all these matters its stance clearly expressed the basic political principles—and prudence—of its pre-war thinking. In the

long run a small power would be most secure in a prosperous, democratically inspired world community living under the rule of law, with adequate provision for peaceful change; but common sense insisted that in the real world there were limits to the influence a small country could exert, and good relations with a friendly great power (or powers) were indispensable.

In this matter World War II brought fundamental changes, and destroyed the simple pattern of external relations. In 1939 Britain was protector, and was overwhelmingly important to economic life: New Zealand was in a real sense a piece of Europe anchored in the Pacific. In 1941 Japanese victories demonstrated clearly that America alone could be the protector in the Pacific; thereafter, though still firmly tied to Britain, as a Pacific country it lived under the American umbrella. During the later years of the war, and in the post-war world, New Zealand's well-being has depended on relations with two great friends, instead of one. Nor is this all. The wartime experience and decline of British world power, followed by Britain's entry into the European Economic Community, forced New Zealand governments to recognise its status as a Pacific country, its close links with Australia, and the fact that its trading interests were world wide. In the new situation, problems, dangers, and opportunities which would one day have been perceived distantly, became matters for New Zealand's own policy-making and action.

Concern with the Pacific environment has a part—though a tenuous one—in New Zealand's historic tradition. From the earliest days there were persistent trading links with the Pacific islands, and mission fields overlapped. New Zealand politicians—Vogel, Grey, and Seddon vocally among them—thought it right and proper that the Pacific should become as far as possible a British lake, with New Zealand as a leader of Imperial activity. The Cook Islands and Niue were in fact placed under New Zealand's jurisdiction, and in 1914 Seddon's ambitions were partially fulfilled with the capture of German Samoa. The initially stormy tale of New Zealand's control of Western Samoa, first as a mandate and then as a trust territory, culminated in Samoan independence and a Treaty of Friendship in 1962, which illustrated a sincere attempt to apply in a pioneering way New Zealand's basic social policies, reinforced by belief in the principle of self-determination.

There has long been in New Zealand's attitude towards island peoples a growing element of concern for social welfare. This was expressed, for example, in her support for the South Pacific Commission—the most positive result of the controversial Canberra Pact of 1944 between Australia and New Zealand. In some contexts New Zealand regards itself—and is regarded by others—as the major Polynesian community; and indeed Auckland houses the world's largest group of Polynesian people.

Among island communities, New Zealand is the largest and most fully developed. Among the powers active in the Pacific area, including the Asian hinterland, it remains small and vulnerable, and faced with the necessity to frame its own policy in a complex and fluid situation. In its quest for security it can no longer count on immediate and effective protection from Britain, as in the old days, nor from the United States as during the war against Japan. However favourably disposed, Britain might not have the power, and the United States might remain uncommitted till the eleventh hour or beyond. Nor, after these changes, were these two great powers the only ones concerned. Japan, Russia and China all had active interests in the Pacific area; and the unsettled state of South-East Asia raised endless possibilities of rivalries and conflict.

Hopes for a world-wide system of security dissolved in the tensions of the 'cold war'. In this situation New Zealand's interests seemed increasingly identical with those of Australia; and its policy crystallised in the ANZUS Treaty, linking it in a defensive alliance with Australia and America. SEATO soon followed, involving commitments in mainland Asia, and the transference of New Zealand's obligations, in the event of a major war, from the Middle East to the Commonwealth countries in South-East Asia.

New Zealand continued to insist that the long-term solution to world insecurity lay in the strengthening of collective security and in the United Nations; but in the Pacific area regional arrangements, consistent with the Charter, were thought to be essential in the short run, even if the nature of the possible threats to security were not always clearly defined. In the years following World War II there was naturally uneasiness about the possible renewal of Japanese militarism; more recently fear of 'communism' played its part, as it did from time to time in domestic politics. In practice this line of thinking meant that, as throughout its history, New Zealand needed a powerful protector and was willing to pay the price in active and sometimes costly co-operation—witness Vietnam, and 'forward defence' in Malaysia.

This strategy was challenged by minority groups—by those who judged American policy wrong and asserted New Zealand's right to a different judgment, and by those who stressed alternative methods of dealing with the problems of Asia. Indeed, since 1950 the Colombo Plan combined New Zealand's general humanitarian impulses (economically controlled) with the calculation that the promotion of welfare in poor and developing communities was a better way of dealing with Asian communism than the mailed fist, even if the fist be American. Again economic considerations received a sharp stimulus through Britain's entry into the European Economic Community, by which New Zealand was faced with the necessity to diversify its interests and its markets. The closest relationships remained with Australia, but Asia (and to some extent the Pacific islands) seemed to offer opportunities for trade and for New Zealand's experts in developing countries, as well as for humanitarian activities such as Volunteer Service Abroad. In terms of hard, economic calculations, New Zealand's trade remains predominantly with Europe and North America, despite the development of mutually advantageous relations with Japan, more recently with Latin America, and, somewhat tentatively, with China.

Despite its European commitments, New Zealand is a Pacific country, a neighbour to South-East Asia. These are facts of which it is increasingly conscious, and which may well influence its community's development far more deeply than in the past.

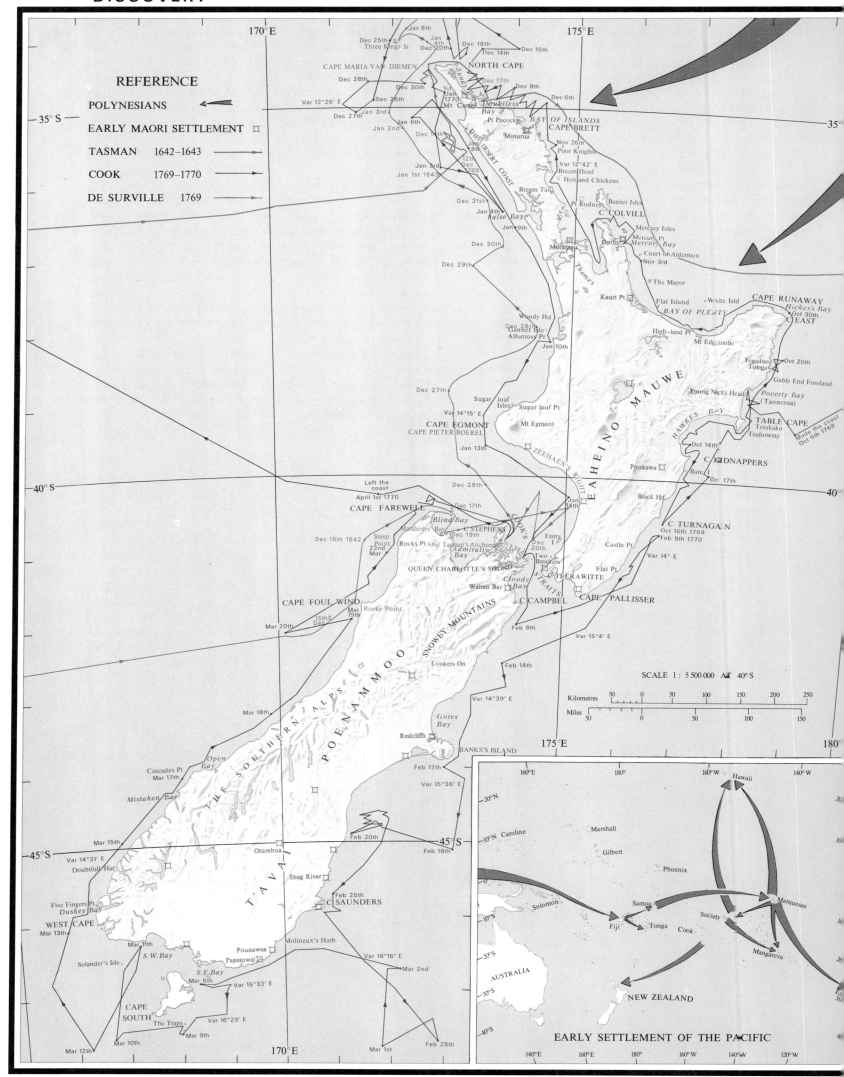

EARLY SETTLEMENT OF THE PACIFIC

DISCOVERY

Janet Davidson

New Zealand was first discovered and settled by Polynesians, ancestors of the present Maori people. More recently it was re-discovered and subsequently colonised by Europeans. The European discoveries are better known because they were described in accounts written at the time, whereas the earlier discovery and settlement must be reconstructed from the varied evidence of Maori tradition and the findings of pre-historians.

By the time the Polynesians reached New Zealand most other Pacific islands of any size were already occupied. New Guinea and Australia had been settled for many thousands of years. Slowly people spread eastwards across the Pacific, discovering and colonising smaller and more remote islands. The ancestors of the Polynesians reached Tonga about 1000 BC and gradually settled all the islands of Tonga and the Samoan group to the north-east. From these islands, and particularly from Samoa, some people moved eastwards, early in the first millenium AD, to the Society, Marquesas and Cook islands. Present evidence suggests that the remote Marquesas rather than the more central Society Islands may have been the first to be settled in this area. Once the eastern islands were occupied there was little or no contact between them and the Samoan and Tongan groups. The eastern groups share many features of language and culture which are not present in the west, and to this eastern group the language and culture of the New Zealand Maori belong.

Maori traditions attribute the discovery of New Zealand to several different persons. Some stories relate how Maui fished up the North Island from the depths of the sea, so that it became known as Te Ika a Maui. The exploits of Maui, however, are known throughout Polynesia and similar stories can be found in many other islands. The voyager whose name is best known to most New Zealanders is Kupe. It has been shown, however, that Kupe was known only to certain tribes. Others had different versions of the discovery and settlement of New Zealand. Moreover the Kupe traditions are now known to have been embroidered and enlarged in European times. The primacy of Kupe or of any other single Polynesian explorer cannot be proved.

In the case of European exploration, the discoverers were not the first settlers, although their reports ultimately led to the arrival of settlers. In the Polynesian case it is not certain whether the discoverer sailed away again, leaving New Zealand as empty of people as he found it, or whether the first discoverer became, perforce, the first settler. Archaeology has uncovered much information about the early settlers, but if there were in fact earlier visitors who returned whence they came, no trace of them has yet been found.

There has been much debate about the nature of Polynesian voyaging. Some theorists have held that the ancient Polynesians were capable of deliberately navigating from tropical East Polynesia to New Zealand and back. It has even been suggested that climatic conditions were more benevolent in the remote period when these voyages are believed to have taken place. Others have advanced the view that most or all long-distance voyages were inadvertently undertaken by fishermen or short-distance travellers blown off course. Between these extremes lies the possibility that the first settlers of New Zealand deliberately set out to find and colonise a new land, loading their canoe with all the provisions they might need for a long voyage and deliberately steering in a particular direction without then being able to return the way they had come, or to make known their discoveries or their fate to their kinsfolk at home. Certainly, New Zealand was settled by men and women who had dogs and food plants in their canoes—hardly the normal equipment of fishing parties.

The evidence of archaeology has shown that the first people to establish a continuing population in New Zealand were Polynesians who had come from the cluster of East Polynesian islands which includes the Society, Marquesas and Cook groups. Excavations in settlements strung out along the coast of New Zealand from Houhora in the north to Foveaux Strait in the south have revealed a great deal about the culture of these early New Zealanders. Many of their artifacts, including fish-hooks, ornaments and stone adzes, are very similar to those used at similar periods in the Society and Marquesas islands. Burial customs were also similar and one of the most impressive proofs of relationship between New Zealand and the Society Islands is the identical nature of a burial ground at the Wairau bar in Marlborough, and one on the island of Maupiti in the Society Islands. Another important early site, at Hane on Uahuka in the Marquesas, contained other artifacts similar to some found in early sites in New Zealand, but not yet known from the Society Islands. It is thus not possible to say with certainty from which islands the first New Zealanders came.

Theoretically, New Zealand need have been settled only once, by a single canoe containing both men and women. From these settlers the entire population could have arisen. But both the evidence of traditions and the extent of Polynesian dispersal to so many far-flung islands make it unlikely that only one group reached New Zealand. It is more probable that the country was settled by a number of separate groups arriving from various closely related islands. After a time the population would grow to a point where new arrivals would have to be very numerous or vastly better equipped to make any significant impact on the people already here. It should be noted that despite numerous 'migration' traditions there is at present no archaeological evidence to support the theory of a second and culturally distinct migration after the initial settlement.

Maori traditions describe the initial landing of most canoes somewhere between North Cape and East Cape. All early archaeological sites so far investigated have contained obsidian (volcanic glass) from Mayor Island, showing that the discovery of Mayor Island preceded the occupation of all these sites. The only early site yet found which contains an artifact probably brought from tropical Polynesia is at Tairua on the east coast of the Coromandel Peninsula. Here a pearl-shell lure shank was found in a deposit, radiocarbon dated to the eleventh century AD. Since pearl-shell does not occur in New Zealand, either the artifact itself or the shell from which it was made must have been brought from a tropical island. However, as other items in the site were of local manufacture, the lure shank may have been carried a long way around the New Zealand coast before being lost at Tairua. All that can be said at present is that there is a distinct possibility that the first landfall may have been somewhere in the Bay of Plenty.

By about the thirteenth century AD, on the basis of carbon dating, New Zealand had been thoroughly explored and the population was already sufficiently large to have left considerable evidence for archaeologists to study. At what date the first settlers arrived is unknown; it was probably as early as the tenth century AD but perhaps not much earlier. By the thirteenth century, however, the first era of discovery, exploration and settlement was over. Thereafter the inhabitants continued to increase and their culture gradually developed and changed, so that the relationship with the cultures of tropical East Polynesian islands, although still recognisable, grew more distant.

The first European explorer known to have visited New Zealand was Abel Janszoon Tasman, who sighted the west coast of the South Island on 13 December 1642. Tasman, an experienced seaman employed by the Dutch East India Company, was charged with opening up new trade avenues in the South Pacific. He commanded two small ships, the *Heemskerck* and the *Zeehaen*. With him as pilot-major was Frans Jacobszoon Visscher, one of the ablest Dutch pilots of the time. Tasman crossed the sea which now bears his name from Tasmania, which he had also discovered and which he named Van Diemen's Land. On sighting New Zealand he turned northwards up the coast and on 17 December rounded the point later named Cape Farewell. The coast here appeared more hospitable, signs of human habitation were seen, and on the evening of the following day the ships anchored. Trumpet blasts and shouts were exchanged between those on the ships and the occupants of a canoe which came out to them. On the following day, 19 December 1642, the first real encounter between Maori and European took place. A number of canoes approached, apparently with friendly intentions. The occupants of one, however, fell upon the *Zeehaen's* cockboat, killing four men. The Dutch in return fired on the canoes but without apparent effect. Tasman abandoned hope of obtaining water and supplies at this place, which he named Murderers' Bay. For several days the ships were held up by bad weather. Then they sailed northwards up the west coast of the North Island, charting parts of it. By 4 January 1643 they were off Cape Maria van Diemen which Tasman named. Only one other sight of the Maori was obtained—at the Three Kings Islands where men of apparently enormous stature were seen on the hilltops. Tasman tried twice to obtain water and supplies here but was frustrated on each occasion. On 6 January 1643 he sailed away to the north-east.

For more than a century after Tasman's discovery New Zealand remained unvisited by Europeans. The existence of a land of unknown extent, with war-like inhabitants, was placed on record. The name of New Zealand was given to it by the Dutch authorities in place of Tasman's name of Staten Land. It remained for the next explorer to define its extent and describe its inhabitants and resources in detail. In the interval Maori life continued unaffected by Tasman's fleeting visit. The inhabitants of Murderers' Bay themselves succumbed to hostile attacks and all memory of Tasman's appearance passed out of traditional memory.

On 6 October 1769 the *Endeavour,* commanded by James Cook under instructions from the British Admiralty, approached New Zealand from the east. Land was sighted by a boy, Nicholas Young. Cook had been instructed to observe the transit of Venus at Tahiti and then to explore the southern ocean. Among those who accompanied him were two Fellows of the Royal Society, Joseph Banks and Daniel Solander; an astronomer, Charles Green, and an artist, Sydney Parkinson.

In a little less than six months, Cook circumnavigated both islands of New Zealand, mapping 2400 miles of coastline with remarkable accuracy. His first landfall was in Poverty Bay. From here he sailed south for a short distance, then turned and sailed north up the east coast, pausing for several days at Tolaga Bay, Mercury Bay (where he observed the transit of Mercury) and the Bay of Islands. He rounded North Cape in December and sailed down the west coast without landing, resting for some time at Queen Charlotte Sound. Passing through Cook Strait in early February 1770 he completed the circumnavigation of the North Island by sailing up the Wairarapa coast to within sight of Cape Turnagain—the southernmost point reached in October of the previous year. He then proceeded to circumnavigate the South Island, sailing along the east coast and back up the west coast, mistaking Banks Peninsula for an island and Stewart Island for a peninsula. At the beginning of April 1770 he turned his back on Cape Farewell and set his course towards Australia.

At Mercury Bay and Queen Charlotte Sound, Cook formally took possession of the places and adjacent land in the name of King George III. He was the first European to take formal possession of any part of the country for a European sovereign; Tasman had made no such claim.

As soon as he approached the coast of the North Island, Cook became aware that it was inhabited. Canoes, hutments and people on the shore were easily visible. The first encounters between the British and the Maori were unhappy. On the first landing, one Maori was shot when his party attempted to capture a ship's boat. Later a group of Maori tried to snatch arms and other possessions and again one was killed. An unfortunate fracas took place the following day when several more Maori were killed. Three, however, were taken on board and befriended. Thereafter, Cook tried wherever possible to establish friendly relations with the people. Usually he was successful, although other incidents took place, such as that at Cape Kidnappers, where several Maori were killed or wounded when they attempted to capture a Tahitian boy from the *Endeavour*. Both Cook and those who accompanied him were able to make numerous observations on the appearance of the country and the manners and customs of its inhabitants. These descriptions are invaluable to students seeking to study New Zealand as it was after seven centuries or more of Polynesian occupation, but before the effects of the European discovery had been felt.

Cook returned on his second and third voyages, using Queen Charlotte Sound as a rendezvous and refreshing place on each occasion. His journals and those of his companions document some of the changes in Maori life at Queen Charlotte Sound during that period. Already other Europeans were visiting New Zealand. In December 1769 Cook narrowly missed meeting another European, the French adventurer, Jean de Surville, near North Cape. Before Cook returned in 1773 another French expedition, that of Marion du Fresne, had spent three months in the Bay of Islands, a visit which ended with the tragic deaths of du Fresne himself and other Frenchmen, and fierce reprisals by the French against the Bay of Islands Maori. But these events could add little to the story of discovery.

The journals of Cook and those who accompanied him did much to make New Zealand known to the European world. He found the country rich in resources and ideally suited for settlement. Soon it began to attract other European visitors, first explorers, then traders and eventually missionaries and settlers. Later explorers made notable contributions to knowledge of its geography and resources but the fundamental task of discovering and making known had been accomplished.

PATTERNS OF SETTLEMENT

Raewyn Dalziel

The settlement of New Zealand has been predominantly the work of two peoples—Polynesian and British. The Polynesians arrived more than a thousand years ago and held undisturbed tenancy of the country until the seventeenth century. British migration, following the discovery of the country by Cook, was slow at first but gathered momentum after 1840 and reached its greatest numbers in the 1870s. From that time the population has grown more by natural increase than by immigration.

One of the few statements that can be made with certainty about the first settlers of New Zealand is that they were Polynesian, and from eastern Polynesia. It seems likely that their homeland was the Society Islands and that they arrived in New Zealand some time before AD 1000 as the result of accidental voyages or of forced or voluntary exile following economic or political trouble at home. There may have been subsequent landfalls.

The story of Polynesian migration to New Zealand has been recounted in legends, speculated about by amateur enthusiasts, and is slowly being reconstructed by anthropologists, archaeologists, linguists and ethno-historians.

The legends that have passed into common usage provide a highly imaginative account of the first landfalls. Many of them tell of Kupe who, around AD 925, discovered New Zealand. Some of the Kupe legends report that he saw signs of settlement, others that there was no human habitation. They agree that Kupe sailed round the country and returned home with directions for a return voyage. These directions were remembered and used many years later by Toi, another Maori hero. Toi allegedly reached New Zealand about 1150 and found the country inhabited by a people known as the 'tangata whenua'. Their presence is unexplained. Some generations later the main group of Polynesian migrants reached New Zealand in a convoy of canoes known as the 'great fleet'. Each tribal group has its own ancestral canoe, the most famous being Aotea, Te Arawa, Horouta, Mataatua, Tainui, Takitimu and Tokomaru.

Whatever the explanation of arrival, archaeology has revealed a number of facts about early settlement. Polynesian sites dating to the eleventh and twelfth centuries have been discovered along the length of New Zealand, in sheltered harbours in the North Island and at river mouths and tidal estuaries in the South. These sites show that there were marked differences between the life styles of the early Polynesian settlers and those living in New Zealand at the time of European discovery. Initially, the settlers appear to have been a peaceful people, living in open villages and organising their economy around local food resources which then included the moa. By the eighteenth century, with the favoured locations not only occupied but often in dispute, warfare had become endemic, fortified villages or pa had increased greatly in number, and existence was finely balanced between the need to produce food and the obligation to fight.

European discovery of New Zealand in 1642 and then re-discovery in 1769 brought the first challenge to Polynesian possession. Even then European settlement lagged considerably behind discovery. In the late eighteenth and early nineteenth centuries there were sporadic visits from officials of the nearby British convict settlement of New South Wales, by trading vessels, whalers and sealers, but only the odd individual—an escaped convict or runaway sailor—and a few sealing gangs actually took up residence. The first important, permanent settlement did not occur until 1814 when the Church Missionary Society established a small mission station at the Bay of Islands. Forced to rely largely on the goodwill of the people they had been sent to civilise and convert, the early missionaries led a frustrating and disturbed existence. However, reinforced from time to time by members of their own and competing denominations, they spread further inland and became firmly established in the North Island.

Missionary endeavour, combined with a never-ending search for new sources of trade goods and a growing population in New South Wales, brought New Zealand firmly within the European, and in particular the British, world view. The British population of New Zealand grew steadily. Whaling stations, financed and run by Sydney merchants, were dotted round the southern coast of the South Island; in Hokianga the great kauri trees attracted small settlements of sawyers; the Bay of Islands became a service centre for vessels trading, whaling and sealing in the South Pacific, and the mission stations grew. In 1826 the first British company with the aim of colonising New Zealand was founded and sent out two shiploads of would-be colonists. Only a few of these decided to brave the supposed hostility of the Maoris and most departed rapidly for Australia. The missionary Henry Williams, who attempted a head count in 1839, estimated that there were more than 1300 Europeans in the North Island. There were possibly 200 in the South Island at the same time.

The first large influx of European settlers took place in the 1840s consequent on the British decision to annex New Zealand. The settlement of this period, although of a diversified sort, is inextricably linked with Edward Gibbon Wakefield. Wakefield was an imaginative idealist, a superb but unscrupulous propagandist. Opposed to the 'shovelling out of paupers' that appeared to be the British solution to the problem of surplus population, Wakefield tried to bestow upon emigration some form of organisation. His aim was to administer emigration from Great Britain efficiently and humanely, and to transplant to the new lands of the South Pacific a 'vertical slice' of British society divorced from both the unlovely and divisive aspects of industrial Britain and the uncivilised, democratic aspects of the United States.

Wakefield wanted to establish a closely integrated, stratified agricultural society, in which the classes were kept in balance by a sufficiently high price for land. His ideas were adopted by four colonising companies—the New Zealand Company formed in 1839, its short-lived subsidiary the Plymouth Company, and the Otago and Canterbury Associations. These last two were backed respectively by the Free Church of Scotland and the Church of England. These four companies sent more than 15 000 persons to the six settlements of Wellington, Wanganui, Nelson, New Plymouth, Canterbury and Otago.

The 'vertical slice' theory did not work out in practice. It was difficult to persuade gentlemen with means to emigrate to New Zealand. Most of those who purchased land preferred to stay at home and allow their investment to appreciate. At Nelson three-quarters of those who bought land had no intention of emigrating. In Wellington, where more landowners did settle, a large number returned to Britain in the first decade. Only Canterbury managed to attract a fair share of landed gentry—almost a quarter of the early settlers there came out as cabin passengers. The

53

result was that although New Zealand received a cross section of British society it was not well balanced. The great majority were steerage passengers—artisans, farm workers, labourers and domestic servants. At first they found the life hard and suffered many disillusionments. Within a couple of decades, however, some had taken up small farms ringing the main settlements, others had travelled further afield to work on the large sheep runs while the majority settled to their various occupations in the developing towns.

All the Wakefield settlers were British except for two small German groups recruited by a Hamburg colonisation company. Most of the Germans were Lutherans, vine dressers and farm labourers from the Rhineland and Hanover and artisans from Bremen and Hamburg. They settled on farms in the Nelson area where they were in the forefront of experiments with new crops such as hops and tobacco. They remained culturally distinct and had their own churches and schools until the 1870s. A solid core of these families remains in Nelson and among those who spoke High German the language is still extant. They have produced several descendants who have gained professional distinction.

Organised settlement was only one way in which New Zealand was peopled in the forties and fifties. The capital, Auckland, grew up in a spontaneous, disorganised way. Once this area had been chosen by Governor Hobson as the site of government, it became the home of government officials, land speculators from the Bay of Islands and Australia, merchants, skilled and unskilled artisans, small farmers and aspiring but dissatisfied immigrants from the southern settlements. Other groups of people reached New Zealand independently. At Akaroa there was a small settlement of Frenchmen, sent out by a French trading company before New Zealand was formally taken by Great Britain. James MacAndrew, later a prominent Dunedin citizen and politician, brought a group of Free Church capitalists, closely connected by marriage, to Dunedin. The Parkhurst prison boys, ninety of whom were sent to Auckland, were one, not very welcome, example of Great Britain's attempts at rehabilitating juvenile offenders. Military settlement also took place. The 'fencibles', discharged soldiers of good character, were located in four villages around Auckland and were on call for military service when required. Group settlement was the case in Waipu where several parties of Scots finally made their home after a long trek from the Highlands via Nova Scotia and Australia. They formed a tight, Gaelic-speaking community. So close were their connections that a lack of surnames and a proliferation of children made it usual to identify people by their occupation—'Butcher McKays'; by their personal appearance—'Duncan Bar' (white Duncan); or by their place of residence—'Bridge McLeans'.

After the granting of the Constitution of 1852 the Provincial Councils took over the responsibility for settlement. Each province tackled this in its own way and according to its own needs, but the determining factor was usually the quantity of land at each council's disposal. In the South Island there was a good supply of such land, and consequently agricultural labourers were much in demand and eagerly recruited overseas. In the North Island, where land was more difficult to acquire, and where Maori and European were at war in the sixties, less attention was paid to settlement although even the northern provinces offered assisted passages to domestic servants and artisans. Auckland also had a scheme which offered forty-acre (16.2 ha) grants of land to emigrants who paid their own passages. The Bohemian settlers at Puhoi give an example of one group to take advantage of this. Persuaded to emigrate by Martin Krippner, who had visited New Zealand in 1859, they struggled for years on the infertile acres he had chosen and still exist as a community with its own religious and social character.

The Maori Wars had their offshoot in settlement. To defend the European towns and outlying farms from possible attack, the central government began a series of military settlements in 1863 which stretched from Raglan to Tauranga. Settlers were recruited from Australia and from other parts of New Zealand. They were required to enrol in the Auckland militia and received, in return, pay, rations and allowances and, eventually, a land grant according to their rank. The land needed back-breaking work before it could be brought into production and by 1867 most of the settlers had abandoned or sold their acres and moved to more congenial areas.

Settlement of this sort was small scale compared with what was going on in the South Island at the beginning of the sixties. In 1861 it was discovered that the river beds and valleys of Otago were rich in the greatest of all magnets—gold. The population of Otago at the beginning of the rushes was some 12 600—by September 1863 it was estimated at 60 000. From the gold fields of California and Victoria and from the rest of New Zealand, miners, storekeepers, clerks, publicans and campfollowers joined in the crowds flocking to Otago. In one month alone, March 1863, 14 000 people landed at Dunedin. Most of the newcomers were men, the ratio of women to men in the gold fields being 1:100 in 1861 and reaching only 18:100 in 1864. Most came from Australia and moved on from Otago when news of discoveries further north arrived. A large number however did stay and by the end of the decade Otago was the most populous and prosperous of all the provinces.

Westland also benefited from the discovery of gold. When payable gold was found there in 1854 thousands arrived in the previously unsettled territory, from Australia and Otago. The Australian element was dominant—the west coast could be reached more quickly from Sydney by boat than from Christchurch by land—and the isolation of the region meant that the gold fields style of life lingered on years after the gold ran out.

The dwindling of the gold supplies brought a new group of settlers—the Chinese. Chinese were rarely in the fore of the gold rushes. Instead they arrived late, to scour abandoned claims and worked-out tailings for remaining specks of gold dust. By 1867 there were more than 1100 Chinese in Otago. This led to some European hostility and to the restriction of the entry of further Chinese into the country by means of a poll tax imposed in 1881, but in 1971 there were 12 818 Chinese in New Zealand.

By the end of the sixties the gold, except for alluvial which needed heavy machinery to extract it, was almost worked out. The heady prosperity of the early years of the decade gave way to dull stagnation. In all the provinces, immigration and land development slowed almost to a stop. It needed government action to dispel the gloom. The central government, spurred on by Julius Vogel, responded in 1869 by investigating possible schemes of immigration and in 1870 it embarked on an ambitious programme of development through public works and settlement.

Under this impetus the New Zealand population almost doubled during the 1870s. More than 190 000 people immigrated to the country and of these more than half were assisted financially by the government. The remainder were attracted by extensive public works which provided many extra jobs and by the economic opportunities resulting from large-scale borrowing in both the public and private sectors of employment.

The assisted immigrants of the seventies in the main reinforced the existing ethnic and cultural patterns in New Zealand. An overwhelming majority came from England, Scotland and Ireland and were dispersed around the main areas of population. Otago and Canterbury took the largest numbers—29 000 and 27 000 respectively. With these immigrants, most of whom were agricultural labourers or, in the case of women, housewives or domestic servants, there were few problems of assimilation until decreased borrowing and falling overseas prices brought recession and unemployment.

Assisted immigration was not all 'more of the same'. In the early stages of the programme, when immigrants from Great Britain were difficult to recruit, the government made efforts to get people from other European countries, and attempts were made to settle people away from the main centres of population.

The two main foreign groups assisted to migrate came from Germany and Scandinavia. There were 3034 Germans, nearly 2000 Danes and a smaller number of Swedes and Norwegians. The policy with these settlers was to locate them together in small bush communities in the southern part of the North Island. Each village had a certain area of land set aside for churches, reserves, schools and town lots, with the rest divided into twenty-acre (8.1 ha) sections to be paid off over three years. During this time the settlers could work on road and railway construction for three or four days a week. Although the work was hard and progress slow, these immigrants persisted and turned the bush around Palmerston North, in the Wairarapa and Hawke's Bay, into profitable farms and prosperous small towns.

Smaller numbers of French and Italians were also assisted to migrate. They were not such a success. The Italians, many of whom were sent to the inhospitable Jackson Bay settlement, pined for a hotter climate and did not take kindly to the pioneering jobs the government expected them to accept. The French, too, wished to remain in the towns and were not content with the lot assigned to them. A group which migrated as mechanics converted itself into a ballet troupe, thus earning governmental, and critical, disapproval.

The special settlements of the seventies owed something to both government and private enterprise. The government sponsored settlements in Westland, Stewart Island and Nelson as well as in the Great Bush, between Maurice-ville and Norsewood. Only the latter were a real success. Probably the most successful private settlement was that at Katikati and Te Puke which George Veysey Stewart, a landowner from Northern Ireland, took the initiative in organising and where, at Katikati, he himself settled.

The peak year for immigration for the seventies, and indeed the year of the highest net migration New Zealand has ever experienced, was 1874. In that year, 43 965 immigrants arrived in the country. After this the numbers declined steadily, but in 1879 still reached 24 000. The eighties, a time of severe economic depression, saw a dramatic change. In the years of the 'exodus', 1886 to 1890, 8702 more people left New Zealand than arrived.

From the 1880s New Zealand's population has grown more as a result of natural increase than of immigration, and settlement patterns, with one or two notable exceptions, have largely been determined by internal migration. The opening up of North Island dairy lands in the late eighties and nineties was responsible for the growth of numerous

small towns as service centres and in turn these developments drew people northwards. The 1901 census showed that the North Island had finally overtaken the South in population. This trend has continued and accelerated until in 1971, 2 051 363 people lived in the North Island compared with 811 268 in the South.

One new ethnic group appeared in the late nineteenth century, that of the Dalmatian kauri gum diggers of North Auckland. The descendants of these people, together with more recent Yugoslav immigrants, have remained in the same area and have been largely responsible for the burgeoning vineyards and the improvement in the quality of home-produced wines.

Immigration in the twentieth century has fluctuated, mainly in response to economic conditions. The government sponsored limited immigration from 1906 until 1927 when this was suspended. In 1947, in an attempt to offset labour shortages, assisted passages were re-introduced for people in certain occupational and age groups. Until 1950 this scheme was confined to Great Britain; after 1950 it was extended to other countries and taken advantage of extensively by the Dutch. Between March 1946 and March 1974, 7738 Dutch people came to New Zealand on assisted passages, the Netherlands government itself having given assistance since 1963. Many have settled on farms, especially in the Taranaki region, where they have turned marginal holdings into profitable ones, and others have contributed significantly in metropolitan areas in both the professions and trades and by opening numerous small delicatessen shops.

In addition, after World War II the government, in co-operation with the International Refugee Organisation, arranged for more than 4500 European refugees to come to New Zealand. The largest numbers came from Rumania and Poland. All these Europeans brought special skills and cultural accomplishments that have done much to open the minds of New Zealanders to a richer way of living.

Most of the recent migrants have settled in the large towns. Urban areas have increased most rapidly in size. Whereas in 1874 two-thirds of the population lived in settlements of less than 500, in 1966 more than seventy-seven per cent lived in communities with populations greater than 1000. The trend has been for the large towns to grow larger and for people to move north in search of employment and greater opportunities.

A notable development in recent years has been the arrival and settlement of large numbers of Polynesians. Before the 1950s, apart from the Maori people, there were few Polynesians in New Zealand. Indeed, by requiring possession of a permit, the Undesirable Immigrants Exclusion Act of 1919 made it difficult for them to enter. After World War II a growing sense of responsibility for, and involvement with, the Pacific region led to a more lenient administration of the regulations. In 1956 there were 8781 people born in the Pacific Islands living in New Zealand. The 1971 census shows that there were 45 413 Polynesians, not of New Zealand origin, living in this country, of whom 42 442 were in the North Island, with 27 589 in central Auckland. They are a much more youthful group than the population as a whole and the majority are engaged in semi-skilled or unskilled jobs. This presents a number of social and economic problems for the government and the community. This most recent development is one that has brought New Zealand's immigration and settlement pattern to a full circle.

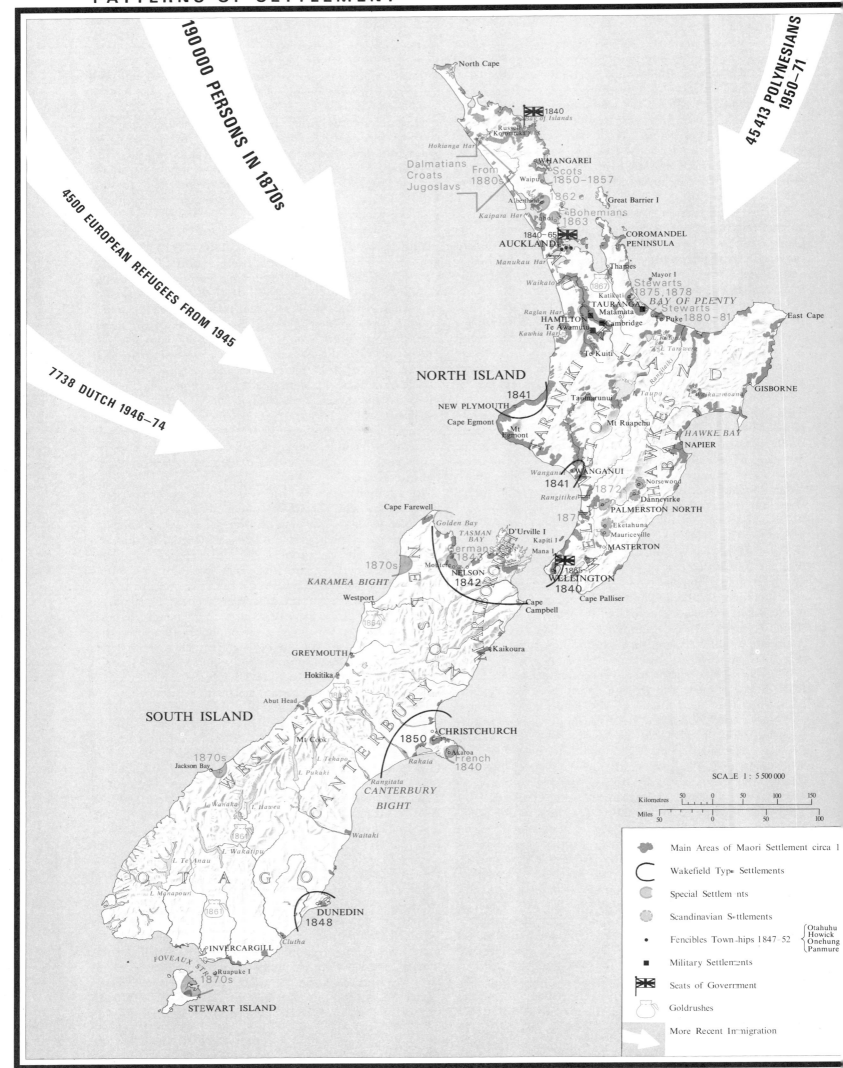

190 000 PERSONS IN 1870s

4500 EUROPEAN REFUGEES FROM 1945

7738 DUTCH 1946–74

45 413 POLYNESIANS 1950–71

North Cape

1840
Bay of Islands
Russell
(Kororareka)
Hokianga Har.

Dalmatians
Croats
Jugoslavs
From
1880s

WHANGAREI
Scots
1850–1857
Waipu
1862
Albertland
1863
Bohemians
Great Barrier I

1840–65
AUCKLAND
Kaipara Har. *Puhoi*
Manukau Har.

COROMANDEL
PENINSULA

Thames

Waikato
1867
Katikati
TAURANGA
Matamata
HAMILTON
Te Awamutu Cambridge
Raglan Har.
Kawhia Har.
Te Kuiti

Mayor I
Stewarts
1875, 1878
BAY OF PLENTY
Stewarts
Te Puke 1880–81
East Cape

L. Rotorua
Tarawera
Rangitaiki

NORTH ISLAND

1841
NEW PLYMOUTH
Cape Egmont
Mt
Egmont
Taumarunui
Mt Ruapehu
L. Taupo
L. Waikaremoana
GISBORNE

HAWKE BAY
NAPIER

Wanganui WANGANUI
1841
Rangitikei
1872
Norsewood
Danneyirke

PALMERSTON NORTH
Eketahuna
Mauriceville
MASTERTON

Cape Farewell

Golden Bay
TASMAN BAY
D'Urville I
Kapiti I
Mana I

Germans
1842
Moutere
NELSON
1842

1870s
KARAMEA BIGHT
Westport
Cape
Campbell
1855
WELLINGTON
1840
Cape Palliser

1864
GREYMOUTH
Kaikoura

Hokitika

Abut Head
1864

SOUTH ISLAND

WESTLAND

CANTERBURY

Mt Cook
L. Tekapo
L. Pukaki

1850
CHRISTCHURCH
Akaroa
French
1840
Rakaia

Jackson Bay
1870s

Rangitata
CANTERBURY
BIGHT

L. Wanaka
L. Hawea
Waitaki

1861
OTAGO

L. Te Anau
L. Wakatipu
L. Manapouri

1861
DUNEDIN
1848

INVERCARGILL
Clutha

FOVEAUX STR.
Ruapuke I
1870s

STEWART ISLAND

SCALE 1 : 5 500 000

Kilometres 50 0 50 100 150
Miles 50 0 50 100

Legend

Main Areas of Maori Settlement circa 1

C Wakefield Type Settlements

Special Settlements

Scandinavian Settlements

• Fencibles Townships 1847–52   { Otahuhu Howick Onehunga Panmure }

■ Military Settlements

Seats of Government

Goldrushes

More Recent Immigration

GOVERNMENT

Mary Boyd

New Zealand is an independent state in the South Pacific which has grown into nationhood as a self-governing community within the British Commonwealth of Nations. New Zealanders are both British subjects and New Zealand citizens.

The Queen of the United Kingdom and Head of the Commonwealth is the Queen of New Zealand. Her personal representative is the Governor-General whom she appoints for a five-year term on the advice of the New Zealand Government. The Governor-General is the formal head of the Executive Council, but he is bound to accept its advice. The Executive Council, meeting without the Governor-General, that is as the Cabinet, administers Government business; it is composed of ministers of the Crown presided over by the Prime Minister and is responsible to the majority party in the House of Representatives, from which it is chosen. The eighty-seven members of the House of Representatives are elected by New Zealanders of twenty years and more who have resided for at least one year in the country and three months in the electorate. Since the Upper House or Legislative Council was abolished in 1950, the House of Representatives has had full legislative powers.

New Zealand's parliamentary system is essentially British, except that it is unicameral. The way in which it works has been largely determined by local needs and precedents, and in this sense it has sprung from the native soil.

A STATELESS SOCIETY

In pre-historic times, New Zealand was inhabited by small, numerous, dispersed, highly mobile groups of people whom the European has called the Maori. The effective political unit was the sub-tribe or hapu, a group of kinsmen with common rights in an area of land. Related hapu formed a tribe, iwi, while tribes sharing a common founding ancestor were loosely associated as a canoe, waka. The mana (power or prestige) of tribal and sub-tribal chiefs depended on their personal ability as well as on geneological seniority. Decisions were made after discussion and debate on the marae, where only chiefs and elders had the right to speak, but as they always consulted their families, government was largely by consensus. The authority of the chiefs was supported by the institution of tapu (prohibitions). Disputes between tribes and hapu were customarily settled by taua (war parties) to exact utu (recompense), or by muru (legal plundering). Old New Zealand was indeed 'a stateless society' of rival, warring hapu and shifting political alliances. The country was so sparsely settled, with tribal and sub-tribal groups so fluid, that no one chief or group had any prospect of becoming politically dominant.

By the 1820s and 1830s competition for European trade goods, especially muskets, had intensified tribal warfare, but no warrior-chief, or musket-trader, succeeded in becoming a pocket-Napoleon. Christianity and literacy helped to inspire the Maori King Movement, which was too late to create the kind of 'missionary kingdom' that emerged elsewhere in Polynesia.

AN IMPERIAL FRONTIER

Early European settlements in New Zealand were similarly small, numerous and dispersed. By the late 1830s, mission stations studded the populous Maori districts, a 'beach community' had grown up in Kororareka, with timber depots on other northern harbours, and shore-whaling stations through Cook Strait and down the east coast to Foveaux Strait. Missionaries and traders depended on chiefly protection and were subjected to Maori customs until they established their economic independence.

The Church and Wesleyan Missions were supervised by local committees and their parent societies, the Roman Catholics by their bishop. Each whaling bay had its own law or custom and the head man maintained 'discipline almost as good as that of a man-of-war'. Responsible residents at Kororareka formed themselves into an association to maintain law and order and to protect lives and property. Colonists going out to the New Zealand Company's first and principal settlement at Port Nicholson agreed to provisional machinery for government by committee in which local Maori chiefs were to participate. Nonetheless, the problem of lawlessness grew, and men-on-the-spot, governors in New South Wales and interested bodies at home put pressure on the British Government to intervene.

British statesmen and officials were generally ignorant of or indifferent to what was happening in New Zealand and, moreover, they preferred informal methods of controlling unruly British subjects, in their rapidly expanding empire of trade and Christianity, to colonial rule. In New Zealand, these methods included general orders to shipping, Vice-Admiralty jurisdiction, visits by naval vessels and the appointment of a British Resident, James Busby, but none was effective. Busby's attempt to form the northern tribes into an independent state under the designation of the 'United Tribes of New Zealand' also failed, for the Maori had no indigenous institutions on which to build a strong, effective central government. The British government reluctantly concluded that annexation was necessary.

A CROWN COLONY

While the formalities of annexation were being completed, New Zealand was attached to the colony of New South Wales, 'an ingenious device' to provide Hobson (as lieutenant-governor) with a few officials, a little revenue and some advice. In 1841, New Zealand was erected into a separate colony. Hobson, now governor, had full power and authority directly from the Colonial Secretary. He was advised and assisted locally by an executive council of officials and a legislative council with an official majority empowered to pass ordinances for peace, order and good government. This crown colony system of government was intended to provide strong, benevolent rule on the spot for new settlements 'struggling with the first difficulties of their new situation'. Yet the early governors were denied the men and money they needed to establish law and order in the six separate settlements which had been founded, let alone in the Maori districts.

Security of life and property depended largely on friendly chiefs, on missionary mediators and on the Protectorate Department, established to safeguard Maori interests. A sub-protector aptly described himself as a portable fire engine going around extinguishing small outbreaks before they became major conflagrations. Fortunately, many of the Maori had embraced peace and Christianity and were busy producing foodstuffs for a growing European market. Even so, there was some primary resistance, in the north to British sovereignty, and around the Company settlements to attempts to survey and occupy land before ownership was determined. Grey, third governor, with greater resources at his command, coerced the resisters, appointed resident magistrates in the mixed settlements to bring the Maori under British law, and laid the foundations for unified government.

THE MOVEMENT FOR SELF-GOVERNMENT

Self-government was a cardinal point of British policy, but some officials believed that the protection of the Maori and peaceful association of the races were essential prerequisites. Nevertheless, practical problems of governing from a distance, agitation from the Company and its supporters, as well as local pressure from the settlers led to the 1846 Constitution Act. This provided for elected municipal corporations in the six main settlements, and representative legislatures for two provinces and for the whole country. Areas inhabited principally by the Maori could be proclaimed native districts in which Maori custom would prevail.

Grey, convinced that the Act was too soon, persuaded the British Government to suspend it for five years. The country, however, was divided into two provinces—New Ulster and New Munster—each with a nominated council. Outraged Wellington and Nelson settlers formed constitutional associations to agitate for self-government, with support coming from the other settlements and from the colonising bodies in England.

The 'battle' for self-government was led by young radicals with education, good home connections and small amounts of capital, who sought public office. Instructed by J. R. Godley and E. G. Wakefield, they espoused the idea of 'responsible' government, in which men who could command a majority in an elected assembly served as members of the executive council.

PROVINCIAL GOVERNMENT

Grey was the chief architect of the 1852 Constitution Act. He described New Zealand at that time as consisting of nine principal European settlements besides smaller dependencies, with about twenty-six thousand souls scattered over a distance of about nine hundred miles and separated from each other by wide intervals. Communication, even for persons on horseback, was between only three of the settlements. The wide intervals between were occupied by a native race, estimated to consist of one hundred and twenty thousand souls.

The new Act made provision for a General Assembly, consisting of the Governor, an appointed Legislative Council and elected House of Representatives, and for six provinces with elected councils and superintendents. Grey recommended a low property franchise for voters because 'every well conducted family, however humble their circumstances may originally have been, acquire here in a few years property of their own'. This allowed an early historian, A. S. Thomson, to comment that men who influenced elections in England by brick-bats were voters in New Zealand.

Grey had wide discretionary powers which he used to bring in the constitution 'provincially, head hindmost'. The General Assembly handed over to the provincial governments all the land revenue, not less than three-eighths of customs revenue and the administration of land purchased by the Crown from the Maori, a commonsense arrangement in 1856, but increasingly inequitable as times changed. The provinces best endowed with land, sheep and gold, and thus able to borrow money, forged ahead of the rest. Outlying districts which complained of neglect were permitted to form themselves into new provinces, which weakened the whole system.

The vested interests of the provinces in a fixed share of the colony's revenue impeded self-reliance in Maori affairs and local defence, and, later, in Vogel's policies of national development. The provincial system collapsed financially during the recession of the late sixties and was abolished in 1876. Provincialism was transmitted into localism, which defeated the creation of a uniform, national system of local government as provided for in the Municipal Corporations and Counties Act of 1876. County, city and borough councils, town boards and numerous other local authorities with special functions proliferated, until by April 1971 they numbered 640.

To small, scattered, isolated settlements in absolute want of everything, multiplication and specialisation in local body administration must have seemed the quickest way to get anything. Nonetheless, the need for consolidation and amalgamation grew as the country developed, and was confirmed by various committees and local government commissions. Since 1967 a reconstituted commission has been preparing area schemes to set a general pattern, while an Auckland regional authority has been established. (*See p 67*). Although localism remains a formidable force, it is gradually being broken down by urbanisation and the demand for more adequate, efficient and economical services and facilities.

RESPONSIBLE GOVERNMENT AND DOMINION STATUS

The 1852 Act was silent about responsible government, but Wakefield mobilised overwhelming support for it in the Wellington Provincial Council and in the House of Representatives. The British Government raised no objections and Henry Sewell formed the first responsible ministry in 1856. To preserve internal tranquility, the Governor arranged to retain control temporarily of native affairs. This suited ministers, for it meant that when war broke out they could depend on the imperial troops and commissariat—until Britain, in 1867, insisted on all troops being withdrawn, and the Governor relinquished the control of native affairs.

New Zealand's reluctance to accept total self-reliance notwithstanding, it had no hesitation in whittling away the governor's powers. John Ballance, by persuasion, in 1891 and the Colonial Office, by instruction, in 1892, established precedents that the governor must accept the advice of his ministers in exercising his prerogative of mercy and in the appointment of new members of the Legislative Council. The Royal Instructions of 1917 left the governor-general discretionary power to reserve legislation affecting imperial interests, but, by convention, he had already become a figure-head.

Although external affairs were still essentially an imperial matter, New Zealand again had no hesitation and made its voice heard whenever its national interests were at stake. Being largely content with imperial partnership, it saw no need for the Balfour Declaration of 1926 defining dominions as:

> autonomous Communities within the British Empire, equal in status, in no way subordinate to one another in any aspect of their domestic or external affairs, though united by a common allegiance to the Crown, and freely associated as the British Commonwealth of Nations.

Similarly it did not immediately adopt the Statute of Westminster passed by the Imperial Parliament in 1931 to remove remaining legal inequalities. 'We had all the self-government we wanted,' said Sir Carl Berendsen. 'We could control our own tariffs, choose our future fellow-citizens, and do all the other things we wanted to do . . .

We were doing all right without it.' However, getting the Imperial Parliament to legislate by 'advice and consent' on imperial matters, which included the form of New Zealand's constitution, proved inconvenient, and the Statute was adopted in 1947 when the abolition of the Legislative Council was proposed. Meanwhile the Second World War had forced New Zealand to turn from Britain to the United States for protection and accelerated the exercise of independence in external affairs. Dominion status now meant, in the memorable words of Peter Fraser, 'independence with something added and not independence with something taken away'.

SPECIAL INSTITUTIONS FOR THE MAORI

For the Maori, responsible government meant a change of masters, not of policy. Although the political objective was still amalgamation, four separate Maori electorates were established in 1867. Contrary to humanitarian intentions, most Maori voters had been disqualified at earlier elections by the 'peculiar nature' of their land tenure. Resident magistrates enforced the law in Maori districts until 1893, when they were replaced by stipendiary magistrates on the same basis as elsewhere.

War, defeat and punishing land confiscation strengthened Maori opposition to amalgamation which, in fact, meant European domination. Supporters of the Maori King now practised local autonomy, other protestors looked to religious prophets for deliverance from the pakeha. Maori parliaments, largely supported by those who had freely sold their land through the Native Land Court, met annually from 1892 to 1903 to administer their own affairs. However, the tide was turning against political separatism. The Young Maori party and later the Ratana religious movement sought State assistance for their people by winning the Maori seats in Parliament.

In the present century, beginning with the Maori Councils Act of 1900 which provided machinery for improving standards of health in Maori villages, attempts have been made to encourage the Maori to assume more responsibility for his own economic and social affairs as well as to participate more actively in both local and national politics. The Maori Social and Economic Advancement Act of 1945 (consolidated and amended by the Maori Welfare Act of 1962) made provision for tribal and district committees and executives. In 1961 the New Zealand Maori Council of Tribal Executives, its members elected by the District Councils, was formed. Finally, in 1973 a White Paper reviewed many matters affecting the Maori, with the aim of producing amending legislation to give them 'the fullest opportunity of genuine consultations on any legislative proposals affecting them.'

DEMOCRATIC GOVERNMENT

A radical political heritage, combined with local opportunities for self-betterment, encouraged the growth of democracy as well as of self-government. After 1852, New Zealanders were well represented numerically, although plural office-holding was common. Manhood suffrage was early introduced, for the Maori in 1867 and for Europeans in 1879. New Zealand, in 1893, became the first state not part of a Federation to give women the vote. Plural voting had been abolished in 1889. Parliamentary proceedings have been broadcast since 1935. New Zealanders clearly believe that government should be carried on in the sight and hearing of the people and not behind closed doors. They expect individual ministers and politicians to be freely accessible to their constituents and acutely sensitive to public opinion. They take it for granted that in times of need or hardship government will provide. The advance of democracy has made government a benign as well as a powerful, omnipresent institution to remedy grievances and to promote general happiness and welfare.

POPULATION

Miriam G. Vosburgh

In the 1971 census, the New Zealand population was enumerated at 2.86 million people and the monthly abstract for April 1974 showed that the three million mark had been passed by 42 800. The people are mainly of European origin, the largest distinct minority being that of the Maori who constitute approximately eight per cent of the total population. Pacific Islanders represent just over one per cent and all other non-European races combined contribute less than one per cent of the total. Some eighty-five per cent of the people are New Zealand-born. Although the economy is based largely on agriculture, most New Zealanders live in towns or cities. In the 1971 census, 81.5 per cent were classified as urban, that is living in towns of more than 1000 people, leaving a rural proportion of only 18.5 per cent. The North Island is more densely settled than the South, with some seventy-two per cent of the population.

The numbers of males and females in the population are approximately equal. However, the ratio varies considerably by age. Amongst children under sixteen years, there are 104 boys to every 100 girls, numbers equalise just before age fifty and in the age group 65+ years, there are only seventy-four males to 100 females.

The total population contains a substantial proportion of children. However, there is also a high enough proportion of people of 65+ years for the population to be considered 'aged' according to United Nations definition. If those in age groups 0–14 and 65+ are considered to be economically dependent on those in age group 15–64 years, there is a high dependency ratio in New Zealand as compared with that in most countries with predominantly European populations.

The Maori population is much 'younger' than the total population. In fact, it is one of the youngest in the world, due to very high birth rates and rapidly decreasing infant and childhood mortality rates. Further, even if numbers of births per woman decrease, there is every reason to expect that the population will continue to contain high proportions of children for several decades at least, as the continuing decreases in mortality at younger ages ensure that the great majority of children already born will reach reproductive age.

The age and sex structure of the population at the end of 1971 is shown below:[1]

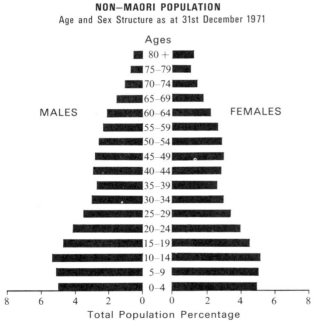

NON–MAORI POPULATION
Age and Sex Structure as at 31st December 1971

MAORI POPULATION
Age and Sex Structure as at 31st December 1971

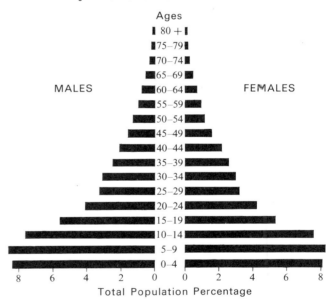

POPULATION GROWTH BEFORE 1936

The New Zealand European population increased from the 26 707 people enumerated in the first general census of 1851, to just under 1.5 million in 1936.[2] As would be expected, growth rates during the colonisation period were very high by today's standards, the average annual increase varying from some seven to fourteen per cent from the 1850s to the 1880s. The major part of this increase came from continuing immigration, predominantly from the British Isles and Australia, but natural increase was also substantially higher than at present. Rates of natural increase are determined by the difference between death rates and birth rates, the latter being dependent on the proportion of the population bearing children and on the average number of births per woman. The higher rates of natural increase in the early period of settlement were due solely to the large numbers of children per married woman, averagely between two and three times the present number. Death rates were higher and a smaller proportion of the population was married. Most women married, but pioneer conditions and a relative scarcity of potential brides resulted in a large proportion of men remaining single

A severe economic recession in the 1880s depressed population growth by its influence on both migration and birth rates. Migrant inflow diminished in the early 1880s and actual losses through net migration were recorded between 1886 and 1890. Slow economic recovery, together

---

[1] Maoris are defined for census purposes as those with half or more Maori blood.

[2] Technically these statistics relate to non-Maoris but here and throughout the paper the term 'European' is used and includes the very small number of non-Maori who are not European.

with the effects of depression conditions in parts of Australia, brought renewed increases through migration in the 1890s and substantial numbers arrived in the first quarter of the twentieth century. The onset of another major economic depression again diminished and reversed the flow. Birth rates also began to decrease in the 1880s but, unlike migration rates, showed no recovery as economic conditions improved. Once begun, the decline in birth rates continued for more than fifty years, the lowest point being reached in the depression years of the 1930s. In marriages contracted in the 1920s and early 1930s the average number of live births was 2.5 or less. Regardless of fluctuations in migration rates, the main source of population growth since the 1880s has been natural increase, for although birth rates were declining, the population base was increasing sufficiently to prevent a severe decrease in actual numbers of births, and death rates were slowly declining.

Although information on the size of the Maori population during the nineteenth century is less reliable than that on the European, it is well known that Maori numbers were decreasing. The decline was associated with such factors as European-introduced epidemics, defeat in war and struggles over land, which often separated husbands and wives for long periods. At the end of the century, the Maori population was enumerated at a little more than 40 000 people. Subsequently, under conditions of greater stability and a slow decrease in mortality rates, it began to increase and in the 1936 census was enumerated at 82 326.

POPULATION GROWTH AFTER 1936

Total population growth from the end of the depression years in the 1930s, starting at 1936 as the nearest census year, is shown below:

Date of Census	Total Population	Average Annual Percentage Increase
1936	1 573 810	
1945*	1 747 679	1.1
1951*	1 941 366	1.9
1956*	2 176 224	2.3
1961*	2 417 543	2.1
1966*	2 678 855	2.1
1971*	2 864 113	1.3

*Includes members of New Zealand armed forces overseas at census date.

The low rate of growth between 1936 and 1945 can be attributed mainly to the effects of World War II, namely an increase in mortality, a low level of immigration and a disruption of marriage and family life, which all prevented birth rates from recovering to the extent that might otherwise have occurred as economic conditions improved in the late 1930s. The greater rate of increase between 1945 and 1951 represents a resumption of gain through net migration and the beginning of high birth rates after the war. Growth rates between 1951 and 1966 were substantial for a country where birth control was widely practised. The main factors in the increase were continuing high birth rates to 1961, with a gradual decline to 1966, and a sustained gain from net migration. The considerable decline in the growth rate between 1966 and 1971 resulted mainly from a net migration loss over three years but decreased birth rates made some contribution.

The changes in fertility, mortality and migration rates, which have caused these swings in rates of population growth, are examined below.

FERTILITY

Trends in the birth rate from 1936–40 to 1971 are shown below:

Number of Births per 1000 Mean Population from 1936–40

Years	Rate	Year	Rate	Year	Rate
1936–40	18.36	1961	26.99	1966	22.44
1941–45	23.21	1962	26.21	1967	22.43
1946–50	26.70	1963	25.49	1968	22.62
1951–55	25.77	1964	24.12	1969	22.50
1956–60	26.58	1965	22.83	1970	22.06
				1971	22.59

After recovery from the effects of a major economic depression and World War II, birth rates remained high between 1946 and 1961, despite a consistent decline in the proportion of women of reproductive age in the population, as those born during the period of low birth rates in the 1920s and 1930s entered into this category. The high birth rates were sustained through an increase in proportions married, through higher fertility within marriage and, to a lesser extent, through an increase an ex-nuptial birth rates.

Increasing proportions of women in each age group, including those of maximum reproduction, 20–29 years, were recorded as being married at each census date between 1936 and 1961 and the trend has continued to the present. It has resulted from changes in social, economic and other conditions which have lessened constraints on marriage. Such conditions include a period of relative economic prosperity and security and, after 1945, the absence of major wars. However, the change which has exerted the greatest influence has undoubtedly been the rapid increase in the employment of married women since World War II, especially in the proportion continuing to work for a period immediately after marriage.[3] This has become quite customary and acceptable for urban women, at least, and has encouraged earlier marriage on the basis of two incomes.

Although, from the early 1950s, the increase in the proportion of wives working for a period after marriage tended to lengthen the average interval between marriage and first birth, there was until 1962 an increase in fertility rates of married women. The fertility rates of married European women were eleven per cent higher in 1951 than in 1945, seventeen per cent in 1956 and twenty-one per cent in 1961. During this period, a long-term trend continued towards a decrease in the fertility rate of married women of more than thirty years of age, so that the increase derived from the increased fertility of younger women. In part, the increase represented an overall acceleration of family building after the first child, in part a small increase in the average family size of those married in the late 1940s and the 1950s as compared with the average in the marriages of the two previous decades.

From an examination of the decline in birth rates from 1962, it appears that this has occurred despite a gradual increase in the proportion of the population in the reproductive ages, a greater percentage married and an increase in ex-nuptial birth rates. It must be attributed solely to a decrease in the fertility rates of married women, which are expected to result in a slight reduction in average family size. This may slow population growth on a long-term basis.

During the period under examination, Maori birth rates have been about twice as high as those of the non-Maori population. Nevertheless, a slow but fairly consistent decline in the rates began in 1962, the same year in which they began to fall throughout the total population. There is little evidence of a conscious attempt among the Maori

---

[3] No nationally-based estimates of the increase in the proportion of women who have continued in employment upon marriage is available, but a survey of non-Maori families in Wellington City in 1967 found a continuing increase in the proportion, from 17 per cent of women married in the period 1927–32 to a projected 79 per cent of those married between 1962 and 1967.

people to restrict fertility before the 1960–70 decade, but the recent decrease in birth rates suggests that increasing numbers are practising birth control. This is undoubtedly associated with the progressive urbanisation of the Maori people.

MORTALITY

The mortality rate which relates to population growth is the crude death rate, the number of deaths per thousand population. Although some fluctuations in this rate have shown since 1936, they have been minor in comparison with those in fertility and migration, and so have made relatively little contribution to variations in population growth. The rate, however, is not an adequate measurement of the changes in mortality which affect the age–sex structure of the population, and these deserve some comment.

Official life tables, prepared according to the mortality rates in a period around a census date, show that there has been a continuous but decelerating increase in life expectancy at birth for European females, from 68.5 years in 1934–38 to 74.8 years in 1965–67. For males, there was a very gradual increase, from 65.5 years in 1934–38 to 69.2 in 1960–62, followed by a slight decrease to 68.7 years in 1965–67. The difference between the trends for males and females results in an increase in their differential life expectancy from three years in 1934–36 to six years in 1965–67.

Increases, however disproportionate, in life expectancy for both sexes derived from improvements in infant, childhood and young adult mortality rates. Even at these ages, improvement has begun to slow down and, for males, except for infant mortality, showed a slight reversal between 1960–62 and 1965–67. Mortality rate improvement in the middle and older age groups has been less and will probably not occur to any large extent until there is a breakthrough in the prevention or the treatment of organic complaints such as cancer and heart disease, major causes of death. The decreased mortality rates for younger rather than older ages is a major contribution to the trend towards a 'younger' population.

Since World War II, Maori mortality rates have experienced a spectacular decline, a trend which has accelerated population growth both directly and indirectly, as more children have survived to the reproductive stage. Life expectancies at birth, 61.4 for males and 64.8 for females in 1965–67, are still lower than those of non-Maoris but the differences are narrowing. A major reason for mortality rate improvement has been the increased availability of medical services, the implementation of the medical provisions in the Social Security Act, the extension of government health services and the continued urbanisation of the Maori people. An important feature of the improvement was an advance in the diagnosis and treatment of tuberculosis, for many years a major cause of death amongst them.

MIGRATION

Rates of immigration have been largely determined by the economic conditions prevailing in New Zealand compared with those in other countries, notably Britain and Australia, and by the presence or absence of major wars. Government immigration policies have also exerted an influence, through certain restrictions, through the implementation of preferences for migrants with various occupational skills, particularly in the trades and technical fields, and through the funding of assisted passage schemes.

Migration to New Zealand, after a virtual cessation during World War II, recommenced gradually towards the end of the 1940s and until 1967, net migration gains contributed nearly a quarter of the population increase. After that year, an economic recession resulted in a net migration loss over a three-year period and was the main reason for the decrease in the population growth rate during the 1966–71 intercensal period. Net migration gains resumed in 1970.

Following long-standing practice, the great majority of immigrants in recent years have come from Britain, Australia and other Commonwealth countries with populations of European origin. Post-war migration, however, has also included substantial numbers of people from the Netherlands and other European countries, together with small groups of displaced persons and refugees from a variety of countries. There has also been an acceleration of immigration from the Pacific islands, especially the Cook Islands, Niue, Fiji and Western Samoa. The implementation of a government scheme to bring to New Zealand most of the inhabitants of the Tokelau Islands, where population growth was fast outstripping resources, has been undertaken. Immigrants from the Pacific islands, however, have been relatively few, constituting only some four to five per cent of the total number of immigrants intending permanent residence in New Zealand. Immigration of groups of people with few industrial skills leads to certain problems of integration, which will be discussed later.

POPULATION DISTRIBUTION

A brief examination of the maps reveals two key features of the population distribution; firstly, that most people live in urban concentrations and, secondly, that the North Island is more heavily populated than the South. These features represent the effects of long-term trends.

In 1881, forty-two per cent of the population was classified as urban, fifty-eight per cent as rural. By 1971, the rural percentage had declined to 18.5; 81.5 per cent being recorded as urban, of which 82.7 per cent lived in twenty-four larger urban concentrations, classified in the census as Urban Areas. Urbanisation has been occurring from the early years of settlement and, by the time of the 1911 census, just over half the population were town dwellers. Until that time, urbanisation had been almost entirely the result of population growth, but since then the major source has been population movement to the towns. At first, this movement was both to existing cities and smaller towns as industrial and commercial functions grew, and to new towns such as the service towns which were established in the first two decades of the century in the dairying areas in the North Island. After the early 1920s the establishment of new towns became much less frequent and population movement became increasingly directed towards the larger towns and cities, where industries and services were experiencing greater expansion. For the most recent intercensal period, 1966–71, the population increase in the smaller towns was 7.6 per cent whereas the increase in urban areas was 10.4 per cent. The rural population showed a 4.6 per cent decrease, the first time that an absolute decrease has been recorded for rural areas. The differences in these growth rates were almost entirely the result of residential movement.

Population redistribution has been largely a response to redistribution of employment opportunities. Changes such as amalgamation of holdings, and increased mechanisation have reduced the amount of work available in many rural areas, while industrial expansion has increased urban employment opportunities, especially in the larger cities.

In recent years, the Maori population has been particularly affected by these changes. They had been mainly country dwellers and, further, were concentrated in areas with few employment opportunities, notably the Northland and Gisborne areas. Since the end of World War II the urbanisation of the Maori people has been remarkably rapid. In 1951, twenty-nine per cent was classified as urban, in 1971, seventy per cent.

Population build-up in the urban areas has encouraged the process of suburbanisation, which, though under way by the 1920s, has accelerated markedly since World War II. During this time, the largest urban areas have been experiencing a loss of population from the city centres, a decreasing gain in the outer sections of administrative cities and major gains on the peripheries. Initially, the peripheral settlements were largely commuter suburbs, but more recently some of the newer living areas, around Auckland and Wellington particularly, have achieved a degree of administrative independence from the major city.

From the 1860s, population growth rates have been higher in the North than in the South Island. In 1901, the census recorded that half the population lived in the North and half in the South Island. By the time of the 1971 census, seventy-two per cent lived in the North. More recently, the predominant movement has been not to just the North Island but to its northern half, where the rapid build-up of industry in Auckland and other major cities, notably Hamilton and Rotorua, has attracted in-migration. Industry has continued to grow more rapidly in the north than elsewhere. This has been partly because the greater volume of industry, which already existed by the 1950s, offered increased efficiency to new ventures through industrial interdependence, better transport and other services; partly because the larger population provided a larger ready market and a wider range of labour skills. It appears that this trend of population movement is unlikely to be reversed in the near future.

IMPLICATIONS OF POPULATION CHANGE

Demographic changes have combined with certain economic and other social changes to encourage the increase in the proportion of married women in employment. In 1936, only four per cent of married women were in the labour force, by 1966 the percentage had increased to twenty. The main reasons for this increase were the growth of occupational opportunities, a continuing decrease in the proportion of single women of working age and changes in family patterns which have made employment outside the home possible for larger numbers of married women.

While a further increase is probable, there are several trends, such as the rising proportion of the population in the work-force ages and an extension in the average length of female education, that are likely to dampen the rate of increase.

The growth of commuter suburbs and major settlements on the margins of cities has been accelerated by continuing urbanisation and, in a society where couples typically set up their own households upon marriage, by increasing marriage rates. These demographic changes have reinforced various economic, technological and institutional causes of suburban growth. Some of the more important of these have been increases in urban employment, improvements in transport, the policy of building state housing settlements at the periphery of cities and the policies of lending institutions which favour the granting of loans for new rather than already-built houses.

Certain social problems have typically been associated with the growth of suburbs and particularly with the larger, faster growing state housing settlements like Otara, outside Auckland, and Porirua, outside Wellington, which were conceived as satellite cities rather than as commuter suburbs. The provision of services and facilities has lagged behind population growth and industrial development has been slow, forcing many to commute to work and making employment virtually inaccessible to others, such as women with young children. Resulting problems have been so widely publicised that housing authorities will be expected to try to minimise them in future housing developments of this type.

The rapid urbanisation of the Maori people has been accompanied by the problems typically associated with the integration of a rural people into urban economic and social life. One major difficulty is the relatively low educational qualifications and lack of urban occupational skills amongst the in-migrants. This has led to their being over-represented in semi-skilled and unskilled manual jobs and under-represented in jobs of higher occupational status. This distribution is unsatisfactory in two main, interrelated ways. Firstly, it adversely affects social status, and secondly, it results in an economic disadvantage in earnings and in job security, for, as mechanisation and industrialisation advance, manual labour becomes increasingly marginal to the labour force. Stimulated, in part, by special programmes and other educational incentives, Maori educational achievement is slowly providing a remedy.

The problems associated with immigrants from the various Pacific islands are similar to those associated with Maori urbanisation. Further, mainly because of their similarity in financial and migrant status, they tend to be residentially concentrated in inner city areas and in the newer state housing settlements in suburbs outlying the larger North Island cities. Because there is little common identification between the two groups, in spite of their Polynesian ancestry, their close physical contact and their competition for jobs have already provoked some conflict. This could increase, especially in a time of economic recession.

It is increasingly necessary to provide for the care of greater numbers of aged people, with special attention to the growing proportion of older widows, a feature of the increasing differential in male–female mortality rates.

A healthy and expanding economy will be needed to provide enough employment for the increases in the numbers in the work-force ages, which are expected throughout the 1970s as the result of the high birth rates in the 1947–61 period.

Adjustments in educational facilities and staffing continue to be necessary, both nationally and locally, to accommodate the rapid changes in numbers of children at each educational level. These changes have resulted from trends in birth rates and in urbanisation and suburbanisation since World War II.

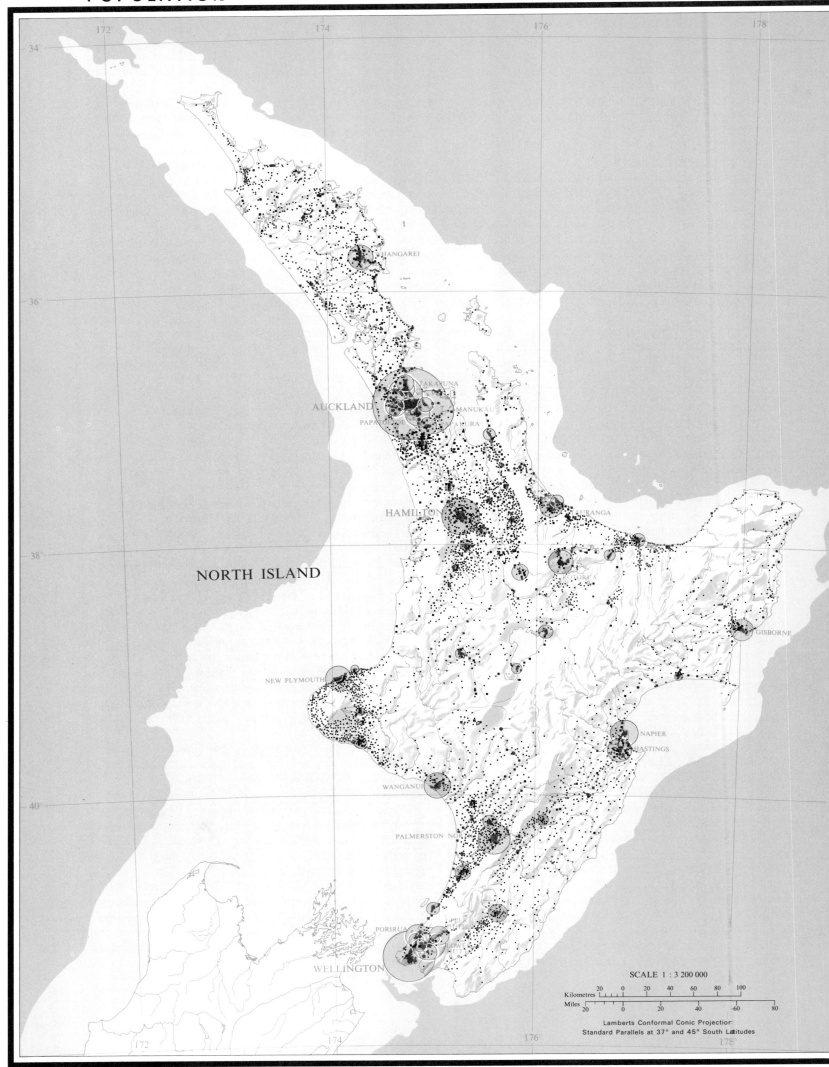

NORTH ISLAND

WHANGAREI

AUCKLAND
TAKAPUNA
MANUKAU
PAPATOETOE
PAKURA

HAMILTON
TAURANGA

ROTORUA

GISBORNE

NEW PLYMOUTH

NAPIER
HASTINGS

WANGANUI

PALMERSTON NORTH

PORIRUA
UPPER HUTT
LOWER HUTT

WELLINGTON

SCALE 1 : 3 200 000

Kilometres 20 0 20 40 60 80 100

Miles 20 0 20 40 60 80

Lamberts Conformal Conic Projection
Standard Parallels at 37° and 45° South Latitudes

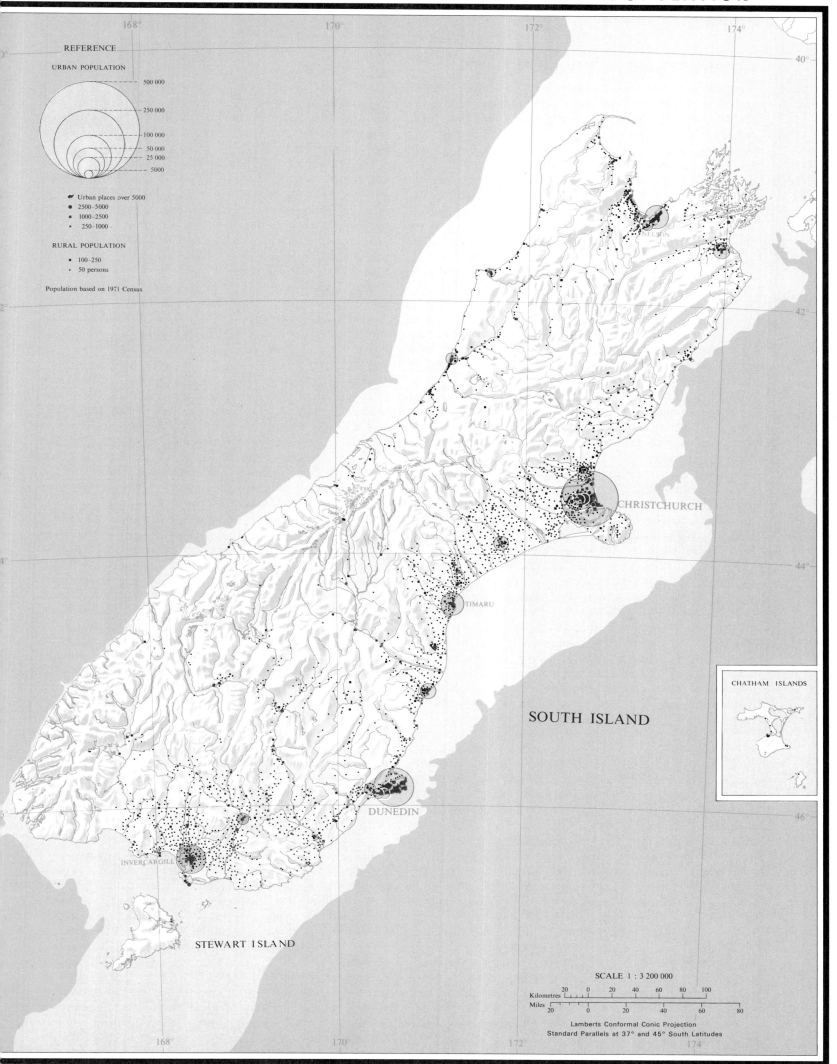

REFERENCE

URBAN POPULATION

— 500 000
— 250 000
— 100 000
— 50 000
— 25 000
— 5000

Urban places over 5000
● 2500–5000
■ 1000–2500
▪ 250–1000 ·

RURAL POPULATION
■ 100–250
· 50 persons

Population based on 1971 Census

NELSON

CHRISTCHURCH

TIMARU

SOUTH ISLAND

DUNEDIN

INVERCARGILL

STEWART ISLAND

CHATHAM ISLANDS

SCALE 1 : 3 200 000

Kilometres 20 0 20 40 60 80 100
Miles 20 0 20 40 60 80

Lamberts Conformal Conic Projection
Standard Parallels at 37° and 45° South Latitudes

ADMINISTRATIVE DIVISIONS

R. J. Lowe

New Zealand today has many regional divisions in central and local government administration, and there are other divisions for the administration of sporting and youth organisations, churches, political parties, industry and marketing, and so on. Here we consider only local and central government administrative divisions.

Administrative divisions for local government purposes date from 1846, when New Zealand was divided into two provinces. Legislation in 1852 introduced a system of six (later ten) provincial councils which functioned as the chief, regional administrative bodies until 1876, when they were abolished. Their founding dates are still celebrated by annual public holidays, and the provincial boundaries persist as widely recognised reference points.

The present local government system, which replaced provincial governments in 1876, comprises both territorial and *ad hoc* authorities. Territorial authorities (counties, boroughs, cities and town districts), provide the basic structure of local government, performing a wide range of functions in any one area. An *ad hoc* authority provides one service only, such as electric power supply. The county town and county borough forms of administration, both relatively recent additions to the local government structure, operate within the framework of counties. The more independent county borough is restricted to areas with more than 1500 persons, the normal lower limit for borough status. The town of Tokoroa, much the largest town without a borough council, presents an anomaly; it remains technically a county town (within Matamata County), but unlike other county towns is administered by a county borough committee and a mayor.

The Auckland Regional Authority, established in 1963, constitutes a second tier of the territorial local authority structure, providing several dissimilar services (such as transport, drainage, water supply, airport, regional planning, reserves) on a regional basis for more than twenty smaller territorial local authorities. Unique, it is important for servicing such a large proportion of New Zealand's population, and as a possible pointer to future administrative forms for other metropolitan areas. Regional Planning Authorities are quite different in form and principle, performing the single function of regional planning.

Education Boards (*p 67*) are descended from the pre-1876 provincial councils. They provide primary level education services in all public schools, train and employ teachers and allocate Department of Education grants for building, equipment, and maintenance of schools. The members of local school committees elect the board members. Education boards provide services to secondary education where district high schools are involved, but generally the secondary school boards and the Department of Education are responsible in this field.

Hospital Boards, which date from 1885, provide the majority of institutional medical services, including psychiatric hospitals. Board members are locally elected, but since 1957 government has been fully responsible for finance.

District Roads Councils were constituted under the National Roads Act 1953. They consist of appointed central and local government representatives, and of representatives of motoring interests, under the chairmanship of the District Commissioner of Works. They advise the National Roads Board about roading needs and expenditure in their respective districts.

Electric Power Boards provide most of the electric power distribution services at retail level, though a decreasing number of the territorial local authorities also perform this function. Some of the electricity retailed is generated by some boards, but most is purchased wholesale from the national grid.

Other matters too are dealt with by *ad hoc* local authorities. Several different types deal with rivers and drainage control. Legislation in 1941 led to the establishment of catchment boards and catchment commissions (differing in composition rather than function) over a large portion of the land area of New Zealand, performing many soil conservation and river control functions; these were joined in 1956 by the Waikato Valley Authority, performing similar functions. Under more recent legislation, all catchment boards, commissions and the Waikato Valley Authority have become Regional Water Boards with even wider responsibilities, such as the allocation of rights to utilise water sources and control of discharge into rivers and lakes.

Regional Planning Authorities, including the Auckland Regional Authority (*p 67*), are responsible for the preparation of regional planning schemes under the Town and Country Planning Act 1953, to co-ordinate the local planning of their constituent local authorities. The Dunedin Regional Planning Authority (1947) is the longest established, although planning authorities were established in Taranaki and Wanganui under earlier legislation, but have lapsed through lack of interest.

Examples of government administrative divisions defined by statute are Land Districts, Health Districts (*pp 67 & 68*), Transport Licensing Districts and Industrial Districts. Such districts reflect the internal organisation of the responsible government department under which they operate. For example, the Ministry of Works has seven districts, below which are more than twenty residencies, controlled by resident engineers who are responsible to the district commissioners of works, who in turn are responsible to the permanent head of the Ministry. In some departments there are only single offices, each servicing a prescribed area, such as the Department of Labour's Employment Districts and the Customs Districts.

Statistical Areas are not, strictly speaking, administrative divisions, for they are defined by the Government Statistician solely for the purpose of publishing breakdowns of statistics by areas.

Land Districts are constituted under the Land Act 1948, each having a Chief Surveyor and Commissioner of Crown Lands, both members of the Lands and Survey Department. With the same boundaries, Land Registration Districts are constituted under the Land Transfer Act 1952, and are under the control of the District Land Registrar, a member of the Justice Department. All property titles define a property as being part of such and such a Land District.

Health Districts, constituted under the Health Act 1956, are each in charge of a Medical Officer of Health responsible for public health, such as public hygiene and the quarantining of persons, places, buildings, ships and animals.

Works Districts (*p 68*) are simply the internal organisational arrangement of the Ministry of Works, although their controlling officers (district commissioners) are referred to as such in various acts of Parliament. The Ministry of Works lower administrative tier, the residencies, follows District Roads Council boundaries; in some cases there is more than one residency for each Roads Council District.

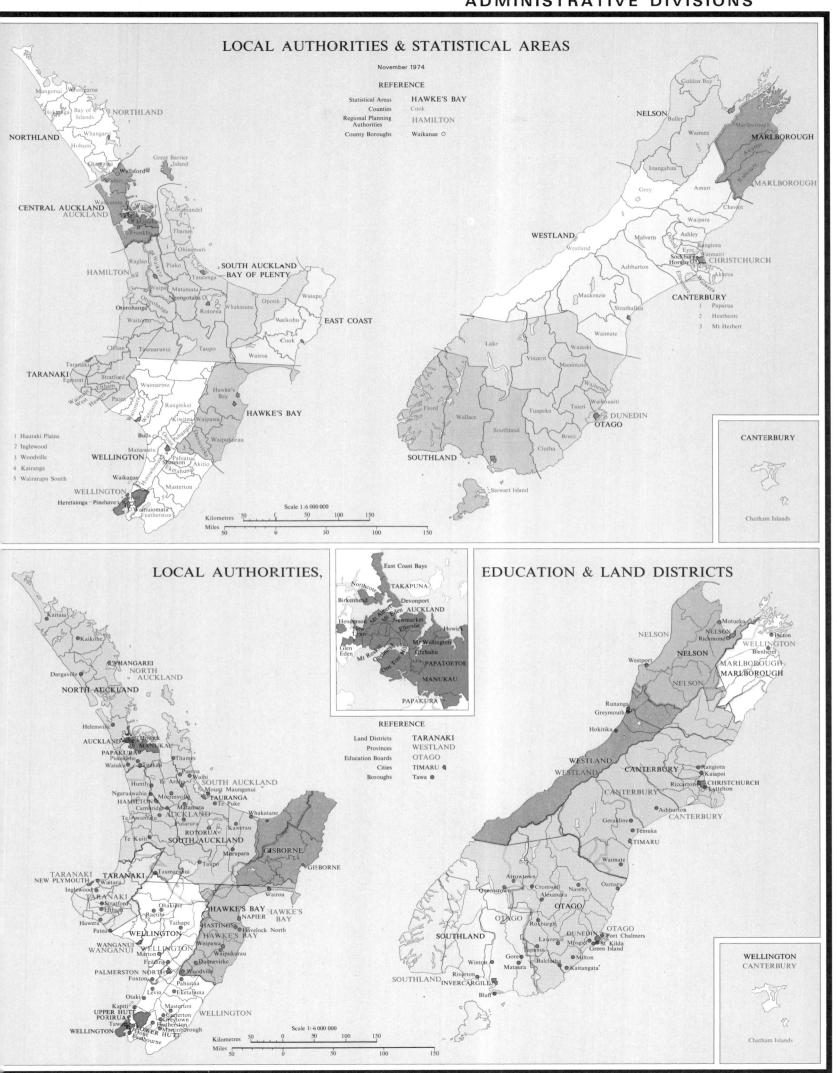

LOCAL AUTHORITIES & STATISTICAL AREAS

November 1974

REFERENCE

Statistical Areas	HAWKE'S BAY
Counties	Cook
Regional Planning Authorities	HAMILTON
County Boroughs	Waikanae ○

Scale 1:6 000 000

LOCAL AUTHORITIES, EDUCATION & LAND DISTRICTS

REFERENCE

Land Districts	TARANAKI
Provinces	WESTLAND
Education Boards	OTAGO
Cities	TIMARU
Boroughs	Tawa ●

Scale 1:6 000 000

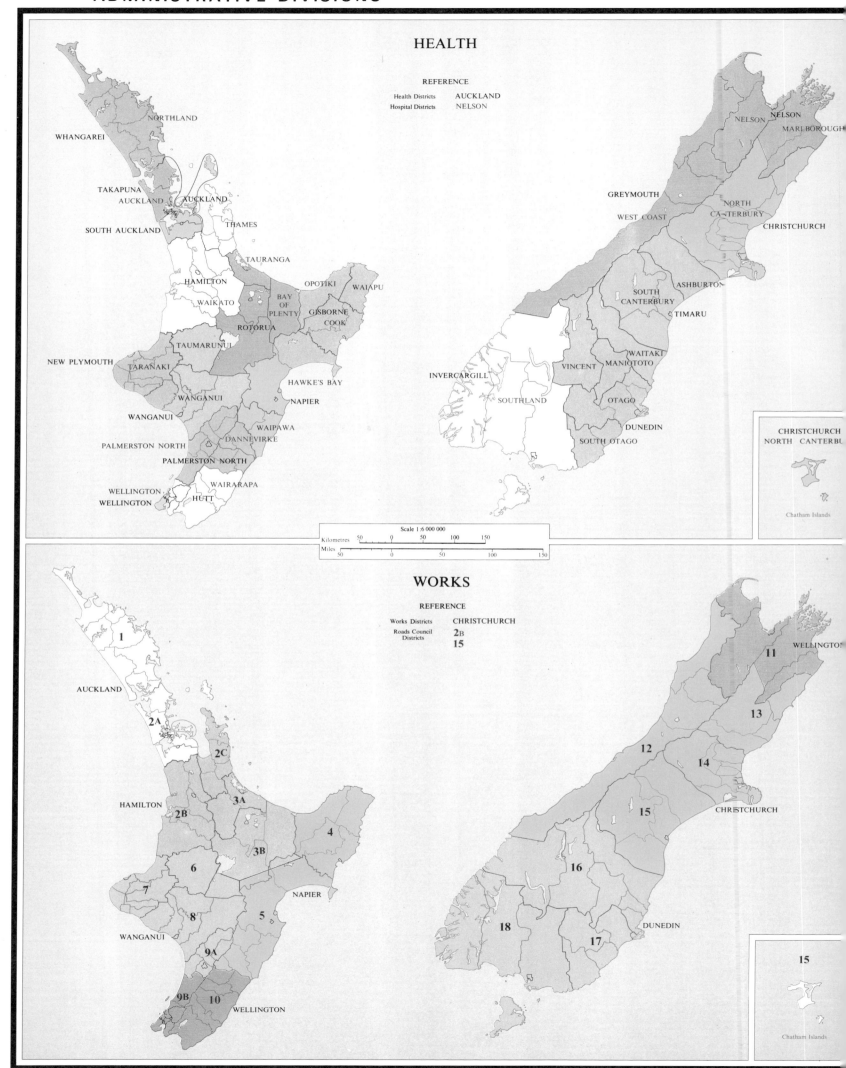

HEALTH

REFERENCE

Health Districts AUCKLAND
Hospital Districts NELSON

NORTHLAND

WHANGAREI

TAKAPUNA
AUCKLAND   AUCKLAND

SOUTH AUCKLAND

THAMES

TAURANGA

HAMILTON   OPOTIKI   WAIAPU

WAIKATO   BAY
OF
PLENTY   GISBORNE
COOK

ROTORUA

TAUMARUNUI

NEW PLYMOUTH

TARANAKI   HAWKE'S BAY

WANGANUI   NAPIER

WANGANUI

WAIPAWA

PALMERSTON NORTH   DANNEVIRKE

PALMERSTON NORTH

WELLINGTON   WAIRARAPA
WELLINGTON   HUTT

NELSON   NELSON
MARLBOROUGH

GREYMOUTH   NORTH
WEST COAST   CANTERBURY
CHRISTCHURCH

ASHBURTON
SOUTH
CANTERBURY   TIMARU

WAITAKI
INVERCARGILL   VINCENT   MANIOTOTO

SOUTHLAND   OTAGO

DUNEDIN
SOUTH OTAGO

CHRISTCHURCH
NORTH CANTERBU[RY]

Chatham Islands

Scale 1:6 000 000

Kilometres 50 0 50 100 150
Miles 50 0 50 100 150

WORKS

REFERENCE

Works Districts CHRISTCHURCH
Roads Council   2B
Districts   15

1

AUCKLAND

2A

2C

3A

HAMILTON

2B

3B

4

6

7

8   NAPIER

5

WANGANUI

9A

9B   10

WELLINGTON

11   WELLINGTON

13

12

14

15

CHRISTCHURCH

16

18

17   DUNEDIN

15

Chatham Islands

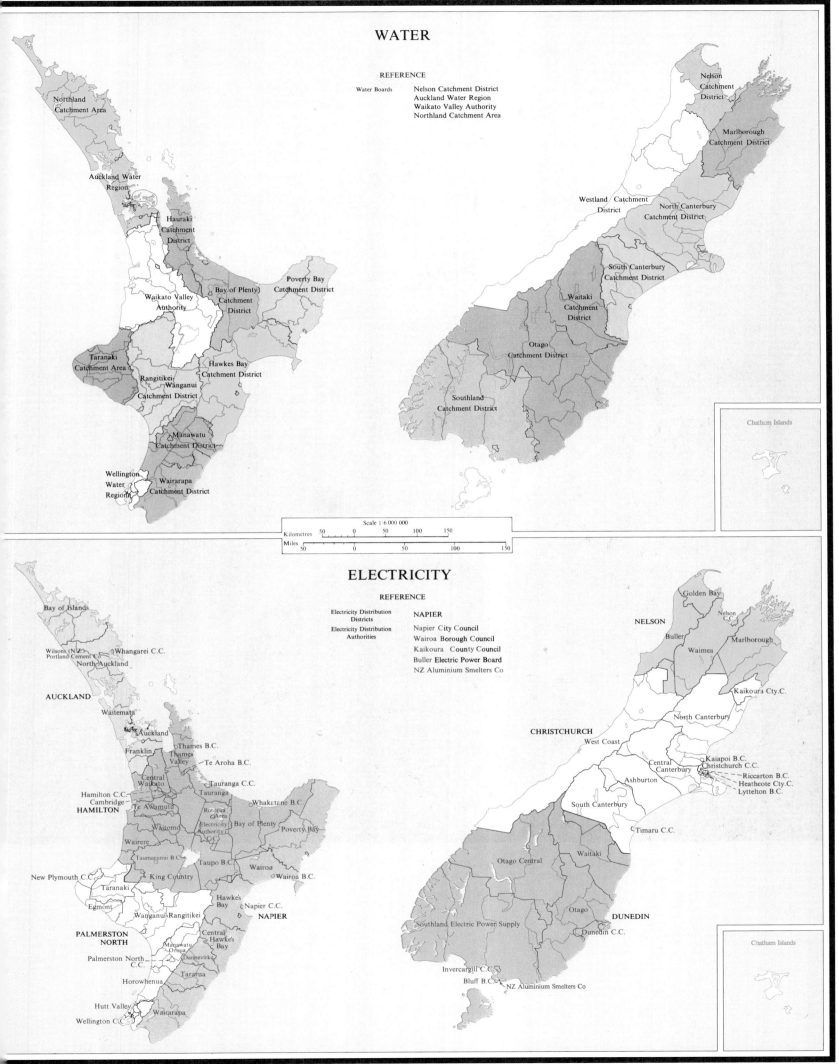

WATER

REFERENCE

Water Boards
Nelson Catchment District
Auckland Water Region
Waikato Valley Authority
Northland Catchment Area

Northland Catchment Area

Auckland Water Region

Hauraki Catchment District

Waikato Valley Authority

Bay of Plenty Catchment District

Poverty Bay Catchment District

Taranaki Catchment Area

Rangitikei-Wanganui Catchment District

Hawkes Bay Catchment District

Manawatu Catchment District

Wellington Water Region

Wairarapa Catchment District

Nelson Catchment District

Marlborough Catchment District

Westland Catchment District

North Canterbury Catchment District

South Canterbury Catchment District

Waitaki Catchment District

Otago Catchment District

Southland Catchment District

Chatham Islands

Scale 1:6 000 000
Kilometres 50 0 50 100 150
Miles 50 0 50 100 150

ELECTRICITY

REFERENCE

Electricity Distribution Districts
Electricity Distribution Authorities

NAPIER

Napier City Council
Wairoa Borough Council
Kaikoura County Council
Buller Electric Power Board
NZ Aluminium Smelters Co

Bay of Islands

Wilsons (N.Z.) Portland Cement Co

Whangarei C.C.

North Auckland

AUCKLAND

Waitemata

Auckland

Franklin

Thames B.C.

Thames Valley

Te Aroha B.C.

Central Waikato

Tauranga C.C.

Tauranga

Hamilton C.C.
Cambridge
HAMILTON

Te Awamutu

Rotorua Area

Whakatane B.C.

Waitomo

Electricity Authority C.C.

Bay of Plenty

Poverty Bay

Wairere

Taumarunui B.C.

Taupo B.C.

Wairoa

New Plymouth C.C.

King Country

Wairoa B.C.

Taranaki

Egmont

Hawke's Bay

Napier C.C.

Wanganui-Rangitikei

NAPIER

PALMERSTON NORTH

Manawatu Oroua

Central Hawke's Bay

Dannevirke

Palmerston North C.C.

Tararua

Horowhenua

Hutt Valley

Wairarapa

Wellington C.C.

Golden Bay

Nelson C.C.

NELSON

Buller

Marlborough

Waimea

Kaikoura Cty.C.

North Canterbury

CHRISTCHURCH

West Coast

Central Canterbury

Kaiapoi B.C.
Christchurch C.C.

Riccarton B.C.
Heathcote Cty.C.
Lyttelton B.C.

Ashburton

South Canterbury

Timaru C.C.

Otago Central

Waitaki

Otago

DUNEDIN

Southland Electric Power Supply

Dunedin C.C.

Invercargill C.C.

Bluff B.C.

NZ Aluminium Smelters Co

Chatham Islands

LANDFORMS AND RESOURCES

D. W. McKenzie

New Zealand offered its first European settlers two dominant characteristics which were to direct its development and guide its future; the first was a close juxtaposition of physical variety in a small country of sharp relief and the second was a climate–vegetation complex which offered firstly, opportunity, secondly, problems of continued use and thirdly, the promise of permanent future productivity.

The mountain building which is still shaping the New Zealand of today—the block movement, the faulting and warping which continues to deform its surface, the massive volcanoes of the geologically immediate past, their activity not yet over—has taken place in a climatic situation the result of which is a deep and extremely fine dissection of a mosaic of landscape types. The dominant characteristic of physical New Zealand is diversity.

These physical characteristics of the country leap to the eye from the remarkable and unusual maps which are associated with this general introduction. The classic maps of land relief show altitudes by colours, either by variations in the intensity of one single colour, or by colour combination, the whole frequently brought to life by oblique shading, as though a light from the top left were illuminating the landscape. Our presentation abandons such a colour procedure and the detailed oblique shading has a colour variation designed to show how the land would look to the eye of an observer in space. Thus the expanse of the Kaingaroa plains is shown to be completely different from the dissected hill country of eastern Taranaki, though both are of comparable altitude; the grassed, consolidated dunes of the western Manawatu are clearly shown to be of a different green from the adjacent alluvial plains to the east, though again both are of exactly the same altitude and would be indistinguishable on a map of more conventional type.

These maps show, then, the widespread deep dissection of the greater part of the country. The section of the Atlas dealing with geology will describe the origins of the landscape and its continuing development. It is still in active tectonic movement. The major faults reflect New Zealand's position on the margin of the great plate of the earth's surface on which lie peninsula India and Australia. The dominantly transcurrent movement of the major faults of New Zealand are part of the northward movement of that plate. Thus New Zealand in its continued movement, so vividly reflected by these maps, is a tiny part of the world structural situation.

The dissection evident on the maps has two other major components. The first is the contrasting mountain systems; that of the South Island with its spectacular glacial, lake-holding valley systems and the deeply drowned fiords of the south-west as opposed to the dominantly river-dissected hill country of the North Island. The second is on a smaller scale: the fineness of the dissection and the steepness of the slopes of small valleys in the North Island and the northern part of the South Island is most surprising considering the lithology, the original vegetation and the climatic variables.

The general picture which emerges is one of a landscape of extreme complexity and diversity, with sharply juxtaposed variation in landscape types. For example, the sweep of Ninety Mile Beach close to the complexity of the inlets and harbours of the Auckland area; Lake Taupo, renowned for its trout fishing, in close proximity to the barely-leashed energy of the thermal steam bore at Wairakei; the boiling mud and geysers of Rotorua

juxtaposed with the ice fields of National Park; Egmont suddenly arising from the Taranaki plains; the lush green dairyland of Taranaki and the tussock land of the 'Desert' plateau; the uplifted areas of the Wellington peninsula in contradistinction to the drowned valleys of Marlborough twenty-six kilometres across Cook Strait; the hiatus of the Strait itself; the broad sweep of the agricultural flat lands of the South Island between the alpine Main Divide culminating in Mt Cook (3764 metres) to the west and the ocean reaches to the east; the glaciers from the alpine range dropping down to the West Coast rain forests; the southern fiords, more extensive in area, more spectacular in their mountain surrounds, than their northern counterparts, abutting the pastoral lowlands of the fertile Southland plains.

The maps show too the limited extent of the lowlands, either outwash plains or alluvium-filled depressions, and their sharp separation from the uplands. These were the first areas to be farmed by European settlers. The Canterbury plains in particular, with no dense forest covering them, came early under the plough, with a rapid initial deterioration of the soil-cover.

It is easy to generalise that, in the oceanic mid-latitude position of New Zealand, the sequence of anticyclones and depressions will produce a tree-growing climate of surprising uniformity. These maps show why this would be an over-simplification. They not only indicate the dominance of the central mountain areas of both islands, with a separation of the wetter west from the relatively drier east, but they also show the complexity of the landscape which produces an accompanying sharp juxtaposition of climatic differences. The interior basins of Central Otago, with a climate almost continental by New Zealand standards, are hard against the wet west coast of the South Island. The widespread sharp dissection produces a ridge–valley situation in which aspect further complicates matters, with sun slopes and shade slopes which produce differences in grazing patterns, forest regeneration and vegetation stability.

Generalisation about New Zealand as essentially a forested land is further complicated by the fact that at the time of European colonisation a considerable proportion of it was in tussock grassland and scrub. As investigations proceed it is becoming clearer that much of this early vegetation pattern was induced—by fires started either by man, intentionally or accidentally, or by volcanoes, especially in the North Island. There is no doubt that climatic changes would have helped in the resultant vegetation changes, but opinion is hardening that they were not by themselves the dominant factor. Such spectacular changes as the present vast forestry developments on the Kaingaroa plains, formerly tussock and scrub-land, show that the pre-European vegetation was controlled not only by climate.

Maori settlement, as indicated on the Settlement map, was concentrated in areas providing both low relief, to aid the simple agricultural practices of the Maori, and water access, for communication purposes. European farming and settlement also spread first on to the areas of low relief, and a comparison of the maps with that of rural population distribution will show the persistence of this pattern. Early pastoralism used the native tussock grassland, especially of the South Island, with sometimes disastrous effect on the quality of the vegetation cover, which only modern patterns of stocking and land treatment have alleviated. A more drastic vegetation change was the introduction of grass and clover on to land cleared by the burning of the forest. The success of this, with its accompanying problems, was to change one major component of the resources available for New Zealand's development.

The essential factor, so easily overlooked, was that man was growing grass in a climatic situation in which nature would favour forest. The result was that grass grew vigorously and was not subject to the annual severity of either drought or cold which would inhibit growth. Not only was there winter growth of grass, but animals were able to graze outdoors throughout the year, though with some supplementary feeding, mostly of grassland products. Recent trends towards restricting the use of the movement of stock for pasture management have not been the result of climatic stress but are directed towards achieving a maximum yield from pasture.

The other side of this use of grass and clover in an essentially tree-growing climate is the tendency for the forest, through succession, to re-assert its dominance. Farming practice on gentle slopes can control this easily; on steeper slopes the problem has not been so simple, particularly in the past. The large areas of deep dissection shown on these maps have, when sown to grassland after forest, produced slopes fundamentally unstable, where soil loss on hills is coupled with massive aggradation in lower valley systems. Where the soil loss is not severe enough to form gullying, numerous small, quickly healed slips may herald a topsoil loss which is associated with the invasion of scrub, sometimes native, sometimes exotic, which is the precursor of forest return.

The answer lies in farming practices producing essentially strong pasture, together with balanced stocking. In the sustaining of grass on dissected hill country the breakthrough was in the field of aerial topdressing, where the aeroplane, as a farming instrument, overcame the limitations of the steep terrain. The result was spectacularly successful. Some hill farmers, formerly supplying only wool and store sheep for lower country fattening, could now enter the field of cattle and fat lamb production directly for market. This was the result of farsighted direction and experiment in a farming community prepared to share in experiment and to change.

A similar situation arose in the dairy industry where mechanisation resulted in the consolidation of dairy factories after important changes in the transport of whole milk and butterfat, and with a change to products other than the traditional butter and cheese, following sensitivity to the requirements of overseas markets. The result was greater productivity in line with that of the sheep and cattle industries. The limitations of the area of land available for dairying are illustrated by the dissection pattern shown on these maps.

These farming patterns have arisen from the practice of growing grass in an essentially forest-growing climate. Initially the use of such magnificent timber trees as the kauri and totara focussed attention on the economic advantages of the native forest, but the demand for land created such pressure to remove forest and to plant grass that destruction of forest, mainly by fire, went on apace. The process was carried far beyond necessity and large areas of steep country whose apparent dense forest cover gave an illusion of soil fertility were burned and sown to grass, mainly to depasture sheep. The degree of fertility, however, depended on the continuous tree cover and was not maintained on unstable slopes subject to excessive soil erosion by the subsequent grass cover. The pressure of introduced animals on a forest developed in an absence of grazing added other dimensions. Deer, goats, pigs, opossums in forest and rabbits in either introduced grassland or native tussock country, brought profound disturbances to the ecological balance, one direct effect being a change in slopes adjusted to the existing vegetation condition. The introduced animals cannot be completely eradicated, but their numbers can be partly controlled.

The tree-growing climate of New Zealand encourages the development of another industry, forestry. The management of timber-producing native forests is possible, though on a necessarily long-term basis. The planting of high-yielding, quick growing, exotic trees to capitalise on the climate is, however, already yielding remarkable returns. Trees as a crop now form an accepted part of the country's economy. The trees themselves, and their part in New Zealand's commerce, are detailed in other sections, particularly in the article on forestry. Their presence is a direct result of the climatic situation, and though much of the indigenous forest was destroyed when timber was a glut on the market, New Zealand can now capitalise on its climate in a world hungry for timber.

The practice of the first European settlers in New Zealand was to use the obviously abundant resources of the land and to establish a variety of communities and organisations in apparently stable situations. That some resources could be exhausted and that others, while not directly expendable, were in a state of delicate ecological balance, was not then generally recognised, and sometimes is not recognised even today, though recent changes in public attitude point to a more hopeful future. Early physical changes took place in country where farming developments were extended into sharply varied slope situations which meant that grassland, succeeding forest cover, was pushed on to slopes too steep to maintain it. This was particularly evident in areas with rock of weak stability, as in the region north of Hawke's Bay in the North Island. It was even more critical when remedial techniques of today, like aerial topdressing, were far in the future and farmers were using variations in stock handling to fight the spread of second growth on steep country formerly under forest, and sometimes failing in the attempt.

Again and again the re-grading of slopes occurred in conditions of soil instability under vegetation change. This happened not only on steep slopes formerly under forest, but also on tussock grassland slopes where the vegetation change was frequently initiated by repeated burnings. The resultant situation was a soil loss which might be spectacular on steep South Island slopes, or the more easily eroded of the North Island slopes where shingle slips or extensive gullying offered dramatic evidence. Or the soil loss might be less spectacularly present on moderately steep slopes where accelerated soil creep and many slight slips gave evidence of its widespread existence. The re-grading of slopes under accelerated erosion, whether dramatically obvious or more general over a greater area, was linked with the disturbance of the valley systems of the rivers. These rivers, usually in balance with the prevailing degree of erosion, were then overloaded with the waste of excessive, induced, rapid erosion, and responded by aggrading their beds, generally destroying or modifying the valuable farmland of river flood-plains.

These events took place in a climate of opinion in which 'use' was the word, rather than 'continued use' which is the key phrase of conservation, with its implication of permanent or renewable resources. Though many profound studies came from some farmers, from ecologists, geographers and foresters, land use and land development frequently proceeded unwisely under the pressure of monetary return. That land and water had other uses which transcended monetary return was an idea which for a long time was in the future, an idea which is fighting for full recognition even today.

On these two maps is evident another of the dominant features in the early development of New Zealand and its continued expansion, a factor which is far more vulnerable than the early settler foresaw and which is clearly limited in quantity. This is the presence and the availability of water.

New Zealand is dependent in many ways upon the abundance and the quality of the waters that prevail throughout and around it. Its position in the world dictates its reliance on seaways for trade and communication; its inland waters, whether lakes, rivers or snowfields, supply an almost unlimited range of tourist and recreational facilities, from ski-ing and skating to sailing and angling; its beaches, too, provide recreation for thousands.

The sea and its products have always been important to New Zealand's development and economy, from pre-colonisation days when whalers and sealers were among its first contacts with the rest of the world. With settlement, the sea provided a source of food and today the fishing industry supplies home and overseas markets as well as employment for hundreds of people. Deep sea fishing, as a sport, is a minor industry in the north while fresh water fishing too is important in the tourist industry.

The existence of plentiful water, however, is accompanied by increasing hazards. This rugged land, with an abundant and regular rainfall, can be seen to be traversed by steep, flowing rivers, many of which have their origins in lakes; and whether these lakes are in recently glaciated valleys, as in the South Island, or in areas of collapse associated with volcanism, as Lake Taupo in the North Island, they are nearly all at comparatively high altitudes and are therefore storage lakes whose flow can be regulated for hydro-electric development in the valleys that drain them. The rosy dreams of abundant hydro-electric power, however, have been dispelled by greatly increased demand. Successive available areas are being used up, with associated lowering of lake storage levels, the latter a subject for bitter controversy between advocates of increased commercial usage and those determined to retain the aesthetic qualities of an unspoiled natural landscape.

Equally, the abundance of pure water in early New Zealand has been suddenly shown to be susceptible to the by-products of urban settlement and of industry, and to the run-off from rural grassland subject to the chemical topdressing today so essential a feature of intensive pastoral production. The fresh water supply is thus vulnerable, as is the purity of sea water at many coastal situations near urban centres, where deterioration of marine life has been shown. New Zealand is slowly beginning to face the massive problems of the organisation of population pressure on resources, small by world standards though that population

and therefore those problems may be. Remedies which would ensure the continued health of water resources are not easy but their pursuit is essential to avoid permanent ecological and aesthetic damage to lakes, rivers and seaboards.

The Population map reveals another facet of New Zealand's economy. The rural population seems sparse when seen against the high pastoral production and the position of New Zealand in world trade in such products. This reflects the extremely high agricultural production per unit engaged in farming and the accompanying rise in city and town growth. A study of the maps also shows the physical situation which led to the establishment and growth of Auckland, Wellington, Christchurch and Dunedin, as ports, and to the subsequent rise of centres such as Hamilton and Palmerston North, each initially a service centre for an agricultural area. The establishment of further port facilities nearer agriculturally productive areas led to the development of ports where the physical characteristics were not so suitable, such as New Plymouth, Napier and Timaru. These maps show that what might be ideal harbour situations sometimes do not lie near productive hinterlands, so that coasts offering less in harbour facilities must be used because of their position. New ports and harbours have been established to handle new export products. The demand for New Zealand's forest products overseas has led to the establishment or expansion of port facilities at Whangarei, Tauranga and Nelson.

A characteristic of settlement, that based on the prevalent New Zealand ideal of a dwelling house on an individual plot of land, shows in the photographs. Even the major cities sprawl over areas far greater than the numbers of their populations would lead one to expect. The use of a special symbol on the Population maps for the small population centres in rural areas shows their importance as service centres in the economy, an importance far greater than the number of people in them would indicate.

Increasingly, New Zealand is placing itself under self-scrutiny and closely questioning continued economic growth and the continued utilisation of natural resources. The first was long regarded as being such an essential part of national development that its rate and directions were beyond question. It is only now being realised that the direction of growth may result in a disturbance of the national resources themselves, and that what seem to be simple developments may have profound and sometimes unforeseen effects. Planning, in the past, was looked at askance by New Zealanders; today it is seen to be essential not only to widely-directed development but also to the continued existence of living standards at the present level.

Thus the movement for the preservation of the landscape has become almost a crusade in New Zealand. That some of it should go beyond reality in the demand for preservation is inevitable. That the productivity of this country, either lowland, gently rolling or steeply sloped, shall be adjusted to a permanent balance of resources is essential. To this end New Zealand is moving.

The photograph on *page 70* shows the deep and extremely fine dissection of the ridges of the southern Richardson mountains in Central Otago.

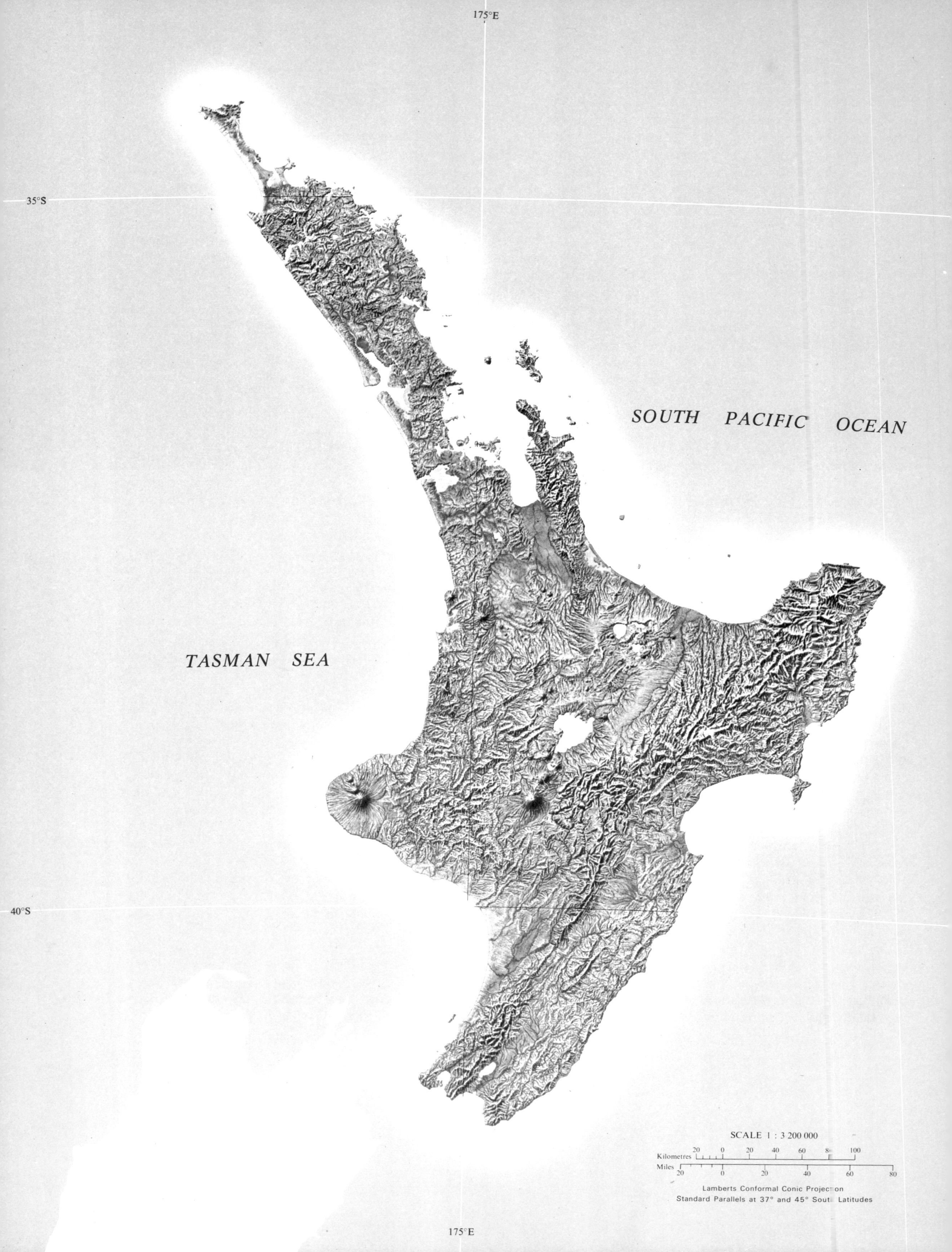

175°E

35°S

SOUTH PACIFIC OCEAN

TASMAN SEA

40°S

SCALE 1 : 3 200 000

Kilometres 20   0   20   40   60   8   100
Miles   20   0   20   40   60   80

Lamberts Conformal Conic Projection
Standard Parallels at 37° and 45° South Latitudes

175°E

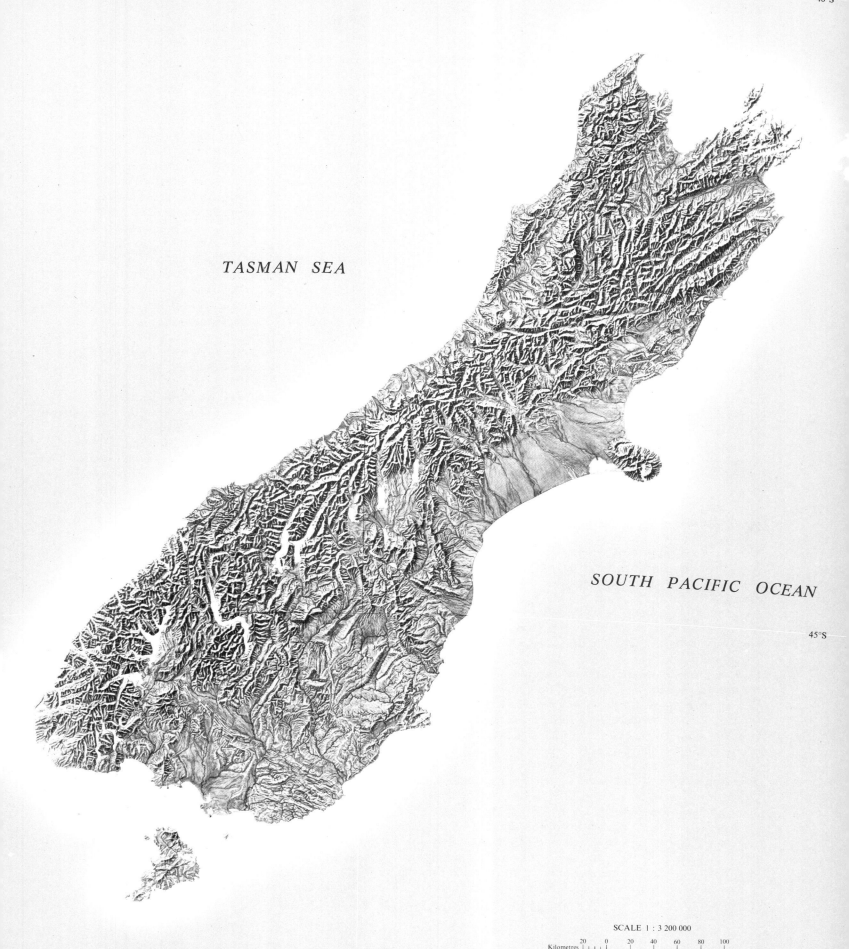

170°E

40°S

TASMAN SEA

SOUTH PACIFIC OCEAN

45°S

SCALE 1 : 3 200 000

20   0   20   40   60   80   100
Kilometres

20   0   20   40   60   80
Miles

Lamberts Conformal Conic Projection
Standard Parallels at 37° and 45° South Latitudes

170°E

GRAVITY, MAGNETISM AND SEISMICITY

G. A. Eiby & W. I. Reilly

The Gravity Field in New Zealand

The map which follows is based on many thousands of measurements of the Earth's gravitational attraction in New Zealand. Since this attraction depends markedly upon height above sea level, it is not feasible to show observed values on a small map. Instead, the map shows contours of the value (in mN/kg)[1] that gravity would have if the land surface were everywhere at sea level. To obtain the actual value at a given place, find its height from a topographic map and subtract 1.97 mN/kg from the value shown for each kilometre of elevation. On the surface of the ocean, subtract 0.67 mN/kg for each kilometre of ocean depth. For points above the surface of either land or sea, subtract a further 3.09 mN/kg for each kilometre of additional height.

The Magnetic Field in New Zealand

The map shows the smoothed regional pattern expected in 1975, with localised effects due to surface rocks removed. It is based on continuous records of the Earth's magnetic field made at Amberley Observatory, and on measurements repeated every few years at many points throughout New Zealand. The intensity of the magnetic field[2] is given by contours at intervals of $4\mu T$; its value is at present decreasing by $0.05\mu T$ per year. The direction of the field is given by its inclination to the horizontal, at intervals of $4°$, and by its easterly declination, the angle between the compass direction and true north, at intervals of $1°$. The angle of inclination is increasing at a rate of less than one minute of arc per year, and the declination angle is increasing (that is, the compass direction is moving to the east) at a rate of three minutes of arc per year.

Gravity and Magnetic Anomalies

Localised differences of the observed gravity, or magnetism, from the regional pattern are due to variations of rock density in the outermost 100 kilometres of the Earth, or of rock magnetisation in the upper twenty kilometres. Detailed comparison of these anomalies with the surface geology yields a fuller picture of the three-dimensional structure of the region.

The map shows contours of isostatic gravity anomaly. These are found by comparing the observed values of gravity with those calculated for a model Earth in which the thickness of the lighter crustal rocks is assumed to vary in a regular manner. Beneath elevated regions they become thicker, and thinner beneath the deep ocean floors. These lighter rocks may be pictured as floating on a denser substratum, which has been shown by seismological investigations to lie at a depth of thirty to forty kilometres beneath New Zealand.

Both positive and negative anomalies of up to 1.5 mN/kg are found in New Zealand, comparable in amount to the largest anywhere. The most notable zone of gravity deficiency, which may indicate either a greater thickness of light crustal rocks, or a region of lower than normal density in the underlying mantle, extends from East Cape to Cook Strait, and is roughly coincident with the zone in which deep-focus earthquakes occur. The centre of the anomalous mass cannot lie deeper than fifty kilometres.

Zones of negative anomaly experience an upward hydrostatic pressure, and consequently have a tendency to rise. There is no large anomaly associated with the Southern Alps, which, although young, must therefore be close to equilibrium. The small area of large positive anomaly in Fiordland, on the other hand, indicates a complex and unstable geological situation, reflected also in the high seismicity. Minor positive anomalies follow the belts of dense ultrabasic and basic igneous rocks in Otago.

Some of the gravitationally anomalous areas are also magnetically anomalous. Areas in which the strength of the magnetic field is $0.2\mu T$, or more, above the normal are shown in red. Observational coverage is less complete than for gravity. Many of the magnetic anomalies are caused by rocks associated with active or recently extinct volcanoes. Others, such as those in the west of the North Island, in Nelson, Otago and Southland mark the positions of ancient volcanoes that have long since been eroded away. In some cases the rocks responsible are exposed at the surface, but in others they are concealed beneath younger formations.

The Seismicity of New Zealand

There is no part of New Zealand in which earthquakes have never been felt, but the frequency of occurrence varies. Only very restricted areas remain in which no shocks have been instrumentally detected and located, and in the present state of knowledge seismologists expect every locality to experience large earthquakes from time to time.

The earthquakes of New Zealand are not isolated, but form part of a belt of activity that parallels the greater part of the perimeter of the Pacific Ocean. This activity is not strictly continuous, and its character changes from section to section, so that even within New Zealand it is possible to identify several different, though related, systems.

The largest of these is the *Main Seismic Region*, which covers the North Island (except the Northland peninsula), and the northern half of the South Island. Within this region, a shock of magnitude 7 or more can be expected about once a decade, one of magnitude 6 or more once a year, and one above magnitude 5 some ten times a year. For the *Fiordland Region*, covering the south-west part of the South Island, the figures are similar, but the area is much smaller, and there is reason to think that the proportion of large shocks may be greater. In neither case, however, does the level of activity approach that in such other parts of the circum-Pacific system as Japan, Chile or the Philippines, and New Zealand may in fact be regarded as an area of only moderate seismicity.

Between the Main and Fiordland Seismic Regions lies a less active *Central Seismic Region*. Here the average level of activity is markedly lower, but it has an intermittent character, and, during an active period, a district within this Region may experience shocks with a frequency approaching that in the Main Region, while other places

---

[1] The intensity of the gravitational attraction on an object is expressed as the force in newtons exerted on each kilogram of its mass. A body allowed to fall freely in a gravitational field of strength 1 N/kg will accelerate at a rate of one metre per second per second. mN is a millinewton $(10^{-3}N)$.

[2] The intensity of the magnetic field is expressed in teslas (T). A field of intensity 1T would produce a torque of 1 newton-metre on a magnetic dipole of moment 1 ampere-turn square metre. μT is a microtesla $(10^{-6}T)$.

remain quiescent. Shocks here, and also in *Northland*, which has the lowest average level of seismicity in New Zealand, have sometimes reached damaging intensity.[3]

Earthquake activity does not stop at the coast, but to the west it does not extend beyond the 500 metre depth-contour, except in Fiordland, where deep water is very close to the coast, and the activity continues to the foot of the continental slope. Few shocks have been placed further east than the axis of the Hikurangi Trench, and it seems probable that almost all of these have been mis-located. Between these limits, the whole region is active.

Submarine earthquakes also occur along the northern flank of the Chatham Rise, and near the Chatham Islands. To the north-east, activity continues towards the Kermadec Islands and beyond, becoming increasingly vigorous. Activity along the Macquarie Ridge continues the circum-Pacific system to the south-west.

Most earthquakes occur within the earth's crust, which has in New Zealand an average thickness of a little more than thirty kilometres, but in tectonically active regions deep-focus earthquakes originate at depths as great as 700 kilometres. New Zealand's deepest known earthquakes (under northern Taranaki) had depths of about 600 kilometres, but very deep shocks have been infrequent and none in the range 400–600 kilometres is known. Most New Zealand earthquakes below the crust might therefore be termed 'intermediate' rather than deep.

In the Main Seismic Region, the deep shocks occupy a restricted volume dipping to the north-west, away from the Hikurangi Trench. The maximum depth of occurrence (if the small group of shocks at 600 kilometres is neglected) diminishes from about 400 kilometres beneath the Bay of Plenty to less than 100 kilometres beneath Nelson and Marlborough. The maximum depth beneath Fiordland is about 160 kilometres, but the series of observations available is much less extended, and the configuration is not accurately established. The system clearly dips eastwards, away from the Tasman Basin. Outside these regions, only shallow shocks are known.

For most seismological and engineering purposes, it is important that maps and lists of earthquakes should be complete above some stated lower magnitude. Without instrumental data, it is difficult to determine reliable magnitudes. Formally accurate lists may therefore differ in detail, and exclude shocks whose nearness to centres of population has given them social or historical importance. In the Main and Central Seismic Regions it is unlikely that

any shock above magnitude 7 (the approximate lower limit of destructiveness) has gone unobserved since European settlement began, but recent instrumental data suggest strongly that records for the Fiordland Region are incomplete. For the whole country, about sixteen destructive shocks are known, and some hundreds have caused minor damage. Only the south-west Wairarapa earthquake of 23 January 1855 is believed to have reached magnitude 8, and only the magnitude $7\frac{3}{4}$ Buller (17 June 1929) and Hawke's Bay (3 February 1931) earthquakes have caused more than isolated deaths and casualties.

Because of the more limited area in which they occur, deep earthquakes dominate the pattern whenever both deep and shallow shocks are shown on a single map. Since depth reduces the maximum intensity experienced at the Earth's surface, shallow shocks have more practical significance for engineering and civil defence purposes. Separate maps are therefore presented.

Although the broad pattern of activity becomes apparent in any map covering a period of a year or more, the less active parts of the country may be without shocks for long periods. A period has been chosen for the map of shallow shocks that enables at least a few to be shown in most active areas. A different period has been used for the deep activity, as it has only recently become possible to determine the depths of shocks in the Fiordland Region with acceptable accuracy.

In the cross-sections, all crustal earthquakes are assigned arbitrary depths of twelve or thirty-three kilometres, as it is impossible to obtain exact values when the depths are small. Shocks within this range are more common than those between ten kilometres and the surface. The positions and magnitudes of earthquakes before instrumental recording was introduced, in the first decades of this century, are necessarily uncertain. No historic earthquake shown is likely to have had a magnitude of less than $6\frac{1}{2}$. All those in the Main Region reaching magnitude 7 are believed to have been included, but the status of a few shocks remains doubtful. The distribution of instrumentally located shocks of more than magnitude 6 shows the historic data for Fiordland to be incomplete. Shocks more than 150 kilometres from the coast are not shown.

The recording network enables all shocks of magnitude 4 and above, within 150 kilometres of the coast, to be detected and located. Every station has a short-period vertical component seismograph, and about a quarter of them have several additional instruments. There are also stations under New Zealand control in Samoa, Rarotonga and Fiji, on Raoul, Chatham and Campbell islands, and at Scott Base in the Antarctic. A network of strong-motion recorders for engineering purposes is also in operation.

[3]The *magnitude* of an earthquake is a figure related to the total energy liberated. It is determined by instrumental measurement, and should not be confused with the *intensity*, which is based on a non-instrumental assessment of the degree of shaking experienced at a given place.

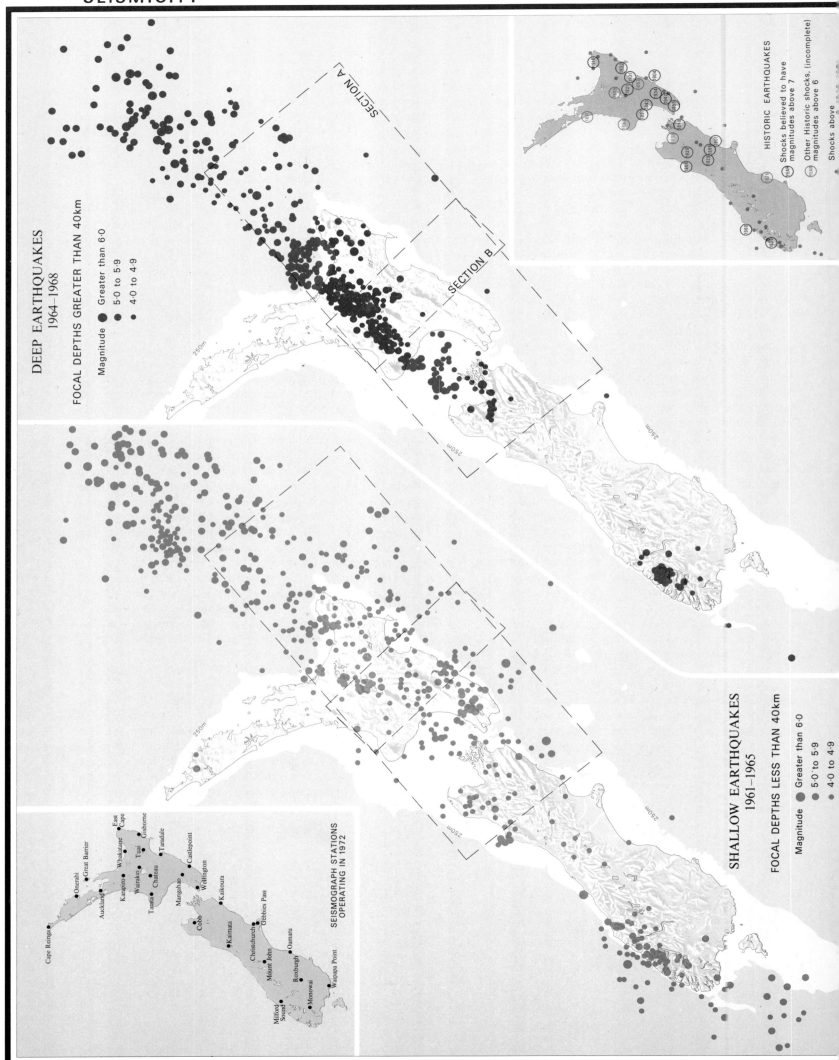

DEEP EARTHQUAKES
1964–1968

FOCAL DEPTHS GREATER THAN 40km

Magnitude
● Greater than 6·0
● 5·0 to 5·9
· 4·0 to 4·9

SECTION A

SECTION B

HISTORIC EARTHQUAKES

● Shocks believed to have magnitudes above 7
● Other Historic shocks, (incomplete) magnitudes above 6
· Shocks above

SHALLOW EARTHQUAKES
1961–1965

FOCAL DEPTHS LESS THAN 40km

Magnitude
● Greater than 6·0
● 5·0 to 5·9
· 4·0 to 4·9

SEISMOGRAPH STATIONS
OPERATING IN 1972

Cape Reinga
Onerahi
Great Barrier
Auckland
Whakatane
East Cape
Karapiro
Wairakei
Gisborne
Tuai
Chateau
Taradale
Turaia
Castlepoint
Mangahao
Wellington
Cobb
Kaikoura
Kaimata
Gebbies Pass
Christchurch
Mount John
Oamaru
Roxburgh
Milford Sound
Monowai
Waipapa Point

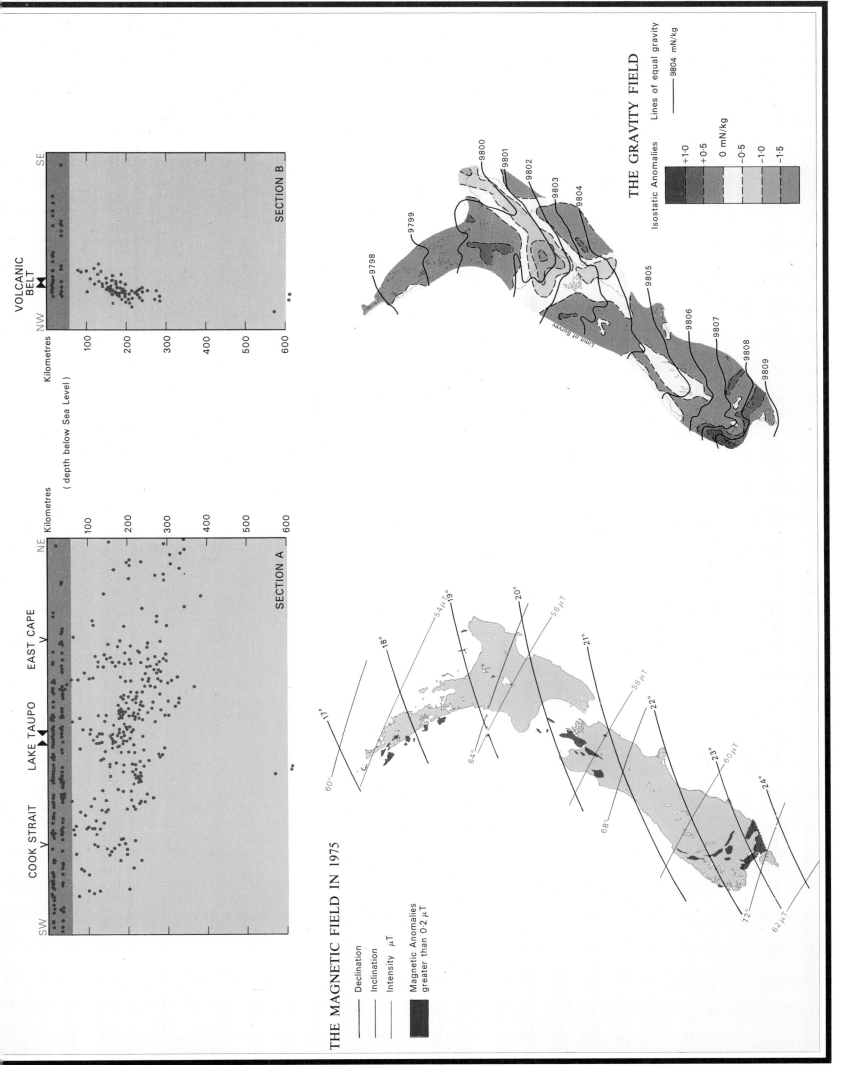

SECTION B

SECTION A

VOLCANIC BELT

NW   SE

Kilometres
(depth below Sea Level)

100
200
300
400
500
600

COOK STRAIT   LAKE TAUPO   EAST CAPE

SW   NE

Kilometres

100
200
300
400
500
600

THE MAGNETIC FIELD IN 1975

- Declination
- Inclination
- Intensity μT

Magnetic Anomalies
greater than 0·2 μT

THE GRAVITY FIELD

Isostatic Anomalies   Lines of equal gravity

9804 mN/kg

+1·0
+0·5
0 mN/kg
−0·5
−1·0
−1·5

Limit of Survey

9798
9799
9800
9801
9802
9803
9804
9805
9806
9807
9808
9809

17°
18°
19°
20°
21°
22°
23°
24°

54 μT
56 μT
58 μT
60 μT
62 μT

60°
64°
68°
72°

THE SEA FLOOR
D. J. Cullen

The New Zealand landmass, small in extent and isolated within an oceanic environment, is merely the emerged portion of a broad segment of abnormally thick submarine crust of quasi-continental type. This segment contrasts with and separates expanses of thin oceanic crust in the Tasman Sea and south-western Pacific Ocean. The differences in crustal thickness determine the bathymetry of the region, New Zealand lying at the 'hub' of a complex of submarine plateaus and ridges with intervening basins and troughs and associated deep trenches.

Genetically, these features are of two distinct types. To the south-east and north-west of New Zealand, Campbell Plateau, Chatham Rise, Lord Howe Rise, Norfolk Ridge and Three Kings Rise are considered to be remnants of the former continental margin and peripheral geosynclinal belt of the ancient supercontinent, Gondwanaland. In terms of modern geological concepts, the submarine ridges and plateaus thus represent crustal strips separated from one another and from Australia and Antarctica by rifting, with the consequent formation of new sea floor beneath the Tasman Sea and south-western Pacific Ocean continuing since late Cretaceous times.

In contrast, the Kermadec–Colville and Macquarie ridges, which trend respectively north-north-east and south-west from New Zealand, are seismically-active, volcanic island arcs, formed concurrently with the new sea floor during the Cenozoic era. Deep oceanic trenches, such as the Kermadec and Puysegur trenches, denote subduction zones, where the edge of one crustal plate is forced under its neighbour. Volcanism is now extinct on Macquarie Ridge, but, at the southern end of Kermadec Ridge, recent underwater volcanic activity has been detected in a group of seamounts aligned with the active White Island volcano and the North Island geothermal centres.

THE CONTINENTAL SHELF AND SLOPE

The New Zealand landmass is surrounded by a shallow, well-defined submarine platform, the continental shelf, sloping gently downward from the intertidal zone to depths of approximately 180 metres. Below this level, the sea floor gradient increases abruptly and passes into the continental slope, which plunges to depths usually greater than 1000 metres.

The width of the continental shelf varies considerably. At its widest, west of Cape Egmont, the shelf is 110 kilometres across, whereas off the Fiordland coast it is often reduced to three kilometres or less. The shelf is essentially an erosional feature, cut across inclined or folded Tertiary and pre-Tertiary strata by marine transgressions. Traces of former shorelines, related to episodes of lowered sea level during the Pleistocene Ice Age and now represented by local minor steepenings of the shelf profile, are recognised on the New Zealand shelf. One such submerged shoreline occurs at the eastern entrance to Foveaux Strait, associated with the inundated remnants of an ancient coastal lagoon, morphologically similar to modern lagoons along the northern margin of the Strait.

The extension into recent times of localised folding and uplift within the shelf area, comparable with movements measured on land, has been demonstrated in Hawke Bay where three recently-active anticlinal fold axes have been identified striking north-north-east to south-south-west. Large-scale submarine slumps, emanating from the top of the continental slope between Cape Kidnappers and Cape Turnagain, are attributed to earthquakes associated with this folding. The upper part of the slope is normally characterised by much thicker sediment accumulations than occur on the shelf, and the inherent instability of these deposits undoubtedly contributed towards triggering the slumps.

Deeply-incised submarine canyons traverse the shelf and slope, usually where the shelf is narrow or adjacent to a mountainous coast as in the vicinity of the Otago and Kaikoura peninsulas and off the south-east coast of the North Island. The canyons are erosional features, cut by mud-laden 'turbidity currents' and serving as channels for the dispersal of sediment to deeper regions. Their configuration often suggests control by structures in the underlying rock basement.

SEA-FLOOR SEDIMENTS

A heterogeneous assemblage of sediments occurs on the sea floor around New Zealand. On the shelf and upper slope, the sediments consist of land-derived detritus ranging from boulders to clay, mixed with varying amounts of biogenic calcareous material such as molluscan shell. Certain current-swept areas where present-day sedimentation is inhibited, as in parts of Foveaux and Cook straits, are floored by ancient fluviatile gravels submerged during the post-Glacial sea level rise and reworked in the marine environment. Fine-grained terrigenous sediments may extend to deeper sea floor areas fed by submarine canyons, as in the Hikurangi Trench.

Much of the remaining sea floor around New Zealand is covered by pelagic oozes, composed largely of the skeletal remains of microscopic organisms that originally lived in the topmost oceanic layers and accumulated on the bottom after death. Calcareous foraminiferal tests and coccoliths are the commonest particles, but siliceous radiolaria and diatoms are also widespread. The latter are especially abundant on the subantarctic sea floor.

Because of the tendency of organic carbonate to dissolve in depths greater than 4000–5000 metres, the deepest parts of the south Fiji, south-western Pacific and Tasman basins are floored by non-calcareous, residual red clay composed of fine volcanic ash and aeolian dust.

Coarse to fine volcanic debris, including primary ejectamenta and redeposited material, is widespread on the sea floor close to recent eruptive centres in the Bay of Plenty and along the Kermadec Ridge. Submarine cores, recovered from the shelf and deeper regions east of the North Island, contain ash layers that can be related to specific eruptive phases on land. Pumice particles are found in oceanic sediments as far south as the Chatham Rise and Bounty Trough.

Mixed assortments of faceted and striated boulders, that sporadically appear on Chatham Rise and Campbell Plateau, are glacial erratics deposited by melting icebergs from Antarctica. Unusual concentrations of the minerals glauconite (a silicate of iron, potassium and aluminium) and phosphorite (calcium carbonophosphate) are also prominent on the Chatham Rise. The minerals developed *in situ* and have been concentrated by the winnowing action of bottom currents. Manganiferous concretions are reported on Campbell Plateau and Aotea Seamount, and on the deep floor of the southern Tasman Sea.

80

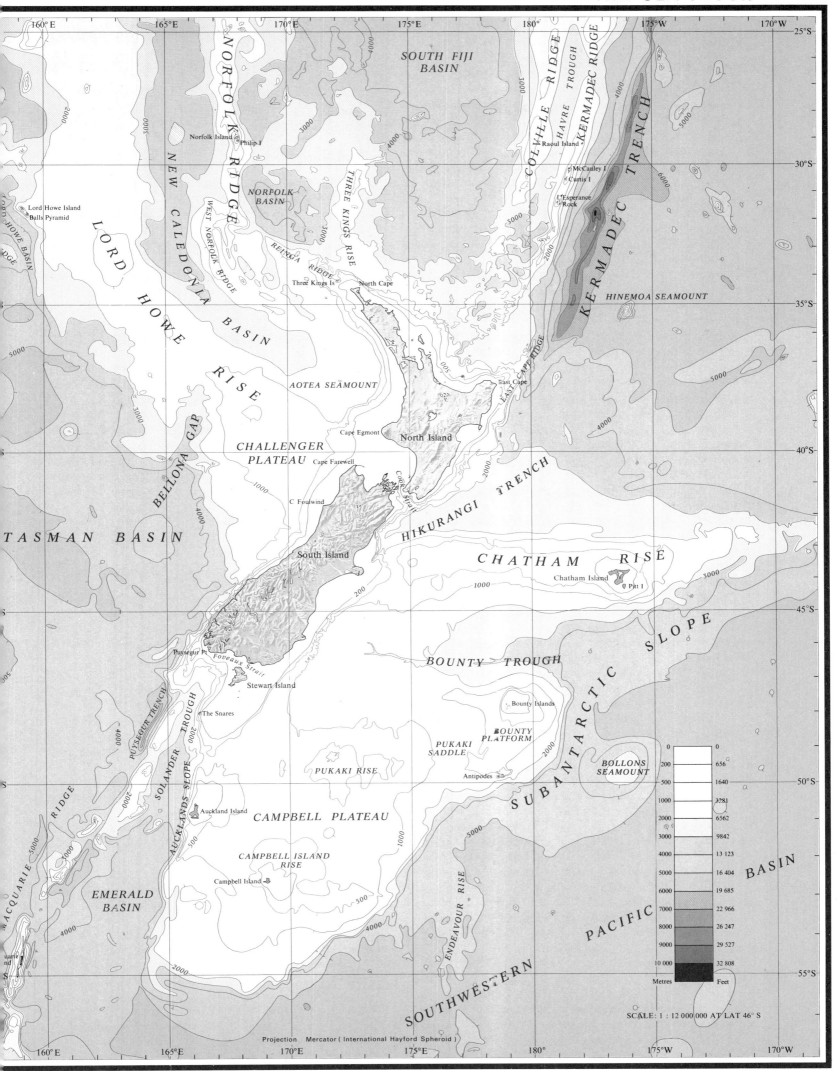

25°S
160°E 165°E 170°E 175°E 180° 175°W 170°W

SOUTH FIJI
BASIN

NORFOLK RIDGE

COLVILLE RIDGE
HAVRE TROUGH
KERMADEC RIDGE

KERMADEC TRENCH

Norfolk Island Philip I

NORFOLK
BASIN

NEW CALEDONIA BASIN

WEST NORFOLK RIDGE

THREE KINGS RISE

Raoul Island

McCauley I
Curtis I

L'Esperance
Rock

30°S

LORD HOWE BASIN

Lord Howe Island
Balls Pyramid

LORD HOWE RISE

REINGA RIDGE

Three Kings Is   North Cape

HINEMOA SEAMOUNT

35°S

AOTEA SEAMOUNT

East Cape

EAST CAPE RIDGE

CHALLENGER
PLATEAU

Cape Egmont

North Island

Cape Farewell

BELLONA GAP

TASMAN BASIN

C Foulwind

Cook Strait

HIKURANGI   TRENCH

40°S

CHATHAM   RISE

South Island

Chatham Island   Pitt I

45°S

SUBANTARCTIC   SLOPE

Puysegur Pt
Foveaux Strait

BOUNTY   TROUGH

PUYSEGUR TRENCH

Stewart Island

The Snares

Bounty Islands

BOUNTY
PLATFORM

PUKAKI
SADDLE

BOLLONS
SEAMOUNT

SOLANDER TROUGH

PUKAKI RISE

Antipodes Is

50°S

MACQUARIE RIDGE

AUCKLANDS SLOPE

Auckland Island

CAMPBELL PLATEAU

CAMPBELL ISLAND
RISE

ENDEAVOUR RISE

PACIFIC   BASIN

Campbell Island

EMERALD
BASIN

Metres	Feet
0	0
200	656
500	1640
1000	3281
2000	6562
3000	9842
4000	13 123
5000	16 404
6000	19 685
7000	22 966
8000	26 247
9000	29 527
10 000	32 808

SOUTHWESTERN

55°S

SCALE: 1 : 12 000 000 AT LAT 46° S

Projection Mercator (International Hayford Spheroid)

160°E 165°E 170°E 175°E 180° 175°W 170°W

CLIMATE

A. I Tomlinson

The lower layers of the thin skin of air surrounding the earth move, on the average, in six large systems. Each has its associated characteristic weather pattern. From the equator to the latitudes of about 30° North and South are the north-east and south-east trade winds. Between the latitudes of about 30° and 70°, mid-latitude westerly winds blow around both hemispheres. Poleward from about 70° there are predominantly easterly winds.

New Zealand lies within the mid-latitude, westerly zone and the climate is very much influenced by this predominant wind flow. The isolation of the country in a large area of ocean ensures that the winds arriving here have had ample opportunity to become moisture-laden, and, accordingly, humid conditions are common. Moreover, the passage over vast areas of ocean effects a moderating influence on the temperature of the air.

Within this band of mid-latitude westerlies is a succession of anticyclones and depressions. Generally, the depressions lie to the south of the anticyclones in the Southern Hemisphere, and the average position in New Zealand of the anticyclones goes through an annual cycle from about latitude 26° South in the winter to latitude 36° South in the summer, though there is considerable variability in all seasons. This predominantly eastward-moving sequence of anticyclones and depressions, with their associated cold and warm fronts, produces much of the day-to-day weather over New Zealand. On *p 83* is an example of this sequence with associated cloud pictures taken from the weather satellite ESSA 8 at a height of 1400 kilometres. There is a major trough of low pressure over and to the east of New Zealand in this figure, with two cold fronts and a depression contained in it. Anticyclones lie over eastern Australia and the south Pacific Ocean.

The interval of time between the successive troughs of low pressure passing over the country is very variable. On a seasonal basis, only about one season in two experiences a regular progression with a fairly constant interval between troughs of low pressure, and when this occurs the interval is usually between five and eleven days, with a marked preference for eight to ten days. There is no apparent seasonal variation throughout the year.

While the country's location in the mid-latitude westerlies determines the general nature of the climate, its orography has a very dominant effect on the variation of the climate and wind flow within the country. The main ranges of the North and South Islands extend in a north-east/south-west line and provide a barrier to the prevailing westerly winds. This is most noticeable in the South Island where the Southern Alps provide a barrier of greater height than 1000 metres for about 750 kilometres. As the maritime air from the Tasman Sea rises to cross this barrier, it often cools enough to produce clouds and rain to the west of the main divide. These western slopes of the main ranges receive very high annual rainfall totals, sometimes in excess of 6000 millimetres, while just to the east of the main divide there are some areas of very low rainfall and high sunshine duration.

WINDS

Winds from a westerly quarter prevail in all seasons, with a general tendency to increase in strength from the north to the south of the country; at the same time, considerable local modifications to the general air flow occur during its passage across the mountainous terrain. A considerable number of south-westerlies in Westland and a predominance of north-westerlies in inland districts of Otago and Canterbury result, often as strong gales, in spring and early summer. On the Canterbury coast, however, north-easterlies are almost as frequent as the predominant south-westerlies, mainly as a result of persistent sea breezes during the summer. To the north of Taranaki the general air flow is more south-westerly and there is a noticeable reduction in windiness in summer. Cook Strait, the only substantial gap in the main mountain chain that forms the backbone of both Islands, acts as a natural funnel for the air flow and is a particularly windy locality afflicted by gales from the south as well as from the north-west (*see map on p 87*). This 'funnel' effect is also much in evidence about Foveaux Strait.

Sea breezes, occasionally enhanced by the general wind flow and funnelled by the local orography, are the predominant winds in summer in many coastal places. Calm conditions are common in inland areas in autumn and winter. At such times dispersion of smoke from industrial plant and domestic chimneys is poor.

High wind gusts occur over exposed parts of the country. Instantaneous gusts of up to 130 knots have been measured in the Southern Alps and are probably not uncommon there. The instantaneous gusts which are equalled or exceeded with an average frequency of once in two, and once in twenty, years are given below for a selection of stations:

Gust Speed (knots) to be expected once every:

	2 years	20 years
AUCKLAND	56	68
GISBORNE	55	65
NEW PLYMOUTH	62	79
WELLINGTON	73	92
HOKITIKA	55	67
CHRISTCHURCH	59	74
DUNEDIN	57	71
INVERCARGILL	64	76

RAINFALL

The average rainfall and number of days with rainfall of one millimetre or more are represented on *p 85*. The average rainfall ranges from as little as 350 millimetres in a small part of Central Otago to more than 7000 millimetres in the Southern Alps. The average for the whole country is high, probably more than 2000 millimetres, but for a large area it lies between 600 and 1600 millimetres. The only areas having less than 600 millimetres are found in the South Island, to the east of the main ranges, and include Central and North Otago and most of South Canterbury. Areas of Hawke's Bay, Wairarapa and Manawatu, with rainfalls of 700–1000 millimetres a year, are the driest parts of the North Island. The remainder has more than 1000 millimetres, while much valuable farm land has upwards of 1500 millimetres, chiefly in North Taranaki and Northland. In both islands there is a sizeable area with more than 2500 millimetres a year but, with the exception of Westland, this land is mountainous and unoccupied, much of it being forest-covered.

Over most of the North Island there are between 100 and 150 days a year on which one millimetre or more of rain falls. In the South Island the corresponding figures are of more than 200 days in the Alps, 150 to 200 days on

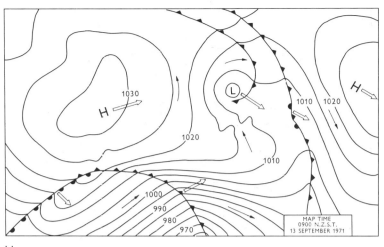

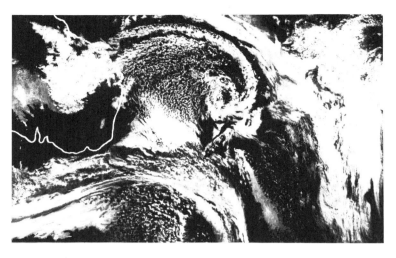

H .... Anticyclone

L .... Depression

1030 .... Isobaric Pressure in Millibars

▲▲▲ .... Cold Front

●●● .... Warm Front

→ .... Wind Flow Direction

⇨ .... Movement of Weather System

MAP TIME
0900 N.Z.S.T.
13 SEPTEMBER 1971

A TYPICAL WEATHER MAP FOR THE NEW ZEALAND AREA WITH THE ASSOCIATED SATELLITE CLOUD PICTURE (the white areas in the satellite picture are cloud)

CLIMATE DISTRICTS

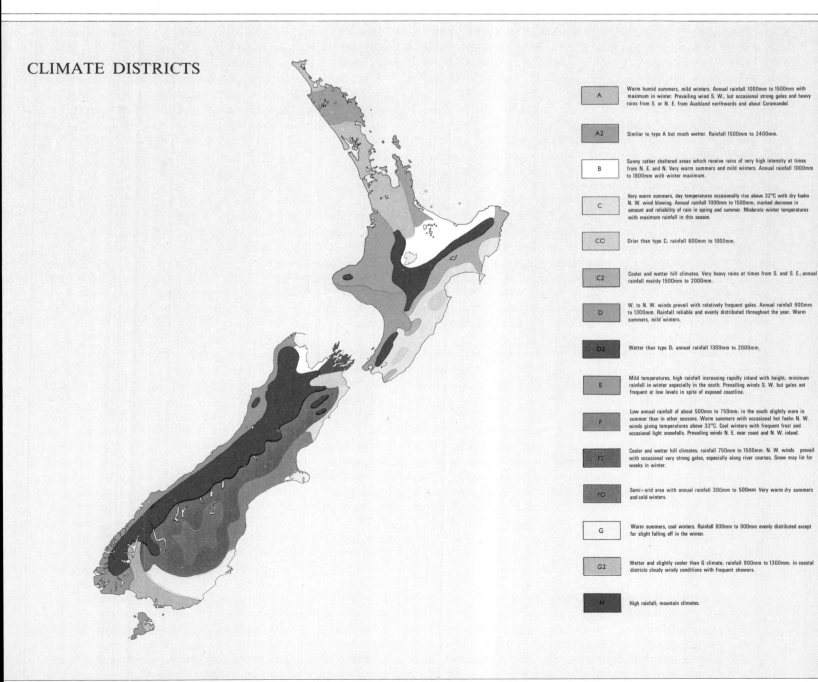

A — Warm humid summers, mild winters. Annual rainfall 1000mm to 1500mm with maximum in winter. Prevailing wind S. W., but occasional strong gales and heavy rains from E. or N. E. from Auckland northwards and about Coromandel.

A2 — Similar to type A but much wetter. Rainfall 1500mm to 2400mm.

B — Sunny rather sheltered areas which receive rains of very high intensity at times from N. E. and N. Very warm summers and mild winters. Annual rainfall 1000mm to 1800mm with winter maximum.

C — Very warm summers, day temperatures occasionally rise above 32°C with dry foehn N. W. wind blowing. Annual rainfall 1000mm to 1500mm; marked decrease in amount and reliability of rain in spring and summer. Moderate winter temperatures with maximum rainfall in this season.

CC — Drier than type C; rainfall 600mm to 1000mm.

C2 — Cooler and wetter hill climates. Very heavy rains at times from S. and S. E.; annual rainfall mainly 1500mm to 2000mm.

D — W. to N. W. winds prevail with relatively frequent gales. Annual rainfall 900mm to 1300mm. Rainfall reliable and evenly distributed throughout the year. Warm summers, mild winters.

D2 — Wetter than type D; annual rainfall 1300mm to 2000mm.

E — Mild temperatures, high rainfall increasing rapidly inland with height; minimum rainfall in winter especially in the south. Prevailing winds S. W. but gales not frequent at low levels in spite of exposed coastline.

F — Low annual rainfall of about 500mm to 750mm; in the south slightly more in summer than in other seasons. Warm summers with occasional hot foehn N. W. winds giving temperatures above 32°C. Cool winters with frequent frost and occasional light snowfalls. Prevailing winds N. E. near coast and N. W. inland.

F2 — Cooler and wetter hill climates; rainfall 750mm to 1500mm. N. W. winds prevail with occasional very strong gales, especially along river courses. Snow may lie for weeks in winter.

FO — Semi—arid area with annual rainfall 300mm to 500mm Very warm dry summers and cold winters.

G — Warm summers, cool winters. Rainfall 600mm to 900mm evenly distributed except for slight falling off in the winter.

G2 — Wetter and slightly cooler than G climate; rainfall 900mm to 1300mm; in coastal districts cloudy windy conditions with frequent showers.

H — High rainfall; mountain climates.

the West Coast and between 60 and 100 days over much of Central and North Otago, Canterbury and eastern Marlborough. The figure for the remainder of the South Island lies between 100 and 150 days.

Heavy rain is most frequent in the west and the north of the country. At Hokitika there are, on the average, forty-eight days a year with a rainfall of more than 20 millimetres, while Dunedin averages only six such days (p 85). Rainfalls of durations of one, six, twenty-four and seventy-two hours, expected to be equalled or exceeded on the average of once every two, and once every twenty years, are given below:

Rainfalls (mm) to be expected once every 2 (20) years in the durations given:

	1 hour	6 hours	24 hours	72 hours
KAITAIA	30(65)	60(110)	90(150)	110(195)
AUCKLAND	30(70)	60(130)	90(200)	125(250)
TAURANGA	35(80)	70(155)	110(195)	140(245)
NEW PLYMOUTH	30(65)	50(105)	90(235)	115(265)
NAPIER	20(50)	45(105)	80(180)	105(230)
WELLINGTON	15(25)	40(65)	75(135)	100(180)
NELSON	20(45)	50(90)	70(120)	95(145)
HOKITIKA	25(50)	60(100)	111(195)	165(275)
MILFORD SOUND	35(55)	130(215)	255(470)	375(685)
CHRISTCHURCH	10(20)	30(45)	55(95)	75(135)
INVERCARGILL	10(20)	25(49)	40(65)	60(90)

Generally speaking, Northland, Auckland and the Bay of Plenty receive the heaviest short-period rainfalls (in convective showers and thunderstorms) while the West Coast receives the heaviest longer-period rainfalls (from active troughs of low pressure crossing the South Island).

Over a large portion of the country the rainfall is distributed very uniformly throughout the year. The greatest contrast in seasonal rainfall occurs in the north, where winter has almost twice as much rain as does summer. This predominance of winter rainfall diminishes progressively southwards, to become slightly reversed over the southern part of the South Island. Here, the summer maximum becomes even greater inland due to the effect of convective showers.

On the whole, seasonal rainfall does not vary greatly from year to year, the reliability of falls in spring being particularly advantageous for agricultural purposes. It is least reliable in late summer and autumn, when very dry conditions can develop east of the ranges, particularly in Hawke's Bay. This variability is clearly shown in the rainfall graph for Napier at the foot of p 85.

Annual rainfall variability over New Zealand is shown on p 89. The areas of greatest variability are generally in the east and north. In parts of North Otago, Canterbury, Marlborough, Hawke's Bay, Gisborne, Coromandel and Northland the standard deviation is twenty per cent of the mean. Accordingly, these are the areas most susceptible to unusually dry or wet years. When many years of rainfall totals are studied, it is found that the variations from year to year, at any place, are erratic and lack any clear upward or downward trend, and also that abnormally dry or wet years do not usually afflict many areas of the country at once.

WATER BALANCE

These erratic variations of annual rainfall generally represent deviations of less than thirty per cent from the average value. Seasonal, monthly, weekly and daily rainfalls are progressively more variable. Because of this and the large variations in evapotranspiration (the combined processess of evaporation from the earth's surface and transpiration from vegetation), the water available from day to day for plant growth varies appreciably. To assess

this availability of water it is assumed that the soil can hold a fixed amount of plant-available water. It is then possible to calculate each day whether the rainfall, plus the water stored in the soil, is sufficient to meet the evapotranspiration and if it is not, the amount of deficit is noted and this is accumulated through the years. The map on p 89, showing the Average Annual Water Deficit, summarises the results of this procedure carried out over several years at a network of stations, on the assumption that the soil can hold 76 millimetres of water.

A comparison of the Average Annual Rainfall and Average Annual Water Deficit maps reveals that those areas of New Zealand with low rainfall are generally those of high water deficit. The same areas are those which suffer most when rainfall is below average, and they have a high frequency of drought conditions compared to the remainder of the country where droughts are relatively rare.

THUNDERSTORMS AND HAIL

Thunderstorms are not numerous. The average number of days per year on which thunder is heard (map on p 89) is greatest in the north and west at fifteen to twenty days and least in the east, commonly less than five days.

The distribution of reported tornadoes shows a similar pattern, apart from a maximum in the Waikato and Bay of Plenty districts. An average of about twenty tornadoes and waterspouts is reported each year in New Zealand but most of these are small.

Hail falls are generally less frequent than thunderstorms. Only a few places have more than ten days a year on which hail falls. However, hail, though infrequent, does occasionally cause damage (mainly to crops) and about ten such storms occur each year throughout the areas shown on the map on p 89.

TEMPERATURE

The distribution of the mean temperature (not reduced to sea level) is mapped on p 87. An approximation to sea level temperature may be gained by adding 0.5°C per hundred metres of altitude for inland places. Sea level temperatures decrease from 15°C in the far north to 12°C about Cook Strait and 9°C in the south of the South Island. Also on p 87, a series of temperature graphs presents detailed temperature summaries for eighteen selected places.

January and February, with approximately the same mean temperature, are the warmest months of the year; July is the coldest. Coastal districts in the west or southwest have a relatively small range of temperature. Inland, and to the east of the mountains, the range is substantially greater. Maximum temperatures show little latitudinal influence; both Dunedin and Invercargill have recorded temperatures of 32°C which equals the highest ever recorded at Auckland.

The frequency of warm days is shown on p 88 in a map of days per year with a temperature greater than, or equal to, 25°C. It is apparent that this figure is higher in the north, on the west side of the country, but in the east (where a Foehn wind operates from time to time) there is no such latitudinal variation.

The highest recorded temperature in New Zealand occurred on 7 February 1973, when Christchurch and Rangiora both recorded 42°C in strong Foehn wind conditions. The lowest minimum temperature was recorded on 2 July 1943, that of minus 20°C at Ophir in Central Otago.

Excluding the relatively uninhabited mountainous areas, the most severe winter conditions are experienced in

AVERAGE ANNUAL RAINFALL
(1941-1970)

DAYS OF RAINFALL

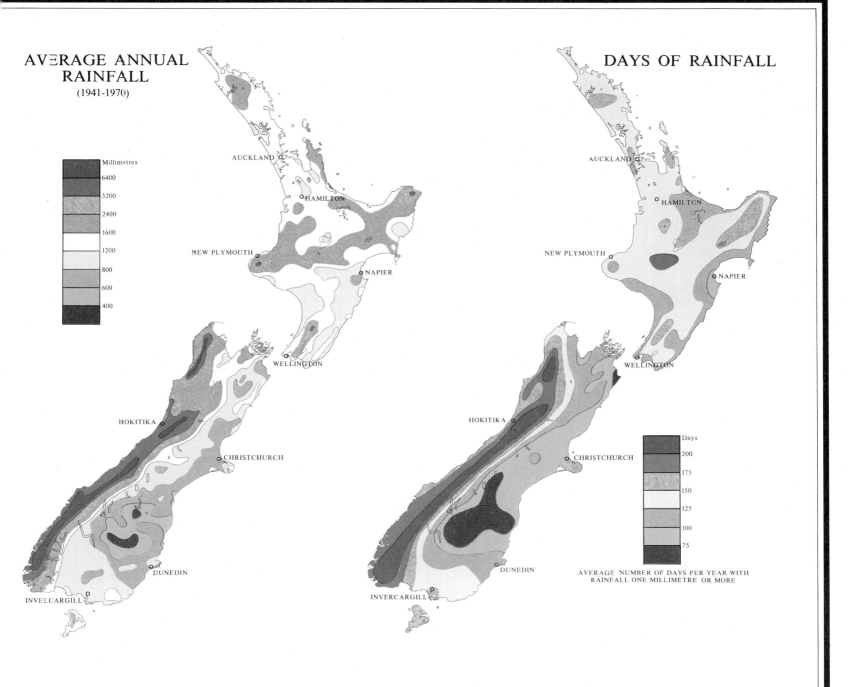

Millimetres
6400
3200
2400
1600
1200
800
600
400

Days
200
175
150
125
100
75

AVERAGE NUMBER OF DAYS PER YEAR WITH
RAINFALL ONE MILLIMETRE OR MORE

ANNUAL VARIATION OF RAINFALL

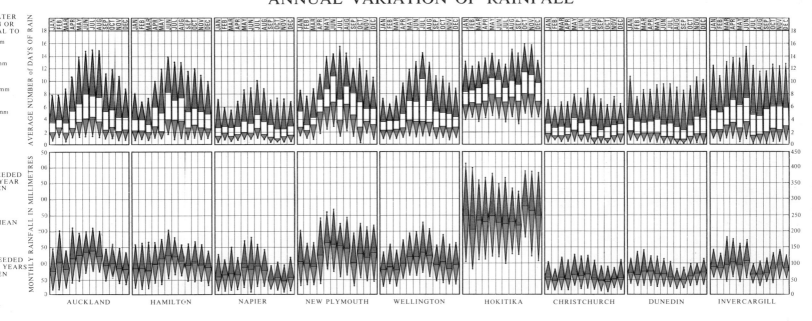

AVERAGE NUMBER of DAYS OF RAIN

MONTHLY RAINFALL IN MILLIMETRES

AUCKLAND HAMILTON NAPIER NEW PLYMOUTH WELLINGTON HOKITIKA CHRISTCHURCH DUNEDIN INVERCARGILL

Central Otago, in the Mackenzie Basin of inland Canterbury and on the central plateau of the North Island, though even in these areas night temperatures rarely fall as low as minus 10°C. Apart from on the central plateau, the North Island winters are very mild and pastures maintain continuous, though greatly reduced, growth. In both Islands, sheep and cattle remain in the open the year round.

There have been changes in the mean temperature over New Zealand in the last hundred years, the period during which temperatures have been recorded at Auckland, Wellington, Christchurch and Dunedin. The diagram on *p 88* was produced by adjusting the long-period temperature records to readings at the current recording sites. The values shown are ten-year averages of mean temperature and have shown variations of about 1°C during the hundred-year period. The random nature of the graphs obviously makes extrapolation difficult but the changes which have occurred relate to the general weather over the country. For example, between 1895 and 1908 there was a succession of winters with severe snowfalls in the South Island, yet none from 1945 to the late 1960s.

RELATIVE HUMIDITY

Relative humidity is commonly between seventy and eighty per cent in coastal areas and about ten per cent lower inland. Very low humidities—of less than twenty-five per cent—occur at times in the lee of the Southern Alps where the Foehn effect is occasionally very marked. In summer, the hot, dry 'Canterbury Nor'wester' is generally a most unpleasant wind. Cool south-westerlies are also at times very dry when they reach eastern districts. In Northland, the humid mid-summer conditions are inclined to be rather oppressive, though temperatures rarely reach 30°C. Dull, humid spells are generally not prolonged anywhere, but their frequency is greater in the south.

FROST AND SNOW

It is well known that local variations in frostiness are considerable, even within quite small areas. On a calm, clear night the cold air in contact with a sloping surface gravitates slowly downhill, to collect in valleys and depressions, and it is these 'katabatic' drifts which are mainly responsible for local temperature variations. Gently sloping ground with a northerly aspect tends to be least affected by frost. Favourable sites in coastal areas of Northland are free of frost, although further inland frosts occur frequently in the winter months. At Albert Park, Auckland, the screen minimum thermometer (1.2 metres above the ground) has registered below 0°C only once in nearly seventy years, yet across the harbour at Whenuapai Aerodrome there are, on the average, eight screen frosts per annum.

On *p 88* is a map showing the average number of days per year on which there is a screen frost (air temperature below 0°C). This is dependent on both latitude and altitude.

For areas below 300 metres, in the North Island there are generally fewer than thirty days of frost per year, while in the South there are twenty to sixty days.

The North Island has a small, permanent snow field above about 2400 metres on the central plateau, but the snow-line rarely descends below 500 metres even for brief periods in winter. In the South Island, snow falls on a few days a year in eastern coastal districts and in some years may lie for a day or two even at sea level. In Westland it does not lie at sea level. The snow-line on the Southern Alps is at around 2100 metres in summer, being slightly lower on the western side where the Franz Josef and Fox glaciers descend through heavy forest to within 300 metres of sea level. In inland Canterbury and Otago, snow falls are heavier and more persistent. Serious losses of sheep can occur during severe winters on the considerable areas of grazing lands above 300 metres. Only rarely, however, does the winter snow-line remain below 1000 metres for longer than a month.

RADIATION AND SUNSHINE

The relevant maps appear on *p 88*. The annual average radiation received on a horizontal surface varies from just over 380 calories per square centimetre (langleys) per day to about 280 langleys per day. The amount of radiation received is quite closely related to the sunshine, though differing cloudiness characteristics cause variations—Napier and Blenheim with the same average radiation differ by nearly 200 hours in their average annual sunshine.

The sunniest areas are to be found near Nelson and Blenheim and just in the lee of the Southern Alps near Mount Cook. In these areas, the average annual bright sunshine exceeds 2400 hours, and a large portion of the remainder of the country receives at least 2000 hours. Even parts of Westland, despite the high rainfall, have 1900 hours. Southland, where sunshine hours fall sharply to 1600 per year, lies on the northern fringe of a broad zone of increasing cloudiness. At Campbell Island, 650 kilometres farther to the south, the average sunshine hours decrease to the extremely low value of 650 per year. A pleasant feature of the New Zealand climate is the high proportion of sunshine during the winter months, as shown on the diagram on *p 88*.

On *p 89* is a map of Heating Degree-Days, based on the level of 18°C. The values are accumulated temperature deficits below 18°C and represent both the amount and the duration of those temperatures in an average year. They indicate the relative amount of heat required to keep the temperature above 18°C, without allowing for the heating effect of direct solar radiation.

CLIMATIC DISTRICTS

The map on *p 83* summarises the main characteristics of the climate in New Zealand. The map is self-explanatory, but it should be noted that the change in climate from one district to the next is gradual, except where the boundaries coincide with some marked orographical feature.

MEAN ANNUAL TEMPERATURE

WIND FLOW CHARACTERISTICS

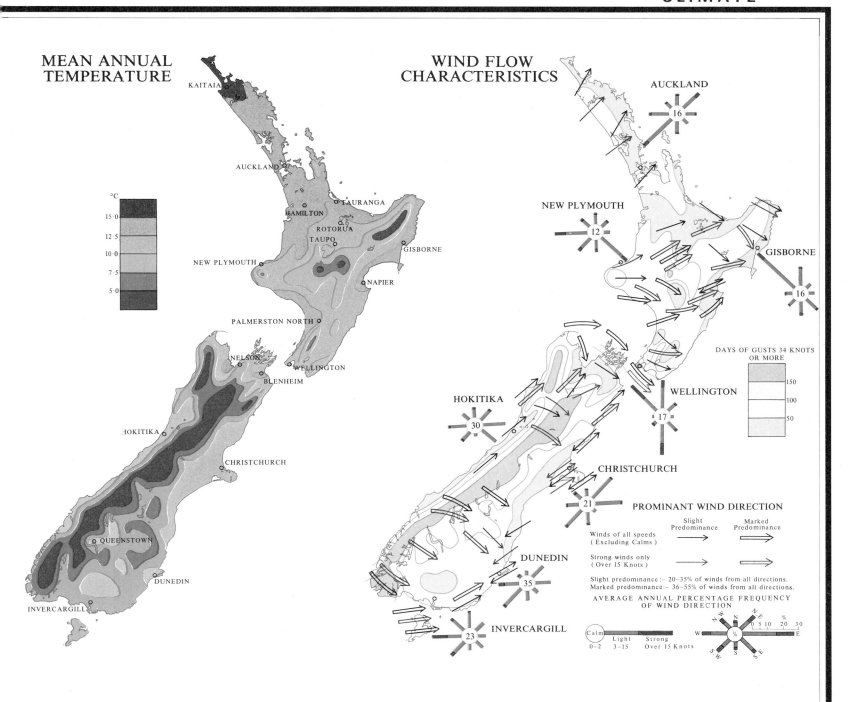

°C
15·0
12·5
10·0
7·5
5·0

KAITAIA
AUCKLAND
TAURANGA
HAMILTON
ROTORUA
TAUPO
NEW PLYMOUTH
GISBORNE
NAPIER
PALMERSTON NORTH
NELSON
WELLINGTON
BLENHEIM
HOKITIKA
CHRISTCHURCH
QUEENSTOWN
DUNEDIN
INVERCARGILL

AUCKLAND 16
NEW PLYMOUTH 12
GISBORNE 16
HOKITIKA 30
WELLINGTON 17
CHRISTCHURCH 21
DUNEDIN 35
INVERCARGILL 23

DAYS OF GUSTS 34 KNOTS OR MORE
150
100
50

PROMINANT WIND DIRECTION

Slight Predominance
Marked Predominance

Winds of all speeds (Excluding Calms)

Strong winds only (Over 15 Knots)

Slight predominance :− 20−35% of winds from all directions.
Marked predominance :− 36−55% of winds from all directions.

AVERAGE ANNUAL PERCENTAGE FREQUENCY OF WIND DIRECTION

Calm
0−2
Light
3−15
Strong
Over 15 Knots

% 0 5 10 20 30

ANNUAL VARIATION OF TEMPERATURE

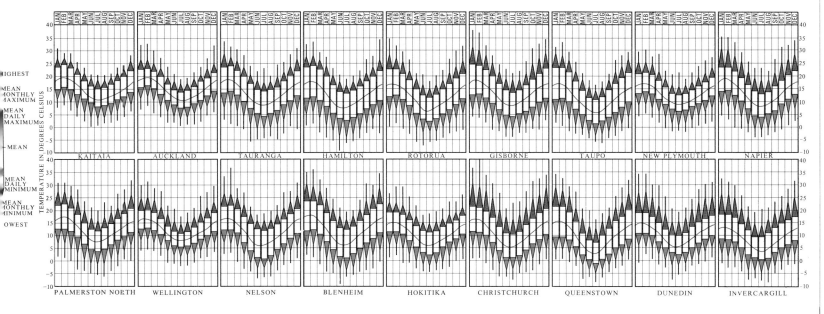

HIGHEST
MEAN MONTHLY MAXIMUM
MEAN DAILY MAXIMUM
MEAN
MEAN DAILY MINIMUM
MEAN MONTHLY MINIMUM
LOWEST

TEMPERATURE IN DEGREES CELSIUS

KAITAIA AUCKLAND TAURANGA HAMILTON ROTORUA GISBORNE TAUPO NEW PLYMOUTH NAPIER

PALMERSTON NORTH WELLINGTON NELSON BLENHEIM HOKITIKA CHRISTCHURCH QUEENSTOWN DUNEDIN INVERCARGILL

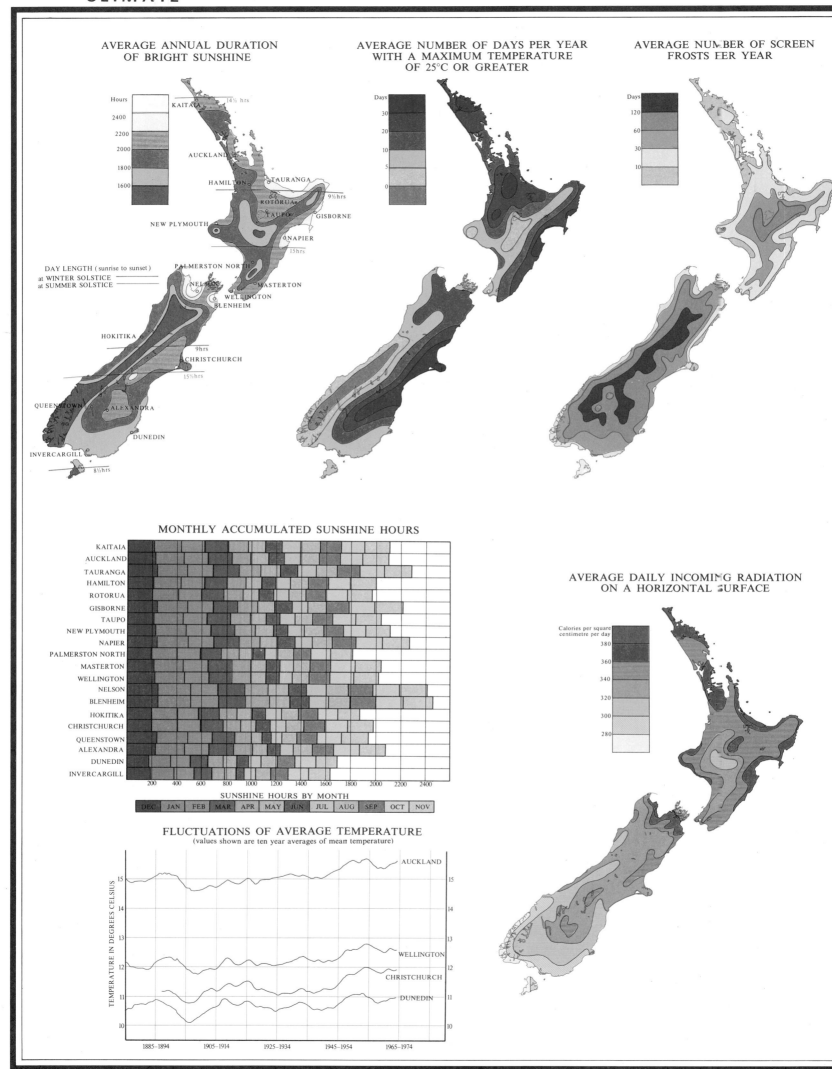

AVERAGE ANNUAL DURATION
OF BRIGHT SUNSHINE

AVERAGE NUMBER OF DAYS PER YEAR
WITH A MAXIMUM TEMPERATURE
OF 25°C OR GREATER

AVERAGE NUMBER OF SCREEN
FROSTS PER YEAR

DAY LENGTH (sunrise to sunset)
at WINTER SOLSTICE
at SUMMER SOLSTICE

MONTHLY ACCUMULATED SUNSHINE HOURS

AVERAGE DAILY INCOMING RADIATION
ON A HORIZONTAL SURFACE

SUNSHINE HOURS BY MONTH

| DEC | JAN | FEB | MAR | APR | MAY | JUN | JUL | AUG | SEP | OCT | NOV |

FLUCTUATIONS OF AVERAGE TEMPERATURE
(values shown are ten year averages of mean temperature)

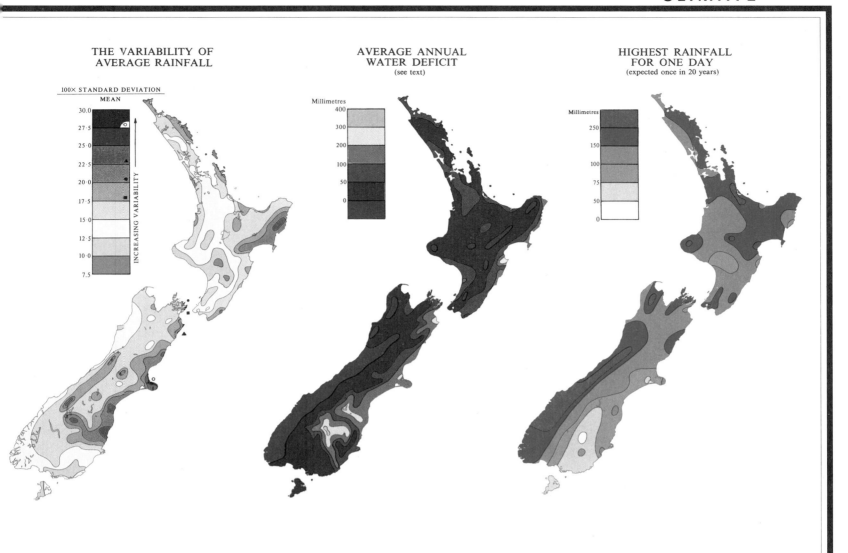

THE VARIABILITY OF AVERAGE RAINFALL

100× STANDARD DEVIATION / MEAN

INCREASING VARIABILITY

30.0
27.5
25.0
22.5
20.0
17.5
15.0
12.5
10.0
7.5

AVERAGE ANNUAL WATER DEFICIT
(see text)

Millimetres

400
300
200
100
50
0

HIGHEST RAINFALL FOR ONE DAY
(expected once in 20 years)

Millimetres

250
150
100
75
50
0

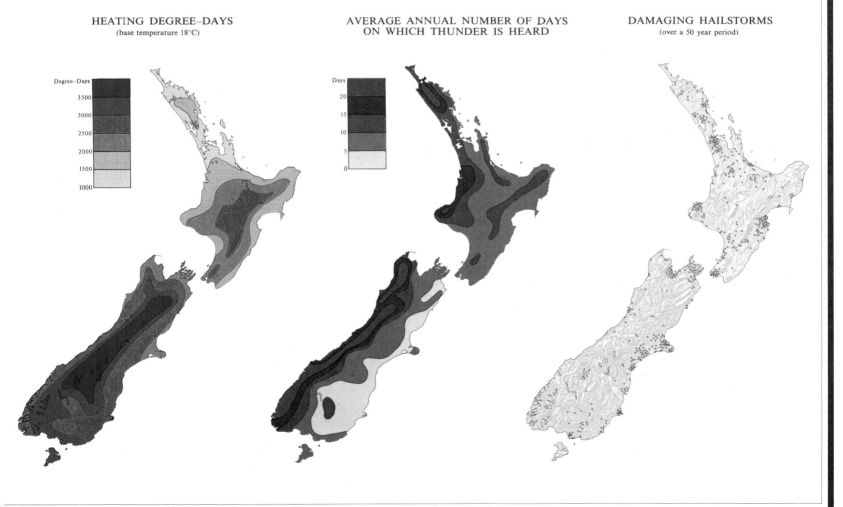

HEATING DEGREE–DAYS
(base temperature 18°C)

Degree-Days

3500
3000
2500
2000
1500
1000

AVERAGE ANNUAL NUMBER OF DAYS ON WHICH THUNDER IS HEARD

Days

20
15
10
5
0

DAMAGING HAILSTORMS
(over a 50 year period)

GEOLOGY

R. P. Suggate & P. M. Riddolls

The islands of New Zealand, rising above the Pacific Ocean, are fragments of the whole region of the south-west Pacific, and as such have taken part in its complex geological history. The present-day coastline is only a temporary boundary; off-shore drilling for oil and the land distribution of the rocks indicate that the past coastline has been very different. The geological history recorded in the rocks on land is a long and complex one, but primarily indicates that land, of changing shape and size, has existed in the vicinity of present-day New Zealand for at least 500 million years. Further, the position of that land relative to its continental neighbours, Australia and Antarctica, has probably greatly changed. The geological changes that have taken place are indicated by the different types, ages, distribution and deformation of rocks.

ROCK TYPE

The rock units shown on the geological map are divided into three major categories based on their modes of formation:

The first category, sedimentary rocks, results from deposition and consolidation of particles eroded from an adjacent land area. Different sources of material and depositional environments result in different types of sedimentary rock, such as sandstone, siltstone and limestone. Most New Zealand sedimentary rocks are siltstones and sandstones that were deposited beneath the sea.

The second category consists of igneous rocks, formed when molten rock (magma) from deep within the earth's crust cooled after being intruded into existing rocks or sediments, or after being extruded on to the surface. Acid (silica-rich) igneous rocks are light in colour whereas the basic (silica-poor) igneous rocks are dark. The plutonic igneous rocks are intruded at depth, cool slowly and are coarse-grained. Granite is an example of an acid plutonic rock, whereas diorite and gabbro are basic. Volcanic igneous rocks are extruded on to the land surface or beneath the sea, cooling quickly to form fine-grained rocks. The acid volcanic rocks include rhyolite, ignimbrite and pumice, the last two being formed when the lava was particularly gaseous and explosive in nature. The intermediate and basic lavas include andesite and basalt. A sedimentary rock which is derived from volcanic fragments is called a tuff.

In the third category are the metamorphic rocks (schists and gneisses) which have been re-crystallised under conditions of very high temperature, pressure or both. They vary in type depending on the nature of the parent rocks (either sedimentary or igneous) and the intensity and type of metamorphism. Characteristic minerals form under certain conditions of temperature and pressure. Thus chlorite is characteristic of a low degree of metamorphism, and garnet and oligoclase of a high degree of metamorphism. Gneiss forms under conditions of the highest temperatures and pressures.

GEOLOGICAL PROCESSES

The processes of rock formation are never-ending. Sedimentation is cyclical, particles being continually eroded, transported, deposited and cemented to form new rock that may later be uplifted so that erosion starts the cycle again. The uplift and erosional periods of the sedimentary cycle make it impossible for any one area to have a rock sequence representing the whole of geological time. Only when an area is totally submerged beneath the sea can there be continuous sedimentation providing a complete time record, and even then there may be gaps resulting from removal of sediments by strong bottom currents. When an area is above sea level the time interval is represented only by minor terrestrial deposits, such as coal measures, or igneous rocks that may have formed both being usually restricted in extent.

Compressional and tensional forces produce movement of the earth's crust (tectonism), causing it to buckle, warp or crack. Long-continued downwarping may occur and form very extensive troughs in the sea called geosynclines, in which many thousands of metres of sediments can accumulate. The deepest sediments are heated to high temperatures and become metamorphosed. In contrast, slight downwarping allows the sea to extend over the land, producing shallow shelves close to the land and deeper basins further off shore. When compression forces the crust and overlying sediments upwards, mountain chains may be formed, the periods of mountain building being called orogenies. Severe folding and fracturing of the rocks accompanied by igneous activity often occur during the period of climax of orogeny. The effect of orogeny varies from place to place and locally the rocks may be only gently tilted.

New Zealand's geological history is made up of successive depositional phases and orogenies, which have resulted in a constantly changing pattern of land and sea. An example of this is shown in the reconstruction of the changes that occurred during the Cenozoic Era (*Fig 1*).

AGE OF NEW ZEALAND

In terms of the international geological time scale (*Fig 2*) New Zealand is a 'young' country with a great proportion of the surface rocks less than 100 million years old. A brief inspection of the geological maps shows that in the North

Figure 1 THE NEW ZEALAND COASTLINE
THROUGHOUT THE CENOZOIC ERA

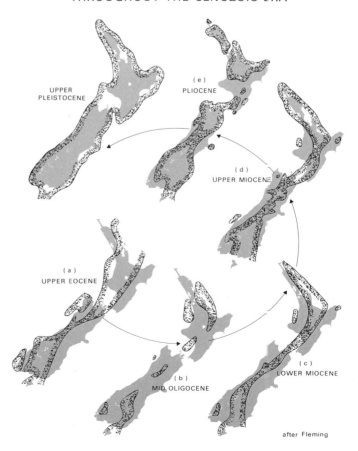

UPPER PLEISTOCENE

(e) PLIOCENE

(d) UPPER MIOCENE

(a) UPPER EOCENE

(b) MID OLIGOCENE

(c) LOWER MIOCENE

after Fleming

Island younger rocks are more widespread than in the South Island, the oldest rocks being of Permian age, but the majority being Tertiary, or younger. In the South Island, rocks of all ages from late Precambrian to the present are represented. The oldest rocks are present only in Westland, and by world standards even these are not very old, probably no more than 600–700 million years. In contrast, the oldest known rocks in the world have been dated at between 3600–3900 million years. Thus the rocks of New Zealand represent only a fraction of the total geological history of the earth.

Figure 2   GEOLOGICAL TIME SCALE

MILLIONS OF YEARS	ERA	PERIOD	EPOCH	N.Z. EVENT
0	CENOZOIC	QUATERNARY	HOLOCENE	KAIKOURA OROGENY
			PLEISTOCENE	
			PLIOCENE	
		TERTIARY	MIOCENE	
50			OLIGOCENE	
			EOCENE	DEPOSITIONAL PHASE
			PALEOCENE	
100	MESOZOIC	CRETACEOUS	UPPER	
			LOWER	RANGITATA OROGENY
150		JURASSIC	UPPER	
			MIDDLE	
			LOWER	
200		TRIASSIC	UPPER	
			MIDDLE	DEPOSITION IN NEW ZEALAND GEOSYNCLINE
			LOWER	
250	PALEOZOIC	PERMIAN	UPPER	
			LOWER	
300		CARBONIFEROUS		
350				TUHUA OROGENY
		DEVONIAN	UPPER	
			MIDDLE	
400			LOWER	
		SILURIAN		
450		ORDOVICIAN	UPPER	
			MIDDLE	
			LOWER	DEPOSITIONAL PHASE
500		CAMBRIAN	UPPER	
550			MIDDLE	
			LOWER	
600		PRECAMBRIAN		?

THE GEOLOGICAL TIME SCALE

The international geological time scale was established in Europe and is based on the stratigraphy (sedimentary sequence) there. The time intervals have been dated using radiometric methods (based on the radioactive decay rates of certain elements) applied mainly to igneous rocks whose stratigraphic position is accurately known. Each time unit is characterised by certain fossil groups and assemblages found in the rocks. These fossils can be used for correlating one set of rocks with another in a different area. However correlation is not always easy, as some fossil groups did not achieve a global distribution. A local time scale based on New Zealand rocks and fossils has had to be established and tied in with the international geological time scale, using radiometric dates and matching fossils where possible.

The periods in European geological history were originally defined by a marked break in sedimentation (unconformity) or a change in rock type. These criteria may not be evident elsewhere and the time boundaries can only be determined by use of fossils. In New Zealand, for example, there was a continuous period of sedimentation throughout the Upper Paleozoic and most of the Mesozoic. These rocks are mainly hard sandstone (greywacke) and large areas contain relatively few fossils, so that it can be difficult to divide them accurately into periods. Thus the natural divisions of New Zealand rocks do not necessarily correspond with those of the time scale. Indeed, the New Zealand rocks are more naturally divided into periods from late Precambrian to Devonian, from Carboniferous to Lower Cretaceous, and from Upper Cretaceous to the present day.

Late Precambrian to Devonian

The environment of the earliest major recorded period of rock formation in New Zealand was that of a geosyncline adjoining a land area with off-shore volcanic islands. Little detail can be inferred because most of the rocks are covered by younger ones and are thus not visible at the surface. Further, many of the original sedimentary and volcanic rocks have been so changed by metamorphism, and so disrupted by successive earth movements over many millions of years, that their original nature and distribution are only imperfectly known. The rocks are exposed in the south-west and north-west of the South Island. Formerly probably contiguous, the rocks are now separated as a result of horizontal movement at the Alpine Fault (*see Map*). The rocks also extend off shore to the north as proved by schist found at the bottom of an oil-prospecting well to the west of Taranaki.

The oldest rocks are found in Westland and adjoining areas of Nelson. They comprise an extensive area of gneiss in the Paparoa Range and great thicknesses of interbedded sandstone and mudstone, now highly indurated and in places semi-schistose. They are tentatively thought to be of youngest Precambrian age, though they may range into the oldest Paleozoic. In north Westland, mineral fragments in sandstone are more than 1100 million years old, giving the oldest known record of land (from which the fragments were eroded) in the New Zealand region.

The oldest fossiliferous rocks—Cambrian in age—are in west Nelson. They, and probably the Precambrian rocks too, are part of a sequence of conglomerate, sandstone, mudstone, limestone and volcanic rocks of which the youngest are Devonian. Although the geosynclinal environment lasted as a whole at least 250 million years, the sequences of rocks in west Nelson indicate substantial variations in detail. In all, these Paleozoic rocks are at least 10 000 metres thick.

Cambrian rocks, both sedimentary and volcanic, are varied in lithology. The oldest are thick andesitic lavas and intrusions with minor tuffaceous sediments; in places they are metamorphosed to green schists and are intruded by ultrabasic rocks. The younger Cambrian rocks, although predominantly sandstone and siltstone or their metamorphic (schistose) equivalents, also include marble and conglomerate. Middle Cambrian fossils have been found in limestone lenses in the Cobb valley.

The Ordovician and Silurian rocks of west Nelson, of which most are Ordovician, are generally finer-grained than the Cambrian rocks. The older rocks are not calcareous but the younger ones include thick lenses of marble. Most of the older rocks are semi-schistose phyllite (originally a siltstone) and sandstone, but in the far north-west there is slaty argillite which is less altered and contains fossils (graptolites) that give ages ranging through almost the whole of the Ordovician. The younger Ordovician rocks and the Silurian are quartzite (indurated quartz sandstone), argillite and marble, plus their schistose metamorphic equivalents. The marble is resistant to erosion so that it forms the prominent mountains of Mts Arthur and Owen. At the Takaka Hill, solution of the marble by water has resulted in deep caves and a characteristic rough topography.

Devonian rocks are adjacent to the Silurian in north-west Nelson, but to the south near Reefton the Silurian is missing alongside faulted slivers of Lower or Middle Devonian. These slivers are mainly calcareous argillite, limestone and quartzite, and locally contain many fossils including reef corals in limestone.

In Fiordland almost all of the rocks were altered by greater heat and pressure than were the Nelson rocks, so that they were almost molten. They are now gneisses of various compositions, giving little indication of their original sedimentary lithologies. They have been interpreted, however, as representing the whole Nelson sequence. In the extreme south-west, sandstone, siltstone and tuffaceous rocks are less metamorphosed and locally contain Ordovician graptolites.

THE TUHUA OROGENY

The name 'Tuhua Orogeny' is applied to the tectonic episode that followed the late Precambrian–Devonian geosynclinal phase and preceded the development of the New Zealand Geosyncline. The severe folding and faulting, together with plutonic intrusion, that took place in late Devonian and early Carboniferous times mark the climax of a long period of deformation and intrusion.

Details of the orogenic movements are imperfectly known, as the effects are widely obscured by those of subsequent deformations. Further, in some areas the deformed rocks are obscured by younger sediments, or have been eroded away to expose plutonic rocks that were intruded into the lower layers of the deformed rocks.

In north-west Nelson, complex folding has produced steeply-dipping sequences, and in places rocks have been turned upside-down. Major faulting, some involving large-scale thrusting of one group of rocks over another group, has brought together belts of rocks of dissimilar lithology or age. Most of the plutonic intrusions in this area are granitic but some are dioritic. Over extensive areas in north-west Nelson the Paleozoic rocks have been metamorphosed by the heat from the intrusions, but further south-west the areas affected are much smaller. The deformation within the Fiordland gneisses is poorly understood but, as in north-west Nelson, the rocks were intruded by granites.

Carboniferous to Lower Cretaceous

During the early part of the Carboniferous, the New Zealand Geosyncline began to evolve; it continued until the beginning of the Cretaceous, and so extended over a period of about 200 million years. In it, enormous thicknesses of sediments accumulated, and at its maximum development it is thought to have extended from New Zealand to as far north-west as New Caledonia, and to a considerable distance beyond the South Island. It is probable that a land mass existed to the west of the Geosyncline, and that this land mass was close to, or adjoining, the continents of Australia and Antarctica. The rocks deposited in the Geosyncline have a very wide distribution. They constitute the highest mountains of the Southern Alps and form the main axial ranges of the North Island and, as well, underlie younger rocks in much of the less mountainous country.

In the South Island the rocks are exposed in a north-east trending belt which curves round to trend in a south-easterly direction in the far south. Except in the Nelson–Marlborough area, they are confined to the east of the Alpine Fault, movement along which has been a major factor influencing the distribution of the rocks in the South Island. The movement on the fault took place after the end of deposition in the New Zealand Geosyncline, and by correlating similar rocks on the east side of the fault in north-west Otago with those on the west side in Nelson, it has been estimated that there has been a lateral movement of 450 kilometres along the fault. The curvature of the present distribution of rocks is emphasised by the presence of similar rocks in the Chatham Islands. Like the faulting, the development of the curvature is thought to have been caused by a later tectonic event and the original Geosyncline was probably far straighter.

Sediments of the New Zealand Geosyncline now form the oldest rocks in the North Island. They are exposed in Northland, Coromandel, on the west coast as far south as northern Taranaki, and from Wellington through the main ranges to East Cape. Oil-prospecting wells, for example in eastern Taranaki, have proved the presence of these rocks beneath Cenozoic sediments and it is assumed that they form a 'basement' for most of the North Island.

The non-metamorphic rocks can be divided into two facies (associations of related rock types) that reflect the major differences of depositional environment within the Geosyncline. The deposits of the western facies indicate a shelf environment bordering a land mass. The rocks are characterised by being generally more fossiliferous and having a greater content of volcanic detritus than rocks of the eastern facies. The eastern facies was deposited further away from the land mass and mostly in deeper water. The rocks form a very thick monotonous sequence, now intensely deformed and containing very few fossils.

The shelf deposits of the western facies are found in synclinal (downfolded) structures in Southland, Nelson and south-west Auckland and are up to at least twenty kilometres thick. The Southland Syncline contains rocks ranging in age from Permian to Jurassic, with some that may be Carboniferous along the north-east flank. The Permian sedimentary rocks are sandstone, siltstone, and limestone with some tuffaceous sandstone. During the Permian, lavas were erupted from submarine volcanoes on the western margin of the Geosyncline and ultrabasic rocks—serpentinite, peridotite and gabbro—were intruded at about the same time. Volcanic activity continued well into the Triassic, beds of tuffaceous sandstone being common even though no lavas are found. Conglomerate, sandstone and siltstone are the other Triassic rock types. In the Jurassic, deposition of marine sandstone and siltstone continued and was followed in the Upper Jurassic by freshwater deposition of sand, silt and plant beds, indicating the end of the geosynclinal environment in this region.

In Nelson on the west side of the Alpine Fault, the sequence is incomplete as a result of deformation, and among the younger rocks only the Upper Triassic is represented, by a narrow faulted belt of sandstone and conglomerate. The Permian sedimentary rocks are similar to those in Southland and have a similar relationship to volcanic rocks and ultrabasic intrusives, which include dunite, an all-olivine rock. The sequence continues to the north, to be exposed again around Kawhia Harbour in south-west Auckland, but there are no Permian rocks at the surface, only Triassic and Jurassic. However, an Upper Triassic conglomerate contains large igneous boulders at least as old as Permian, indicating the previous existence of an igneous belt not far away. Tuffaceous sandstone and siltstone are the main rock types in the Triassic and Jurassic, and, as in Southland, there are Upper Jurassic freshwater deposits and plant beds.

The rocks of the eastern facies have a wide distribution. They are very uniform in both Islands throughout their age range, consisting almost entirely of sequences of greywacke and argillite, with some chert and volcanic bands. Greywacke and argillite are the most common rock types and are found as thin alternating beds, or as graded beds in which the greywacke layer grades upwards into the overlying argillite layer. These rocks have undergone intense deformation and are usually extremely fractured and folded; they are also very hard, and in some places are slightly metamorphosed, some re-crystallisation having taken place. The age range is from the Carboniferous to the Upper Jurassic and, in the eastern part of the country, probably into the Lower Cretaceous. However, in many areas, especially in the North Island, fossils are sparse and the age is uncertain. The sequences are undoubtedly very thick but it is difficult to estimate the exact thickness because of the folding and faulting that has taken place; estimates have varied from ten to twenty-eight kilometres. Being hard and resistant to erosion, these rocks generally form rugged, high topography and they make up the highest mountains in the Southern Alps.

Many of the sediments within the Geosyncline were depressed into zones of high temperature and pressure where they were intensely deformed and metamorphosed. They are now represented by the wide band of semi-schist and schist in the south of the South Island, curving round to follow the Alpine Fault, and becoming narrower to the north. On the western side of the Alpine Fault, schist is exposed in Marlborough and continues northwards beneath younger rocks in the North Island, where semi-schist is known to the east of Mt Ruapehu and at the bottom of an oil-prospecting well north-east of Wanganui. In the South Island the greywacke passes gradually through semi-schist into schist so that it is difficult to draw boundaries; the intensity of metamorphism increases towards the Alpine Fault where the rocks are garnet–oligoclase schist and gneiss.

THE RANGITATA OROGENY

The episode that disrupted the New Zealand Geosyncline and ushered in a new tectonic environment is known as the Rangitata Orogeny. The main period of tectonic movements was the Lower Cretaceous, but in parts of the Geosyncline the movements began earlier, and over most of the New Zealand region they continued into the Upper Cretaceous. The two main divisions of the Geosyncline, in which rocks of the western and eastern groups were deposited, were deformed differently.

The western rocks lying furthest from the Alpine Fault were folded generally into broad, open folds, well exemplified in Southland and south-west Auckland. In north-west Otago and in Nelson the degree of deformation increases as the fault is approached, faulting being common and steep dips being usual. The 450 kilometres of horizontal displacement is inferred mainly from the matching of Permian sequences, including ultramafic rocks. Most of the displacement took place during the late stages of the Rangitata Orogeny, although some geologists assign it to the Kaikoura Orogeny (see p 95).

The eastern rocks of the Geosyncline were much more severely deformed and have been uplifted more than the western rocks, either during the Rangitata Orogeny, as in Otago, or during the Kaikoura Orogeny, as along the Alpine Fault. The schists were uplifted most, and it is known from studies of details of the patterns of schistosity that they have been deformed in several successive phases. It is thought that the Otago schists were metamorphosed during compression of sediments into a stack of folds now lying on top of each other. Structures in the greywackes differ from area to area, but are everywhere so complex as to be difficult to decipher. Clearly, however, the deformation involved much vertical and probably also some horizontal movement.

There was little plutonic igneous activity during the Rangitata Orogeny, but some granites in western Nelson, for example that at Separation Point, are probably of Cretaceous age.

Cretaceous to Present Day

Following the disruption of the New Zealand Geosyncline, most of the present-day area of New Zealand was above sea level, and marine sedimentation was restricted to the east and north. The mountains that were formed in the Rangitata Orogeny were gradually eroded over a long period of time to such an extent that a surface of low relief (peneplain) began to form in some places towards the end of the Cretaceous and became more widespread by the Upper Eocene. At the surface of the peneplain the rocks became deeply weathered. In the late Cretaceous and early Tertiary the sea started to invade the low-lying areas and *Figure 1* shows that the marine transgression over the land reached a maximum in the Oligocene, with subsequent regression until all of New Zealand was above sea level late in the Quaternary. Locally, marine sedimentation continued into the Quaternary, particularly in the south of the North Island, but most Quaternary deposition was terrestrial. In the South Island especially, the advent of the Quaternary Ice Age had a major effect and, although the climate was not continuously cold, many deposits are glacial in origin. Volcanism, sporadic in the Cretaceous and early Tertiary, increased later with widespread andesitic eruptions in the Miocene in Northland and Coromandel, and continued with a sequence of dacitic, rhyolitic and basaltic eruptions in that area until late in the Quaternary. Rhyolite domes and vast ignimbrite sheets were formed in the Taupo Volcanic Zone in the Quaternary and active volcanoes in Tongariro National Park and White Island have erupted andesitic lavas during this century. In the South Island, Cenozoic volcanism was restricted to the east coast, and on land ended in the early Quaternary.

Throughout the late Cretaceous and Tertiary, sedimentation took place in one region or another, even though rapid changes of environment resulted in many local breaks in the rock sequences; the fossil record is generally good, with marine microfossils, Foraminifera, being particularly useful for age subdivision.

The rocks of this period have attracted the most interest in the search for oil and gas. Although there are oil seeps within these rocks in the east of the North Island and north-west of the South Island, no oil or gas has been found, despite intensive prospecting and drilling. However, gas and condensate from an Eocene sandstone 3000 metres beneath the surface in Taranaki have been commercially exploited and gas and some oil have been found in off-shore wells.

CRETACEOUS

In Northland, eastern North Island and Marlborough, the sediments deposited after the climax of the Rangitata Orogeny were marine sandstone and siltstone. Marine deposition continued in these areas throughout the Cretaceous and into the Tertiary. The younger Cretaceous rocks tend to be finer-grained sandstone and siltstone, and the youngest deposits are commonly greensands and very siliceous mudstone, with bedded flint in the south-east of the North Island and in Marlborough. In scattered areas in the west and south of the South Island, terrestrial breccia-conglomerate was deposited in the mid-Cretaceous.

Later, sedimentation became more widespread, the first sediments being deposited in low-lying swampy areas to form coal measures, now containing valuable coal seams that have been extensively mined, particularly in the Greymouth, Kaitangata and Ohai coalfields. Many of the Cretaceous coal measure areas were not reached by the marine transgression until the Tertiary but in some areas of Canterbury and east Otago, Cretaceous marine sandstone was deposited.

PALEOCENE–EOCENE

The sea continued its transgression in the Lower Tertiary. In the east and north of the North Island, marine sedimentation continued on subsiding shelves with fine-grained, mainly calcareous sediments. In Northland, the main rock types are mudstone and muddy limestone with greensand beds; similar rocks are found on the east coast together with bentonitic mudstone. In the north-east of the South Island, greensand and calcareous mudstone are flanked to the east by chalky limestone, the result of the accumulation of vast numbers of Foraminifera. Sedimentation in the south and west continued in deepening basins, and freshwater coal measures were followed by marine calcareous siltstone and sandstone, with some carbonaceous beds. In the Oamaru area lavas from basaltic volcanoes are interbedded with the Eocene sediments. Central North Island, and the central and southern South Island, were still above sea level at the end of the Eocene (*Fig 1a*), with local swampy conditions suitable for the formation of coal measures.

OLIGOCENE

The maximum of the marine transgression was reached in the Oligocene (*Fig 1b*) and most of the country was submerged. Characteristically, the deposits are calcareous and include some pure limestones that are of economic importance.

In Northland, muddy limestone and minor pure crystalline limestone were deposited; on the east coast of the North Island the Oligocene deposits consist of calcareous mudstone and sandstone. South of Auckland, the Eocene coal measures were covered by a thin sequence of limestone, siltstone and calcareous sandstone, deposited in a gradually deepening basin. In the north and west of the South Island, crystalline limestone or calcareous mudstone predominate although sandy beds including thin greensand are found locally; the sequences vary greatly in thickness. Similar deposits are found in the east, and in Marlborough and north Otago they are accompanied by basaltic volcanics. In the Waiau valley of western Southland, thick deposits of sandstone, mudstone and limestone were deposited in a subsiding basin to the west of a remaining land mass, where thin greensand accumulated at the height of the transgression.

MIOCENE

In the Miocene, the land started to emerge (*Figs 1c, 1d*) and the sea began to retreat as a result of preliminary earth movements of the Kaikoura Orogeny. The result of these movements was a complex of small, isolated sedimentary basins sinking, filling and rising again. Volcanism became widespread in the north of the North Island but in the South Island was mainly in the isolated volcanic centres of the Otago and Banks peninsulas.

Lower Miocene deposits in Northland consist of sandstone, tuff, conglomerate and some greensand. By the mid-Miocene, the sea had retreated from the area and, except for minor incursions, has not returned since.

Andesite volcanoes to the east and west formed Coromandel Peninsula and the Waitakere ranges. Sandstone accumulated from north of Auckland southwards to north Taranaki until the area emerged in the mid-Miocene, while in south Taranaki calcareous siltstone with thin limestone beds was followed by increasingly sandy formations with tuff beds. On the east coast of the North Island, Lower Miocene mudstone and sandstone were originally widely deposited but are now preserved only in the East Cape region and south of Hawke's Bay, later, during the Miocene, local high areas had the effect of isolating small depositional basins, and active faulting during deposition resulted in rapid changes of environment. Thus the distribution of different sediment types is complex, with sandstone and thin conglomerate predominating over siltstone and limestone.

In the Lower Miocene, calcareous siltstone and sandstone were deposited in the east of the South Island, together with some limestone in the north and greensand in the south. As the land area extended and the sea retreated, the marine sediments became coarser and less calcareous. Freshwater conglomerate and coal measures were deposited in south Canterbury. In Marlborough, a coarse conglomerate containing large angular blocks of pre-Tertiary rocks was deposited first in the sea and later on land in the mid-Miocene, the material resulting from movement at the developing major faults along the Awatere and Clarence valleys. Basaltic eruptions took place in Canterbury and Otago and built the Otago Peninsula. Near Christchurch, eruptions of rhyolite followed by andesite started the Banks Peninsula volcanic complex, the development of which was mainly completed by the end of the Miocene. In the north and west of the South Island, siltstone and fine sandstone are the predominant Lower and Middle Miocene sediments but, as the sea retreated, freshwater and estuarine sandstone and mudstone with coal beds became predominant inland. In the south-west, shallow water limestone and sandstone were deposited.

PLIOCENE

Tectonic activity increased during the Pliocene. The principal mountain ranges were being uplifted and the land began to take the shape we know today. The South Island was above sea level except for a narrow strip along the west coast and around Banks Peninsula. Deep basins developed, however, across the southern and eastern parts of the North Island, except where the main ranges were rising.

In the South Island, sand, silt and conglomerate were deposited in low-lying land areas, south-west from Nelson to Reefton, in inland Canterbury and in Southland, while marine siltstone and coarse sandstone were confined to a few areas close to the east and west coasts. The final eruptions on Banks Peninsula were of andesite and basalt.

In the southern North Island, great thicknesses of fine-grained sandstone and siltstone were deposited in the main Wanganui basin, but to the east, in shallow water, unconsolidated shelly limestones (coquina) interbedded with siltstone were laid down. Extensive volcanic activity took place in the Coromandel region, rhyolite and andesite being erupted; in Northland, sporadic activity was mainly basaltic.

QUATERNARY

The Quaternary deposits of New Zealand are more varied than those of any other period, as is to be expected during a time of great climatic fluctuations and extensive volcanic activity. Adding complexity to the Quaternary rocks was the rapidly-changing depositional environment, the result of the progressive tectonic activity that led to the formation of the major landscape features found today.

The sedimentary rocks can be divided into an older group deposited in continuity with Pliocene rocks, and a younger group formed in a physiographic environment rather similar to that of the present day. The older group has been considerably deformed by tectonic movement, whereas the younger group has mainly been uplifted rather than deformed, but in some areas a sharp line cannot be drawn between the two groups.

In the North Island, the older group of rocks was deposited in subsiding basins in the Wanganui, Hawke's Bay and Wairarapa areas. Except close to the rising Tararua and Ruahine ranges, most deposits are marine—sandstone, siltstone and, in the east, coquina limestone. In the South Island, vast amounts of rock were eroded from the Southern Alps and other rising ranges, with the resultant accumulation of thick gravel deposits. In the west of the South Island, glacial deposits within the gravel resulted from the first known glaciation in New Zealand.

The younger group of rocks consists of deposits that underlie dunes, coastal and river terraces, alluvial plains, glacial moraines, lakes and other physiographic features of the present landscape. As a result of uplift of the land, many of these features are now high above the level at which they were formed. In the late Quaternary there were four major cold periods during which glaciers advanced and formed moraines, mainly in the South Island. During these cold periods, rivers built up terraces in many valleys outside the glaciated area, and spread thick deposits of gravel beyond the mountains to form the Canterbury and Southland plains. Fine dust, blown off gravel terraces, plains and hills devegetated by cold, was deposited as loess over large areas, especially in the eastern South Island and in the south-eastern North Island. Between each cold period there were warm intervals, in which the glaciers retreated and the sea, which had dropped in glacial times, rose again. In many areas, the rise in sea level caused the coastline to be eroded, forming coastal benches, underlain by sand and gravel and backed by cliffs that have now been abandoned. Elsewhere, great amounts of dune sand accumulated, notably on the west coast of Northland.

The Quaternary volcanic rocks, of acid, intermediate and basic composition, are found mainly in the centre of the North Island, with some around Auckland and in Northland. The most impressive features involved are the andesitic central volcanoes (Ruapehu and Ngauruhoe) and Mt Egmont, and also the great sheets of ignimbrite west and east of the volcanic zone that extends north-east from Lake Taupo. Volcanic ash, both rhyolitic and andesitic, thrown high into the air during eruptions, now thickly mantles much of the central North Island.

THE KAIKOURA OROGENY

The Kaikoura Orogeny, which continues today as shown by the surface displacements at times of earthquakes, began slowly in Miocene time and the cumulative effects have resulted in the development of the major features of of the present physiography. In comparison with earlier orogenies, the Kaikoura Orogeny has not resulted in particularly complex deformation, except where soft rocks have been disrupted by squeezing or sliding on a huge scale, especially as in the Gisborne and Northland regions. Folds are generally fairly gentle and, in many areas, differential vertical movement has resulted from block-faulting rather than folding. Steeply-dipping sequences are mainly associated with major faults, both those with predominantly vertical movement and those with predominantly horizontal movement.

An outstanding result of vertical movement was the formation of the Southern Alps, where the rocks may have risen by as much as twenty kilometres, although their height has been constantly reduced by erosion during uplift; the greatest uplift has been immediately east of the Alpine Fault. Other major ranges also developed, for example the Kaikoura ranges in the South, and the Tararua and Ruahine ranges in the North Island. In contrast to these areas of uplift, other areas subsided. One such area, Cook Strait, has been submerged by the sea, whereas over the Canterbury plains and southern Wairarapa lowlands, the gravel eroded from the ranges has kept the sea back.

Less prominent in the landscape, but equally characteristic of the Kaikoura Orogeny, are the horizontal movements along major faults in the north-east of the South Island and the south-east of the North Island. Several faults have horizontal displacements of twenty kilometres or more, with the north-western side moving to the north-east relative to the south-eastern side.

Volcanic activity in the North Island has been closely connected with the developing orogenic movements. In the late Miocene a volcanic zone developed in Coromandel, and subsequent uplift and erosion have exposed deposits strongly altered by high temperatures and hot water. The youngest, still continuing, volcanism is in the Taupo Volcanic Zone, which is subsiding relatively to the regions to east and west.

The tectonic movements of the Kaikoura Orogeny are generally typical of those along the whole western margin of the Pacific, and are characterised by great local variations. In many particular details, however, they are strongly influenced by older tectonic trends derived from the earlier Tuhua and Rangitata orogenies—the Kaikoura movements are superimposed on a region of the earth's crust with a long geological history, although this is imperfectly recorded in the rocks. That long history contrasts with the youth of the New Zealand landscape, a landscape being constantly but slowly changed as a result of erosion by seas and rivers, and more rapidly changed as a result of earthquakes and volcanism that indicate the continuation of the Kaikoura orogeny in the present day.

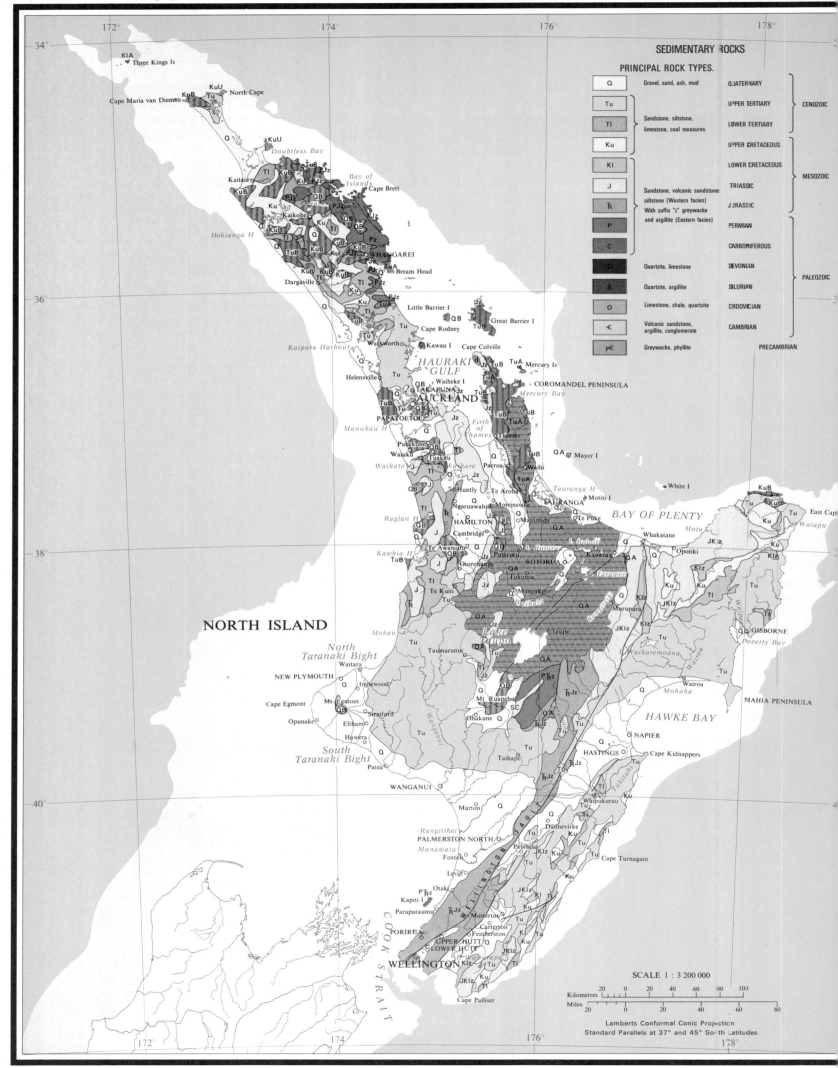

SEDIMENTARY ROCKS

PRINCIPAL ROCK TYPES.

Q	Gravel, sand, ash, mud	QUATERNARY
Tu	Sandstone, siltstone, limestone, coal measures	UPPER TERTIARY
Tl		LOWER TERTIARY
Ku		UPPER CRETACEOUS
Kl		LOWER CRETACEOUS
J	Sandstone, volcanic sandstone, siltstone (Western facies) With suffix "z" greywacke and argillite (Eastern facies)	TRIASSIC
Ŕ		JJRASSIC
P		PERMIAN
C		CARBONIFEROUS
D	Quartzite, limestone	DEVONIAN
S	Quartzite, argillite	SILURIAN
O	Limestone, shale, quartzite	ORDOVICIAN
Є	Volcanic sandstone, argillite, conglomerate	CAMBRIAN
pЄ	Greywacke, phyllite	PRECAMBRIAN

CENOZOIC
MESOZOIC
PALEOZOIC

NORTH ISLAND

SCALE 1 : 3 200 000

Lamberts Conformal Conic Projection
Standard Parallels at 37° and 45° South Latitudes

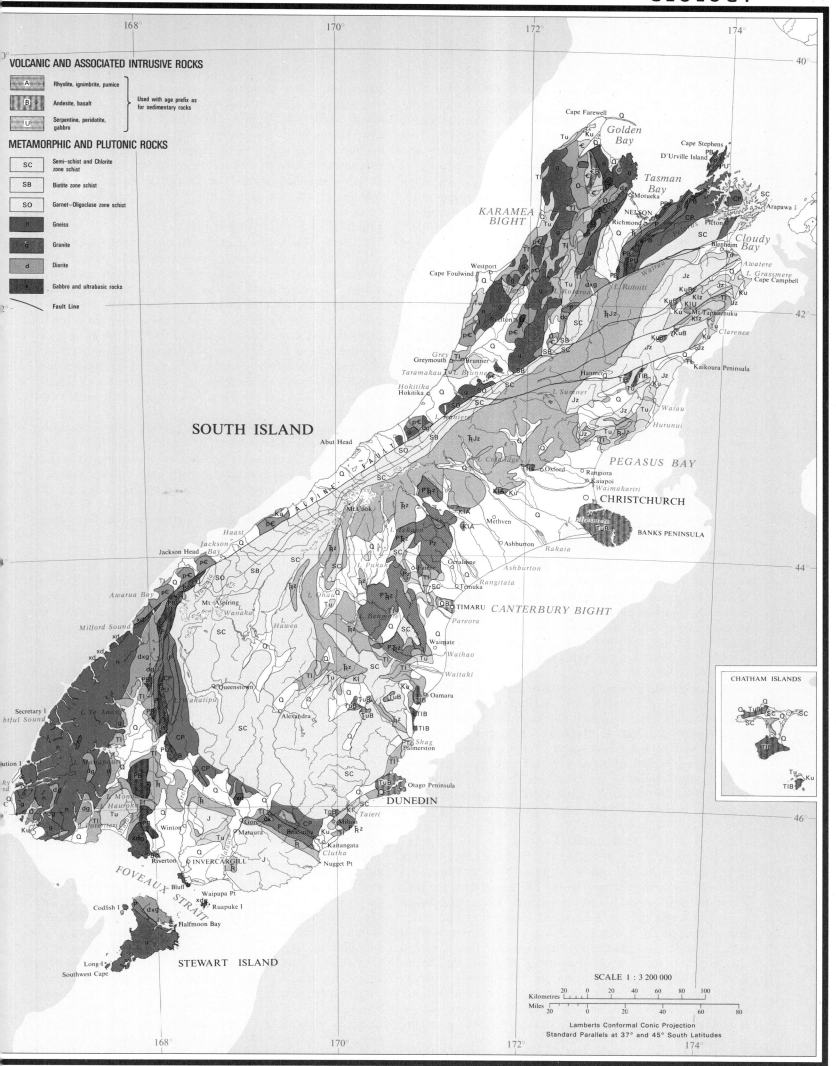

VOLCANIC AND ASSOCIATED INTRUSIVE ROCKS

A	Rhyolite, ignimbrite, pumice
B	Andesite, basalt
U	Serpentine, peridotite, gabbro

Used with age prefix as for sedimentary rocks

METAMORPHIC AND PLUTONIC ROCKS

SC	Semi-schist and Chlorite zone schist
SB	Biotite zone schist
SO	Garnet–Oligoclase zone schist
n	Gneiss
g	Granite
d	Diorite
x	Gabbro and ultrabasic rocks
	Fault Line

SOUTH ISLAND

KARAMEA BIGHT

Golden Bay
Cape Farewell
Cape Stephens
D'Urville Island
Tasman Bay
Motueka
NELSON
Richmond
Arapawa I
Cloudy Bay
Blenheim
Picton
Westport
Cape Foulwind
Awatere
L. Grassmere
Cape Campbell
Buller
L. Rotoroa
L. Rotoiti
Reefton
Mt Tapuaenuku
Greymouth
Brunner
L. Brunner
Hanmer
Clarence
Taramakau
Kaikoura Peninsula
Hokitika
L. Sumner
Waiau
Hurunui
L. Kaniere
Abut Head
L. Coleridge
PEGASUS BAY
Oxford
Rangiora
Kaiapoi
Waimakariri
CHRISTCHURCH
Mt Cook
Methven
BANKS PENINSULA
Ashburton
L. Tekapo
Rakaia
L. Pukaki
Geraldine
Jackson Head
Jackson Bay
Temuka
Haast
L. Ohau
Rangitata
CANTERBURY BIGHT
Mt Aspiring
TIMARU
Awarua Bay
L. Wanaka
Pareora
Hawea
Waimate
Milford Sound
Waihao
Waitaki
Benmore
Secretary I
Doubtful Sound
L. Te Anau
Oamaru
Queenstown
L. Wakatipu
Shag
Palmerston
Resolution I
Alexandra
L. Manapouri
Mt Hauroko
DUNEDIN
Taieri
L. Poteriteri
Winton
Gore
Mataura
Balclutha
Otago Peninsula
Milton
Kaitangata
Clutha
Riverton
INVERCARGILL
Nugget Pt
Bluff
FOVEAUX STRAIT
Waipapa Pt
Ruapuke I
Codfish I
Halfmoon Bay
STEWART ISLAND
Long I
Southwest Cape

CHATHAM ISLANDS

SCALE 1 : 3 200 000

Kilometres   20 0 20 40 60 80 100
Miles   20   0   20   40   60   80

Lamberts Conformal Conic Projection
Standard Parallels at 37° and 45° South Latitudes

FORESTS

W. J. Wendelken

Forests have always been an integral part of the New Zealand landscape. At the time of European settlement they covered some 14 million hectares and their protective cover is still a factor in the shaping of the country and its image. As well, they provide a source of both wealth and recreation.

Today there are two forests, the residual indigenous forests, largely occupying steep land in remote places with, elsewhere, depleted remnants scattered throughout occupied farmlands, and the exotic forests, much less extensive but now producing more than eighty per cent of the country's wood products. The two are quite distinct in composition, in function and in degree of acceptance by sectional interests in the community. Apart from historical and emotive differences, the main contrasts are now in area and economic importance.

From the original cover of fifty-three per cent of the land, indigenous forests now cover only twenty-three per cent. Some once-extensive associations of species have become very reduced in area, for example the northern kauri forests and the lowland kahikatea swamp forests; others, such as the upland beech forests, have remained almost unchanged. Much of the remaining native forest is either preserved from exploitation or is not suitable for traditional sawing purposes.

The exotic forests are concentrated for production in but few localities and, although increasing annually in area at a rate of more than six per cent (40 000 ha), still cover only two per cent of the land surface. This contrast in area is even more remarkable when compared with the volume and value of products derived from each category of forest. Most of the small volume of indigenous wood produced today is used for building and general purposes, with better quality material providing finishing grades for board and panel products, joinery and furniture. Its annual volume and value is 700 cubic metres (3 000 000 board ft), worth $560,000, approximately two per cent of the total production. Very little is exported and only as made-up components.

The increase in volume and value of exotic wood products is remarkable and has had a twofold effect. Increased usage for an ever-widening variety of products has significantly reduced exploitation of indigenous forests and demand for imported wood. Surplus production has been exported, particularly as pulp and paper products, with considerable economic gain. In the last six years, the annual value of exported exotic wood products has risen fourfold, and now exceeds $80 million.

Indigenous Forests

The section on Flora describes the botanical composition of the main plant formations found in New Zealand, in a relatively undisturbed state, at the beginning of systematic European settlement, taken as around 1840. Four broad classes of forest may be recognised in the rich and varied indigenous forest types and associations, the extent of which is shown on the accompanying maps. That for 1840 also indicates the general occurrence of grasslands, scrub lands and other types of vegetation. The forests typically grade into scrub forms at coastal sites, towards the upper altitudinal limits of tree growth and around the margins of regions where climates are more suitable for drier grassland communities.

Rarely was an area occupied by a single tree species and commonly both conifers (*gymnosperms*) and leaf-trees (*dicotyledons*) were intimately associated. There are only twenty species of conifer, all endemic, of which seven are large trees, while the pygmy pine is one of the smallest conifers in the world. The range of families represented among the leaf-trees is much more varied, and commonly all have smallish leaves, an evergreen habit and small flowers.

KAURI–PODOCARP–HARDWOOD CLASS

The giant kauri was scattered throughout the area north of latitude 38° and below 800 metres altitude being locally intermixed in diverse associations of podocarps and hardwoods. The kauri grew mostly on ridges and its common associates were the podocarps rimu, miro, totara, tanekaha, toatoa, and the hardwoods rewarewa and tawari, but it also occurred with almost any one or more of the indigenous tree species found in its range, for example with pohutakawa in coastal situations. Southern rata and kaikawaka are found with kauri on the crest of the Coromandel Range, and hard beech and northern rata occur locally with kauri at lower levels.

Some eighty per cent of the remaining forest containing kauri has been at least partially logged or affected by fire, and a high proportion of the known and mapped stands now comprises much second growth kauri ('ricker stands'). Large stands of unlogged kauri, containing some of the largest specimens ever known, still occur in the Waipoua, Omahuta and Manaia forest sanctuaries and in other reserves.

PODOCARP–HARDWOOD CLASS

This broad group contains a large number of forest tree types. In extant forests, over relatively small areas, podocarps are abundant and completely dominant, the hardwoods confined to an understory. These types are most common on recent volcanic soils in the central North Island and on alluvial soils and exceptionally fertile hill soils elsewhere, and this was largely true for former extensive tracts now cleared. It is mainly on such sites that the podocarps, matai, totara and kahikatea, and the hardwoods, pokaka and maire, are characteristic; all are rare elsewhere.

Below 900 metres most podocarp–hardwood forest has only scattered podocarps, with rimu the commonest, but the hardwood stocking is usually high. In general, the hardwood composition changes from north to south, with distance from the sea and with increasing altitude. Because several species have remarkably distinct geographical distribution, the pattern of forest types is complicated. The most widespread trees are the hardwoods rata, tawa, hinau, rewarewa, pukatea, kohekohe and kamahi. Taraire and puriri are increasingly abundant at low altitudes, from the lower Waikato and Thames districts northwards, and kamahi is replaced by the closely related towai. Mangeao, at lower altitudes, and tawari, in the higher forests, are common in the Waikato and Bay of Plenty podocarp–hardwood forests. As many of the forests which have been logged for prime podocarp timber were left in a cutover state, subsequent regrowth, masking the scars of logging, restored a forest cover which has become accepted by the public as 'native forest'. On rugged terrain, on boggy ground, above 900 metres and in the absence of beech where this class reaches the timber line, the podocarp–hardwoods include a wide variety of types. Characteristic species in these situations are miro, Hall's totara, tanekaha, toatoa and mountain toatoa, kaikawaka, pink pine, silver pine, yellow-silver pine, kamahi, broadleaf and tawheowheo.

In the South Island this class was suppressed or hindered in its full development by the more extensive beech forests. Apart from the absence of some of the main tree species restricted to a more northern distribution, such as hinau, taraire, puriri, pukatea, kohekohe and rewarewa, the southern podocarp–hardwood forests are generally comparable with those in the North Island although southern rata, kamahi, Hall's totara and kaiwaka are more common, and extend to quite high altitudes, in the upland forests. The Westland *quintinea* is abundant in the lower and middle level forests between Collingwood and Hokitika, locally extending into montane forests where beech species are not present. The larger areas of beech forest outlined on the South Island maps do not distinguish this class where it occurs locally within them, because of the difficulty in defining the complex sub-classes at so small a scale.

On the Contemporary map, standing logged forest and secondary forest, developed after burning of high forest in Maori or early European times, have not been shown separately. In most districts, these modified types occur as small pockets or strips along or near the main forest margins. Appreciable areas of logged podocarp–hardwood forest occur within a radius of forty kilometres from Rotorua, in the south-west quarter of the Urewera forest tract, between Lake Taupo and the main trunk railway, in the Ohakune district and on the south-west side of the Tararua Range. The secondary forest stands are most extensive in the Bay of Plenty and Upper Waikato districts. In Westland, the extensive areas of cleared terraces along main rivers now have degraded soils, with high water tables, leading to the typical *pakahi* formation. Though young podocarps are locally abundant, hardwoods predominate generally; rewarewa, hinau, kamahi and kanuka are the common species. Except in reserves and managed State forests, many of the secondary forest types are giving way to the rapid development of agriculture and commercial exotic afforestation.

PODOCARP–HARDWOOD–BEECH CLASS

In the North Island, most of this forest class occurs below 750 metres in the Taranaki and East Cape districts. It was probably not much more extensive in 1840 than it is today; in the intervening 130 years logging and clearing has been confined to comparatively small areas, chiefly in the Ohakune district and northern Hawke's Bay. In the South Island, where a broadly similar class may be recognised, clearing took place in Nelson/Marlborough, along the mountain fringes through Canterbury and Otago and, to a limited extent, in the Buller, Grey and Taramakau catchments. Large tracts still remain in western Southland, Westland and north-west Nelson.

To the north there is a botanically fine complex of enormously varied stands, although beech species are most abundant on steep ridges, with tawa and other hardwoods in gullies. The most common beech in North Taranaki, and west of the main divide in the East Cape tract, is hard beech; in South Taranaki, and east of the Raukumara Range, it is black beech. The same broad type of podocarp–beech forest with tawa occurs locally elsewhere, especially in northern Hawke's Bay, and red and silver beech are locally present. Above 750 metres on the upper flanks of the main axial ranges and on Mt Ruapehu are abundant red beech or red with silver beech, with frequent rimu, miro and Hall's totara, over understories of kamahi and

broadleaf, with tawari and tawheowheo from the Mohaka River northward. A similar pattern is evident to the south, but the North Island hardwoods are largely absent. Podocarp–hardwood–beech forest above 900 metres is rare and with increasing altitude red, silver and mountain beech are associated with kaikawaka, mountain toatoa, pink pine and broadleaf on parts of the Raukumara, Huiarau and Ruahine ranges and on Mt Ruapehu.

In the South Island, the class comprises a simpler range of forest types, with common North Island species, such as rewarewa and tawa, extending only into the Nelson region, the South Island tawheowheo taking over from its North Island counterpart, and the southern rata replacing the northern species. The beeches become more common and dominant, with silver and mountain beech extending to the upper timber line, mixed with southern rata, kamahi and kaikawaka; at lower levels kamahi is the dominant associate. Remnants of what was probably once a more extensive grouping of beech forest associations with podocarps and hardwoods occur along the Kaikoura coast, as residual pockets in the eastern foothills of the Southern Alps and in other favourable climatic pockets, indicating that, like the beech forests of the central North Island, this class suffered from fires over centuries of time in the low rainfall, inland, high country areas.

BEECH FOREST CLASS

The genus, comprising four distinct species and a subspecies, mountain beech, was probably the most common forest type before human occupation and still occupies extensive tracts of rugged and mountain terrains. There were anomalies in the distribution of beeches, still evident today; they were absent from Mt Egmont and between the northern Ruahine and southern Tararua ranges. There was a marked distribution gap along the west coast of the South Island between the Taramakau and Paringa rivers, and, perhaps less surprisingly, no beech occurs across Foveaux Strait on Stewart Island.

In the north, pure beech forest occurs mainly on the highest parts of the Huiarau Range, over most of the Kaweka and Kaimanawa ranges, at the northern end of the Ruahine Range and along the southern crest of the Tararua Range. Although only red, silver and mountain beech are present in this montane forest, there is a complex pattern of forest types. Large tracts are mono-specific; others include every possible mixture of the three species with their associated secondary hardwood species and large shrub tiers. Silver beech is rare on the Kaweka Range and the southern half of the Kaimanawa Range, and extremely rare on the Ruahine Range. Mountain beech is seldom found to the north of the Kaweka Range and is absent on the Tararua Range and minor ranges around Wellington. On a few highlands to the north of the main axial ranges of the North Island, pockets of beech occur in the podocarp–hardwood class, as on the Mamaku plateau and Mt Te Aroha.

In the south, beeches occupied a variety of sites, from the wet, rugged fiordland coast and adjacent mountains to the dry inland valleys of the eastern Southern Alps, adapting to a range of climates from super-wet coastal, through an annual rainfall variation of 6100 millimetres, to dry, cold, near-continental. Although silver and red beech provide quite high quality timber from defect-free, mature trees, and black beech was used locally, as in Canterbury where podocarp forests were scarce or distant from early settlements, beech forests as a class have suffered less impact from logging than have the other three classes. Locally, extensive fires have decimated or destroyed important protection forests, as throughout the Marlborough Sounds, the upper Wairau Valley, parts of North Canterbury and around the Central Otago basin.

Soils under beech forests tend to be poorer than under podocarp–hardwood forests, and slopes are commonly steeper. Although marginal areas were latterly cleared by logging and for agriculture, few former beech forest sites today provide areas of permanent and productive agriculture. In Nelson, for example, the extensive Moutere gravel formation is now largely planted with exotic pines, established on what were previously hill-country grazing areas developed in the ashes of burnt forest. Today, northwest Nelson, northern Westland and Fiordland, and the flanks of both sides of the Southern Alps contain extensive tracts of beech, still largely on original sites, although many of the associated species have been subject to considerable modification and reduction as a result of a century of browsing by deer. Many beech forest types offer an unparalleled opportunity among the indigenous forests for intensive management, for the production of wood and for other important functions, such as soil and water conservation, and the provision of recreation and wildlife habitats.

In summary, the indigenous forests are still prominent in many of the less populated areas of New Zealand, flanking most of the inland mountain areas, steep valleys and fiords, and, even though some tracts have been unwisely cleared for agriculture, they still present a full, albeit locally restricted, spectrum of the many botanical and ecological complexes that evolved before humans occupied this land. From the magnificent kauri in the north, through the dense, high-volume podocarp stands found on fertile sites in lower valleys, to the extensive range of the beeches, New Zealand has been endowed with a wealth of forest types. This has only recently been recognised, by the bulk of its people, as being worthy of preservation rather than, as in the past, as being a resource to be utilised or even destroyed as a hindrance to agricultural pursuits.

Forest Clearing

With the foregoing in mind, a brief outline of the events of, and the reasons for, the clearing of the forests may be given, concurrently with an outline of the development of a national forest policy and Forest Service. This leads to, indeed considerably overlaps, the beginnings of exotic forests in New Zealand, forests not only for the production of timber but also as an important landscape factor. The early colonists promptly set about clearing the forest, to provide the wood products and fuel required for settlement and for trading purposes. Rapid clearance took place near centres of settlement to prepare land for agriculture. The sawmilling which developed was largely incidental to a strong desire for settlement land, except where extensive tracts of natural grassland existed, as in the Canterbury and Otago–Southland plains and to a lesser extent the inner valleys of the mountain ranges. Here, early provincial governments encouraged planting of exotic species in the early 1870s, by the provision of free land grants. Elsewhere, sawmilling-based communities moved inland into the uncut forests, keeping ahead of agricultural development.

The highly-prized kauri timber, concentrated in the Northland, Coromandel and Great Barrier Island forests, was soon produced in large quantities, firstly by handsaws operated from pits. Many wooden buildings, from Auckland to Dunedin, still stand as century-old monuments to the quantity and quality of wood produced in the first thirty years of settlement. The old Government Building in Wellington, built in 1876, is an outstanding example covering more than 9 300 square metres.

The agricultural potential of soils, under kauri forest in particular and of low mineral content under some other forest associations, was not understood and, although early attempts were made to develop grassland and cropland on such sites, it was soon recognised that the most fertile land and the greatest opportunity for agricultural production were provided by the mixed podocarp–hardwood forests of the lowland valleys and younger volcanic soils. Consequently, although the large kauri reserves that existed remained available for cutting, it was the other forests that were wastefully cleared to satisfy the demand for agricultural land.

The Crown attempted, in the early days, to reserve for itself forested areas, passing legislation (the Forest Bill 1874, promoted by Julius Vogel) to protect forests, but the lack of sympathy for forestry as an integral part of land-use, coupled with an intense hunger for agricultural or pastoral land, nullified these praiseworthy and far-sighted proposals. In 1876, I. Campbell-Walker was appointed the first Conservator of Forests and soon produced a valuable description of forest conditions and proposals for management which, had both he and the proposed Bill been more popular with provincial governments and settlers, could have markedly influenced the pattern and use of Crown forests today.

In the Land Act 1877, the first conservation seeds sown by Campbell-Walker began to take root in government thinking, and Crown forests came under the provisions of the Act, thus regulating the cutting of timber on proclaimed land.

Governments debated and voted on forestry throughout the 1880s; in 1885 the State Forest Act was passed and a second Conservator of Forests appointed. Administration of Crown forests continued, under various Lands Acts, but, in the absence of either political support or knowledge of the limitations of permanent agricultural practices, forest clearing continued with wasteful land utilisation and much loss of valuable wood and forest cover. The innate instability of many of the country's steepland soils was another factor little understood. In 1885, Vogel introduced a second major piece of forest legislation, aiming to set aside areas of forest land in an attempt to safeguard one of the elements which might influence climate.

Thomas Kirk, indefatigable botanist, geologist and scholar, became Chief Conservator of Forests in 1885, and by 1887, when a change of government curtailed forest reservation and other forest activities, 560 000 hectares had been reserved. Large bush fires, particularly in Northland where in 1887 375 million board feet of kauri were destroyed, also encouraged, albeit temporarily, the reservation of lowland forests. However, the conflict between responsibilities for settlement and for reserving forests, in the administering Forest and Agriculture Branch of the Lands Department, resulted in little further effective action to save production forests.

By the beginning of the twentieth century it was mandatory for State forest land to be logged of its merchantable timber before clearing and settlement for agriculture were permitted. State forests in areas open for mining could be cut, under control of the Mining Wardens, and this led in some instances to further wasteful use of the merchantable forests.

Early Policy

Early botanists, scientists and foresters accumulated much descriptive material on indigenous forests and began to assess the volume of usable timber remaining. A Royal Commission on Forestry in 1913 defined some of the main forest management and timber problems of the day, and the Commission's findings led to the formation of an independent State Forest Service in 1919. A new State Forest Act was passed in 1921–2 and remains in its essential features unchanged to this day.

By 1890, the Forest Branch of the Lands and Survey Department had established exotic plantations near Whangarei, in association with a School of Forestry, and other plantings had been started in the Waikato and at Kaingaroa, while by 1896 planting had extended to sites at Hanmer and Maniototo. By the time the Forest Service became a separate Department in 1919, 15 500 hectares had been planted, with many mixtures of species including wattle, eucalyptus and a wide variety of conifers. The Service then controlled 2 124 000 hectares of provisional forest, land held as Crown land until the native forest was logged, at which time a decision would be made to allocate land, where appropriate, to agriculture; a further 690 000 hectares was held as State forest, or permanently dedicated forest land.

Despite the varying results from planting on a wide variety of sites, an expanded afforestation programme was urged as it became obvious that the indigenous timber resources were being expended at an alarming rate. In 1909 it was estimated that 6 880 000 hectares of forests remained, of which 607 000 hectares was merchantable. This contained 198 million cubic metres (35 000 million board ft) and current usage was 2.3 million cubic metres (414 million board ft). Demand for timber was expected to rise, while production from the merchantable forests was not expected to last for much more than forty years. The area of forests in 1909 was 3 268 000 hectares of Crown forests, containing 108 million cubic metres (19 180 million board ft) of timber. The areas concerned comprised Crown land, State Forest and Forest Reserve. Permanent forests containing only 7.3 million cubic metres (1 300 million board ft) covered 850 000 hectares, with private and native forests estimated to contain 82 million cubic metres (14 600 million board ft) occurring on 2 896 000 hectares. By this time the earlier emphasis on reservation for conservation was matched by determined efforts to increase the permanent forest areas for timber supply, to prevent wastage of native timbers and to increase the rate of exotic afforestation.

Sawmilling

The first sawing of native timber probably took place in Dusky Sound in 1773 when the crew of the *Resolution* cleared a site for an observatory and some of the trees were pitsawn into planks. Later in the same century kahikatea and kauri were pitsawn and, as spars and masts, were exported from the Coromandel to Tahiti. Early in the nineteenth century pitsawn timber was exported to Australia, and houses and boats were being constructed at several coastal stations in Northland and Auckland and at other settlements, including whaling stations. By 1838 water power had been introduced to drive saws at Mercury Bay and bullocks introduced to haul logs to mills, thereby widening the range of terrain that could be worked and supplementing the flotation systems of bringing in the logs.

From these early beginnings, the logging and sawmilling industries grew rapidly wherever settlers concentrated and forests were available for cutting, particularly where ports or rivers facilitated movement of timber, both round the coasts by scows, commonly made from native timbers, and to export markets. The main market was Australia, but many other Pacific countries bought prime kauri and podocarp timber, and many shipments were made to Britain. The growth of the industry continued throughout the last century; in 1886, there were 220 mills employing 3890 men and cutting 164 million board feet; by 1909, 423 mills employed 7410 men and cut 414 million board feet.

Many early settlements depended on the local sawmills and associated industries for work, and the transport of logs to mills helped to stimulate the development of roads, opening up further areas for settlement. The source of supply moved steadily inland as the accessible and better forests were cut, and this created a demand for better roads and railways to serve the increasing, predominantly coastal-oriented population of the young country; the Rimutaka road constructed in 1856 gave access not only to extensive land easily cleared for agriculture in the Wairarapa but also to a plentiful supply of cheap timber for Wellington's rapid development. Railways soon followed the roads; again using the Wellington example, by 1878 rail access had been provided to Featherston, markedly decreasing the price of timber in the capital yet increasing the financial return to sawmillers, by substantially reducing transport costs.

Although the early sawmilling industry did contribute to the growth of many small settlements, the general pattern of development was for small mills of low capital cost to move quickly onward to uncut forests as local supplies became exhausted. Re-location was common, although the advent of bush trams hauling logs for long distances ensured sawmills a longer life in one location and encouraged investment in larger, integrated plants. Some cutting concessions required bush trams to be built to railway specifications, as at Port Craig in western Southland where large unused viaducts and easily graded routes are today silent testimony to a once large industry planned with ambition and vigour. Elsewhere, the provision of employment in isolated areas, from which sawmills moved on, was found in industries servicing agriculture, but even today there are communities still dependent on sawmilling, as in the King Country, Westland and eastern Southland.

SAWMILLERS FEDERATION

The forest industry, like agriculture, is susceptible to fluctuations in demand. With the development of comprehensive fiscal policies in the last seventy years, it has experienced wide changes both in demand for its produce and in its economic viability, not always directly associated with changing economic circumstances overseas. In 1917, after the 1913 Royal Commission on Forestry, a Dominion Federated Sawmillers Association was formed, with seventy-five companies represented. The association's aims were to provide cheaper timber and to promote co-operative principles in marketing, in procuring supplies and in accident and fire insurance. It is interesting to speculate how the forestry industry might have developed had this association been as successful as the Dairy Co-operative movement which came into being at the same time.

Exotic Forests

Early in the 1920s the first formal enunciation of the policy which the new Forest Service was to implement on behalf of the government was made by Sir Francis Bell, the first Minister of Forests. He attached considerable importance to the prior claims of indigenous forestry, stating that he wanted to initiate first and foremost conservation and use of existing forests and secondly, and far behind, plantation. The emphasis on conservation, which was much wider than merely rationing the amount of native wood cut, was continued throughout the next fifty years, and has only recently been taken up widely as a public issue. Aspects of conservation included protection of forests, the creation of permanent reserves, the gazetting of sanctuaries, all emphasising the value of the mountain forests to soil and water conservation.

LARGE SCALE AFFORESTATION

Later in the 1920s, the State Forest Service undertook large-scale exotic afforestation on the pumice soils of the Kaingaroa plains, with more modest programmes on the poor gravel soils south of Nelson, on phosphate deficient soils at Maramarua, at Karioi on the slopes of Mt Ruapehu and on the Canterbury plains. Private afforestation companies stimulated public interest in afforestation and from 1925 to 1936, coinciding with a serious shortage of work in other sectors, a planting boom resulted in 172 000 hectares being planted in the centre of the North Island by State and private interests. The year 1928 saw a peak of planting when 40 000 hectares were planted, a figure not again reached until 1973.

DWINDLING INDIGENOUS RESOURCES

In 1923, a National Forest Inventory indicated that nine per cent of the country carried merchantable forest containing 351 million cubic metres (62 000 million board ft). Like previous estimates, this contained gross errors, due in part to changing standards in utilisation as well as to wide variations in commercial acceptance of the various species. Predicted usage led to a forecast that by 1952 the resource should be 181 million cubic metres (32 000 million board ft). A detailed survey was carried out and the 1952 estimates showed that the resource was in fact only about one-fifth of this, leading to great concern for future timber supplies. Despite this, there was little effective action to correct the position for about a decade.

Between 1936 and 1960, afforestation proceeded at a modest pace, the State being the major contributor. During the years of the Second World War, annual planting fell to 400 hectares and the total area planted during the whole twenty-five years was only 30 500 hectares.

A survey in 1960 indicated once more that a vigorous afforestation effort was needed. The impetus of this planning has continued to the present day, and provides sound justification for further expansion of exotic forests because of their role in catering for domestic needs, in the diversification of New Zealand's trade, in the provision of employment in both forest growing and product processing and in regional economic and social development. More recently the role of exotic plant species has been recognised in providing a protective cover on badly eroded soils in the high country where the native vegetation has been destroyed.

After the flush of post-war land development, following a vigorous farm settlement scheme, it became obvious that many farms contained some land which could more profitably be used for forestry, and land managers began to think in terms of integrating forestry with pastoral farming. In 1960, the government announced that the timber value of trees on private land would be exempted from estate duty, and a prompt public reaction initiated a minor planting boom. The National Farm Forestry Association, which originated in 1958, took heart from this development, and the passing of the Forestry Encouragement Act in 1963, whereby loans with suspensory clauses were granted to farmers, further stimulated farm forestry plantings.

At this stage, planning for the future included the planting by the State of another 405 000 hectares by the end of this century, in order to meet the demand expected to be brought about by a population which is forecast to reach five million. This would entail an average annual planting rate of 10 000 hectares.

The recognition of forestry as a land use and in industrial production culminated at the end of the 1960s in a government-sponsored Forestry Development Conference, a preliminary to an all-sector National Development Conference, which affirmed forestry's important role in the economy. The 1960 targets were increased to an annual planting target of 23 000 hectares. The already expanding private contribution to the productive exotic forests was further stimulated by the Forestry Encouragement Grants Regulations in 1970 and by the sudden upsurge of interest from Japanese buyers in logs from exotic forests. This demand for raw wood in Japan meant that many small growers were, for the first time, not only able to sell their timber stands but to sell them at a price several times higher than local sawmillers were formerly prepared to pay. Today, the interest in afforestation is such that businessmen as well as farmers are interested in investing in forestry and some companies are promoting schemes whereby investors may participate in forestry ventures backed by sound management and marketing expertise.

The annual planting rate has risen from 6070 hectares in 1960 to 43 300 hectares in 1973, divided approximately equally between State and private sectors.

This second, post-war, planting boom has resulted in the extension of forests to new sites and to regions not previously considered for major afforestation. Important forests have been developed on the Manawatu sand dunes, and on the coastal dunes north from Auckland City to Ninety Mile Beach. Afforestation with a valuable protective role has been carried out in the headwaters of river catchments in the Gisborne—East Cape region. Highly productive sites in Hawke's Bay are being afforested, and forests in the South Otago region are now forming the nucleus for important wood-processing industries. On a smaller scale, forests are being established on the Coromandel Peninsula, in the Wairarapa, in Marlborough, Canterbury and Southland.

As exotic forests matured, the Forest Service took the initiative to develop the cutting and marketing of exotic sawntimber; there is marked difference in log size and apparent quality between indigenous and exotic sawlogs. State sawmills were established at Waipa, near Rotorua, in 1939 and at Conical Hill, in south Otago, ten years later. The sawing and preservative treatment techniques developed by these sawmills laid the basis for the regional development of exotic sawmilling. The output of exotic timber has increased from 80 000 cubic metres (34 million board ft) in 1935 (11% of total exported timber), to 1 673 000 cubic metres (710 million board ft) in 1973 (81% of total).

PULP AND PAPER AND TRADE

The first commercial pulping of radiata pine in New Zealand began in 1939, with the production of paperboard from a mill established at Whakatane.

In 1952, New Zealand Forest Products began production of kraft paper and pulp at Kinleith and in 1955 at Kawerau, the Tasman Pulp and Paper Company established its plant to produce chemical and mechanical pulp. By 1962, newsprint was also being produced. Radiata pine proved to be suitable for a wide range of mechanical and chemical pulping processes, and these two integrated processing units expanded and diversified so that today their parent companies are amongst the largest commercial enterprises in New Zealand. Since 1953, total wood pulp production has increased from 35 000 tonnes a year to 600 000 tonnes a year (1973) and paper and paperboard production from 28 000 tonnes a year to 453 000 tonnes. This growing industry has brought very rapid development to towns, transport industries and ports in the Bay of Plenty, and increased employment opportunities and prosperity to both the region and the nation. A further pulp industry has recently been established near Napier, and another unit is currently being built for the Nelson region.

Panel industries have also developed and diversified since the war, and their products complement sawn timber in domestic usage. Fibreboard (softboard and hardboard), plywood and particle board are produced in plants at Auckland, Kinleith, Taupo, Rotorua and Christchurch. Further developments are occurring at Thames and near Rangiora. These industries provide a valuable means of utilising wood material which would otherwise be wasted, either in forests or at sawmills. In 1970 panel industries produced about 17 million square metres of panels of various kinds.

With the development and diversification of New Zealand's forest processing industries, the volume of imports has steadily declined. Commodities now required to be imported are mainly hardwood timbers for furniture, speciality wood pulps and high quality papers. The total value of these imports in 1972 was $19 million. A wide range of products is exported, earning essential overseas exchange; included are logs and poles, sawn timber, veneer and panels, wood pulp, paper and paperboard, having a total value to New Zealand in 1972 of $82 million. This represents six per cent by total value of all export products.

PRODUCTION AND GROWTH

As the forests planted after 1960 mature, forest roundwood will be available in increasing quantities for further industrial development and trade diversification. In 1972, the total production of roundwood from New Zealand forests amounted to 8.2 million cubic metres. Projections of future production, prepared in 1973, indicate that the roundwood yield of the country's forests will reach 15 million cubic metres by 1985, 20 million cubic metres by 1995 and more than 25 million cubic metres by 2005, depending on the maintenance of a high rate of afforestation.

In little more than a century, the country's forests and forest industries have shown a remarkable change, progressing from small, pioneering, frequently transient industries wastefully cutting the best of the native forests, to large, integrated plants drawing supplies of exotic wood from sustained-yield forests. The ability of these exotic forests to produce large quantities of wood, with wide utility, on relatively small areas frequently not suited for intensive agriculture, has meant that many native merchantable forests under Crown ownership could be preserved from massive exploitation. Because alternative wood supplies, from exotic forests, have reduced industries' demands for native wood, careful and methodical management of some indigenous forests has been attempted. Today, extensive podocarp forests in south Westland are managed on a selection system, ensuring the perpetuation of both the forests and their timber. In Southland, silver beech forests have been managed to regenerate the forest after logging, and sawmills can plan for a longer life with security of supplies, steady employment and a sustained social contribution to their district.

In Westland, the hill country podocarp–hardwood forests are not suitable for sustained management and the existing mills are rapidly approaching the end of their resources. In this area, a pioneer type of industry still exists, with wasteful cutting of logs and, because of the small and scattered nature of the units, unable to integrate and use sawmill residues and lower-quality logs. In Westland and western Nelson, large areas of unlogged beech forests still occur over extensive hill and lower mountain slopes. Present plans are to combine the opportunity for integrating a larger scale, and more efficient utilisation of this resource with the existing small industries and the people dependent on them for their livelihood. This Beech Forest Scheme has been the subject of public debate reminiscent of the early controversies concerning forestry of the late nineteenth century. Inevitably the proper use of these beech forests must proceed, rather than the perpetuation of what is virtually the last of the early pioneering sawmill days.

Forestry Today

Today many people are taking an interest in the native forests, from those demanding complete preservation to those advocating wise multi-purpose management. With large areas either permanently reserved in National Parks, Scenic Reserves and dedicated State Forests, including sanctuaries, or protected in State forest parks, the country is well situated to ensure the continuance of its native forests. In the mountains, the associated scrub and grasslands which make up the protective forest mantle guarding the lowlands against flooding and damage are similarly considered for management. While the increasing exotic forests have already made an impact on the landscape and play an important role in providing protection, recreation and amenity functions, as well as wildlife habitats for many native birds, the native forests have both a greater appeal and a more important role. Wise management and protection of these forests can meet many demands, including some that at first sight seem incompatible, such as the production of wood and the maintenance of a native forest structure. This blending of uses has already been demonstrated in the terrace rimu forests of south Westland and in the beech forests of Southland. The government's policy of perpetuating kauri, as a species in managed forests, is another example of recent policy re-emphasis, which contrasts strongly with the pioneering tradition of removing obstructing forest for agricultural development. Some small changes in forest policy are required in order fully to meet the needs of New Zealanders in the rest of this century and beyond; these include partial logging of all the remaining indigenous forests in such a way as to maintain the forest structure and to perpetuate the supply of valuable native woods, a development made possible largely by the substitution of exotic for indigenous timbers in many traditional uses. Increased planting rates on the many thousands of hectares of marginal or reverted farmland, and increased production from existing pastoral land can facilitate and hasten this, thus avoiding the further clearing of logged, indigenous forests.

It is doubtful whether the early settlers and pioneers who brought seeds of exotic trees to this country could have envisaged the effect these were to have, or whether the early planners and planters who promoted the massive plantings of the 1925–35 decade appreciated just how much influence exotic forestry could have on conserving the native forests. The scene is now set for further development; past mistakes in land use and forest clearing have been recognised; new generations of New Zealanders have learnt, as their European forebears learned and forgot in the enthusiasm of settlement, that forests are an integral part of the country and an important factor in the lives and well-being of all the people.

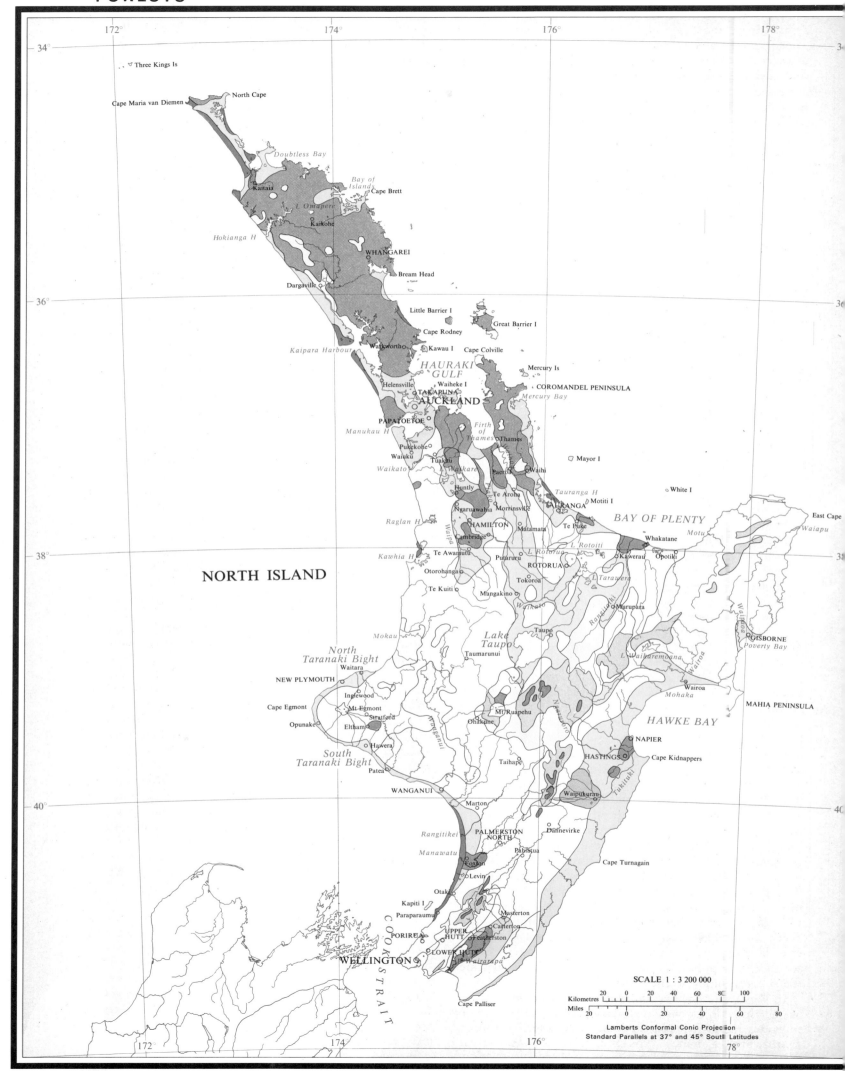

NORTH ISLAND

SCALE 1 : 3 200 000

Kilometres 20 0 20 40 60 80 100

Miles 20 0 20 40 60 80

Lamberts Conformal Conic Projection
Standard Parallels at 37° and 45° South Latitudes

VEGETATION *circa* 1840

REFERENCE

- Kauri–softwood–hardwood: kauri–beech
- Softwood–hardwood or purely either
- Softwood–hardwood–beech (lowland types only)
- Softwood–hardwood–beech (montane types only); hardwood–beech; pure beech
- Lowland short tussock grassland
- Subalpine grassland and scrubland
- Lowland tall tussock grassland
- Scrubland and fernland
- Swampland
- Duneland
- Alpine barrens

SOUTH ISLAND

STEWART ISLAND

SCALE 1 : 3 200 000

Kilometres

Miles

Lamberts Conformal Conic Projection
Standard Parallels at 37° and 45° South Latitudes

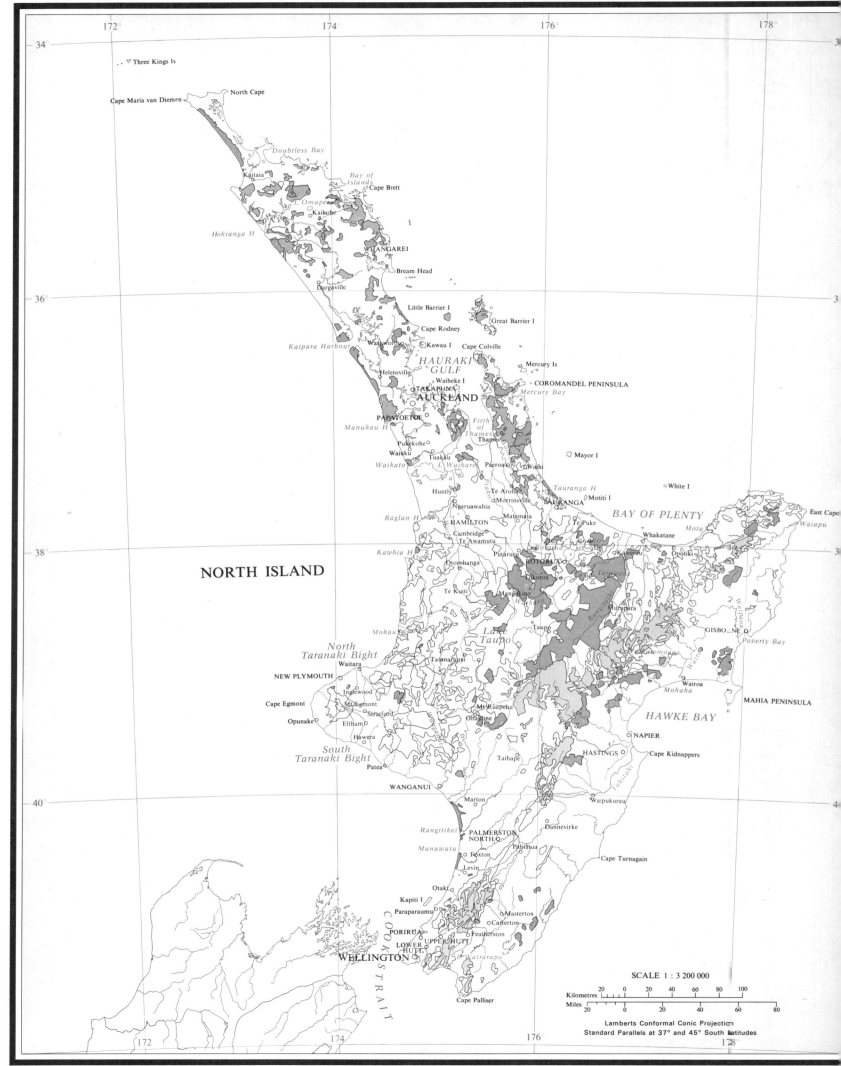

NORTH ISLAND

SCALE 1 : 3 200 000

Kilometres
Miles

Lamberts Conformal Conic Projection
Standard Parallels at 37° and 45° South Latitudes

CONTEMPORARY FOREST COVER

REFERENCE

Kauri–softwood–hardwood;
kauri–beech

Softwood–hardwood or purely either

Softwood–hardwood–beech
(lowland types only)

Softwood–hardwood–beech (montane types only) ;
hardwood–beech; pure beech

Exotics (area planted or held for planting)

• Small area of exotics

SOUTH ISLAND

STEWART ISLAND

SCALE 1 : 3 200 000

Lamberts Conformal Conic Projection
Standard Parallels at 37° and 45° South Latitudes

E. J. Godley

The native plants of New Zealand are descended from those which came over the sea during some 60 million years of isolation, and from those which earlier arrived overland when ancient New Zealand formed part of a great southern continent. Long isolation has led to a flora which is not rich in species of higher plants but which has a high percentage of species found nowhere else. This endemism is particularly marked in the species of seed plants (85%) but less so in the ferns (41%). Native species which are not endemic are shared predominantly with Australia.

On the generic level New Zealand has only one endemic genus of ferns (*Loxoma*) and only thirty-nine of flowering plants. Although many typical Australian genera are not native to New Zealand, the relationship in the reverse direction is still close, with seventy-five per cent of the genera of New Zealand seed plants and eighty-five per cent of the fern genera also found in Australia. The equivalent figures for New Zealand genera in Chile are forty-three and forty per cent. Genera are also shared with South-east Asia and the Pacific islands, the relationship being more obvious at higher altitudes, as in New Guinea, Tahiti and Hawaii.

In New Zealand there are 138 native families of higher plants (flowering plants 109; conifers 3; ferns and their allies 26) but none is endemic. However the degree of endemism on the specific and generic levels, and the important development of certain genera in this country, is considered sufficient to give New Zealand the status of a distinct Botanical Region. This Region consists of the three principal islands, North, South and Stewart, as well as the Kermadec, Chatham, Snares, Antipodes, Auckland, Campbell and Macquarie islands. This range in latitude, from sub-tropical to subantarctic, as well as the wide range of altitudes, particularly in the South Island, provides environments for a rich variety of vegetation types.

LIFE FORMS AND LEAVES

The native plants of New Zealand are mainly evergreen and perennial. Deciduousness in varying degrees is seen in species of *Sophora, Fuchsia, Plagianthus, Hoheria, Muehlenbeckia, Discaria,* and *Aristotelia.* In lowland vegetation, summer-green or winter-green herbs are of little importance, being represented by small terrestrial orchids such as *Thelymitra* and *Pterostylis,* or by plants of minor special habitats, for example the raupo, *Typha orientalis* (fresh-water swamps) or the sedge, *Scirpus americanus* (salt swamps). At higher altitudes and latitudes however, several important species are summer-green. In montane tussock-grasslands there are species of *Coriaria* (tutu) and *Bulbinella* (bog lily); in alpine meadows *Ranunculus lyallii* and *Senecio scorzoneroides* (snow groundsel); and most of the unique scree species of the Southern Alps are summer-green, for example *Anisotome carnosula* and *Ranunculus haastii,* as well as two important species of the southern islands, *Bulbinella rossii,* and the daisy, *Pleurophyllum criniferum.*

Annual plants are uncommon in the native flora and are insignificant in vegetation.

Divaricating shrubs, with their dense tangled branches and small leaves, are represented by some fifty-one species in sixteen families. Common lowland examples are *Plagianthus divaricatus* (shrubby ribbonwood) of coastal salt swamps, *Coprosma rhamnoides* of forest, *Melicope simplex* of coast and forest, and *Corokia cotoneaster* of open hillsides and scrub. Some trees such as *Pennantia corymbosa* (kaikomako) and *Hoheria angustifolia* (narrow-leaved lacebark) possess divaricating juvenile forms which persist long after adult foliage is produced.

Mat and cushion forming species are characteristic of two endemic genera of the daisy family, *Raoulia* and *Haastia,* and the large cushions of *Raoulia eximia* and *Haastia pulvinaris* have been aptly termed 'vegetable sheep'. Also notable are the large toetoes (*Cortaderia* sp.), relatives of the pampa grass; the tuft trees or 'cabbage trees' of the genus *Cordyline*; the tree ferns (*Cyathea, Dicksonia*); and the slender stem and rigid deflexed leaves of the juvenile lancewood (*Pseudopanax crassifolium*).

The largest leaves are found in the ferns and monocotyledons, the latter including the New Zealand flax, *Phormium tenax,* still cultivated for its fibres. The trees and shrubs have relatively small leaves. Amongst the herbs, *Ranunculus lyallii* with round leaves up to thirty centimetres in diameter has been called the largest buttercup in the world. Herbs with even larger leaves are *Myosotidium hortensia,* confined to the Chatham Islands, and *Stilbocarpa polaris* and *Pleurophyllum* sp. confined to the southern islands.

FLOWERS

Spring and summer are the main flowering seasons, winter-flowering trees like *Pseudopanax arboreum* and *Vitex lucens* being exceptional. The attractive 'brush'-flowers of the genus *Metrosideros,* as seen in the scarlet mid-summer displays of the pohutukawa (*M. excelsa*) or the southern rata (*M. umbellata*), are striking, but not typical of lowland flowers. Nor are the golden blossoms of the kowhai (*Sophora* sp.). A great many lowland flowers are small and inconspicuous and the predominant colours are white or green. However, as in *Coprosma,* inconspicuous flowers may be just as characteristic of the genus outside New Zealand.

In the alpine flora conspicuous flowers are common, with white and yellow predominant colours. Even the gentians have white petals with rarely a trace of red, although in the southern islands the amount of red pigmentation increases.

A striking feature of the native flowering plants is that some twelve to thirteen per cent are dioecious (with male and female flowers on separate plants) as compared, for example, with some two per cent in the British flora. It would be erroneous, however, to claim that this dioecism has all evolved in New Zealand. Many of the genera have brought their dioecism with them.

COASTAL PLANTS

On the northern off-shore islands is a remarkable group of species with tropical affinities: *Meryta sinclairii,* one of the few native trees with large leaves, grows abundantly on the Three Kings and the Hen and Chicken islands and represents a genus centred on New Caledonia; *Xeronema callistemon,* common on Poor Knights and the Hen islands, is related to *X. moorei* of New Caledonia; *Tecomanthe speciosa,* a woody climber, known from only a single plant in Great Island (Three Kings) is most closely related to *T. hillii* of Queensland; *Elingamita johnsoni,* a monotypic endemic genus of about a dozen trees on West Island (Three Kings), resembles *Tapeinosperma* of New Caledonia; and *Pennantia endlicheri* of Norfolk Island is represented by a single tree on Great Island (Three Kings).

Other species with tropical affinities follow the mainland coast southwards until factors such as frost or terrain halt their advance. On the east coast, the mangrove, *Avicennia resinifera*, is characteristic of muddy tidal estuaries from near North Cape to near Opotiki (38° S), but on the west coast reaches only the Manukau Harbour (37° S). The pohutukawa (*Metrosideros excelsa*) forms coastal forest on off-shore islands and mainland to about 38° S on each coast. The karaka, *Corynocarpus laevigata*, crosses to the South Island, extending down the east coast to Banks Peninsula. The nikau palm (*Rhopalostylis sapida*) becomes coastal in the south, extends to Banks Peninsula on the east coast, to just beyond Greymouth on the west, and reaches its southern limit on Pitt Island (44° 18′) in the Chatham group.

On salt marshes of both main Islands the austral glasswort, *Salicornia australis,* is prominent. Salt swamps throughout are characterised by *Juncus maritimus* var. *australiensis* and by the jointed rush, *Leptocarpus similis,* except in the southern South Island, where only the latter species is found. On dunes, the sandbinders (*Spinifex hirsutus* and *Desmoschoenus spiralis* (pingao)) occur as far south as Blenheim, beyond which there is only pingao.

On southern coasts there are important tree daisies such as *Senecio reinoldii* and *Olearia lyallii*. Both grow on Stewart Island and the nearby 'mutton-bird' islands, while the latter species is found in the Snares and the north of Auckland Island. In the sheltered harbours of the Auckland Islands, the southern rata, *Metrosideros umbellata,* forms a coastal belt reminiscent of pohutukawa forest in the north.

Indigenous Forests

A little more than a century ago the early settlers found most of the North Island under forest, except for areas recovering from the effects of volcanic activity or where Maori fires or other activities had changed the landscape. In the South Island, forest predominated in the wetter north, west and south but in the drier east there were extensive areas of indigenous grassland at lower elevations. However, evidence in the form of surface logs, wind-throw hummocks and hollows, buried wood and charcoal, buried soils and relics of earlier vegetation showed that a good deal of the lowland east had been under forest in the not too distant past, but that this had been destroyed by a sequence of natural and Polynesian fires.

New Zealand forests are dominated by various combinations of gymnosperms and angiosperms. The first group are conifers or 'softwoods' in the families Araucariaceae (*Agathis*), Cupressaceae (*Libocedrus*) and Podocarpaceae (*Podocarpus, Dacrydium*). The second group are flowering plants or 'hardwoods', such as the beeches (*Nothofagus*).

Most of the forest can be divided into two major types (which the article on Forests further groups into four classes), the first dominated by one or more species of the native conifers usually in association with hardwoods and the second dominated by one or more of the four native species of beech (*Nothofagus*). But beeches and conifers are not mutually exclusive, and podocarps, *Libocedrus* or even *Agathis,* can be found intermixed with *Nothofagus*; and podocarp or *Agathis* communities are connected with forests of hardwood trees by many intermediate combinations.

CONIFER—HARDWOOD FORESTS

The vegetation in these forests is generally extremely luxuriant, with small trees, shrubs, ferns, bryophytes and epiphytes plentiful. However, this forest does not compare in diversity of species of trees with that of the tropics. The greatest diversity is in the low altitude forest of the far north where fourteen species occur constantly.

The following are the most important trees. None extends to the Kermadec or Chatham islands, and only *Metrosideros umbellata* to the Auckland Islands.

1. *Agathis australis* (Araucariaceae), the kauri, is perhaps the most famous timber tree of New Zealand and was prominent in forests of North Auckland, the Barrier Islands and Coromandel. It extends to 38° S.

2. *Beilschmiedia tarairi* (Lauraceae), the taraire, is one of the commonest trees of northern forests but disappears at about 38° S.

3. *Beilschmiedia tawa*, the tawa, is of great importance in North Island forests from near North Cape and occurs locally in the eastern South Island to 42° S.

4. *Metrosideros robusta* (Myrtaceae), the northern rata, overtops most forest trees in the North Island, and extends to about Greymouth in the South Island. It begins life as an epiphyte.

5. *Metrosideros umbellata*, the southern rata, is a smaller tree than *M. robusta* and important in montane forests in the western South Island. It also grows in the Auckland Islands, and sparingly in the North Island.

6. *Weinmannia racemosa* (Cunoniaceae), the kamahi, is the commonest forest tree, extending from about 38° S to Stewart Island, and is important in both lowland and montane vegetation. North of 38° S is the less important *W. sylvicola*.

7. *Podocarpus totara* (Podocarpaceae), the totara, is widely distributed and particularly prominent in the central North Island. Most of the totara of Westland is the closely related *P. hallii* which is widespread elsewhere, and ascends to higher altitudes than the true totara.

8. *Podocarpus dacrydioides*, the kahikatea, or white pine, is widely distributed in the North and South Islands but is rare on Stewart Island. It grows on fertile soil, and pure stands in wet low-lying areas form the kahikatea swamp forest.

9. *Podocarpus spicatus*, the matai, is widely distributed in the North and South Islands but rare on Stewart Island.

10. *Podocarpus ferrugineus*, the miro, is common throughout the three main Islands, with a distribution similar to that of rimu. It has a very local occurrence in parts of the eastern South Island.

11. *Dacrydium cupressinum* (Podocarpaceae), the rimu, or red pine, is widespread, but absent from the forests of Banks Peninsula.

12. *Libocedrus bidwillii* (Cupressaceae), the kaikawaka, is prominent in subalpine forests.

Important small trees and shrubs are: *Elaeocarpus dentatus* (hinau), *Litsea calicaris* (mangeao), *Hedycarya arborea* (pigeon wood), *Carpodetus serratus* (putaputaweta),

Aristotelia serrata (wine berry), *Plagianthus betulinus* (ribbon wood), *Melicytus ramiflorus* (mahoe), *Fuchsia excorticata* (kotukutuku), *Schefflera digitata* (pate), *Pseudopanax crassifolium* (lancewood), and *P. arboreum* (five-finger), *Griselinia littoralis* (broad-leaf), and *G. lucida* (puka), *Myrsine australis* (mapou), *Coprosma lucida* (karamu), *C. robusta* (glossy karamu). Common ground plants are species of *Microlaena*, *Astelia*, *Cardamine*, *Ranunculus*, *Uncinia*, *Carex*, *Epilobium*, *Nertera* and *Hydrocotyle*. Ferns are abundant, with the following genera well represented: *Asplenium*, *Blechnum*, *Adiantum*, *Histiopteris*, *Hymenophyllum*, *Grammitis* and the tree ferns *Cyathea* and *Dicksonia*.

Some fifty species in New Zealand forests are habitually epiphytic, and have been classified as follows: semi-woody pteridophytes (3), filmy ferns (20), tufted ferns (7), creeping ferns (5), succulent herbs (2), orchids (7), tussock plants (2) (*Collospermum hastatum*, *Astelia solandri*), and shrubs (4) (*Senecio kirkii*, *Griselinia lucida*, *Pittosporum kirkii* and *P. cornifolium*). Also prominent are the following lianes and climbers: *Freycinetia banksii* (kie-kie), *Ripogonum scandens* (supplejack) and species of *Passiflora*, *Parsonsia*, *Rubus* and *Clematis*. Of particular interest are a group of climbing *Metrosideros* species, a habit apparently rare in the Myrtaceae.

BEECH FORESTS

These may be dominated by one or more of the four native species of *Nothofagus* (all of which are evergreen), often in association with certain podocarps. Beech forest may occur from sea level to timberline and in regions with annual rainfall as low as 600 millimetres or greater than 7000 millimetres. *Nothofagus truncata* (hard beech) is the only species found north of about latitude 37°. It was common on small islands near Auckland and isolated patches are known in the North Auckland area. It is important in the southern Tararua Range, in the Marlborough Sounds and western Nelson and reaches the Taramakau River in Westland. *N. fusca* (red beech) is closely related to *N. truncata* and extends from about 37° S to Lake Manapouri (45° 30′ S). *N. menziesii* (silver beech) ranges from about 37° S to the southern limit of the genus in New Zealand and is the only beech found in the forests of the south-east South Island. It is the species found most frequently at timberline. *N. solandri* var. *solandri* (black beech) grows at lower altitudes from near Lake Taupo to the northern half of the South Island, while *N. solandri* var. *cliffortioides* (mountain beech) tends to higher altitudes from the latitude of Taupo to the southern limit of the beeches, although absent from the Tararua Range. *Nothofagus* is not found on Stewart Island.

Libocedrus bidwillii, *Dacrydium cupressinum* and *Podocarpus dacrydioides,* are commonly associated with beech forests.

The interior of *Nothofagus* forest is in general more open than that of the conifer–hardwood forest. In the driest areas there is a paucity of vegetation under the canopy. Common shrubs and small trees are: *Pseudowintera colorata* (pepper tree), *Coprosma foetidissima* (hupiro), *C. pseudocuneata*, *Pseudopanax colensoi* (mountain ivy tree), *P. simplex*, *Phyllocladus alpinus* (mountain toatoa), *Myrsine divaricata* (wiry matipo), and small-leaved species of *Pittosporum*. Given sufficient moisture the forest floor may be thickly carpeted with bryophytes and dotted about will be such species as *Microlaena avenacea* (bush rice-grass), *Luzuriaga parviflora*, species of *Nertera* and ferns such as *Blechnum discolor*, *Hymenophyllum multifidum* and, in drier areas, *Polystichum vestitum*. Lianes and epiphytes (except mosses and lichens) are not important.

The Indigenous Grasslands

These are dominated by species with a tussock (bunchgrass) habit and were found from near sea level to the alpine zone. There are two main types, short tussock-grassland and tall tussock-grassland, but the dominant species of each are not mutually exclusive.

About a century ago, short tussock-grassland covered considerable areas of the eastern South Island from sea level to 800–900 metres, and soon invaded areas of cleared beech forest in many places. Large areas of induced short tussock-grassland also occur to the east of the central plateau of the North Island. Common dominants are *Festuca novae-zelandiae* and *Poa caespitosa*, growing to about half a metre in height and yellow-brown in colour. There are relatively few larger plants present—examples are the spiny shrub, *Discaria toumatou* (matagouri) and the cabbage-tree, *Cordyline australis*—but between the tussocks this grassland is floristically quite diverse. Common herbs are the small daisies *Raoulia monroi*, *Lagenophora pumila* and *Vittadinia australis*, and adventives such as *Trifolium arvense*, *Rumex acetosella* and *Hypochoeris radicata*.

The original short (and tall) tussock-grassland has been modified in greater or lesser degree during a century of grazing. The extreme was seen in the driest areas such as Central Otago and the upper Awatere Valley, in the southern and northern South Island respectively. Here stocking and burning opened up the association and made an ideal home for rabbits, whose depredations accelerated the vegetation changes. Deserts of the scab-weed *Raoulia australis*, a composite mat-plant, were induced. Attempts to reverse the trend have involved extermination of rabbits, control of burning and reduction of grazing by sheep.

Tall tussock communities are found on Mt Egmont and from the central North Island southwards through the high country of both islands, either above forest or above low tussock-grassland. At lower elevations tall tussock-grassland may be found on coastal hills, as on Banks Peninsula, or on the Southland plain.

Chionochloa rubra (red tussock) dominates large areas in the central North Island originally devastated by volcanic eruptions. In the South Island it is not uncommon on poorly drained terraces and was particularly abundant in Southland. *C. pallens* is important in the north of the North Island mountain chain, and in the Tararua Ranges is joined by *C. flavescens*. In the South Island various combinations of *C. pallens*, *C. rigida* and a relative of *C. flavescens* dominate most tall tussock-grasslands. *C. crassiuscula*, a smaller grass, forms communities through most South Island high mountains and, with *C. pungens*, forms the meagre high altitude grassland found on Stewart Island. In the northern South Island, *C. australis*, a lax species with smooth leaves lying downhill forms a slippery 'carpet' grassland.

Like the short tussock-grassland, the tall tussock is floristically diverse, but with adventive species usually less common. Important species of *Chionochloa rigida* grassland are *Celmisia spectabilis* (common cotton plant) and *C. lyallii*, *Aciphylla aurea*, *Cyathodes colensoi*, and *Pentachondra pumila* (little mountain heath).

Scrub and Timberline

Perhaps the most important lowland scrub genus in the country is *Leptospermum* (Myrtaceae) with either *L. scoparium* (manuka), or *L. ericoides* (kanuka) growing singly or mixed, three to ten metres high. Both are important 'nurses' for forest trees, and in northern New Zealand, for example, protect the early life of the kauri.

At high altitude, *Nothofagus* forest often stretches

uninterrupted to the alpine vegetation, but where the forest is not beech there is usually a belt of subalpine scrub forming an almost impenetrable barrier of prostrate trunks and stiff interlocking branches. A main type, classified as 'shrub-composite', is dominated by species of *Senecio* and *Olearia*.

New Zealand is no exception to the general rule that the upper limit of continuous woody vegetation is lower in the southern than in the northern hemisphere. In the North Island it drops from 1500 metres near East Cape to 1350 metres in the Ruahine Range and is down to 1200 metres in the Tararua Range (41° S). In the western South Island, at 41° S the timberline is at about 1200 metres, declining to about 900 metres at 45° S, while in the central and eastern South Island the timberline can be up to 300 metres higher than at a similar altitude in the west. On Stewart Island (47° S) the timberline is about 740 metres and on Campbell Island (52° S) it is 150 metres.

Swamps and Bogs
In swamps the most striking plants are the New Zealand flax (*Phormium tenax*), the raupo (*Typha orientalis*), *Carex secta* the giant grasses (*Cortaderia* spp.) and the cabbage-tree *Cordyline australis*. Under drier conditions *Podocarpus dacrydioides* may form swamp forest.

Sphagnum is not an important bog plant in New Zealand. Common bog genera are the sedges *Schoenus* and *Cladium*, the fern *Gleichenia*, and the rush *Calorophus*. Shrubs of the genera *Dracophyllum*, *Hebe*, *Dacrydium* and *Leptospermum* are common. In the wet mountains and lowlands of the south are bogs in which predominate cushion plants of the genera *Oreobolus*, *Phyllachne*, *Gaimardia*, and *Donatia*. *Sporadanthus traversii* (Restionaceae), a member of the monotypic endemic genus, is found in localised bogs in northern New Zealand and the distant Chatham Islands.

Alpine Vegetation
New Zealand is well isolated from other lands, particularly from any with a mountain system of similar height or extent. This mountain system supports some 500 species which do not extend to the lowlands; the main diversity is in the South Island but alpine vegetation is found throughout the North Island mountain chain, and isolated patches occur on the Coromandel Range some fifty miles east of Auckland.

Subalpine scrub, cushion bogs and grassland at high altitudes have already been mentioned. Composites are important in the alpine vegetation, and pride of place is taken by *Celmisia*, a predominantly herbaceous genus, which has evolved more than fifty species in New Zealand and a few in Australia. In *C. coriacea* the leaves may be sixty centimetres long, oblong-lanceolate, with a silvery pellicle and in large tufts, while in *C. laricifolia* at the other extreme the leaves are tiny and needle-like. Other composites are *Helichrysum*, *Leucogenes* (the native edelweiss) and the previously noted *Haastia* and *Raoulia*.

The largest genus of the Scrophulariaceae in New Zealand is *Hebe*, which is well represented at higher altitudes. Particularly interesting are the 'whip-cord' hebes, with leaves reduced almost to scales, for example *H. lycopodioides* and *H. cupressoides*. *Ourisia*, *Euphrasia*, *Gentiana* and *Ranunculus* all contribute attractive species to the alpine vegetation, and all have an important centre of evolution in New Zealand.

The Shelf Islands
The Kermadec Islands have some 117 species of ferns and flowering plants, twelve per cent of which are endemic and seventy-six per cent found also in New Zealand. There are no endemic genera. *Metrosideros kermadecensis* dominates the lower altitude dry forest, in which also grow *Cyathea milnei*, *Myrsine kermadecensis*, *Coprosma petiolata* and the mainland species *Corynocarpus laevigata* and *Myoporum laetum*. In the higher wet forest above are found *Ascarina lanceolata*, *Cyathea kermadecensis*, *Rhopalostylis cheesemanii* and the mainland species *Melicytus ramiflorus*.

The one endemic genus of the subantarctic islands is *Pleurophyllum*, a large-leaved herbaceous composite with three species. There are about 193 species, of which thirty-one per cent are endemic and sixty-three per cent found in New Zealand proper. The Snares has low forest of *Olearia lyallii* and *Senecio stewartiae*, and grassland dominated by *Poa litorosa* and *Poa foliosa*. On the Auckland Islands, a narrow belt of *Metrosideros umbellata* coastal forest in sheltered eastern inlets is replaced by a tangled scrub of *Myrsine divaricata*, *Cassinia vauvilliersii*, *Coprosma* spp., *Pseudopanax simplex*, *Dracophyllum longifolium* and stunted *M. umbellata* to about 300 metres. Above this is *Chionochloa antarctica* grassland. Campbell Island has a belt of *Dracophyllum* scrub to about 130 metres in sheltered situations, above which is *Poa litorosa* grassland. *C. antarctica* grassland, now diminished in area, is found in the floors of certain valleys. On Antipodes Island, *Poa litorosa* is the dominant tussock, and of the fifty-seven species only the three species of Coprosma are woody. There are no woody plants on Macquarie Island, which supports only thirty-one species of flowering plants, three ferns, and one lycopodium. *Poa foliosa* grassland is common.

The Chatham Islands support some 300 species of ferns and flowering plants of which fourteen per cent are endemic and eighty-five per cent found in New Zealand. The one endemic genus is *Myosotidium* (Boraginaceae). There are no gymnosperms or other large mainland trees, and much of the original forest has been destroyed by fire. In coastal forest *Corynocarpus laevigata* and *Rhopalostylis sapida* were common but did not extend to the 'tableland' forest where the endemic *Dracophyllum arboreum* was dominant.

Adventive Plants
Some 1700 species not native to New Zealand have now been recorded in the wild, but only about 560 can be regarded as fully naturalised, with some 240 more or less common throughout the country. There are more than eighty adventives which are so aggressive that they are listed as noxious weeds. Some of the most notorious are blackberry (*Rubus fruticosus*); californian thistle (*Cirsium arvense*); ragwort (*Senecio jacobaea*); and sweet brier (*Rosa rubiginosa*). Also listed is the native *Cassinia leptophylla*, a composite bush particularly aggressive on open hillsides in the southern North Island and north-eastern South Island.

Other physiognomically prominent species are the widespread gorse, *Ulex europaeus*; the broom, *Cytisus scoparius*; *Hakea sericea* in the north; *Lupinus arboreus* on dunes and river beds; and *Ammophila arenaria* on dunes. In the eastern South Island there is a serious infestation of *Nassella trichotoma*, an unpalatable South American tussock grass, and special legislation has been necessary to combat this pest of pastoral land.

This extensive introduction of plants by accident or design, and the extensive clearing of native vegetation, particularly in the lowlands, means that in many areas the visitor may notice little that is native to the country. The plants of pastures, fields, hedges, plantations, roadsides, parks and gardens may be all from other lands.

7 and 8

9 and 10

11 and 12

13 and 14

15 and 16

17 and 18

Lancewood, *Pseudopanax crassifolius*

Mount Cook Lily *Ranunculus lyallii*

ee Daisy, *Senecio laxifolius*
ild Spaniard, *Aciphylla horrida*
karamu, *Coprosma robusta*
aori Onion, *Bulbinella hookeri*
aast's Buttercup, *Ranunculus haastii*
hatham Island Forget-me-not,
yosotidium hortensia
acophyllum fiordense
ax, *Phormium tenax*
elmisia traversii
anuka, *Leptospermum scoparium*
etoe, *Cortaderia fulvida*
phekohe, *Dysoxylum spectabile*
abbage Tree, *Cordyline bankaii*
heki Fern, *Dicksonia fibrosa*
cebark, *Hoheria populnea*
lery Pine or Tanekaha, *Phyllocladus*
chomanoides
upata, *Coprosma repens*
chid, *Thelymitra longifolia*

Southern Rata, *Metrosideros umbellata*

113

FAUNA

R. A. Falla

If an account of the fauna of any region is to be usefully contained in a short summary, a decision must be made whether to use the opportunity to present an outline of hypotheses about the origins of the fauna or to concentrate on a rapid survey of the nature of the existing fauna. The second alternative has been chosen here, because an understanding of beginnings rests in part on geological studies, and that background can be found in the general articles dealing with them.

Zoologists sometimes attempt, by analysing an existing fauna and estimating its potential in locomotion or evolutionary change, to construct retrospectively a pattern of origins for the existing animal groups of the selected area. There comes a point at which they are restricted by what geologists can concede. The degree of this concession has changed even in the last decade. Ten years ago it was still orthodox to postulate land bridges joining continents believed to be fairly static, except for tectonic movement and erosion which then eliminated the bridges and left some organisms isolated from the rest of the parent stock. As the breakaway group carries its own discrete genetic composition, further evolutionary modifications are both directed and limited by its potential. Thus the relationships between the separated sections of the original stock may, and usually do, become more difficult to recognise with the passage of time. This biological process is, of course, independent of the history of the land masses, but the origins of any fauna can be much better understood as the earth sciences progress.

One notable recent advance has been consolidation of support for theories of continental drift. When the 1959 Descriptive Atlas was published, the majority of earth scientists regarded the theory, if not as a heresy, at least as unsupported by sufficient evidence. With deep core research and related studies, the emphasis has changed to an impressive structure of support, and the biologist finds that the land-bridge theories can give way to a more comforting concept. This in brief is that in Palaeozoic times a super-continent, Gondwanaland, straddled much of the Southern Hemisphere. The segment that can today be identified as New Zealand lay integrated with what is now the Victoria coast of Antarctica, and the present State of Victoria in Australia, Tasmania being conveniently out of the way further west. In the long term, the detached fragment in which we are presently interested drifted east and south, but not in its present form, very little of it being above the sea surface. Subsequent volcanic action and upthrusting produced most of the New Zealand of today.

The above suggests that the vagrant land mass could have brought from its point of origin very little in the way of flora and fauna; and this, except for the presence of a few puzzling relict forms, is borne out by any study of the present day faunal composition. The fossil record is rich in marine animals, especially invertebrates. Paleontologists derive from the study of mollusca and other marine orders abundant material for recognising the relationships of the present fauna and even evidence of past climatic changes. An important factor here is the extent and direction of surface ocean currents, which are themselves a secondary result of conditions existing in different climatic zones. The East Australian warm current has an effect on the whole of the western shore of New Zealand, and another, of tropical origin, on seas to the north-east. At the other extreme of the temperature gradient, cool waters of the West Wind Drift and several upwellings of cold bottom waters bring a subantarctic element.

Marine Life

All this is reflected in the composition of marine life. The mollusca and other marine groups have elements of both tropical and sub-polar fauna, with a predominance of cool temperate forms. There has been long enough isolation, however, for the development of endemic species, and the varied nature of the long coast line, extending through thirteen degrees of latitude, provides suitable conditions for a comprehensive variety in which nearly all the main orders are well represented. In mollusca alone about 2000 indigenous species, including terrestrial forms, have been described.

It is not only invertebrates which are abundant and varied in the marine fauna. Wide-ranging tropical surface fish make regular seasonal incursion and the giants of such families as the swordfishes, spearfishes, tuna and surface sharks are all common. There are also large populations of smaller surface predators, like the local barracouta, which have discontinuous distribution in cool temperate seas in the Southern Hemisphere. The whole pelagic fauna of New Zealand seas would be rated as rich by any standard.

This richness is further emphasized by a consideration of the oceanic birds. Of the principal orders and families of these, the albatrosses and petrels are represented by sixty species on the local list, penguins by twelve of the eighteen known species and marine cormorants by a similarly high proportion. Many of them breed here, and are able to maintain high levels of population because they frequent the many island outliers which are little modified, and often have reserve status. Tropical gannets (boobies) are rare vagrants, but the cool-temperate gannets proper are well established, with a vigorous breeding stock.

In the fossil record also, vertebrate remains of any antiquity are marine forms, and these include penguins in the Oligocene, swimming reptiles in the Cretaceous and toothed whales in the Triassic. Sea temperatures today are too cold for marine reptiles, and the turtles and sea snakes which regularly wander south remain moribund if they survive at all. Whales of all kinds are well represented, and some of the coastal porpoises are endemic. Fur seals and sea-lions are the breeding representatives of the eared seals, the latter an endemic species with headquarters at the Auckland Islands. Earless seals are represented by sea-elephants, breeding on the subantarctic fringe, with a few stragglers of the Antarctic species as visitors.

Terrestrial Fauna

Organisms of the fluid environment thus have a long and well-documented association with the New Zealand land masses, and the marine fauna lacks few of the forms suited to the physical conditions. Terrestrial fauna, by contrast, has had to build up from fragmentary beginnings. In the original separation from Gondwanaland, the departing fragment either lacked, or subsequently lost, any terrestrial fauna; for example, at least three Australian insect families existing at that time are not found in New Zealand. With increasing isolation from neighbouring land masses, the number of land-based forms that could get here by such dispersal agencies as air, water or attachment to flying vertebrates, was restricted and selective. The new fauna was impoverished in the sense that it was not comprehensive.

Land masses in this category are classed as oceanic islands, and the New Zealand archipelago conforms to this, with the qualification that its surface features have most of the variety and complexity found on any continent. Under such conditions, the handicaps of an impoverished start are largely overcome by the propensity of organisms to undergo a process of adaptive radiation, whereby a comparatively limited original stock eventually occupies a variety of vacant niches. Under such conditions there is usually an increase in the tempo of evolution. This process probably accounts for the high proportion of endemic forms, some of them divergent from ancient stock to the point of being difficult to relate, and others tending to conditions of giantism, or wing reduction or some other modification. It is manifested to a greater or lesser extent in all classes of the terrestrial fauna, and is a conspicuous characteristic of the birds.

Available habitat is an all-important factor in determining the distribution and variety of any fauna. By the time most of the land mass had assumed its present form, surface soils were able to support a changing vegetation, in climatic conditions which encouraged profuse covering of forest on much of the country at altitudes below 1000 metres. Abundant rainfall provided a network of rivers and a system of lakes of practically every known kind, from deep lakes of glacial origin to the comparatively shallow wetlands of coastal plains.

Waterfowl

Ever since the country had a bird fauna at all, waterfowl have been well represented. The relationship with the waterfowl of Australia is close, and, as ducks in particular are very mobile, many of the species are identical on both sides of the Tasman. An aberrant endemic, the blue duck of mountain streams, is one exception, and there was also at the Auckland Islands, until it recently became extinct, a merganser whose ancestors must have overshot from the northern hemisphere. On the other hand, a surprising number of the aberrant endemic ducks of Australia occurred in New Zealand in the recent past, as their sub-fossil remains testify, although they are not now found here. In those days there were also swans, geese, and coots now extinct, but in the last century all 'vacancies' have been re-filled by the establishment of geese introduced from North America, black swans from Australia and coots self-introduced from the same source.

In addition there are herons, bitterns and grebes, all of Australian affinity or cosmopolitan. Modification of some habits to permit survival under local conditions is apparent in a few cases. The large white egret is extra-limital in this zone of high winds, and apparently finds a sheltered swamp–jungle habitat suitable for successful nesting only in one spot in Westland, from which in winter the whole population, of about 100 birds and twice as many young, disperses to all parts of the country. The almost cosmopolitan great crested grebe, likewise, finds the ancestral habit of building a floating nest ill-adapted to the rapid fluctuations of lake levels in areas of high and erratic rainfall, so that the less typical, solid-based nest site is quite often used.

Rails and gallinules, which get their food not so much in the water as from feeding round its edges, are an interesting group in the New Zealand context. The world-wide distribution of the family, even to remote islands, suggests that they have a potential for wide-ranging dispersal, but no inclination to be regular migrants once they have found a suitable niche. A further trend under these conditions has then been to loss of flight. Many of the now extinct rails of the early fauna in New Zealand and the Chatham Islands

were flightless, as are the two surviving genera, *Gallirallus* and *Notornis*. The former range of both of these is now much reduced but whereas the weka, in its restricted habitats, maintains vigorous populations to the point of being a minor nuisance, the takahe, in its last remaining habitat re-discovered only in 1948, does not present the same picture. The area, in the heart of Fiordland National Park, is under strict protection, but nevertheless a good deal of regular investigatory work has shown that, with some fluctuations, there has been a marked tendency to a decline in numbers since an overall estimate of about 200 pairs in 1969. The two genera just mentioned may be regarded as obsolete models of the stronger, flying and less clumsy rails and gallinules, of which three ralline species and the pukeko, a gallinule, are later arrivals, now occupying most of the former territory of the old-timers.

The Kiwi

Kiwis may be conveniently mentioned at this time, although there is very slender evidence to connect them with the rails or anything else. Because of some structural peculiarities they are classed as ratites, along with the much larger, flightless ostriches, rheas, cassowaries, emus and the extinct moa, but the question whether these ratites are more closely related to one another than to other groups of birds has not been resolved. Found in New Zealand only, there are several species of kiwi. Brown kiwis have three sub-species, found respectively in the three main Islands. The South Island has two additional species, the great spotted kiwi and the little spotted kiwi. Except for the last-mentioned, which has proved elusive in recent years except on Kapiti Island where it was introduced, they are all plentiful.

That these quaint endemics should be resistant to the factors that are supposed to have caused the decline of so many other endemic birds is a mystery. Their nocturnal habits have made it difficult to learn the simplest outline of their life-histories, and most of the available information has been derived from study of birds in captivity. The female, which exceeds her mate in size, takes very little part in the incubation of the disproportionately large egg, and the male, after sitting for about eighty days, still has to guide the early steps of the chick. From recent field studies it seems likely that, at least in certain circumstances, kiwis are polyandrous, and that a female will lay as many eggs as she can find broody males with burrows to incubate. Such extreme emancipation of the female in New Zealand's national bird must provoke sobering reflection.

Birds of Forest and Shore

The luxuriant and denser forest areas are not today 'alive with birds'. It is probable that, except in more open situations, they never were, for few species adapt to high rainfall conditions in a cool climate. Nevertheless, adaptive radiation has here again produced a varied fauna from a limited stock of original families. A surprising proportion of the insectivorous small birds of the bush are in origin flycatchers. Their vernacular European names reflect diversity, designating them variously as fantails, grey warblers, tits, robins and so on. The creeper is not a creeper and the wren is not a wren, but they behave like their Old World namesakes. Vocally, the small birds range from good singers to those uttering single faint notes. Bursts of wild music come from the honey-eaters, the flamboyant tui and the ubiquitous bellbird, both of which are common. One honey-eater which became rare is the stitchbird, now found only on the sanctuary island of Little Barrier.

Of the fruit-eating birds frequenting the forest canopy

115

and ranging widely, the large native wood pigeon, once present in vast numbers, still occupies what is left of its former habitat. A large brown parrot, the kaka, once shared the same niche, but it is a comparatively rare bird today. Other parrots present some interesting anomalies. The kea, restricted to a mountain environment, has proved more adaptable than the kaka to which it is related, and has survived a period of persecution for real or imagined misdeeds in sheep country. The kakapo has survived from the period when it was fashionable to be fat, overgrown and flightless; but it has only just survived, for it has now a precariously small population. More conventional-looking parrots, the active parakeets of the genus *Cyanorhamphus*, persist only where their normal habitat is relatively undisturbed.

Some families of birds which have large species groups on all continents are sparsely represented. There are only two owls, one kingfisher and two birds of prey; two cuckoos which winter on islands of the south-west Pacific are endemic breeders. But natural colonisation continues, and in the past half-century, six or more species have established themselves after crossing what has been called 'the selective filter of the Tasman Sea'. Of these, one, the swallow, adds a new family to the fauna. The annual influx of migrants, apart from the two cuckoos and some seabirds, consists almost entirely of waders or shorebirds from near the Arctic Circle and they occupy the wetlands and estuaries along with flocks of the local waders.

Reptiles

Reptiles as a class have found the 'filter' very restrictive. There are no crocodiles, tortoises or snakes; and of the five families of lizards found in Australia, only two, the skinks and the geckos, are represented in New Zealand. Amongst the dozen species of gecko, however, are some of the most colourful known anywhere. There are seventeen species of skinks, of which the largest is about twenty-three centimetres long. Until recently it was thought that all the local skinks, like the geckos, produced their young alive, but it has recently been recorded that one of the species on islands off the northern coasts lays eggs. It also, incidentally, eats berries as well as insects.

One other native reptile, however, has a classification order to itself. The tuatara (*Sphenodon*) is the only living representative of the order *Rhynchocephalia*, of which all other members became extinct after the Mesozoic, in which age they had flourished. The term 'living fossil', often applied to the tuatara, is thus not inappropriate. It was formerly thought to be some kind of lizard and it is not difficult to imagine it as one of the Australian dragon lizards in disguise, but such a theory, which would be equivalent to regarding the kakapo as being only a budgerigar in disguise, has not been seriously advanced. The orthodox theory of its ancient origin is supported by much structural and anatomical evidence, and is handicapped only by the absence of any known fossil links for the genus, and the difficulty of reconstructing how it got here. All evidence of its former abundance on the New Zealand mainland is in sub-fossil bones in surface deposits, often in the middens of man. Today it occurs on several groups of islands between North Cape and East Cape, and in Cook Strait. The largest of these islands, though it has probably the fewest tuataras, is Little Barrier, but there is a greater density on a number of small islets not exceeding four or five hectares in area. Much of the occupied habitat is on surfaces bare of ground cover because of seabird traffic, while at Stephens Island in Cook Strait, formerly grazed, the population is several thousand. Optimum conditions seem to require an abundance of insects and lizards.

Tuataras live in burrows, and emerge to feed at night. Burrowing petrels also nest on all the tuatara islands, and there is seasonally some joint occupancy of burrows. The leathery-shelled eggs are laid in shallow trenches in light soil and covered. They incubate without further care for a period which averages twelve months, but apparently varies with the temperature conditions. Reaching physical maturity is a slow process, taking about fifty years, and how long a tuatara survives after this nobody knows. Recent and continuing field work on life-history and population studies has disclosed a correlation between the apparent breeding success of tuataras on islands with or without the Polynesian rat. It has not progressed far enough to be conclusive, but the indications are that the presence of rats depresses the breeding rate.

Amphibia

The only indigenous amphibian, a genus of small frog, is, like the tuatara, of obscure affinity, though it has structural similarity with genera as far away as North America. There are three species and they have very restricted distribution. One occurs in hilly, forested country in several separate areas from just north of Auckland to East Cape; another inhabits the mist line on the ridge of the Coromandel peninsula, while the South Island species occurs on two island outliers bordering Cook Strait. In the last localities, and at Coromandel, there is no permanent running water. The frogs live under stones, and what would normally be the tadpole stage is completed within the egg, before the young frog emerges. Elsewhere in New Zealand, ponds have good stocks of introduced frogs, two species from Australia.

Freshwater Fish

The indigenous freshwater fish comprise only a few genera and, except for eels and lampreys, most of the species are of small size. The only one with a size range averaging or exceeding thirty centimetres was the native grayling which is now rare, and may be extinct. The rest are found in all freshwater habitats, and as a common characteristic retain a link with the sea, markedly so in the case of eels and lampreys, but strongly also in the genus *Galaxias* and most of the others. Where spawning has occurred in or near the sea, there is always the seasonal run upstream of post-larval young. The commercialised whitebait fishery is based on the annual run of one of the *Galaxias* species.

In any realistic assessment of total freshwater vertebrate fauna, the dominance of introduced species of salmon and trout must be taken into account. The success of this acclimatisation venture has been so spectacular that, in the estimation of the public and not a few biologists, fish are exempt from the strictures, amounting sometimes to resentment, with which the presence of other introduced vertebrates is regarded. Most of these introduced fish have been here for more than a century, but there has been little sustained study of their integration into ecosystems, or their significance in the biomass, of which they now form a large part. It may well be another hundred years before New Zealanders finally accept that the only realistic faunal study is of what you have, rather than of what you would like to have.

Mammals

The integration of introduced terrestrial mammals into the New Zealand biosystem is the sharpest area of debate, accentuated by the fact that the only indigenous mammals are two species of bat, which almost justifies the claim that this was a land without mammals. The bats, of which one must have been an early arrival and the other a late-comer, are now rare and localised, and their life histories little known. The naturalised mammals include ten species of deer from three continents, thar, chamois, goats, several wallabies and an opossum from Australia, two rats and their Polynesian forerunner, mice, stoats, weasels and polecat-ferrets, hares, rabbits and hedgehogs. Except for cats, feral farm and domestic animals such as cattle, sheep and dogs are insignificant in number in a wild state. It has recently been found that one of the marsupials, the parma wallaby, is now extinct in its original homeland, and some have been sent back to Australia, raising the problem, no doubt, as to what is the effect of re-introducing mammals.

Inevitably this brief survey leaves sections of the fauna with scant mention, or none at all. All the major invertebrate groups are well represented in New Zealand. Studies of the main orders of insects have been carried out for many years, and some have been monographed, as have spiders, earthworms, myriopoda and many more. The general picture emerging from such specialist studies is the same as that attempted here for the vertebrates, namely a derived fauna from more than one point of origin, with some gaps due to difficulties with the 'filter'; remarkable adaptive radiation filling the vacant niches; giantism, melanism, loss of flight and other marked trends; and finally a small percentage of enigmatic archaic forms. It all adds up to a rich and varied fauna which is almost entirely insular, but has also much of the variety associated with that of the larger continents.

Tuatara, *Sphenodon punctatus*

Snail, *Paryphanta lignaria annectens* Powell

Kakapo, *Strigops habroptilus*

New Zealand Sea Lion (female), *Otaria hookeri*

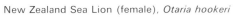

Takahe, *Notornis mantelli*

118

Kea, *Nestor notabilis*

Katipo, *Latrodectus katipo*

Stephens Island Frog, *Leiopelma hamiltoni*

119

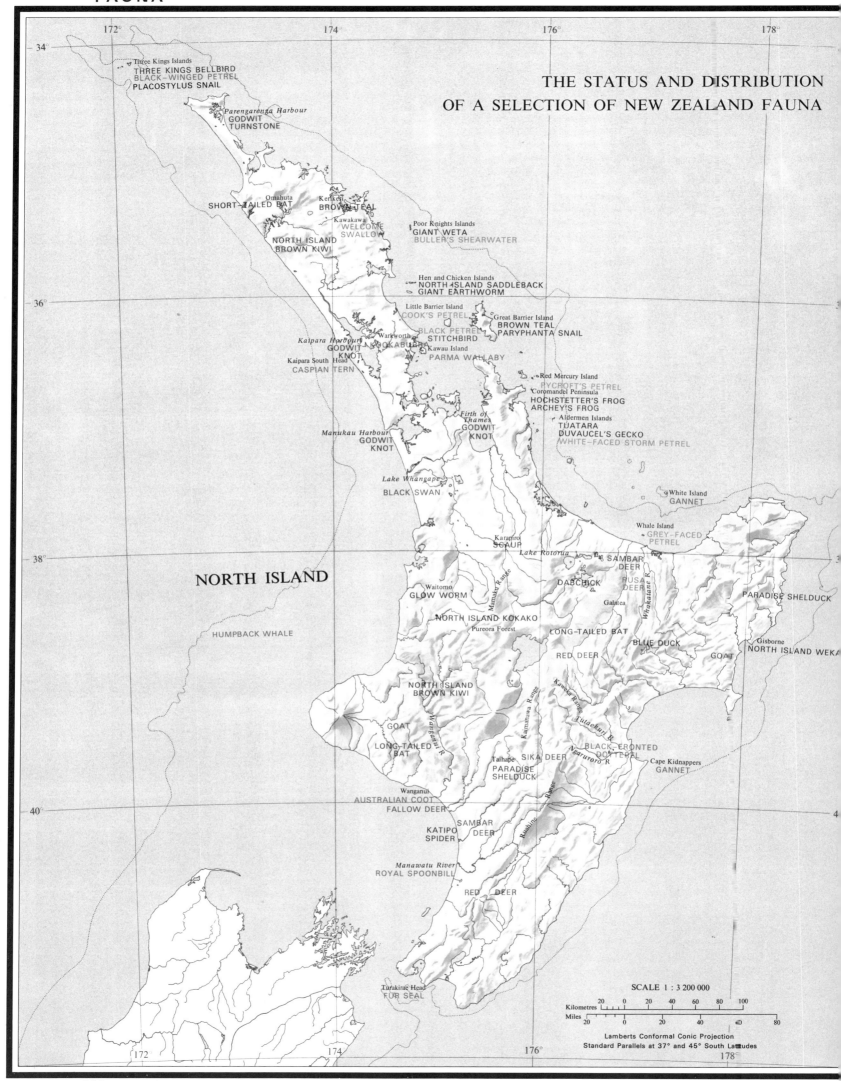

THE STATUS AND DISTRIBUTION
OF A SELECTION OF NEW ZEALAND FAUNA

Three Kings Islands
THREE KINGS BELLBIRD
BLACK-WINGED PETREL
PLACOSTYLUS SNAIL

Parengarenga Harbour
GODWIT
TURNSTONE

Omahuta
SHORT-TAILED BAT
Kerikeri
BROWN TEAL

Kawakawa
WELCOME
SWALLOW

Poor Knights Islands
GIANT WETA
BULLER'S SHEARWATER

NORTH ISLAND
BROWN KIWI

Hen and Chicken Islands
NORTH ISLAND SADDLEBACK
GIANT EARTHWORM

Little Barrier Island
COOK'S PETREL
BLACK PETREL
STITCHBIRD

Great Barrier Island
BROWN TEAL
PARYPHANTA SNAIL

Kaipara Harbour
GODWIT
KNOT

Warkworth
KOOKABURRA

Kawau Island
PARMA WALLABY

Kaipara South Head
CASPIAN TERN

Red Mercury Island
RYCROFT'S PETREL
Coromandel Peninsula
HOCHSTETTER'S FROG
ARCHEY'S FROG

Manukau Harbour
GODWIT
KNOT

Firth of Thames
GODWIT
KNOT

Aldermen Islands
TUATARA
DUVAUCEL'S GECKO
WHITE-FACED STORM PETREL

Lake Whangape
BLACK SWAN

White Island
GANNET

Whale Island
GREY-FACED
PETREL

Karapiro
SCAUP

Lake Rotorua

SAMBAR
DEER

DABCHICK

RUSA
DEER

PARADISE SHELDUCK

NORTH ISLAND

Waitomo
GLOW WORM

HUMPBACK WHALE

NORTH ISLAND KOKAKO
Pureora Forest

LONG-TAILED BAT

Galatea

RED DEER

BLUE DUCK

GOAT

Gisborne
NORTH ISLAND WEKA

NORTH ISLAND
BROWN KIWI

GOAT

LONG-TAILED
BAT

Wanganui R.

Kaimanawa Range

Kaweka Range

Tutaekuri R.

BLACK-FRONTED
DOTTEREL

Ngaruroro R.

Cape Kidnappers
GANNET

Taihape
SIKA DEER

PARADISE
SHELDUCK

Ruahine Range

Wanganui
AUSTRALIAN COOT
FALLOW DEER

KATIPO
SPIDER

SAMBAR
DEER

Manawatu River
ROYAL SPOONBILL

RED DEER

Turakirae Head
FUR SEAL

SCALE 1 : 3 200 000

20   0   20   40   60   80   100
Kilometres ┣━┫━┫━┫━┫━┫━┫━┫━┫

20   0   20   40   80
Miles ┣━┫━┫━┫━┫━━┫━━┫━━┫

Lamberts Conformal Conic Projection
Standard Parallels at 37° and 45° South Latitudes

KING SHAG	Occurs naturally only in the New Zealand region and only at the location shown
BROWN TEAL	Occurs naturally only in the New Zealand region, particularly, but not only, at the location shown
BLACK PETREL	Breeds only in the New Zealand region but ranges further afield
GODWIT	Occurs naturally but does not breed in the New Zealand region
FUR SEAL	Occurs naturally and breeds in the New Zealand region but also occurs and breeds elsewhere
RED DEER	Introduced, occurs in the New Zealand region particularly but not only at location shown
RUSA DEER	Introduced, occurs in the New Zealand region only at location shown
Banks Peninsula	Locations of species
	Forests

Farewell Spit
GODWIT
KNOT
SOUTH Collingwood
ISLAND
WEKA
RED
DEER Tasman
Mountains
GREAT SPOTTED KIWI
Karamea River
BLUE DUCK
Mt Kendall
LONG-TAILED BAT

Stephens Island
TUATARA
STEPHENS I FROG
FAIRY PRION

PARYPHANTA SNAIL

Cook Strait
KING SHAG
KILLER WHALE
COMMON
DOLPHIN

Lake Rotoiti
CHAMOIS
Durville Valley
GOAT
Paparoa Range FALLOW
DEER
WESTLAND ORANGE-FRONTED PARAKEET
BLACK PETREL

HECTOR'S
DOLPHIN

Seaward Kaikouras
HUTTON'S
SHEARWATER

Kaikoura
FUR SEAL

Lake Kaniere
RED DEER

Okarito Lagoon
ROYAL SPOONBILL Hanhari
WHITE HERON LITTLE SPOTTED KIWI
Waimakariri River
THAR
CHAMOIS

Motunau Island
WHITE-FLIPPERED
PENGUIN

Jackson Bay
FIORDLAND
CRESTED PENGUIN

Canterbury Riverbeds
BLACK-BILLED GULL
Canterbury-
Nth Otago Riverbeds
WRYBILL

Banks Peninsula
SPOTTED SHAG
WHITE-FLIPPERED PENGUIN

Lake Ellesmere
WELCOME SWALLOW

CANADA GOOSE
BLACK SWAN

Lake
Alexandrina
CRESTED GREBE
Lake Ohau
CANADA Lake Pukaki
GOOSE PARADISE SHELDUCK
Lake Hawea
THAR
CHAMOIS
McKenzie Basin
BLACK STILT Hunter Hills
RED-NECKED
WALLABY

HUMPBACK WHALE

Cleddau
Catchment
KAKAPO Homer
Tunnel
ROCK
WREN
Wanaka
CHUKOR
Mt Pisa
MOUNTAIN
JUMPING SPIDER
Richardson Mountains
GOAT
Harris Mountains
Lake Hayes Cromwell
AUSTRALIAN CALIFORNIA
COOT QUAIL
Lake Wakatipu Alexandra
CHAMOIS
FALLOW DEER

SOUTH ISLAND

WAPITI
RED DEER
TAKAHE
BROWN
TEAL
Murchison
Mountains
BLUE DUCK
Wet
Jackson Arm
Hunter
Mountains
GOOSE RED DEER
Cameron Mountains Heath
Mountains
SOUTH ISLAND
BROWN KIWI

Shag River
GREY TEAL

GIANT
SKINK

FALLOW DEER

Blue Mountains

Otago Peninsula
YELLOW-EYED PENGUIN
NORTHERN ROYAL ALBATROSS

SHEPHERD'S BEAKED WHALE

Invercargill North
SPUR-WINGED PLOVER

Solander Island
BULLER'S
MOLLYMAWK

Muttonbird Islands
SOUTH ISLAND
SADDLEBACK

Stewart Island
STEWART ISLAND BROWN KIWI
NEW ZEALAND SEA LION
WHITE-TAILED DEER

SCALE 1 : 3 200 000

Kilometres 20 0 20 40 60 80 100
Miles 20 0 20 40 60 80

Lamberts Conformal Conic Projection
Standard Parallels at 37° and 45° South Latitudes

SOILS, LAND CLASSIFICATION AND USE

M. L. Leamy & M. Fieldes

Production from the land is essential to the economy of New Zealand. More than twelve per cent of the working population is directly engaged in primary production, which provides the basis for the country's internal needs and for up to ninety per cent of its overseas earnings. The appraisal, classification, management and conservation of land is thus a matter of national importance.

Relation of Soil to Land Use

The number of agencies established to foster wise land-use includes the Department of Lands and Survey; the Ministry of Works and Development, responsible, among other activities, for water and soil conservation and administration of the Town and Country Planning Act; the Department of Internal Affairs; the Valuation Department; the Ministry of Agriculture and Fisheries; the New Zealand Forest Service; the National Parks Authority; the Nature Conservation Council; the National Roads Board; regional planning authorities; the Local Government Commission; city, borough and county councils; catchment boards and authorities; several divisions of the Department of Scientific and Industrial Research and many others. Each agency is concerned with aspects of the proper use of the nation's essential primary resources—water, rocks, soils, plants, animals and people.

The various agencies have in recent years increasingly recognised the importance of planned multiple use of the land so that their activities can be co-ordinated to preserve amenities and to provide for long-term sustained production. These objectives have always been important but with increasing population pressures they have assumed urgency, and basic information on the distribution, kinds and amounts of the primary physical resources must be available for national land-use planning of this description.

Soil information is fundamental to such planning for a number of reasons. *Firstly,* soils are essential components of land. *Secondly,* the description of each soil takes account of water (in the moisture regime of the soil), of the kind of rock, of the vegetation, and of animal life within and on the soil, so that a description of a soil is in effect an inventory of primary physical resources for land at the site described. *Thirdly,* the boundaries of mapping units of different kinds of soil are established with care in the field. The resulting soil maps provide an inventory of the location, disposition and nature of primary physical resources and also provide information about the precise areas involved and their distribution. *Fourthly,* interpretations of soil maps are developed with the co-operation of land-use experts so that specialist knowledge is implicit in them. *Fifthly,* data on the mapping units provide many facts concerning components of the ecological cycle including water and soil–plant–animal relationships that are immediately useful in complex land-use and environmental studies. Soil maps of adequate detail are therefore unique as a source of basic data for classifying land for many different uses.

The Nature of Soil

Soil is the product of its environment—of the rock waste which is the parent material, of the climate under which that waste weathers, of the kind of topography upon which it is situated, of the vegetation under which it develops, and of the length of time during which it has been developing. The complex soil pattern in New Zealand is due to many different kinds of rock and to the variety of conditions under which they are transformed into soil. New Zealand, which is some 27 million hectares in area, is about 1600 kilometres long, and embraces such climatic extremes as subtropical North Auckland, the cold uplands of the alpine regions, the semi-arid basins of Central Otago, and the very wet mountains and lowlands of Westland. The topography is varied; approximately fifty per cent of New Zealand is steep, twenty per cent is moderately hilly, and only thirty per cent is either flat or rolling. The natural vegetation under which the soils were formed ranged, in more humid areas, from kauri forests in the north to mixed podocarp–broadleaved and beech forests further south, with subalpine scrub and fellfield in more elevated situations; in the drier areas tussock grassland was the dominant vegetation. In addition, from time to time such events as the flooding of rivers over alluvial plains, the drifting of sands, and the fall of ash from erupting volcanoes have in places interrupted soil development. It is no wonder, then, that the pattern of New Zealand soils is complex. What is wondrous is that through the complexity there is a clear pattern of soil variation in response to fluctuations in one of the main causal elements in the soil environment—the climate.

Soils and Climatic Zones

Very marked differences have been observed between the kinds of soil occurring in different major climatic zones of the earth. Russian scientists in particular, in the latter part of the nineteenth century, were early to appreciate the occurrence of characteristic soils corresponding to the different climatic zones. The soil differences were seen in differences of colour, structure, thickness and arrangement of horizons (horizontal layers apparent in vertical sections of a soil) which make up the soil profile.

LATITUDINAL ZONATION

The Russian scientists recognised that in traversing areas of low relief from north to south across lines of latitude one passed successively through arctic, temperate, and tropical climatic zones, with corresponding latitudinal zones having characteristic soils and vegetation.

The principal profile features of the tundra soil, characteristic of the arctic zone, are a horizon of peat on bluish-grey mineral soil with poor aeration and drainage over permanently frozen subsoil. Features of the podzol, characteristic of the moist, cold, temperate, forested zone, are a horizon of dark, raw humus on a strikingly pale grey horizon overlying a strongly-coloured horizon commonly brown. Features of the chernozem, characteristic of the grasslands and steppes of the semi-arid temperate zone, are an upper horizon of high humus content, considerable thickness, and uniform very dark colour. Other climatic zones are characterised by chestnut soils, brown desert soils, grey desert soils, and so on.

The soil zones in the Russian sectors of Europe and Asia are hundreds of miles wide and extend latitudinally for thousands of miles. Their counterparts are recognised in the American continent and other parts of the world.

ALTITUDINAL ZONATION

Effects corresponding to altitudinal zonation were recognised in addition to the latitudinal zonation of soils described. Where the low relief, chernozem zone of the steppes was interrupted, for instance by the Ural Mountains, chernozems gave place successively, with increasing altitudes and corresponding changes in precipitation and temperature, to podzols and tundra soils.

Soil Zonation in the New Zealand Soil Pattern

There is evidence that the planners of settlement may have anticipated that New Zealand soils would resemble soils of tropical Pacific islands of volcanic origin. Climatic differences and the limited extent of soils from volcanic materials were to give such assumptions little validity.

Early attempts by soil scientists of the 1920s to apply Russian concepts of soil zonality to this country appear to have suggested that the generally moist, cool, temperate, forested conditions would produce a zone of soils akin to podzols. Podzols are identified in New Zealand, although they differ in certain ways from their Russian counterparts because here the insular, oceanic, climatic conditions differ greatly from those of the vast continental podzol zones. The idea of a podzol zone nevertheless laid the foundation for the concepts of soil zonation which were evolved subsequently in the classification of New Zealand soils.

Continuing research has led to recognition here of a soil pattern in which major soil groups have characteristics of distinctive climatic zones.

Climate is, of course, only one of the important factors in soil formation. Throughout New Zealand, perceptible soil differences can be related to all or any of the following: changes in the parent material, as expressed by both the nature of the parent rock and its degree of weathering; variations in the vegetation and soil fauna; differences in the nature of the terrain and fluctuations in the length of time the soil has been forming. Climate remains, however, a factor which dominates the pattern of New Zealand soils, particularly in widespread areas where the nature of parent materials is relatively uniform, and flat and undulating terrain minimises the varying influences of topography.

Soil parent materials over much of New Zealand are relatively uniform because the geological pattern is dominated by ordinary siliceous rocks, neither markedly acidic nor basic. The greywackes, argillites and schists of the mountain ranges throughout most of the country provide soil parent materials on downs, terraces and plains from the weathered rock itself, or from drift materials such as alluvium, colluvium, solifluction debris and loess. Recent research in many areas has demonstrated the similarity of the mineralogy of the drift materials to that of neighbouring parent rock.

Over areas of similar topography and parent material, changes in vegetation and soil fauna, in most cases in response to climatic changes, leave their imprint on the soils. In a mountainous country such as New Zealand, the importance of steepening slope as a parameter differentiating both soils and land use is almost self-evident. Most New Zealand soils are Quaternary soils—that is, they have formed over about the last million years—and many have been developing only over the last 10 000 years or so. Thus, compared with the soils of many continental areas, such as Australia and Africa, New Zealand soils are young. Even so, the clear effects of the amount of time available for soil formation are identifiable in age sequences of profiles in many parts of the country.

Recognition of the principles of soil zonation in New Zealand is the basis of the New Zealand genetic soil classification.

Soil Classification

The soils of New Zealand may be grouped into three major divisions:—

Zonal groups embrace soils from ordinary siliceous rocks. Their main differentiating characteristics are due to processes controlled by the climate and vegetation of the zone.

Intrazonal groups have distinguishing characteristics reflecting the strong influence of some local factor, such as a particular kind of rock or high water table.

Azonal groups have characteristics dominated by such factors as instability associated with steepness of slope, or intermittent burial by flooding, both of which shorten the time of soil development.

ZONAL SOILS

Ordinary siliceous rocks in New Zealand include greywacke, argillite, schist, granite and quartzo–feldspathic sandstones, mudstones and conglomerates. At varying stages of weathering, these rocks, together with the loess,

CLIMATIC PARAMETERS FOR THE ZONAL SOILS OF NEW ZEALAND

Temperature Regimes *figures indicate the average and range of mean annual temperatures*	Moisture Regimes *figures indicate the range of mean annual rainfalls*				
	Semi arid 330–500 mm	Subhumid 500–1000 mm (seasonally dry)	Humid 1000–2000 mm	Humid to superhumid 1500–2500 mm (Mor forming vegetation)	Superhumid 2000–2500 + mm
Warm (Northern) 14°C 13°C–15°C			Northern yellow-brown earths (Auckland, North Auckland)	Northern podzolised yellow-brown earths and podzols (North Auckland)	
Mild (Central) 12°C 11°C–13°C		Central yellow-grey earths (Marlborough, Wairarapa, Hawke's Bay, Manawatu)	Central yellow-brown earths (Marlborough, Nelson, Wellington, Wairarapa, East Coast, King Country)	Central podzolised yellow-brown earths and podzols (western Nelson, Westland)	Gley podzols
Cool (Southern) 8°C 7°C–10°C	Brown-grey earths (Central Otago, North Otago and inland South Canterbury)	Southern yellow-grey earths (Southland, Otago, eastern Canterbury)	Southern yellow-brown earths (Southland Otago, western Canterbury)	Southern podzolised yellow-brown earths and podzols (Southland, Stewart Island)	
Cold to cool (High country) 5°C 4°C–7°C			High country yellow-brown earths (inland South Island)	High country podzolised yellow-brown earths and podzols (inland South Island)	High country gley and organic soils (Westland, Fiordland, Stewart Island, North Island main ranges)

gravels, sands, silts and clays derived from them, are widespread throughout the country and form the parent materials of the zonal soils.

Within characteristic climatic and vegetational zones, well-developed soils on flat and rolling sites from such parent materials have similar morphological features.

Zonal soils of New Zealand comprise brown-grey earths; southern and central yellow-grey earths; high country, southern, central and northern yellow-brown earths; high country, southern, central, and northern podzolised yellow-brown earths and podzols; high country gley[1] and organic soils; and gley podzols. *Table 1* summarises features of the climatic zones under which these soils develop.

The main zonal soils on flat and rolling terrain and their corresponding hilly soils occupy approximately 6½ million hectares.

INTRAZONAL SOILS

Intrazonal soils comprise yellow-brown sands; yellow-brown pumice soils; yellow-brown loams; brown granular loams and clays; red and brown loams; organic soils and gley soils. These soils occupy nearly 4 million hectares.

AZONAL SOILS

Azonal soils occupy 14½ million hectares. The azonal soils comprise recent soils from alluvium, recent soils from volcanic ash, and steepland soils related to zonal soil groups.

The Main Soil Regions

Aspects of the range of environments under which agriculture is conducted are indicated by the range of climatic moisture and temperature zones shown in *Table 1* for the zonal soils.

Moisture and temperature affect many components of the environment. Some of the effects are reflected in the very different morphology and physical properties of zonal groups (brown-grey earths, yellow-grey earths, yellow-brown earths, podzols, and gley podzols) associated with different ranges of rainfall and temperature.

In general, the presence of adequate water in a soil induces fertility by stimulating biological turnover and by increasing the rate of weathering of primary minerals. Primary minerals such as feldspars and micas are converted by hydration to clay-size minerals and colloids and in the process they release calcium, potassium and other chemical elements. With time, the increasing amounts of clay formed alter the capacity for retention both of water and of chemical elements by the soil, in ways that, according to circumstances, may be beneficial or detrimental. Excess water tends to reduce fertility by leaching soils of desirable elements and, in poorly-drained situations, by limiting aeration. Other things being equal, rising temperature tends to increase rates of chemical and biochemical processes, and to result in increased clay contents of soils together with decreased reserves of essential elements in primary minerals.

Because of the close link between the climates of different regions, the form of the soils and factors affecting fertility and management, it is valuable for soil classification and for comparison of land use to consider both in four regions which include the four principal zones of climate and weathering.

The *northern* region includes the warm zone of the Coromandel, Auckland and North Auckland districts where the rate of mineral weathering is fast, the stage of weathering commonly advanced and many soils are

strongly weathered.

The *central* region includes the mild, coastal lowlands north of about the Waiau River on the east coast and Franz Joseph on the west of the South Island, extending in the North Island to as far north as and including the Waikato and Bay of Plenty districts. In this zone the rate of mineral weathering is moderate, and most soils are moderately weathered.

The *southern* region includes the cool, coastal lowlands of the South Island south of about the Waiau River and Franz Joseph. Here the rate of mineral weathering is slow and most soils are weakly weathered. Similar conditions and soils have been recognised in the north-western part of the South Island at elevations from 300 metres.

The *high country* region includes the cool to cold, humid to superhumid, elevated inland zone of the South Island, where the rate of mineral weathering is very slow, resulting in very weakly weathered soils.

Soils and land use are considered according to these regional groupings. The soils below are treated in order of regions of decreasing temperature and weathering.

SOILS OF THE NORTHERN REGION

Northern yellow-brown earths are extensive on the rolling and hilly lands of the North Auckland peninsula and northern parts of South Auckland and form mostly from weathered sedimentary rocks under dominantly mull-forming forest. They are heavy soils, greyish-brown to grey clay loam in the topsoil and yellowish-brown compact clay in the subsoil.

Weakly leached northern yellow-brown earths occupy small areas in hilly land and are commonly relatively shallow soils over less weathered rock; moderately leached northern yellow-brown earths are also associated with less weathered parent materials. Both soils, with light to moderate application of lime and phosphate, support excellent pastures for dairy cattle or sheep.

Strongly leached northern yellow-brown earths commonly occur on strongly weathered parent materials. They are extensive on lower hill slopes and rolling land, frequently associated with weakly podzolised yellow-brown earths and their vegetation was podocarp–broadleaved forest with kauri. In contrast with the less leached soils they have increased mottling in the subsoil, higher amounts of clay, increased acidity and decreased levels of macro-plant and micro-plant nutrients.

Northern podzolised yellow-brown earths and podzols are commonly found on gently sloping low ridges or on lower slopes of rolling land and are developed from deeply weathered sedimentary materials. Mor-forming trees such as kauri, rimu and kamahi dominated their original vegetation and accelerated the leaching process. Under natural conditions, available plant nutrients were mainly cycled between the vegetation and the upper soil horizons and were retained by the organic mor horizon. Where trees were removed, however, the mor horizon oxidised rapidly to expose a surface horizon of very low natural fertility.

Weakly, moderately and strongly podzolised soils and podzols commonly occur in complex mosaics. Weakly and moderately podzolised northern yellow-brown earths have formed from deeply weathered sedimentary rocks under podocarp–kauri forest. Topsoils are brownish-grey to grey silt loam with weakly developed, very soft, granular aggregates. Subsoils are very firm yellow clay with coarse, blocky aggregates combined into large prisms. The soils are strongly acid, low in nutrients and, because of their coarse subsoil structure, aeration and moisture contents fluctuate widely. Fertility is low and heavy topdressing

---

[1]The term gley implies yellow and grey mottling in the soil produced by partial oxidation and reduction of iron caused by intermittent waterlogging.

with phosphates and lime is required to maintain pastures.

Strongly podzolised northern yellow-brown earths have developed under mor-forming vegetation. Structure and drainage are poor. They have distinct subsoil clay horizons, in some cases with marked accumulations of organic carbon and of aluminium and iron. With fertiliser application they maintain good pastures for dairying or sheep farming, but stocking in winter must be kept at a low density to prevent pugging.

Well developed podzols are formed on slightly consolidated sands. They have thin, grey topsoils with little or no structure, and indurated silica, humus and iron pans that cause wide fluctuations in moisture and limit plant growth. Their very low plant nutrient levels, with problems of control of ground water levels, limit their productive use. In North Auckland they contain numerous kauri stumps and kauri gum and are commonly known as 'gumlands'.

Northern brown granular clays are derived from andesitic rocks and volcanic ash and are formed under forest with an annual rainfall greater than 1250 millimetres. They are extensive on hilly land and rolling plateaus at elevations from sea level to 600 metres or more, and occur mainly on the western side of the North Auckland peninsula. They are commonly clay soils with greyish-brown to brown, friable topsoils and brown to yellowish-brown, firm to compact subsoils and have moderately to strongly developed granular and nutty structures in the topsoil, grading into blocky to prismatic structures in the subsoil. They are commonly used for pastoral production. Natural fertility and management differ with the degree of leaching and weathering.

Weakly leached, brown granular clays, which occupy small areas, mainly of hilly land, were developed under broadleaved trees. They have high natural fertility and when cleared may carry pasture for many years without topdressing. Moderately leached, brown granular clays formed under broadleaved-podocarp forest are extensive and require light dressings of superphosphate and potash to maintain pasture.

Strongly leached soils developed under mixed podocarp–kauri forest and have higher fertiliser requirements: very strongly leached soils developed under kauri-dominant forest at low elevations and require heavy topdressing with phosphate, potash, lime and trace elements to establish and maintain pasture.

Northern red and brown loams are formed under annual rainfalls of 1250 to 2000 millimetres and support in their natural state subtropical forest. They are not very widespread but show some interesting characteristics. Red loams are developed from basaltic rocks which are scoriaceous and easily weatherable, but brown loams are from denser basalt flows. Both soils generally occur in close association and are weathered to clays of low plasticity that consist of oxides of aluminium and iron. Although clay content may be greater than fifty per cent, the soils are so friable that they have properties more comparable to loams than to clays. Topsoils are very friable, range in colour from red to brown and have a fine granular structure. Subsoils range from very friable to very firm in consistency, are also red or brown and have fine, nutty or blocky structures. High phosphate retention results from the considerable amounts of iron and aluminium oxides and this, together with a tendency to droughtiness resulting from free drainage, can be a handicap to realising the substantial agricultural potential of these soils. The time of application and the kind of fertilisers are particularly important.

The red and brown loams may be arranged into soil development sequences according to leaching. Weakly leached red loams are commonly derived from basaltic ash and scoria, under broadleaved forest. They have excellent physical properties and are of high natural fertility. Total phosphorus is high but its availability is low. These weakly leached soils are found on the sloping sides of volcanic cones and are used for growing vegetables or for dairying. They are, perhaps, the closest correlatives in New Zealand to the soils characteristic of the young, high islands of the Pacific. Moderately leached brown loams are commonly derived from scoriaceous basalt, are less friable and granular than red loams, and are slightly lower in natural fertility. If topdressed with phosphate, and in many cases potassium as well, these soils can give moderate to high yields of vegetable crops or pastures for dairying. Production is limited to some extent by the high retention of phosphorus. Strongly leached brown loams are developed on basalt under mixed or podocarp-dominant forest. They are soils of low natural fertility for pastoral purposes and require lime as well as phosphate for high production. Similar soils are used for citrus farming at Kerikeri. Brown loams of very low fertility occur on undulating to flat plateaus in the Bay of Islands district. They were formed under mixed podocarp–kauri forest and have friable, granular topsoils overlying tightly-packed, fine, nutty and blocky aggregates with numerous iron concretions. They are known locally as 'ironstone' soils and have developed on strongly weathered basalt, which is a poor source of nutrients. The soils thus require heavy applications of fertiliser, particularly of phosphate and potassium, while some minor elements such as molybdenum and cobalt may be deficient. Small areas have been developed for dairy farming and sheep fattening.

Northern yellow-brown sands are formed on sand dune complexes with intervening peaty plains. They occupy an extensive strip along the western coast of North Auckland. The degree of soil development increases inland with the age of the sand deposit, as with yellow-brown sands throughout New Zealand. The youngest soils have surface horizons of humus-stained sand held together by a mat of roots overlying unconsolidated brown sand; the oldest soils have topsoils ranging from sandy to sandy-clay loam overlying a range from slightly to moderately compact sandy-clay loam to sand.

Although summer drought limits pasture growth, free drainage allows grazing at times when heavier soils in the vicinity are liable to pugging. With regular applications of phosphate and potash, the more developed soils hold excellent pastures which are used for fattening stock and for dairying. Moderate pastures can be maintained on the young soils, which are also used in part for forestry.

Northern recent, gley and organic soils, on flood plains and swamp lands, are of limited area, but because they are above average in fertility and well suited to mechanical improvement, they provide valuable agricultural land. They are derived from either alluvium or peat, and major differences between them are related to wetness and to conditions of accumulation.

The soils are deep, loamy and fertile on the narrow strips of free-draining flats bordering rivers and streams. On wider flood plains, drainage is generally slow and soils are clay-textured, with coarse structures and pale grey, mottled subsoils. In places where the water table is permanently high, organic soils have developed on peat. When carefully drained and topdressed with phosphate, potash, lime and copper, such soils carry valuable summer pastures for dairying.

SOILS, LAND CLASSIFICATION & USE

Northern steepland soils occur on isolated ranges where hard rocks have resisted erosion. They are derived either from andesitic rocks or greywacke and have thin topsoils subject to rapid sheet and slip erosion when used as pasture. They are well suited to forestry.

SOILS OF THE CENTRAL REGION

Central yellow-grey earths and associated intergrades are formed on flat to undulating terraces and on rolling and hilly land in the Manawatu, Hawke's Bay, Wairarapa, Marlborough and Nelson districts where the average annual rainfall ranges from 500 to 1000 millimetres. The climate is also characterised by a well-defined dry season. Most of these soils are formed on loess or weakly consolidated alluvial or marine sediments. Accessions of volcanic ash can be seen near the central North Island volcanic region. Most soils formed originally under tussock grassland, but the moister soils of the Manawatu district developed under forest.

The dominant morphological feature of most of these soils is a massive, compact and, in the northern part of the zone, cemented subsoil horizon. This 'fragipan' is commonly penetrated by widely-spaced vertical cracks and is overlain by pale yellow and brown horizons which which may be mottled or gleyed, and by grey and greyish-brown silt loam friable topsoils with granular and nut structures.

In general these soils are moderately weathered and moderately leached, of low natural fertility, low in available phosphorus and with the ratio of calcium to magnesium decreasing down the profile. The moister soils in the Manawatu district require drainage to remove excess water which accumulates in winter, while the drier soils in the Marlborough district may require irrigation. The main fertiliser requirements are phosphate, potassium and lime. Erosion is a hazard to land use, particularly on hilly land in the drier areas where disastrous tunnel-gully erosion has occurred in the past.

Central yellow-grey earths are developed predominantly for pasture although cash cropping, supplementary feed cropping and fruitgrowing are other significant uses.

Central yellow-brown earths occur on the west coast to the south of Auckland, in the King Country, East Coast, Manawatu, Hawke's Bay, Wellington, Marlborough, Nelson and West Coast districts. They are formed on undulating, rolling and hilly land under evenly distributed mean annual rainfalls of 1150–1500 millimetres. Most soils are derived from greywacke materials, in some places directly from rock and in others indirectly, from water-laid or wind-blown deposits derived from greywacke. Adjacent to the volcanic region, there are important soil differences related to accessions of volcanic ash. In eastern sectors of the North Island, these soils are formed from sediments ranging from claystones to conglomerates and from soft bentonitic mudstones to hard greywacke sandstones. In the East Coast district they have been severely affected by accelerated erosion. In the Nelson and West Coast districts, yellow-brown earths are commonly formed on weathered Pleistocene gravels.

These soils developed under broadleaved, podocarp and beech forests, and are characterised morphologically by greyish-brown to brown, friable silt loam topsoils over yellowish-brown, friable to firm silt to clay loam subsoils, with moderately developed, medium nutty structures and rarely any mottling.

In general, drainage is free and under the moderately high rainfall there is a continual loss of plant nutrients. Most soils have low natural fertility but good physical conditions and they respond well to fertilisers. Applications of lime, phosphate, molybdenum and in some cases potassium have resulted in moderately to highly productive pastoral land on these soils. Under cultivation, soil aggregates break down rapidly and the yellow-brown earths are thus not very well suited to regular cropping. Exotic forests have been established in the South Island on these soils, and correction of a number of recorded nutrient deficiencies, such as phosphorus, calcium and magnesium, would probably further enhance the success of these operations.

Gley podzols are commonly known as 'pakihi soils'. They occur in Westland, predominantly on flat land but also on rolling and hilly terrain, where the annual rainfall normally exceeds 2500 millimetres and is almost always in excess of plant needs. They are intensely leached and have developed under podocarp forest which, where cleared and burnt, has reverted to low scrub, rushes and fern. Characterised by peaty topsoils, they overlie strongly gleyed, massive, very slowly permeable, grey, silty horizons resting on gravels cemented with iron oxide. The silty horizons overlying the gravels range from less than thirty centimetres to more than two metres in depth. Massive nutrient deficiencies, and the necessity for large-scale drainage, render these soils extremely difficult to use. However, pasture has been established following drainage and heavy application of lime, phosphate, potash, copper, molybdenum and sulphur. Exotic trees have been established on a trial basis. It is not likely that these isolated and hard-won successes will be followed by large-scale land development on gley podzols.

Yellow-brown pumice soils comprise a soil group with unusually distinctive mineralogical, physical and chemical properties. This situation results from the combination of a limited geographical distribution, a restricted range of parent materials and a comparatively brief period of soil development.

They occupy most of the Central Volcanic Region of the North Island, and are formed on young, rhyolitic parent material, most of which originated violently as two eruptions of pumice, estimated to have fallen 800 and 1800 years ago. In most places topsoils are very dark, sandy and friable and overlie yellowish-brown, weakly structured pumice sands and gravels. Soils derived from the deposits of distinctive volcanic events, such as the Taupo eruptions of about 1800 years ago, can be arranged in sequences of profile development that are correlated with differences of climate and vegetation. Such sequences are characterised by an increase in leaching and by the onset of podzolisation with increasing rainfall. These soils are formed under an annual rainfall range of about 1250–2000 millimetres and under forest, scrub and tussock vegetation.

Yellow-brown pumice soils are unusual in that the development of their horizons, in response to the effects of vegetation, is out of step with the low degree of weathering of the mineral material of the soil. An important feature of this weathering is the formation of allophane, a clay mineral which absorbs organic matter and phosphorus, but which does not retain potassium. Large quantities of phosphatic fertiliser are therefore needed in the early stages of pasture establishment, with subsequent and frequent applications of potash. Magnesium responses have been obtained from both pasture and pine seedlings grown under these conditions. Cobalt is low and small quantities must be added to prevent bush sickness—a stock malady which crippled early attempts at pastoral development in this region. Deficiencies of other trace elements may occur under intensive farming, because the soil particles are coarse and have only a limited surface area exposed to weathering and to plant roots. However, the restoration of nutrient balances is much easier than in other more weathered soils with higher clay content; in general, the chemical disadvantages of the yellow-brown pumice soils are readily corrected with fertilisers, permitting full use of their excellent physical properties.

Pastoral development in recent years has been afflicted by rapid and destructive gully erosion in some areas of pumice soils, probably a natural consequence of the change from forest to pasture. Both remedial and preventive soil conservation practices are being employed. Considerable areas of yellow-brown pumice soils have been planted in exotic forests and the activity resulting from the harvesting and replanting of these forests imparts a special character to the whole region.

Central yellow-brown loams are formed either on the older, more weathered, rhyolitic pumice sand that lies beyond the boundary of the yellow-brown pumice soils in the Bay of Plenty and Waikato districts, or, as in Taranaki and the central North Island, on deposits of fine-textured andesitic ash such as originated from Mt Egmont and the central volcanoes. They are older and more weathered than yellow-brown pumice soils but younger and less weathered than brown granular loams. They occur on flattish, rolling and hilly land under a wide range of annual rainfalls of 1000 to 4000 millimetres. In some places they still support broadleaved and podocarp forests.

The soils are friable and free-draining, with black to brown silt loam topsoils with soft, granular and crumb structures. Subsoils are brown to yellow silt loam, are very friable and have weakly developed nutty structures. They are not sticky, absorb large amounts of water without swelling and have a high requirement for phosphate and potash. Because they occur under a wide range of rainfalls, leaching sequences are quite common and the most strongly leached soils commonly display some morphological evidence of this, such as the occurrence of subsoil iron pans. In the southern part of the North Island, soils formed on mixtures of volcanic ash and loess are less friable, with lower phosphate fixation and greater potassium retention, than typical yellow-brown loams, but resemble them more than the yellow-brown earths towards which they grade. The distinctive physical and chemical properties of the yellow-brown loams are attributed to the dominance of allophane in the clay fraction.

These soils are both productive and versatile. Their light texture, good aeration and drainage under the warm climate of the Waikato and Taranaki districts result in rapid spring growth, quick response to summer rains and high pastoral production. New Zealand's dairy industry is legitimately regarded as one of the most efficient, competent and soundly based in the world. The productivity of the yellow-brown loams is not the least of the several factors which contribute to this situation.

Central brown granular loams are derived from old deposits of andesitic and rhyolitic ash which either have not been covered by younger ash or have been exposed by erosion. Thus they are older than the yellow-brown loams. They are extensive on rolling country, south of Auckland to the Hamilton area, where they are developing under mean annual rainfalls of 1250–1500 millimetres. They originally supported a native vegetation of broadleaved forest.

Topsoils are greyish-brown to brown, friable silt to clay loam and pass downward into brown to yellowish-brown clay loam to clay. Aggregates are moderately to strongly developed granular to nutty in the topsoil, grading to blocky in the subsoil where, although they are tightly packed, they separate easily. The brown granular loams are sticky when wet owing to their high content of kaolinitic clays. In this they differ from yellow-brown loams, which are high in allophane. The moisture range is quite wide, and summer dryness can be a limitation to high production. Irrigation can be beneficial for dairying, fattening, market gardening or grape growing, which are the main uses for these soils. They exhibit high phosphate retention and respond to phosphate topdressing. Lime and molybdenum are also required on the more developed soils, while relatively low rates of potassium are often beneficial.

Brown granular loams also occur on the basic and ultra-basic volcanic rocks that crop out extensively on the hills surrounding the Nelson lowland and, to a lesser extent, in North Canterbury. They are derived from massive intrusions of basaltic materials into sedimentary rocks and thus have complex parent materials. They are developed under broadleaved forest and an annual rainfall of 1000–1250 millimetres, and have greyish-brown granular to nutty silt loam topsoils on reddish-brown to brown, firm, blocky, clay loam subsoils. Soils formed under podocarp-beech forest and an annual rainfall of 1250–1500 millimetres are browner in the topsoil, yellower in the subsoil, and more variable in texture. They are of moderate fertility and, with fertilisers, hold pastures well, although pasture production on the drier soils is restricted by seasonal droughts. Considerable areas of these soils are covered with manuka, fern and gorse.

Soils developed on ultrabasic dunite and serpentine rocks under annual rainfalls of 1150–1500 millimetres and low scrub vegetation occur on the steep to moderately steep slopes of parts of D'Urville Island, on the eastern hills of the Nelson district and on the Red Hills range of the Upper Wairau valley. Topsoils are greyish-brown, friable sandy or silt loams, and subsoils are yellowish-brown to greenish-brown, friable stony clay loams. They are soils of very low fertility, with a very high content of magnesium, chromium and nickel but very low of calcium, phosphorus and potassium. On present knowledge, these unusual soils are unsuitable for either agriculture or forestry.

Central yellow-brown sands, like their Northern counterparts, are formed on coastal sand drifts. They cover about 100,000 hectares in the Wanganui, Manawatu and Wellington districts. Areas of these soils consist of complexes of dunes, sand plains and peat swamps with a very wide range of drainage conditions developing in accordance with the age of the sand deposit. Soils on the younger sand drifts bordering the coast show little or no profile development and, except on sand plains where the water table is high, they are droughty and unstable. Further inland, the soils formed on older sand drifts are more weathered and slightly to moderately leached. To grow plants, leaching losses are more than offset by an improved physical condition due to increases in organic matter and accumulation of fine particles of dust that increase both the moisture-holding capacity and resistance to erosion. The more weathered soils, and those with high water tables, are capable of maintaining high-quality pastures for dairying and fat-lamb farming. Regular dressings of phosphate and potash are required, and the wetter soils need draining. Trace-element deficiencies of copper, cobalt and selenium have been reported on some farms. On the more excessively drained soils, exotic forestry is preferable to pastoral farming.

Yellow-brown sands characteristically have a dark grey to black, very friable topsoil over yellowish-brown, slightly firm sand, which grades down into grey, loose sand. This morphology is varied in places by more strongly developed B horizons[1] and by features induced by wet conditions in inter-dune depressions. Drainage sequences and age sequences both occur within the yellow-brown sand group.

Central recent soils from volcanic ash occur adjacent to the active or recently active volcanic centres of Mts Ngauruhoe, Ruapehu, Egmont and Tarawera and Lake Rotomahana. Deposits of andesitic sand thicker than eight centimetres, which have resulted from intermittent eruptions over the last 400 years from Ngauruhoe and Ruapehu, occur in an oval-shaped area around the two mountains. The resultant soil is deep and friable with high levels of organic matter in the subsoil from the burial of successive topsoils. Continual accession of ash has suppressed horizon development. Under cool, wet conditions, mineral weathering is slow, as is the decomposition of organic matter and accumulation of nitrogen. The native vegetation is red tussock. Deep deposits of sandy ash are susceptible to wind erosion. Accessions of ash occur in a wide zone beyond the mapped area. They contribute mineral elements such as cobalt to the soils, so that the normal deficiency is not present in soils derived principally from Taupo pumice in the southern Taupo region.

Recent soils are also developed on the gravelly and sandy andesitic materials erupted from Egmont between 200 and 400 years ago, mainly in the Egmont National Park.

Soils developed from the rhyolitic sand, silt and gravels violently ejected from Lake Rotomahana in June 1886 occupy about 13 000 hectares of rolling and hilly land between Lake Rotorua and Mt Tarawera. Apart from limited incorporation of organic matter into the topsoil, very little soil development has occurred. Hydrothermal weathering of minerals prior to eruption has enhanced the fertility of this soil. Some soils have been cultivated and sown to grassland for dairy farming, and, by using phosphate fertiliser, excellent pastures have been established and maintained.

Gravelly soils are developed on the predominantly basaltic material erupted from Mt Tarawera in June 1886. These deposits cover about 91 000 hectares of hilly and rolling land to depths greater than about eight centimetres. The soils comprise dark greyish-brown gravelly sand over greyish-brown and black gravel and sand. The coarse particles are scoriaceous and include glassy basalt showing few external signs of weathering; soil nutrients are derived principally from the small amounts of rhyolitic dust and Rotomahana mud erupted at the same time. Drainage and decomposition of organic matter are rapid and the combined effects of low moisture and nutrient-content make pastures difficult to maintain. These soils are suited to growing exotic trees that can root deeply and obtain benefit from old soils buried below the Tarawera lapilli.

Central recent, gley and organic soils occur throughout the North Island and northern South Island on flood plains and swamps, where the dominant process is accumulation or where the water table is close to, or at, the surface.

The soils are derived from alluvium deposited by rivers, streams or lakes, and have little horizon development but a wide range of texture and organic-matter content. Soil characteristics change frequently over short distances, and a detailed map would be required to show the pattern of soil types. Major soil differences are related to the conditions of accumulation, and on this basis three sets of soils are separated—recent soils on free-draining flood plains, gley recent and gley soils in the slow-draining parts of the plains, and organic soils in swampy depressions once permanently covered with water.

Recent soils are commonly friable, deep, brown to yellowish-brown sand and silt loams, with little horizon development. They are highly fertile and suited to a wide variety of cropping or pastoral uses. The closely associated gley soils range in texture from sandy loam to clay, with a fairly distinct change in colour downward from greyish-brown topsoil to grey subsoil. The subsoil shows a variable amount of rusty-coloured mottling. Nutrient status is high, and, with adequate drainage, the soils make highly productive land for pastures or annual cropping. Surface drainage is slow, and the surface becomes puddled with heavy stocking. Organic soils have developed in swampy places from dead vegetation which may have been mixed with some fine-textured mineral alluvium deposited during floods. They may be moderately fertile but require careful drainage before they become useful for crops or pasture. With drainage and use, the surface gradually sinks and soils formed from forest peats expose successive layers of stumps and logs that are costly to remove. Some areas which have been over-drained now dry out severely in summer. However, many organic soils that have been drained and stumped make excellent land for dairying or market gardening. In Westland, recent, gley and organic soils are widely distributed on flood plains and low terraces of major rivers under annual rainfalls of 1500–3750 millimetres. They are moderately fertile and, where adequately drained, are used for dairying.

Central steepland soils are extensive throughout the region and occur predominantly in association with yellow-brown earths, yellow-brown loams and yellow-brown pumice soils.

Steepland soils related to yellow-brown earths are generally shallow, and many have a B horizon over weathering rock. They are free-draining, friable soils with differences related chiefly to parent rock and to climate.

Soils formed on Tertiary rocks, mainly siltstones and sandstones, were developed under forest where annual rainfalls were 1150 to more than 1500 millimetres. They are widespread in the East Coast, Wanganui, Manawatu and Wairarapa districts. Accessions of volcanic ash are common adjacent to the Central Volcanic Region. On the drier soils, run-off is rapid under pasture and the soil–moisture conditions for pastoral growth are uneven. Nutrients other than phosphorus are moderate to high, and, with topdressing, excellent pastures for sheep and cattle grazing can be obtained. The chief farming problem is instability, caused in part by the effects of replacing forest with grass, and both slip and slump erosion are common. Careful pastoral management is required to lessen the occurrence of slips and gullying in stream channels. In the upper reaches of the Rangitikei and Wanganui valleys, where annual rainfalls exceed 1500 millimetres, the pastoral problems are increased by the lower level of soil nutrients and by the more aggressive growth of fern and manuka on surfaces exposed by erosion.

The effects of climate and vegetation on steepland soils are considerable. Soils developed on steep slopes under mull-forming, broadleaved–podocarp forest are moderately leached and, with topdressing, make excellent pastoral land. Soils developed under the mor-forming beech and podocarp forests of higher rainfall areas with lower temperatures are strongly leached, have very low fertility and are difficult to maintain in pasture, although they grow excellent crops of timber. On these soils the growth of vegetation is slow, and they are best retained for protection forest to conserve water supplies.

Steepland soils occur on Mt Egmont and adjoining

[1] The horizon categories are: A – Topsoil; B – Subsoil; G – Waterlogged; O – Organic; a figure following the category designation, as in A₂, indicates a subdivision.

ranges, and also extensively in the eastern half of Taranaki. The latter areas were once covered by ash showers, but the deposits have been removed, by erosion, from many steep slopes, exposing to soil formation underlying weathered marine sandstones or siltstones. On Egmont and adjacent ranges these rocks are andesitic lavas, the soils are stony and rocky, and they are best retained in protection forest.

Except for a low level of available phosphorus, steepland soils related to yellow-brown loams, as in east Taranaki, are moderately well supplied with plant nutrients. Their main problem is not fertility but stability, for the boundary between soil and rock is distinct, bonds between them are weak, and susceptibility to slip erosion increases with conversion from forest to grassland. Where grazing can be rotated in conjunction with the adjacent yellow-brown loams, pastoral farming has generally been successful. These steepland soils are capable of growing excellent crops of timber trees.

Steepland soils related to yellow-brown pumice soils are common throughout the Taupo and Bay of Plenty districts, where steep land has been smothered by showers of volcanic ash. The thick, porous mantle of the little-weathered Ngauruhoe and Tarawera ashes, or Taupo pumice, has been protected by forests that either survived the eruptions or were re-established quickly afterwards and allowed little run-off or surface erosion. The underlying rocks contribute to the soils where recent landslides have removed the ash mantle, or where deposits are shallow and roots penetrate into the underlying weathered materials. Generally this contribution is small, except on the Coromandel Peninsula where the ash deposits are quite weathered and eroded and the strongly weathered rhyolitic rocks are more exposed. Native forests are mainly podocarp–broadleaved on the lower slopes, grading into beech on higher slopes, and provide a shallow, mor humus layer to the soils. Small areas have been cleared for farming, but the general deterioration to low fertility after the initial flush from the forest burn, together with the aggressive invasion by ferns and shrubs, has resulted in general abandonment. Exotic forests have been established on areas of lower altitude, but for the most part these steepland soils are best kept under protection forest for water and soil conservation.

SOILS OF THE SOUTHERN REGION

Brown-grey earths occur in the driest parts of the Central Otago and southern Mackenzie basins. Profiles are characterised by platy, thin, brownish-grey topsoils and pale, yellowish-brown subsoils with a distinct claypan. Accumulations of calcium carbonate are common in the deep subsoil, and high concentrations of soluble salts may occur throughout the profile.

Most brown-grey earths occupy flat, sloping, undulating, rolling and hilly terrain on schist, colluvium and alluvium, with a thin surface layer of schist loess, under annual rainfalls of about 330–500 millimetres. They support scattered hard tussock and scabweed. The soils on schist are predominantly shallow, but in some places, largely on associated loess and colluvium, deep soils are developed with clay and calcium carbonate accumulations in the subsoil. Associated soils formed on Tertiary clays, sands and deeply weathered schist have heavy textures, blocky structures and contain soluble salts.

Deep soils on terraces and fans have dark grey, sandy loam topsoils overlying compact, olive, silt loam subsoils with coarse, prismatic structure and calcium carbonate accumulations at depths below one metre. Shallow soils

are mainly loamy sands over gravels with irregular calcium carbonate accumulations.

Brown-grey earths include some of the most fertile soils in Otago, as well as some of the least productive. With irrigation, the deep soils support intensive sheep farming and fruitgrowing. Careful and efficient irrigation is needed to increase productivity and to avoid deleterious effects such as waterlogging or contamination of nearby fertile soils by the flushing of soluble salts.

Southern yellow-grey earths are the dominant soils of the sub-humid downlands of the east coast of the South Island. Where relief is gentle, the loess mantle is continuous, but with steeper relief it becomes thinner and the soils are formed in part from the underlying Tertiary sandstones and mudstones. At the time of European settlement the yellow-grey earths supported mainly hard and silver tussock grassland. Today the arable downlands are under cultivation and used for mixed farming, incorporating pastoral and cereal cropping. Productivity is limited by the compact subsoils, which induce waterlogging in winter and accelerate summer drought. Topsoils are uniformly silt loam with fragile aggregates and the soils are accordingly prone to sheet erosion. In some places tunnel-gully erosion is also a hazard.

Genetic relationships of yellow-grey earths and their associated intergrades are expressed in the subsoil characteristics of soils developed on loess. Under low rainfalls of 500–575 millimetres, subsoils are pale and have weak horizon development and mottling; those under moderate rainfalls of 500–750 millimetres have distinct iron staining and mottling and a weakly structured B horizon over a massive fragipan; and those under higher rainfall have more clay, a nutty structured B horizon, and an underlying fragipan with coarse prismatic structure and distinct grey veins. Characteristics of subsoil and fragipan are also influenced in part by local variations in the thickness of the loess deposits and by the nearness of buried soils to the surface.

Shallow and stony soils associated with southern yellow-grey earths are extensive on flattish and sloping surfaces of older fans and terraces, particularly on the Canterbury plains and in the Waitaki valley. They have developed on coarse, greywacke gravels mantled with loess which is up to about forty centimetres thick. Under the sub-humid climate they are droughty and susceptible to wind erosion when cultivated. However they can be raised to moderate productivity under dryland farming techniques or to high pastoral production under controlled irrigation.

Southern yellow-grey earths are successfully used for intensive mixed farming. They respond to application of fertilisers containing phosphate, sulphur and molybdenum. *Southern yellow-brown earths* are widespread on the humid downlands and hills of Southland, Otago and Canterbury. They occur under annual rainfalls ranging from about 625 to 2000 millimetres.

Under lower rainfalls, southern yellow-brown earths are of low natural fertility and are typified by soils which are extensive on the schist uplands of Otago at altitudes ranging from 215 to 600 metres. They formed under annual rainfalls of 625–900 millimetres and a red fescue or silver tussock vegetation. They have profiles of dark greyish-brown, friable silt loams on yellowish-brown, friable silt loams. Unlike yellow-grey earths, they are free-draining and do not dry out in summer. At present they are used for extensive grazing and, with appropriate fertilisers and pasture management, are becoming more productive.

Southern yellow-brown earths developing under an annual rainfall of 1125 millimetres or more are extensive on the loess-covered, undulating terrace land between the Mataura and Waiau valleys in Southland. They supported red tussock and some podocarp–broadleaved forest at the time of European occupation. They are friable to firm silt loam with free drainage and, after applications of lime, phosphate and potash, are widely used for fat-stock production. The soils are strongly leached but show little clay or iron illuviation. Cobalt deficiency in Southland was first discovered in these soils.

Southern yellow-brown earths developing under high annual rainfalls of up to 2000 millimetres are represented by soils derived from mudstones and sandstones on the rolling and hilly land in western Southland. They are developed under mixed beech and podocarp forest. The surface soil is a thin, peaty loam, which rests on greyish-brown and yellowish-brown clay loam with nutty to blocky structures. They are strongly leached soils with some podzolised profiles in better drained sites.

Southern yellow-brown earths are well suited to pastoral farming when nutrient deficiencies are corrected, and to production forestry under the higher rainfall conditions, mainly in western parts of the region.

Southern podzolised yellow-brown earths and podzols in Southland are widespread on wet, coastal hills under podocarp–broadleaved forest with annual rainfalls of 1250–1500 millimetres. Parent materials range from greywackes in the east to Tertiary sediments in the Waiau Valley in the west and diorite and granite in Stewart Island. Soils form a sequence from weakly to moderately podzolised yellow-brown earths, with thick O_2 horizons, bleached A_2 horizons, and moderate to strong clay, iron and humus illuviation. These soils are largely under milled native forest which is slow to regenerate.

Soils resembling gley podzols derived from basic greywackes occur on the moderately steep, cold, wet Longwood Range of Southland under silver beech and subalpine scrub and tussock. They are best left in native vegetation.

Podzolised yellow-brown earths also occur in the cold, moist areas of eastern Otago. They are formed under tall tussock and subalpine herbs on schist uplands above 800 metres. A profile on an easy rolling slope shows dark grey, firm silt loam, on pale grey, mottled silt loam, separated by a six-millimetre red iron pan from yellowish-brown, silty clay loam. This soil is very strongly leached, has very slow drainage and is not suitable for pastoral or forestry production.

In general, southern podzolised yellow-brown earths and podzols have severe limitations for pastoral farming, and are best retained in native vegetation, or carefully managed for limited forestry production.

Southern yellow-brown sands occur in coastal locations in Canterbury, Otago and Southland. Yellow-brown sands formed on coastal sand dunes associated with gravelly beaches are extensive to the north and south of Banks Peninsula, and occur in coastal bays as far south as Dunedin. Soils vary widely in development but commonly have dark grey, loamy sand over olive-grey, loose sand. They are very droughty and of doubtful value for farming, but in places may be suited for commercial forestry. On some dunes, burning of the original tussock and shrubs has caused severe wind erosion and has necessitated the planting of marram grass for stabilisation.

Similar soils occupy a discontinuous strip of old beachlands along the southern coast of the South Island. The annual rainfall is 1150–2000 millimetres, and the natural vegetation is tussock, scrub and forest. There is a range of soil development, profiles varying widely from loose, yellow sands with a thin, grey topsoil to more weathered and leached loamy sands with a distinct brown B horizon. The natural fertility is low to very low, but in places pastures have been established by topdressing. Wind is a serious problem since it causes erosion after cultivation, and malformation of exotic trees.

Southern yellow-brown loams have developed on moraines from granite, gneiss and diorite of the last glaciation, in the upper Waiau valley, under rainfalls of 1000–1500 millimetres. Vegetation is stunted fern and scrub, with patches of beech forest that was more widespread in pre-European times. These soils are mostly stony and sandy loams with dark, greyish-brown, very friable, granular topsoils, bright brownish-yellow to yellowish-red, very friable, granular subsoils and hard, cemented pans. They are very strongly leached, their clay content is low, and allophane, hydrous micas and vermiculite have been identified. They have affinities with strongly leached yellow-brown earths.

Similar soils occupy stony outwash terraces and have gravelly subsoils. They support hard tussock and manuka but with heavy dressings of fertiliser maintain pastures for sheep and cattle.

Southern brown granular clays are of limited areal extent and occur as isolated pockets under a wide range of environments. They include some soils identifiable as brown granular loams.

Brown granular soils are developed from the basaltic lavas of Banks and Otago peninsulas, and are capable of intensive pastoral production, especially if topdressed. Other small outcrops occur elsewhere in the eastern part of the South Island, as, for example, in north Otago where such soils are derived from basaltic tuffs under a sub-humid climate and an annual rainfall of 500–625 millimetres. They are black, nut-structured clays, very sticky when wet, and are known locally as 'tarry soils'. In summer these north Otago soils dry out and fissure deeply. They must be cultivated during optimum moisture conditions to obtain a fine tilth, but their fertility is high and with suitable management they are highly productive for market gardening. Intergrades to rendzina soils are common where the tuffs are interbedded with limestone deposits.

Soils formed on the basalts of Otago Peninsula under broadleaved–podocarp forest and an annual rainfall of 625–900 millimetres have profiles of dark brown, friable silt loam on brown, nutty clay loam containing pieces of basalt. These soils are principally on hilly land and, when farmed with associated loess-derived soils on rolling land, are capable of intensive pastoral production.

Soils formed from basaltic rocks on the moister hills of the Dunedin district under podocarp forest up to about 900 metres, and under snow tussock above this altitude, have dark brown, firm silt loam with basalt stones on reddish-brown, stony clay. With topdressing, these and associated soils derived from loess and solifluction deposits are successfully used for sheep and cattle breeding and fattening.

Similar soils are formed on the steep slopes of Banks Peninsula under an annual rainfall of 1000–1250 millimetres. They have similar profiles and a high natural fertility. High yields of cocksfoot seed have been produced and, without fertilisers, these soils still support fair pastures after more than 100 years of farming. With fertilisers they become highly productive. Associated soils are derived from loess and underlying basalt, with profiles of yellowish-brown, silty subsoils, and they are related to yellow-brown earths. They need fertilisers to maintain good pastures.

Soils south of the Takitimu range in Southland are on hills of basic volcanic rocks and are formed under tussock and broadleaved shrubs and rainfall of 1000–1150 millimetres. Topsoils are friable, dark brown, granular stony loam to very dark reddish-brown, nutty silt loam and subsoils are dark brown, nutty, heavy silt loams. The soils are weakly leached, but are very low in available phosphorus. They are used for range grazing.

Similar soils occur mainly on the low terraces of the Southland plains between the Oreti and Aparima rivers, and in the Waiau valley. They are derived from thin, loess-like drift on gravels and are developed under a moist climate and predominantly tussock vegetation. Topsoils are dark brown, very friable silt loams with fine, nut to granular structure and subsoils are dark brown to yellowish-brown, friable silt loams with nutty to blocky structures. They are used largely for fat-stock production but are cropped more frequently than other Southland soils and are well suited for intensive mixed farming.

Southern recent, gley and organic soils are widely distributed over the flood plains and low terraces of the numerous rivers of the region. Recent soils are formed on alluvium ranging in texture from gravel to silt, derived from greywacke, tertiary sediments and loess. Fertility and use vary accordingly.

Recent and gleyed recent soils on the Southland plains commonly have dark brown A horizons merging into pale brown mottled B horizons and greenish-grey G horizons with yellow mottles. The native vegetation consisted of sedges, rushes and in places red tussock, flax and swamp forest. The older soils are moderately leached and have a higher base saturation in the G horizon than in the topsoil. Clay content increases down the profile and commonly iron content is highest in the B horizon.

Some of these soils occur on freely-draining parts of flood plains of the Ashley, Waimakariri, Selwyn, Rakaia, Ashburton, Hinds, Rangitata, Opihi, Waihao, Waitaki, Taieri and Clutha rivers. They range in texture from stony sand to deep silt loam, and have corresponding fertility and usefulness. Some soils have accumulated more slowly and have a greyish-brown topsoil that grades into a yellowish-brown, friable subsoil. Where the soils are deep, fine sandy and silt loams they are highly fertile and widely used for cropping.

Soils on free-draining intermediate terraces of the river valleys of the region receive small deposits of dust from the river beds. Profiles are mostly silt to sandy loam in texture and are dark greyish-brown in the topsoils, grading into pale yellowish-brown in the subsoils, which are firm rather than friable. The deep silt and sandy loams are widely used for mixed crop and pastoral farming and some have been successfully irrigated. The shallow silt and sandy loams have limited use for dryland cropping because of droughtiness and require irrigation for intensive use.

Soils occupying swampy parts of flood plains and low terraces are mainly of silt loam texture, of high natural fertility and, with drainage, capable of intensive use for mixed cropping and pastoral farming, or for dairying.

Recent soils also occur in narrow strips bordering river banks where wind-blown dusts have accumulated at the rapid rate of some two millimetres yearly. They are fine, sandy or silty soils with weakly developed structure and when cultivated are susceptible to wind erosion. They are used for pastoral farming with occasional cropping.

The gley soils occupy depressions of the coastal lowlands where ground water is close to the surface for most of the year. With increasing wetness they grade into organic soils.

Typical gley soils are formed from poorly-drained, silty alluvium with some organic matter from the native raupo and flax vegetation. They have profiles of dark grey silt loam over bluish-grey silt or clay loam, with orange mottles common in both horizons. The natural fertility is high as is production when the soils are suitably drained. However, the improved soils dry out in summer and spray irrigation is used on some dairy farms.

Some gley soils occur on saline marshes near the coast, particularly around Lake Ellesmere in Canterbury. In their natural state, the soils support salt-tolerant plants, but with drainage they can be converted to pastoral land with some cropping on less saline areas. Textures range from silt to sandy to peaty loams in topsoils and from silt loam to sand in the subsoil.

Organic soils in Canterbury and Otago are restricted to very swampy sites on the coastal lowlands where water tables are permanently at the surface and where decomposing organic matter has accumulated above the mineral soil. Typically they are derived from decomposed remains of sedges, rushes and flax, mixed with some silt and clay alluvium. The soils are very dark greyish-brown to dark brown peaty loams with granular structure on very dark brown loamy peat. When the swamps are carefully drained and managed, they become moderately to highly productive market-garden or dairying land. Additions of copper are required for onions, and to offset the high molybdenum content in the pasture.

In the southern part of the region, organic soils occur in peat bogs near Bluff and on Stewart Island. The surface layers are raw and at present unsuitable for agricultural use, but the more decomposed layers below might be made suitable for pasture if the surface layers were removed.

Southern steepland soils are widespread and are mainly associated with brown-grey earths, southern yellow-grey earths, southern yellow-brown earths and southern podzolised yellow-brown earths and podzols.

Soils related to brown-grey earths, occurring on the steep slopes of the dry inland ranges under rainfalls of less than 500 millimetres, are formed on schist and greywacke, and support depleted hard tussock and ephemeral introduced grasses. Widespread rock outcrops are a characteristic feature. Topsoils are sandy, with weakly developed platy structures, and overlie pale yellow or olive-brown stony subsoils with a pan of rock fragments in a matrix of clay. These soils are used for very extensive sheep grazing, but over-grazing and rabbits caused widespread erosion in the past.

Steepland soils associated with yellow-grey earths are derived from greywacke and schist on steep slopes under annual rainfalls of 425–900 millimetres. They support mainly hard tussock, with some silver tussock in damp sites and scrub in gullies. They are shallow and stony, with a weak, compact subsoil developed where there is deep loess or fine alluvium. Sheet and gully erosion is moderate to severe, some soils bearing spectacular screes. They are used for extensive sheep grazing, and topdressing and oversowing greatly increase yields of clover and pasture grasses.

Steepland soils which occupy the steep slopes of the drier coastal country, and the drier lower slopes of the foothills under silver and hard tussock grassland, have profiles comprising dark greyish-brown, stony silt loam on shattered greywacke. Deeper profiles on colluvial deposits are less droughty and their pastures respond well to superphosphate. They grade into the steepland soils on the flanks of the greywacke foothills which form the western boundary of the Canterbury plains, and have a higher annual rainfall.

Steepland soils associated with yellow-brown earths are extensive and are characterised by those occurring on steep and hilly foothills along the western edge of the Canterbury plains. These soils are developed from greywacke under an annual rainfall of 900–1150 millimetres and under mixed vegetation. Silver and hard tussock is extensive on drier areas and manuka, fern and beech forest grow in higher-rainfall areas. Forest was probably widespread before clearing by extensive burning began. A common profile on talus shows fifteen centimetres of dark grey, stony silt loam with nutty structure over brownish-yellow, stony silt loam. These soils have moderate natural fertility, are slow to erode and, with aerial oversowing and topdressing, make excellent pastoral land for sheep breeding.

Steepland soils related to podzols and podzolised yellow-brown earths are extensive on steep to very steep slopes from the coast inland to the axial ranges, from sea level to 900–1250 metres elevation, under rainfalls of 2–5000 millimetres. Soils derived from schist and greywacke support mainly rata–kamahi–rimu forest grading into subalpine scrub. Under a thin, fibrous litter, soils are characterised by shallow, dark brown sandy loam topsoils, very shallow, grey sandy loam A₂ horizons with rock fragments, and yellowish-brown, blocky, stony loam B horizons resting on schist. These soils are subject to sheet and slip erosion on very steep slopes where the forest cover has been weakened by the activities of introduced opossums and deer. Soils developed on greywacke, granites, sandstones and conglomerates under beech–podocarp (rimu) on lower slopes, and under mountain beech on higher slopes, have topsoils under forest litter which are shallow, greyish-brown sandy and silt loams, resting on yellowish-brown, blocky, stony and silt loams. Severe earthquakes have caused much slip and slump erosion on very steep granite and sandstone slopes, especially in the neighbourhood of Murchison and Karamea. These soils should be maintained in protection forests.

SOILS OF THE HIGH COUNTRY REGION

High country yellow-brown earths extend from Marlborough to Otago, commonly at elevations greater than 600 metres, and in many places between 900–1850 metres. They have developed on greywacke or schist parent materials, under annual rainfalls ranging from 1–2000 millimetres. The native vegetation was mainly tall tussock, with some mountain beech forest in places. Profiles have brown or greyish-brown, very friable, crumb silt or sandy loam topsoils and yellowish-brown, very friable, crumb or nutty subsoils. The soils are periodically covered with snow and are subject to numerous frosts. The friable, crumbly topsoils are protected against frost heave and accelerated erosion by the litter from decayed tussocks or from trees, but the destruction of tussocks and their litter, by fires and browsing animals, has led to widespread erosion shown by extensive screes. In many places on easy rolling to flattish terraces much topsoil has been removed by wind erosion, and a stony pavement is exposed.

Most high country yellow-brown earths have been used for extensive sheep farming, but the subalpine environment, their very low natural fertility, and their susceptibility to erosion indicate very clearly that in the interests of watershed protection, animal grazing should be strictly controlled.

High country podzolised yellow-brown earths and podzols are grouped on the map with high country gley and organic soils because they form part of a complex mosaic of soils that occupy wetter and higher subalpine regions, mainly in the South and Stewart Islands, but also in some small areas in the North Island.

High country podzols and podzolised yellow-brown earths are found under a wide range of vegetation, including subalpine scrub, rata, beech and cedar forest, and on a wide range of parent rocks, including schist, greywacke, granite, gneiss and sandstone. They occur predominantly in Nelson, Westland and Fiordland, generally above about 900 metres. The principal profile features of these soils are dark grey silt loam topsoils with crumb to nut structures grading downwards into grey to pale grey, nutty structured silt loam, sometimes with bluish-grey mottles, abruptly changing to a thin wavy iron pan up to five millimetres thick. The iron pan overlies a subsoil of yellowish-brown, friable, blocky structured silt loam merging to rock. Many variations occur in the soil profile, a number of which resemble gley podzols.

These soils are of little potential value for agriculture or commercial forestry, but they are important for water and soil conservation and for recreation.

High country gley and organic soils occur in complex association under rainfalls probably always in excess of 2000 millimetres. They are associated with high country podzols but generally occur under higher rainfalls and at higher altitudes. They are found on the flattish to rolling summits of non-glaciated mountain ranges in the central and southern parts of the North Island, in Otago and in Stewart Island. They also occur along the western flanks of the Southern Alps and in Fiordland where there is evidence of the gley process operating under a blanket of peat.

Organic soils are formed over granite, schist and a variety of other rocks, in places with very high rainfall, under snow grass, sedges and subalpine scrub. They are typified by soils occurring on steep mountain slopes in south Fiordland (annual rainfall more than 2500 millimetres), on Stewart Island and on the easy rolling slopes of the Blue Mountains in south-west Otago (more than 1500 millimetres rainfall). Their profiles have 1–1.5 metres of dark brown to black, well-decomposed, crumbly peat containing fragments of wood from *Dracophyllum* species and other woody plants, resting on bluish-grey, gleyed silt.

These soils are of no agricultural value, but they are important as reservoirs of water and therefore play a role in regulating run-off and maintaining flow in streams.

High country steepland soils are related mainly to high country yellow-brown earths, and to a lesser extent high country podzols, and are associated with them, from Marlborough to Otago. They occupy steep to very steep slopes (27° to more than 40°) on greywacke and schist at altitudes between 600 and 1850 metres, under rainfalls of 900–2500 millimetres. Vegetation ranges from tall tussock to forest. Steepland soils related to yellow-brown earths have thin, greyish-brown, friable, stony silt loam topsoils on yellowish-brown, friable silt loam subsoils overlying fragmented greywacke or schist. They are prone to erosion, screes being extensive. In the interests of soil and water conservation it is desirable that these soils should be maintained in protective vegetation.

Steepland soils related to high country podzols are extensive under high rainfall and forest cover near the Main Divide. Profiles are characterised by bright yellowish-brown subsoils and thin, discontinuous, bleached A₂ horizons. They are susceptible to erosion if disturbed and are therefore suitable only for protection forests.

OTHER SOILS

New Zealand's soil spectrum is too diverse to be shown comprehensively on a small-scale map. Important soils not recognised or described separately here, because of their limited areal extent, include rendzinas formed on limestone and other calcareous rocks, which occur in all regions except that of the high country; soils showing properties which intergrade between two main groups, such as intergrades between yellow-grey earths and yellow-brown earths, or between gley soils and recent soils; saline gley soils formed in coastal locations where drainage is poor; solonetzic soils which occur in semi-arid Central Otago and are formed where high levels of soluble salts accumulate; and recent soils on unconsolidated sand, which are related to yellow-brown sands.

Land Classification

Land can be quite readily classified for some specific purpose, such as pastoral farming, exotic forestry, fruit-growing or urban use, because such uses have defined and restricted needs in terms of the basic elements which make up land.

But because all the purposes for which land may be used require a multitude of diverse and, in some cases, conflicting conditions, it is very difficult to portray on one small-scale map an all-purpose land classification. Probably the best that can be achieved is to group those basic elements of land which are most relevant to most uses.

In the Land Classification map shown here, the surface of New Zealand has been considered simply in five broad landform categories, subdivided on the basis of broad climatic conditions, which are equated with the main soil zones. Indications of the range and intensity of land use are given in the description of each of the soil groups in the text, as in turn they are discussed.

The Land Utilisation map depicts the location and extent of the predominant types of current land use, and the legend to this map indicates the soil groups on which each activity is based.

It is important to appreciate that on small-scale maps such as these, considerable generalisations need to be tolerated in order to make a useful pattern. In particular, important variations which occur over short distances cannot be shown; for example, the Heretaunga plains consist predominantly of fertile, alluvial land but they also contain important areas of stony pumice, peat and saline lands, all of which have different land uses. Only one category can be shown on a small-scale map. Furthermore, certain liberties have had to be taken with the strict interpretation of the various categories in order to avoid unacceptable complications; for example, the Waikato peat lands are not true bottom lands in the sense used, but it was considered sensible to group them with the peat lands of the Hauraki plains and the Bay of Plenty.

The soil resources of New Zealand are diverse and bountiful. But although soil properties are generally advantageous for most land-based activities, they may impose limitations on specific uses in certain places and it is important that this is recognised in land-use planning. Productive land-use and environmental harmony can both be achieved by the balanced management of our soil resources.

THE DIVERSITY OF NEW ZEALAND SOILS
Four Soil Type Identifications
Scales are in metres and in centimetres

Northern Red Loam

Identification: Red colour; friable consistence; well-developed structure.

Environment: Formed on basaltic scoria under a warm, humid climate.

Main limitations for use: High phosphate retention and a tendency to droughtiness.

Predominant uses: Market gardening and dairying.

Central Yellow-Brown Sand

Identification: Sandy textures; weak structures; dark-coloured topsoil over yellowish-brown subsoil.

Environment: Coastal sand drifts under a mild subhumid climate.

Main limitations for use: Droughty on dune ridges and susceptible to wind erosion; poorly drained in depressions; deficient in phosphate and potash and some trace elements.

Predominant uses: Pastoral farming for dairying and for lamb production; exotic forestry on the excessively drained soils.

Northern Podzol

Identification: Organic rich topsoil underlain by leached, ash-grey horizon which overlies a dark-coloured, clay textured subsoil grading into paler coloured weakened rock.

Environment: Warm humid to superhumid climate under kauri vegetation.

Main limitations for use: Very low plant nutrient levels; firm and massive subsoils; poorly drained.

Predominant uses: Semi-extensive pastoral farming.

Central Recent Soil from Alluvium

Identification: Uniform colour, texture, consistence and structure throughout the profile apart from slight darkening in the topsoil.

Environment: On river floodplains under a mild, humid climate.

Main limitations for use: Flooding.

Predominant uses: Cropping, market gardening, horticulture, intensive pastoral farming.

Above, an oblique aerial photograph of Reefton with below, the divisions of the area into Soils and Land Use.

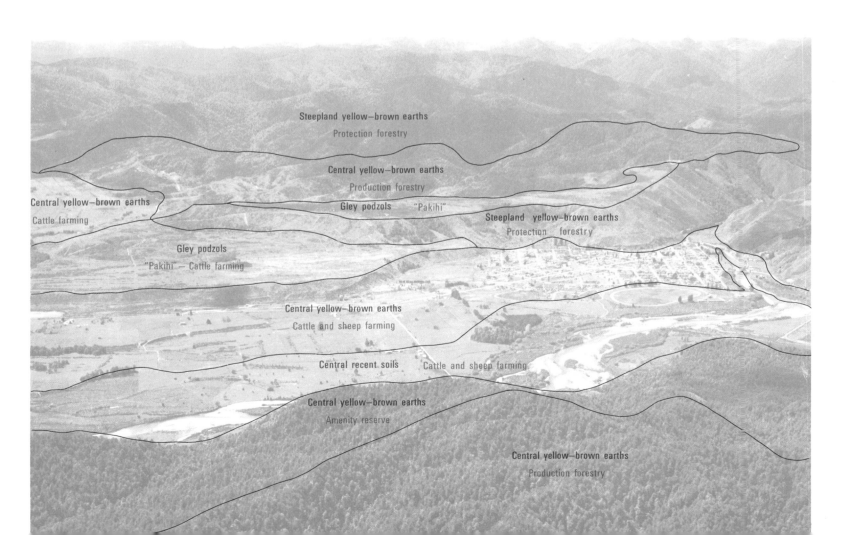

Steepland yellow—brown earths

Protection forestry

Central yellow—brown earths

Production forestry

Central yellow—brown earths

Cattle farming

Gley podzols   "Pakihi"

Steepland yellow—brown earths

Protection forestry

Gley podzols

"Pakihi" — Cattle farming

Central yellow—brown earths

Cattle and sheep farming

Central recent soils   Cattle and sheep farming

Central yellow—brown earths

Amenity reserve

Central yellow—brown earths

Production forestry

Satellite imagery is being employed increasingly in the collection of land resource data. Soil surveys are being compiled from these aids in some parts of New Zealand. The photograph shows a tract of North and Central Otago in false colour as derived from the Earth Resources Technology Satellite on 8 December 1973. From this photograph land classes comprising soil zones and landforms have been derived for the figure below. The symbols are those used for the Land Classification map on page 141.

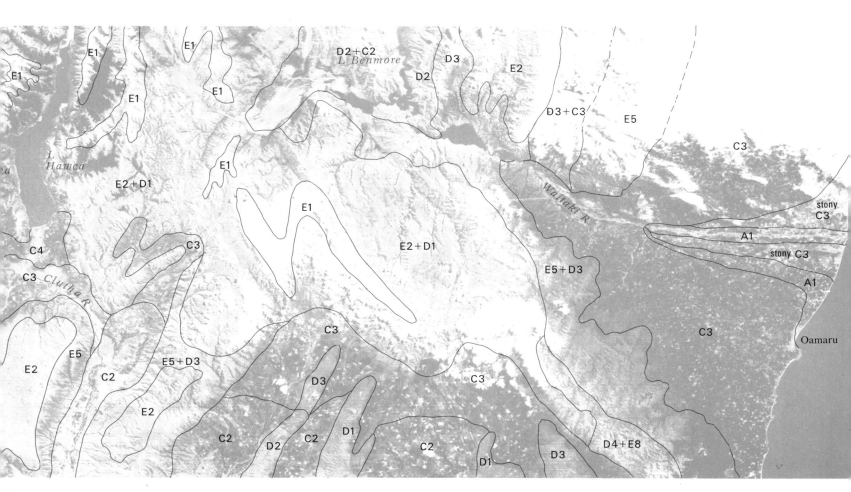

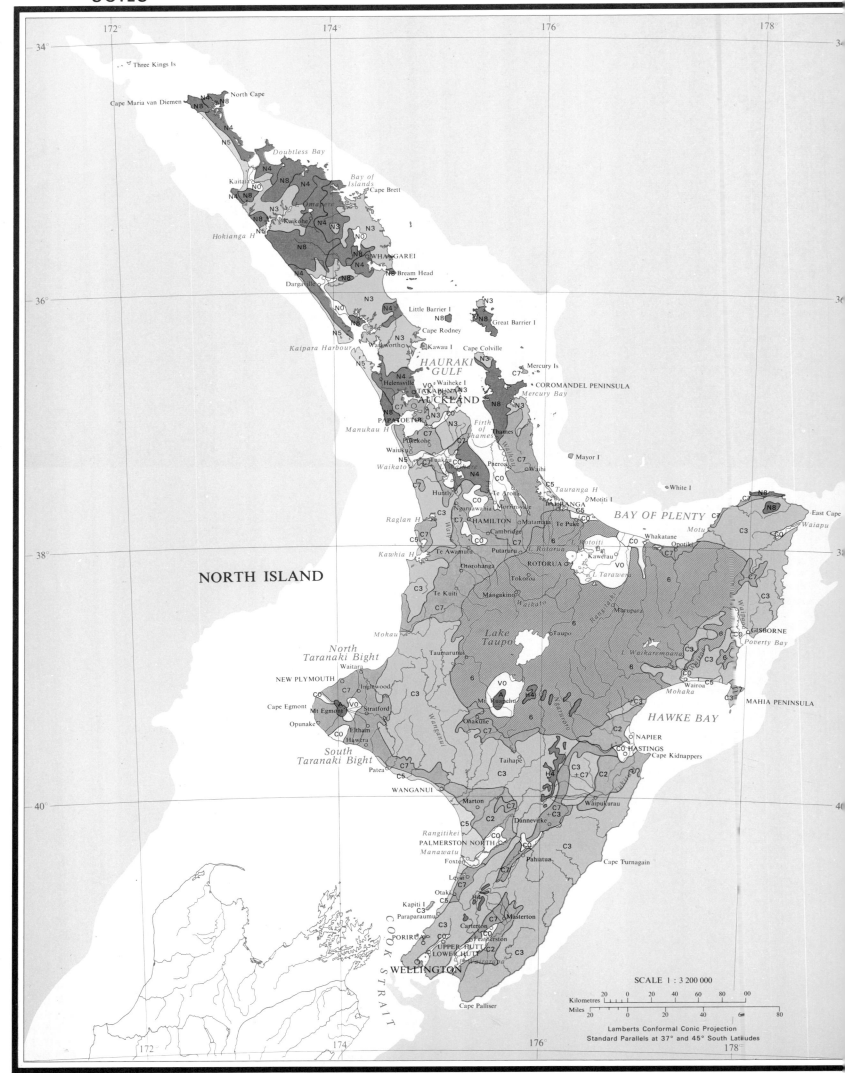

NORTH ISLAND

SCALE 1 : 3 200 000

Kilometres
Miles

Lamberts Conformal Conic Projection
Standard Parallels at 37° and 45° South Latitudes

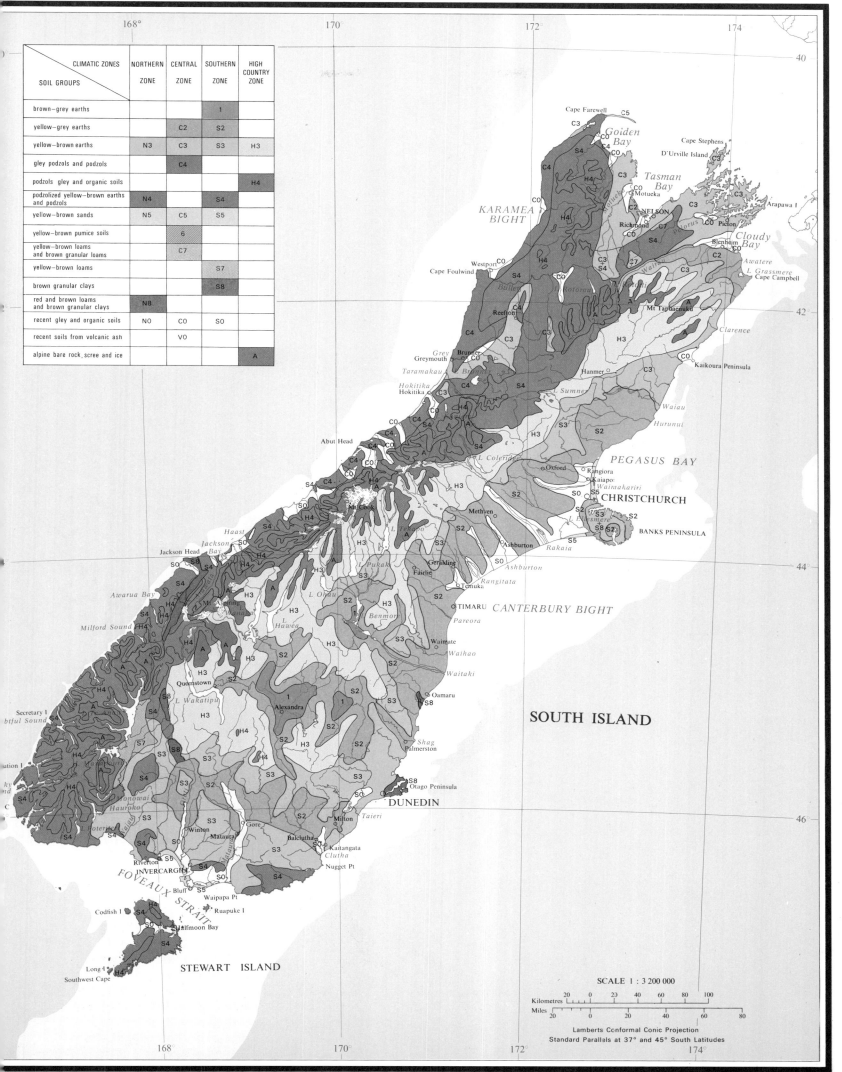

CLIMATIC ZONES / SOIL GROUPS	NORTHERN ZONE	CENTRAL ZONE	SOUTHERN ZONE	HIGH COUNTRY ZONE
brown–grey earths			1	
yellow–grey earths		C2	S2	
yellow–brown earths	N3	C3	S3	H3
gley podzols and podzols		C4		
podzols gley and organic soils				H4
podzolized yellow–brown earths and podzols	N4		S4	
yellow–brown sands	N5	C5	S5	
yellow–brown pumice soils		6		
yellow–brown loams and brown granular loams		C7		
yellow–brown loams			S7	
brown granular clays			S8	
red and brown loams and brown granular clays	N8			
recent gley and organic soils	NO	CO	SO	
recent soils from volcanic ash		VO		
alpine bare rock, scree and ice				A

SOUTH ISLAND

STEWART ISLAND

SCALE 1 : 3 200 000

Lamberts Conformal Conic Projection
Standard Parallels at 37° and 45° South Latitudes

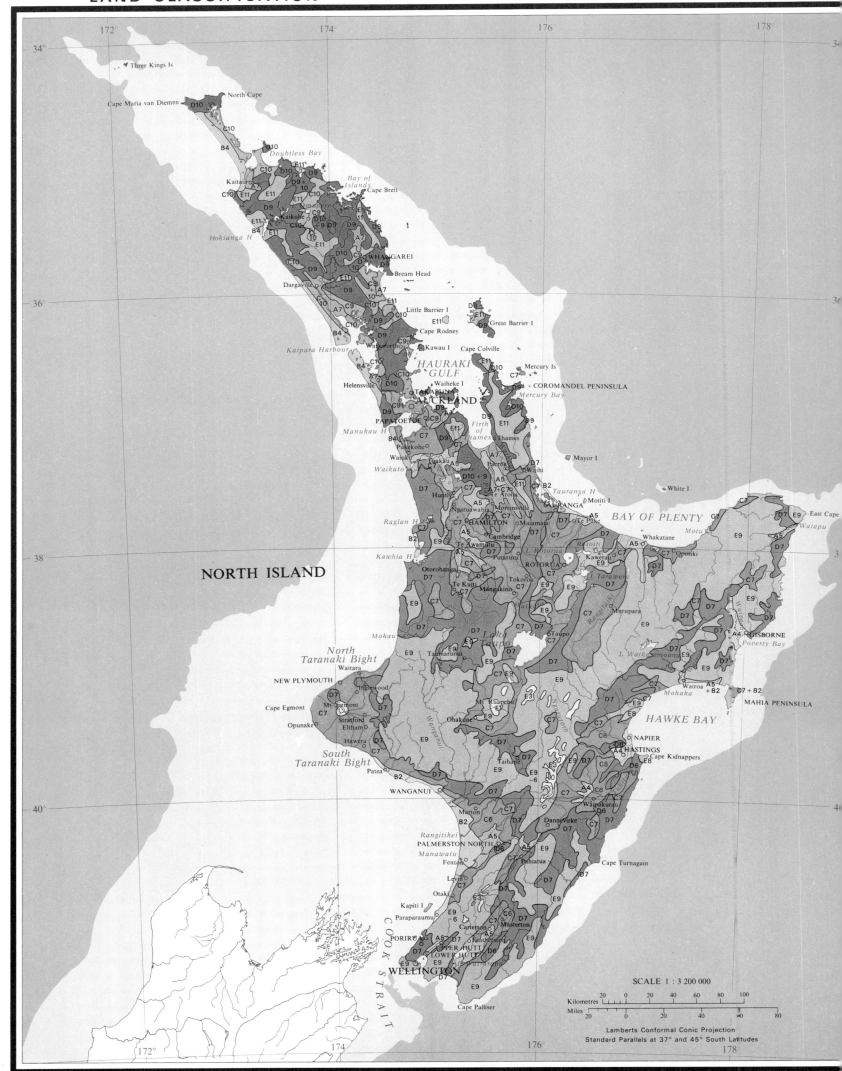

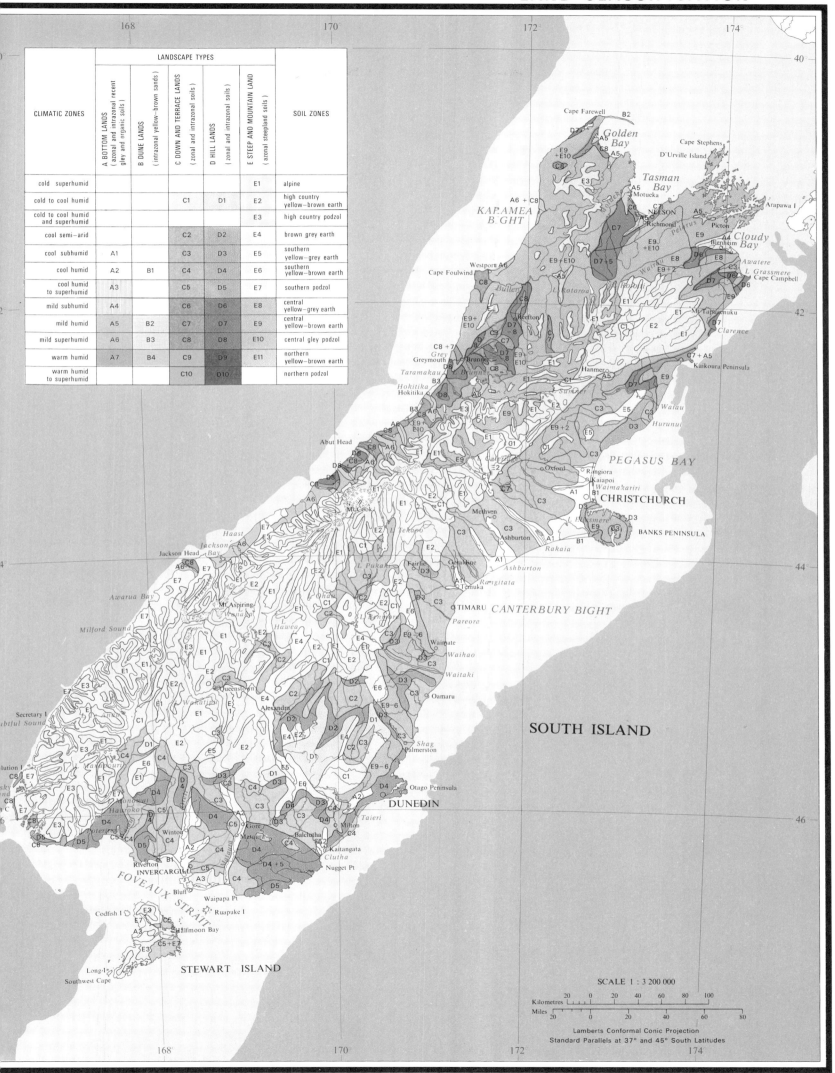

CLIMATIC ZONES	LANDSCAPE TYPES					SOIL ZONES
	A BOTTOM LANDS (azonal and intrazonal recent gley and organic soils)	B DUNE LANDS (intrazonal yellow–brown sands)	C DOWN AND TERRACE LANDS (zonal and intrazonal soils)	D HILL LANDS (zonal and intrazonal soils)	E STEEP AND MOUNTAIN LAND (azonal steepland soils)	
cold superhumid					E1	alpine
cold to cool humid			C1	D1	E2	high country yellow–brown earth
cold to cool humid and superhumid					E3	high country podzol
cool semi–arid			C2	D2	E4	brown grey earth
cool subhumid	A1		C3	D3	E5	southern yellow–grey earth
cool humid	A2	B1	C4	D4	E6	southern yellow–brown earth
cool humid to superhumid	A3		C5	D5	E7	southern podzol
mild subhumid	A4		C6	D6	E8	central yellow–grey earth
mild humid	A5	B2	C7	D7	E9	central yellow–brown earth
mild superhumid	A6	B3	C8	D8	E10	central gley podzol
warm humid	A7	B4	C9	D9	E11	northern yellow–brown earth
warm humid to superhumid			C10	D10		northern podzol

SCALE 1 : 3 200 000

Kilometres 20 0 20 40 60 80 100

Miles 20 0 20 40 60 80

Lamberts Conformal Conic Projection
Standard Parallels at 37° and 45° South Latitudes

SOUTH ISLAND

STEWART ISLAND

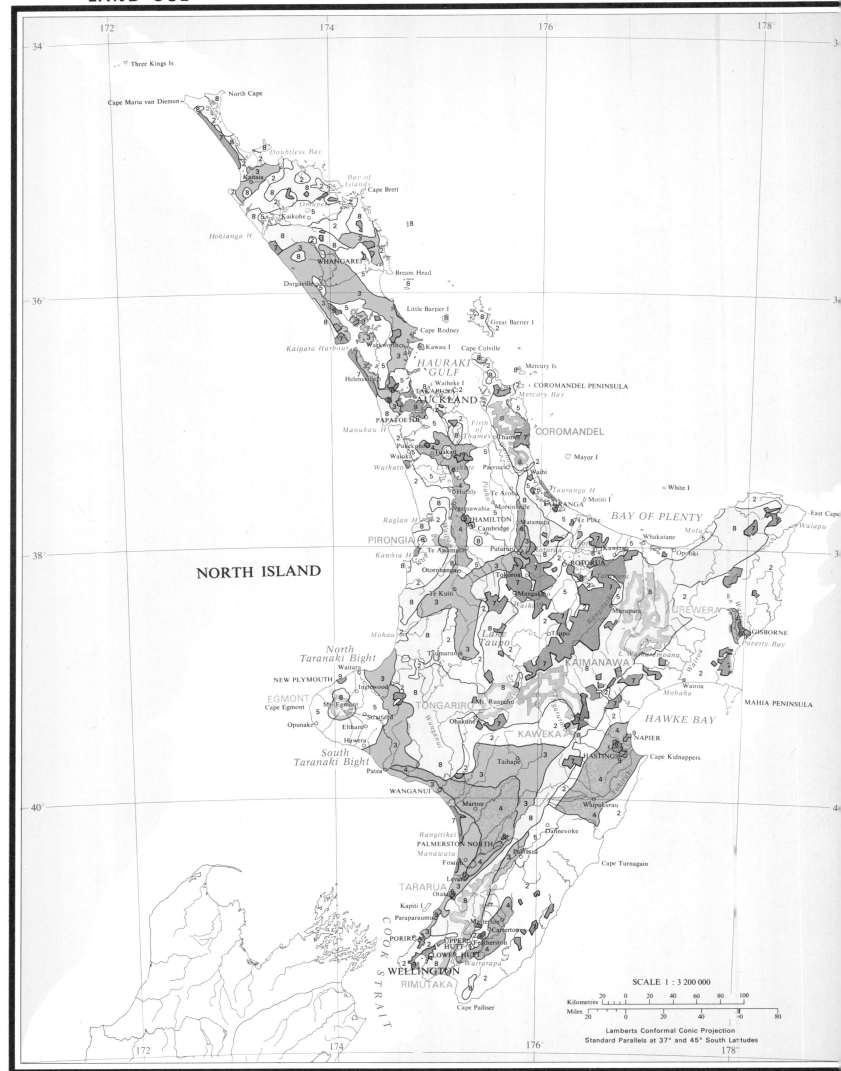

NORTH ISLAND

SCALE 1 : 3 200 000

Kilometres 20 0 20 40 60 80 100
Miles 20 0 20 40 80

Lamberts Conformal Conic Projection
Standard Parallels at 37° and 45° South Latitudes

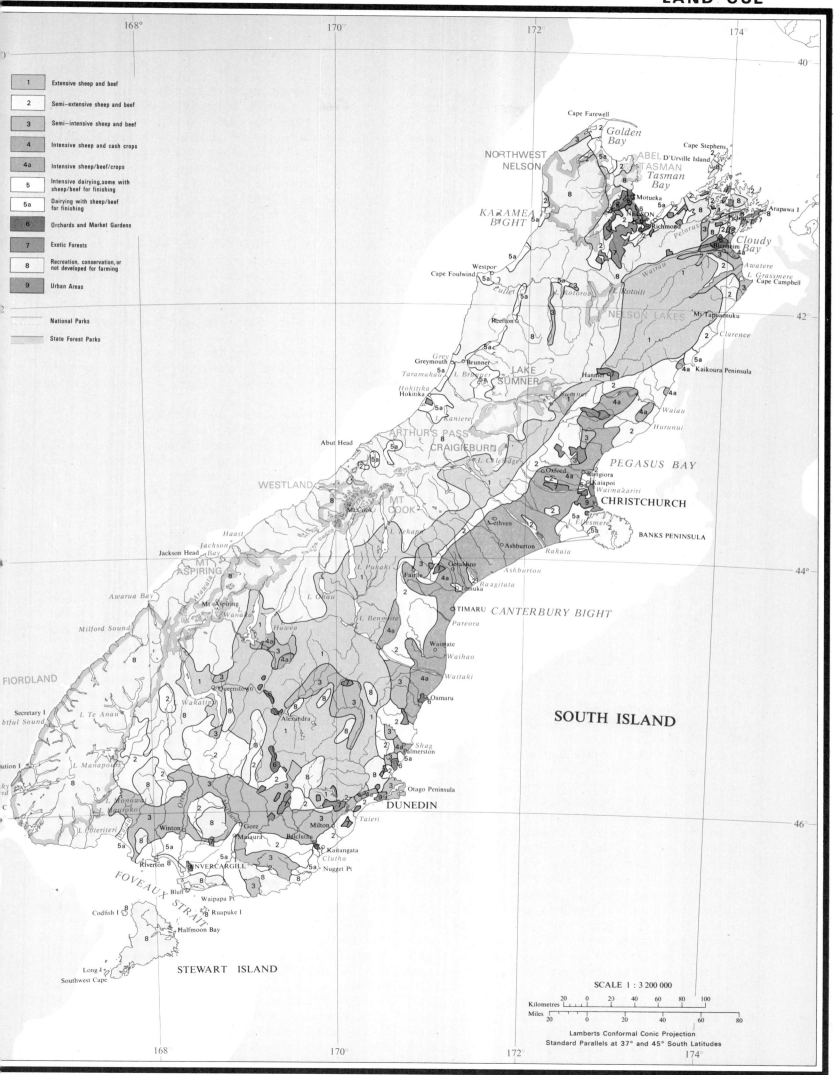

Legend:

1	Extensive sheep and beef
2	Semi-extensive sheep and beef
3	Semi-intensive sheep and beef
4	Intensive sheep and cash crops
4a	Intensive sheep/beef/crops
5	Intensive dairying, some with sheep/beef for finishing
5a	Dairying with sheep/beef for finishing
6	Orchards and Market Gardens
7	Exotic Forests
8	Recreation, conservation, or not developed for farming
9	Urban Areas

National Parks

State Forest Parks

SOUTH ISLAND

STEWART ISLAND

SCALE 1 : 3 200 000

Kilometres   20   0   20   40   60   80   100
Miles   20   0   20   40   60   80

Lamberts Conformal Conic Projection
Standard Parallels at 37° and 45° South Latitudes

FARMING

P. R. Stephens

No account of New Zealand agriculture would be complete without full description of its organisation and structure. Not only is agriculture of vital importance, providing more than eighty per cent of export income, but the system of farming that has been evolved is, in many respects, unique. High levels of productivity are attained, and output per person engaged is as great as anywhere in the world.

A distinctive feature of New Zealand agriculture is that the major pastoral industries have been developed for export markets and have had to adapt themselves to the requirements of those markets. This state of affairs creates instability, but it also imposes a discipline upon producers.

Of a total land area of about twenty-seven million hectares, only some two-thirds is occupied and less than half is in established pasture. The area of really productive land amounts to about four million hectares, and much of this is not naturally very fertile. Its present productive capacity has been built up by heavy application of fertiliser and by careful grazing management.

The topography, climate and soil types of New Zealand are discussed in other articles. The significant fact here is not only that the climate is suited to pasture production, but also that systems of farm management have been adapted to exploit this situation. A well distributed rainfall and an absence of extremes of heat and cold enable pasture growth to be maintained for the greater part of the year in much of the country, so that animal production does not require a large area of fodder crops and costly feed grains, and animals do not have to be housed in winter. These latter factors keep labour requirements to a minimum, capital does not have to be tied up in plant or buildings, and feed costs are low. Obviously there are many qualifications and modifications: for example, in some districts lack of soil moisture in the late summer virtually brings pasture growth to a halt, and management must be adapted to such conditions.

The Pioneers

Europeans on their arrival in New Zealand were initially dependent on Maori food producers. The latter had evolved a system of agriculture well attuned to their primitive technology, but were not slow to adopt new crops, particularly fruit, potatoes and maize, to breed pigs and to use European steel tools. For their part the European settlers, particularly in the Wakefield settlements, consciously tried to re-create the pattern of rural England, but the futility of such efforts very soon became apparent. New Zealand, like Australia, could develop in the early stages only on the basis of extensive sheep farming. Old world skills, modified by Australian experience, could be further adapted to local needs. To some extent, the 'squatters' age' represented a narrowing of the range of opportunities open to the prospective settler because of the need for capital for stock purchase, but there seemed no alternative.

Between the mid-1840s, when squatting began in the Wairarapa, and the 1860s, practically all the open country suitable for grazing in both the South Island and the southern half of the North Island was occupied and stocked, and some extensive flocks had been built up. Managerial processes suited to extensive sheep farming had already been evolved in Australia; in New Zealand they were readily adapted to a climate not dissimilar to that in England and Scotland. A ready supply of Merino breeding stock was available from Australia, although its suitability, under New Zealand conditions, was sometimes questionable.

Progress was naturally slower in the bush-covered areas of the North Island, the task of clearing and burning them not really getting under way until the 1870s when the Maori wars were over, labour more plentiful and roads of a sort built. In the space of some thirty years, millions of acres of forest were cleared, to be replaced by pastures of varying quality. At the time few queried the desirability of such changes; in fact many demands were made to the government for them to be hastened.

Much of the North Island was cleared and burned by the 1880s. The advent of refrigeration then provided a needed boost to the country's economy, for the system of extensive sheep farming had gone about as far as was possible in the light of existing knowledge. None the less, depressed prices for wool in the same period countered the effects of the increasing meat, and later dairy, exports. Refrigeration's main contribution was the creation of a better economic basis for closer settlement, a development coinciding with increasing population and political change.

Consolidation and Development

In the South Island during the 1890s, closer settlement was assumed to be a step towards the establishment of a system of mixed farming on the British model, and to a greater or lesser extent this objective was achieved; in the North Island these traditional concepts proved much less satisfactory. Climate and soil were such that attempts to establish mixed farms generally ended in dismal failure. By virtue of necessity, farmers had to adopt novel approaches to management, including the wholly new concept that the growing of grass should be considered the primary objective. This change of approach did not come about abruptly and it was not until after the First World War that New Zealand agriculture came to depend mainly on the effective exploitation of pastures, with arable and other fodder crops of secondary importance.

Another factor encouraging the evolution of grassland farming was the growth of the dairy industry. With some help from government, as dairying provided a good economic basis for closer settlement, dairy farming and dairy factories increased in number in the North Island, from the 1890s onwards in Taranaki and more slowly in the Waikato. It was in the latter area that farmers, whether they were dairying or not, were compelled to review their traditional methods. Here more than elsewhere large land companies had undertaken the initial development of much of the open scrub and fern covered country, with the objective of eventually disposing of it on profitable terms. The failure of many of these companies forced those occupying the land to look to new methods and gradually many of them must have become aware that the only crop that grew well was the grass around the stock yards or in paddocks that had been manured to give a boost to turnips or other fodder crops.

In the years before 1914 the more far-sighted farmers in the Waikato and Taranaki were applying basic slag with the straightforward objective of boosting pasture growth. They were also beginning to see that it might be possible virtually to dispense with the plough and annual crops and to rely almost entirely on grass supplemented by hay or perhaps silage. Dairy farmers were the first to adopt new management techniques along these lines, much assisted by the development of home milk separation, milking machines and improvements in milking shed. design. The pace of development, particularly in the Waikato, quickened after the First World War.

The re-organised Department of Agriculture, after 1918, created the machinery to disseminate scientific ideas and to adapt them to local needs and situations. It was in this period that the present form and structure of New Zealand agriculture emerged, based on the intensive utilisation of pastures to produce meat, milk and wool, even if much of the wool was derived from hill country where the newer techniques then had little relevance. Heavy applications of superphosphate, which became much cheaper with the exploitation of the rock phosphate on Nauru Island and the establishment of large works in New Zealand, closer sub-division and careful grazing management helped to build up fertility and to allow a higher carrying capacity. The increase of phosphate in the soil allowed clover to be established, thus further improving fertility. Inevitably progress was uneven, but a basic change had been made in the approach to livestock production and a system had been developed which enabled New Zealand to exploit its major natural asset, grassland. At the same time, the already traditional absence of a need for a large force of agricultural labourers was confirmed.

Over the forty years from 1930 to 1970 the evolution of New Zealand farming consisted very largely of refinements and adaptations of the techniques worked out in the 1920s. These techniques were improved and developed on land which was accessible to wheeled vehicles, but on the steeper hill country little could be accomplished. In the North Island areas where the bush had been cleared the farmer had also to struggle against the land's reversion to fern and second growth, particularly if he lacked enough capital to fence his property adequately and to carry sufficient stock.

Low returns from wool and store stock throughout the 1930s and, later, shortages of labour and materials during the Second World War limited further major advances in farming techniques, until local experiments showed that light training aircraft could be used to drop fertiliser from the air. After the War there was no lack either of suitable aircraft or of pilots, and improved revenues from wool and meat from the late 1940s enabled farmers to meet the costs involved. Gradually the fertility of millions of acres of previously inaccessible hill country was built up. Aerial topdressing has been followed by better sub-division, the construction of access tracks, the building of stock water dams and the introduction of higher-producing pasture strains.

The application of scientific research to agriculture began even before 1900, but it was at first on a very limited scale. In the 1920s an organised programme of research was initiated by the government, attention being directed to the study of fertiliser responses and to the improvement of pasture strains. Much less was undertaken in the broad field of animal production, as it was correctly assumed that the immediate objective was to ensure that animals were better fed. Men such as Cockayne and Levy developed the study of pasture ecology, and were as concerned with animal grazing as with actual plant associations and successions. The identification of higher-producing strains of rye grass, the emphasis on the key role of clover and the need for the phosphate status of the soil to be raised to enable it to be established, were significant. Subsequently, superior strains of various pasture species have been evolved, some designed to meet particular seasonal requirements. Advances along these lines were the more effective when they were associated with improved management practices.

Investigations and correction of trace element deficiencies have been particularly important. 'Bush sickness', or cobalt deficiency, in the centre of the North Island and in parts of Nelson first attracted the attention of research workers to this field.

Types of Farming

New Zealand farmers now run about 60 million sheep, including 43 million breeding ewes, about 3 million dairy cattle and 5–6 million beef type cattle. From these flocks and herds are produced more than one million tonnes of meat, 320 million kilogrammes of wool, 280 kilogrammes of butterfat and 240 000 tonnes of butter, 100 000 tonnes of cheese and about 200 000 tonnes of milk powder and casein. Farmers also grow about 200 000 hectares of cereals, sufficient for local needs; 20 000 hectares of vegetables; 9000 hectares of fruit, from which apples and pears are used for both local and export markets. Pig farming produces up to about 40 000 tonnes annually; poultry yields some 85 million dozen eggs and a broiler production of about 25 000 tonnes annually. Some 2000 hectares of land are used for viticulture, producing 284 000 litres of wine.

Despite the growth in home demand resulting from a larger population, the proportion of total farm production exported has remained high, with that for beef having risen. The country's ability to maintain its position in overseas markets has been dependent upon its adaptability and capacity to keep its prices fully competitive; to do this successfully various management systems have been evolved, most based on intensive exploitation of pastures, though varying according to climate and topography.

DAIRY FARMING

Dairy farming is largely confined to flat to rolling land in the North Island where the rainfall is more than 120 centimetres annually—the Waikato, Northland, Bay of Plenty, Taranaki and Manawatu districts. The typical dairy farm has an area of from forty to sixty hectares and in recent years carries 100–120 cows. Ten years ago the same property might have carried 80–100 cows. No permanent labour is employed, but jobs such as hay baling and spreading fertiliser are done by contractors who may be called in for other tasks as well. The farmer's wife probably assists with the milking and receives payment for doing so. A good deal of attention will have been given to sub-division, with the farm being divided into twenty or thirty paddocks, as many as possible of these being directly accessible from a central race. An ample supply of water in each paddock is important.

The herd is moved around the farm to make the most effective use of the new growth in each paddock, with the replacement calves preceding the herd to ensure that they get the best feed. In the late spring and early summer a number of paddocks are closed up for hay or silage, about twenty bales of hay per cow being adequate insurance for the winter or for a dry spell in late summer. The greater part of the farm is topdressed each year with a super-phosphate–potash mixture at about 3–400 kilogrammes per hectare, but unless a pasture has obviously deteriorated it is not ploughed up. Implements other than a light tractor are few. The milking shed is designed for speed in handling the cows and at the same time for ease in cleaning. About ninety per cent of the total milk produced is collected by tanker, home separation now being confined to the few areas where tanker collection is uneconomic. The construction of better designed milking sheds from the mid-1950s onwards enabled farmers to handle more cows and encouraged them to stock their properties more heavily.

About one dairy farm in five is operated by a sharemilker, the most common arrangement being for the sharemilker to own the herd and to receive fifty per cent of the receipts from milk products in return for the use of the land.

A distinctive feature of the New Zealand dairy industry is its wholly co-operative character. The co-operative system existed from the earliest period in the industry's history, and gradually expanded, possibly because proprietary companies did not find the business very profitable. There was no class of large farmers, as in the meat industry, with sufficient capital to invest in processing facilities, nor did overseas companies evince much interest in the manufacture of dairy products. On the other hand, in the industry's earlier stages, neither cheese nor butter factories, of the capacity that were generally built, required a capital investment beyond the scope of local resources. Factory size and the collection area were determined in fact by the time it took a horse and cart to reach the factory by, say, 9.0 a.m.

Cream collection by truck began in the early 1920s; the development of the dairy industry has always been closely associated with improvement in roads, and tanker collection of whole milk began in the early 1950s, although cheese factories adopted it rather later. Whole milk collection by tanker and the expansion of skim powder and casein manufacture have enabled the industry to rationalise its production, eliminate small, uneconomic factories and introduce a greater degree of mechanisation. Yet in 1973 there were still about ninety dairy companies in the country, ranging in size from the New Zealand Co-operative Dairy Company in the Waikato with an annual output valued at $150 million, to some small cheese companies in the South Island with an output valued at $200,000 per annum. Scope for further rationalisation therefore remains, though strong local loyalties may continue to delay seemingly desirable amalgamations.

FAT-LAMB AND CATTLE FARMING

Management practices on dairy farms do not vary to any great extent from one district to another, although feed conservation requirements may; ground rules are much the same. With sheep farming, whether or not it is combined with the running of beef cattle, the situation is very different. Apart from the final product, there are few points of similarity between an intensive lamb-and-beef production unit in the North Island, on land that could also be used for dairy farming, and a high country sheep station in the South Island. In the mixed farming areas of the South Island, livestock production is dovetailed into a system of cropping not dissimilar to that carried out in the United Kingdom.

The fat-lamb farmer's objective, like the dairy farmer's, is to take full advantage of the rapid pasture growth in the spring and early summer; the aim of his management is to ensure that his ewe flock has sufficient feed to enable the lambs to be fully fattened before they are weaned so that he does not have to provide them with any special feed. But he also has to deal with his beef herd, which has a production cycle of at least two years. He needs, therefore, a fair amount of supplementary feed both for his sheep and cattle in the winter and for his ewe flock in the late summer when pastures may have dried up. Generally only in times of drought or flood will he think in terms of feeding grain meal to his animals. In the South Island he will have to grow more fodder crops, partly because he will plough up his land more frequently anyway and partly because the period when pasture growth is dormant is longer.

HIGH COUNTRY FARMING

Hill country farms in the North Island are usually on land that was cleared of forest in the last three decades of the nineteenth century or was covered in heavy fern. Guthrie Smith's 'Tutira' was one of the latter: the process of breaking it in was largely one of trying to find enough stock to trample and chew down the fern. If pastures are not properly established on hill country that has been cleared of bush, fern will quickly take over to be replaced by second growth—a complex association of native species—that may provide the cover for the ultimate regeneration of native forest. Just how long this process of regeneration may take, if left undisturbed, is a matter that plant ecologists have studied closely and, although much data on plant associations and successions has been accumulated, it is still a subject of controversy.

A combination of low natural fertility and the pressure towards reversion meant that hill country farming was always something of a struggle—many men were forced to give up after the First World War and in the depression of the 1930s. Then the advent of aerial topdressing changed the picture. Many hill country properties have been developed until they are able to fatten a proportion of their stock and to build up their cattle numbers, which in turn allows more scientific grazing management. Yet farmers on these properties still depend heavily on the sale of wool and store stock; the recession in wool prices from 1967 to 1971 hit them severely.

High country sheep stations in the South Island have always seemed to have glamorous qualities, perhaps because of their remoteness and size. They are much larger than most other farms; wool and store stock as well as some cattle are practically the only products; most of the land is held on Crown lease and scope for change or development is rigidly limited. Comparatively few sheep can be carried through the winter; with a shorter growing season and little capacity to produce supplementary crops, this limitation must be accepted. Flocks are generally Merino or halfbred; they seem to be well adapted to the system of extensive management and move readily up to the higher country in summer.

Probably the bulk of the fine wool produced on these properties is sold to local manufacturers and would amount in total to not more than two to three per cent of New Zealand's total production. The economic contribution made by the high country must be seen in this context, and the desirability of continuing to graze some of it may be called into question on the grounds of conservancy.

CATTLE FARMING

The most significant development over the past twenty years has been the great increase in the number and proportion of cattle run in association with sheep. Up until the Second World War, the greater part of the beef produced was sold in the local market; that exported fetched a low price. Just before the War, the establishment of the chilled beef trade promised better returns, but the risks were always high and the trade, interrupted by the war, was not resumed until the early 1950s. Wartime prices for beef were not particularly encouraging. Any description of the management system up to the mid-1950s always laid stress on the fact that cattle were used as cultivating implements—to trample fern and second growth on hill country and to keep down rank growth on the better-class land. Here each beast might be kept for three or four years, as the older animals were more efficient and heavier implements than younger ones.

With the opening up of the American market for manufacturing grades of beef in the mid-1950s, the position changed rapidly, and beef cattle numbers expanded steadily. Dairy farmers have also gained a useful income supplement as cull dairy cows have increased considerably in value. Large numbers of cattle demanded improved sub-divisional fences, better water supplies and more winter feed. Additional revenue from beef was a major factor in countering the fall in wool prices between 1966 and 1972. Export sales of beef equalled those for lamb in 1971. The rise in wool and lamb prices in 1972 slowed down the growth in cattle numbers, although the growth is expected to continue.

CEREAL PRODUCTION

In New Zealand, cereal production has never occupied the key position that it has in Western Europe and North America. On the heavier land in the South Island, where annual rainfall is between seventy-five and eighty-five centimetres, most of the country's wheat and barley is grown. Some farmers specialise in cash crops and obtain the bulk of their revenue from this source, though they must make a considerable investment in both cultivating and harvesting machinery. Others grow a more limited and changing area and are more influenced by the returns from wool and lamb. Barley is a spring-sown crop that allows more flexibility than wheat, and its increased production over the past decade has been associated with an expanding demand for various stock feeds, including poultry compounds. Oats are now reduced to an area of less than 15 000 hectares a year, a substantial change from the situation early this century when ten times that area was harvested. Maize is confined largely to Poverty Bay, the Bay of Plenty and the Waikato. High yields have been obtained in these latter areas from land used for many years for intensive dairying.

PIG FARMING

Pig production was developed as a side line for dairy farmers, the pigs being fed on skim milk which then had no other uses. With the steady increase in skim milk powder production over the past twenty-five years, the pig industry has become more specialised and animals are fattened on meal.

POULTRY FARMING

Changes have also taken place in the poultry industry, egg production and broiler production now being organised as separate entities. The typical egg production unit has grown larger and total output has reached the point at which steps have been officially taken to discourage further expansion.

VITICULTURE

The history of the New Zealand wine industry has been chequered and for many years it suffered from both a lack of official encouragement and an absence of real discrimination on the part of its customers. Production has increased rapidly during the past decade, with attention now being paid to light table wines suited to the climate in grape growing districts, as in the Henderson and Gisborne areas in the North Island and more recently the large area planted near Blenheim in the South Island.

HORTICULTURE

Most branches of the horticultural industry have developed to meet local needs, but an export trade in apples began just before the First World War. After 1918, expansion was more rapid, many people taking up fruit growing, even if usually without the requisite technical knowledge. By 1938, some 1.5 million cases of apples were being exported annually and, despite the interruption caused by the Second World War, production continued to expand, to reach a total of about seven million bushels in recent years, of which approximately three to four million are exported. The industry's problem has always been to sell profitably a product for which freight rates are very high in relation to the final selling price. Its advantage is that it can land fruit in the United Kingdom and Western Europe in their off-season.

Vegetable production for processing has also become an export industry in the last twenty years, with the establishment of modern processing plants and the development of a consumer preference for processed vegetables. Fresh vegetables and fruit other than apples and pears are produced for local or regional markets only, although some strawberries are exported and overseas markets for sub-tropical fruit look promising. Despite progress made with mechanisation, horticulture remains fairly labour-intensive and special organisation of labour for harvesting is always needed.

Land Tenure and Farm Credit

Forms of land tenure, structural reform in agriculture, the problem of the uneconomic unit, regional imbalance, are all issues that excite interest in Western Europe and even Australia, but they do not assume any real magnitude in New Zealand. The freehold–leasehold controversy was carried on with great vigour at the beginning of the century, but it died down in 1911 with the victory of the Reform Party, champion of the right to freehold. The controversy is not yet buried; arguments in favour of a system of leasehold tenure are probably as valid as they ever were, but freehold proved to be the political winner at a time when forms of land tenure were ceasing to be a major political preoccupation. Indeed, statistics showing the area of land held under various forms of tenure are collected only occasionally. The latest available figures, for 1960, show that some 9 million hectares were then freehold, 7.4 million were Crown land and 1.4 million were leasehold. The freehold would include practically all the better class land; much of the Crown land would be high country in the South Island. There are few limitations on an owner's right to dispose of land as he wishes, although a foreigner wanting to buy will need official approval, which may or may not be granted unless he intends permanent residence. The owner of one fully economic unit may not be permitted to buy another, though if he establishes a company he may be able to get round this restriction. This type of legislation was enacted to ensure that land would be available for ex-servicemen of the Second World War.

New Zealand farmers have enjoyed one advantage for a long period, a relatively straightforward system of land transfer. This has helped to prevent the emergence of a class of quasi-peasant proprietors unable to finance the improvement of their own farms and unable to sell for a figure sufficient to establish themselves elsewhere. Farm properties have always changed hands readily in New Zealand; so readily in fact that the ease of transfer has sometimes been blamed for helping to push up land values. Nevertheless, the system does at least help to ensure that those who want to get out of the business can do so without undue delay or financial loss.

FARM CREDIT

The New Zealand farmer is reasonably well-provided with sources of credit and has ample opportunity to make contact with the local representatives of the organisations that supply it. The government has provided long-term credit since 1894, when the Advances to Settlers Department (later the State Advances Corporation and now the Housing Corporation and the separate Rural Banking and Finance Corporation) was created. For many years it financed farm purchases only, as settlement was its primary aim. In the last decade, however, a fair proportion of resources have been devoted to financing farm development and restructuring, types of lending which other agencies tend to avoid.

Short-term or seasonal finance is provided by banks and stock-and-station agents. The latter usually lend on the condition that they handle the wool and surplus stock, but the extent to which this obligation can be imposed depends on the farmer's overall financial position. Stock firms also hold interest-bearing deposits on behalf of clients. From the farmer's angle the stock firm may be the most flexible source of credit, as the decision on the limits of an advance may be made quickly and with minimum red tape, the stock firm's agent probably having a fair knowledge of the client, of his stock and of his managerial capacity. Banks provide a substantial volume of short-term credit, but are less directly involved.

The seasonal credit requirements of the dairy farmer are fewer because he receives a regular payment from his company for most of the year; his need for additional finance is largely to meet special situations. Stock firms do not, as a rule, lend on any scale to dairy farmers; some finance is, however, provided by dairy companies.

Marketing

Experience with bulk purchase arrangements during the First World War showed that a departure from the traditional marketing pattern was practicable; the fact that the post-war slump, in meat and then in dairy prices, followed fairly closely on the termination of the bulk purchasing arrangements prompted both the government and the industry to look for methods to reform the organisation of marketing. The Meat Export Control Act 1921–22 and the Dairy Export Control Act 1924 both set up bodies with power to regulate shipments, to enter into freight contracts and to undertake promotion. These measures improved the farmers' position by helping to ensure that the flow of produce to the United Kingdom, the only significant market, was regulated to avoid periodic gluts and shortages.

Such forms of rationalisation could, however, do little to counter longer-term price movements, a fact starkly emphasised during the depression of the 1930s. In the mid-1920s the Dairy Board did endeavour to play a more active marketing role, but lack of unanimity within the industry and hostility on the part of the United Kingdom merchants defeated its efforts. During the depression New Zealand exporters continued to compete against each other almost as much as they did with their overseas rivals. Within the industry, however, the concept of a minimum price gained support, despite the contention of the sceptics that the consumer or the taxpayer would have to carry the final burden. Though meat and wool prices fell relatively further in the depression than did dairy prices, the demand for action to stabilise returns came largely from the dairy industry.

The Primary Products Marketing Act 1936 established a guaranteed price for butter and cheese and created a single marketing authority which obtained its working capital at concessional rates from the Reserve Bank. Though the Act made it clear that other products could be included within its provisions, there was no move to extend its range to include meat and wool. The dairy industry's co-operative structure facilitated the task of a centralised marketing agency; sheep farmers, then as well as later, showed themselves to be more distrustful of change. Although the concept of a guaranteed, or basic, price for butter and cheese remains, nearly forty years' experience has brought about a number of modifications. It has been accepted that the producer cannot, and should not, be insulated from the market; but the basic price must at least ensure him a minimum standard of living while he adjusts to the processes of change.

In this respect, the system which has been established for the dairy industry must be regarded as being reasonably successful. It has not been used to insulate the producer, but it has, in the face of a good many difficulties, given him a measure of stability. The industry has sometimes run deficits for several years at the Reserve Bank, but these have always been paid off. If non-fat products, insignificant in 1936 but today considerably more important than cheese, were covered by the basic price mechanism, the deficits recorded would have been fewer. In this respect the dairy industry's pricing arrangements must still be regarded as evolving; it seems that ultimately a single price for milk, whatever its end uses, will be paid.

Meat and wool marketing policies have followed a totally different course, with a large number of producers still continuing to reject the concept that a centralised marketing system would improve their bargaining power. Floor prices for wool were introduced in 1951, the system being financed by funds accumulated following the disposal of wartime stocks and the proceeds of a special levy. Minimum price for export meat came into effect in 1955, backed by reserves accumulated as a result of the wartime, and immediate post-war, system of bulk purchase by the United Kingdom. The objective of each system is to ensure that the producer receives at least a minimum return during periods of price recession, but both have shortcomings.

It is now more apparent, though perhaps it was always true, that no system of price support by itself can ensure a reasonable standard of life to producers in a country dependent upon export markets. Any such system must be associated with an active selling programme, with detailed marketing and product research, and must help to encourage sufficient flexibility in production to ensure that market requirements can be readily met. It is equally important to increase the number of markets.

Marketing arrangements for other produce have evolved along varying lines. As in most other countries, wheat was the first product to be subjected to some degree of control, but, as New Zealand seldom produces an export surplus, the task is largely one of matching imports with local production, a statutory marketing authority performing this function. Policy over the last decade has aimed at self-sufficiency, subject to the qualification that a local price should not diverge far from the world price nor inefficient patterns of land use be encouraged. Wheat competes with livestock products and if the returns for these are favourable wheat acreages will tend to contract, just as they will tend to expand when prices for wool and lamb decline. No formal marketing arrangements have been established for other cereals.

About half the apple and pear production is exported and the marketing organisation that has been set up is similar in character to that for the dairy industry, and growers have developed co-operative forms of organisation. Statutory marketing organisations have also been established for liquid milk, citrus fruit, eggs, tobacco, potatoes and honey, but apart from the last none of these products is exported.

Vegetables, whether fresh or for processing, and stone and berry fruit continue to be handled either through produce markets or by direct contact between grower and processor.

The Roles of Government and Education

From the moment that the sovereignty of New Zealand was acquired, the government played a role in agriculture through its right to dispose of land to incoming settlers. The sale of Crown land and the management of that not sold became major activities of government; to these were later added the provision of advisory and research services, the establishment of machinery to enforce minimum quality standards, and the provision of long-term credit. The Department of Lands and Survey absorbed the provincial waste lands administrations in 1876, the nucleus of a separate Department of Agriculture was established in 1892 and two years later the Advances to Settlers Department was created. The Department of Scientific and Industrial Research was formed in 1926, by which time there was at least an awareness of the need for agricultural research and of the inefficiency of leaving it to gifted and enthusiastic amateurs.

Yet, despite the complexities of agriculture and agricultural marketing today, the major tasks of decision-making are still undertaken by the individual farmer. He determines how his land should be utilised and reaps whatever financial rewards or penalties flow from his decision. Production quotas, standard quantities and other manifestations of bureaucratic control do not exist in New Zealand, nor have controls over imports much relevance to an industry involved almost entirely in production for export. The government, then, has relatively few powers to influence the pattern of land use, nor has it sought to acquire them by indirect methods such as the determination of price support levels or the allocation of credit. Government advisory services have not been used to promote any objective other than that of helping a farmer to help himself.

The Ministry of Agriculture and Fisheries is the main body for providing farmers with advice, and its work is reinforced by the Dairy Board, by private consultants and by improvement clubs which are simply co-operative groups of farmers banding together to engage a professionally qualified adviser. Techniques associated with advisory work are much the same in all developed countries— the adviser's task is not to tell a man how to run his farm, but to assist in solving particular problems, whether technical or managerial. Direct contact with farmers, radio and television programmes and newspaper articles, field days and demonstrations are all methods used. Obviously direct contact is the most productive, but it is also the most expensive. Yet without it little may be done for those farmers who most need help. Although no absolute yardstick can be utilised in assessing the effectiveness of advisory work, the contribution that dynamic extension workers have made over the past fifty years or so to the country's economic growth could hardly be over-estimated.

Formal teaching of agriculture at the tertiary level started at Lincoln College in the South Island in 1880, but for the first two or three decades did not succeed particularly well. Massey in the North Island did not open its doors until nearly fifty years later, in 1930, by which time research and advisory services had been built up by the government, the system of intensive grassland farming was being established and there was available a body of scientific knowledge which could be adapted to New Zealand's needs. Farmers themselves became receptive to new ideas; a substantial number has now taken one of the diploma courses offered by the colleges.

Agricultural instruction at the secondary school level has never been of much importance despite the work of a few enthusiasts. More attention is now being given to the role of training institutes and on-the-job training, such as that provided by the Federated Farmers' cadet scheme. There is an increasing emphasis on the need for those taking up farming to receive some training in management and it may indeed become a prerequisite to any government assistance in farm purchase.

Land Use Administration and Land Development

The largest single area of Crown land is the 4 million hectares or so of tussock country in the South Island, most of which is divided into extensive sheep farms. The limited value of the land, and the fact that the terms of Crown leases are reasonably satisfactory to the occupier, make it unlikely that there will be any demand for change in the form of tenure. Some of the high country blocks may be retired from farming for ecological reasons.

A major change in land administration policy came about in 1930 when the government began to develop other Crown land prior to its sale. The large area of pumice country in the central North Island had attracted settlers as soon as it was opened up, but until the means to overcome cobalt deficiency became known in the mid-1930s little economic return was possible. It was apparent that, quite apart from the correction of trace element deficiencies, the capital investment, particularly in fertiliser, to get the land in grass was beyond the resources of the individual farmer and could be undertaken much more effectively if large blocks were tackled. In the 1930s such work also provided a means to absorb the unemployed. After the Second World War the whole process of Crown land development was speeded up to help with the settlement of returned servicemen, a major achievement in itself.

Since the mid-1960s there has been some slowing down in the development of land by the government, those blocks that can still be brought into production offering greater physical difficulties. The uncertain outlook for pastoral products makes it harder for the farmer established on a new block to meet his financial commitments, as the price he paid for the land was designed also to cover the capital cost of development. There will always be dispute that some of the capital devoted to bringing virtually unproductive land into grass could have been utilised more effectively had it been used to improve land already being farmed. More sophisticated techniques for project evaluation may help to answer such queries.

Growing urbanisation makes necessary the preservation of high-quality land on the outskirts of some city areas and, like other countries, New Zealand has no complete answer to the problem. Local authorities' planning schemes aim to conserve better-class land, but the rise in land values on the perimeter of urban areas inevitably creates pressure for further sub-division.

Farmers' Organisations

Farmers generally have preferred to exert pressure through existing political parties and their loyalties, since early this century, have been with the Reform, or later National, Party. This preference has proved fairly successful, as, from 1912 when William Massey took office on a programme designed to meet farmers' needs, political parties not so directly committed to defending farmers' interests have been in office for less than a third of the period. Farmers' political views have thus usually been in a position to command a fair amount of weight.

The Farmers' Union was formed at the beginning of the century, but its problem for many years was the lack of both an effective central organisation and financial resources. Up to 1914, local agricultural and pastoral societies were regarded as the forums where farmers' views at the local level could be expressed.

Federated Farmers, the present national organisation, was formed in 1944 with the amalgamation of the Farmers' Union and the Sheep Owners' Federation, the latter rather more an employers' organisation concerned with the negotiation of industrial awards. Federated Farmers has always professed to be non-political, and is organised on the basis of twenty-two provinces and some hundreds of branches. Recently it has acquired, as of right, a source of revenue from meat levies, intended to finance its head-quarters' activities. Farmers are also represented at the national level through the producer boards. Election to these is on an indirect basis: to the Dairy Board through a system of local wards, to the Meat and the Wool boards by an electoral committee also elected on a district basis. As a rule, changes in representation are few and the large-scale transformation of the Electoral Committee in 1973 was quite without precedent.

Farm workers still largely lack industrial organisation, despite increasing pressure towards unionism from other labour groups. This may be a reflection of the fact that many of them have family links with farm owners; many of the rest are fairly young men who do not regard farm work as a lifetime career. In itself this is one of the industry's basic problems in that many farm workers leave in their mid-twenties, at their most useful age. Reasons advanced for this state of affairs are many and various, but include uncertainty about future advancement, difficulties in the way of a worker acquiring his own house, lack of employment opportunities for other members of the farm worker's family and perhaps the conviction that he and his wife are not fully accepted socially. After three decades of full employment, it has been accepted by farmers that they cannot recruit men at sub-standard wages, but hours of work remain an issue not really resolved.

Traditionally it has been assumed that the keen farm worker would obtain his reward when he took over his own property and many continue to have this as their goal. A liking for the life, a desire to be independent, a conviction that a farm represents the best investment, all motivate those who seek to become farm owners. Farms in New Zealand continue to change hands freely and the majority of farm owners are men under fifty, but the individual farm worker, without access to additional capital, is finding the task of financing himself into a property more and more difficult unless he can be helped by a government settlement programme.

Sometimes it is claimed that the modern farm is too complex to be managed on the basis of the typical family business and that a larger corporate form of organisation is needed. Evidence to back up such claims is hard to come by; in fact, such indications as are available might suggest the reverse. It would seem that with efficient advisory and research services, the ready availability of specialised contractors and the continuation of the present pattern of livestock production, the family unit is likely to remain the dominant form in the foreseeable future.

Agriculture today provides more than eighty per cent of New Zealand's export earnings. Faced with the dangers arising from dependence on its single traditional market, that of the United Kingdom, New Zealand has diversified to such an extent that more than seventy per cent of its exports now go elsewhere.

The demand overseas for animal protein and animal fibres remains brisk. The pattern of production in this country has not materially altered, other than through the steady increase in the number of beef cattle, with a growing proportion of export receipts coming from beef sales. This trend towards more beef cattle can be expected to continue, despite new and profitable markets for sheep meats.

Change in the individual farmer's pattern of land use is not likely to be marked in any other respect in the immediate future. No major technological innovation, like those of the 1920s' revolution in grassland management or the 1950s' advent of aerial topdressing, appears to be imminent. Progress seems more likely through the attainment of higher standards of management expertise by farmers seeking to narrow the gap between what has been reached by the highly efficient and that accomplished by the majority.

The accumulated knowledge of New Zealand farmers in both pasture and livestock management is being increasingly called upon by developing countries with a similar farming potential. Dissemination of such knowledge could well be New Zealand's major contribution to the essential increase in world food production in the years ahead.

FISHING

V. T. Hinds

The Maori peoples who settled in these islands after long and hazardous trans-Pacific migrations in small boats brought with them traditional fishing skills, and handed down the legend of Maui the great fisherman who, using the South Island as his canoe, pulled the North Island from the deep ocean on his line. Thus, according to the ancient legend, were these islands formed.

When Captain James Cook circumnavigated these islands, he and his companions recorded in their journals several species of fish which the crew had seined in local bays to supplement monotonous rations of salt beef and hard tack.

Then, later, adventurous pioneers established small fishing ventures, and from these early endeavours developed the whaling and sealing, the trawling and seine netting, the long-lining and rock lobster potting, the set netting and oyster dredging that are the foundations of today's fishing industry. This industry employs 5890 fishermen, manning 3487 vessels around 7000 kilometres of coastline. In 1973, vessels fishing full-time and earning more than $4,000 per annum numbered 1074 and employed 2286 men; 167 vessels earned more than $30,000 each. The total value of the main fisheries resources harvested in 1973 exceeded $21 million, with earnings from rock lobster and wetfish landings forming the greatest return.

QUANTITY AND VALUE OF THE PRINCIPAL CLASSES OF FISHERIES PRODUCTS MARKETED IN 1973

	QUANTITY kg	VALUE $
Wetfish	44 752 609	8,546,180
Whitebait		
West Coast, South I.	44 648	196,896
Waikato	10 210	45,024
Oysters		
Dredged Bluff	125 910 *sacks*	1,825,695
Dredged Nelson	4696 *sacks*	63,396
Rock (Ministry and private farms)	9558 *bags*	212,174
Mussels	2 363 733	209,642
Paua	811 886	241,007
Scallops	2 532 013	542,020
Squid	373 892	88,551
Other Shellfish (cockles, octopus, pipis, sea eggs, tuatuas)	336 254	43,312
Rock Lobsters	4 769 981	9,487,779
Southern Spider Crab (experimental only)	23 517	41,470
Prawns	152	409
Seaweed	82 286	569
TOTAL VALUE:		$21,544,124

QUANTITY AND VALUE OF EXPORTS OF FISHERIES PRODUCTS FOR 1973

	QUANTITY kg	VALUE $
WETFISH		
Fresh, frozen or chilled	10 990 571	7,093,085
Smoked or dried	136 982	120,677
Canned or otherwise processed	150 980	124,206
ROCK LOBSTER		
Fresh, frozen or chilled	1 745 773	10,669,281
Canned or otherwise processed	161 979	606,504
OTHER CRUSTACEAN AND MOLLUSCS		
Fresh, frozen or chilled	272 965	240,613
Canned or otherwise processed	662 914	1,239,756
TOTAL	14 122 164	20,094,122

Administration, Research and Development

The Ministry of Agriculture and Fisheries administers and encourages the development of all fisheries resources. Stock assessment, evaluation of optimum yields, regulatory monitoring, inspection and advice are effected; teams of scientists with technical assistants investigate pelagic, demersal, shellfish and freshwater fisheries throughout New Zealand, working both ashore and afloat from a technological and two research vessels. Sea and shore patrols enforce conservation and other regulations of the Fisheries Act, principally by encouragement and advice but by prosecution if necessary.

The Fishing Industry Board in New Zealand is charged with the promotion and expansion of the fishing industry, with increasing the catch and improving the quality of the products, with training fishermen and with investigating new methods and new fisheries. Increasing pressure on overseas fisheries resources has given rise to an increasing awareness of the relatively under-exploited fish stocks around New Zealand and many long-range vessels now operate close to its exclusive fishing zone twelve nautical miles from the coast. This is a matter of concern to the New Zealand fishing industry, and the government, by participating in international discussions and negotiations at the Law of the Sea Conference hopes to achieve greater safeguards for its fisheries resources. These could be effected by the consolidation of exclusive fishing limits and the establishment of a fisheries management zone of 200 nautical miles which would include most of the continental shelf.

Pelagic Fisheries

The development locally of a small but growing tuna industry has been based principally on the harvesting of albacore tuna (*Thunnus alalunga*), mainly by surface trolling but also by pole and bait fishing. The major effort has been concentrated at the ports of Greymouth and Westport and off the west coast of the South Island. A small but effective fleet also operates from Whakatane in the Bay of Plenty, where regular landings of skipjack tuna (*Katsuwonus pelamis*) are made. Currently, tuna is frozen for export to foreign-based canneries.

A fresh appraisal of the commercial purse seining of tuna, mackerel and other surface-swimming species, including trevally (*Caranx lutescens*) and kahawai (*Arripis trutta*), was inaugurated late in 1973. That year, an American-type purse seiner began a year-long survey of these stocks in New Zealand waters to assess the viability of bulk fishing, initially for export but eventually for local processing. This project, conjointly sponsored by the New Zealand government and a major American tuna cannery, soon demonstrated the efficiency of purse seining for skipjack tuna when this fish formed seinable schools; however, before the overall success of the survey can be determined, these early successes must be related to the variables of coastal sea and weather conditions and to the continuing studies of school fish behaviour during the relatively short tuna season.

A recent innovation has been the coastal box net. Fish moving along the coast in season are diverted into the trap net by a net leader set at right angles to the shore line, and are held alive until removed for processing ashore. This method of culling part of a migrating school of fish in prime condition has opened hitherto unexploited overseas markets for selected quality fish, mainly yellowtail kingfish (*Seriola grandis*), trevally and kahawai. Less valuable English blue mackerel (*Scomber australasicus*) is processed and utilised as a food supplement for eel cultivation and farming enterprises. As yet in its early stages in New Zealand, box netting is closely monitored by scientists of the Ministry of Agriculture and Fisheries. This method would appear to have a rewarding future in New Zealand when established as a total box net fishery, with integrated fin fish and shellfish cultivation developments, canning and further improved fish handling facilities.

Shellfish Fisheries

OYSTER AND MUSSEL

In Foveaux Strait, extensive beds of the dredge oyster (*Ostrea lutaria*) continue to yield a valuable seasonal (four month) harvest, in 1973 amounting to 125 910 sacks valued at $1,825,695. Quotas and surveys maintain optimum harvests. Increased spat settlement of existing beds and the development of special sites on Stewart Island have been carried out, with the aim of developing a greater export for this product, until now restricted by regulation to home consumption and limited export to a few Pacific island territories.

Rock oyster (*Crassostrea glomerata*) farms in the bays and inlets north of Auckland continue to increase with assistance from government demonstration farms. Nearly half the 9558 bags produced in 1973 were exported to Pacific island territories and to Australia.

A by-crop of rock oyster farming is the blue mussel (*Mytilus edulis aoteanus*), which is, however, mainly culled from natural wild stocks. The green mussel (*Perna canaliculus*) is farmed by rope cultures suspended from rafts, a form of mariculture which, backed by induced spawning of seed spat by local commercial enterprises, shows promise.

PAUA

A traditional food much esteemed by the Maori, the paua (*Haliotis iris*) has suffered serious encroachments in recent times, as a result of the strong demand for this delicacy from buyers in the South-east Asian market. Recently strict control was effected by regulation and improved management measures, such as farming based on artificial propagation, are being investigated.

TOHEROA

Until 1972, the toheroa (*Paphies (mesodesma) ventricosa*) was taken from beaches north of Auckland, west of Wellington and west of Bluff on a limited basis, mainly by the public and also by a small cannery. The numbers of legally sized toheroa have diminished to a low level in all areas, and a closed season has been enforced until annual surveys recommend further harvesting. A small colony of toheroa, transplanted to a suitable site in the Chatham Islands, continues to thrive.

Rock Lobster Production

Landings of rock lobster consist principally of the red spiny lobster (*Jasus edwardsii*) supplemented by steady catches of the packhorse rock lobster (*Jasus verreauxi*). Until 1965, supplies came mainly from the southern coast of the South Island, including Stewart Island and Fiordland, but then very rapid expansion developed in this fishery following the discovery of large stocks of rock lobster at the Chatham Islands. In 1968, New Zealand was second only to Australia in world production, but had lost this position by 1970 and in 1973 held only fourth position. Exports have established the rock lobster fishery as the highest money-earner amongst the New Zealand fisheries.

Commercial Eel Fisheries

Two species of freshwater eels are widely distributed throughout New Zealand and the adjoining islands: the long-finned eel (*Anguilla dieffenbachii*) and the short-finned eel (*Anguilla australis schmidtii*). The long-finned eel occurs only in New Zealand and is one of the largest freshwater eels, reaching twenty kilogrammes in weight; the other, short-finned, species occurs also in Australia and some Pacific islands.

During the 1960s a commercial fishery rapidly developed, first for the European and then for the Japanese market. In 1966, eel production amounted to 50 000 kilogrammes, expanding thereafter to reach a peak of 2 million kilogrammes, with an export value of $1.6 million in 1972. The 1973 figures showed a drop to 1.5 million kilogrammes, with an export value of $1.2 million.

The wild eel stocks are not expected to sustain heavy fishing pressures for much longer and eel farming is being encouraged by the government.

Trawling and More Recent Developments

Trawling and Danish seining still remain the principal methods of taking the fish most popular with the New Zealand consumer, and account for seventy-nine per cent of all fish landings. Of some fifty-four species landed, snapper (*Chrysophrys auratus*), trevally (*Caranx lutescens*) and tarakihi (*Cheilodactylus macropterus*) represent fifty-seven per cent of the entire production from these traditional methods. Improvements are still being made in demersal trawl fishery and may lead the way to increased landings. Mid-water trawling trials have indicated interesting possibilities in fishing for pilchard (*Sardinops neopilchardus*), anchovy (*Engraulis australis*), sprat (*Sprattus antipodum*) and barracouta (*Thyrsites atun*) in season. Trials with Japanese squid angling machines have also been carried out aboard a chartered New Zealand fishing vessel during the 1973–74 squid season and commercial pot fishing for the southern spider crab (*Jacquinotia edwardsii*) has been tried experimentally.

Angling

BIG GAME FISHING

Big game fishing in New Zealand shows a steady growth and is an important tourist attraction in the Bay of Islands, Whakatane in the Bay of Plenty, Mercury Bay and Kawau Island. In 1972 and 1973, 1580 yellowtail kingfish, 878 mako shark, 644 yellowfin tuna, 245 striped and 26 black marlin and 185 hammerhead sharks were landed. Of this total, 1184 landed game fish were recorded at Whakatane, 828 at the Bay of Islands and 299 at Tauranga.

FRESHWATER FISHERIES

Inland sport fisheries are based upon introduced fishes which have been successfully acclimatised in New Zealand. Anglers in the 1967–68 season fished for 1.25 million days to take 0.9 million fish, weighing a total of 1060 tonnes.

Rainbow trout (*Salmo gairdneri*) is the principal fish in the North Island, from south of Hamilton down to a line drawn from southern Hawke's Bay to north Taranaki. To the south of this line the brown trout (*Salmo trutta*) predominates, as it does in the South Island. Here, there is also the quinnat salmon (*Oncorhynchus tshawytscha*) mainly in east coast rivers, with small runs in some west coast rivers. The South Island lakes have brown trout, rainbow trout and, in some, landlocked stocks of quinnat salmon. Commercial fishing for all these species is prohibited.

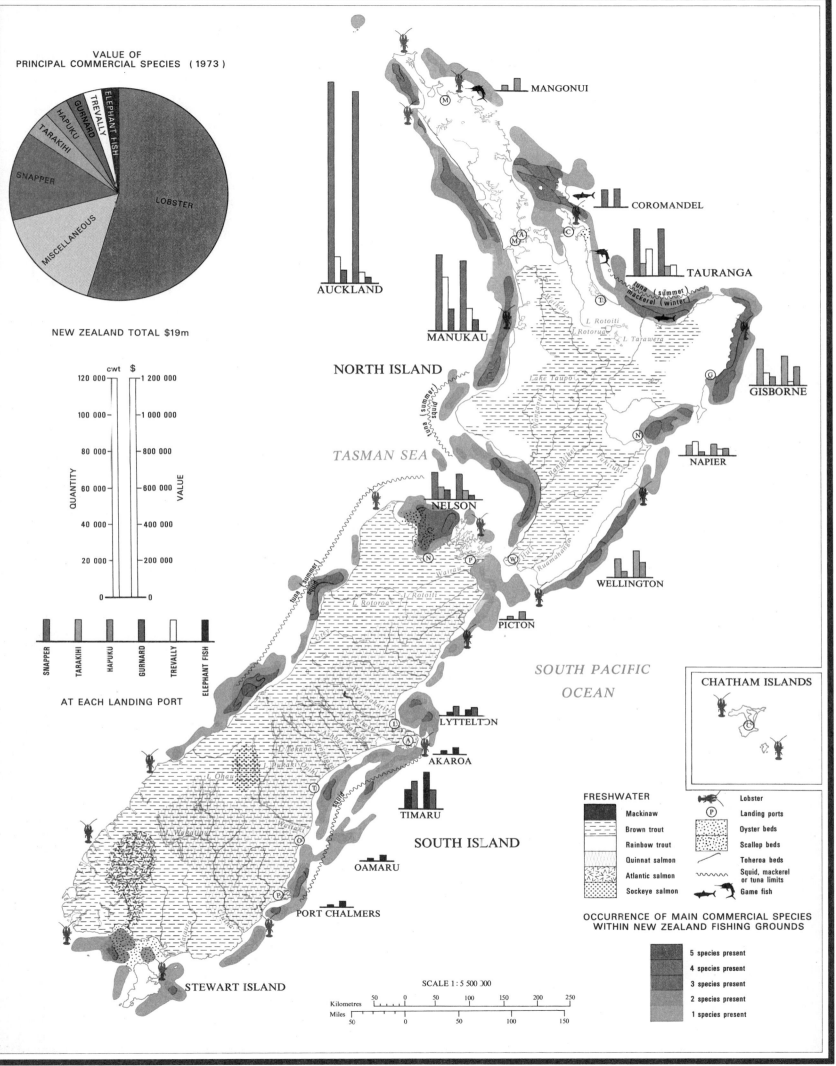

VALUE OF
PRINCIPAL COMMERCIAL SPECIES (1973)

TREVALLY
ELEPHANT FISH
GURNARD
HAPUKU
TARAKIHI
SNAPPER
LOBSTER
MISCELLANEOUS

NEW ZEALAND TOTAL $19m

cwt $

120 000 — 1 200 000
100 000 — 1 000 000
80 000 — 800 000
60 000 — 600 000
40 000 — 400 000
20 000 — 200 000
0 — 0

QUANTITY
VALUE

SNAPPER
TARAKIHI
HAPUKU
GURNARD
TREVALLY
ELEPHANT FISH

AT EACH LANDING PORT

MANGONUI
COROMANDEL
TAURANGA
tuna (summer)
mackerel (winter)
GISBORNE
NAPIER

AUCKLAND
MANUKAU

NORTH ISLAND

TASMAN SEA
tuna (summer)
squid

NELSON
WELLINGTON
PICTON

SOUTH PACIFIC
OCEAN

LYTTELTON
AKAROA
TIMARU
SOUTH ISLAND
OAMARU
PORT CHALMERS
STEWART ISLAND

CHATHAM ISLANDS

FRESHWATER

Mackinaw
Brown trout
Rainbow trout
Quinnat salmon
Atlantic salmon
Sockeye salmon

Lobster
Landing ports
Oyster beds
Scallop beds
Toheroa beds
Squid, mackerel
or tuna limits
Game fish

OCCURRENCE OF MAIN COMMERCIAL SPECIES
WITHIN NEW ZEALAND FISHING GROUNDS

5 species present
4 species present
3 species present
2 species present
1 species present

SCALE 1 : 5 500 000

Kilometres 50 0 50 100 150 200 250
Miles   50 0   50   100   150

MINERAL RESOURCES

B. N. Thompson

In Maori culture the most important mineral elements were rocks sufficiently hard and dense for hammering and for cutting, and natural pigments for colouring and ornamentation. The hardened argillite from Nelson was used for adzes, greenstone from the West Coast for ornaments and North Island obsidian for cutting; the natural pigments included black manganese oxide, blue vivianite (pukepotu — iron phosphate) and red and yellow ochres (kokowai — iron oxides).

During the last century, gold production was the most valuable mineral operation in New Zealand until it was replaced by coal, which was in turn superseded, in 1960, by constructional materials. In 1973, mineral production was valued at $75 million.

Fuels

COAL

Coal remains the major fuel mineral produced in New Zealand despite increased consumption of natural gas and oil fuels. Coal still has major uses in cement and steel works and in electricity generation.

There are four types of coal mined in New Zealand, from seams that are mostly between two and six metres thick though some are up to thirty metres. *Lignite*, which is mined opencast in Canterbury, Otago and Southland (where there is the greatest potential) produced 144 799 tonnes in 1973; some lignites, and the Chatham Island peat, contain an appreciable quantity of montan and peat wax. *Sub-bituminous coal* is mined in all North Island and four South Island fields and in 1973 yielded 1 901 541 tonnes; the large opencast and underground deposits at Huntly, which contain 67 and 130 million tonnes respectively, and at Maramarua (20 and 52 million tonnes) are used mainly for steam raising at the Meremere power station and at dairy factories and hospitals. Some mines ceased operation in the 1970s, while the yield from Murchison and Reefton is small, the coal being either relatively inaccessible or distant from markets.

Bituminous coal, used for making gas and coke, is restricted to the South Island west coast. Production, which was 422 084 tonnes in 1973, is increasing despite difficult terrain and distorted seams.

Anthracite coal, which gives the greatest heat of all coals, is found in the Fox River area and in the metamorphosed lignite at Acheron, Canterbury. None was produced in 1973.

OIL AND NATURAL GAS

New Zealand's first oil field at Moturoa, New Plymouth, was discovered in 1866, and closed in 1972 after producing 215 518 barrels of crude oil and millions of cubic metres of gas for local use. A large gas condensate field discovered at Kapuni in 1959 first produced gas in 1970, and now supplies much of the North Island.

Oil is generally found in near-coastal and marine sedimentary rocks, areas of which, in Northland, Gisborne, Hawke's Bay, Westland, Canterbury and Southland, have been prospected with little success and only the Taranaki region, on-shore at Kapuni and off-shore at Maui, has so far proved 'productive'. The Maui field is reported as being amongst the largest gas fields in the world.

Oil shale, which may possibly be economic when oil prices are high, is known at Nevis Valley (Otago) and at Orepuki (Southland).

Metallic Minerals

GOLD

In New Zealand, gold is found in two main host rocks, quartz lodes and alluvial sand and gravel which has been either deposited by ancient rivers that drained the quartz lode areas or eroded from these old gravels and reconcentrated in the richer, younger gravels of the present-day river beds. The once high-yielding quartz lodes are now worked out and by 1973 the single commercial alluvial operation was that of the Kanieri dredge on the Taramakau River. Gold recovered from all sources in 1973 amounted to 354 kilogrammes.

SILVER

Silver is alloyed with gold in all fields, but is most common in the Hauraki field where the silver to gold ratio averages 1:2, but rises to 8:1 locally near Waihi. Silver mines as such, at Puhipuhi in Northland, Great Barrier Island and Collingwood, have been generally uneconomic. Most South Island mineral-bearing reefs contain little silver. In 1973, a total of 1530 kilogrammes of silver was recovered, most of it, 1298 kilogrammes, from the Maratoto mine, to the north-east of Paeroa.

IRON MINERALS

Ilmenite is common in the South Island west coast sand from Karamea to Bruce Bay, and in the western North Island titanomagnetic sand. The richest deposit is between Greymouth and Westport, where 5–10 million tonnes of ilmenite concentrate near Westport contain 44–47 per cent titanium oxide and some zircon.

Limonite has been worked from a number of small deposits in Northland. At Onekaka, north-west Nelson, a larger deposit contains nearly 10 million tonnes with forty per cent iron.

The North Island west coast *titanomagnetite* sands derived from andesitic (volcanic) rocks, form young beach and dune deposits from Kaipara Harbour southwards to Wanganui. More than 500 million tonnes of concentrate, containing 53–57 per cent iron, 7–9 per cent titanium oxide and 0.36–0.4 per cent vanadium oxide, is available. Present mining is at Waiuku State Forest for the steel industry, twenty per cent of the sand there containing 90 million tonnes of concentrate, and at both Taharoa (55%: 200 million) and Waipipi, South Taranaki (16%: 60 million), for export.

LEAD AND ZINC

The Tui mine, New Zealand's only lead–zinc mine, ceased production in 1973. Up to then it had produced concentrate containing mainly lead (4400 tonnes) and zinc (7250 tonnes), but also cadmium (54 tonnes), copper, gold and silver. At the Broadlands geothermal area, lead and zinc materials are forming today at a temperature of about 280°C at a depth of about 1500 metres. They are also known at a number of Coromandel gold mines, at north-west Nelson and at Fiordland, but no deposit is economic.

Non-Metallic Minerals

Clay, from a variety of sources, is used in brick, tile and pipe manufacture. Fireclay is commonly found immediately beneath coal seams, and has been worked at Kamo, Maramarua, Huntly and Gore. Halloysite clay, for pottery manufacture, is quarried from hydro-thermally-altered, rhyolite volcanic cones in north-eastern Northland.

Bentonite is used as drilling mud and as a filler, and was used as a binding agent for ironsand pellets. Sodium bentonite, in a low grade form that swells on wetting, has been worked at Porangahau on the east coast of the North Island for thirty years. The much purer, but non-swelling, calcium–magnesium bentonite, quarried at Coalgate, Canterbury, can be made to swell by chemical treatment.

Constructional materials are the most important group of the non-metallic minerals. They include rock aggregate and sand for roading, harbour work, ballast and concrete, and facing stone such as Coromandel granite, Hinuera and Oamaru stone. Production in 1973 was 30 million tonnes, valued at $36,642,648. Suitable rocks include hard sandstone (greywacke), which forms part of the mountain ranges and the gravels in rivers that drain them, some Fiordland gneisses and young basalts in the Northland, Auckland and Dunedin districts. Lower grade rocks have been used locally for concrete, for road making and for fill.

Diatomite, formed from the siliceous skeletons of small plants, occurs widely in both marine and terrestrial sediments. The marine diatomite at Oamaru has potential use for insulation, and, after treatment, as an abrasive. Much of that in ancient lakes near Kaikohe, Auckland, Mercer, Tauranga and Rotorua has been worked spasmodically for a cement additive and for dry cleaning, filtration and abrasives. Diatomite from a very large deposit, not now working, at Middlemarch, Otago, was used for filtration and as a filler in asbestos board.

The main *dolomite* deposit at Mt Burnett, Collingwood, contains possibly more than 50 million tonnes. Since 1947 dolomite has been used in fertiliser manufacture, and since 1962 in glass manufacture at Whangarei.

Greenstone, which was used extensively by the Maori for ornaments and adzes, is in two mineralogical forms: nephrite (jade), the Maori pounamu, and the less hard bowenite or tangiwai. Nephrite occurs principally as boulders in the gravels of the Taramakau River, in Douglas Creek, a small tributary of the Haast River, and in Caples Valley in north-west Otago. Semi-nephrite is found in the Dart and Routeburn valleys. Bowenite forms veins in a band of ultramafic rock extending from Anita Bay to Sutherland Sound in Fiordland.

High-grade *limestone*, used with marl for cement manufacture (1.78 million tonnes in 1973), and limestone for industry, including paper fillers (238 315 tonnes in 1973), is in scattered outcrops near Whangarei, Te Kuiti, north-west Nelson, Westport, Canterbury and Fiordland. The more widespread, lower grade limestone, used mainly for agriculture (1.69 million tonnes in 1973), is found in south-west Auckland, Gisborne, Hawke's Bay and Southland.

Magnesite and talc: talc–magnesite and quartz–magnesite rocks occur at the Cobb River dam site near Nelson and in Southland. As the largest deposits are 800 metres wide and 1700 metres long, the quantity of rock is large, but because the separation of talc from magnesite is not yet economically possible, the rock is used, without treatment, principally as a magnesium-rich fertiliser and as a filler.

Perlite, a natural volcanic glass which, on heating, expands up to ten times its original size, forms the surface layers of some rhyolite volcanoes at Rotorua–Taupo, on the Coromandel Peninsula and Great Barrier Island: quantities available are large. Perlite is used as an inert insulator, a filler in wallboard and for horticultural purposes.

Pumice was erupted extensively during the last 40 000 years in the Rotorua–Taupo area; it was also carried by rivers and deposited in valleys up to several hundred kilometres from the eruption point. Commercial grade pumice in its natural state should be moderately well graded, loosely compacted for easy excavation and with few contaminents. Usable material includes coarse 'airfall' material from near Rotorua, pumice erupted from the Taupo area about 1800 years ago and carried as both lump and sand by the Waikato and Wanganui rivers almost to their mouths, and from the older pumice sand near Hunua, Auckland. Pumice sand is used in sandsoap and as a wallboard filler; lump pumice is used for insulation and in lightweight concrete.

Bedded *salt* deposits are unknown in New Zealand, but sea water, evaporated in basins at Grassmere in Marlborough, produces about 40 000–100 000 tonnes annually.

Serpentine, which is used mainly as an additive to superphosphate fertiliser to aid spreadability, is found in long, discontinuous, narrow belts from D'Urville Island to Red Mountain in north-west Otago and Mossburn; as massive complexes at North Cape, Cobb River and Bluff; as a diapiric intrusion at Piopio near Te Kuiti and in small isolated masses associated with slumped sediments in Northland.

Silica, from ten square kilometres of dunes at Parengarenga Harbour, Northland (64 269 tonnes in 1973) and from the sand in the coal measures at Mt Somers, Canterbury (15 667 tonnes), is used for the glass industry. Lower grade deposits are found in Westland, Otago and Southland.

Most other *industrial sand* is won from Kaukapakapa, Auckland (27 523 tonnes in 1973), various Wellington localities (3057 tonnes) and from near Tarakohe, Golden Bay, for the cement works (33 136 tonnes). Natural moulding sand is scarce. The most suitable for iron casting is from mid-Canterbury, and for non-ferrous casting from Fairfield in Dunedin, but other sand can be used after sieving, grading and mixing with kaolin or bentonite.

Geothermal *steam* is used for electric power generation at Wairakei, for industrial processing at Kawerau, Rotorua and Taupo and for domestic heating at Rotorua and Taupo. There appears also to be ample available for small industrial and domestic uses at other hot spring areas.

Elemental *sulphur* is common around fumeroles in thermal areas on White and Whale islands and in the Rotorua–Taupo district. Sulphur and gypsum mining at White Island stopped in 1914 after all the miners were killed in a collapse of the crater, but was continued in 1925 until 1929, when production finally ceased. A recently discovered deposit at Lake Rotokawa, near Taupo, containing 30 million tonnes of sediments with twenty per cent sulphur is being investigated.

Pyrite-bearing rocks with seven to eight per cent sulphur at Kauaeranga, Thames, and Copperstain Creek near Takaka are too low in grade for economic mining, although the raw rock might help sulphur-deficient soils.

Ground water collects in the joints and pores of many fresh volcanic and sedimentary rocks. Large quantities of water can be extracted from young river gravels on the Canterbury and Heretaunga plains and in many valleys, from well-jointed basalt in Northland, from ignimbrite in the Rotorua–Taupo area, and from moderately hard sandstone and limestone.

Mineral wax is found in some brown coal, lignite and peat. On the Chatham Islands, wax, with a melting point of 73°C, constitutes about nine per cent of the peat; it is also known in the lignite beds of Southland and in south Otago.

Minor Minerals

METALLIC

Antimony sulphide is associated with silicified crush zones in greywacke or argillite at Waikare Inlet in the Bay of Islands, Endeavour Inlet in Marlborough, Reefton, Stillwater, Lawrence and Hendon, Otago, and also forms small deposits in volcanic rocks on Great Barrier Island and the Coromandel Peninsula. More than 4000 tonnes was extracted between 1872 and the 1940s.

Bauxite, consisting mainly of the clay gibbsite, is developed by deep, tropical weathering of flat-top remnants of the older basalt lava flows in the Kaeo–Kaikohe area. More than 20 million tonnes of rock containing thirty-seven per cent aluminium oxide was proved near Matauri Bay.

Chromite crystals are disseminated through serpentinite between D'Urville Island and Red Hill in the Wairau Valley, and at Red Mountain in north-west Otago. Although about 6000 tonnes of chromite were mined between 1859 and 1900 from Dun Mountain and Croisilles Harbour, Nelson, the possibility of finding commercial grade ore is low.

In Northland, several attempts at working *copper sulphides* from gossans (superficial covers of oxidised iron sulphide) in sediments associated with marine volcanics of Cretaceous age produced about 2600 tonnes of concentrate. About 2500 tonnes of ore were mined from each of Kawau and Great Barrier islands between 1849 and 1869, but both are worked out. Copper sulphides of the 'porphyry' type, disseminated along joints of altered diorite and in andesitic–dacitic breccia pipes, and associated with andesite volcanism, are usually low in grade, as at Doubtless Bay, Coppermine Island and Paritu, Coromandel. Copper mineralisation is also associated with granitic stocks in north-west Nelson and Stewart Island, with serpentine in Nelson, Westland and Southland and with metamorphic rocks in Fiordland.

Manganese, as the oxide, usually accompanied by chert, is a persistent associate of the volcanic 'red rock' suite of rocks in greywacke, as manganese garnet at Macetown, Taieri, and as rhodonite at Skippers and at Akatore, Taieri. About 19 600 tonnes of oxide were mined from the area between the Bay of Islands and Kawau Island between 1878 and 1911, and about 6800 tonnes from the Otaua–Bombay area up to 1960.

Mercury, as cinnabar, has been produced only from hydrothermal areas. Most of it was extracted from Puhi-puhi between 1917 and 1925, and smaller amounts from Ngawha Springs in Northland in the 1930s and from Mackaytown, Waihi, in 1910.

Platinum group minerals have been reported in many areas of mafic and ultramafic rocks. At Orepuki, Southland, twenty-three kilogrammes of platinum concentrate, presumably derived from ultramafic rocks of the Longwood Range, were recovered as a by-product from gold mining.

Rutile (titanium oxide) is present in many beach sands at Westport and in very small quantities in the southern South Island rivers.

Minor minerals known to exist, but in uneconomic quantity or value, include *beryl*, in granitic pegmatites at Charleston and Stewart Island; *molybdenum* sulphide, along the west coast of the South Island; *nickel*, as a nickel–iron alloy (awaruite) or as sulphides, in the Upper Takaka and Graham valleys; *scheelite* (calcium tungstate); *tin* (cassiterite). Prospects for *uranium* are best in the Buller and upper Porarari river areas, and detrital grains of *uranothorite* and *monazite*, also radio-active minerals,

have shown on Westland beaches and at Port Pegasus.

NON-METALLIC

Asbestos is found principally in ultramafic rocks, such as serpentinite and pyroxenite, in South Island areas. About 5800 tonnes of rock, averaging six to seven per cent asbestos, was mined between 1941 and 1963 in the Takaka valley, and a new deposit is being prospected in the Pyke River area of western Otago.

About 3000 tonnes of *barite*, together with *fluorite*, form several lodes, up to 0.5 metres thick, cutting marble at Thomson Hill in north-west Nelson.

Small quantities of potentially useful *feldspar* are widespread in granitic rocks from Nelson to Westland, in Fiordland and in Stewart Island; the nearby coastal and coal measure sands are rich in potash feldspar. Possible sources of calcium feldspar include Northland's east coast beach sand, where sand derived from the rhyolitic rocks of the central North Island has been deposited.

During the Second World War, about 1.5 tonnes of *mica* was recovered from muscovite–pegmatite sills at the north end of the Mataketake Range, South Westland. The yield is about 0.1 per cent of the rock.

Phosphate sand production near Clarendon, Otago, in 1902–24 and 1942–44 totalled 193 000 tonnes (twenty-five per cent phosphorous pentoxide), but no other economic deposit is known.

Silica, as quartzite, at Reefton and the Acrere Valley, Nelson, and at Landslip Hill, Southland, where roughly 10 million tonnes of rock contain about 98.4 per cent silica, 0.13 per cent alumina and 0.8 per cent ferric oxide, is marginally suitable for the manufacture of ferrosilicon and silicon.

Future Demands

The most rewarding policy for mineral exploration is aimed at the discovery of minerals which are imported or which may yield foreign exchange through export. Initially, specific items of high value or volume, such as oil and iron, are probably best to investigate. To help in the exploration, regional geological and specialist paleontological services are used in the search for oil, and regional and detailed geological mapping in the ironsands survey for the steel industry.

The exploitation of some minerals already available in sufficient quantity, for example ferro alloys and silicon metal, now depends upon the development of new processing techniques or a cheap power supply. Others, too low in grade or of insufficient quantity for economic exploitation at current prices, such as gold, silver, copper and manganese, could become economic with a favourable price change. New industries might require some other minerals, for example uranium for nuclear power stations, while the low yield of some minerals can be increased by special methods of beneficiation, such as the magnetic separation of titanomagnetite grains from raw sand, or chemical treatment, for example conversion of non-swelling calcium–bentonite to the swelling variety.

The demand for minerals for new uses is always present; recent examples include the halloysitic clays of Northland for pottery, limestone of industrial grade for steel and paper manufacture, and the use of natural gas as a fuel for electricity generation.

A constant assessment of the technical advances in processing, in the light of both quality and quantity of mineral deposits, is required to meet the changing demands of the consumer.

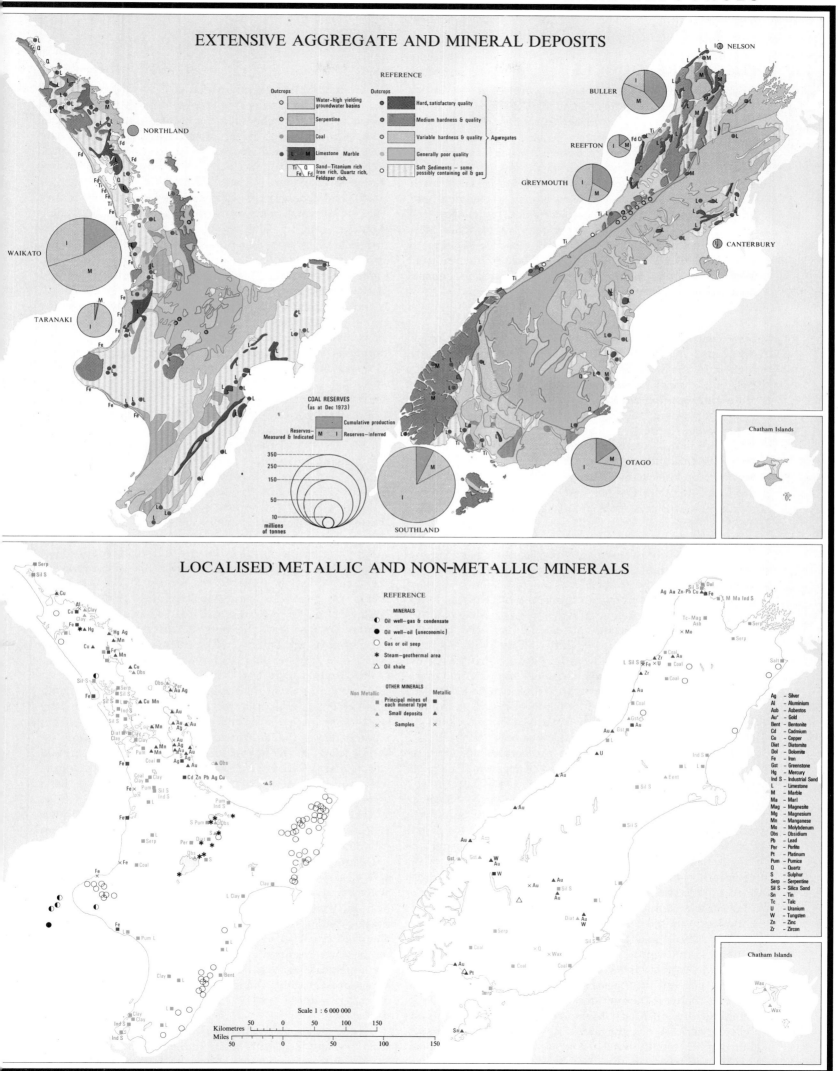

EXTENSIVE AGGREGATE AND MINERAL DEPOSITS

REFERENCE

Outcrops

- Water–high yielding groundwater basins
- Serpentine
- Coal
- L M Limestone Marble

Ti Q — Sand–Titanium rich, Iron rich, Quartz rich, Fe Fd — Feldspar rich,

Outcrops

- Hard, satisfactory quality
- Medium hardness & quality
- Variable hardness & quality — Aggregates
- Generally poor quality
- Soft Sediments – some possibly containing oil & gas

NORTHLAND

BULLER

REEFTON

GREYMOUTH

NELSON

WAIKATO

TARANAKI

CANTERBURY

COAL RESERVES
(as at Dec 1973)

Reserves— Measured & Indicated

M I

Cumulative production

Reserves— Inferred

350
250
150
50
10
millions of tonnes

SOUTHLAND

OTAGO

Chatham Islands

LOCALISED METALLIC AND NON-METALLIC MINERALS

REFERENCE

MINERALS

- ◐ Oil well–gas & condensate
- ● Oil well–oil (uneconomic)
- ○ Gas or oil seep
- ✳ Steam–geothermal area
- △ Oil shale

OTHER MINERALS

	Non Metallic	Metallic
Principal mines of each mineral type	■	▲
Small deposits	■	▲
Samples	×	×

Ag – Silver
Al – Aluminium
Asb – Asbestos
Au – Gold
Bent – Bentonite
Cd – Cadmium
Cu – Copper
Diat – Diatomite
Dol – Dolomite
Fe – Iron
Gst – Greenstone
Hg – Mercury
Ind S – Industrial Sand
L – Limestone
M – Marble
Ma – Marl
Mag – Magnesite
Mg – Magnesium
Mn – Manganese
Mo – Molybdenum
Obs – Obsidium
Pb – Lead
Per – Perlite
Pt – Platinum
Pum – Pumice
Q – Quartz
S – Sulphur
Serp – Serpentine
Sil S – Silica Sand
Sn – Tin
Tc – Talc
U – Uranium
W – Tungsten
Zn – Zinc
Zr – Zircon

Chatham Islands

Scale 1 : 6 000 000

Kilometres 50 0 50 100 150
Miles 50 0 50 100 150

ENERGY RESOURCES

Alison D. Allen

In the industrial and technological world of the seventies, energy is a basic component of society, and the availability of adequate resources of energy is vitally important to a nation's standard of living. New Zealand has been fortunate in having some resources of its own, which have played a most important role in ensuring the supply of energy essential to its way of life and its industrial growth. Technological advances and consumer preferences are, however, leading to increasing demands for energy, and although New Zealand has large reserves of some fuels, careful planning and utilisation of resources is already required. As all New Zealand's oil requirements come from overseas, changing patterns of supply and demand on a world-wide scale must be taken into account.

Electricity

New Zealand is very electricity-minded, with consumption per capita by domestic consumers being amongst the highest in the world. Industrial usage is growing—as the pulp and paper industry, the steel industry and the aluminium smelter at Bluff illustrate.

The topography of the country, and of the South Island in particular, is ideally suited for hydro-electric generation. Swift-running, fast-falling rivers ensure a continuous supply of fuel and numerous lakes provide natural storage. New Zealand has an extensive hydro-electric system which produces almost eighty per cent of its electricity, having a total generating capacity of 4100 megawatts, with a planned 4500 by June 1975.

Hydro-electricity has great advantages. Although stations are costly to build, running costs are low, the fuel is self-replenishing and the process pollution-free. As well as realising the tremendous benefit to the country of a cheap and reliable power supply, the building of hydro stations has also opened up previously inaccessible country, helped to control flooding and extend irrigation, and has provided new recreational facilities. The giant Benmore project in the South Island has become a tourist attraction in itself. The Waitaki River feeds not only Benmore but three other stations with a further four planned.

It has become government policy over the years to make electricity available on a nation-wide basis, and there are few populated areas in the country not now served. Hydro stations are usually distant from the centres of electricity usage and consequently an extensive and complex reticulation system has been developed. Basically, it is a 220 000 volt system, capable of moving large blocks of energy. An advanced part of the system is the direct current link between the Benmore dam on the Waitaki River and the Haywards substation in the Wellington area of the North Island. The link comprises forty kilometres of sea cable and 570 kilometres of overhead line, together with a rectifier station at Benmore and a convertor station at Haywards to link the DC line in to the AC system. On its completion in 1965, the scheme was the largest of its type outside Russia and technically ahead of any other such system in the world.

The hydro-electric system is supplemented by coal, natural gas, oil and geothermal generating stations. At present, there are thermal stations at Meremere (coal-fired), Otahuhu (gas/oil-fired), Marsden (oil-fired) and Wairakei (geothermal). A 600 megawatt station at New Plymouth, burning oil initially but later to use natural gas, generated its first electricity in 1974, and work has begun on a 1000 megawatt station at Huntly which will use coal and natural gas. This latter station, which will be New Zealand's largest to date, is scheduled to produce its first power in 1978. A further 1400 megawatt station is planned for the Auckland area and a 220 megawatt station at Stratford, both to be gas-fired, and a further oil-fired, 250 megawatt station at Marsden.

Thermal generating capacity, now approximately twenty per cent of total generating capacity, will reach twenty-eight per cent by June 1975. Hydro generation appears almost to have reached its peak, at least in the North Island, and there are now few suitable economic hydro sites left. Large thermal stations will be used progressively to add blocks of energy to the system, particularly in the North Island. Thermal stations are usually built fairly close to the area they are to serve, to avoid wasteful, long and costly transmission lines, but they have potential pollution problems, and are less efficient and generally more expensive in operation than hydro stations.

GEOTHERMAL STEAM

Wairakei was one of the first major geothermal plants in the world to generate electricity. Power was first produced in 1958, by 1963 the installed capacity had reached 192 megawatts and at present the Wairakei station produces 5.5 per cent of New Zealand's electricity supply. Considerable interest has been shown overseas in power generation from geothermal sources, and the success at Wairakei has been instrumental in the rapid development and exploitation of many other geothermal areas in the world. Under the auspices of the United Nations, New Zealand has provided technical assistance and personnel for many overseas projects, for example to the governments of Indonesia and Mexico, and many overseas engineers and scientists have visited this country.

Investigations into the potential of several other geothermal areas are being actively pursued. Hot springs are found in a number of places in the northern half of the North Island, including North Auckland and the East Cape, and also along the Alpine Fault in the South Island. The region of main interest as a source of economically exploitable energy is the thermal belt of the North Island, ranging from the mid-island volcanoes northwards to White Island in the Bay of Plenty. The potential energy in this region is estimated at between 1000 and 2000 megawatts, over about a dozen sites, ranging in status from 'proved' to 'inferred'. The Broadlands field, north of Wairakei, has already been selected as a site for another geothermal power station and studies indicate a production capability of 150 megawatts.

In addition to its large-scale use for electricity generation at Wairakei, and by the Tasman Pulp and Paper Company at Kawerau, geothermal energy is used for space and water heating, timber drying, plywood manufacture, glasshouse heating and other minor industrial uses in the Taupo–Rotorua area. Usage in these ways is very small in relation to the total resource available and other possibilities for the large-scale use of geothermal energy are being evaluated at the present time. One such possibility is the production of heavy water.

Coal

Coal is New Zealand's main indigenous fuel. Measured recoverable reserves amount to 189 million tonnes, with a further 112 million tonnes indicated and 551 million tonnes inferred. Annual consumption at present is 2.5 million tonnes, but new steps being taken to increase production, and an upsurge in demand, are expected to increase consumption substantially.

There are four different types of coal found in New Zealand. The most abundant reserves are found in the low-quality, lignite deposits in Southland, which amount to fifty per cent of the country's total reserves. These deposits can be mined by opencast methods at relatively low cost, but so far production from this area is only 4.5 per cent of the total. It is favourably placed for the export of derivatives from Bluff, and for large-scale power generation in the Southland area.

The main reserves of sub-bituminous coal are found in the Waikato, and there are four South Island fields. This is an all-purpose coal, low in sulphur, which can be burned without modification. It is suitable, and well-placed geographically, for industrial use in the North Island, and for large-scale power generation and domestic use.

The West Coast in the South Island is the traditional coal-mining area of New Zealand. With Acheron, in Canterbury, it has the only deposits of anthracite and it is the only source of bituminous coal, which is particularly suitable for gas manufacture as well as for general industrial and commercial use. Production costs tend to be high owing to the difficult terrain, and over the years traditional markets have declined. No anthracite was produced in 1972–3 from either source.

Traditional markets over the years have been for ships' bunkers, railways, gas manufacture, household use and general industry. The first market to decline was that for ships' bunkers, as more oil-fired ships and motor vessels came into use. The replacement of steam by diesel locomotives reduced another market, and domestic and industrial use fell because of an increasing preference for more convenient fuels. The use of petroleum feedstocks for gas manufacture and the reticulation of natural gas pipelines from New Plymouth to Auckland and Wellington have drastically reduced the demand for coal for town gas supplies.

Industrial consumers have recently begun to show a renewed interest in the use of coal as a fuel, and it appears that the industry will win back some of its previous share of this market. Coal is also becoming increasingly important as a fuel for electricity generation. Substantial improvements in productivity to meet this increased demand are being made by the growing use of mechanical methods of production. Because coal is an indigenous and abundant fuel, it has an important part to play in supplying future energy demands.

Manufactured Gas

The first gasworks in New Zealand was established in Auckland in 1862, and by 1916 there were fifty-six in the country. The industry was based on the coal carbonisation process and provided a ready market for West Coast coal, but owing to technical difficulties and competition from electricity and oil, the number of gas undertakings has decreased over the years. By 1974, the industry consisted of twelve undertakings providing less than one per cent of the country's energy requirements.

Although the contribution to the energy market is small, manufactured gas is still a valuable alternative fuel, especially in the South Island. Over the years, the industry has received considerable government support in the form of subsidies, mainly to strengthen the West Coast gas-coal industry, but also to avoid the large capital expenditure

necessary to provide the alternative, electricity.

In the last few years, traditional methods of gas manufacture have become increasingly uneconomic and updating, the use of coal substitutes and re-organisation have become necessary. In 1972, a detailed study of each gas undertaking, and of the industry as a whole, was made in order to determine a policy which would achieve this. As a result of the study, the industry now receives increased subsidies on domestic sales, and a policy of loans to update equipment has been implemented.

Natural Gas

A major event in the energy sector in recent years has been the discovery of large quantities of natural gas. This had long been produced in commercial quantities on a small scale from the Moturoa field near New Plymouth. The first well in this field was sunk in 1866, which made it one of the first producing fields in the world. Production from its last well ceased in 1972. During 1971, the final full year of production, 286 000 litres of crude petroleum and 0.04 million cubic metres of natural gas were produced.

Drilling in the Kapuni field, south of Mt Egmont, by the Shell BP and Todd Consortium, between 1959 and 1962 confirmed the presence of substantial quantities of natural gas and condensate. This discovery led to a flurry of prospecting both off shore and on shore, and in 1969 the Maui field, thirty miles off the Taranaki coast, was discovered.

Studies showed that the maximum benefit from Kapuni gas would be obtained by its use as a premium fuel for industrial and domestic purposes. The gas has a high carbon dioxide content, approximately 40 per cent, which is removed before it is transmitted. In 1967, the Natural Gas Corporation was formed, to buy gas from the consortium, process it and sell it to the distributors. The first customers were supplied in 1970, and by 1972 the corporation was selling gas to distributors in nine North Island centres, for retailing to domestic, commercial and industrial consumers.

Since the original discovery of the Kapuni field, reserves have been revised progressively and are now estimated to be about 485 300 terajoules (460×10^{12} BTUs). The clean-burning qualities and high efficiency of the gas make it a sought-after fuel. Expansion of the processing facilities is at present under way to increase production from 2 million to 6 million cubic metres per day.

In April 1973, the government and the oil consortium reached agreement on the terms of a joint venture for the ownership and development of the Maui field, with the government purchasing a half share. Development of the Maui field is the largest single undertaking entered into by the State in the history of New Zealand, with immense importance in planning future energy policies.

The Maui field covers an area of 785 square kilometres and is one of the twenty largest fields in the world. Gas from the field will be used initially for the generation of electricity, as this provides the large, early and stable market necessary to justify the very high capital costs involved in gas recovery. The feasibility of establishing industries based on natural gas is also being studied. The development of the field is of great importance in that it ensures a vital supply of hydrocarbons at a time of world shortage and high prices.

Petroleum Products

Continued drilling activity indicates that there may be further oil and gas discoveries, but in the meantime New Zealand is not self-sufficient in oil and oil products. Fifty-nine per cent of the energy market is provided by oil products, of which nearly half is to meet motor gasoline requirements. The demand for power-station and industrial fuel oils is relatively light compared to that in other industrialised countries, but has increased rapidly in recent years. Very large advances in oil prices, however, could mean that this demand will increase only slowly.

In 1964, the New Zealand Refinery Company began production at Marsden Point, Whangarei. The refinery, with a rated capacity of 60 000 barrels per day, was designed to meet all New Zealand's then requirements for motor gasoline, gas oil or diesel fuel oil and bitumen, totalling about ninety per cent of the demand for all petroleum products previously imported. The refinery is currently working at its maximum capacity of 23.5 million barrels a year, but demand has outrun supply and up to 30 per cent of refined product supplies have still to be imported. Crude oil and partly refined products are imported mainly from the Persian Gulf, while fully refined products to meet the balance of demand come from Australia, Singapore and the Persian Gulf. Demand in 1973 for the principal petroleum products was:

Motor gasoline	–	2256 million litres per annum
Gas oil	–	1150 million litres per annum
Fuel oil	–	1310 million litres per annum

Plans for the expansion of the existing refinery to double its capacity are under discussion, and plans for a second have also been mooted. Condensate from the Maui and Kapuni fields is likely to supply ten to fifteen per cent of the feedstock for the present refinery, but, subject to a crude oil find, New Zealand will continue to rely largely on overseas supplies.

Nuclear Power

The 1964 Power Planning report suggested that increased demand in the Auckland area would necessitate a large thermal station in the 1970s, but that consideration should be given to a nuclear station. Committees were established to study possible sites, together with manpower requirements, safety criteria and licensing arrangements, and staff of the Electricity Department attended overseas courses. The 1968 Power Planning report recommended a unit, rating 250 megawatts, to be in operation in 1977, with three similar units following at regular intervals. The report pointed out that this programme could be significantly affected by large-scale discoveries of natural gas, but recommended that plans for a nuclear station should proceed on the assumption that natural gas would not be available. In 1969, overseas consultants were engaged to report on all aspects of nuclear generation and its economics in relation to hydro and thermal generation. The purpose of the study was to verify that a nuclear station, north of Auckland, would be the most economical means of meeting the load growth in the North Island in the seventies, and to obtain specific recommendations for the type of nuclear system most suitable.

By 1970, however, it had been firmly established that the Maui field contained substantial quantities of natural gas. It seemed that electricity generation alone would make its recovery economic, and the consultants accordingly preferred a gas-fired to a nuclear-powered station. The nuclear station was, therefore, omitted and a 1000 megawatt thermal station substituted in the Power Plan. It was not until 1974, when the forecast growth in demand for electricity had still further increased, that a nuclear power station was re-introduced in the Plan; but the decision to 'go nuclear' will not be made until 1977 at the earliest.

Alternative Sources of Energy

Two new sources of energy currently being considered in New Zealand are wind power and solar power. New Zealand's wind power potential is one of the highest in the world and its utilisation is being studied by both university and government scientists. As well, a study of solar energy, particularly for use in domestic water heaters, is being made.

Organisation of the Energy Sector

In 1972, the Ministry of Energy Resources was established to develop and co-ordinate energy policies and to act as a focal point on energy matters. In advising the government, it must take social, economic, local and national factors into account. Its establishment has aroused considerable interest overseas.

There is too the Energy Research and Development Committee, created by the Prime Minister and independent of existing government agencies, to further research in other than established fields of energy resources. As well, the National Research Advisory Council, the universities and the Department of Scientific and Industrial Research all carry out research on a wide range of energy and energy-related topics. Other government departments involved in energy matters include the Ministry of Works and Development, which is responsible for the design and construction of power stations; the Department of Trade and Industry, because of the energy requirements of industries, and Treasury, which is responsible for the financial aspects.

The New Zealand Electricity Department is responsible for almost all the electricity generation and bulk trans-mission in the country, the remainder being generated by stations operated by industrial establishments and local supply authorities. The Department supplies the electricity supply authorities, which in turn distribute to the final consumers. It is also responsible for servicing the committee that produces the annual Power Planning Report.

The Mines Department, with the prime responsibility for coal, its production and distribution from the State Coal Mines, also advises the government on policies affecting prospecting and mining; issues licences for mining and petroleum prospecting; maintains inspections to ensure compliance with licensing conditions and safe operation, and provides financial assistance where it will stimulate worthwhile work. It has already been described how natural gas is the responsibility of an exploration consortium and a distribution corporation. Final distribution is effected by both municipal and private authorities, which are also concerned with manufactured gas where no reticulation of natural gas is yet possible.

The oil industry is the only energy industry in New Zealand which is totally privately-owned. There are six oil companies operating, all of them now overseas-owned and with international associations; one of them, Europa Oil, was wholly New Zealand-owned until its sale to British Petroleum (NZ) in 1972. The Marsden Point refinery is operated by the New Zealand Refinery Company, in which approximately one-third of the shares are held by the New Zealand public and the remainder by the oil companies.

The future for the supply of energy, in the beginning of 1975, is complicated by the high price of oil throughout the world. New Zealand has the advantages of its own great water, natural gas and coal resources but will continue its search for its own crude oil to supply gasoline.

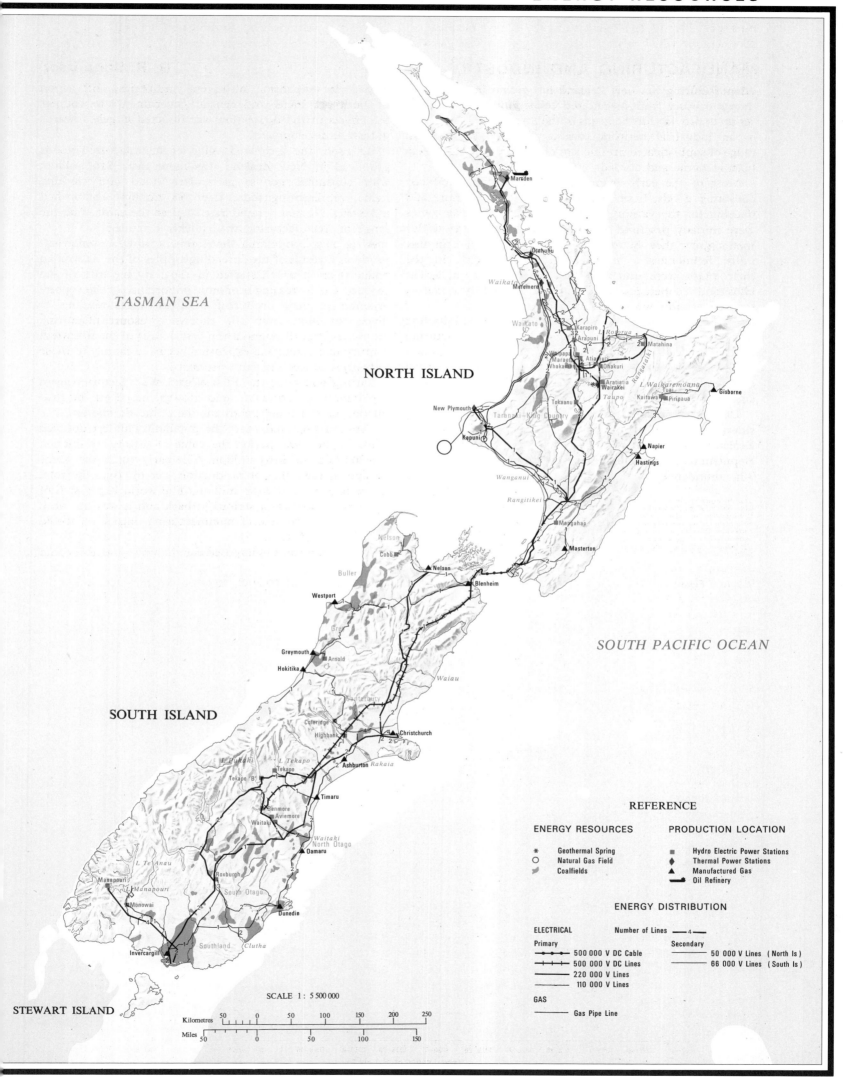

TASMAN SEA

NORTH ISLAND

Waikato

Waikato

Marsden

Otahuhu

Meremere

Karapiro
Arapuni
Waipapa
Maraetai
Whakamaru

L Rotorua

Matahina

Atiamuri
Ohakuri

Aratiatia
Wairakei
Taupo

Tuai
Kaitawa
Piripaua

L Waikaremoana

Gisborne

New Plymouth

Tokaanu

Taranaki-King Country

Kapuni

Napier
Hastings

Wanganui

Rangitikei

Mangahao

Masterton

Nelson

Cobb

Buller

Nelson

Blenheim

Westport

SOUTH PACIFIC OCEAN

Grey

Greymouth
Arnold

Hokitika

Waiau

Canterbury

Coleridge
Highbank

Christchurch

Rakaia

Ashburton

L Pukaki
L Tekapo

Tekapo

Tekapo 'B'

Timaru

Benmore
Aviemore
Waitaki

Waitaki
North Otago

Oamaru

L Te Anau

SOUTH ISLAND

Roxburgh

South Otago

Manapouri

L Manapouri

Manowai

Dunedin

Southland   *Clutha*

Invercargill

STEWART ISLAND

REFERENCE

ENERGY RESOURCES   PRODUCTION LOCATION

✳ Geothermal Spring   ◼ Hydro Electric Power Stations
◯ Natural Gas Field   ◆ Thermal Power Stations
   Coalfields   ▲ Manufactured Gas
                              ▬ Oil Refinery

ENERGY DISTRIBUTION

ELECTRICAL   Number of Lines ————4————

Primary   Secondary
•━━• 500 000 V DC Cable   ——— 50 000 V Lines (North Is)
━┼━┼ 500 000 V DC Lines   ——— 66 000 V Lines (South Is)
━━━ 220 000 V Lines
——— 110 000 V Lines

GAS

——— Gas Pipe Line

SCALE 1 : 5 500 000

Kilometres 50 0 50 100 150 200 250

Miles 50 0 50 100 150

MANUFACTURING AND INDUSTRY

G. R. Sanderson

Manufacturing[1] in New Zealand has grown in little more than a century from a scattered collection of local trades, set up to provide for the needs of the first European settlers, to an industrial network turning out a comprehensive range of sophisticated products to meet the needs of markets both at home and abroad.

Most of the early manufacturing industries produced consumer goods, basic needs such as food, clothing and housing for the various small communities. These trades were initially practised as home crafts, but as the settlements grew they became factory-based. Flour and flax mills, fellmongeries and ropewalks established in the early 1840s were quickly followed by breweries, brick-kilns and cooperages, lime kilns, ship and boat yards, soap and candle works and tanneries.

Statistics of factory production were collected for the first time in 1867, by which time the range of manufacturing had been extended to include grain milling, the production of biscuits, bone-manure, coaches, scoured wool, cordial and aerated water as well as engineering workshops, sash and door factories and a woollen mill.

Despite a world depression in the early 1870s, considerable manufacturing expansion took place in New Zealand during the decade, boosted by a rapid rise in population and a gradual improvement in communications. The abundance of cheap labour created by the depression

[1] This discussion conforms to the definitions in the United Nations International Standard Industrial Classification of All Economic Activities (1958). Single person establishments, and persons engaged in distribution are excluded, which restricts the total labour force to some 86% of the recorded grand total. Statistics, unless otherwise indicated, are for the year ended 31 March 1972, with value of production based on the factory selling price of all articles manufactured, assembled or processed, and comprising total costs of materials, salaries and wages, general expenses and factory profit margin. Net output or net value added represents salaries and wages, interest on borrowed capital, and factory profit.

helped the expansion of several industries, and action by both provincial and central governments to counter the effects of the depression was directed largely towards industrial development.

By 1890, the estimated value of manufactured goods produced in New Zealand was more than $16 million, with consumer goods, particularly food and clothing items, representing more than $8 million. Established industries grew at a rapid rate, and at the same time the range of manufacturing was quickly extended.

After 1890, industrial development slowed somewhat, partly as a result of the spreading ripples of the Australian financial crash which started in 1893. By the turn of the century, the increasing economic importance of the export-oriented primary producing industries was tending to divert attention from the expansion of manufacturing industries, and throughout the first decade of the twentieth century manufacturing expansion occurred mainly in those industries processing farm products.

During and after the First World War, factories again experienced a period of rapid growth, based on the production of consumer goods for the domestic market.

Between 1890 and 1920, the population almost doubled while in the same period the value of factory production rose tenfold, to $164 million. The early 1920s saw some decline in the value of production, yet by 1930 the total figure had risen to $180 million. The world depression of the early 1930s was a serious setback and it was not until 1935 that the volume of manufacturing output recovered to the level of 1930.

Import control was imposed for the first time at the end

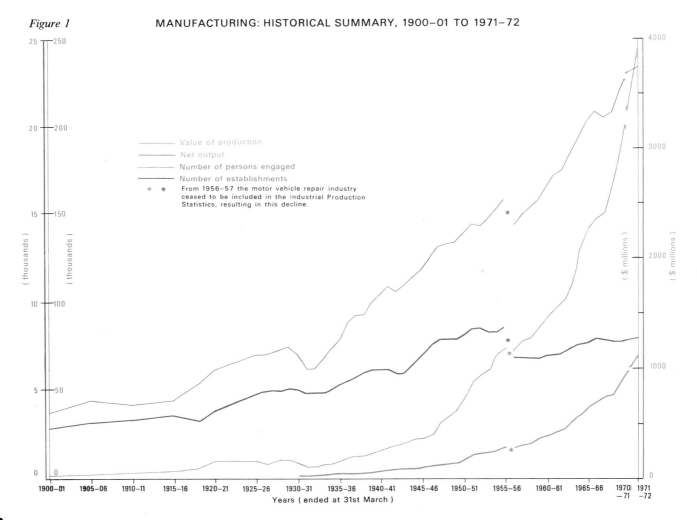

Figure 1   MANUFACTURING: HISTORICAL SUMMARY, 1900–01 TO 1971–72

Value of production
Net output
Number of persons engaged
Number of establishments
*   *   From 1956–57 the motor vehicle repair industry ceased to be included in the Industrial Production Statistics, resulting in this decline.

Years (ended at 31st March)

of 1938, largely to counteract the country's unfavourable balance of payments. Its effects were rapidly overtaken by the outbreak of the Second World War, which stimulated demand and created shortages of all kinds, notably of consumer imports. These conditions gave a considerable boost to New Zealand manufacturing; many industries, assured of a substantial part of the domestic market, were able to grow to optimum size quickly, without having to struggle through a difficult period of competition with established overseas producers. In the six years to the end of 1945, net output of manufactured goods expanded by almost one third. Continued protection against imports and an excess of demand over supply maintained expansionary conditions until the end of the 1940s.

The removal of a considerable degree of import control in 1950 and the substantial imports resulting from high export receipts for wool during the Korean war, tended to slow industrial development. However, the rapid growth of the manufacturing industries as a whole was carried on into the mid-1950s because of rapid population growth and high internal liquidity.

Export prices, particularly for dairy produce, fell sharply towards the end of 1957, with no compensating reduction in the high level of imports. Tumbling overseas reserves brought the re-imposition of import and exchange controls in the following year and fairly comprehensive import control remained during most of the decade. A minor recession in the years immediately after 1967, largely a result of international financial uncertainties, was followed by returning stability, permitting a significant degree of reduction and rationalisation of protective control. From 1960 to 1970, the number of people employed in manufacturing increased by almost fifty per cent, while the value of production more than doubled, to $3,153 million.

The high prices commanded by beef and wool exports in the early 1970s had slumped by 1974, and increased prices for many essential imports, especially oil, again brought about a deficit in the balance of payments and slowed the growth of manufacturing.

The history of the development of manufacturing in New Zealand is therefore characterised by a series of relatively long periods of stable growth, checked by crises frequently related to external factors affecting the balance of payments. It is nevertheless apparent that, since the depression of the 1930s, New Zealand's manufacturing industry has been sufficiently established, diversified and competitive to sustain much of its own impetus.

The Face of Industry

The principal concentration of manufacturing activity is around and immediately south of Auckland, with other major areas in Wellington and the adjoining Hutt Valley, and in a zone radiating from Christchurch. Most factories are of single-floor construction, and few are more than two-storeyed, reflecting the hitherto comparatively modest price of industrial land. Although prices are now rising rapidly and land availability cannot always be taken for granted, there are few signs that New Zealand factories are about to grow higher or closer together.

The larger cities are still characterised by a core of old factories, built up to eighty years ago, often of brick or stone. Conforming to urban renewal trends long observed overseas, the inner city factories are steadily giving way to high-rise offices or warehouses, the flour mill in down-town Auckland, for example, having recently disappeared. Old factories are being re-located and new plants built in industrial areas either towards the fringes of the cities or in industrial ribbon developments along the main access routes. Factories in the new industrial zones are sometimes able to draw workers from neighbouring residential areas. In the largest cities, however, labour remains scarce despite improved factory locations, and manufacturers frequently provide transport for workers living many miles from their employment. The search for an adequate and stable labour force is leading a growing number of city-based manufacturers to set up satellite factories, in nearby towns and in more remote districts.

Small-town industry retains, in many cases, much the same appearance that it had a century ago. The smallest locality on a map of New Zealand may not feature a hotel or even a general store, but it is very likely to be marked by a service station and workshop. The village blacksmith remains alive and well in the guise of the local garageman, a jack-of-all-trades who repairs cars as well as trucks, tractors and a variety of farm and other machinery. When the need arises he will also modify equipment to suit his customers or design and construct machinery for specialised purposes.

Among the industries characteristic of many small towns are bakeries, grain processors, sawmills and joineries, dairy factories, wool scours and clothing factories. Each town is likely to possess only one or two such factories but, because the small towns are usually agricultural service centres rather than centres of manufacturing activity, these industries tend to be important in their own localities. Some of the activities of the stock and station agent are classified as manufacturing, among them stock feed preparation, seed cleaning, sack and bag production, the moulding of concrete fence posts and other items, and the fabrication of sheet metal products.

Some industries have developed away from towns: sawmills, quarries and cement works are obvious examples. New Zealand's few 'mill towns', largely dependent on a single industry, are typically associated with coal mining, forest products and hydro-electric power projects. The most notable example is probably Tokoroa, in the centre of the North Island, serving the pulp and paper mill at nearby Kinleith; Kawerau in the same region, with its two paper mills, and Waiuku in the South Auckland region with its steel mill, are perhaps equally obvious. Nevertheless, in such cases, existing townships were transformed by the major industries, not built around them as with a number of power projects. Deliberate efforts have been made to create a balanced economy within the towns. Knitwear, clothing and light electrical industries integrate well with very large industrial plants, since they not only help to diversify the range of activity but also provide employment for women.

Control of Industry

Britain enjoyed a clear start in establishing ownership over industries in this country, particularly those producing machinery and metal products, foodstuffs and household goods. After the Second World War, American influence became increasingly strong, particularly in the rapidly growing chemical and electrical industries, where imported technology was needed. Several large European firms also have significant shares in these industries. Since the 1960s, more and more technology has come from Japan, particularly in the chemical, electronic, optical, mineral and automotive industries.

Australian companies have a substantial stake in New Zealand's glass, plastics and sugar refining industries, besides in fields such as metal products manufacture, where the transfer of moulds, dies and jigs between associated companies on either side of the Tasman permits reductions in some manufacturing overheads. Many American, British and European manufacturers have indirect interests through Australian subsidiaries.

In 1964, just over five per cent of the factories in New Zealand were described as overseas owned. These factories employed twenty per cent of the manufacturing labour force and the value of their production represented almost twenty-six per cent of all manufactured goods.

Almost all dairy factories are New Zealand owned, and New Zealand retains very substantial control in vegetable and fruit processing, brewing, textile and apparel, paper, pulp, timber and wood products industries, as well as in the manufacture of mechanical engineering products.

Cultural Influences

Overseas influences do not come only from those countries whose manufacturers operate subsidiaries in New Zealand. Several industries owe much to the skills of immigrants: Eastern European vintners helped to develop the New Zealand wine industry; the woollen milling industry still employs many men with Yorkshire accents; Scandinavians contribute their expertise to the timber and pulp industries; leathergoods, ski apparel, women's top-quality blouses and coats, and other specialised products are amongst the goods made in New Zealand by immigrants, particularly from Europe. Many enterprises which started as one-man or one-family businesses now employ sizeable staffs and add to New Zealand's export trade.

In designs, New Zealand industry has been enriched by contributions from its own culture. Traditional Maori patterns are now used in consumer industries alongside motifs from the Americas; woodware may be fashioned in Polynesian or in European styles; and jewellery may reveal Pacific or Baltic origins. The quality of industrial design is emphasized by the government-supported Industrial Design Council.

Industrial Development

A summary of the history of manufacturing reveals three major trends: first, the growth of basic consumer industries producing goods for the local market; secondly, the development of factories producing substitutes for imported goods; and thirdly, the emergence of fully independent and competitive industries utilising New Zealand resources. The trends may overlap, and many industries exemplify all three. The textile industry provides a good example. Small-scale woollen mills weaving cloth for the townsfolk grew and diversified to provide goods that could not be imported, because of wartime conditions or shortages of overseas funds. More recently, the industry assumed major economic importance as a producer of carpet yarn and carpets using New Zealand wool.

The first trend requires no further comment. The second trend, import substitution, developed from the end of the 1930s, has aided both the establishment and the diversification of New Zealand industry and remains the basis for much manufacturing activity. However, the scope for its application is limited. If much of the raw material must be imported, prospects for developing manufacture are restricted. Moreover, the small size of the domestic market and New Zealand's relatively high standard of living mean that New Zealand production costs tend to be high. Perhaps most significantly, import substitution tends to make manufacturing in New Zealand a micro-copy of that in highly industrialised countries, often limiting opportunities for the development of industry on lines particularly suited to New Zealand conditions.

The third trend, the emergence of distinctively New

Zealand industries, was becoming apparent during the 1950s, and has intensified since the mid-1960s. In this category are the industries processing indigenous resources into finished products, instead of exporting them in raw or semi-processed states. Greasy wool, for example, is being turned into yarn and carpets, logs into pulp and paper, ironsand into steel and meatworks by-products into base materials for pharmaceuticals.

An industrial sphere of particular significance is the design and construction of equipment for the mass markets represented by the primary industries. New Zealand is a leading producer of dairy machinery, ranging from milk stimulators to automated cream freezing tunnels, together with much machinery for handling or processing meat, wool, timber and horticultural produce.

Industries based on home-grown expertise represent a further important group. Farming needs led to the production of aircraft for topdressing, and this was followed by the development of small aircraft for training purposes. Recreational pursuits prompted the manufacture of climbing and boating equipment now well known overseas. New Zealand's contributions to medical equipment are exemplified by artificial heart valve supports, portable heart monitors and binaural sensory aids for the blind. Several nuclear accelerators in overseas countries use polarised ion sources and ion beam handling systems of New Zealand origin. Expertise in specialised fields is also leading to the marketing of pure technology rather than of products: civil engineering programmes and project evaluations are prominent examples.

Regional Distribution

Manufacturing activity is markedly concentrated in the North Island, which contains three-quarters of New Zealand's factories, factory employees and manufactured goods by value. The Central Auckland region, with a quarter of the total New Zealand population and a third of the manufacturing work force, has factories and value of production representing a little more than thirty per cent of the national total.

The Auckland employment district contributed precisely a third of the net output of all New Zealand factories, while the next highest district, Christchurch, was responsible for only one eighth. However, if the net output of factories in the Wellington and Lower Hutt districts were combined, the total would be slightly higher than that for Christchurch. Separately, Lower Hutt contributed eight per cent, while Hamilton, Rotorua, Wellington and Dunedin each contributed approximately five per cent of the New Zealand total. Invercargill, at 4.2 per cent, and Palmerston North, at 3.7 per cent, were followed by Whangarei, Napier, Hastings, New Plymouth, Wanganui, Nelson and Timaru, all within the range of 1 1–2.7 per cent. Tauranga, Gisborne, Masterton, Blenheim, Greymouth, Ashburton and Oamaru each contributed one per cent or less.

A number of industries assume special importance in particular regions. Amongst these are Northland's oil refinery and Central Auckland's steel mill; pulp and paper production in the South Auckland/Bay of Plenty region; vineyards and fish, fruit and vegetable processing on the East Coast; the electrical industry in Hawke's Bay; dairy factories and non-ferrous metal production in Taranaki; motor vehicle assembly in the Wellington region, machinery manufacture in Marlborough, tobacco and cement production in Nelson, sawmilling and mineral processing on the West Coast, rubbergoods manufacture and grain milling in Canterbury, woollen milling and tanning in

Otago and aluminium smelting in Southland.

The increasing regional and national costs of continued rapid growth in the major urban centres, and the economic and social consequences of flagging development in many provincial towns, attracted considerable attention in the late 1960s, leading in the early 1970s to the establishment of a comprehensive government programme to help counteract imbalances in regional growth rates. Regional Development Councils, effecting a programme that, while applicable to a wide variety of projects, is primarily geared to the expansion of manufacturing, had been set up in ten areas by early 1975.

The Scale of Industry

New Zealand manufacturing is characterised by small-scale enterprises. In 1972, fifty-three per cent of all factories employed no more than ten people each, practically the same percentage as that recorded a decade earlier. Factories employing more than a hundred workers accounted for only 5.24 per cent of all establishments. The average number of persons engaged in each establishment was 29.86 in 1971–72, compared with 24.50 in 1961–62.

The high percentage of factories with staffs of fewer than six contributed less than three per cent of the total value of production, compared with the thirty-four per cent from the considerably fewer factories employing more than 200; ten or more per cent of total production value came from the fourteen plants with staffs of at least a thousand. The small size of so many New Zealand factories is attributable in part to the geographic characteristics of the country and its consequently fragmented markets, and in part to its comparatively short manufacturing history.

industries accounted for twenty-four per cent of the total labour force, with those in agriculture, forestry and fishing together contributing only half that percentage.

Industrial Groups

In the year ended 31 March 1972, there were 7783 factories employing 232 424 people. The total value of production was $3,873 million, and the value of net output reached $1,437 million. There were sixteen statistically distinguished industrial groups.[2]

FOOD, BEVERAGES AND TOBACCO

The processing of foodstuffs was New Zealand's largest single manufacturing industry. With a value of production totalling $1,234 million, the food manufacturing industries surpassed in value the output of any other manufacturing group, and accounted for thirty-two per cent of all factory output. Yet the 541 factories engaged in food processing constituted only about five per cent of the total number of factories in New Zealand.

The average factory output in the group was worth $2.28 million annually. Of the sixty-two plants with a production valued at $5 million or more, thirty-two were freezing works, and twenty-one dairy factories.

In the food manufacturing group, three in every ten factories were co-operatively owned dairy factories engaged in the production of butter, cheese or other milk products. Meat freezing and preserving works accounted for one factory in every twelve.

The beverage-making industries employed just over 3000 people and had 137 factories with production valued at $76 million. Almost half of the establishments were concerned with winemaking, and of these, two out of

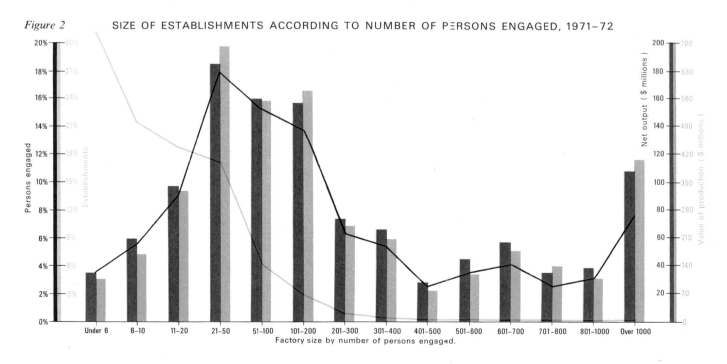

Figure 2 SIZE OF ESTABLISHMENTS ACCORDING TO NUMBER OF PERSONS ENGAGED, 1971–72

Factory size by number of persons engaged.

Economic Role of Manufacturing

In the year ended 31 March 1972, manufacturing industry contributed almost twenty-one per cent of domestic output. As a proportion of gross national product, the value of manufacturing production, in unadjusted monetary terms, remained fairly constant throughout the 1960s, with annual percentage growth rates following very closely those of gross national product, although those for the farming sector fluctuated considerably in response to changes in overseas markets.

In October 1973, workers engaged in manufacturing

three were located in the Central Auckland area. Having achieved volume, the industry is now concentrating on quality production based on classical varieties of grapes. The next largest group of beverage-making industries produced aerated water and cordials. These factories are concentrated in the major cities. The breweries, with only fifteen plants, had a value of production of $48 million. Gin and vodka are distilled and blended in Auckland, while the first officially distilled New Zealand whisky was

[2] The industrial groups considered below conform to those in the New Zealand Industrial Production statistics, but several of the headings have been shortened or summarised.

distributed from Dunedin at the beginning of 1974.

The tobacco industry comprised five units, with a total output valued at $28 million. Some 1200 workers were employed, a comparatively high proportion of them being women. Three of the factories, in Central Auckland, Hawke's Bay and Wellington, were engaged in the manufacture of tobacco, cigars and cigarettes from imported and New Zealand leaf, with a fourth factory being set up in Masterton. The Hawke's Bay plant was the largest, employing more than 600 people. Two other factories in this sector, both located in Nelson, carried out drying and shredding of New Zealand leaf, which accounted for forty per cent of all leaf used.

TEXTILES

The New Zealand textile industry remains strongly oriented towards the use of wool. By value, almost ninety per cent of fibre purchased by spinning and weaving mills was wool. Although the knitting sector made considerable use of cotton and man-made fibres (nylon accounted for more than a third of the value of yarn used), wool still made up thirty per cent of the cost of yarn.

The 197 factories in the textile group represented 2.5 per cent of all the factories in the country; yet the industry's value of production, amounting to $254 million, was equivalent to 6.5 per cent of the national total. The export-oriented sectors, particularly wool scouring and the manufacture of carpet and carpet yarn, made a substantial contribution. Employment in the textile industry totalled 16 000, forty-five per cent being women.

Most mills in the textile industry were involved in the manufacture of knitted goods, including hosiery. These mills are located for the most part either in or near the main urban centres, almost half of them in the Central Auckland area, as are half of the establishments in the 'other spinning and weaving' sector. Woollen mills, concentrating on the production of woven fabric, totalled twenty-three, with eleven situated in Otago and Canterbury. The twenty-six wool scours are distributed evenly through the country.

Rationalisation, diversification and expansion modified the nature of the woollen milling industry during the fifteen years to 1973, with the number of companies reduced by mergers and the range of cloth expanded, particularly in light-weight and synthetic fabrics. Two mills, south of Auckland and near Levin, produced polyamide (nylon) and polyester yarn and fibre, while others, notably in Christchurch, extruded polypropylene flat yarn and wove it into sacks and bags. The recent installation of much modern machinery has improved production and productivity.

New Zealand wool, being of predominantly cross-bred classes with relatively coarse counts, is well suited to the production of carpets, where its durability and resilience confer the properties desired in high-quality floor coverings. Drysdale wool, possessing many of the characteristics of Scottish Blackface wool, was specially developed in New Zealand for carpet manufacture. The volume of carpet yarn spun in New Zealand doubled between 1965 and 1969, and doubled again in the following four-year period to approximately 14 million kilogrammes. Wool carpet production also doubled between 1965 and 1970, rising to 9 million square metres in 1973.

APPAREL

This group comprised 925 factories manufacturing footwear, clothing apparel accessories, gloves, hats and all kinds of made-up textile goods. The total value of all goods produced was $186 million and the total number of people employed was 29 000, of whom more than eighty per cent were women. Outerwear accounted for forty per cent of all factories in the group. Many small clothing factories have been set up in smaller provincial centres in order to take advantage of the local female labour force.

A characteristic of the clothing sectors is the prominent role of sub-contractors, known as 'cut, make and trim' (CMT) establishments. These factories produce garments from materials supplied by their customers, often large retail chains.

The most widely used material in the clothing sectors was woven cotton, followed by woven fabric of man-made fibres. Wool and wool blends occupied an important place in clothing produced from woven cloth, but was much less significant in the production of knitted goods. The most numerous products were trousers and dresses. Two pairs of women's shoes were manufactured for every one pair of men's.

TIMBER PRODUCTS

The establishments in this group comprised sawmills, board mills, joineries, and factories making a very wide range of wood products, from clothes pegs to gates. Logging activities and furniture making were excluded. In total, 982 establishments produced goods valued at $198 million. More than 14 000 people were employed, ninety-five per cent of the total work force being men.

Joineries represented the most numerous sub-group, with sawmills not far behind. Planing mills and timber preservation plants, both frequently operating within general timber merchants' premises, made up the third main sub-group, while plywood and veneer mills, and fabricators of wooden containers represented the only other distinguishable bodies of manufacturers within the group.

The manufacture of timber-based building boards has expanded spectacularly since the late 1960s. Particleboard was first manufactured in New Zealand in 1965, when annual output was 550 000 square metres, and production grew rapidly. A plant starting production at Kumeu, north of Auckland, in 1972, doubled the previous New Zealand output to a total of 6.5 million square metres, while other major expansions have taken place or are planned at Taupo and Thames. Hardboard and softboard production has also risen, and a large fibreboard plant is to begin manufacture at Rangiora in the late 1970s.

Besides rough-sawn timber, which may later be dressed by planing mills, sawmills produce such items as fence posts and railway sleepers. Timber preservation techniques now permit the ubiquitous radiata pine to be used for these and other demanding purposes for which Australian hardwoods were formerly needed.

Regionally, sawmills and joineries are well spread. Small mills of this type are a feature of many New Zealand townships, particularly in Northland, Nelson, Otago and Southland, while the large sawmills tend to attract their own servicing settlements. On the other hand, most of the timber merchants operate in or near the larger towns. It is significant that fifty-seven per cent of the manufacturing labour force in Westland was employed in timber production (excluding logging), compared with a national average of only six per cent. Similarly, even in the much more populous areas of South Auckland and the Bay of Plenty, the timber products industry was the largest single employer, taking twenty-two per cent.

FURNITURE

Domestic, commercial and other furniture and fittings were the principal items produced by this group, including products made from all kinds of materials, and embracing French-polishing, upholstering and the manufacture of wooden television cabinets and laminated sink benches. Minor sections produced mattresses (of material other than foam rubber), pillows, quilts and other bedding, venetian and roller blinds. There were 407 factories, the total value of their production reaching $58 million.

PAPER

The manufacture of pulp, paper and associated products is one of New Zealand's largest industries in terms of its contribution to the national economy. Although this group comprised only 114 establishments and some 9000 people, its production was valued at $195 million. The industry is based on the large exotic forests of the central North Island, statistically represented by the South Auckland/Bay of Plenty area, where one in every seven factory workers was an employee of the paper industry. Although one dollar in five paid out in factory salaries and wages within this area was earned by a paper industry worker, salaries and wages throughout the industry represented only sixty-one per cent of net output. In the Rotorua employment district, in the heart of the exotic forest region, the industry contributed half the value of goods manufactured.

The principal products of the paper mills included pulp; newsprint; printing, writing, wrapping and tissue paper and paperboard and fibreboard. Other factories produced corrugated board, boxes, cartons, and containers of many kinds. More specialised manufacturers concentrated on goods such as envelopes, cigarette paper, carbon paper, sensitised paper, wallpaper and mill cores.

During 1973, New Zealand Forest Products' pulp and paper mill at Kinleith commissioned a new kraft pulp mill, doubling output to 425 000 tonnes, and completed the installation of a sixth paper machine. These developments, along with extensions of the company's activities at Whakatane and Penrose, comprised an expansion programme originally estimated in 1969 to cost $105 million, the largest ever undertaken by an individual company in New Zealand's industrial history. The Tasman Pulp and Paper Company's mill at Kawerau in the early 1970s embarked on a 120 per cent increase in sulphate pulp production, and the installation of a third newsprint machine. Literally across the road from Tasman, Caxton Paper Mills, in the mid-1970s, extended pulp capacity and set up a third paper machine for the manufacture of tissue grades. The year 1973 also saw the establishment of a new mill at Whirinaki, north of Napier, by Carter Oji Kokusaku Pan Pacific, processing sawn timber and refiner groundwood pulp for the Japanese market. During the mid-1970s, a number of smaller companies initiated plans for the production of refiner groundwood pulp.

PRINTING

Printing and publishing houses were principally involved in the production of newspapers, periodicals, magazines and books. The sector used 94 000 tonnes of newsprint and received $47 million from daily newspaper sales. The number of delivery boys handling these sales was not recorded. Sales for the whole printing group totalled $132 million from 512 establishments.

The general printing sector included contract and commission work, as well as bookbinding and the printing of calendars, cards, account books and other commercial items. Sales of greetings and Christmas cards reached an incredible $3.8 million in 1971–72, an increase of fifty per cent in only two years. The service industries sector covered companies specialising in type-setting and photo-engraving, as well as in more diversified work.

LEATHER

Of the 115 factories in this group, only seven were public companies, the rest being privately owned. The 2500 people employed produced goods worth $26 million.

Until 1970, a very high proportion of New Zealand's sheep and cattle skins was sold overseas in virtually unprocessed form. Since then, spurred partly by international shortages of raw material and increasingly serious pollution problems in industrialised countries overseas, there has been a marked upsurge in efforts to carry out more processing in New Zealand. Several existing tanneries have expanded, and new groups are establishing large plants in various parts of the country to produce crust-tanned and fully-finished leathers. Tanneries, producing leather from sheep skins and cattle hides, as well as the popular woolly sheepskins, numbered eighteen, four being in Central Auckland and a similar number in Otago. The tanneries used twice as many sheep skins as cattle hides.

Saddlery and harness sales of $700,000 may indicate something about life in New Zealand.

RUBBER

Small firms engaged primarily in retreading tyres predominated in the rubber industry, with seventy-four factories from the total 109 units. Although tending strongly to concentrate near the large urban areas, tyre retreaders operated at least one plant in every statistical area of New Zealand. The other sectors, engaged in tyre and general rubber goods manufacture, had factories located in Central Auckland, Wellington and Canterbury. Three of them, tyre and tube manufacturers, had the greatest influence in the group. Motor tyres were the largest single item manufactured, having a sales value of $18 million, equivalent to one third the value of all goods produced by the group.

The rubber industry's labour productivity, measured in net value per employee, reached $5,760, almost twenty per cent above the national average.

CHEMICALS

The chemical industries represented one of the most diverse groups of New Zealand manufactures, despite the fact that they comprised only 224 factories with a total value of production of $183 million. The factories are concentrated in the Central Auckland, Wellington and Canterbury areas, but some chemical works are to be found in virtually every area. Although most plants were small and only sixteen employed more than 100 people, the typical turnover was high in relation to the numbers employed. Sales of more than $200,000 each were recorded by fifty-eight per cent of all plants.

In the whole group, which employed 7000 people, salaries and wages covered only forty-eight per cent of net output, one of the most efficient ratios for any manufacturing industry.

Manufacturers of miscellaneous chemical products comprised the largest sector in the group, with ninety establishments turning out goods worth $50 million. Their products included cleaners, polishes, detergents, disinfectants, adhesives, weedkillers, insecticides and a very wide variety of industrial chemicals and gases. The thirty-six paint and varnish manufacturers, whose products include automotive and marine paints, had a total turnover of $23 million.

The pharmaceuticals, toiletries and cosmetic sector comprised thirty-seven factories with an output of $27 million. An important step occurred in the early 1970s

167

with the formation of a company near Palmerston North to manufacture a range of pharmaceutical materials from animal bile or gall, previously exported in dehydrated form. The potential pharmaceutical value of a New Zealand plant species is currently being studied by other companies.

Other sectors processed vegetable and animal oils and fats, and made soap and ink. There were fifteen chemical fertiliser manufacturers, of vital importance to New Zealand's primary production. Half of the $41 million spent on raw materials was for phosphate rock from overseas, while ninety-four per cent of the $55 million worth of fertiliser manufactured was superphosphate.

OIL AND MINERALS

The oil and coal sector stands out in both its own group and in the whole manufacturing field. With a base index of 1000 in the year ended 31 March 1962, oil and coal products reached an index figure above 10 000 for the value of production, compared with an overall average of 2500. In terms of output per employee, the sector achieved a production value of $134,000, no other topping $28,000. The fifty-two plants had a total production value of $91 million, with total employment less than 700, almost all men.

The sector's main activities were oil refining, blending lubricating oils and greases, and producing foundry coke, coal tar, creosote and carbonettes (gasworks products are excluded from this sector). The principal product was premium grade petrol, of which 1200 million litres were refined; other important products included diesel, fuel and bunker oils, bitumen, bituminous road mixes and bituminous building products.

Despite the numerous consumer goods manufactured by the 457 factories in the mineral products sector, most factories were located close to their raw materials rather than to their markets. Consequently, the sector makes a considerable contribution towards regional development.

Cement and concrete were amongst the most important materials produced. The four cement works turned out more than 840 000 tonnes of cement valued at $16.3 million. Concrete blocks, posts, tanks and other items were manufactured in 216 plants scattered throughout the country, with the seventy-two companies in the ready-mixed concrete business enjoying sales of $20 million, representing an increase of more than forty per cent in two years. Most of the eighty lime works were on sites in Northland, Canterbury and Southland. Glass, produced by three large manufacturers, was processed by forty-four further companies into window panes, bottles, light fittings and other items, worth $24 million. Other mineral products were fibrous plaster; bricks, pipes and tiles; crockery, insulators and sanitary ware. The ten manufacturers of pottery items did not include the many craftsmen whose individual wheels and kilns are tucked away in many communities and whose distinctive wares are sold overseas as well as in New Zealand.

METALS AND METAL PRODUCTS

The plants in the basic metal industry were engaged in the smelting and refining of iron, steel, brass, lead and other metals, including precious metals; the drawing of wire and the casting and forging of bars, angles, rods, sheets and other metal materials.

Since the mid-1950s, the basic metals sector has enjoyed one of the fastest growth rates of any industry in New Zealand. The 110 factories turned out goods worth $96 million, just over eighty per cent of that total being contributed by six plants. More than eighty per cent of all

factories are located in Central Auckland, Wellington and Canterbury.

New Zealand Steel's mill at Glenbrook started processing a variety of steel products in 1968, and commissioned its own steel-making plant in 1970, using indigenous ironsands. Fully commercial operation was delayed by problems arising from the specialised processes and equipment needed to cope with feedstock in this unusual form. The mill now produces ingots, billets, galvanised sheet, pipe and sections. Another mill south of Auckland converts steel scrap into bars and steel products.

At Tiwai Point, near Invercargill, New Zealand Aluminium Smelters operates a primary smelter, commissioned in 1971. Initial capacity of 70 000 tonnes had been raised to 112 000 tonnes by 1974, with a further increase to 152 000 tonnes planned for 1976. Aluminium from this plant supplies several factories in other parts of the country manufacturing electrical conductor redraw rod, plus a wide range of extrusions, rolling mill products and fabricated items.

The metal products sector is extremely important in the Central Auckland area, involving almost one in every seven factories and more than one in eight of the area's work force. Almost a tenth of the area's value of all manufactured goods and an eighth of the total net output were produced in metal products factories. The only other statistical area in which the sector played such an obvious role was Canterbury, where more than twelve per cent of all factories manufactured metal products. However, in other than numerical terms, the industry was less significant in the southern area.

In all, the sector comprised 923 factories turning out metal products worth $241 million. The sheet metal-working division was prominent, with 238 factories producing goods worth $93 million. One of the most important products was tin-plated cans, worth $15 million. The wide range of other products included steel drums, tanks and cisterns; cooking utensils and sink benches; carcases for stoves, refrigerators, washing machines and driers, and stainless steel buckets, vats and tanks for the dairy industry.

The wire-working division's total production worth $14 million comprised barbed wire, fencing wire and fabricated wire fencing; reinforcing rods, metal strapping and baling and springs. Other units made structural and reinforcing steel valued at $51 million, as well as numerous items of builders' and plumbers' hardware—in fact, everything from needles to anchors.

MACHINERY

The manufacture, assembly and repair of all classes of machinery except electrical and transport equipment is included in this group, which comprised 835 factories. Total value of production was $201 million. The group is characterised by a large number of small units widely dispersed throughout New Zealand. Only twenty per cent of the factories had staffs of more than twenty. In Taranaki, Marlborough, Southland and South Auckland, machine shops accounted for fourteen to sixteen per cent of the total number of factories in the area.

Farm machinery production included the manufacture of ploughs, combine harvesters and much other equipment, some of it made or modified to order. Production of milking machinery was valued at $1.4 million. In the machinery group as a whole, principal items included road construction machinery ($4.8 million), forklift trucks ($7.1 million), front-end loaders ($2.9 million), industrial heating, refrigerating and air conditioning plant ($15.4 million) and fire fighting equipment ($2.6 million).

ELECTRICAL PRODUCTS

Factories in this group numbered 343, and included twenty-one establishments making radio and television sets, and six making electric ranges and other goods. The total value of goods produced was $123 million, to which the radio and television sector contributed $23 million. The manufacture of cables and connections was worth $22.8 million. In relation to the typical size of plants, the average value of production from each unit in the group was fairly high. Sales of $100,000 to $1 million were recorded by each of 105 factories, and five radio and television manufacturers were amongst those above the $2 million mark. The total number of people employed was 10 000, of whom a third were women.

TRANSPORT EQUIPMENT

Establishments involved in the transport equipment industry (excluding those engaged in motor vehicle repair) totalled 305 and achieved a production value of $255 million. The fifteen motor assembly plants produced vehicles worth $177 million, an increase of more than fifty per cent in two years. Imported components accounted for more than eighty per cent of the value of all materials used by the sector, which was concerned principally with the assembly of vehicles from 'completely knocked down' (CKD) units.

Recently, there has been considerable progress towards increasing the level of domestic content in the motor vehicle assembly industry, particularly by rationalisation of component manufacture between Australia and New Zealand. A large manual transmission and chassis component machining plant was opened at Wiri, south of Auckland, in 1972, while in 1974 it was decided to set up a factory in Palmerston North to manufacture rear axles and manual and automatic transmission systems. Recent major expansion by several motor vehicle assemblers includes the establishment at Porirua, north of Wellington, of the largest single assembly plant in New Zealand.

While net output in 1972 was still only seventeen per cent of the production value in the motor vehicle assembly sector, it represented thirty-nine per cent of the value of production in the motor body building sector, whose eighty-one plants had sales totalling more than $16 million. Bodies for buses, vans and trucks were built to both standard and individual specifications, with some firms specialising in fire engines and ambulances. Easily the most valuable single line was that in caravans, worth $5.4 million.

New Zealand had 110 establishments connected with boatbuilding and ship repairing, their production earning $20 million, of which more than half came from marine engineering. The sector constructed a considerable variety of craft, including dinghies, fishing boats, pleasure launches, yachts, barges and tugs.

Aircraft manufacture, maintenance and repair was carried out by forty-five establishments whose value of production totalled $20 million.

Statistical publications interpret transport equipment very widely, and include even dolls' prams, the manufacture of which took $134,000 from the nation's parents.

MISCELLANEOUS

The most substantial sector within the group of miscellaneous manufacture is the plastics industry, whose 195 factories recorded a gross output of $77 million. These figures, however, excluded many factories whose products were classified in other groups, such as apparel or electrical goods. If these lines were included, the total value of production for the plastics industry would reach just under $110 million. Plastic bags for packaging would account for eleven per cent of this latter figure.

The miscellaneous industrial group includes the jewellery and silverware sector and the manufacture of toys and sports goods. Each of these two sectors produced goods worth close to $8 million. Production of brushes and brooms was valued at $4.6 million and included three million toothbrushes.

New Zealand's thirty-two manufacturers of optical, surgical, dental and laboratory equipment achieved a fifty-four per cent sales increase in two years to bring their total output to a value of almost $3.3 million.

Research and Development

The economic significance of manufacturing to New Zealand is considerably greater than is suggested by the number of factories or by their contribution to the national income. Manufacturing provides a degree of stability in an economy basically dependent on agricultural exports, both by creating a substantial measure of internal self-sufficiency and by helping to diversify external trade. Government, therefore, has set up or supports a comprehensive range of organisations for the assistance and guidance of industry.

The Development Finance Corporation, now a wholly government-owned autonomous body, has a special responsibility for the needs of smaller manufacturing businesses, together with the encouragement of regional development, the increase of export earnings and new technology.

The Productivity Centre, under the guidance of the Productivity Advisory Council, promotes efficiency in manufacturing and servicing industries, with special emphasis on optimum utilisation of resources. The Centre offers a wide range of techniques and services and has grown rapidly in importance since its establishment in 1973.

The Inventions Development Authority provides financial and advisory services for the promotion of inventions likely to extend the range, quality or efficiency of goods or services. Complementary assistance is available under the Industrial Research and Development Grants Scheme, which financially encourages new or expanded research by industry.

The Standards Association of New Zealand, a statutory body under the control of the Standards Council, while having wider functions, also serves to develop and maintain the quality of New Zealand-made products. Many functions are performed by the Manufacturing Development Council, which is concerned with long-term development.

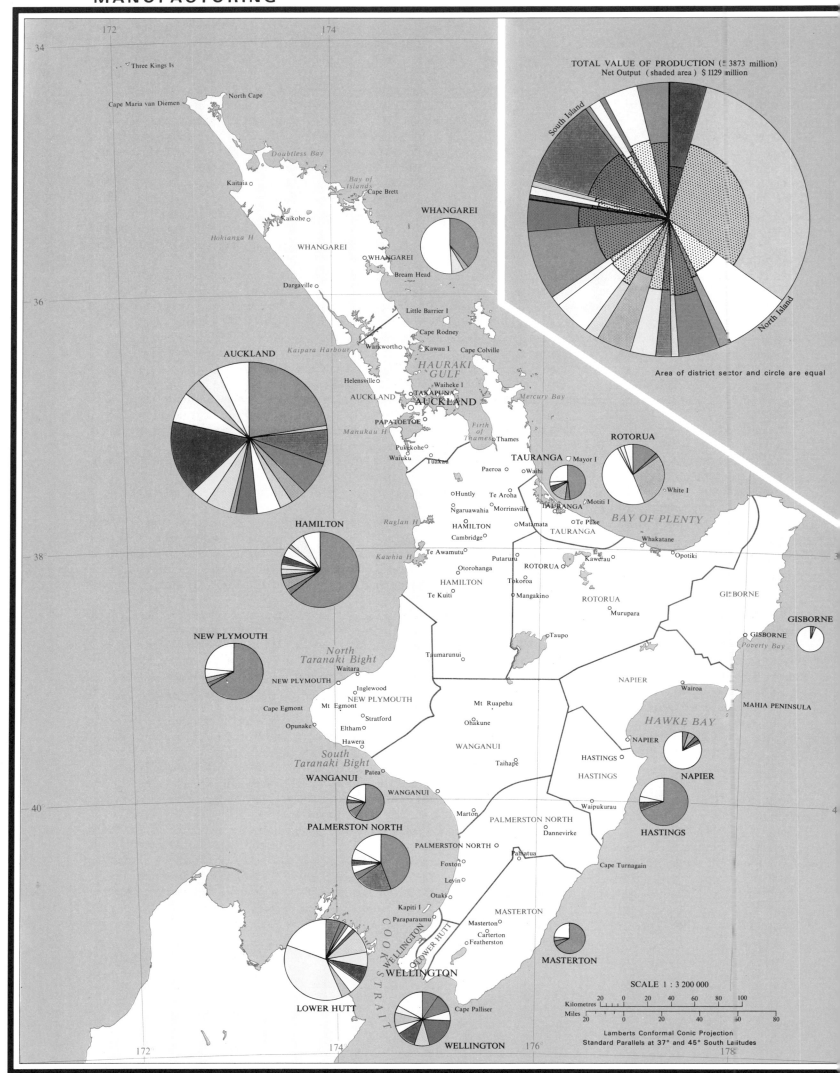

TOTAL VALUE OF PRODUCTION (£ 3873 million)
Net Output (shaded area) $ 1129 million

Area of district sector and circle are equal

WHANGAREI

AUCKLAND

HAMILTON

NEW PLYMOUTH

WANGANUI

PALMERSTON NORTH

WELLINGTON

LOWER HUTT

TAURANGA

ROTORUA

GISBORNE

NAPIER

HASTINGS

MASTERTON

SCALE 1 : 3 200 000

Kilometres 20   0   20   40   60   80   100
Miles   20   0   20   40   60   80

Lamberts Conformal Conic Projection
Standard Parallels at 37° and 45° South Latitudes

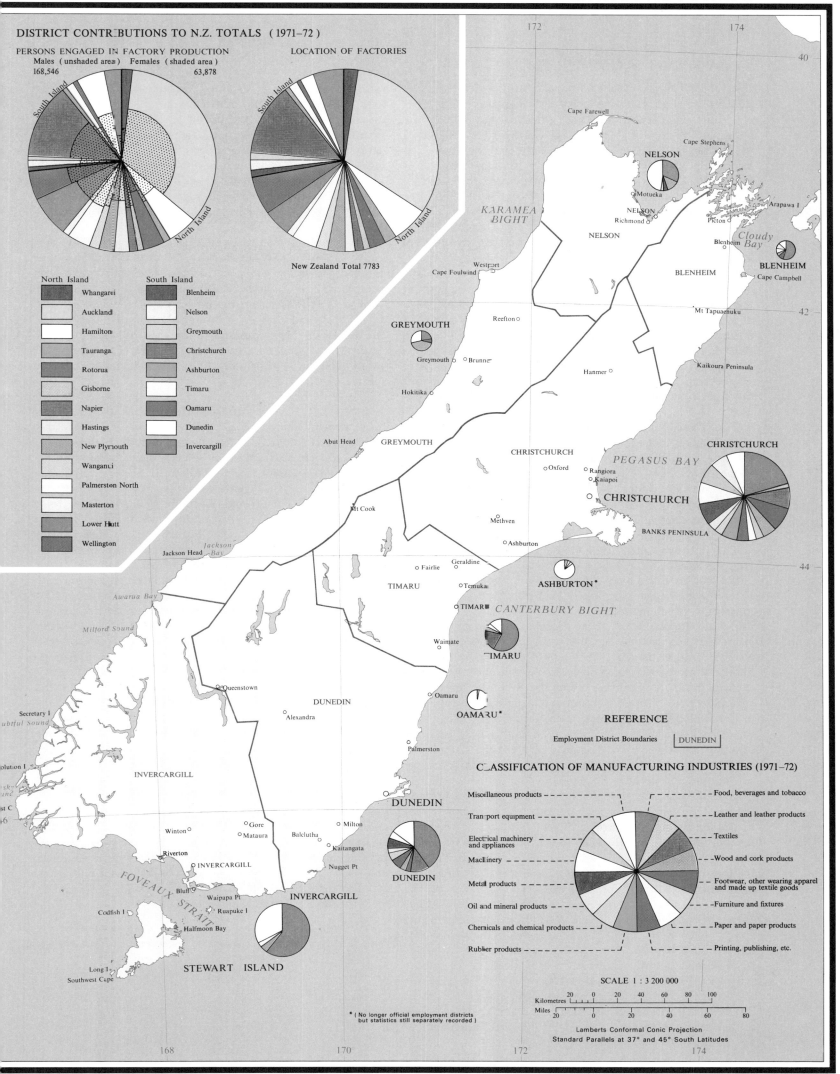

DISTRICT CONTRIBUTIONS TO N.Z. TOTALS (1971–72)

PERSONS ENGAGED IN FACTORY PRODUCTION
Males (unshaded area)   Females (shaded area)
168,546   63,878

LOCATION OF FACTORIES

New Zealand Total 7783

North Island

	Whangarei
	Auckland
	Hamilton
	Tauranga
	Rotorua
	Gisborne
	Napier
	Hastings
	New Plymouth
	Wanganui
	Palmerston North
	Masterton
	Lower Hutt
	Wellington

South Island

	Blenheim
	Nelson
	Greymouth
	Christchurch
	Ashburton
	Timaru
	Oamaru
	Dunedin
	Invercargill

REFERENCE

Employment District Boundaries   DUNEDIN

CLASSIFICATION OF MANUFACTURING INDUSTRIES (1971–72)

- Miscellaneous products
- Transport equipment
- Electrical machinery and appliances
- Machinery
- Metal products
- Oil and mineral products
- Chemicals and chemical products
- Rubber products
- Food, beverages and tobacco
- Leather and leather products
- Textiles
- Wood and cork products
- Footwear, other wearing apparel and made up textile goods
- Furniture and fixtures
- Paper and paper products
- Printing, publishing, etc.

* (No longer official employment districts but statistics still separately recorded)

SCALE 1 : 3 200 000

Lamberts Conformal Conic Projection
Standard Parallels at 37° and 45° South Latitudes

KARAMEA BIGHT
Cape Farewell
Cape Stephens
NELSON
Motueka
Arapawa I
NELSON
Richmond
Picton
Blenheim
Cloudy Bay
NELSON
BLENHEIM
Westport
BLENHEIM
Cape Campbell
Cape Foulwind
Mt Tapuaenuku
Reefton
GREYMOUTH
Kaikoura Peninsula
Greymouth   Brunner
Hanmer
Hokitika
Abut Head
GREYMOUTH
CHRISTCHURCH
PEGASUS BAY
CHRISTCHURCH
Oxford
Rangiora
Kaiapoi
CHRISTCHURCH
Mt Cook
Methven
Ashburton
BANKS PENINSULA
Jackson Head   Jackson Bay
Fairlie   Geraldine
Awarua Bay
TIMARU   Temuka
ASHBURTON *
Milford Sound
TIMARU   CANTERBURY BIGHT
TIMARU
Waimate
TIMARU
Secretary I
Doubtful Sound
Queenstown
DUNEDIN
Oamaru
Alexandra
OAMARU *
Resolution I
Palmerston
Dusky Sound
West C
INVERCARGILL
Winton   Gore   Milton
Mataura   Balclutha
DUNEDIN
Riverton   Kaitangata
INVERCARGILL   Nugget Pt
DUNEDIN
Bluff
Waipapa Pt
FOVEAUX STRAIT
Codfish I   Ruapuke I
INVERCARGILL
Halfmoon Bay
Long I
Southwest Cape   STEWART ISLAND

TRANSPORT AND COMMUNICATIONS

R. J. Polaschek

Transport has always been costly to provide in New Zealand because of its geographic features. Remote from any continental land mass, New Zealand is a long, narrow country; the combined length of the two main Islands is more than 1600 kilometres, with neither wider than 320 kilometres at any part. Rugged mountains provide a longitudinal spine to both Islands, which are separated by a narrow but turbulent seaway. At least three-quarters of the land surface is more than 200 metres above sea level, and seventy-three rivers longer than forty kilometres, as well as many smaller, flow swiftly to the surrounding Pacific Ocean and Tasman Sea.

Despite its extended coastline, New Zealand has few natural harbours, although four, Auckland, Wellington, Lyttelton and Otago, are particularly fine. The west coast does not have even many anchorages and its bar-bound estuaries are exposed to frequent high winds. The east coast is not a great deal better endowed by nature for sea transport operations. Nevertheless, skilful but costly engineering has ensured that New Zealand has a network of harbours capable of handling its large volume of overseas trade.

The Maori found landing places adequate for entry into New Zealand and for limited coastal journeys. Apart from that, they relied on porterage and on a few waterways for freight movement. Their ability to transport and exchange goods was therefore severely limited. The European colonists brought horses and bullocks and the vehicles they drew, and quickly began to build roads and tracks on which these vehicles could be used.

The railways, introduced in the 1860s, offered the first effective means of opening up the country, and by the 1880s had become a major factor in economic development. From the mid-1920s, the motor truck played an increasingly important supplementary role, and was a key element in the rapid expansion of dairy farming. Ultimately, roads surpassed the railways as the most important means of internal freight-haulage, although railways continued to handle most of the long-distance cartage and the movement of bulk commodities. Since the Second World War, agricultural avaiation has become an indispensable tool of the hill-country farmers, with aeroplanes being used for topdressing, for spraying crops and weeds and for other agricultural work. Passenger and freight aircraft too have assumed an important, though subsidiary, role throughout the country.

In the last twenty years, the private motor car has become the most popular, and overwhelmingly the most important, means of passenger travel, with air services in demand for medium and long-distance journeys. As a consequence, travel by bus, train and ship has declined. While the total volume of passenger and freight movement has increased in recent years, the proportion of work undertaken by the various forms of transport has changed significantly. What is required is a total system which will move passengers and freight from point of pick-up to destination quickly and efficiently, using whatever mode or combination of modes is most appropriate. Because of this need, a Transport Advisory Council was set up in 1968 to advise the Minister of Transport on any transport problems placed before it. The Council, of which the Minister is chairman, consists of representatives of those who provide transport, of those who use it and of transport workers.

The Council is serviced by the Ministry of Transport which administers government legislation relating to sea, road and air transport. The Ministry is also responsible for undertaking research into all aspects of transport and for advising the Minister on the development of an efficient national policy, including investment.

In 1972 a group of overseas consultants, Wilbur Smith and Associates, with the assistance of New Zealand experts, undertook a comprehensive review of transport policy in New Zealand and the government is currently studying its detailed recommendations.

Developments in transport have been paralleled by improvements in other forms of communication. The first telegraph system was inaugurated in the 1860s, to be followed by telephone exchanges in 1881; the first internal airmail service was in 1935 and the first regular overseas airmail in 1940. In 1925, the Radio Broadcasting Company of New Zealand undertook to develop and maintain an efficient broadcasting service throughout the whole country, while the first experimental television service began in 1959.

Ports and Shipping

New Zealand harbours are vested in and operated by locally-elected boards. In recent years, most of these have embarked on extensive re-development programmes, which include a new wharf at Whangarei for the Marsden Point Oil Refinery; new overseas passenger terminal buildings at Auckland and Wellington; facilities for roll-on/roll-off vessels at Auckland, Wellington, Picton, Lyttelton and Otago; the installation of all-weather mechanical loaders at Timaru and Bluff and extensions to the Port of Tauranga to serve the growing timber industry in the Bay of Plenty. Auckland, Wellington, Lyttelton and Port Chalmers will soon handle all containerised cargo.

Harbour development has taken place under the general supervision of the New Zealand Ports Authority, which is charged with fostering an efficient and integrated ports system, and with stimulating research into cargo handling, education and training.

In 1973, legislation was approved by Parliament to authorise the establishment of the Shipping Corporation of New Zealand. This is a wholly State-owned company which will operate ships on the New Zealand coastal route and to other countries.

OVERSEAS SHIPPING

The following table shows the number of overseas vessels entered and cleared at the main ports for the year ended 31 December 1973. For the purpose of this table, an overseas vessel calling at more than one New Zealand port during a single voyage has been recorded as entered and cleared at each port visited. The cargo tonnages are given in manifest or measurement tons of one cubic metre or, by weight, of 1000 kilogrammes per tonne.

	Arrivals		Departures	
PORT	VESSELS	TONNAGE	VESSELS	TONNAGE
Whangarei	132	3 659 355	124	56 020
Auckland	1136	2 926 360	1139	845 194
Tauranga	526	427 333	533	2 040 524
Napier	234	346 386	232	416 916
Taranaki	128	399 277	124	156 470
Wellington	542	1 222 094	540	398 035
Nelson	115	54 897	116	496 166
Lyttelton	475	816 112	478	177 537
Timaru	111	94 382	115	182 872
Otago	210	240 948	213	223 182
Bluff	210	542 995	211	307 820

During 1971–72 the Pacific America Container Express Line, the Columbus Line and the Farrell Line introduced container services between North America and New Zealand. The British Associated Container Group, in co-operation with the Australian National Line, began a container service between the United Kingdom and this country in 1972. This is a revolutionary and extremely costly innovation, the all-round effect of which is not yet fully known.

The Union Steam Ship Company of New Zealand, formerly owned by the Peninsular and Orient Company of London, was taken over on 31 December 1971 by a consortium of private Australian and New Zealand interests. This company uses some roll-on/roll-off vessels and has an expanding 'sea freighter' container service operating between Australia and New Zealand. The introduction of container and roll-on/roll-off services to and from New Zealand makes available modern shipping techniques and involves changes in internal transport methods.

COASTAL SHIPPING

Movements of coastal vessels have declined since the introduction of the Cook Strait rail-road ferries in 1962. Since 1967, additional roll-on/roll-off freighters, specialising in unit cargo loads, have operated between all major ports, gradually superseding the more traditional trading vessels. Specialist ships designed to carry cement and other bulk cargo are now in service. Coastal shipping has advanced to the stage where about half the general cargo is carried in unit loads (including containers).

At 16 August 1974, there were fifty-seven ships owned or chartered by New Zealand companies working on the home or foreign trade. Of this number, thirty-four were owned or operated by the Union Steam Ship Company, the New Zealand Railways operated four vessels, while three each were registered by the Northern Steam Ship Company, the oil industry and the Shipping Corporation of New Zealand. The companies appearing on the register as each operating two vessels were Tarakohe Shipping, New Zealand Cement Holdings, Wilson's Portland Cement, Karamea Shipping and the New Zealand Shipping Line.

FERRIES

Ferries offer an essential link between the two Islands. The New Zealand Railways operates four ferries, the *Aranui*, the *Aramoana*, the *Arahanga* and the *Aratika*, between Picton and Wellington. The *Rangatira*, formerly operated on regular services between Wellington and Lyttelton by the Union Steam Ship Company, is at present maintained by the government, as size and operating costs combined to make private operation uneconomic. Private operators provide ferry services in the Hauraki Gulf and inlets of North Auckland, as well as on Lake Wakatipu. The Ministry of Transport operates a ferry service between Bluff and Stewart Island.

Roads and Road Transport

New Zealand has a widespread network of 95 000 kilometres of formed roads, many of which, because of climatic, geological and topographical conditions, have been difficult to construct. Some 39 000 kilometres of road are sealed, of which 11 160 kilometres have been gazetted as motorways and State highways.

Responsibility for local roads and streets is vested in city, borough and county councils, which receive subsidies and grants from the National Roads Board. The Board constructs and maintains motorways and State highways,

and also assists local authorities to develop a satisfactory and comprehensive roading system. The Board was established in 1954 to replace the Main Highways Board, and comprises ten members, representing the Ministry of Works, the Ministry of Transport, the New Zealand Counties and Municipal Associations and the owners of motor vehicles, with the Minister of Works as chairman. The Board receives its revenue from taxation and government grants. Total income for the year ended 31 March 1974 amounted to $104,787,393, comprising primarily:

Petrol tax	$85,302,296
Heavy traffic fees	$11,520,643
Mileage tax	$5,691,421
Contribution from Consolidated Revenue Account	$700,000
Interest	$97,250
Miscellaneous receipts	$1,475,783

The net expenditure for the same period was $98,761,521. This is summarised under five main headings as follows:

State highway maintenance	$16,702,366
State highway construction	$35,913,058
Payments to counties	$23,528,555
Payments to municipalities	$15,814,680
Other expenditure	$6,802,862

In addition to payments from the National Roads Fund, local authorities spent $44,447,513 on roading during the year ended 31 March 1974. The total expenditure on roading by all public agencies for that year was $143,209,034

Despite this substantial expenditure, it was necessary to impose or continue weight restrictions on 297 bridges and, with varying degrees of severity, on roads generally.

MOTOR VEHICLES

The number of motor vehicles registered in New Zealand has increased from 106 449 in June 1925 to 1 438 815 (excluding trailers) in December 1973. The main classes of vehicles included in the latter figure are cars 1 052 410; goods service vehicles 195 101; omnibuses 2516; taxicabs 3087; rental cars 5215; vehicles exempt from some taxation 97 859; motor cycles 52 593 and 24 081 power cycles. New Zealand, with one motor car for every 2.3 people, has the highest ratio of motor vehicles to population of any country other than North America.

The rapid growth in the use of motor vehicles has thrown an increasing strain on the roading system, giving rise to demands for greater maintenance in rural areas and causing congestion at peak hours in the larger cities. To cope with the latter problem, almost all of the big cities have undertaken transportation surveys in an attempt to predict traffic volumes and flow patterns and the changes that will be necessary to enable the roading system to cope with future demands.

URBAN TRANSPORT

Urban public passenger transport is provided by a Regional Authority in Auckland, by a Transport Board in Christchurch, by municipal councils, by limited liability companies (in the case of Auckland controlling sea as well as road services) and by the Railways Department road and rail services.

In recent years, urban passenger transport operators have been faced with rising costs and, as a result of the increasing use of private cars, with declining patronage. As a consequence, almost all of the State and local body services run at a substantial loss. In an attempt to remedy the situation, the government in 1972 established a New Zealand Urban Public Passenger Transport Council to conduct research and to advise it on problems associated with urban passenger transport. The Council was also to offer loans and grants towards capital expenditure to those who provide urban passenger services. It consists of the Secretary for Transport (chairman), the Secretary to the Treasury, the Secretary for Internal Affairs and three non-government members appointed by the Minister of Transport.

In some of the major cities, transportation surveys, which have been concerned primarily with roading, have been supplemented by special studies into passenger transport requirements. In Auckland and Wellington, consultants have recommended extensions and improvements to the urban railway system. Detailed planning for the introduction of a combined bus and rapid-rail service in the Auckland metropolitan area is well advanced.

TRANSPORT LICENSING

A licensing system regulates the carriage in a motor vehicle of passengers and goods for hire or reward as well as competition between road and rail for freight haulage. It is primarily an economic measure designed to achieve better co-ordination between road and rail transport and to prevent excessive competition and duplication of services within the road transport industry.

New Zealand is divided into sixteen transport licensing districts which are administered by five full time, one man, licensing authorities appointed by the Minister of Transport. In addition, where regional authorities are set up, the transport licensing authority for the area is augmented by the appointment of two other persons, one of whom is recommended by the regional authority when passenger service or harbour ferry services are being considered. This system now operates in Auckland. Transport licensing authorities adjudicate on applications for a licence to enter the industry, on transfers and renewals of licences and on requests to change or withdraw transport services.

Civil Aviation

Because of its ability to overcome the barriers to rapid movement created by Cook Strait and New Zealand's mountain ranges, air transport, particularly for passengers, has proved popular over even short distances. The bulk of the very extensive internal air services is provided by the New Zealand National Airways Corporation, which uses Boeing 737, Viscount and Fokker F27 (Friendship) aircraft. Valuable secondary services are run by smaller, privately-owned airlines, of which the most important is Mount Cook Airlines. Specialised freight transport between the North and South Islands (and also freight and passenger transport to the Chatham Islands) is available from Safe Air Limited, formerly owned mainly by United Kingdom interests, but now a subsidiary of the National Airways Corporation. Safe Air has made important contributions to aviation through its development of a passenger capsule for use in freight aircraft and (in conjunction with the Railways Department) of devices for the rapid loading and unloading of air freight.

During the year ended 31 December 1973, the major domestic airlines flew 22 511 974 revenue kilometres. This involved 75 762 revenue hours of flying, during which 1 992 573 revenue passengers and 66 109 tonnes of revenue freight were carried.

Airports at Auckland, Wellington and Christchurch link New Zealand to Australia and through Australia to the Far East and Europe. From Auckland International Airport, several airlines provide services to the Pacific, the United States of America and Europe. New Zealand's own international airline, Air New Zealand, flies to Sydney, Melbourne, Brisbane, Hong Kong, Singapore, Norfolk Island, New Caledonia, Fiji, American Samoa, Tahiti, Honolulu and Los Angeles. Its fleet is made up of Douglas DC10 and DC8 aircraft.

Other services include: Pan American World Airways, from the United States via Tahiti, Honolulu and Pago Pago to Auckland, thence to Sydney and around the world; British Overseas Airways Corporation, from the United Kingdom through the Far East and Sydney to Auckland; the Union de Transport Aeriens (French), from Los Angeles via Tahiti to Auckland and on to Noumea; American Airlines, from the United States to Auckland, and Qantas (Australian), offering a full range of services across the Tasman Sea linking with regional and around the world carriers at Sydney and Melbourne. Air transport now provides the main means of international passenger travel. During the year ended 31 December 1973, 1 017 260 passengers (excluding through traffic) entered or left New Zealand by air to the 70 807 passengers by sea.

AERODROMES AND ADMINISTRATION

New Zealand has eighty public, and approximately 230 private aerodromes and authorised landing grounds, including nearly one hundred water-alighting areas. There are many uncounted agricultural aviation airstrips. Twenty-seven airports are used for regular scheduled air services; eighteen of them have paved runways and night-flying facilities, while precision approach equipment has been installed at the three international airports, at Auckland, Wellington and Christchurch. Runways at Auckland and Wellington have recently been extended to accommodate larger aircraft; a new terminal is under construction at Auckland and one is planned for Wellington. Work is in hand to extend the terminal building at Christchurch, while a new international airfield and terminal came into operation at Rarotonga in the Cook Islands late in 1973. General upgrading programmes are being carried out at a number of secondary airports.

The development and operating costs of the more important airports are shared as a joint venture by central and local government, usually on an equal partnership basis, although the central government makes a larger contribution in respect of the three international airports. The local authorities manage the airports, while the Civil Aviation Division of the Ministry of Transport is responsible for aviation safety and for the provision and maintenance of air navigation facilities in New Zealand, its island territories and the Cook Islands.

The Civil Aviation Division also operates an airport crash fire service (using a hovercraft at Auckland) and maintains ground-to-air communications for both local and airfield control and control throughout the whole route, as well as communications between airports. The Division co-ordinates Search and Rescue operations.

Railways

New Zealand Railways is a State owned and operated enterprise, without private competition. Its railway system, constructed to a track guage of 1067 millimetres has as its backbone a north–south main line extending from Auckland to Wellington in the North Island and in the South Island from Picton to Christchurch and thence to

Invercargill. This is supplemented by secondary main and branch lines in all totalling 4797 kilometres, a rail-ferry service between Wellington and Picton and an extensive network of road services employing more than a thousand buses, coaches and trucks. The Railways, in fact, is the largest commercial user of motor vehicles in New Zealand. Air transport is also used for the conveyance of some commodities between the North and South Islands.

A staff of about 21 000 is controlled by a General Manager, who is responsible to the Minister of Railways.

Although predominantly a freight carrier, the Railways has, since the late 1960s, improved several of its inter-city passenger services by introducing new and upgraded trains and railcars. The map shows the relative density of traffic on different parts of the system and highlights the importance of the main trunk line between Auckland and Wellington. During the year ended 31 March 1974 total gross tonne-kilometres amounted to 9942.8 million and the average number of route kilometres in use during that period was 4799. The average weight or density of traffic moved over the entire system during those twelve months was thus 2072 million tonnes.

The Post Office

The New Zealand Post Office offers a wide range of services to those who wish to communicate orally or in writing with persons within New Zealand or in other countries. With a staff of approximately 34 600, the Post Office is the largest employer of labour in New Zealand. Post Office employees are located in 1430 offices which are equipped with a total of 4352 motor vehicles.

As well as providing surface and airmail postal services within New Zealand and to other countries, the Post Office offers telecommunication services including telephone, telegraph, telex, phototelegraph and data transmission facilities. Ninety per cent of telephone subscribers receive automatic service and toll-free calling within their own town or city centre.

Overseas telecommunication links are maintained by undersea cable and via satellite through the satellite earth station at Warkworth. These links carry the telecommunication services named above. In the overseas service, live television broadcasts are transmitted and received via satellite. A radio service is operated by the Post Office for ships at sea as well as a land mobile radio service which enables drivers of road transport vehicles to keep in contact with their headquarters.

The Post Office Savings Bank provides a large range of banking services including personal loans, money transmitting facilities and personal cheque accounts.

In its capacity as agent for other government departments the Post Office handles transactions such as the issuing of television and motor vehicle licences and social security benefits.

Post Office Communication Statistics for the year ended 31 March 1974

TYPE OF SERVICE	NUMBER
Articles posted	668 560 000
Telephone subscribers	933 883
Telephones (all types per 1000 population)	475
Toll calls	73 905 370
Outward International telephone calls	586 380
International telex calls	644 796
Telex connections	1824
Telegrams	4 897 374

Broadcasting

Broadcasting in New Zealand was restructured by statute late in 1973, abolishing the New Zealand Broadcasting Corporation and the New Zealand Broadcasting Authority which had been set up in 1961 and 1968 respectively. The new structure consists of a Broadcasting Council and three operating corporations—Radio New Zealand, Television Service One and Television Service Two. Three of the six Council members are appointed by the Governor-General on the advice of the Minister of Broadcasting, while the remaining positions are filled by the chairmen of the operating corporations. The general powers of the Council include the collection and allocation of licence fees; the establishment and operation of transmitters and micro-wave links; the acquisition and disposal of property; the holding of shares in companies intending to carry on broadcasting or to provide programmes, and the conduct of technical and audience research surveys. The Symphony Orchestra is to be managed by Radio New Zealand while the *New Zealand Listener* will be published by the Council.

The new structure has been designed to achieve decentralised administration. To this end, TV 1 production is to be centred on Wellington and Dunedin, TV 2 on Auckland, Christchurch and Hamilton. Radio New Zealand's facilities are to be spread throughout both Islands but are to be focussed in the Wellington complex. The headquarters of the Broadcasting Council are to be in Christchurch.

At present there are a number of privately owned and operated radio stations in New Zealand, but no new warrant to operate will be granted. However, applications for the renewal of warrants will be received by the Director-General of the Post Office, who may advise that they be renewed.

Radio New Zealand provides an overseas service with two short-wave transmitters and nineteen assigned frequencies. In addition there are fifty-one medium-wave transmitting stations, twenty-six of which are commercial.

Television programmes on a black and white 625 line system are currently available from studios at Auckland, Wellington, Christchurch and Dunedin. A subsidiary studio is located at Hamilton. Because of the problems created by the geographic configuration of the country, television programmes are relayed by the NZBC through 139 transmitting stations. Ten of these stations are transmitters, while 129 are repeaters or translators. In addition, there are 210 repeaters and translators which are operated by private individuals. Even so, there remain some areas without television reception. The full network of stations was in operation by October 1973. Also at this time colour television was introduced, operating from Auckland, Wellington and Christchurch and serving some fifty-three per cent of the population. Other installations will be converted progressively. At the end of August 1973, eighty-six per cent of homes within New Zealand were equipped with television sets.

The majority of the Corporation's income was derived from two sources: advertising services on both radio and television and sales of the *New Zealand Listener*, and from annual television licence fees. During the year ended 31 March 1974, income from these sources amounted to $18,499,729 and $13,873,818 respectively, as against a total expenditure of $31,587,897.

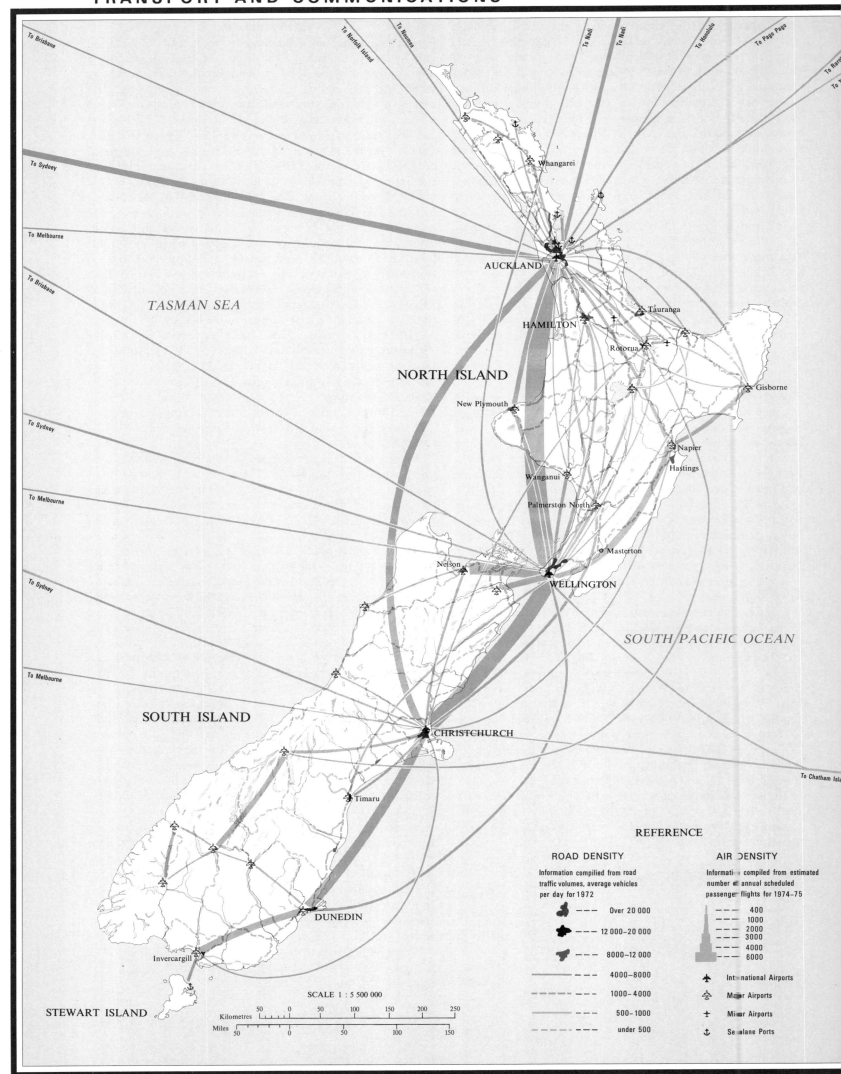

To Brisbane
To Sydney
To Melbourne
To Brisbane
To Sydney
To Melbourne
To Sydney
To Melbourne

TASMAN SEA

To Norfolk Island
To Noumea
To Nadi
To Nadi
To Honolulu
To Pago Pago
To Rarotonga

Whangarei

AUCKLAND

Tauranga

HAMILTON

Rotorua

NORTH ISLAND

Gisborne

New Plymouth

Napier

Hastings

Wanganui

Palmerston North

Masterton

Nelson

WELLINGTON

SOUTH PACIFIC OCEAN

SOUTH ISLAND

CHRISTCHURCH

To Chatham Islands

Timaru

DUNEDIN

Invercargill

STEWART ISLAND

SCALE 1 : 5 500 000

Kilometres 50 0 50 100 150 200 250

Miles 50 0 50 100 150

REFERENCE

ROAD DENSITY

Information compiled from road traffic volumes, average vehicles per day for 1972

	Over 20 000
	12 000–20 000
	8000–12 000
	4000–8000
	1000–4000
	500–1000
	under 500

AIR DENSITY

Information compiled from estimated number of annual scheduled passenger flights for 1974–75

	400
	1000
	2000
	3000
	4000
	6000

✈ International Airports

⍦ Major Airports

✢ Minor Airports

⚓ Seaplane Ports

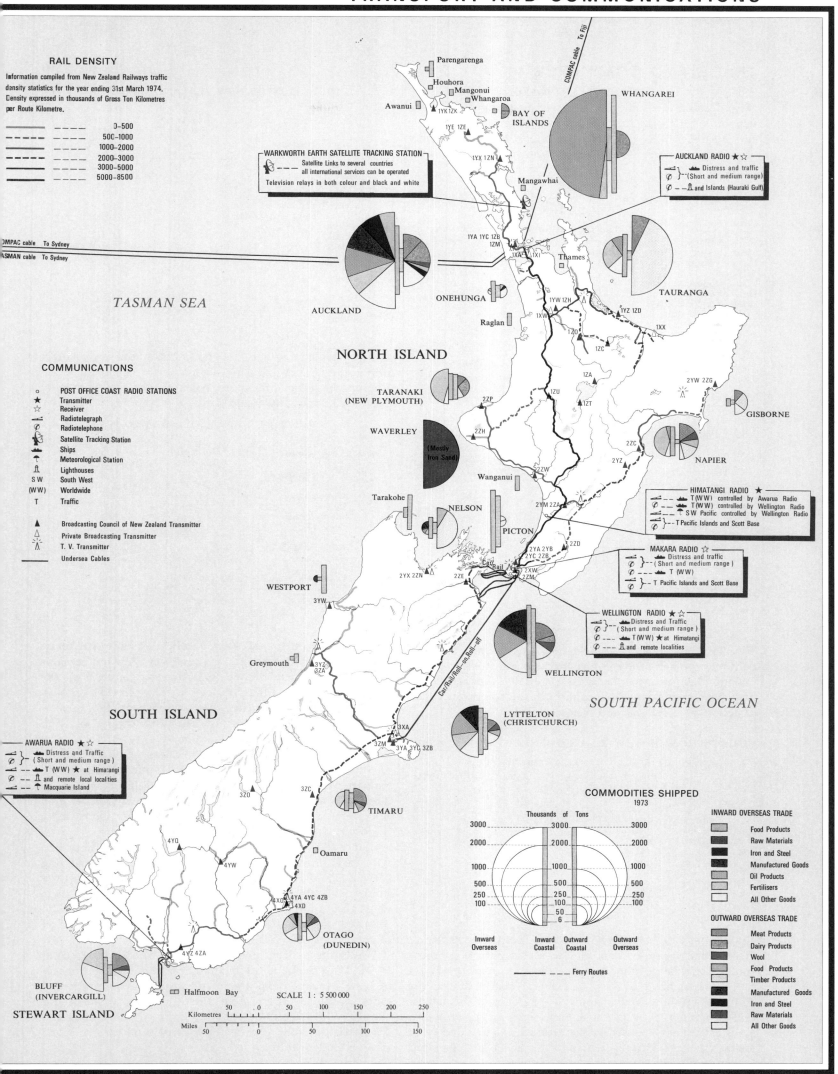

RAIL DENSITY

Information compiled from New Zealand Railways traffic density statistics for the year ending 31st March 1974. Density expressed in thousands of Gross Ton Kilometres per Route Kilometre.

0–500
500–1000
1000–2000
2000–3000
3000–5000
5000–8500

COMPAC cable   To Fiji

Parengarenga
Houhora
Mangonui
Awanui   Whangaroa
1YK 1ZK
BAY OF ISLANDS
WHANGAREI
1YE 1ZE
Mangawhai
1YX 1ZN

WARKWORTH EARTH SATELLITE TRACKING STATION
Satellite Links to several countries all international services can be operated
Television relays in both colour and black and white

AUCKLAND RADIO ★ ☆
Distress and traffic
(Short and medium range)
and Islands (Hauraki Gulf)

COMPAC cable   To Sydney
TASMAN cable   To Sydney

1YA 1YC 1ZB 1ZM
1XA 1XI   Thames
ONEHUNGA
TAURANGA

TASMAN SEA

AUCKLAND

Raglan
1YW 1ZH
1XW
1ZO
1YZ 1ZD
1XX

NORTH ISLAND

1ZC
1ZA

2YW 2ZG

COMMUNICATIONS

o	POST OFFICE COAST RADIO STATIONS
★	Transmitter
☆	Receiver
	Radiotelegraph
	Radiotelephone
	Satellite Tracking Station
	Ships
	Meteorological Station
	Lighthouses
S W	South West
(WW)	Worldwide
T	Traffic
▲	Broadcasting Council of New Zealand Transmitter
△	Private Broadcasting Transmitter
	T. V. Transmitter
	Undersea Cables

TARANAKI
(NEW PLYMOUTH)

1ZU
1ZT
2ZP
2ZH

GISBORNE

WAVERLEY
(Mostly Iron Sand)

2ZC
2YZ

2ZW
Wanganui

NAPIER

Tarakohe
NELSON
2YM 2ZA

HIMATANGI RADIO ★
T (WW) controlled by Awarua Radio
T (WW) controlled by Wellington Radio
S W Pacific controlled by Wellington Radio
T Pacific Islands and Scott Base

PICTON
2YA 2YB 2YC 2ZB
2ZD

MAKARA RADIO ☆
Distress and traffic
(Short and medium range)
T (WW)
T Pacific Islands and Scott Base

2YX 2ZN
2ZE
Car Rail
2XW 2ZM

WESTPORT
3YW

WELLINGTON RADIO ★ ☆
Distress and Traffic
(Short and medium range)
T (WW) ★ at Himatangi
and remote localities

SOUTH PACIFIC OCEAN

Greymouth
3YZ 3ZA

WELLINGTON

SOUTH ISLAND

Car/Rail/Roll-on.Roll-off

LYTTELTON
(CHRISTCHURCH)

3XA
3ZM
3YA 3YC 3ZB

AWARUA RADIO ★ ☆
Distress and Traffic
(Short and medium range)
T (WW) ★ at Himatangi
and remote local localities
Macquarie Island

3ZC
3ZO

COMMODITIES SHIPPED
1973
Thousands of Tons

3000	3000
2000	2000
1000	1000
500	500
250	250
100	100
	50
	6

Inward Overseas | Inward Coastal | Outward Coastal | Outward Overseas

Ferry Routes

INWARD OVERSEAS TRADE
Food Products
Raw Materials
Iron and Steel
Manufactured Goods
Oil Products
Fertilisers
All Other Goods

OUTWARD OVERSEAS TRADE
Meat Products
Dairy Products
Wool
Food Products
Timber Products
Manufactured Goods
Iron and Steel
Raw Materials
All Other Goods

TIMARU
4YO
4YW
Oamaru

4XO 4YA 4YC 4ZB
4XD
OTAGO
(DUNEDIN)

4YZ 4ZA

BLUFF
(INVERCARGILL)
Halfmoon Bay
STEWART ISLAND

SCALE 1 : 5 500 000
Kilometres 50 0 50 100 150 200 250
Miles 50 0 50 100 150

TRADE AND COMMERCE

J. C Mosley

EXTERNAL TRADE

New Zealand is dependent on its export earnings from the sale of a relatively limited number of products, mainly agricultural, for the purchase and import of a large variety of plant, raw materials and semi-manufactured and manufactured goods.

COMPOSITION OF NEW ZEALAND EXPORTS BY CLASSES 1973

Commodity	Value NZ$ (million) f.o.b.	Percentage Value of Total Exports
Meat	589.0	30.91
Dairy products	332.4	17.44
Wool	432.0	22.67
Forest products	99.5	5.22
Hides and skins	94.3	4.94
Crude animal material	25.0	1.31
Fruit and vegetables	33.9	1.77
Fish	20.1	1.05
Machinery and transport equipment	38.1	1.99
Other, including re-exports	241.0	12.70
Total Exports	**1,905.3**	**100.00**

f.o.b. = free on board

COMPOSITION OF NEW ZEALAND IMPORTS BY CLASSES 1973

Commodity	Value NZ$ (million) c.d.v.	Percentage Value of Total Imports
Machinery and transport equipment	500.0	33.73
Manufactured goods	468.0	31.57
Chemicals	196.0	13.22
Mineral fuels	99.8	6.73
Food and live animals	63.9	4.31
Crude materials inedible, except fuels	86.9	5.86
Beverages and tobacco	27.0	1.82
Animal and vegetable oils and fats	19.3	1.30
Other	21.2	1.46
Total Imports	**1,482.1**	**100.00**

c.d.v. = current domestic value

Twenty years ago, New Zealand's dependence on agricultural exports was even more marked than it is at present. During the past two decades, especially the last, there have been significant changes in both the composition and direction of New Zealand's export trade.

COMPOSITION OF NEW ZEALAND EXPORTS BY CLASSES

Commodity	Percentage Value of Exports					
	1951	1956	1961	1966	1971	1973
Meat	11.04	23.82	25.85	26.19	33.04	30.91
Dairy products	25.52	29.70	24.11	24.54	21.93	17.44
Wool	51.58	32.94	35.30	30.16	16.02	22.67
Forest products	0.34	1.68	2.54	3.15	6.55	5.22
Hides and skins	5.18	3.87	4.26	5.63	4.55	4.94
Sausage casings	1.57	1.76	1.28	1.49	1.20	0.79
Fruit and vegetables	0.62	1.17	1.23	1.35	1.68	1.77
Fish	0.32	0.60	0.42	0.76	1.69	1.05
Other, including re-exports	3.83	4.46	5.01	6.73	13.34	15.21
Total Exports	100.00	100.00	100.00	100.00	100.00	100.00

Traditionally, the United Kingdom has been New Zealand's main market for exports and the largest supplier of imported goods. Its relative importance as both a customer and a supplier has, however, declined over recent years, as the tables below show, as the result of the policy of diversification promoted by successive New Zealand governments and pursued assiduously by the producer boards and other major exporters. Britain's entry to the European Economic Community lent urgency to such policies.

DIRECTION OF NEW ZEALAND EXPORTS

Country	1973 % of Total Exports	1961 % of Total Exports
United Kingdom	27.10	51.02
United States	15.59	14.53
Japan	13.17	5.26
Australia	8.24	3.89
West Germany	3.07	2.84
Canada	2.75	1.33
Netherlands	2.57	1.41
Belgium and Luxembourg	2.35	2.93
France	2.35	6.16
USSR	2.33	0.54
Greece	2.10	0.14
Italy	1.69	2.39
Chile	0.95	0.01
Poland	0.92	0.34
Fiji	0.89	0.39
Hong Kong	0.89	0.14
China	0.88	0.47
Other	12.16	6.21
	100.00	100.00

Other smaller nations are now becoming increasingly important to New Zealand as markets; they include the Philippines, Peru, Singapore, Malaysia, French Polynesia, New Caledonia and Yugoslavia.

SOURCE OF NEW ZEALAND IMPORTS

Country	1973 % of Total Imports	1961 % of Total Imports
United Kingdom	30.52	44.73
Australia	27.03	16.23
United States	14.85	9.42
Japan	11.20	2.93
West Germany	3.59	3.46
Hong Kong	1.98	0.19
Canada	1.78	3.76
Netherlands	1.07	1.96
Switzerland	0.97	0.88
Italy	0.79	0.79
Sweden	0.68	0.90
France	0.62	1.01
Singapore	0.60	0.79
Other	4.32	12.92
	100.00	100.00

The Development of New Zealand Trade Patterns

For certain key agricultural exports New Zealand remains particularly dependent on the British market. In the trade year ending June 1973, eighty-six per cent of New Zealand's exports of butter, sixty-six per cent of its exports of cheese and seventy-two per cent of its exports of lamb were sold in the United Kingdom.

In the first years after the colonisation of New Zealand, its most important trade link, based initially on gold and timber, was with the east coast of Australia. However, as land was brought into production trade with the United Kingdom, especially in wool, assumed an increasingly important role.

The 1880s saw the advent of refrigerated ships, and with their introduction came the possibility of diversifying New Zealand's exports of agricultural products. Pastoral industries were developed—wool retained its importance, while the export of frozen mutton and lamb grew rapidly, followed, after the turn of the century, by a great expansion of exports of dairy products.

Under the bulk purchase agreements during the Second World War, the United Kingdom became the sole purchaser of New Zealand's exportable surpluses of wool, meat and dairy products, apart from the quantities required for supply to the United States under the Lend-Lease Act. The bulk purchase contracts for dairy products and meat were extended until 1954.

There were two main advantages accruing to New

178

Zealand in the export of the bulk of its butter, cheese and lamb to the United Kingdom: first, an assured market, able constantly to absorb the increasing quantities of foodstuffs that New Zealand produced; secondly, unrestricted entry and preferential tariff treatment for these and other products entering the United Kingdom.

These duty and tariff rights were guaranteed by the Ottawa Agreement of 1932. The basic provisions were continued and extended by the United Kingdom–New Zealand Trade Agreements of 1959 and 1966.

However, the agreements, which provided the framework within which trade between New Zealand and the United Kingdom was conducted, were incompatible with the provisions of the Treaty of Rome, the basic document establishing the European Economic Community. Therefore, while New Zealand recognised the value and importance of wider European integration in the interests of peace and stability, it viewed with concern the first British moves to join the EEC in 1961. It was immediately apparent that the implications for New Zealand's trade were extensive, and that, without adequate safeguards, the application of the EEC's agricultural import policy would lead very rapidly to the erosion of New Zealand's position as a major supplier of foodstuffs to the British market. The New Zealand government sought special arrangements which would enable New Zealand to continue to find in the United Kingdom an adequate and remunerative market for at least the key agricultural exports. It also looked for new markets to absorb both the goods which would inevitably be displaced from the British market and the new exports which were becoming increasingly important.

When the negotiations between the United Kingdom and the EEC were renewed late in the 1960s, the New Zealand government decided that emphasis should be placed on obtaining special arrangements for the three key agricultural products—butter, cheese and lamb—for which there were no adequate alternative markets outside the United Kingdom. The New Zealand Government listed the requirements which it regarded as essential for safeguarding the two major pastoral industries, which together provided more than sixty per cent of New Zealand's total export earnings, as follows:

(a) that New Zealand should be able to continue to sell, at remunerative prices, the quantities of butter and cheese for which, before the British entry into the EEC, it had received assured access;

(b) that guarantees of access should not terminate with a transitional period, but that there should be continuing arrangements subject to periodic review;

(c) that, in the event of the Community's adoption of a common regulation for sheepmeats, New Zealand should continue to have special access for lamb.

After protracted discussions, often at Ministerial level, in which New Zealand was actively involved, agreement was reached in Luxembourg in June 1971. The British delegation and the delegation of the Community agreed on a special arrangement to protect New Zealand's trade in butter and cheese.

The main elements of the arrangement are guaranteed access and sale for specified quantities of New Zealand butter and cheese on the British market for the years 1973 to 1977, a guaranteed minimum price for these quantities, and a review in 1975 to establish conditions of access for New Zealand butter after 1977. This special arrangement was incorporated into the Treaty of Accession (by which

Britain joined the EEC) as Protocol 18.

The British government also stated publicly that it was confident that there would continue to be adequate and remunerative access into Britain for lamb from traditional sources of supply after the enlargement of the EEC.

Coupled with these efforts to safeguard New Zealand's trade were efforts to diversify New Zealand's markets. At government level, such efforts have taken the form of involvement in international organisations, the negotiation of bilateral trade agreements and consultative mechanisms, and the promotion of exports to New Zealand's traditional, as well as more recent, markets.

New Zealand Participation in International Forums

The international organisations and commodity agreements with which New Zealand is associated vary greatly in their size, scope and objectives, and range over all political, economic and trade considerations. For New Zealand, the most important of the organisations concerned primarily with trade is the General Agreement on Tariffs and Trade (GATT).

Originally intended as an interim agreement to serve until a proposed International Trade Organisation could be formally established, GATT was negotiated in 1947 and is still the only multilateral agreement which sets down agreed rules for the fair conduct of world trade. The principal objective of GATT is the encouragement of multilateral, non-discriminatory trade, through the progressive removal of tariff and non-tariff barriers. The Agreement is now accepted by countries responsible for four-fifths of total world trade, the major exceptions being USSR and China. New Zealand was one of the twenty-three original signatories.

Although it takes a keen interest in all aspects of the work of GATT, New Zealand is particularly active both in the Agriculture Committee, set up in 1967 to consider the outstanding problems of world trade in agricultural products, and in the Working Party on Dairy Products, which was established in the same year. A price arrangement, setting a floor price for skim milk powder, came into force in May 1970 and was extended to cover anhydrous milk fat early in 1973.

Another large, multilateral, trade organisation to which New Zealand belongs is the United Nations Conference on Trade and Development (UNCTAD), a forum for the consideration of measures to assist less developed nations. Here, New Zealand's activities have centred on the work of the Committee on Commodities, which encourages the conclusion of international agreements aimed at increasing the stability of the commodity trade, as well as the formulation and adoption of a scheme for extending tariff preferences to developing countries. New Zealand also has an active interest in the work of the Committee on Shipping, in which national shipping policies and world trade expansion programmes are discussed.

Other international trade and economic organisations to which New Zealand belongs include the Economic Commission for Asia and the Far East (ECAFE), the Economic Co-operation Centre for the Asian and Pacific Region (ECOCEN) and the United Nations Food and Agriculture Organisation (FAO).

After participating for several years in the work of the Committee for Agriculture of the Organisation for Economic Co-operation and Development (OECD), and in the OECD Gentlemen's Agreement on Wholemilk Powder, which was established in 1963 to set a floor price for world trade in that product, New Zealand became a full member of the OECD early in 1973. Since that time

New Zealand has reviewed its policies with other members.

BILATERAL APPROACHES

New Zealand entered into a number of bilateral trade agreements during the 1960s and early 1970s, as part of its efforts to diversify its markets. Most of these agreements were with countries in Eastern Europe or the Pacific. However, a bilateral trade agreement between New Zealand and West Germany, superseding the earlier trade agreements between the two countries, had come into effect on 1 April 1959. In the terms of this agreement, West Germany undertook to try to give expanding access to the German market for a number of New Zealand agricultural exports.

New Zealand concluded trade agreements with the following Eastern European countries during the period 1960–70: USSR (1963), Poland (1965), Bulgaria (1967), Rumania (1969) and Hungary (1970). The five trade agreements are similar in that they each provide for the mutual extension of most-favoured-nation tariff treatment on goods entering into trade between the two countries and for consultations on request on any matters affecting the operation of the agreements. Pacific countries with which New Zealand concluded trade agreements during this period are Malaysia (1961), Australia (1965), Korea (1967), the Philippines (1967) and China (1973).

In the terms of the trade agreement with Malaysia, duties on certain goods are held to a minimum, and preferential treatment on other goods is reciprocally extended. The trade agreements with Korea and the Philippines provide for full reciprocal most-favoured-nation tariff treatment.

The New Zealand–Australia Free Trade Agreement came into effect on 1 January 1966. The basis of NAFTA is the progressive removal of import duties on goods included in Schedule A, the list of products that will eventually be traded duty-free between New Zealand and Australia. Other provisions of the Agreement, and subsequent undertakings, relate to the rationalisation of industry between the two countries, consultation on tariff changes, the development (under Article 3: 7, including the Schedules B, C and D) of special arrangements for intercompany trade in goods which would be difficult to add to Schedule A, and the use of industry panels to review production and marketing problems in sensitive areas, such as sawmilling products and frozen peas and beans.

Since the inception of NAFTA, total two-way trade has increased from $175 million in the calendar year 1965 to the record figure of $401.5 million in 1973. The total number of tariff items covered by Schedule A increased from 990 at the time the Agreement came into force to 1760 at 1 January 1974. Principal Schedule A items among New Zealand's exports are newsprint, wool, pulp and timber; major items of trading interest remaining outside Schedule A include motor vehicles, carpets, domestic freezers, clothing and synthetic yards and fibres.

Since the introduction of Article 3: 7 arrangements in 1967, about 239 proposals have been approved, as at 1 March 1974, with a total trade value of about $92.3 million, $59.2 million representing New Zealand exports and $33.1 million imports from Australia. Motor vehicle components and domestic electrical (whiteware) products are the principal goods involved. Of late, both Australia and New Zealand have laid greater emphasis on Article 3: 7 arrangements involving trade in related products, goods resulting from complementary industrial development and goods to be considered for Schedule A.

Following the Ministerial review of NAFTA held in March 1973, it was agreed that a twelve-month survey of the objectives and operation of the Agreement should be undertaken and that new initiatives should be developed to expand trade. Particular attention was to be given to the development of secondary industry in the two countries and high priority placed on the complementary use of resources as a means of developing the economy of both. As a result of this survey, Ministers in Canberra on 27 November 1973 signed an Exchange of Letters which provides for a more flexible use of Article 3:7 by establishing the three new Schedules B, C and D to complement Schedule A. This provides for increased trade and will enable industry to enter into longer-term arrangements than were in general available under the original Article 3: 7 procedures.

An interim agreement on tariff rates and margins of tariff preference between Australia and New Zealand, following Britain's entry into the EEC on 1 February 1973, was finalised in an Exchange of Letters dated 7 May 1973. The agreement was designed to preserve, to the fullest possible extent for each country, the benefits of the British preferential tariff system, formerly derived from the trade agreements both countries had had with the United Kingdom. This was an interim agreement, intended to last until 30 September 1974, unless it was earlier agreed that it should be extended. In June 1974, New Zealand and Australian officials met to consider a new agreement. Another agreement was concluded with Canada to maintain preferential tariff arrangements on an interim basis, and the government decided to continue preferences for all Commonwealth countries (other than the United Kingdom), pending a future review of policies in this field.

BILATERAL MECHANISMS

In recent years, export credits have assumed an increasingly important role in international trade, with buyers in less-developed countries coming to rely more and more heavily on their overseas suppliers for credits and financial assistance. New Zealand has granted bilateral credits to Peru and Indonesia in an effort both to foster the economic growth of countries concerned and to establish and maintain trade. New Zealand has also agreed to engage in bilateral conversations with Canada, the United States, Russia, China, Italy and Korea, to discuss on a regular basis relevant trading patterns and problems.

Trade Publicity

Promotion is another aspect of trade diversification. Once the formal framework for the development of trade has been established, customers must be found for the goods. Over recent years, the government has become increasingly involved in promotional activities both within New Zealand and abroad.

Within New Zealand, the government, through the Department of Trade and Industry, tries to ensure that all potential exporters are made aware of the opportunities open to them, and of the particular characteristics and requirements of specific markets. To this end, export seminars are arranged, and publications prepared and circulated to all firms and organisations known to have export interests. The Export Guarantee Office, established in 1965, is designed to assist exporters to become established in new markets.

The government encourages the exhibition of products at trade fairs in a number of countries, and in recent years has arranged fairs in Australia, Fiji, Indonesia, the United States, France and Germany. A number of smaller displays and promotions have been mounted in other countries, including Malaysia and Italy. In Europe particularly, the government, generally in conjunction with the New Zealand Meat Producers Board, has been involved in a number of lamb promotion ventures.

Participation in fairs and promotions serves not only to focus attention on New Zealand as a source of supply of both its traditional agricultural products and its newer exports, but also to provide an opportunity for New Zealand exporters to test market reaction to their products.

The government's network of Trade Commissioners is constantly being expanded. There are at present thirty-one trade posts.

Trade with the Pacific

Increasingly, New Zealand has been looking to the countries of the Pacific both as markets for exports and as sources of imports. As the tables below show, trade with the United States, Australia and Japan, which are three of New Zealand's four largest single markets and sources of supply, has increased markedly over the past decade, both in relative and absolute terms.

EXPORTS

	1961		1973	
	NZ$(000) f.o.b.	% of total exports	NZ$(000) f.o.b.	% of total exports
USA	84,302	14.9	287,581	15.6
Australia	21,934	3.9	151,969	8.2
Japan	29,658	5.2	242,939	13.2

IMPORTS

	1961		1973	
	NZ$(000) c.d.v.	% of total imports	NZ$(000) c.d.v.	% of total imports
USA	54,400	9.4	220,524	14.9
Australia	93,878	16.3	401,537	27.0
Japan	16,656	2.9	166,426	11.20

Many of the smaller Pacific nations, especially those in the south Pacific, have become increasingly important to New Zealand as trading partners over the last ten years. Fiji provides New Zealand's largest market among the Pacific islands, buying from New Zealand, in 1973, goods to the value of NZ$16.4 million. The most important items are butter and sheepmeats, together with fruit and vegetables, milk powder, paper, paperboard and machinery. Total New Zealand exports to the islands of the south Pacific, including Fiji, Western Samoa, Tonga, Papua New Guinea and New Caledonia/French Polynesia, amounted in value in 1973 to NZ$37.6 million. A large proportion of New Zealand's total imports from the region came from Fiji, valued at NZ$3.1 million in 1973. Sugar is the main import from Fiji, accounting in 1973 for approximately ninety-two per cent of total imports. Other purchases include fruit and vegetables (largely manioc and bananas), wood, cork and some manufactured goods.

INTERNAL TRADE AND COMMERCE

Wholesale Trade

Wholesale trade in 1973 accounted for $3,455 million. In the 1967–68 Census of Distribution, there were 3778 wholesale stores in New Zealand, 23 per cent dealing with food and drink, 10 per cent with apparel, 7 per cent with furniture, 9 per cent with automotive products, 13 per cent with hardware and 4 per cent with chemicals. Wholesale stores with an annual turnover of less than $40,000 accounted for 18.6 per cent of all stores but only 0.9 per cent of total turnover. Stores with an annual turnover of more than $1 million accounted for 10 per cent of all stores, but for 56 per cent of total wholesale turnover.

The main urban areas, which at 31 March 1968 accounted for 44.8 per cent of total population, had 66 per cent of all stores and accounted for 75.5 per cent of total turnover. Secondary urban areas had 18.4 per cent of the population, 23.3 per cent of the stores and 19.5 per cent of total turnover. Smaller centres, remaining urban and all rural, had 36.8 per cent of population, 10.7 per cent of the stores and 5.0 per cent of total turnover.

Retail Trade

Retail trade for 1973 accounted for $3,050 million. This represented a turnover per head of population of $1,023, compared with $463 in 1960.

There were, in the 1967–68 Census of Distribution, 29 331 retail stores in New Zealand, 48 per cent dealing with food and drink (34% of retail turnover), 14 per cent with apparel (12.5% of turnover), 5.4 per cent with furniture and 4.6 per cent in the automotive field (14% of turnover). Stores with an annual turnover of less than $10,000 accounted for 10.4 per cent of all stores, but only 0.9 per cent of total turnover. At the other end of the scale, stores with an annual turnover of more than $2 million accounted for 1.5 per cent of all stores but for 7.0 per cent of total turnover.

The retail trade is less centralised than the wholesale; the main urban areas, as at 31 March 1968, had only 44.5 per cent of all retail stores, accounting for 47.1 per cent of total turnover; secondary urban areas had 21.3 per cent of the stores and 24.0 per cent of total turnover; small centres had 34.2 per cent of the stores and 28.9 per cent of total turnover.

Trade Movements

The small and widely dispersed population of New Zealand and, in particular, the division of the country by Cook Strait, make internal distribution a significant factor in the commerce of New Zealand.

In 1960, coastal vessels made 10 249 calls and carried 5 million tons (manifest) of cargo; by 1965, the number of calls was reduced to 9766, although tonnage had increased to 7.2 million tons; by 1973, the number of calls was further reduced to 8736 although the tonnage had again increased, to 11.0 million tons. These figures reflect the growth of bulk shipping, and the use of roll-on/roll-off vessels and dry bulk carriers. This has led to the rise of ports handling specialised cargoes and to the virtual elimination of small coastal shipping services. Facilities for roll-on/roll-off vessels are now provided at Auckland, Wellington, Picton, Lyttelton and Otago.

There has been little increase in tonnages carried by railways over recent years. In 1962, 11 million tonnes of goods and livestock were carried; by 1973, this had increased to only 12 million tonnes.

Figures are not available for the tonnage of goods carried by road transport, but the number of goods service vehicle licences, 166 708 in 1966, had increased by December 1973 to 195 101. Freight carried by scheduled commercial air services decreased from 68 173 kilogrammes in 1970 to 67 259 kilogrammes in 1972.

Employment

The commerce sector, as at 31 October 1973, employed 263 700 people of a total labour force of 1 158 000, 153 100 being male and 110 600 female; seventy-three per cent was employed in wholesale and retail trade, and twenty-seven per cent in banking and other financial institutions, and in insurance and real estate. The wholesale and retail trade employed at that time 191 300 people, compared with 143 300 in the agriculture and forestry group, 245 700 in the community and personal services group and 279 300 in the manufacturing industries.

Company Structure

Any number of persons from two to twenty-five may form a private company, while a public company must have at least seven members. Comprehensive legislation relating to companies is contained in the Companies Act 1955.

An important principle in the legislation is the protection of shareholders, creditors and the general public by the requirement that there must be the fullest practicable disclosure of information concerning the activities of companies. The annual financial statements must exhibit a true and complete account of a company's affairs and transactions.

At 31 December 1973, there were 94 233 companies on the companies register, including 519 with more than twenty-five per cent overseas ownership. About ninety-eight per cent of all companies are private companies.

Financial Institutions

The New Zealand financial system embraces a wide variety of institutions whose fundamental role in a modern economy, despite great differences in the nature of the individual activities, is to provide the channels whereby funds, currently surplus to the needs of some persons or institutions, can be transferred to those who wish to borrow. These institutions include trading banks, savings banks, life insurance offices, building, friendly and investment societies, finance companies, the short-term money market, the new issue market, the stock exchange, as well as a host of brokers and other people engaged in the borrowing and lending of money.

Reserve Bank. The functions of the Reserve Bank are to act as the Central Bank for New Zealand, to advise the government on matters relating to monetary policy, banking and overseas exchange and to give effect to the monetary policy of the government. The bank has the sole right of issue of bank notes. It also discounts Treasury Bills, grants advances to the State and to approved public bodies, including the trading banks, and buys and sells government securities.

Trading Banks. There are five trading banks in New Zealand, one, the Bank of New Zealand, being fully State-owned; the others—the National Bank of New Zealand (owned by Lloyds Bank, UK), the Australia and New Zealand Bank (owned by Australia and New Zealand Banking Group, UK), the Bank of New South Wales and the Commercial Bank of Australia—are owned by private shareholders, their shares being traded on the stock exchange. Deposits with the trading banks were $1,835 million (weekly average) in 1973, and advances were $1,015 million, or 55.3 per cent of deposits.

Savings Banks. Savings banks include the Post Office Savings Bank, the trustee savings banks and the savings banks operated by trading banks. At the year ended March 1974, total deposits were $3,157 million. The Post Office Savings Bank operates 1229 branches throughout New Zealand, and offers ordinary savings accounts, special purpose accounts, thrift club accounts, home lay-by accounts, investment accounts and the school savings bank. It also operates the National Development Bonds, the New Zealand Savings Certificates and the Bonus Bonds schemes. There are twelve trustee savings banks in New Zealand, offering a range of accounts similar to those offered by the Post Office Savings Bank.

Stock and Station Agents. Many of the existing stock and station agents began business first as general merchants or retailers in the early days of the country's settlement. However, during the greater part of their history, their main financial operations have been in the supply of merchandise, machinery and implements, and the provision of finance, to the farming community. At 31 March 1974, loans to farmers totalled $178.3 million.

Finance Companies. There are many finance companies in New Zealand. In 1972, 456 of these were surveyed, it being found that twenty-seven of them had eighty-four per cent of the total assets.

Insurance. Many forms of insurance receive government encouragement by way of income tax concessions on premiums paid for life, personal accident or sickness insurance and payments to the National Provident Fund or a superannuation fund. (Compulsory superannuation was introduced in April 1975.) The steady flow of funds to insurance companies by the payment of premiums is in the form of contractual savings (accumulating to considerable capital investment), and the investment of these funds has become a major influence on the financial market.

There are twenty-five life assurance offices in New Zealand. At the end of the 1972–73 year, there were 2.4 million ordinary and industrial life assurance policies in force, with a value of more than $9,444 million.

State Advances Corporation. The State Advances Corporation, constituted in 1936, had two principal activities: the lending of money on farm mortgages and for the building or buying of homes and the financing, letting, administration or sale of State rental houses or flats. In the year ended 31 March 1974, $59 million was authorised for loans in the rural sector and $131 million for loans in the urban sector. There were at that date 52 213 State housing units administered on a tenancy basis, rents received amounting to $22.1 million.

In 1974, the twofold activities of the State Advances Corporation were separated. A Rural Banking and Finance Corporation was established to take over the rural lending activities, those of making loans available for farms and farm support industries, formerly effected by the State Advances Corporation. On the housing side, a new government organisation, the Housing Corporation of New Zealand, was instituted to merge the State Advances Corporation's urban housing activities with those of the Housing Division of the Ministry of Works and Development. These latter comprised State house construction, the planning and development of new Auckland and Wellington urban areas and the erection of houses for government department employees, including those in the armed forces and at major construction jobs. The new Corporation brings under one management the government's major housing activities.

Currency. In July 1967, decimal currency was introduced, with the dollar as the monetary unit replacing the pound. The dollar is equivalent to the previous ten shillings. There are coins for $1 (not in general circulation), 50, 20, 10, 5, 2 cents and 1 cent, and Reserve Bank notes for 1, 2, 5, 10, 20 and 100 dollars. The notes and coins have distinctive New Zealand designs.

Overseas Investment

There are several regulations which apply to overseas investment in New Zealand. The Exchange Control Regulations 1965 provide that the consent of the Reserve Bank is required for both current and capital transactions involving the transfer of money, or having the effect of transferring money, in to or out of New Zealand. The Capital Issues (Overseas) Regulations 1965 provide that the consent of the Reserve Bank is required before any company incorporated outside New Zealand can commence business in New Zealand and before any New Zealand company, whether incorporated or not, can borrow or raise any money overseas. The Overseas Takeover Regulations 1964 are designed to ensure that the government be given notice of the intention of an 'overseas person' to make an offer for the existing shares of a New Zealand company. In 1972, the total overseas, private, direct investment in New Zealand amounted to $NZ97.5 million.

Present government policy is that the prime consideration in assessing investment proposals is the nature of the contribution that the investment will make, both in quantity and quality, to New Zealand's development.

Tourist Trade

Travel between countries in and around the Pacific has boomed in recent years and international jet air services have made New Zealand fairly easily accessible to international tourists of all countries.

The tourist industry is growing rapidly; in 1961, there were 40 924 visitors, including tourist (67 per cent), businessmen (12 per cent) and those on working holidays or here for education (7 per cent), and there were also 36 386 through passengers or visitors on cruise ships. By 1967, there were 112 871 visitors and 72 561 through passengers, and this increased to 254 644 visitors and 83 138 through passengers in 1973.

The visitors are mainly from Australia (49 per cent), the United States of America (25 per cent), the United Kingdom (7 per cent) and Canada (4 per cent). Travel receipts were shown in the Balance of Payments as $78.5 million in 1973, compared with $15.3 million in 1967. The article on Tourism gives further tourist trade figures and a summary of the operation of the tourist hotel industry.

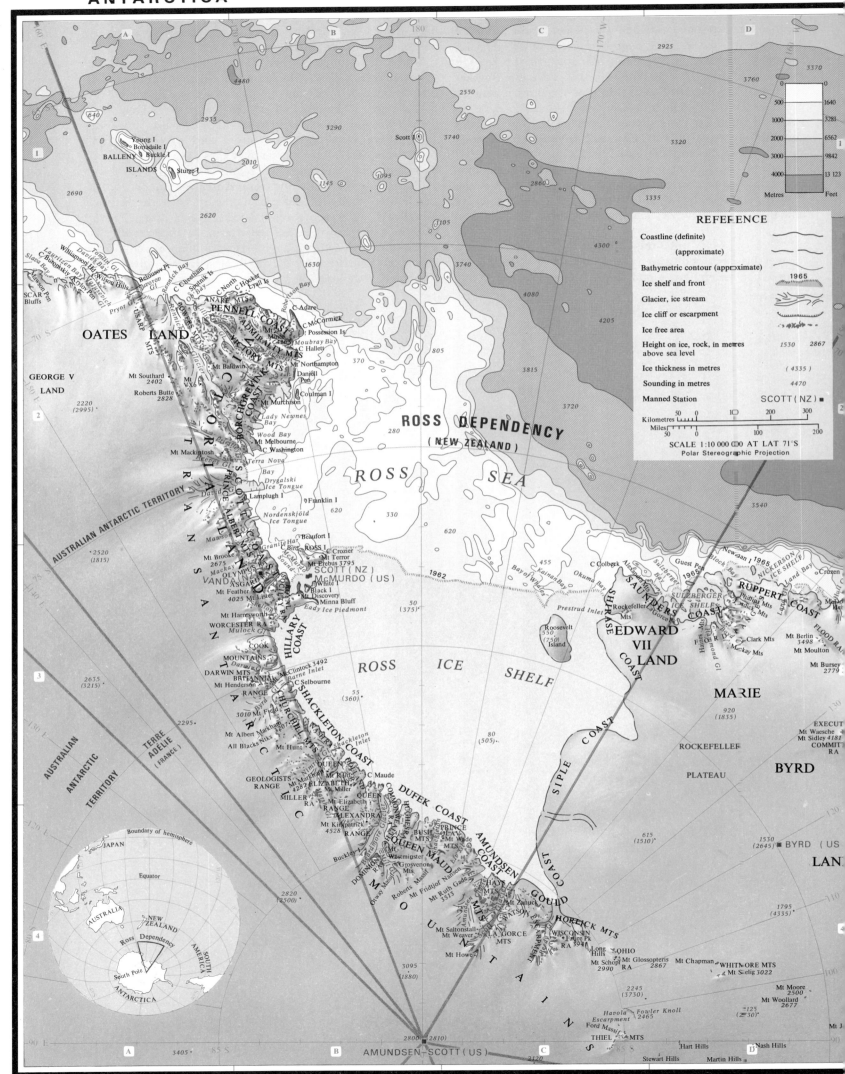

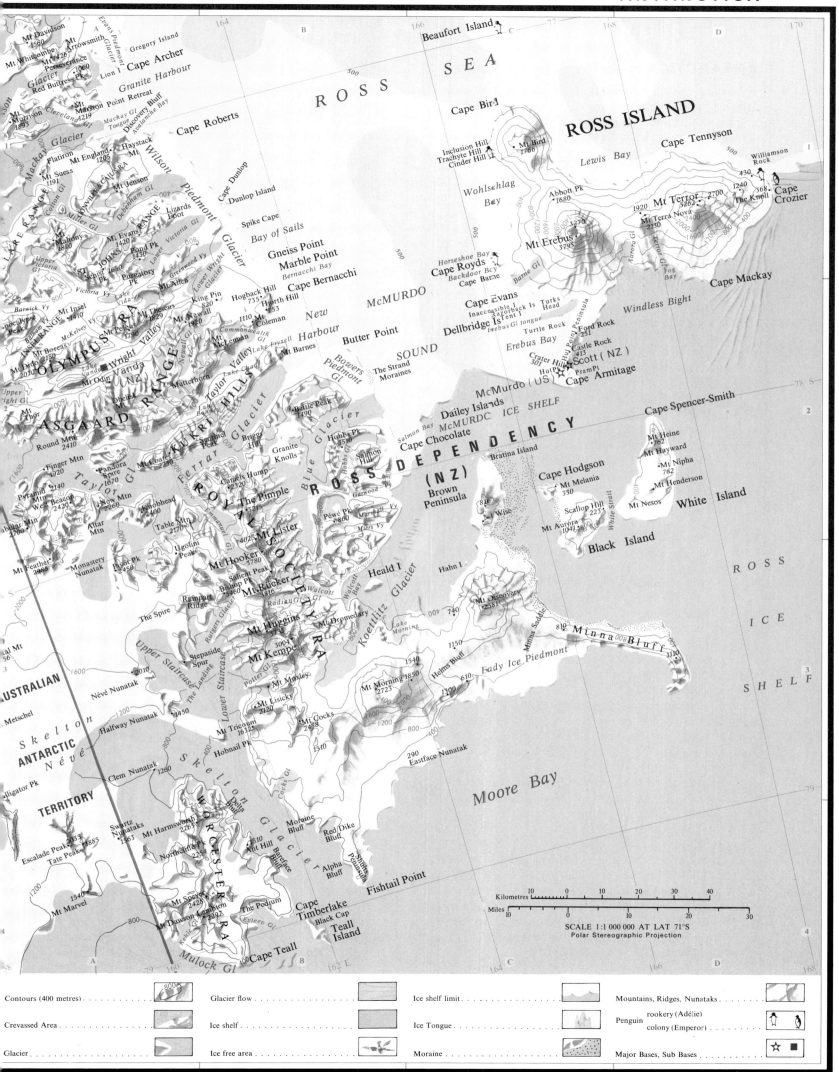

ANTARCTICA

Trevor Hatherton

Following the circumnavigation of the world in the late fifteenth and early sixteenth centuries, Renaissance cartographers speculated on the nature of the earth to the south of the moderate latitudes penetrated on those voyages. They initiated the concept of a large southern continent, *terra australis incognita*, and, remarkably, this notion was not disproved for two centuries. After limited Dutch incursion in the seventeenth century, it fell to the Pacific navigators of the eighteenth and nineteenth centuries, with whom so much of the early European history of New Zealand is linked, to shape the possible extent of the unknown land. James Cook carved great masses from the postulated continent and proved that if land existed at all, it lay in latitudes beyond 60° S. It was along this parallel that he made his circumnavigation in the years 1772–75, though he penetrated as far as 71° 10′ S. By refitting his vessels in New Zealand before heading south in 1773 and 1774, Cook started the long, though for the most part vicarious, association of this country with south polar expeditions.

Who first sighted the Antarctic continent has long been a contentious issue but priority now appears to be given to Thaddeus von Bellingshausen, who in 1819 saw and described, but did not recognise as a land mass, part of what is now called Princess Ragnhild Coast. Bellingshausen sheltered briefly in Queen Charlotte Sound before returning north. The first known landing south of the Antarctic Circle (lat 66° 30′ S) was made by the sealing captain, Freeman, who, on 12 February 1839, briefly landed on Borradaile Island after voyaging south out of Chalky Inlet. But the voyage most significant for New Zealand was that of James Clark Ross who, after leaving Hobart in late 1840, penetrated the pack into the Ross Sea to discover the Great Ice Barrier, the mountains of Victoria Land, Ross Island and McMurdo Bay (now McMurdo Sound), the principal elements of what is today the Ross Dependency. On his return from this journey, Ross spent three months in the Bay of Islands. Just before Ross's voyage, the United States expedition under Charles Wilkes had entered Antarctic waters. 'John Sac, a native of New Zealand' and apparently a petty chief of the Bay of Islands, who had sailed with the expedition from the United States, became perhaps the first New Zealander to cross the Antarctic Circle. The first New Zealander, and possibly the first person, to set foot on the Antarctic continent was the seventeen-year-old Alexander von Tunzelmann, at Cape Adare on 24 January 1895. Von Tunzelmann, nephew of a pioneer Central Otago explorer and settler, was assistant to Borchgrevink, the scientist with Bull's expedition on the ship *Antarctic*.

Exploration of the interior of the continent began at the end of the nineteenth century. The expeditions of Scott and Shackleton between 1900 and 1917 offered opportunities for New Zealanders to take part, though usually in an auxiliary role. Eight New Zealanders were, however, members of the Australasian Antarctic Expedition of 1911–14 under Sir Douglas Mawson.

The official connection between New Zealand and the Antarctic began in 1923, when a United Kingdom Order-in-Council claimed 'all islands and territories' lying between 160° E longitude and 150° W longitude and south of 60° S latitude. This new territory was proclaimed a British 'settlement', named the 'Ross Dependency' and placed under the administrative authority of the Governor-General of New Zealand. During the following thirty years, world events and the disinterest of successive New Zealand governments resulted in little attempt being made at even nominal occupation of the Dependency, though the first three Administrators of the Ross Dependency (who were invariably Nautical Advisers to the Marine Department) went south with whaling fleets. In the meantime, the several American expeditions of Byrd and Ellsworth attracted their share of New Zealanders and New Zealand interest, and some official support came to the British–Australian–New Zealand Antarctic Research Expedition (BANZARE) of 1929–31. Two New Zealand scientists, R. A. (later Sir Robert) Falla and R. G. Simmers, became members of the expedition, again led by Mawson, which was financially assisted by a grant from the New Zealand government.

Enthusiasm aroused by BANZARE and by the Byrd expeditions was responsible for the creation in 1933 of the New Zealand Antarctic Society. For several decades this private organisation carried the burden in New Zealand of promoting interest in the Antarctic. Following the Second World War, public interest began to grow again, especially after the US Navy expeditions of 1946 and 1947 visited New Zealand; 1949 saw the New Zealand Antarctic Society issue its first *Antarctic News Bulletin*, which quarterly has been published continuously for the past twenty-five years (as *Antarctic* from March 1956). In 1952 the Society, in association with A. H. and A. W. Reed, published *The Antarctic Today*, a compendium of Antarctic information which subsequently appeared in Russian and Spanish translations. However it was not until the Society's representations to government were reinforced by those from other, more powerful bodies that New Zealand established itself on the southern continent.

New Zealand Occupation

International Polar Years, during which scientific activities of many nations were concentrated in the higher latitudes, were held in 1882–83 and 1932–33. In 1953, the International Council of Scientific Unions approved a similar, though world-wide, effort, the International Geophysical Year (IGY), for 1957–58. The organising committee, after its Rome meeting in 1954, called 'the attention of the New Zealand Government to the very great desirability of a station at Ross Island or at a suitable site between Ross Island and Cape Adare'. Coincident with the IGY proposal was the British resuscitation of Shackleton's objective, an overland crossing of the continent from the Weddell to the Ross Sea, in which the participation of New Zealand was invited. The combination of these two elements aroused great public interest. In May 1955, the government declared that New Zealand had an inescapable geographic interest in Antarctica and announced its approval of New Zealand's participation in the proposed Trans-Antarctic Expedition (TAE). In August 1955, government also approved New Zealand's IGY programme, which included the establishment of a base in the Antarctic. Further, following discussions with United States authorities, it was announced, in May 1956, that New Zealand would join the United States in the establishment of a second scientific base near Cape Adare for the duration of IGY. This base, Hallett Station, operated continuously from 1957 to 1964 when a fire destroyed most of the scientific equipment.

The New Zealand station erected in McMurdo Sound was named Scott Base. The set of buildings, all joined together by a covered way to permit passage in poor weather, was designed by the Ministry of Works and transported south in the expedition ship HMNZS *Endeavour* and a United States transport ship. The New Zealand flag was formally raised in the presence of Captain Harold Ruegg, the fourth Administrator of the Ross Dependency, on 20 January 1957, and since that date Scott Base, the 'outward and visible sign' of New Zealand's Antarctic aspirations, has remained the operational hub of the country's activities on the continent. The base looks southwards towards the Pole across the Ross Ice Shelf and the polar routes of Scott and Shackleton. Proximity to the United States air and sea transport facilities at McMurdo Sound, though disappointing to those seeking isolation, greatly increased the potential activities of New Zealand in the Antarctic by making extended summer expeditions possible. The two camps are only three kilometres apart.

From Scott Base, supply depots were established during the late summer of 1956–57 and the spring of 1957–58 for Dr (later Sir) Vivian Fuchs's overland party. After laying the depots, a group of five New Zealanders, led by Sir Edmund Hillary and using small tractors as transport, travelled on to the South Pole, being the first to accomplish the feat overland since Captain Scott almost fifty years earlier. On the return of TAE to New Zealand, the New Zealand Government decided that scientific and exploration work in the Ross Dependency should continue indefinitely after the end of IGY. To advise government on appropriate programmes of work, the Ross Dependency Research Committee was formed in April 1958, reporting to the Minister of Science. Meanwhile a Special (later Scientific) Committee for Antarctic Research (SCAR) was formed by the International Council of Scientific Unions to encourage the continuation of general scientific activity in Antarctica after IGY. Response from the twelve nations[1] working in the Antarctic was positive and polar research is now co-ordinated by SCAR which sponsors, through its working groups, collaborative programmes and symposia on all aspects of Antarctic research.

The possibilities of the new bases on Ross Island and of the massive transport facilities associated with them were quickly seen by New Zealand scientists and institutions not connected with IGY or TAE, and universities and government departments began to focus their attention on Antarctic work. Thus a central, independent logistic organisation, to co-ordinate the needs and plans of the growing number of groups with Antarctic ambitions, was required to replace the previous informal methods related to the specific IGY or TAE activities; such a body was also needed to represent New Zealand in the complex logistic discussions with United States authorities. To meet these requirements, an Antarctic Division was set up in 1959 within the Department of Scientific and Industrial Research.

Finally, at the political level, the twelve nations agreed on a treaty 'ensuring the use of Antarctica for peaceful purposes only and the continuance of international harmony in Antarctica', which was signed in 1959 and subsequently ratified by all signatory governments. The Antarctic Treaty and SCAR form the organisational framework within which the individual national research programmes contribute to 'the interests of science and the progress of all mankind'.

The Ross Dependency

The first New Zealand expedition of 1956–58, as well as fulfilling its IGY and TAE obligations, established a broad-based scientific programme developing the work of the British expeditions of the early part of the century; cartography, surveying, geology, upper atmosphere physics, gravity, seismology, meteorology and biology are included in these studies. Since 1958, New Zealanders from the universities and government departments, working in annual summer and wintering-over parties have explored, mapped and studied a considerable part of the Ross Dependency.

The Dependency may be discussed as four separate units, sea, ice, land and atmosphere, which shape the region and determine New Zealand's scientific interests therein.

THE SEA

The greater part of the Ross Dependency is covered by water. The northern boundary of the Dependency is almost coincident with a mid-ocean ridge with water depths of less than 3000 metres. Between this ridge and the Antarctic continent, water depths are greater but, except in the eastern part of the Dependency, never reach the abyssal depths of true ocean basins. Protruding from this ocean cover are some volcanic remnants: Scott Island, which is almost on the 180° meridian, and the Balleny Islands, a linear, south-east-trending group on the Antarctic Circle north of Victoria and Oates Lands.

The sea floor of the continental shelf is gently undulatory, consisting of a series of ridges trending north-north-east. It has a mean depth of about 500 metres, much deeper than the shelves of other continents, and this is characteristic of the whole peripheral shelf of Antarctica. The seaward edge of the shelf, with the exception of the region of Iselin Bank, follows an almost straight line connecting the northernmost parts of Victoria Land and Marie Byrd Land. Zones of glacial erosion and moraines on the sea floor make it probable that the Ross Ice Shelf once reached almost to the continental shelf edge. The geological structure underlying the Ross Sea can be conveniently considered in two parts, separated approximately by the 180° meridian. To the west, the structure is quite complex, whereas to the east there is a broad, deep, sedimentary basin in which the thickness of sediments reaches four kilometres.

The sea is the source, sustenance and habitat of virtually all forms of life in the Dependency. This life depends for its ultimate existence on vegetation (phytoplankton) which in the presence of sunlight can utilise the nutrient salts in the sea water. The cycle of life then proceeds upwards through the small marine animals (zooplankton), squids and fishes, to the penguins, seals, whales and birds which inhabit the southern oceans. Four families represent ninety-five per cent of the plentiful Antarctic fish fauna, with *Nototheniidae* (Antarctic cods) being the most prolific, though the ice, or 'bloodless', fishes (*Chaenichthyidae*) are of major scientific interest. Benthic or 'bottom' fauna of the Ross Sea include a considerable proportion of sponges, crustacea, ophiuroids and mollusca.

Weddell seals are ubiquitous, but the Ross, Crabeater and Leopard seals, because they are creatures of the pack ice, are rarely seen. The toothed Killer whale is the most frequently observed of the whales. Three species of penguins breed in the Dependency, two (Adélie, Emperor) on the mainland and one, the Chinstrap or Ringed penguin, on the Balleny Islands. A bird familiar to all visitors to McMurdo Sound, McCormick's skua, also breeds on the

[1] The twelve nations are Argentina, Australia, Belgium, Chile, France, Japan, New Zealand, Norway, South Africa, USSR, United Kingdom, USA.

continent, as do Wilson's petrel, the Snow petrel and probably the Antarctic petrel. The Silvergrey fulmar, Cape pigeon and Antarctic prion breed on the islands of the Dependency. Some of the species have been seen, by traverse parties, flying hundreds of kilometres inland, presumably on scavenging forays.

THE ICE

For most visitors to the continent, the first truly Antarctic feature encountered is the sea or 'pack' ice. In March, when the temperature begins to drop sharply, ice is formed around the continent by the freezing of sea water and by the addition of superimposed snow. This ice is broken up by wave action and the resulting jostling produces 'pancake' ice. Heavier seas may throw up the small floes, forming rafted ice. By the height of winter, the thick pack is relatively still but, as spring wears on to summer, it loosens and becomes more mobile; by January the Ross Sea is usually clear of pack ice, except in sheltered bays. The pack still determines the timetables of Antarctic supply and relief, except in the case of New Zealand and United States expeditions, where the Christchurch–McMurdo air link provides opportunity to fly over the pack with personnel and equipment at almost any time of the year.

Beyond the pack in the Ross Sea, the next southerly obstacle to progress is the Ross Ice Shelf or 'Great Ice Barrier'. More than one-third of the coastline of Antarctica is fringed by ice-shelves, which are sheets of ice with level or gently undulating surfaces, floating on water and flowing under their own weight. By far the largest of these are in the two major embayments of the Ross and Weddell seas and the greater is the Ross Ice Shelf ($530\ 000\ km^2$) which occupies much of the southern part of the Dependency. The thickness of the shelf varies from 200 metres at the ice front to more than 1000 metres at the junction with land ice some hundreds of kilometres inland. Crevasses are rare except near the periphery and in grounded areas, and the Ross Ice Shelf provided a low-level route for the early explorers to within about $5°$ of the South Pole.

The shelves are nourished by abundant snowfall, together with ice flowing down as great glaciers from the high inland ice cap, and they waste from melting at the ice front and from calving tabular icebergs, some of which achieve huge dimensions. 'Icequakes' or small earthquakes are sometimes produced by the calving; these, and minor shocks probably originating from Mt Erebus, are the only known 'earthquakes' on the Antarctic continent, making it by far the quietest of the five continental regions. This aseismicity is so abnormal that it must be considered when theories of earthquake generation are propounded.

Around the landward periphery of the Ross Ice Shelf, the downslope ice from the vast inland plateau pours down in great rock-walled valley glaciers, of which the 200 kilometre Beardmore Glacier is perhaps the best known, having provided access to the plateau for Scott and Shackleton in their attempts to reach the South Pole.

THE LAND

Antarctica comprises a low-lying continental mass overlain by an ice sheet or 'cap'. The surface of this massive ice cap stands at an elevation of 4000 metres at the centre and generally slopes to the coast. Where the ice is obstructed in its journey to the sea it disgorges down valleys in the form of massive glaciers. One such obstruction forms the entire western boundary of the Ross Sea region—the Trans-Antarctic Mountains which run from Oates Land in the north almost to the Pole itself. These mountains, all of which are in, or very closely bordering, the Ross

Dependency, provide about fifty per cent of the exposed land within the Antarctic Circle, and thus geology has been one of the most popular of New Zealand's Antarctic sciences. The mountains are made up broadly of three major rock units:

1. A Precambrian or Lower Paleozoic basement complex of folded metasedimentary, metamorphic and intrusive igneous rocks;
2. Flat-lying Upper Paleozoic and Lower Mesozoic continental sedimentary rocks intruded by Jurassic dolerite sheets and overlain by flood basalts;
3. Plio-Pleistocene volcanoes and glacial deposits.

This three-fold division remains basically the same from Oates Coast in the north to the Queen Maud Mountains in the south. A major unconformity, the Kukri peneplain, extends completely over the Trans-Antarctic Mountains. The nearly level erosion surface truncates the basement rocks and is overlain unconformably by up to 1500 metres of continental sedimentary rocks known as the Beacon Group. This largely flat-lying sequence ranges in age from Devonian to Jurassic and consists of a wide variety of formations, among which well-stratified buff sandstone is predominant. Siltstones are present everywhere as thin bands within the sandstones, but also occur as formations of wide extent and considerable thickness, in which seams of coal, usually of high ash content and up to ten metres thick, occur. In many places the Beacon formations are intruded by thick horizontal sills of dolerite, their dark colour in striking contrast to the buff-coloured sediments in which they are emplaced. The discovery, in recent years, of fossil remains of freshwater amphibians and land-living reptiles within the sediments of the Trans-Antarctic Mountains has provided key evidence for the connection of Antarctica to other southern continents within the ancient Gondwanaland.

Late Tertiary–Quaternary volcanoes and volcanic remnants stretch from the Balleny Islands down the eastern margin of the Trans-Antarctic Mountains to the Skelton Glacier. The best known and most impressive of these is, of course, the 3800 metre Mt Erebus, an active volcano which dominates McMurdo Sound, but several other, extinct, volcanoes are also visible from Scott Base. Inland from Ross Island are the Dry Valleys, whose accessibility, more pleasant working environment, abundance of rock exposures and unique lakes have attracted scientists of almost all the twelve nations active in Antarctica. The valleys, with their relief of a thousand metres and more, their hanging glaciers and flat, open floors, form striking scenery which is enhanced by the 'layer-cake' geology of the dolerite sills and Beacon sediments. The scientific problems posed by the ice-free valleys, their solar-heated lakes and other climatological and glaciological features, resulted in 1968 in the siting of a small New Zealand base, suitable for both summer and wintering-over parties, near the shores of Lake Vanda in the Wright Valley. One other interesting feature of the region is the occurrence of mummified seals, ranging from fresh carcases to remains some hundreds of years old, on the floors of the valleys at altitudes of up to 700 metres and distances of up to sixty kilometres from the sea.

Terrestrial flora in the Dependency is restricted to mosses, lichens and algae, which usually occur on rock close to some seasonal source of meltwater. Less visible, but living in association with the flora, are minuscule forms of land animals such as springtails and mites.

THE ATMOSPHERE

The climate of Antarctica is more rigorous than that of any other extensive region on earth. Although the Sun—

Earth relationships are similar at both Poles, the Antarctic, with a mean elevation of about 2000 metres, is also the world's highest continent and this elevation alone would make the Antarctic about 12° C colder than the Arctic. Other factors enhance the extreme nature of the climate: the high central elevation and surrounding slopes give rise to strong downslope (katabatic) winds and the frequent blizzard conditions encountered along and at the foot of these slopes. Katabatic effects lead to relatively constant wind direction, giving rise to rippled, dune-like snow surface patterns, called sastrugi, which often make surface travel uncomfortable on the plateau.

Weather conditions at Scott Base and Vanda Station, however, are not unduly severe. Temperatures only rarely fall below −50°C, and then usually in calm conditions, minimising the wind-chill factor. A noticeable seasonal phenomenon is the rapid spring rise in temperature in November and the almost equally rapid fall in late February. Between these times, however, the weather near the coast in the Ross Dependency is often balmy. Striking optical phenomena are frequently observed. Because of the refractive effect of strong vertical temperature gradients which exist in the layers of air nearest the ground, mirages are common. The frequent presence of ice crystal clouds and fogs gives rise to complex halo phenomena including sun pillars, parhelia (mock sun) and other circles and arcs, as well as the common 22° halo. The persistence of the sun at similar elevations for long periods of time at high latitudes, which produces the long, dark winter and nightless summer, also prolongs many beautiful optical and cloud effects.

Weather is produced mainly in the lower atmosphere. Above this, at an altitude of fifty kilometres and higher, is the electrified atmosphere or ionosphere. Because of the role of the magnetic poles in 'collecting' corpuscular radiation from the sun, ionisation of the upper atmosphere in the higher latitudes is often intense. This ionisation has its visible expression during darkness in the auroras, which commonly appear as contorted bands of white, green or red light stretching across the sky; most often the red coloration appears very faintly at the top of a display, although sometimes an aurora may be red from top to bottom. The whole display may often be in violent motion. Superb displays have been seen at Hallett Station, though those at Scott Base are more muted, due to the geometry of the auroral zone. This zone is centred around the geomagnetic pole at latitude 79° S, longitude 110° E; in quiet solar periods, the zone does not extend much beyond Antarctic limits, but in more active periods it may dilate to give auroras visible in New Zealand. Ionospheric disturbance also affects radio communications and the earth's magnetic field more severely in the auroral latitudes. The synoptic study of processes in both ionosphere and lower atmosphere was the scientific impetus for IGY.

Economic Potential

Any possibility of the economic exploitation of Antarctica depends on the resources on the land and in the sea, though there is natural interest in the tourist potential of such an unusual region. The whales and seals of the Antarctic and subantarctic seas have been hunted for two centuries and present little promise for further extensive harvesting in the immediate future. The krill, however, which abound in the cold Antarctic waters, could in the long term provide considerable fish protein yield, and several countries, including Japan and Russia, are experimenting with this resource.

The basement rocks of east Antarctica are the geological correlatives of rocks of South Africa, Australia and South America, that is of ancient Gondwanaland. These other Precambrian shield rocks carry large metallic resources and it is thus logical to expect similar deposits in Antarctic Precambrian basement rocks. So far, geological and geophysical exploration of these exposures in east Antarctica has revealed very little of potential value, though some large, but low-grade, iron deposits occur, notably in Prince Charles Land. The younger sediments, of which there are more extensive exposures, have likewise yielded indications of little other than minor mineralisation. On the other hand, the bedded rocks of the Beacon series contain extensive coal deposits of varying thicknesses that represent, collectively, massive deposits of sub-bituminous coal.

The Antarctic continental shelf is extensive in the Ross and Weddell seas, but around the rest of the coast the shelf is narrow. Marine geological and geophysical exploration in the Ross Sea has revealed large thicknesses of sediments, particularly in the eastern sector. In 1973, two holes drilled for scientific purposes in sediments of the Ross Sea were closed when hydrocarbons were encountered, and the significance of these results was soon perceived by oil interests. It is in dealing with the problems raised by economic mineral discoveries that the peaceful international purpose of the Antarctic Treaty will meet its sternest test.

THE PACIFIC NEIGHBOURHOOD

B. K. Macdonald

Oceania is a region of great diversity. In size the islands range from New Guinea, with a land area of 975 000 square kilometres and a population of 3 000 000, to the Tokelaus with a total of ten square kilometres and a population of 1700. Excluding New Zealand, West Irian and Hawaii, there is a population of about 4 000 000 and a land area of less than 650 000 square kilometres, divided amongst several hundred islands scattered over one-third of the earth's surface. Within this area there are both volcanic and coral islands, some isolated by vast stretches of ocean, others closely clustered; some fertile, others barren; some sparsely populated, others overcrowded and unable to support their populations without external assistance. A few islands are rich in minerals; others, through a favourable combination of physical features and climatic conditions, can support forestry, commercial agriculture, or livestock industries. Most, however, are tied to subsistence farming with, sometimes, a surplus for export.

The origins of the Pacific Islanders are still the subject of controversy, but most authorities agree that they came from the south-east Asian region in migrations of diverse peoples over thousands of years. Intermingling and long periods of isolation then produced a great variety of physical types, languages and socio-political organisations.

The terms Polynesia, Melanesia and Micronesia are commonly used to divide Oceania into broad cultural areas. Of these, Polynesia, which is encompassed by a rough triangle with Hawaii, New Zealand and Easter Island at its angles, is the most homogenous. Most traditional societies within Polynesia were hierarchical; status was determined by descent rather than by achievement. Chiefly *élites* might dispute paramountcy amongst themselves but the paths to power were perpetually closed to persons of common birth. With political and marriage alliances amongst leading members of interlocking hierarchies, it was possible for a high-ranking chief to achieve supremacy over an entire island or island group. Political organisation, like language, had many common elements but was by no means uniform.

Melanesia lies to the north-east of Australia and includes New Caledonia, the New Hebrides, the Solomon Islands and New Guinea. The physical environment in the large islands with densely forested mountains and major river systems made communications difficult, if not impossible, over any significant distances and predetermined a multiplicity of languages, a fragmented society and limited spheres of political influence. Some societies were hierarchical, in New Caledonia for example, but generally status was achieved rather than inherited. The accumulation of wealth was fundamental to political leadership. The payment of others' debts and the 'giving-away' of wealth at ceremonial feasts increased the numbers of those under obligation to the aspiring leader, and they, together with his kin, formed the basis of his support and power.

Fiji, on the Polynesian–Melanesian border, does not fit easily into either pattern. Although by no means a homogenous population in terms of either cultural or physical characteristics, the indigenous Fijians are, generally speaking, physically akin to Melanesians while sharing many cultural traits with their Polynesian neighbours.

Micronesia is comprised of the islands north-east of Melanesia and north-west of Polynesia. Here, as in Polynesia, status was generally ascribed, although social hierarchies were seldom as complex or rigid. Because of the smallness of the islands, and their relative isolation, political units were smaller and hegemony was rarely exercised over more than a single island. The most notable exception was in the southern Gilbert Islands, where community leadership was vested in councils of old men.

European Influences

The arrival in the Pacific of the first visitors from the West a little more than five centuries ago must have been a dramatic event, but with few consequences except the exchange of a few articles and, perhaps, a few ideas. In the late eighteenth and early nineteenth centuries, the beach-combers, and traders seeking provisions, sandalwood, pearl-shell, coconut oil, *bêche-de-mer* and other products, began to cultivate the seeds of change. In time, permanent European settlements were established by traders, planters and missionaries. Christianity was often adopted by the Islanders mainly for political or economic reasons, and conversion, for many, was a matter of outward conformity and rigid laws. Missionaries became the power behind the throne of more than one island 'kingdom' but they also introduced literacy and medicine, and their influence brought peace and stability to many communities and gave a new legitimacy to island governments. For many Islanders, church organisations provided the only effective medical and educational services until well into the twentieth century.

From the mid-nineteenth century plantations were established on many islands, resulting in tension and disorder and a deterioration in race relations in the principal areas of contact. The recruitment of labour from other islands was not always orderly, and the attention of humanitarians in Europe and Australasia became focused on this labour trade. Because foreign settlement produced situations no longer controllable by island governments, western powers began to intervene politically.

The presence and significance of these various agents of change were by no means uniform throughout the Pacific. Generally, however, Polynesia was affected before Melanesia. Although the introduction of epidemic diseases caused some population decline, the nature and cumulative consequences of contact between Europeans and Islanders in this period should not be seen as a 'fatal impact'; rather, the response from the Islanders was a positive one. They sought to benefit from the forces of change accepting some aspects, rejecting others, while making the necessary adjustments to their ways of life.

The quickening interest of the Great Powers in the Pacific after 1850, and the growing problems of lawlessness, led to the establishment of colonies and protectorates. France assumed responsibility for New Caledonia and its dependencies, the eastern islands now known as French Polynesia and, in concert with Great Britain the New Hebrides. Great Britain acquired Fiji, Papua, the Cook Islands, the Tokelaus, Pitcairn, Niue, Ocean Island, the Gilbert, Ellice, Phoenix, Line and Solomon groups. Germany formalised its position in north-eastern New Guinea, New Britain, New Ireland, Bougainville, the Marshalls, Western Samoa and Nauru. Spain 'sold' to Germany its possessions in the Caroline and Mariana islands except for Guam which had already been transferred to the United States at the conclusion of the Spanish-American War. The United States annexed Eastern Samoa and Hawaii. Britain subsequently transferred Papua to Australia and the Cook Islands, Niue and the Tokelaus to New Zealand.

Tonga alone escaped inclusion in the Pacific empires of the powers; under a treaty of amity signed in 1900 Great Britain guaranteed its protection but the control of internal matters remained in Tongan hands.

This patchwork of colonialism was further altered after the First World War when Germany was deprived of its colonies. Under mandates of the League of Nations, the New Guinea possessions were transferred to Australia, Western Samoa to New Zealand and the Marianas, Carolines and Marshalls to Japan. Nauru came under the joint control of Britain, Australia (which was to be responsible for administration) and New Zealand. At the conclusion of the Second World War, the Japanese dependencies became a strategic Trust Territory of the United Nations, administered by the United States; the other Pacific mandates became Trust Territories without a transfer of administrative responsibility.

Before the Second World War, there was very little economic or political development in most islands. Education was left largely in the hands of the missions, health services to Native Medical Practitioners trained in Suva. The war directly or indirectly affected most island groups. The break in the continuity of colonial administration, the presence of foreign troops and evidence of wealth and technological sophistication of a degree hitherto unimagined by most Islanders, caused far-reaching re-appraisals in the island societies.

In the 1930s and 1940s, sovereignty disputes arose between the United Kingdom (with New Zealand) and the United States. Islands in the Tokelau, Northern Cook, Ellice, Line and Phoenix groups—some of them uninhabited—acquired importance for defence purposes and as potential refuelling points on rapidly expanding civil aviation routes. Claims and counter-claims were made, many based on questionable acts of 'discovery' and 'occupation' which ignored subsequent acts of cession and colonial rule. A United Kingdom – United States fifty-year condominium was established over Canton and Enderbury islands in 1939 and the issue has generally lessened in importance: transit stops on Pacific routes have become unnecessary with advances in aeronautical engineering; uninhabited islands are now regarded in international law as *terra nullius* which can be claimed only by colonisation and continuing settlement, and decolonisation, leading to statehood, effectively eliminates external claims to sovereignty.

Self Determination

Partly but not simply because of the war and provisions for international trusteeship in the United Nations Charter, the middle decades of the century saw also policy reappraisals by the administering powers and a new emphasis on the rights of colonial peoples to self-determination. New Zealand and Australia, geographically a part of the region, began to promote 'new deals' for the Islanders. New Zealand moved its territories steadily towards self-government, while in the 1950s Australia favoured 'paternalistic gradualism'. Great Britain declared its intention of guiding its dependencies towards responsible self-government within the Commonwealth. Its Pacific possessions, politically undeveloped in European eyes and economically backward, remained largely free of the forces of change that swept the remainder of the Empire in the 1950s. In the 1960s, aware of the emergence of the powerful and anti-colonial bloc in the United Nations, and reluctant to maintain a commitment to remote, financially dependent and strategically vulnerable territories east of Suez, Britain began to hasten the process of decolonisation. France persisted with its policy of granting colonial peoples citizenship while retaining centralised control through a hierarchy of colonial officials. In 1958, faced with a choice between independence and formal integration with France, its Pacific territories chose the latter. The United States, primarily concerned with the strategic value of its territories, at first took few steps to provide the machinery for self-government.

The United Nations has had only a limited effect on the decolonisation of Oceania. Before 1960 it was little concerned with the Pacific and even since then it has been little involved—able to be invoked but seldom required, because the policies of the metropolitan powers have more than kept pace with local demands for political advancement. Further, the role of the United Nations has been circumscribed by its frame of reference. Apart from seeking information and bringing pressure to bear on administering authorities, the international body has little direct involvement in the formal process of decolonisation of Non-Self-Governing Territories. It has greater scope for influence in the Trust Territories—the former German and Japanese islands—through the preparation of triennial reports by visiting missions appointed by the Trusteeship Council. Also of importance are the attitudes of the administering powers. The dependencies of the United Kingdom clearly fall within the competence of the United Nations while those of France do not, since their integration with the metropolitan country in 1958. The United Nations has been important in a different way with regard to New Zealand's dependencies. New Zealand has deliberately sought the approval of the United Nations for its often unique solutions to the peculiar problems of its territories.

An important factor in decolonisation has been impetus from some of the territories; an impetus resulting from either a deep-rooted and long-standing nationalism or the activities of an *élite*. Although these often coincide in the Pacific, educated leaders have sometimes been opposed by traditional leaders aware of their own declining status; by rural dwellers who, as a result of colonial administration, lack confidence in their capacity for self-rule, or by those closely associated with foreign commercial interests.

Decolonisation has proceeded at an accelerating pace since Western Samoa became independent in 1962. The process has been unmarked by the bitterness and violence that characterised the achievement and early years of independence in many Afro-Asian countries. The tensions implicit in relationships between governors and governed have not, in the Pacific, produced irreconcilable differences and alienation, and the powers have maintained close relationships with their former dependencies after self-government or independence. A continuation of aid has usually been guaranteed, together with markets for produce, thus providing some stability in island economies while removing a potential source of political tension. There has been a willingness to adapt European constitutional models to meet local circumstances but none of the constitutions which have emerged has been purely traditional in nature. The relatively smooth constitutional development which the countries of Oceania have experienced over the past two decades has not, however, removed all the problems which they face as emergent states.

Some of the Difficulties

Most islands suffer from an imbalance between population and resources. Natural population increase is generally high, though it is offset in a few countries by emigration, while urbanisation, education and family planning campaigns are combining to check, and in some cases reduce, birth rates. Urbanisation has been rapid, with people from rural and isolated areas migrating to the towns in an attempt to fulfil rising expectations for education and employment. Most migrants into the urban community are absorbed as a result of traditional kin obligations, but unemployment and problems of social adjustment are still characteristics of Pacific towns. Where opportunity exists, subsequent migration to a metropolitan centre is common. The result of these processes is a rural population bereft of its most productive elements at a time when economic growth can be generated most easily in the agricultural sector.

Resources are limited by a restricted land area, poor soils and an uncertain climate, which limit the range of agricultural products to the ubiquitous coconut and smaller outputs of sugar, coffee, tea, cocoa and bananas. All these are subject to price fluctuations and must compete on an already well-supplied world market. As well, the islands' remoteness makes transport sporadic and expensive.

There are other restraints on economic development. Because dependencies were expected to be self-supporting before the Second World War there was little 'development', except for mining and agricultural ventures which could attract outside capital, and administering powers acted in the belief that, with these exceptions, there was little, if any, potential for economic development in Oceania. Such resources as did exist, therefore, were rarely utilised effectively. Marine resources in particular were seldom investigated, forestry is a recent industry and few attempts were made to render agriculture, for subsistence or cash income, more efficient. In accordance with prevailing attitudes and the desires of the Islanders themselves, improvements in social services were given higher priority.

Recently there have been attempts to correct these omissions through economic planning and investment in agriculture. Moreover, with the growth of air transport, the income from tourism is providing a partial answer for some islands. However, while tourism boosts overseas earnings and creates employment opportunities, it also requires large-scale investment with risks of overseas control of an important sector of the economy.

In addition to having non-viable economies, many Pacific countries lack a natural basis for nationhood. If a nation is defined as people within a specified territory who share a common heritage and common aspirations for the future; and a state as the government and people of an independent territory, then it is clear that in the Pacific the nation and the state do not always coincide. Even where an island group is inhabited by a single race, loyalty to the individual island is commonly stronger than that to the group. The problem is far greater where peoples have been arbitrarily separated or united; where society is fragmented and loyalties localised, or where a large immigrant population has created a plural society.

The Several Communities

In Western Samoa the nation preceded the state. Because authority is not centralised but vested in privileged status groups, and decisions made by consensus under the leadership of titular chiefs, Samoan society has proved particularly resistant to change. During the period of European settlement and colonial rule, *Samoa mo Samoa* (Samoa for the Samoans) became the fundamental principle upon which the Samoans based their often insistent demands for control over their own destiny. The post-war years saw New Zealand accept this view and thereafter constitutional progress proceeded steadily, culminating in independence in 1962. The position of Head of State was vested jointly in the titular leaders of the two dominant lineages with provision for the survivor to remain Head of State for his lifetime; subsequently the office was to be filled by election by the Legislative Assembly. The Prime Minister is appointed by the Head of State and chooses his Cabinet from the Assembly. This has forty-seven members, two elected by universal adult suffrage, and the remainder on a franchise restricted to matai (titled heads of families, themselves chosen from and by leading adults in family groups). Thus the Prime Minister can assume cabinet solidarity but not necessarily a working majority in the Assembly. However, the defeat of a government measure does not force his resignation—he may be removed only by a vote of no confidence passed with a two-thirds majority.

After hurricane damage and disease caused severe setbacks to agricultural production in the mid-1960s, Western Samoa's economy expanded for nearly a decade when, again, disease reduced crop production. Copra, cocoa and bananas are the main exports. External aid plays a significant, but not dominant, role in the economy. The migration of some 1500 Samoans a year to New Zealand helps relieve population pressure, while their remittances provide a substantial boost to the home economy which must now support a remaining population of about 150 000. In the first twelve years of independence there have been only two Prime Ministers—Fiame Mata'afa Faumuina Mulinu'u II (1962–70 and 1973 onwards) and Tupua Tamasese Lealofi IV (1970–73); both are chiefs of high rank, further emphasising the strength of traditional Samoan institutions.

In the 1950s, Cook Islands' aspirations were more for the improvement of living standards than for political progress. Then, in the 1960s, initiative for constitutional advance came from New Zealand. For economic reasons, and because of the value placed on their country's relationship with New Zealand (especially citizenship rights which allowed free entry to the metropolitan country), the Cook Islanders adopted, in 1965, a constitution which gave internal self-government in free association with New Zealand, with the continuing right to self-determination—at that time a unique constitutional experiment. The approach to self-government saw the return to Cook Island politics of Albert Henry who had been politically active in the post-war years before leaving to live in New Zealand. His return re-kindled old loyalties; he established the Cook Islands Party with a strong grass-roots organisation, and emerged as Premier in 1965. Since that time Henry and the Cook Islands Party have dominated politics. Henry's personal style of leadership has been criticised but he has yet to be seriously threatened at the polls. The country is heavily dependent on New Zealand aid. Attempts to generate growth in the agricultural sector have been inhibited by unreliable shipping, low prices for tropical produce, increased opportunities elsewhere for wage employment (especially in Rarotonga) and a high rate of migration from outer islands to Rarotonga and thence to New Zealand. An international airport, intended to foster tourism, may bring increased income but at the cost of further centralising development on Rarotonga, which has over half the total population of 22 000.

Nauru, an island of less than twenty-three square kilometres and with a population of 7000, became a republic and an associate member of the British Commonwealth in 1968. The long and often bitter struggle with Australia, the United Kingdom and New Zealand for political freedom and for control over the phosphates (which are the island's sole economic resource) has been led by Hammer deRoburt, Nauru's Head Chief. An able, well-educated leader, equally acceptable at home and abroad, he became Nauru's first President. Nauru has the highest per capita income in the world, but its leaders are apprehensive of the future. The Nauruans' way of life has been transformed by an intensive

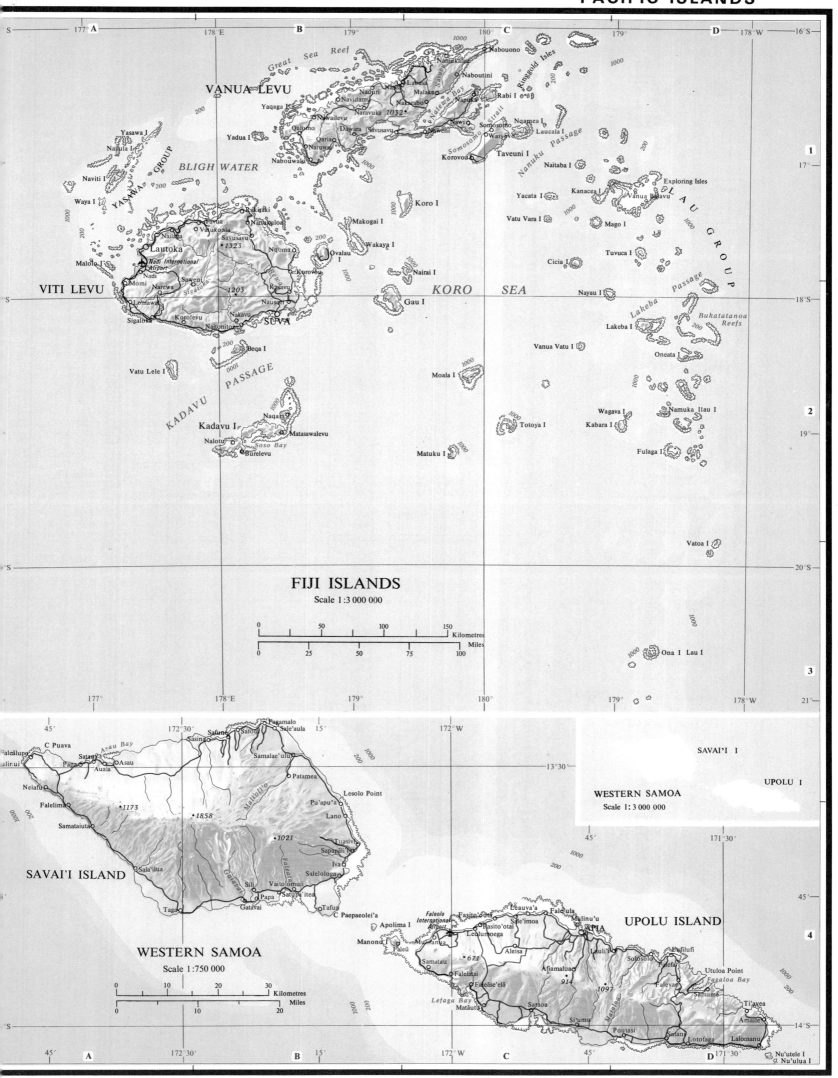

FIJI ISLANDS

Scale 1:3 000 000

VANUA LEVU

Great Sea Reef

Nabouono
Namukalau
Naboutini
Labasa
Nadun
Malake
Navidamu
Nakasabo
Rabi I
Yaqaga I
Naravuka 1032
Ngamea I
Qalomo
Dawara
Savusavu
Nanuka I
Qaria
Nawi
Somosomo
Naruwai
Naweni
Laucala I
Nabouwalu
Waiyevo
Koro I
Korovou
Taveuni I
Naitaba I

BLIGH WATER

Ringgold Isles
Nanuku Passage

Yasawa I
Napula I
Exploring Isles
Naviti I
Makogai I
Yacata I
Kanacea I
Vanua Balavu
Waya I
Wakaya I
Vatu Vara I
Mago I
Rakiraki
Nanukuloa
Nananu
Tavua
Vatukoula
Savusavu
Ovalau I
Cicia I
Tuvuca I
Lautoka
Nailaga
Nqoma
Nadi
1323
Nadi International Airport
Malolo I
Viti Levu
Saweni
Narewa
Sigatoka
Rewa
Nairai I
Nayau I
Lakeba Passage
Momi
1203
Bukatatanoa Reefs
Lomawai
Nausori
KORO SEA
Koroteva
Suva
Gau I
Lakeba I
Sigatoka
Naitonitoni
Vatu Lele I
Beqa I
Vanua Vatu I
Oneata I
KADAVU PASSAGE
Naqara
Moala I
Wagava I
Namuka Ilau I
Kadavu I
Matasawalevu
Totoya I
Kabara I
Nalotu
Burelevu
Matuku I
Fulaga I

Scale 1:3 000 000

0   50   100   150
Kilometres
0   25   50   75   100
Miles

Vatoa I

Ona I Lau I

WESTERN SAMOA

SAVAI'I ISLAND

C Puava
Pagamalo
Sale'aula
Falealupo
Safune
Safotu
Sasina
Uliniui
Sataua
Papa
Auala
Asau
Samalae'ulu
Samalae'ulu
Neiafu
Patamea
Falelima
1173
Lesolo Point
1858
Pu'apu'a
Lano
Samataiuta
1021
Sala'ilua
Tuasivi
Sapapali'i
Iva
Sili
Salelologa
Papa
Vaitoomuli
Taga
Satupa'itea
Gataivai
Tafua
C Paepaeolei'a

SAVAI'I I

UPOLU I

WESTERN SAMOA

Scale 1:3 000 000

WESTERN SAMOA

Scale 1:750 000

0   10   20   30
Kilometres
0   10   20
Miles

UPOLU ISLAND

Faleolo International Airport
Fasito'outa
Leauva'a
Fale'ula
Mulinu'u
Manono I
Fasito'otai
Sale'imoa
APIA
Apolima I
Leulumoega
Aleisa
Laulii
Solosolo
Falefa
Mulifanua
Faleu
Samatau
671
Afiamalua
Fusilufi
Falelatai
Aleisa
914
Falevao
Utuloa Point
Fagaloa Bay
Fatease'ela
Samamea
Lefaga Bay
1097
Saanoa
Ti'avea
Matautu
Amaile
Si'umu
Poutasi
Safata
Lotofaga
Lalomanu
Nu'utele I
Nu'ulua I

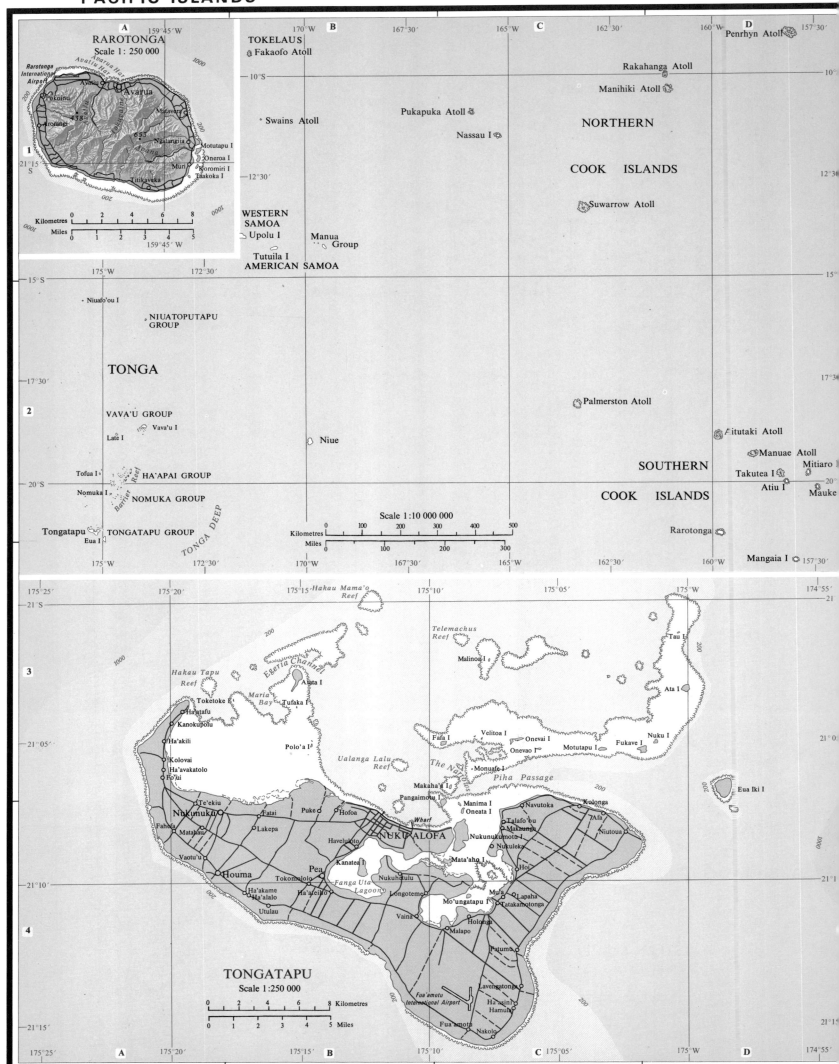

RAROTONGA
Scale 1: 250 000

Rarotonga
International
Airport

Avarua Hat.
Avatiu Hat.

Pokoinu
Avatiu
Avarua
Matavera
Arorangi
Ngatangiia
438
653
Motutapu I
Oneroa I
Muri
Koromiri I
Titikaveka
Taakoka I

Kilometres 0 2 4 6 8
Miles 0 1 2 3 4 5
159°45'W

TOKELAUS
Fakaofo Atoll

Swains Atoll

Pukapuka Atoll
Nassau I

WESTERN
SAMOA
Upolu I
Manua
Group
Tutuila I
AMERICAN SAMOA

Penrhyn Atoll

Rakahanga Atoll

Manihiki Atoll

NORTHERN

COOK ISLANDS

Suwarrow Atoll

Niuafo'ou I

NIUATOPUTAPU
GROUP

TONGA

VAVA'U GROUP
Vava'u I
Late I

Tofua I
Nomuka I

HA'APAI GROUP

NOMUKA GROUP

Tongatapu
Eua I
TONGATAPU GROUP

Barrier Reef

TONGA DEEP

Niue

Palmerston Atoll

Aitutaki Atoll

Manuae Atoll
SOUTHERN
Takutea I
Mitiaro
Atiu I
Mauke

COOK ISLANDS

Rarotonga

Mangaia I

Scale 1:10 000 000
Kilometres 0 100 200 300 400 500
Miles 0 100 200 300

Hakau Mama'o Reef
Telemachus Reef
Tau I
Malinoa I
Ata I

Hakau Tapu Reef
Egeria Channel
Maria Bay
Atata I
Tufaka I
Toketoke I
Ha'atafu
Kanokupolu
Ha'akili
Velitoa I
Onevai I
Nuku I
Fafa I
Onevao I
Motutapu I
Fukave I
Polo'a I
Ualanga Lalu Reef
The Nars
Monuafe I
Kolovai
Ha'avakatolo
Fo'ui
Makaha'a I
Piha Passage
Te'ekiu
Pangaimotu
Manima I
Navutoka
Kolonga
Nukunuku
Fatai
Puke
Hofoa
Oneata I
Talafo'ou
Eua Iki I
Faho'a
Lakepa
Wharf
Makaunga
'Afa
Matakau
Haveluloto
NUKU'ALOFA
Nukunukumotu I
Nukuleka
Niutoua
Vaotu'u
Kanatea I
Mata'aho I
Hoi
Houma
Pea
Nukuhetulu
Mu'a
Tokomololo
Fanga Uta Lagoon
Lapaha
Ha'akame
Ha'ateiho
Longoteme
Takakamotonga
Ha'alalo
Vaina
Mo'ungatapu I
Utulau
Holonga
Malapo
Fatumu
Lavengatonga
Fua'amotu
International Airport
Ha'asini
Hamula
Fua'amotu
Nakolo

TONGATAPU
Scale 1:250 000
0 2 4 6 8 Kilometres
0 1 2 3 4 5 Miles

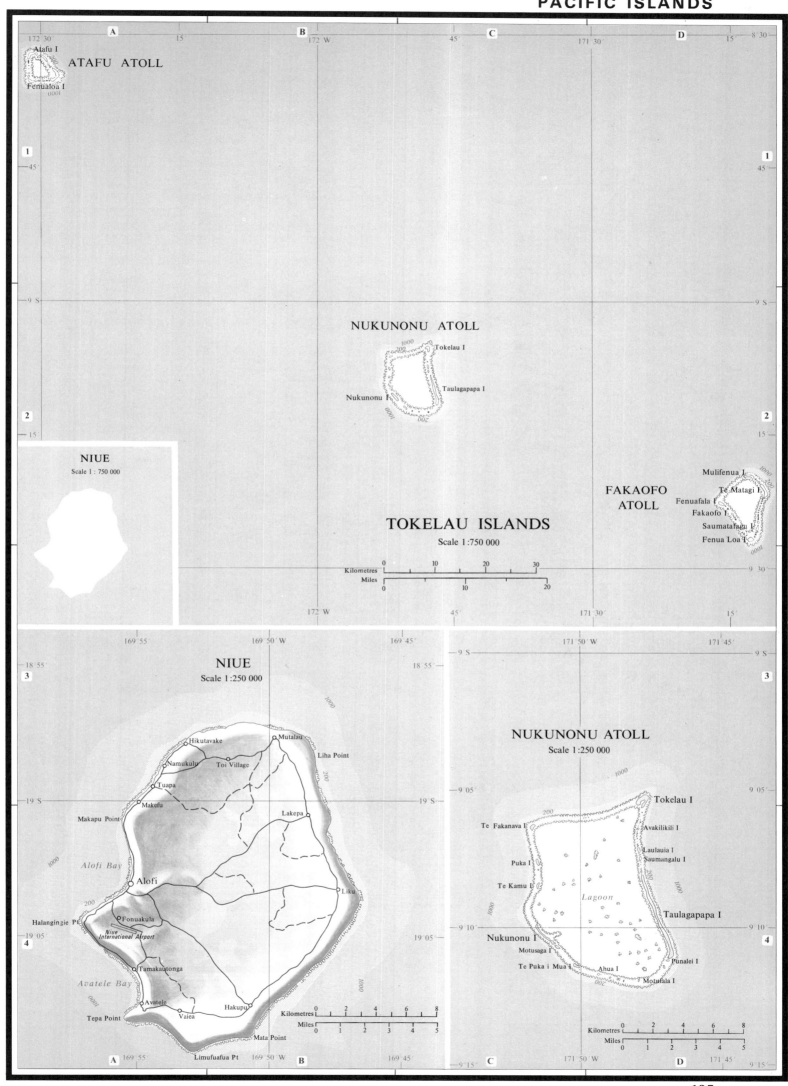

ATAFU ATOLL

Atafu I

Fenualoa I

NUKUNONU ATOLL

Tokelau I

Taulagapapa I

Nukunonu I

NIUE

Scale 1 : 750 000

FAKAOFO
ATOLL

Mulifenua I

Te Matagi I

Fenuafala I

Fakaofo I

Saumatafagu I

Fenua Loa I

TOKELAU ISLANDS

Scale 1:750 000

| Kilometres | 0 | 10 | 20 | 30 |
| Miles | 0 | 10 | 20 |

NIUE

Scale 1:250 000

Hikutavake

Mutalau

Liha Point

Namukulu

Toi Village

Tuapa

Makefu

Lakepa

Makapu Point

Alofi Bay

Alofi

Liku

Halangingie Pt

Fonuakula

Niue
International Airport

Tamakautonga

Avatele Bay

Avatele

Hakupu

Tepa Point

Vaiea

Mata Point

Limufuafua Pt

| Kilometres | 0 | 2 | 4 | 6 | 8 |
| Miles | 0 | 1 | 2 | 3 | 4 | 5 |

NUKUNONU ATOLL

Scale 1:250 000

Tokelau I

Te Fakanava I

Avakilikili I

Laulauia I

Puka I

Saumangalu I

Te Kamu I

Lagoon

Taulagapapa I

Nukunonu I

Motusaga I

Punalei I

Te Puka i Mua I

Ahua I

Motufala I

| Kilometres | 0 | 2 | 4 | 6 | 8 |
| Miles | 0 | 1 | 2 | 3 | 4 | 5 |

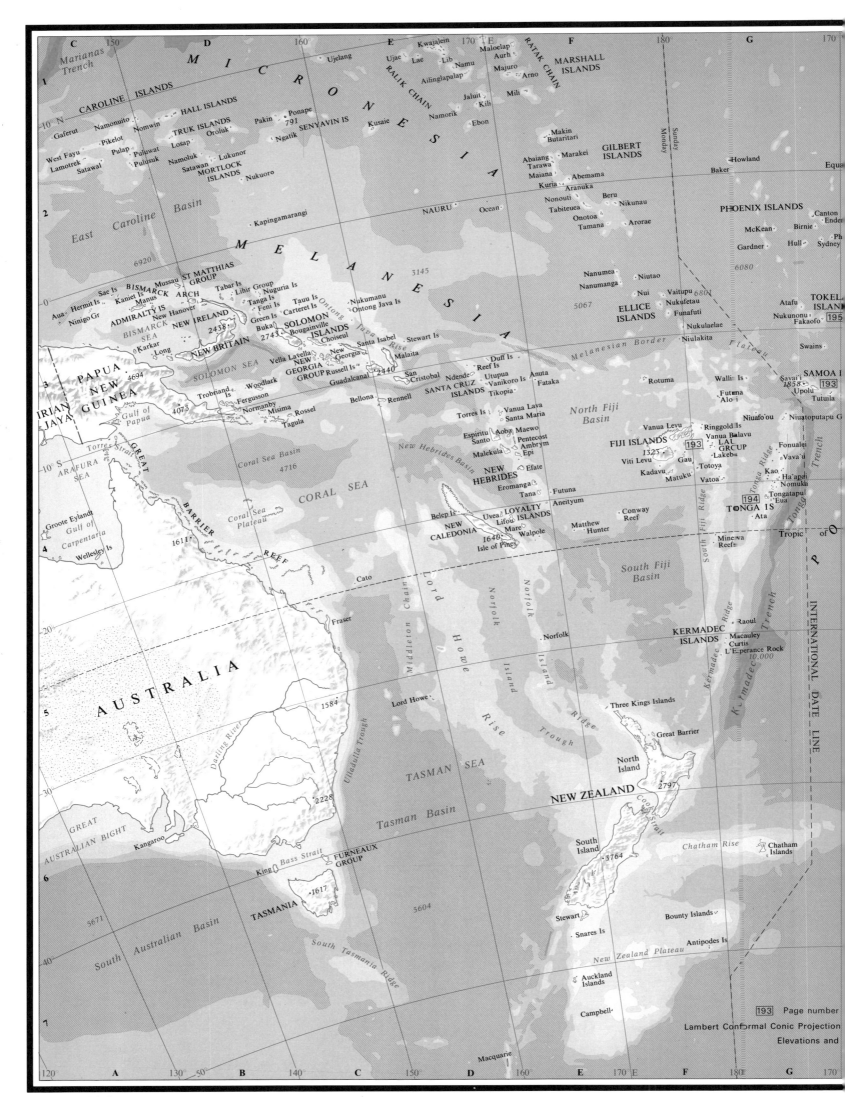

C 150 **D** 160 **E** 170 E **F** 180 **G** 170

Marianas Trench

M I C R O N E S I A

CAROLINE ISLANDS

HALL ISLANDS

Gaferut · Namonuito
Nomwin
TRUK ISLANDS
West Fayu · Pikelot · Pulap Puluwat Losap Oroluk
Lamotrek Satawal Pulusuk Namoluk · Lukunor
MORTLOCK
ISLANDS
· Nukuoro

Ujelang ·

Ujae Lae Lib
RALIK CHAIN
Namu
Ailinglapalap
· Jaluit
· Namorik
Ponape · Ngatik
Kusaie
791 SENYAVIN IS

Kwajalein
Maloelap
Aurh
Majuro
Arno
RATAK CHAIN
MARSHALL
ISLANDS

Kili
Mili
Ebon

Sunday
Monday

· Makin
· Butaritari
Abaiang · Marakei
Tarawa
Maiana · Abemama
Kuria · Aranuka
Nonouti Beru Nikunau
Tabiteuea Onotoa · Arorae
Tamana

GILBERT
ISLANDS

NAURU

Ocean ·

Howland ·

Baker ·

Equa

PHOENIX ISLANDS

McKean · Birnie
Gardner · Hull · Sydney

Canton
Ender
Ph

Kapingamarangi ·

M E L A N E S I A

6920

3145

6080

Nanumea · Niutao
Nanumanga
Nui Vaitupu 6801
5067 Nukufetau
ELLICE Funafuti
ISLANDS
Nukulaelae

Atafu ·
Nukunonu ·
Fakaofo

TOKEL
ISLAN
195

ST MATTHIAS
Mussau · GROUP
Sae Is BISMARCK ARCH Tabar Is
Kaniet Is Manus Lihir Group
Aua · Hermit Is Nuguria Is
Ninigo Gr ADMIRALTY IS Tanga Is
New Hanover Feni Is Tauu Is
BISMARCK New Ireland Green Is Carteret Is
SEA NEW BRITAIN 2438 Buka
· Karkar Bougainville
Long 2743 SOLOMON
ISLANDS
Choiseul
SOLOMON SEA Vella Lavella New Santa Isabel
NEW Georgia
GEORGIA Malaita
GROUP Russell Is
Guadalcanal 2440
PAPUA Bellona
NEW GUINEA 4694
IRIAN Gulf of
JAYA Papua
4073
Trobriand Woodlark
Is
Fergusson
Normanby Misima
Tagula Rossel
Rennell

Nukumanu
Ontong Java Is
Ontong Java Rise

Stewart Is

San · Duff Is ·
Cristobal Reef Is ·
Ndende Utupua Anuta ·
SANTA CRUZ Vanikoro Is Fataka
ISLANDS Tikopia

Niulakita ·

Melanesian Border

Rotuma ·

Walli Is ·
Futuna
Alo i

Savai'i SAMOA I
1858 193
Upolu
Tutuila

Swains ·

Torres Is ·
Santa Maria
Espiritu Aoba Maewo
Santo Pentecost
Malekula Ambrym
Epi
NEW Efate
HEBRIDES
Eromanga
Tana Futuna
LOYALTY
Belep Is Uvea Lifou ISLANDS
NEW Mare Walpole
CALEDONIA 1640
Isle of Pines

Vanua Lava
North Fiji
Basin
Vanua Levu
Viti Levu 1323
FIJI ISLANDS 193
Kadavu Gau
Matuku
Vatoa

Ringgold Is
Vanua Balavu LAU
GROUP
Lakeb
Totoya

Niuafo'ou ·
Niuatoputapu G

Fonualei
Vava'i
Kao
Ha'apai
Nomuka
Tongatapu
Eua

Aneityum
Conway
Reef
Matthew
Hunter

194 TONGA IS
Ata ·

Tropic of O

Minerva
Reefs

South Fiji
Basin

P
South Fiji Ridge A
C
I
F
KERMADEC Raoul · Tonga Ridge
ISLANDS Macauley I
Curtis C
L'E perance Rock Kermadec Trench
10,000

Cato ·

Fraser ·

GREAT
Groote Eylandt
Gulf of
Carpentaria
Wellesley Is

ARAFURA
SEA
Torres Strait

BARRIER

REEF

1611

Coral Sea
Plateau

Coral Sea Basin

4716

CORAL SEA

Lord
Howe
Chain
Ulladulla Trough

Norfolk
Norfolk
Island
Ridge
Trough

Norfolk ·

Three Kings Islands
Great Barrier

North
Island

INTERNATIONAL DATE LINE

AUSTRALIA

Darling River

1584

Lord Howe ·

Island
Rise

TASMAN SEA

NEW ZEALAND
South
Island
· 3764

2797

Cook Strait

Chatham Rise Chatham
Islands

GREAT
AUSTRALIAN BIGHT
Kangaroo ·

King Bass Strait
FURNEAUX
GROUP

2228

Tasman Basin

Stewart

TASMANIA
· 1617

5604

Snares Is ·

Bounty Islands ·

Antipodes Is ·

5671

South Australian Basin

South Tasmania Ridge

New Zealand Plateau

Auckland
Islands

Campbell ·

Macquarie ·

193 Page number

Lambert Conformal Conic Projection

Elevations and

120 **A** 130 50 **B** 140 **C** 150 **D** 160 **E** 170 E **F** 180 E **G** 170

196

THE SOUTH WEST PACIFIC

NORTH   PACIFIC   OCEAN

Palmyra
Washington
Fanning
Christmas

5349
5077

5903

Jarvis

6489

Malden

Starbuck

Penrhyn
Rakahanga
194
NORTHERN
Manihiki
COOK ISLANDS

Pukapuka
Nassau

Caroline
Vostok

Flint

5340

Hatutu · Sable
Eiao
Nuku Hiva · Ua Huka
Ua Pu · Fatu Huku
Hiva Oa
Fatu Hiva

MARQUESAS
ISLANDS

DS
Is
Rose

Suwarrow

5309

KING GEORGE IS

DISAPPOINTMENT IS

Ahe · Manihi
Mataiva Takaroa Tepoto
Tikehau Napuka

TUAMOTU ARCHIPELAGO

Bellingshausen Bora Bora Rangiroa Toau
Motu Iti Aratika Tikei
Scilly Maupiti Tahaa Makatea Njau
Mopelia Raiatea Huahine Fakarava Faaite
Tubuai-Manu Moorea Tetiaroa
Tahiti Mehetia Anaa

Palmerston

Aitutaki
SOUTHERN Takutea Manuae
COOK ISLANDS Atiu Mitiaro
194 Mauke
Rarotonga

Mangaia Maria Rururu
Rimatara

corn

Tubuai

TUBUAI ISLANDS

Raevavae

Raraka
Angatau
Pukapuka
Raroia
Tehuata Fakahina
Tauere Amanu Tatakoto
Reitoru Hao Akiaki
Ravahere Pukarua
Nengonengo Nukutavake Reao
Manuhangi Pinaki
Hereheretue Ahunui
Amanu Raro DUKE OF Vanavana
Amanu Runga Nukutipipi Tureia
GLOUCESTER IS Maturei Marutea
Tematangi Vavao Maria
Mururoa ACTAEON ISLANDS
Fangataufa
Morane
Mangareva
Timoe
GAMBIER
ISLANDS Oeno

SOCIETY ISLANDS

YNESIA

Austral Ridge

Rapa
Bass

SOUTH   PACIFIC   OCEAN

South Western
Pacific Basin

4270

4765

3740

Oeno
Pitcairn Henderson
Ducie

Easter

Pacific Antarctic Ridge

Sea Level		Sea Level
500		1640
000		3281
2000		6562
4000		13123
5000		19685
3000		26246
Metres		Feet

Kilometres 250 0 250 500 750 1000 1250 1500
Miles 250 0 250 500 750 1000

Scale 1 : 25 000 000

rger scale maps

dard Parallels at 0° and 45° S

hs in metres

colonial experience, by Japanese occupation, by the loss of traditional foods and skills, by an almost total dependence on imports, by the presence of Micronesian, Polynesian, Asian and European phosphate-workers whose numbers match their own and by recently acquired wealth. Yet they must face the time, perhaps within two decades, when the phosphates are exhausted. To meet this situation, capital is being invested overseas and a shipping line, intended to provide employment as well as revenue, has been established.

Fiji is a plural society. Of its 550 000 people forty-three per cent are of Fijian and fifty-two per cent of Indian descent, from indentured labour introduced in the nineteenth century for employment in the sugar industry; Europeans, part-Europeans, Chinese and non-Fijian Pacific Islanders make up the five per cent balance. The Fijians were ruled indirectly by Britain, insulated from any effective participation in their own economy or national politics. In the early 1960s when the British government initiated constitutional changes, there was reluctance and sometimes opposition amongst Fijians and Europeans, the former determined to defend their control over the land and doubtful of their ability to compete economically and politically with the more numerous Indians, the latter desiring to preserve their entrenched position of privilege. Indian leaders, however, favoured early independence and a common electoral roll to replace communal rolls.

After negotiation and compromise on both sides, Fiji achieved dominion status in 1970. The constitution provides for both a racial and a national vote for each elector. For the racial vote there are three electoral 'communities'—Fijian, Indian and General (i.e. persons not Fijian or Indian as defined in the constitution) which return respectively twelve, twelve and three members to the House of Representatives. The National roll provides for a further ten Fijian, ten Indian and five General members. The Senate is similarly representative of cultural communities. Complicated as it may be, the system does ensure the protection of racial interests. Since the introduction of ministerial government in 1966, the Alliance party, which generally relies on Fijians and Europeans for its support, has been able to command a parliamentary majority under its leader, the present Prime Minister, Ratu Sir Kamisese Mara.

The period since independence has been one of general racial harmony, in part engendered and preserved by a buoyant economy. Sugar has long been Fiji's main source of overseas earnings, with copra and gold playing lesser but significant roles. The last decade has seen a dramatic increase in tourism, and forestry is also likely to be of increasing importance. In its most recent development plan the government has given priority to projects which will, by moderating personal, racial and regional income disparities, help in the creation of a multi-racial society.

In 1970 Tonga made its 're-entry into the Comity of Nations' as an independent monarchy. By this time the few internal powers exercised by the United Kingdom in earlier years had been surrendered, leaving only foreign affairs and defence to be transferred. Despite the existence of a parliamentary system, power, like land, is concentrated in a few hands. Attempts have been made to 'modernise' Tonga in recent years with the upgrading of social services, increased shipping and the introduction of co-ordinated economic planning, but the country still suffers from a lack of natural resources and a large (90 000) and rapidly increasing population.

With a land area of 475 176 square kilometres and a population of 2 600 000, Papua New Guinea is easily the largest country within the region, yet it is the most fragmented. Socio-political units are small and isolated and there are more than 700 languages. Contact with the West has been uneven and has tended to highlight regional differences. New Britain, New Ireland, Bougainville and the coastal areas of Papua are the most advanced economically and politically, although there has been a substantial investment in plantations in the New Guinea highlands. Partly in response to pressure from the United Nations, the Australian government increased aid grants, allowed greater indigenous political participation in the 1960s and took steps to promote the emergence of an independent state. The introduction of ministerial government in 1972 and the subsequent formation of a coalition dominated by the radical Pangu Pati, led by Michael Somare, saw a dramatic shift of emphasis in policy formation towards the creation of a nation base for the state. Indigenous participation in the economy was stressed, in contrast to earlier concern with capital investment and maximised returns; political education was stepped up, and attempts made to remove the sources of discontent which were motivating regional separatist movements. Social fragmentation, communication difficulties and uneven development have resulted in disparities in political awareness and disputes over the timing of independence, with New Guineans, especially highlanders, taking a conservative approach. As a result of pressures from within the Territory, from the United Nations and from Australia, Papua New Guinea became self-governing at the end of 1973 with independence expected to follow a year later.

In 1974 Niue, a small, remote, raised atoll, votes on the issue of self-government. Niueans, like Cook Islanders, are New Zealand citizens with a right to free entry. Emigration has increased rapidly in recent years and, as a consequence, the population, 4300 in 1974, is suffering a net decline. There are now more Niueans in New Zealand than in Niue. The loss of young adults in particular is leaving an uneven age-distribution in the population, thus inhibiting improvements in agriculture. Before the 1960s Niue was governed under a benevolent paternalism. Lacking confidence in their own ability, and apprehensive about future aid, the Niueans were reluctant to accept the constitutional advances involved in the creation of the Island Assembly. These fears were allayed when the proposed timetable was delayed and assurances given regarding aid and entry to New Zealand. Because of the delay in implementing self-government, the desire of the Niueans for a constitution that would give them something less than independence, and the lack of appreciation of the problems of small countries sometimes shown by the United Nations, the New Zealand government invited representatives of the Committee of Twenty-Four to visit Niue in 1972—the first time a United Nations Mission had visited a Non-Self-Governing Territory before the act of self-determination. The United Nations accepted that internal self-government, with a continuing right to self-determination, would meet the expressed wishes of the people, in conformity with United Nations principles.

The future of the Tokelau Islands has yet to be determined. Dependent on New Zealand aid for eighty-five per cent of their budget, the Tokelau Islands, which have a population of 1700 located on three atolls with a total land area of less than ten square kilometres, can never be self-supporting in a modern world. A resettlement scheme for Tokelauan families, together with private emigration to New Zealand, has caused a gradual decline in population since 1967 but depopulation was not planned and the older people in particular are unwilling to leave.

Britain's remaining territories have little prospect of

becoming economically viable. The Solomon Islands Protectorate is still heavily dependent on aid to supplement an economy based primarily on coconut and forest products. After political development in conformity with the 'Westminster Model', the Protectorate experimented with a 'committee system' and a single Governing Council exercising legislative and executive functions for the period 1970–74. It then reverted to an orthodox ministerial system and is now approaching self-government. The future of the Gilbert and Ellice Islands colony is less certain. The colony will suffer a severe reduction in revenue when the phosphate deposits on Ocean Island are exhausted in about 1978. There are also complications because the 7000 Ellice Islanders, who are Polynesian, fear a loss of cultural identity and domination by the 50 000 Gilbertese who are Micronesian. After a referendum in August 1974, Ellice demands for separation may be met.

France is resisting autonomical movements in New Caledonia and French Polynesia, the former being important as a rich source of nickel and the latter as a testing area for nuclear weapons. France is also blocking Britain's attempts to decolonise the New Hebrides Condominium lest a precedent be set. Strategic interests are at least as important in the American territories. Although Eastern Samoa is no longer critical from a defence point of view, it has a fine harbour and airport, should these be required for military purposes. Swamped with aid, the American Samoans have shown little enthusiasm for political independence. The Trust Territory of the Pacific Islands is still strategically important because of its proximity to Asia. The constitutional future is uncertain; the Micronesians want self-government, if not independence, and guaranteed land rights, which could conflict with the United States military presence on at least some islands.

Towards a Pacific Community

Decolonisation transformed the Pacific in the 1960s. In the past two decades there has been throughout Oceania a growing awareness of developments which has given rise to a regional consciousness. This trend has been assisted by improved communications and transport. But even more important has been the existence of regional organisations where Islanders have met and discussed their common problems and aspirations. The most influential of these organisations has been the South Pacific Commission, which for more than two decades has provided technical assistance to the islands and conducted research into their economic and social problems. Most of the Commission's projects, like its budget, have been modest but they have been vital to the emergence of the modern Pacific. Until 1965 the Commission was dominated by the administering powers—Australia, New Zealand, the United Kingdom, the United States and France—and was used to distribute multi-lateral aid. Then, following strong representations by the island leaders, the advisory South Pacific Conference in which the dependent territories were also represented, became the effective decision-making body for the Commission. The Conference, like the Commission, now meets annually but is still unable to satisfy all the requirements of the new and emerging states.

Political matters cannot be considered by either the Commission or the Conference. In the late 1960s, however, the leaders of the self-governing and independent countries became increasingly aware of political issues which could be discussed for mutual benefit, together with other problems which had arisen as a consequence of their new status. In 1970, after Fiji and Tonga had joined the ranks of the independent countries, island leaders began to voice interest in the establishment of another, less formal organisation which could meet these requirements. The proposal was sympathetically regarded by the New Zealand government, with the result that the first meeting of the South Pacific Forum took place in Wellington in August 1971. Present were the leaders of the Cook Islands, Fiji, Nauru, Tonga and Western Samoa, together with representatives of the New Zealand and Australian governments. Papua New Guinea and Niue were invited to attend the 1973 meeting as observers, which opened the way for other countries to join as they became self-governing.

The meetings of the Forum, for which member countries act in turn as host, are conducted in an atmosphere of informality. Discussions take place amongst government leaders and Forum decisions affecting member countries can be put into effect for mutual benefit. Important issues discussed have included French nuclear testing, sovereignty over the sea, tourism and a host of problems related to shipping, trade and economic development. Reflecting these latter concerns, the South Pacific Bureau for Economic Co-operation was established in November 1972, with its headquarters at Suva, and its services available to countries which are not yet self-governing. Although it has yet to be tested in the face of adversity, the Forum gives expression to the prevailing mood of regional co-operation; New Zealand and Australia sit not as colonial powers but as equals with the countries which are their closest neighbours.

The selection of New Zealand for the first meeting of the Forum was an indication that the island peoples, many of whom had long-standing ties with New Zealand, were seeking a continuation and extension of those relationships. By its distribution of aid and technical assistance, New Zealand had shown itself willing to play a larger role in areas which were not its dependencies or former dependencies. The island leaders were aware that the United Kingdom was withdrawing from the Pacific and that, henceforth, they would need to broaden their contact with developed countries within the region itself. At the same time the New Zealand and Australian governments recognised the need for a new role in the Pacific, due both to developments in Asia, and the entry of the United Kingdom into the European Economic Community. This increased consciousness by New Zealand and Australia of the Pacific environment has been reflected in rapidly increasing aid grants, distributed more widely in the region than previously. In 1973–74, for example, the New Zealand Government gave approximately $12,500,000, which represents more than half of its total overseas aid, to the Pacific Islands.

There has been a similar increase in aid from private agencies, and schemes such as that for the training of Islanders in New Zealand have also served to forge links between Australasia and the Pacific Islands. Within the region itself other organisations, operating at a lower level than the Forum, have encouraged regional ties. There are church and women's organisations, the Fiji School of Medicine and the recently established University of the South Pacific in Suva, which have all emphasised the interdependence of the whole region.

The 1970s represent a culmination of earlier developments, a period in which the microstates of Oceania and their closest metropolitan neighbours are all seeking closer ties with each other. The outcome is regional solidarity and a Pacific consciousness. Countries which have widely differing backgrounds and cultures are, while retaining their individual identities, recognising the common bonds which unite them in a Pacific community.

TOURISM

J. S. McBean

Tourism has become one of New Zealand's fastest-growing industries. The country is well placed geographically to take advantage of the increasing leisure, rising incomes and more rapid transport that make it possible for more and more people, both here and from overseas, to enjoy the pleasures of travel. It has a range of scenery unique for a country of its size, with pleasant cities, green countryside, extensive plains, lakes, every type of river, alpine and thermal regions; it has a mixture of cultures with origins in Europe and Polynesia; it has a politically stable and orderly society with good public health and medical services; it has built up excellent accommodation, transport and tourist services, all well organised and fully supported by both government and people. The objectives of tourism are twofold: to enable New Zealanders to see and enjoy their own country, and to earn foreign exchange by similarly serving overseas tourists.

Development

The variety, beauty and grandeur of the scenery in New Zealand have always made a profound impression on travellers. The Maori, who migrated from the islands of the South Pacific before the fifteenth century, celebrated the new land in a wealth of song and legend. Captain James Cook, carefully and methodically exploring and charting the coast in the late eighteenth century, commented on the grandeur of the snow-clad Southern Alps and on the glaciers which came down so low through the coastal forest that they were clearly visible from the western sea. His name was to be given to the highest peak, called Aorangi or Cloud Piercer by the Maori.

The early settlers were quick to appreciate the potential for tourism and soon developed accommodation houses and tourist facilities in scenic and thermal areas. After his retirement from politics, Robert Graham, Superintendent of the Auckland Province between 1862 and 1865, developed the Waiwera hot springs as a health spa. He went on to build Lake House at Ohinemutu in Rotorua in the early 1870s and at the end of the decade acquired the Wairakei thermal valley near Taupo.

Sir William Fox, an early Premier, published a paper in 1874 in which he saw Rotorua affording the finest conceivable opportunity for establishing a great sanatorium for Indian regiments. Rotorua was initially a stopping place for visitors to the famed pink and white terraces on Lake Rotomahana, destroyed in the great eruption of nearby Mt Tarawera in 1886. By then, Rotorua was well on the way to becoming a tourist centre in its own right, as the government had built and equipped a pavilion with thermal baths. A resident balneologist had been appointed and a start made on laying out and planting large public gardens.

In the South Island, the southern lakes and Fiordland were the first tourist centres to be developed. Anthony Trollope, the English novelist and an indefatigable and discerning traveller, wrote of Lake Wakatipu in 1872, 'I do not know that lake scenery can be finer . . . The whole district around is, or rather will be, a country known for its magnificent scenery.' André Siegfried described the area as: 'Mountainous, picturesque, traversed by lofty mountains . . . the splendid district of the "Sounds" whose fame, long established in Australia, has now penetrated to Europe.' The statement was by no means unfounded since it was in the 1870s that the New Zealand government produced its first tourist brochures and started tourist promotion work, through government offices in London and Australia and through Thos. Cook and Son. Independent travellers were offered a grand tour of New Zealand and could traverse the whole country using public transport, even if this included horse and canoe in addition to rail, sea and coach transport. Regular cruises were available on tiny steamships operating from Dunedin to Milford Sound and other parts of Fiordland

In 1901, the government established a Department of Tourist and Health Resorts and the stage was set for a vigorous and continuing effort to promote and develop tourism. By 1914, when the First World War curtailed tourist travel, government Tourist Bureaus had been established in the main cities and in some tourist centres, with separate offices in Sydney and Melbourne. By 1974, the Department, known as the Tourist and Publicity Department, provided a comprehensive range of services. It has overseas offices in London, Frankfurt, Tokyo, New York, San Francisco, Los Angeles, Brisbane, Sydney and Melbourne, and provides a travel agency service in New Zealand. The Department has its own film unit and publicity studios, it provides information services for the government within New Zealand, it prepares information and publicity material for use abroad; it has its own tourist development and research division and it undertakes tourist promotion work overseas, with a growing budget which reached $1.4 million in 1974–75.

Soon after its inception, the Tourist and Publicity Department operated hotels and ancillary services at national tourist resorts. The hotels have always been noted for their high degree of comfort in accordance with contemporary standards. In 1956, the government established a separate Tourist Hotel Corporation to control these hotels and others that have since been built or acquired. In the past, the hotels were mostly in remote situations where highly seasonal patronage made them unprofitable to operate. However, the economic outlook is improving with the growth of tourism and the extension of operations into more profitable locations. In 1974, the Tourist Hotel Corporation operated hotels or other accommodation at Waitangi, Waitomo, Rotorua, Lake Waikaremoana, Wairakei, Tokaanu, Mt Ruapehu, Mt Cook (2), Franz Joseph Glacier, Twizel near Lake Pukaki, Lake Wanaka, Lake Te Anau and Milford Sound. Where possible, the Corporation has developed a range of accommodation to cater not only for those seeking high quality, but also for other visitors wanting lower-tariff, motel-type accommodation. In the year ended September 1973, the Corporation provided accommodation for a total of 164 110 guests, of whom fifty-six per cent were from overseas. It made an overall net profit of $54,000, the first since it was established.

Under a recent government directive, the Corporation was made responsible for the development of tourist accommodation and related services within National Parks. There are ten National Parks in all, covering 2.1 million hectares, preserved as far as possible in their natural state for public benefit and enjoyment. They are popular tourist attractions and all have developed special centres, with attractive display material, to inform visitors of the nature of each park. The parks are maintained and looked after be a special staff of qualified rangers under the control of National Park Boards, which are in turn responsible to a National Parks Authority.

The Chateau Tongariro on Mt Ruapehu is situated in the Tongariro National Park. The Hermitage, and other accommodation at Mt Cook, are within the Mount Cook National Park and the Milford hotel and hostel are within the Fiordland National Park. In some areas, the Corporation has had to develop power, water and sewerage services. It operates the world-famous Milford Track and provides a wide range of facilities, such as launch services on Milford Sound which carry more than 60 000 passengers a year, guiding services through a subsidiary company at Mt Cook and ski-hire and catering services on parts of Mt Ruapehu. Some of the existing facilities in these areas are provided by private enterprise under the terms of concessions let by National Parks Boards.

Transport

New Zealand has excellent transport links, both internal and with other countries. It has good port facilities and is served by round-the-world passenger shipping services, with cruise vessels calling frequently. However, ninety-five per cent of all overseas visitors arrive by air, sixty-four per cent of them in Auckland, twenty-five per cent in Christchurch and eleven per cent in Wellington. Australian, British, American, French and New Zealand airlines all operate services to New Zealand.

New Zealand has its own international airline, Air New Zealand, based at Auckland and operating direct flights to and from Los Angeles, Singapore, Hong Kong, Australia and the Pacific islands including Tahiti, Rarotonga, Samoa and Fiji. Arrangements have been completed with British Airways for Air New Zealand aircraft to continue on to London, with a British crew, from Los Angeles.

Air New Zealand began operations in 1940 under the name of Tasman Empire Airways Limited—a name later abbreviated to TEAL—running services with British flying boats across the Tasman. The first S-30, Empire-class flying boats carried nineteen passengers and took nine hours for the Tasman crossing. New aircraft were progressively introduced and in 1973 the airline began to re-equip with DC-10, Series 30 tri-jets, carrying 241 passengers and taking three hours. TEAL's name was changed to Air New Zealand in 1965.

Air New Zealand has maintained a distinguished record for safety and efficiency and has rarely failed to make a profit. In 1972–73 it made a net profit of $2.5 million, more than twice the figure for the previous year, and carried a total of 494 769 passengers. The earning of foreign exchange is always important to a trading nation and in 1972–73, Air New Zealand made a useful net contribution of $33.5 million to the foreign exchange earnings of the country.

Internally, New Zealand has good services by road, air and rail, and the two main Islands are linked by frequent roll-on/roll-off ferry services. Private motor vehicles account for by far the greatest proportion of travel, as shown by the following table from a 1970–71 survey.

TRANSPORT USED ON TRAVEL BY NEW ZEALAND RESIDENTS
Percentage Distribution

	BUSINESS & CONVENTION	BUSINESS & PLEASURE	PLEASURE	TOTAL
Private vehicle	59.8	74.1	82.8	79.3
Aircraft	24.8	10.5	3.6	5.8
Scheduled coach	4.4	2.3	4.3	4.8
Rail	3.3	4.2	3.2	3.3
Sea ferry	2.2	4.0	3.0	3.0
Coach tour	1.3	—	0.8	0.9
Rental vehicle	1.3	3.9	0.6	0.9
Other	2.9	1.0	1.7	2.0
	100.0	100.0	100.0	100.0

The National Airways Corporation, which is government-owned, provides frequent services with modern aircraft between both main and secondary centres. Only one major route is operated by private enterprise: the Mount Cook Airlines route between Auckland–Rotorua–Mt Cook–Queenstown–Fiordland–Dunedin. It caters particularly for tourist traffic. The National Airways Corporation has a financial interest in the Mount Cook Company and services its aircraft.

The pattern of transport usage is quite different for overseas visitors and varies according to their country of origin. Whereas eighty-seven per cent of pleasure or tourist travel by New Zealanders is by motor car (including rental vehicles), in the case of Australians this falls to thirty-two per cent and of North Americans to twenty-nine per cent. A 1969–70 survey shows:

TRANSPORT USED BY OVERSEAS VISITORS
Percentage Distribution

	AUSTRALIA	NORTH AMERICA	OTHERS
Coach tour	44.2	16.8	16.8
Scheduled coach	7.0	10.5	15.9
Rental vehicle	25.1	24.7	17.6
Private car	7.4	4.1	18.6
Air	10.1	39.0	21.8
Sea ferry	3.4	2.1	3.7
Rail	1.0	0.4	1.7
Other	1.8	2.4	3.9
	100.0	100.0	100.0

The high proportion of Australians travelling on coach tours is due in part to the relatively low cost of such tours as a result of discounts, and in part to the fact that many Australians visit New Zealand as a destination and find that these tours offer an excellent means of seeing a great deal of the country. American visitors, usually on more comprehensive South Pacific itineraries, use air transport to a greater extent than do other groups because they are usually here for a shorter time. Air transport enables them to visit Rotorua, the Southern Alps, Queenstown and Fiordland, all within the space of a few days.

Accommodation

New Zealand has developed a full range of accommodation in its cities and tourist centres, from modern, top-grade hotels through to low-tariff holiday accommodation in motor camps and youth hostels. A survey by the Tourist and Publicity Department indicated that in 1970–71 New Zealanders spent a total of 37 084 500 person-nights away from home. This is considerably greater than the number of person-nights spent by overseas visitors in the country, estimated in 1969–70 at 2 298 000. All types of accommodation are used by both New Zealanders and overseas visitors, the proportions varying according to the type of accommodation and its location.

ACCOMMODATION USE BY NEW ZEALAND RESIDENTS
Percentage Distribution

	BUSINESS & CONVENTION	BUSINESS & PLEASURE	PLEASURE	TOTAL
Friends & relatives	24.2	56.0	55.8	53.2
Hotels* & motels with restaurant	36.9	11.0	3.4	5.7
Motels without restaurant	11.1	11.0	8.3	8.5
Private hotels & boarding houses	11.2	3.3	1.0	2.0
Other (including camps, cabins, caravans, holiday homes, etc)	16.6	18.7	31.5	30.6
	100.0	100.0	100.0	100.0

*Licensed to sell liquor.

Overseas visitors make proportionately greater use of fully-serviced commercial accommodation than do New Zealanders (1969–70 survey).

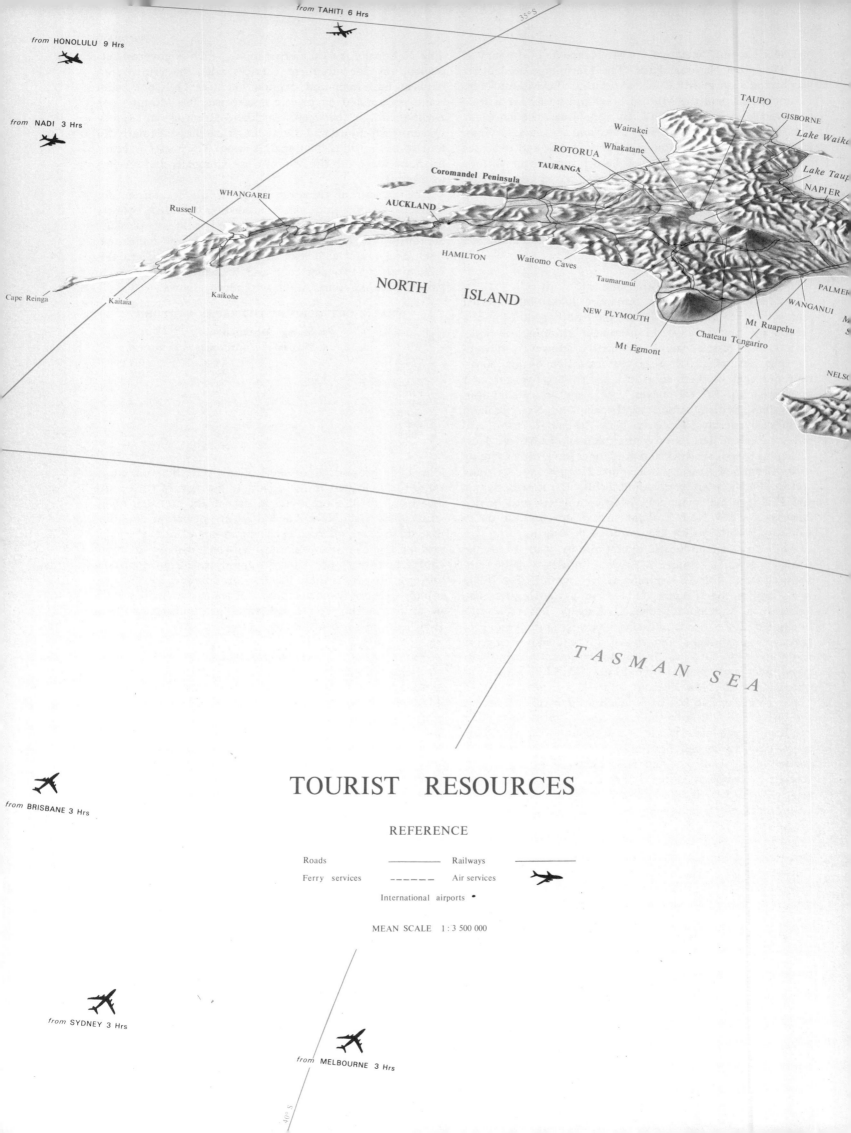

from TAHITI 6 Hrs

from HONOLULU 9 Hrs

from NADI 3 Hrs

TAUPO

GISBORNE

Wairakei

Lake Waika

Whakatane

ROTORUA

Lake Taup

TAURANGA

NAPIER

Coromandel Peninsula

WHANGAREI

AUCKLAND

Russell

HAMILTON

Waitomo Caves

PALMER

Kaikohe

Taumarunui

WANGANUI

Cape Reinga

Kaitaia

NORTH   ISLAND

NEW PLYMOUTH

Mt Ruapehu

NELSO

Mt Egmont

Chateau Tongariro

T A S M A N   S E A

from BRISBANE 3 Hrs

TOURIST   RESOURCES

REFERENCE

Roads	———————	Railways	———————
Ferry services	– – – – –	Air services	✈
International airports	•		

MEAN SCALE   1 : 3 500 000

from SYDNEY 3 Hrs

from MELBOURNE 3 Hrs

SOUTH PACIFIC OCEAN

180°

Chatham
Islands

TINGS

MASTERTON

NORTH

Picton
Blenheim
WELLINGTON

rough

Hanmer Springs

CHRISTCHURCH

SOUTH   ISLAND

Greymouth

Hokitika

TIMARU

Oamaru

Franz Josef Glacier

Fox Glacier

Mt Cook

The Hermitage

DUNEDIN

Haast Pass

Gore

170° E

Milford Sound

INVERCARGILL

Queenstown

Southern

Fiords

Stewart
Island

Lake Te Anau

Lake Manapouri

45°S

TOURISM

Some hotels in arrival cities and tourist centres have specialised in handling group and coach tours and in these instances more overseas visitors than New Zealanders may be accommodated in the course of a year. Staying with friends and relatives is the most popular form of accommodation for New Zealanders, as shown in the above 1970–71 survey. The high proportion of overseas visitors staying in private homes is largely accounted for by visitors from Australia and the United Kingdom who stay with friends and relatives.

Hotels and motels customarily provide rooms or units with their own toilet and bath or shower, although some older hotels still have some rooms with shared facilities, at a lower rate. A feature of many motels throughout New Zealand is the provision of a fully-equipped kitchen in each unit so that guests can prepare their own meals. This is especially the case where there is no restaurant.

ACCOMMODATION USE BY OVERSEAS VISITORS
Percentage Distribution

Hotels and motels with restaurant	45.6
Motels without restaurant	7.8
Private house	34.4
Other	12.2
	100.0

Government policy is directed towards ensuring that the greater part of ownership and control of accommodation remains in New Zealand hands, although in some instances there is a modest degree of participation by overseas interests. Franchise arrangements, a recent innovation, assist with development and promotion whilst retaining ownership in New Zealand.

A range of government incentives and assistance has operated to encourage tourist development by the private sector. Loans totalling $3.9 million and guarantees to the extent of $10.6 million have been provided since 1962 for nineteen hotel or motor hotel projects, under a Tourist Accommodation Development Scheme. In all, these projects provided 3253 beds. Chief requirements of the Scheme have been that a project should be of a standard suitable for overseas visitors, that there should be a proven need for additional accommodation in the particular locality at that time and that finance be not otherwise available. In 1973, the Scheme was revised to enable a wider range of accommodation, including low-tariff, family-type accommodation to be eligible for consideration.

A similar scheme has been in operation for the provision of other tourist facilities but this was used far less and only three projects had been assisted to the end of 1973. In the field of tax incentives, a special twenty per cent depreciation allowance has applied to approved hotel projects of acceptable standard. A one per cent supplementary depreciation allowance, in addition to ordinary depreciation, has applied since 1969 to all types of accommodation. In 1973, the rates were combined and re-organised to permit simpler administration.

Overseas Visitors

In the year ended March 1973, there were 254 644 overseas visitors (excluding through passengers) to New Zealand, more than four times as many as there had been ten years earlier. Australia remained the major source of overseas visitors, providing 49.3 per cent of the total, with North America supplying 25.3 per cent and the United Kingdom 7.2 per cent.

The following table shows growth over the last decade in the numbers of visitors from main countries of origin and expected growth to 1981–82.

VISITOR GROWTH BY COUNTRIES
Years ended 31 March

	1963	1973	1982
Australia	27 032	125 466	248 400
North America	14 841	64 469	193 000
United Kingdom	5835	18 239	23 600
Europe	Not available	8214	17 900
Japan	531	5391	37 900
TOTAL (inc. other)	58 885	254 644	577 400
Through passengers	38 732	83 138	—

Note: Estimates for 1981–82 exclude working holiday and educational purposes visitors.

Although Japanese visitors in 1972–73 numbered only 5391, it is expected that this figure will increase rapidly in future; as with North Americans, most will probably be on organised tours of the South Pacific. The major part of the increase in the next decade is, however, expected to come from Australia and North America.

Targets for future growth are established by the Tourist Development Council. The Council reports to government on progress in achieving targets or on any special measures that may seem necessary to achieve them. It reports similarly on measures that might be necessary to encourage domestic tourism and on the provision of accommodation and facilities in the low-tariff bracket. Care is taken, in setting targets, to consider requirements for accommodation and the capacity of the industry to provide it.

The tourist industry ranks sixth on the list of New Zealand's foreign exchange earners. It is well behind the pastoral farming industries but ranks about the same as forest products, if the overseas earnings of Air New Zealand are added to Reserve Bank travel receipts. These receipts grew in the last decade from $8.7 million in 1962–63 to $78.5 million in 1973–74.

In New Zealand, as in most other countries, there are marked seasonal variations in vacation and holiday traffic. Most New Zealanders take their main holiday in summer and the peak in tourist and holiday resorts occurs between Christmas Day and mid-January, falling off slightly towards the end of that month. There are other, lesser, peaks at Easter, at Queen's Birthday weekend in June, at Labour Day weekend in October and during school holidays in May and at the end of August. North American tourist traffic is spread fairly well outside the summer period. Special incentive fares apply to Australian traffic in the off-season and a promotion campaign undertaken by government and private enterprise has met with appreciable success in encouraging more travel by Australian visitors in spring and autumn.

Tourist Routes and Attractions

The map shows the principal tourist routes and centres throughout New Zealand. The indicators of accommodation use in different centres by overseas visitors and New Zealand pleasure travellers are based on surveys commissioned by the Tourist and Publicity Department. That for overseas visitors was carried out in 1969–70 and that for domestic travellers in 1970–71.

Tourist and recreational centres which are close to main centres of population attract a great deal of regional use. Some, such as Rotorua, Queenstown and Te Anau, attract tourists from within their own region, as well as from other parts of New Zealand and from overseas.

Cape Maria van Diemen

Abel Tasman National Park,
Totaranui

Citrus fruit orchards,
Kerikeri

Ninety Mile
Beach

Marsden Foint Oil
Refinery

Auckland

Pukekohe market gardens and township

Rich Waikato farm land

Esk Valley vineyards

opposite Mature Kauri, Waipoua State Forest

Kaingaroa State Forest
and village

Logs for export, Port Maunganui

Major hill-country erosion, Tarndale slip, Mangatu

overleaf The Poverty Bay plain, looking across the Waipaoa River to Young Nicks Head

Sheep and cattle country, Okawa

Lake Tutira and surrounding farm land

The Tutaekuri River, Hawke's Bay

The coastline at Tongaporutu, North Taranaki Bight

The Lady Knox geyser, Waiotapu

The Wairakei thermal valley

Looking over the craters of Mt Tongariro to the cone of Mt Ngauruhoe and the snowclad peaks of Mt Ruapehu

The terraces of Turakirae Head

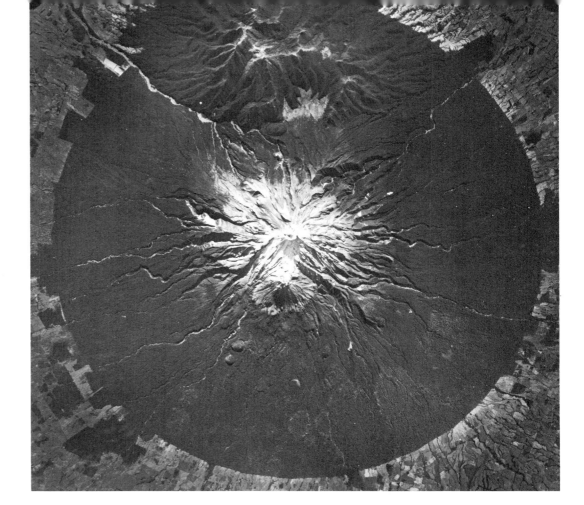

Mt Egmont and the encircling
National Park

Fanthams Peak, *left,* and the summit of Mt Egmont

The Taranaki plains, looking over the coast to the town of Hawera and Mt Egmont

The Wellington fault line along the western side of the harbour and the Hutt valley

The drowned valleys of the Marlborough Sounds

overleaf A West Coast stand of Kahikatea or White Pine

233~234

Nelson City and Port beyond the reclamation and mudflats between the foothills and the Boulder Bank

The Punakaiki rocks skirted by the coastal highway between Westport and Greymouth

Limestone caves at Paturau, north-west Nelson

The Karamea river valley

pp 238–239 The Southern Alps between Mt Elie de Beaumont, *left,* and Mt Cook, the highest peak on the right, lie beyond Westland podocarp forest. The view is from Okarito Trig

River terraces and foothills flank the upper Clutha River

overleaf The Canterbury Plains spread to the sea from the Southern Alps

The Onamulutu valley nestles in the foothills beyond the Wairau River

Christchurch

Dunedin

Benmore, the earth dam and power station, with the great stretch of artificial lake

pp 246–247 Mt Cook, *left,* and Mt Tasman, with the Ball, Hochstetter and Tasman glaciers.

The upper Taieri River flows through tussock grassland

The obelisk on the Old Man Range, Otago

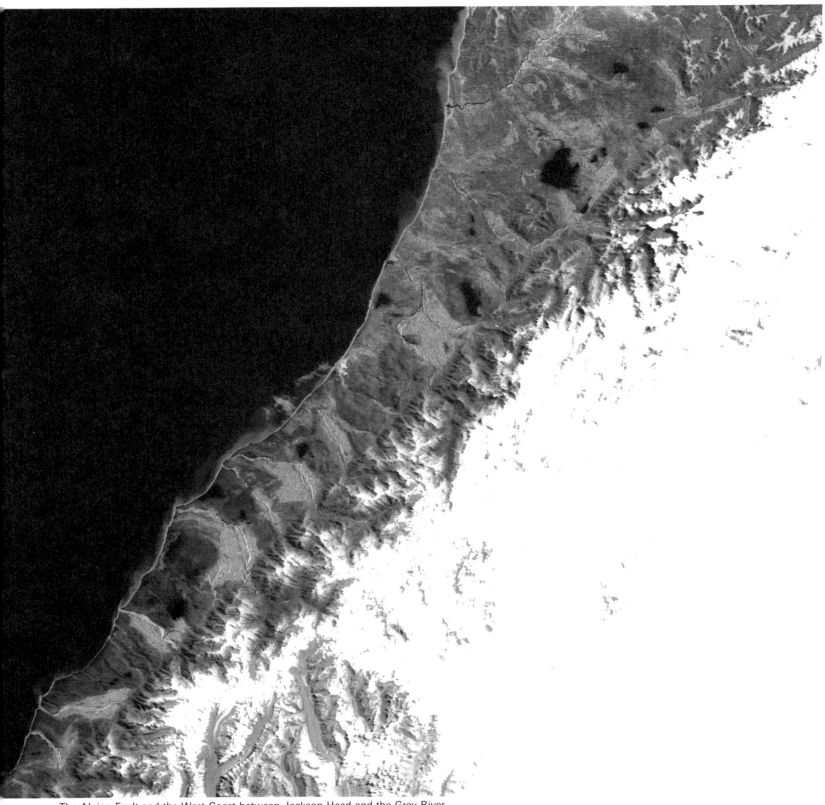

The Alpine Fault and the West Coast between Jackson Head and the Grey River

Milford Sound. The valley lies between the Wick, *left,* and Darran mountains. Mitre Peak is on the left of the Sound

Looking northward over the Lammerlaws

The south fork of the upper Wright Valley

The summit camp, Mt Erebus Expedition 1967–68

Descending the traverse on Axel Heiberg Glacier

Emperor penguins, Cape Crozier

The Wright Valley

Victoria Glacier, Upper Victoria Valley

256

GAZETTEERS

The Gazetteers list only those place names which appear on maps in this Atlas.

The New Zealand Gazetteer gives references for the Topographical, Sectional and Urban maps, the Islands of New Zealand and the Sea Floor. Spellings conform with decisions of the New Zealand Geographic Board.

Names for mapped areas other than New Zealand are listed in the second Gazetteer.

The order of listing is as follows:

First Column: The name. Features, e.g., lakes, mounts, points, ports, rivers, are listed under their proper names, not by the feature, e.g., Mount Cook under 'Cook', not 'Mount'. Where a locality is named after a feature, e.g., Point Dorset, Lake Coleridge, the locality is listed under its feature initial, 'P' or 'L'. Names beginning with 'Mac' or 'Mc' are listed in a phabetical order.

Second Column: A descriptive codeword, as listed below, e.g., GLCR for Glacier.

Third Column: The page reference for the map involved.

Fourth Column: The grid reference, e.g., Mt Cook, grid reference H20. URB indicates urban area map.

Fifth Column: Latitude to the nearest minute.

Sixth Column: Longitude to the nearest minute. For the New Zealand Gazetteer, all longitudes are E unless otherwise indicated.

An asterisk beside a name in the Gazetteer indicates a name that has subsequently been changed by the New Zealand Geographic Board.

Abbreviations

Code	Designation	Code	Designation	Code	Designation
ADM	Administration	GILBERT	Gilbert Islands	PHIL	Philippines
AIR	Airport	GLCR	Glacier	PHOENIX	Phoenix Islands
ALEUT	Aleutian Islands			PITCAIRN	Pitcairn Islands
AM SAMOA	American Samoa			PLAT	Plateau
ARCH	Archipelago	HARB	Harbour	PLN	Plain
ASSOC	Associated		Port	PNG	Papua New Guinea
ATL	Atlantic	HEAD	Head	PNT	Point
ATOL	Atoll		Headland	PORT	Portugal
AUST	Australia			PROT	Protectorate
		IND	Indian	PROV	Province
		INDON	Indonesia		
BASN	Basin	ISLD	Island		
BNK	Bank		Islet	REG	Region
BAY	Bay	ISLS	Islands	REP	Republic
	Bight		Islets	RESR	Reservoir
	Cove			RDGE	Ridge
	Firth				
	Gulf	JAP	Japan		
	Inlet			S	Sea
BCH	Beach				South
BDGE	Bridge	KING	Kingdom	SAD	Saddle
BLDG	Building				Col
BLUF	Bluff			SBNK	Sandbank
BORO	Borough	LAGN	Lagoon	SBRB	Suburb
BR	British	LAKE	Lake	S CRUZ	Santa Cruz
			Pond	S.E.A.	South East Asia
			Pool	SEAF	Sea Feature
C	Central		Tarn	SHEIK	Sheikdom
CANL	Canal	LINES	Line Islands	SHL	Shoal
CARIB	Caribbean	LOC	Kainga	SND	Sound
CAROL	Caroline Islands		Landing	SOLOMON	Solomon Islands
CHAN	Channel		Locality	SP	Spain
	Entrance		Marae	SPMEM	Special Member
CLIF	Cliff		River Bend	STRA	Strait
COL	Colony		River Crossing		Reach (Coastal)
CONT	Continent			STRM	Brook
COOKS	Cook Islands				Burn
C RICA	Costa Rica	MALAY	Malaysia		Creek
COTH	Commonwealth	MARSHALL	Marshall Islands		Reach
CZECH	Czechoslovakia	MBNK	Mudbank		River
		MT	Mount	SULT	Sultanate
		MTN	Mountain	SWMP	Swamp
D'MARK	Denmark	MTNS	Mountains		
DEP	Dependency		Range		
DIS	Disputed			TER	Territory
DOM	Dominion			TOKEL	Tokelau Islands
		N	North	TUNL	Tunnel
		NAT	Nation		
E	East	N CAL	New Caledonia		
ELLICE	Ellice Islands	NETH	Netherlands	U.A.R	United Arab Republic
ESTY	Estuary	N HEB	New Hebrides	URB	Urban Area
		NEWFOUND	Newfoundland	UK	United Kingdom
FED	Federation	NZ	New Zealand	US, USA	United States of America
FIOR	Fiord			USSR	Union of Soviet Socialist Republics
FR	French				
FRST	Forest	O	Ocean	VLY	Valley
		PAC	Pacific		
G	Gulf of	PEN	Peninsula	W	West

NAME	DESC	PAGE	REF	LAT S	LONG E
Abercrombie, Port	HARB	7	T5	36 09	175 19
Aberfeldy	LOC	14	T12	39 47	175 18
Abut Head	HEAD	22	H19	43 06	170 15
Acacia Bay	BAY	10	V10	38 43	176 02
Acheron River	STRM	23	L19	43 24	171 34
Acheron River	STRM	18	N17	42 24	172 58
Acheron Saddle	SAD	18	P16	41 56	173 17
Achilles Point	PNT	31	C5	36 51	174 52
Acton Stream	STRM	26	D24	45 40	168 25
Ada, Lake	LAKE	22, 26	C22	44 43	167 52
Ada Pass	PASS	18, 23	M17	42 18	172 28
Adair	LOC	23	K21	44 25	171 10
Adams Flat	LOC	27	E25	46 07	169 50
Adams Island	ISLD	4	—	50 53	166 05
Adams, Mount	MT	23	J19	43 16	170 32
Adams, Mount	MTN	15, 19	U15	41 19	175 45
Adams Rocks	ROCKS	4	—	50 51	165 55
Addington	SBRB	32	B3	43 33	172 37
Adelaide, Lake	LAKE	22, 26	D22	44 43	168 02
Adele Island	ISLD	14, 18	P14	40 58	173 04
Admiral Hill	LOC	15, 19	U15	41 06	175 40
Admiralty Bay	BAY	14, 19	Q14	40 57	173 52
Adventure, Port	HARB	26	D27	47 05	168 12
Ahaura	TOWN	18, 23	L17	42 21	171 32
Ahaura, Lake	LAKE	18, 23	L18	42 32	171 45
Ahaura River	STRM	18, 23	L17	42 21	171 31
Ahiaruhe	LOC	15, 19	U15	41 05	175 36
Ahimanawa Range	MTNS	11, 15	V11	39 03	176 29
Ahimia	LOC	7, 10	T6	36 51	175 29
Ahipara	TOWN	6	P3	35 10	173 09
Ahipara Bay	BAY	6	P3	35 10	173 07
Ahititi	LOC	10	S10	38 52	174 36
Ahuahu Stream	STRM	14	T12	39 42	175 08
Ahuriri	SBRB	38	D2	39 29	176 54
Ahuriri	LOC	23	N20	43 42	172 34
Ahuriri River	STRM	23	H21	44 30	170 04
Ahuroa	LOC	7, 10	S5	36 29	174 33
Aiguilles Island	ISLD	7	T5	36 03	175 24
Ailsa Mountains	MTNS	22, 26	D22	44 55	168 15
Airedale	LOC	23, 27	J23	45 00	170 56
Aitken, Mount	MT	26	A25	46 08	167 00
Ajax, Mount	MTN	18, 23	M18	42 35	172 04
Aka Aka	LOC	10	S7	37 17	174 47
Akaroa	BORO	23	N20	43 48	172 59
Akaroa Harbour	HARB	23	N20	43 50	172 56
Akaroa Head	HEAD	23	N20	43 54	172 59
Akatarawa	LOC	14, 19	T15	41 00	175 07
Akatarawa River	STRM	34	D4	41 05	175 06
Akatarawa River West	STRM	34	D4	41 04	175 04
Akatere	LOC	6	Q2	34 59	173 38
Akatore	LOC	27	H25	46 07	170 10
Akerama	LOC	6	R3	35 30	174 12
Akina	SBRB	38	C4	39 39	176 50
Akitio	LOC	15	V14	40 36	176 25
Akitio River	STRM	15	V14	40 36	176 25
Akura	LOC	37	D4	40 56	175 38
Alabaster, Lake	LAKE	22	D22	44 31	168 10
Alba, Mount	MT	22	E21	44 10	168 59
Albany	TOWN	30	A3	36 43	174 42
Albatross Point	PNT	10	S9	38 07	174 40
Albatross Point	PNT	4	—	49 43	178 48
Albert Burn	STRM	21	F21	44 22	169 08
Albert Town	LOC	22, 27	F22	44 41	169 11
Albury	LOC	23	J21	44 14	170 53
Aldermen Islands, The	ISLS	7, 10	V6	36 58	176 05
Alert Stack	ISLD	4	—	48 02	166 34
Alexandra	BORO	27	F23	45 15	169 24
Alexandrina, Lake	LAKE	23	H20	43 57	170 27
Alford Forest	LOC	23	L20	43 37	171 30
Alfredton	LOC	15, 19	U14	40 41	175 53
Alfriston	SBRB	31	D7	37 01	174 56
Alice, Lake	LAKE	26	B22	44 58	167 28
Alicetown	SBRB	35	B6	41 13	174 54
Alison, Point	PNT	4	—	43 47	176 53 W
Allandale	LOC	23	J21	44 03	170 52
Allandale	LOC	23	N20	43 38	172 39
Allanton	LOC	27	H24	45 55	170 16
Allen, Mount	MT	26	C27	47 05	167 48
Allenton	SBRB	39	D1	43 53	171 45
Alligator Head	HEAD	14, 19	R14	40 58	174 09
Alma	LOC	27	J23	45 07	170 55
Alpine, Lake	LAKE	22	H19	43 18	170 09
Alta, Mount	MTN	22	E21	44 30	168 58
Alton	LOC	14	R12	39 40	174 27
Amberley	TOWN	23	N19	43 09	172 45
Amberley Beach	LOC	23	N19	43 10	172 47
Amuri Pass	PASS	18, 23	M18	42 31	172 11
Anakiwa	LOC	14, 19	Q15	41 16	173 55
Anama	LOC	23	K20	43 45	171 26
Anatoki	LOC	14, 18	N14	40 57	172 48
Anatoki River	STRM	18	N14	40 52	172 38
Anaura Bay	LOC	11	Z9	38 14	178 19
Anchor Island	ISLD	26	A24	45 46	166 31
Andersons Bay	SBRB	33	C3	45 54	170 32
Anglem, Mount	MT	26	C26	46 44	167 54
Aniseed Valley	LOC	14, 18	P15	41 23	173 09
Annat	LOC	23	L19	43 22	171 59
Annesbrook	SBRB	39	B2	41 18	173 15
Antipodes Islands	ISLS	4	—	49 22	178 48
Anxiety Point	PNT	26	A23	45 06	167 00
Aokautere	LOC	37	B4	40 22	175 40
Aongatete	LOC	10	U8	37 36	175 57
Aorangi	LOC	15	U13	40 14	175 35
Aorangi	LOC	11	Z8	37 57	173 14
Aorangi Mountains	MTNS	14, 19	T15	41 30	175 20
Aorere	LOC	18	N14	40 43	172 36
Aorere Point	PNT	27	J23	45 13	170 53
Aorere River	STRM	18	N14	40 40	172 40
Aoroa	LOC	6	Q4	35 59	173 53
Aotea	LOC	10	S9	38 01	174 50
Aotea Harbour	HARB	10	S9	37 58	174 51
Aotea Seamount	SEAF	81	—	37 40	172 15
Aparima	LOC	26	D25	46 04	168 03
Aparima River	STRM	26	D25	46 20	168 05
Apata	LOC	10	U8	37 39	175 59
Apiti	TOWN	15	U12	39 58	175 52
Apiti Ridge	LOC	15	U13	40 02	175 52
Apotu	LOC	7	R4	37 35	174 17
Appleby	SBRB	40	D2	45 26	168 21
Appleby	LOC	14, 18	P15	41 18	173 08
Arahura	LOC	18, 23	K18	42 42	171 02
Arahura River	STRM	18, 23	K18	42 40	171 01
Arakihi	LOC	11	Z9	38 23	178 07
Aramatai	LOC	10	T9	38 28	175 10
Aramiro	LOC	10	T8	37 53	175 02
Aramoana	LOC	33	D1	45 47	170 42
Aramoho	SBRB	36	D1	39 54	175 04
Aranga	LOC	6	Q4	35 44	173 36
Aranui	SBRB	32	C3	43 31	172 42
Arapae	LOC	10	T9	38 25	175 05
Arapaoa River	STRM	7	R5	36 13	174 18
Arapaoanui	LOC	15	W11	39 16	176 59
Araparera	LOC	7, 10	R6	36 31	174 27
Arapawa Island	ISLD	14, 19	R15	41 11	174 19
Arapito	LOC	18	M15	41 16	172 10
Arapohue	LOC	6	Q4	35 59	173 57
Arapuni	TOWN	10	U9	38 04	175 39
Arapuni, Lake	LAKE	10	U9	38 10	175 40
Ararata	LOC	14	R12	39 31	174 23
Ararimu	LOC	10	T7	37 09	175 03
Ararimu Valley	LOC	7, 10	S6	36 43	174 33
Ararua	LOC	6	R5	36 03	174 10
Arataki	SBRB	36	B1	37 41	176 14
Aratapu	TOWN	6	Q5	36 01	173 54
Aratiatia	LOC	10	V10	38 37	176 10
Aratora	LOC	10	T9	38 30	175 13
Arawata River	STRM	22	E21	44 00	168 41
Arch Hill	SBRB	31	B5	36 52	174 45
Ardgowan	LOC	27	J23	45 04	170 58
Ardkeen	LOC	11, 15	X10	38 56	177 16
Ardlussa	LOC	26	E24	45 48	168 38
Ardmore Aerodrome	AIR	31	D8	37 02	174 58
Arero	LOC	11	Z9	38 13	178 16
Argyll East	LOC	15	W12	39 52	176 32
Aria	TOWN	10	S10	38 34	174 59
Arkles Bay	LOC	7, 10	S6	36 38	174 45
Arkles Bay	BAY	30	B1	36 38	174 45
Arno	LOC	23, 27	J22	44 46	171 00
Arnold, Mount	MT	22	F21	44 20	169 29
Arnott Point	PNT	22	F20	43 43	169 13
Arohena	LOC	10	U9	38 12	175 37
Arowhana	MTN	11	Y9	38 07	177 52
Arowhenua	LOC	23	K21	44 16	171 16
Arrow Junction	LOC	22, 26	E22	44 59	168 51
Arrow River	STRM	22, 26	E22	45 00	168 53
Arrowsmith Range	MTNS	23	J19	43 27	170 55
Arrowsmith, Mount	MT	23	J19	43 21	170 59
Arrowtown	BORO	22, 26	E22	44 56	168 50
Arthur, Mount	MTN	18	N15	41 13	172 41
Arthur Range	MTNS	18	N15	41 15	172 40
Arthur River	STRM	22, 26	C22	44 44	167 50
Arthur's Pass	LOC	18, 23	L18	42 57	171 34
Arthur's Pass	PASS	18, 23	L18	42 54	171 34
Arthurs Point	LOC	22, 26	E22	44 59	168 40
Arthurstown	LOC	18, 23	J18	42 44	171 00
Arthurton	LOC	27	F25	46 07	169 10
Arundel	LOC	23	K20	43 58	171 17
Ascot Park	SBRB	35	B5	41 07	174 52
Ashburton	BORO	39	Urb	43 54	171 45
Ashburton	BORO	23	L20	43 54	171 45
Ashburton Forks	LOC	23	L20	43 45	171 35
Ashburton Gorge	LOC	23	K20	43 38	171 12
Ashburton River	STRM	23	L21	44 03	171 48
Ashburton River, N. Br.	STRM	23	L20	43 53	171 43
Ashburton River, S. Br.	STRM	23	L20	43 44	171 33
Ashcott	LOC	15	V12	39 57	175 21
Ashers	LOC	26	E25	46 28	168 39
Ashhurst	TOWN	15	U13	40 17	175 45
Ashley	LOC	23	N19	43 16	172 36
Ashley Clinton	LOC	15	V12	39 57	176 16
Ashley Downs	LOC	27	F25	46 11	169 30
Ashley Gorge	LOC	23	M19	43 14	172 13
Ashley River	STRM	23	N19	43 17	172 43
Ashton	LOC	23	L21	44 02	171 46
Ashwick Flat	LOC	23	J20	44 00	170 50
Aspiring, Mount	MTN	22	E21	44 23	168 44
Astrolabe Point	PNT	4	—	50 54	165 57
Atapo	LOC	18	N16	41 37	172 47
Atarau	LOC	18, 23	K17	42 20	171 29
Atawhai	LOC	39	B1	41 14	173 19
Athenree	TOWN	10	U7	37 27	175 58
Athol	LOC	26	E24	45 31	168 35
Atiamuri	TOWN	10	V9	38 23	176 02
Atiamuri, Lake	LAKE	10	V9	38 23	176 02
Auckland	CITY	7, 10	S6	36 52	174 45
Auckland	CITY	30, 31	Urb	36 52	174 45
Auckland International Airport	AIR	31	B7	37 01	174 47
Auckland Islands	ISLS	4	—	50 35	166 00
Aucklands Slope	SEAF	81	—	50 50	165 40
Aukopae	LOC	10	T10	38 55	175 07
Auroa	LOC	14	R11	39 29	174 02
Ava	SBRB	35	B6	41 13	174 53
Avalon	SBRB	35	C6	41 12	174 57
Avenal	SBRB	40	C2	46 24	168 21
Aviemore, Lake	LAKE	22, 27	H22	44 37	170 18
Aviemore	LOC	22, 27	H22	44 37	170 13
Avoca	LOC	6	Q4	35 49	173 54
Avoca River	STRM	23	L19	43 11	171 33
Avon River	STRM	19	Q16	41 38	173 40
Avon River	STRM	32	C3	43 30	172 42
Avon River Estuary	ESTY	32	C3	43 33	172 44
Avon Saddle	SAD	18	Q16	41 49	173 30
Avondale	SBRB	31	A5	36 53	174 42
Avonhead	SBRB	32	A2	43 31	172 33
Avonside	SBRB	32	C3	43 31	172 40
Awahou	LOC	11	V9	38 03	176 13
Awahou North	LOC	15	U13	40 10	175 49
Awahou South	LOC	15	U13	40 14	175 48
Awahuri	TOWN	15	U13	40 16	175 30
Awaiti	LOC	10	U7	37 23	175 37
Awakaponga	LOC	11	W8	37 55	176 46
Awakau	LOC	10	S10	38 42	174 41
Awakeri	LOC	11	W8	38 00	176 53
Awakino	LOC	10	S10	38 39	174 37
Awakino Point	LOC	6	Q4	35 55	173 54
Awakino River	STRM	10	S10	38 39	174 37
Awamangu	LOC	27	G25	46 06	169 39
Awamarino	LOC	10	S9	38 16	174 47
Awamate	LOC	11, 15	X10	38 59	177 23
Awamoa	SBRB	39	C3	45 06	170 56
Awamoa Creek	STRM	39	C4	45 09	170 56
Awamoko	LOC	23, 27	J22	44 55	170 52
Awamoko Creek	STRM	23, 27	J22	44 54	170 52
Awanui	TOWN	6	P3	35 03	173 15
Awanui River	STRM	6	P3	35 00	173 16
Awanui Stream	STRM	38	C4	39 41	176 50
Awapuni	SBRB	38	B2	38 40	178 00
Awapuni	SBRB	37	A4	40 23	175 35
Awariki	LOC	15	V13	40 13	176 14
Awaroa	LOC	6	P3	35 16	173 17
Awaroa Head	HEAD	14, 18	P14	40 51	173 03
Awaroa Inlet	BAY	14, 18	P14	40 52	173 01
Awaroa Stream	STRM	10	T7	37 29	175 01
Awarua	LOC	6	Q4	35 34	173 50
Awarua	LOC	40	D3	46 31	168 22
Awarua Bay	BAY	22	D21	44 18	168 05
Awarua Point	PNT	22	D21	44 16	168 03
Awatere River	STRM	14, 19	R16	41 36	174 10
Awatere River	STRM	11	Z8	37 38	178 23
Awatere Valley	LOC	11	Z8	37 41	178 21
Awatoto	SBRB	38	D2	39 32	176 55
Awatuna	LOC	14	R11	39 26	174 03
Awhea River	STRM	15, 19	U15	41 20	175 31
Awhitu	HILL	31	A8	37 04	174 37
Awhitu	LOC	10	S7	37 05	174 38
Awhitu Central	LOC	10	S7	37 06	174 35
Aylesbury	LOC	23	M20	43 32	172 16

NAME	DESC	PAGE	REF	LAT S	LONG E
Bainesse	LOC	14, 19	T13	40 25	175 23
Bainham	LOC	18	N14	40 46	172 34
Balaena Bay	BAY	35	A8	41 17	174 48
Balcairn	LOC	23	N19	43 12	172 42
Balclutha	BORO	27	G25	46 14	169 44
Bald Mountain	MTN	22	D21	44 15	168 30
Balfour	LOC	26	E24	45 50	168 35
Ballance	LOC	15, 19	U13	40 24	175 47
Balls Pyramid	ISLD	81	—	31 50	159 20
Balmoral	SBRB	31	B5	36 53	174 45
Balmoral	LOC	18, 23	N18	42 50	172 44
Banks Peninsula	PEN	23	N20	43 42	172 42
Bankside	LOC	23	M20	43 42	172 05
Bannock Brae Range	MTNS	22	G20	43 44	169 48
Bannockburn	LOC	27	F23	45 05	169 10
Bare Island	ISLD	15	X12	39 50	177 02
Baring Head	HEAD	14, 19	S15	41 25	174 52
Barker, Mount	LOC	22, 27	F22	44 44	169 11
Barn Bay	BAY	22	D21	44 05	168 19
Barnego	LOC	27	G25	46 14	169 44
Barnicoat Range	MTNS	39	B2	41 21	173 16
Barracouta Point	PNT	26	D26	46 33	168 14
Barrett Reef	REEF	35	B8	41 21	174 50
Barrhill	LOC	23	L20	43 40	171 51
Barrier, Cape	CAPE	7	U5	36 21	175 31
Barrier Range	MTNS	22	G21	44 11	169 42
Barrier Range	MTNS	22	D21	44 29	168 24
Barrys Bay	BAY	23	N20	43 46	172 55
Barrytown	LOC	18	K17	42 14	171 20
Barryville	LOC	10	U8	38 30	175 34
Bartletts	LOC	11	Y10	38 51	177 54
Bastia Hill	SBRB	36	D2	39 56	175 04
Batley	LOC	7	R5	36 13	174 19
Baton River	STRM	18	N15	41 17	172 48
Battersea	LOC	14, 19	T15	41 07	175 25
Bauza Island	ISLD	26	A23	45 17	166 54
Bay of Plenty	BAY	11	X8	37 47	177 10
Bay View	TOWN	38	C1	39 26	176 52
Baylys Beach	LOC	6	Q4	35 57	173 45
Bayswater	SBRB	30	B4	36 49	174 47
Beach Haven	SBRB	30	A4	36 47	174 41
Beachlands	LOC	31	D5	36 53	175 00
Beaconsfield	LOC	15	U13	40 05	175 40
Beatrice Peaks	PEAK	26	B25	46 03	167 12
Beaumont	TOWN	27	G24	45 49	169 32
Beaumont River	STRM	27	G24	45 49	169 31
Beautiful River	STRM	18	M15	41 12	172 26
Becks	LOC	22, 27	G22	45 00	169 44
Beddoes, Lake	LAKE	26	C22	44 54	167 33
Beerescourt	SBRB	37	D1	37 46	175 16
Belfast	TOWN	32	B2	43 27	172 38
Belfield	LOC	23	K21	44 06	171 18
Belgrove	LOC	14, 18	N15	41 27	172 58
Bell Block	TOWN	37	B1	39 02	174 09
Belleknowes	SBRB	33	B3	45 53	170 29
Bellevue	SBRB	36	A1	37 41	176 08
Bellona Gap	SEAF	81	—	40 30	165 40
Bells Island	ISLD	39	A2	41 18	173 10
Belmont	SBRB	30	B4	36 48	174 47
Belmont	SBRB	35	C6	41 11	174 55
Belmont	HILL	35	B6	41 11	174 52
Belvedere	LOC	15, 19	T15	41 01	175 30
Ben Bolt	PEAK	26	D25	46 00	168 29
Ben McLeod	MT	23	J20	43 44	170 58
Ben More	MTN	23	L19	43 21	171 43
Ben Ohau Range	MTNS	22	H21	44 00	170 01
Bench Island	ISLD	26	D26	46 55	168 14
Bendigo	LOC	22, 27	F22	44 56	169 21
Benhar	TOWN	27	G25	46 14	169 48
Benhopai	LOC	19	Q16	41 40	173 35
Benio	LOC	27	F25	46 05	169 04
Benmore	LOC	26	D24	45 57	168 21
Benmore Peak	PEAK	22	H21	44 25	170 06
Benmore, Lake	LAKE	22	H21	44 24	170 14
Bennett, Cape	CAPE	4	—	50 49	166 14
Bennetts	LOC	23	N19	43 18	172 17
Bennetts Siding	LOC	15	U12	39 39	175 46
Benneydale	LOC	10	T10	38 31	175 21
Berghan Point	PNT	6	Q2	34 55	173 33
Berhampore	SBRB	35	A8	41 19	174 46
Berlins	LOC	18	L16	41 52	171 50
Berwick	LOC	27	H24	45 57	170 06
Bests Island	ISLD	39	A2	41 18	173 09
*Bethells	LOC	7, 10	R6	36 54	174 27
Bethlehem	LOC	36	A1	37 42	176 07
Bexley	SBRB	32	C2	43 31	172 43
Bexley	LOC	23	M19	43 21	172 04
Bickerstaffe	LOC	7	R5	36 08	174 21
Bideford	LOC	15, 19	U14	40 52	175 51
Big Bay	BAY	31	A8	37 02	174 38
Big Ben Range	MTNS	23	U9	43 22	171 44
Big Hill	LOC	15	V12	39 36	176 25
Big Lagoon	LAGN	14, 19	R16	41 33	174 06
Big Moggy Island	ISLD	26	B27	47 09	167 25
Big Omaha	LOC	7	S5	36 18	174 44
Big Reef Point	PNT	22	D21	44 10	168 14
Big River	STRM	18	L17	42 20	171 32
Big River	STRM	18	M14	40 46	172 16
Big South Cape Island	ISLD	26	B27	47 14	167 24
Binser, Mount	MTN	18, 23	L19	43 02	171 52
Birch Hill	LOC	14, 18	P16	41 39	173 17
Birchfield	LOC	18	L16	41 41	171 48
Birchville	SBRB	34	D4	41 06	175 05
Birchwood	LOC	26	C24	45 57	167 52
Bird Island	ISLD	26	D26	46 46	168 25
Birdlings Flat	LOC	23	N20	43 49	172 43
Birdwood Range	MTNS	23	K19	43 05	171 24
Birkdale	SBRB	30	A4	36 48	174 42
Birkenhead	BORO	30	B4	36 49	174 43
Bishop and Clerks Islands	ISLS	26	C26	46 40	167 48
Bishopdale	SBRB	32	B2	43 29	172 35
Black Head	HEAD	33	B4	45 56	170 26
Black Head	HEAD	15	W13	40 13	176 48
Black Head	HEAD	4	—	50 32	166 08
Black Point	PNT	26	E26	46 41	168 58
Black Range	MTNS	23	K19	43 03	171 29
Black Rock Point	PNT	26	C26	46 41	167 52
Blackball	TOWN	18, 23	K17	42 22	171 24
Blackburn	LOC	15	V12	39 52	176 17
Blackburn, Mount	MT	22	H20	43 45	170 12
Blackmount	LOC	26	C24	45 48	167 41
Blackwater River	STRM	18	L16	41 51	171 47
Blair Logie	LOC	18, 23	P18		173 04
Blairich	LOC	19	Q16	41 42	173 55
Blairich Pass	PASS	19	Q16	41 40	173 48
Blairich River	STRM	19	Q16	41 42	173 56
Blaketown	SBRB	40	A1	42 27	171 11
Blenheim	BORO	14, 19	R16	41 31	173 57
Blenheim	BORO	39	Urb	41 31	173 57
Bligh Sound	SND	26	B22	44 46	167 29
Blind Bay	BAY	7	T5	36 16	175 25
Blind River	LOC	19	R16	41 41	174 08
Blockhouse Bay	SBRB	31	A6	36 56	174 42
Bloxham, Lake	LAKE	26	B23	45 08	167 25
Blue Cliffs	LOC	23	J22	44 31	170 59
Blue Lake	LAKE	4	—	29 15	177 54 W
Blue Mountain	MTN	23	K20	43 55	171 02
Blue Mountain Station	LOC	23	K20	43 51	171 02
Blue Mountains	MTNS	27	F24	45 56	169 21
Blueskin Bay	BAY	33	C1	45 44	170 35
Bluff	BORO	26	D26	46 36	168 21
Bluff	BORO	40	Urb	46 36	168 21
Bluff Harbour	HARB	40	C4	46 34	168 20
Bluff Hill	SBRB	38	D2	39 29	176 55
Bluff, The	CLIF	6	N2	34 41	172 55
Bluff, The	HILL	40	C4	46 37	168 20
Blumine Island	ISLD	14, 19	R15	41 11	174 14
Blythe River	STRM	18	P18	42 56	173 16
Boddytown	LOC	40	A2	42 29	171 13
Boggyburn	LOC	26	D25	46 03	168 23
Bollons Island	ISLD	4	—	49 38	178 49
Bollons Seamount	SEAF	81	—	49 35	176 40 W
Bombay	TOWN	10	S7	37 11	174 59
Bonny Glen	LOC	14	T13	40 03	175 18
Bonpland, Mount	MT	22, 26	D22	44 49	168 18
Borland	STRM	26	C24	45 46	167 36
Bortons	LOC	23, 27	J22	44 53	170 46
Boulcott	SBRB	35	C6	41 12	174 55
Boulder Bank	BNK	39	B1	41 14	173 17
Boulder Beach	BCH	33	C3	45 54	170 37
Bounty Islands	ISLS	4	—	47 43	179 05
Bounty Platform	SEAF	81	—	48 40	179 10
Bounty Trough	SEAF	81	—	46 30	178 30
Bowen Channel	CHAN	26	A24	45 45	166 40
Bowentown	LOC	10	U7	37 28	175 59
Boyle River	STRM	18, 23	M18	42 31	172 22
Braan Mountains	MTNS	26	B24	45 38	167 02
Bradleys Landing	LOC	6	Q4	36 00	173 55
Bradshaw, Mount	MT	26	A24	45 51	166 34
Bradshaw Sound	SND	26	B23	45 17	167 04
Braeburn	LOC	14, 18	N15	41 12	173 00
Braemore	LOC	15	T12	39 52	175 30
Braigh	LOC	7	R5	36 00	174 25
Branch River	STRM	18	P16	41 40	173 11
Breaker Bay	BAY	35	B8	41 20	174 50
Breaksea Island	ISLD	26	A24	45 34	166 37
Breaksea Islands	ISLS	26	D27	47 07	168 12
Breaksea Sound	SND	26	A24	45 33	166 38
Bream Bay	BAY	7	S4	35 56	174 30
Bream Head	HEAD	7	S4	35 51	174 36
Bream Tail	PNT	7	S5	36 03	174 36
Brett, Cape	CAPE	7	R3	35 10	174 20
Brewster	MT	22	F21	44 04	169 27
Bridge Pa	LOC	15	W12	39 39	176 45
Bridge Valley	LOC	14, 18	P15	41 25	173 05
Brig Rock	ROCK	22	C22	44 31	167 47
Brighton	TOWN	33	A4	45 57	170 20
Brightwater	TOWN	14, 18	P15	41 23	173 06
Bristow Point	PNT	4	—	50 45	166 53
Brixton	LOC	10, 14	R11	39 01	174 13
Broad Bay	SBRB	33	C3	45 51	170 37
Broad Gully	LOC	23, 27	K22	44 50	171 03
Broadfield	LOC	23	M20	43 36	172 28
Broadlands	LOC	11	V10	38 31	176 19
Broadwood	TOWN	6	P3	35 15	173 23
Brockville	SBRB	33	B3	45 52	170 28
Broken River	STRM	23	L19	43 13	171 56
Bromley	SBRB	32	C3	43 32	172 42
Brook, The	SBRB	39	B2	41 17	173 17
Brookby	LOC	31	D7	36 59	175 00
Brookdale	LOC	27	J23	45 23	170 50
Brookfield	SBRB	36	A1	37 41	176 08
Brooklands	SBRB	37	A1	39 04	174 05
Brooklands	SBRB	39	B1	41 16	173 18
Brooklands	LOC	23	N19	43 24	172 42
Brooklands	LOC	32	C1	43 22	172 42
Brooklands	LOC	27	G25	46 08	169 59
Brooklyn	SBRB	35	A8	41 19	174 46
Brooklyn	LOC	14, 18	N15	41 06	172 57
Brookside	LOC	23	M20	43 42	172 18
Broomfield	LOC	23	N19	43 07	172 11
Brothers, The	ISLS	14, 19	R15	41 07	174 26
Broughton Island	ISLD	4	—	48 02	166 37
Brown Owl	SBRB	34	D4	41 06	175 06
Brownings Pass	PASS	18, 23	K18	42 57	171 21
Browns	LOC	26	D25	46 09	168 25
Browns Bay	SBRB	30	B2	36 43	174 45
Browns Island	ISLD	30	C4	36 50	174 54
Browns Rock	LOC	23	M19	43 23	172 05
Bruce Bay	LOC	22	G20	43 35	169 35
Brunner, Lake	LAKE	18, 23	K18	42 37	171 27
Brunner Range	MTNS	18	M16	41 54	172 03
Brunswick	LOC	14	T12	39 51	175 02
Bruntwood	LOC	10	T8	37 50	175 26
Bryant Range	MTNS	14, 18	P15	41 16	173 26
Bryce, Mount	PEAK	23	K19	43 04	171 12
Brydone	LOC	26	E25	46 16	168 48
Brynderwyn	LOC	7	R5	36 06	174 26
Bryndwr	SBRB	32	B2	43 31	172 36
Buccleugh	LOC	23	K20	43 41	171 27
Buckland	LOC	10	S7	37 13	174 56
Buckland	LOC	10	U8	37 53	175 39
Bucklands Beach	SBRB	31	C5	36 52	174 54
Bull Rock	ROCK	4	—	52 26	169 11
Buller River	STRM	18	L16	41 44	171 35
Bulls	TOWN	14	T13	40 10	175 23
Bunnythorpe	TOWN	37	B3	40 16	175 38
Burgess Island	ISLD	7	T4	35 55	175 07
Burkes	SBRB	33	C3	45 51	170 34
Burke Pass	LOC	23	J21	44 06	170 39
Burleigh	SBRB	39	A4	41 32	173 56
Burnbrae	LOC	18	M17	42 03	172 15
Burnham	LOC	23	M20	43 37	172 18
Burnham Military Camp	LOC	23	M20	43 37	172 18
Burnside	SBRB	32	A2	43 30	172 33
Burnt Hill	LOC	23	M19	43 22	172 09
Burwood	SBRB	32	C2	43 30	172 41
Busby Head	HEAD	36	D4	35 52	174 32
Bush Creek	STRM	23	J20	43 37	170 53
Bushey	LOC	27	J23	45 28	170 47
Bushside	LOC	23	K20	43 38	171 29
Cable Bay	LOC	6	P2	35 00	173 29
Cable Bay	LOC	14, 18	P15	41 10	173 25
Cairnbrae	LOC	23	L20	43 40	171 41
Callery River	STRM	22	H19	43 20	170 09
Calm Peak	PEAK	26	A23	45 28	166 45
Camberley	SBRB	38	C3	39 37	176 49
Camborne	SBRB	34	B4	41 06	174 52
Cambridge	BORO	10	T8	37 53	175 28
Camden	LOC	19	Q16	41 52	173 41
Camels Back	HILL	7, 10	U6	36 58	175 35
Cameron Mountains	MTNS	26	A25	46 00	166 54
Cameron River	STRM	23	K19	43 29	171 09
Camerons	LOC	18, 23	K18	42 33	171 07
Camp Bay	BAY	32	D4	43 37	172 47
Campbell, Cape	CAPE	19	R16	41 44	174 16
Campbell Island	ISLD	4	—	52 32	169 10

NAME	DESC	PAGE	REF	LAT S	LONG E
Campbell Island Rise	SEAF	81	—	52 15	169 50
Campbell Plateau	SEAF	81	—	50 50	171 10
Campbells Bay	SBRB	30	B3	36 45	174 46
Cannington	LOC	23	J21	44 20	170 52
Canister Cove	BAY	4	—	44 20	176 14 W
Cannons Creek	SBRB	35	B5	41 08	174 52
Canterbury Bight	BAY	23	L21	44 10	172 00
Canterbury Plains	PLN	23	L20	43 40	171 50
Canvastown	TOWN	14, 19	Q15	41 17	173 40
Cape Foulwind	LOC	18	K16	41 45	171 29
Caples River	STRM	22, 26	D22	44 56	168 22
Cardiff	LOC	14	R11	39 22	174 14
Cardrona	LOC	22, 26	F22	44 52	169 00
Cardrona, Mount	MT	22, 26	E22	44 51	168 57
Cardrona River	STRM	22, 27	F22	44 41	169 12
Carew	LOC	23	K20	43 57	171 22
Careys Bay	SBRB	33	C2	45 49	170 37
Cargill, Mount	HILL	33	C2	45 49	170 33
Carleton	LOC	23	M19	43 18	172 16
Carnarvon	LOC	14	T13	40 17	175 22
Carnley Harbour	HARB	4	–	50 50	166 08
Caroline	LOC	26	D24	45 50	168 23
Caroline Bay	BAY	40	B4	44 23	171 15
Caroline Peak	PEAK	26	B24	45 56	167 12
Carrington	LOC	15, 19	T14	40 57	175 30
Carters Beach	LOC	18	L16	41 45	171 33
Carters Mill	LOC	22	E20	43 57	168 52
Carterton	BORO	15, 19	U15	41 01	175 31
Casa Nova	SBRB	39	D3	45 05	170 59
Cascade Point	PNT	22	D21	44 01	168 22
Cascade River	STRM	22	D21	44 02	168 22
Cashmere	SBRB	32	B3	43 35	172 38
Cass River	STRM	23	H20	43 53	170 30
Castle Island	ISLD	7, 10	U6	36 52	175 53
Castle, Mount	MT	22, 26	C22	44 51	167 47
Castle Point	PNT	15, 19	V14	40 55	176 13
Castle Rock	LOC	26	D24	45 44	168 23
Castle, The	ISLD	4	—	44 17	176 21 W
Castlecliff	SBRB	36	C2	39 57	174 59
Castlehill	LOC	15, 19	U14	40 43	175 57
Castlepoint	LOC	15, 19	V14	40 55	176 13
Castor Bay	SBRB	30	B3	36 46	174 46
Caswell Sound	SND	26	B22	44 59	167 08
Cathedral Peaks	PEAK	26	B23	45 27	167 26
Catlins River	STRM	27	G25	46 29	169 43
Cattle Creek	LOC	23	J22	44 31	170 41
Cattle Valley	LOC	23	J21	44 04	170 56
Cavalli Islands	ISLS	6	Q2	34 59	173 57
Cave	LOC	23	J21	44 19	170 58
Cavern Peak	PEAK	4	—	50 45	166 07
Caversham	SBRB	33	B3	45 54	170 29
Cecil Peak	PEAK	26	E23	45 07	168 38
Centaur Peaks	PEAK	22, 26	E22	44 38	168 34
Central Takaka	LOC	14, 18	N14	40 53	172 49
Centre Island	ISLD	26	C25	46 28	167 52
Centre Bush	LOC	26	D25	46 03	168 20
Centre Hill	LOC	26	D24	45 35	168 08
Chalky Inlet	BAY	26	A25	46 03	166 30
Chalky Island	ISLD	26	A25	46 03	166 31
Challenger Plateau	SEAF	81	—	40 00	169 50
Challis	SBRB	33	C3	45 53	170 33
Chamberlain	LOC	23	J21	44 15	170 46
Chambres Inlet	BAY	4	—	50 37	166 11
Channel Island	ISLD	7, 10	T5	36 25	175 19
Chanter Island	ISLD	4	—	29 15	177 51 W
Charing Cross	LOC	23	M20	43 33	172 10
Charles, Mount	HILL	33	D3	45 52	170 42
Charles Sound	SND	26	B23	45 02	167 05
Charleston	LOC	18	K16	41 54	171 27
Charlton	LOC	26	E25	46 09	168 57
Charteris Bay	LOC	32	C4	43 39	172 42
Chaslands Mistake	HEAD	27	F26	46 38	169 21
Chasm Pass	PASS	22	E21	44 15	168 51
Chatham Islands	ISLS	4	—	44 00	176 30 W
Chatham Rise	SEAF	81	—	43 25	179 00
Chatto Creek	LOC	27	G23	45 08	169 31
Chatton	LOC	26	E24	45 59	168 55
Chatton North	LOC	26	E24	45 56	168 58
Cheddar Valley	LOC	18, 23	P18	42 39	173 07
Cheltenham	SBRB	30	B4	36 49	174 48
Cheltenham	LOC	15	U13	40 09	175 41
Chertsey	LOC	23	L20	43 48	171 56
Cheeseman Island	ISLD	4	—	30 33	178 34 W
Chetwode Islands	ISLS	14, 19	R14	40 54	174 05
Chevalier, Point	SBRB	31	A5	36 52	174 42
Cheviot	TOWN	18	P18	42 49	173 16
Christabel, Lake	LAKE	18, 23	M17	42 25	172 14
Christchurch	CITY	32	Urb	43 32	172 37
Christchurch	CITY	23	N20	43 32	172 37
Christchurch International Airport	AIR	32	A2	43 29	172 32
Christina, Mount	MT	22, 26	D22	44 47	168 03
Churchill	LOC	10	T7	37 25	175 05
Circle Hill	LOC	27	G25	46 03	169 58
Clandeboye	LOC	23	K21	44 13	171 23
Claremont	LOC	23	K21	44 23	171 06
Clarence	LOC	19	Q17	42 10	173 56
Clarence River	STRM	19	Q17	42 10	173 57
Clarendon	LOC	27	H25	46 04	170 01
Clareville	LOC	15, 19	U15	41 01	175 33
Claris	LOC	7	T5	36 14	175 28
Clark River	STRM	18	N16	41 34	172 47
Clarke River	STRM	22	F20	43 57	169 30
Clarks Beach	LOC	10	S7	37 08	174 42
Clarks Junction	LOC	27	H24	45 44	170 03
Clarksville	LOC	27	G25	46 08	169 55
Clarkville	LOC	23	N19	43 24	172 38
Claudelands	SBRB	37	D1	37 47	175 17
Clay Point	PNT	14, 19	Q14	40 53	173 59
Clear Stream	STRM	22, 27	H22	44 41	170 10
Clearburn	LOC	22	H21	44 21	170 01
Clearwater, Lake	LAKE	23	K20	43 36	171 03
Clerke, Mount	MT	26	A24	45 41	166 41
Cleughearn Peak	PEAK	26	B24	45 49	167 24
Clevedon	TOWN	7, 10	T6	36 59	175 02
Clifden	LOC	26	C25	46 02	167 43
Clifford Bay	BAY	19	R16	41 41	174 12
Clifton	SBRB	32	D3	43 34	172 46
Clifton	SBRB	40	D2	46 27	168 22
Clifton	LOC	14, 18	N14	40 51	172 53
Clifton	LOC	27	G25	46 12	169 34
Clinton	TOWN	27	F25	46 13	169 23
Clinton River	STRM	22, 26	C22	44 56	167 56
Clive	TOWN	38	D3	39 35	176 55
Cloudy Bay	BAY	14, 19	R15	41 27	174 06
Clutha River	STRM	27	G25	46 21	169 48
Clyde	BORO	27	F23	45 11	169 19
Clyde River	STRM	23	J19	43 27	170 50
Clydesdale	LOC	14	T13	40 17	175 19
Clydevale	LOC	27	G25	46 06	169 32
Coal Creek	LOC	18, 23	K17	42 26	171 15
Coal Creek	STRM	26	E23	45 12	168 59
Coal Creek	LOC	27	F23	45 29	169 20
Coal Island	ISLD	26	A25	46 07	166 38

NAME	DESC	PAGE	REF	LAT S	LONG E
Coal Point	PNT	27	G25	46 18	169 55
Coalgate	LOC	23	L19	43 29	171 58
Coatesville	LOC	7, 10	S6	36 43	174 39
Cobb Reservoir	RESR	18	N15	41 06	172 39
Cobb River	STRM	18	N15	41 06	172 39
Cobb River	LOC	18	N15	41 05	172 44
Cobden	SBRB	40	A1	42 26	171 12
Cobden Hill	HILL	40	A1	42 26	171 13
Cockle Bay	SBRB	31	D5	36 54	174 57
Codfish Island	ISLD	26	C26	46 46	167 38
Colac	LOC	26	C25	46 22	167 53
Coldstream	LOC	23	N19	43 18	172 37
Coldstream	LOC	23	L21	44 09	171 32
Coleridge, Lake	LAKE	23	L19	43 18	171 31
Colliers Junction	LOC	15	U12	39 36	175 35
Collingwood	TOWN	18	N14	40 41	172 41
Collyer	MT	22	E21	44 10	168 36
Colonial Head	HEAD	26	A23	45 08	166 57
Colonial Knob	PEAK	35	A5	41 09	174 48
Colville	LOC	7, 10	T6	36 37	175 28
Colville Bay	BAY	7, 10	T6	36 37	175 26
Colville Cape	CAPE	7, 10	T5	36 28	175 21
Colville Channel	CHAN	7	T5	36 24	175 27
Colville Ridge	SEAF	81	—	28 00	179 25 W
Colyers Island	ISLD	40	C4	46 33	168 19
Colyton	LOC	15	U13	40 14	175 39
Comma Bay	BAY	4	—	48 02	166 36
Command Peak	PEAK	26	B23	45 07	167 05
Company Bay	SBRB	33	C3	45 51	170 36
Conical Hill	LOC	27	F25	46 04	169 14
Conical Peak	PEAK	27	J23	45 16	170 35
Connells Bay	LOC	7, 10	T6	36 50	175 10
Conroys Gully	LOC	27	F23	45 17	169 20
Constance, Lake	LAKE	18	N17	42 05	172 40
Conway Flat	LOC	18	P18	42 37	173 27
Conway River	STRM	18	P18	42 37	173 28
Cook, Mount	MTN	22	H20	43 36	170 09
Cook River	STRM	22	G19	43 27	169 46
Cook Strait	STRA	14, 19	R15	41 20	174 22
Cooks Bay	LOC	7, 10	U6	36 50	175 44
Coonoor	LOC	15, 19	V13	40 25	176 06
Cooper Island	ISLD	26	A24	45 45	166 50
Coopers Beach	LOC	6	P2	34 59	173 30
Coopers Creek	LOC	23	M19	43 17	172 06
Coopers Knob	HILL	32	B4	43 40	172 37
Cooptown	LOC	23	N20	43 45	172 47
Copland Range	MTNS	22	G20	43 34	169 55
Copland River	STRM	22	G20	43 37	169 50
Cornwallis	LOC	7, 10	S7	37 01	174 36
Coroglen	LOC	7, 10	U6	36 55	175 41
Coromandel	TOWN	7, 10	T6	36 46	175 30
Coromandel Harbour	HARB	7, 10	T6	36 47	175 28
Coromandel Peninsula	PEN	7, 10	U6	36 50	175 35
Coromandel Range	MTNS	7, 10	U7	37 03	175 40
Coronet Peak	PEAK	22, 26	E22	44 55	168 45
Corriedale	LOC	23, 27	J22	44 59	170 47
Corstorphine	SBRB	33	B4	45 54	170 28
Cossack Rock	ROCK	4	—	52 31	169 13
Courrejolles Point	PNT	4	—	52 29	169 07
Courtenay	LOC	23	M19	43 28	172 14
Coutts Island	LOC	23	N19	43 26	172 37
Cox River	STRM	18, 23	L18	42 52	171 57
Cradock Channel	CHAN	7	T5	36 12	175 09
Craigieburn Range	MTNS	23	L19	43 12	171 40
Craigmore Downs	LOC	23	J21	44 25	170 58
Crail Bay	BAY	14	Q15	41 10	173 58
Crater Head	HEAD	4	—	34 09	172 07
Crawford, Mount	HILL	35	B8	41 18	174 50
Crawford Range	MTNS	18, 23	M18	42 43	172 05
Crichton	LOC	27	G25	46 08	169 51
Cricklewood	LOC	23	J21	44 12	170 53
Crofton	LOC	14	T13	40 06	175 23
Croisilles Harbour	HARB	14, 19	Q15	41 04	173 40
Cromwell	TOWN	22, 27	F23	45 03	169 14
Cronadun	LOC	18	L17	42 02	171 51
Crookston	LOC	27	F24	45 51	169 20
Crossley, Mount	MTN	18, 23	M18	42 50	172 04
Crow River	STRM	18	M15	41 18	172 28
Crown Hill	SBRB	30	B3	36 46	174 46
Crown Terrace	LOC	22, 26	E22	44 58	168 58
Crownthorpe	LOC	15	W12	39 34	176 34
Croydon	LOC	26	E25	46 03	168 55
Croydon Bush	LOC	26	E25	46 05	168 52
Cuba Channel	CHAN	4	—	43 50	176 53 W
Culverden	TOWN	18, 23	N18	42 46	172 51
Cunaris Sound	SND	26	A24	45 58	166 42
Current Basin	BASN	14, 19	Q14	40 58	173 48
Curtis Island	ISLD	4	—	30 33	178 34 W
Cust	TOWN	23	M19	43 19	172 22
Cuvier Island	ISLD	7	U5	36 26	175 46
Dacre	LOC	26	E25	46 20	168 37
Dagg Sound	SND	26	A23	45 23	166 43
Dairy Flat	LOC	7, 10	S6	36 40	174 38
Dalefield	LOC	15, 19	T15	41 02	175 29
Dallington	SBRB	32	C2	43 31	172 40
Dalmore	SBRB	33	B3	45 51	170 31
Dampier Range	MTNS	18, 23	M18	42 52	172 12
Dampier Ridge	SEAF	81	—	32 45	158 00
Daniells	LAKE	18, 23	M17	42 18	172 17
Dannevirke	BORO	15	V13	40 12	176 06
Dansey Pass	PASS	22, 27	H22	44 57	170 22
Dansey Pass	LOC	23, 27	H22	44 59	170 30
D'Archiac, Mount	MT	23	J19	43 28	170 35
D'Arcy Point	PNT	4	—	29 18	177 55 W
Darfield	TOWN	23	M19	43 29	172 07
Dargaville	BORO	6	Q4	35 56	173 52
Dark Cloud Range	MTNS	26	A24	45 52	166 50
Darran Mountains	MTNS	22, 26	D22	44 39	168 01
Dart River	STRM	22, 26	D22	44 51	168 22
Dashwood	LOC	14, 19	R16	41 38	174 04
Dayrell Island	ISLD	4	—	29 15	177 51 W
Days Bay	SBRB	35	B7	41 17	174 54
De La Bêche, Mount	PEAK	22	H19	43 26	170 16
Deborah	LOC	39	C3	45 07	170 56
Deborah Bay	BAY	33	C2	45 48	170 38
Deborah Bay	LOC	27	J24	45 48	170 38
Deep Cove	BAY	26	B23	45 28	167 09
Deep Creek	LOC	23	K22	44 42	171 04
Deep Creek	STRM	27	J23	45 03	170 30
Deep Inlet	BAY	4	—	50 45	166 12
Deep Stream	STRM	27	H24	45 42	170 18
Deepdale Creek	STRM	18	M16	41 46	172 09
Delaware Bay	BAY	14, 18	P15	41 10	173 27
Denham Bay	BAY	4	—	29 16	177 57 W
Dent Island	ISLD	4	—	52 32	169 02
Devil River Peak	PEAK	18	N14	40 58	172 39
Devonport	SBRB	30	B4	36 50	174 48
Diamond Harbour	LOC	32	C4	43 37	172 44
Diamond Lake	LAKE	22, 26	D22	44 44	168 23
Dick, Mount	MTN	4	—	50 47	166 03
Diggers Valley	LOC	6	P3	35 11	173 19
Diggins	HILL	34	C3	41 02	174 55
Dillmanstown	LOC	18, 23	K18	42 39	171 12

NAME	DESC	PAGE	REF	LAT S	LONG E
Dillon Cone	PEAK	18	P17	42 16	173 13
Dillons River	STRM	18	P17	42 24	173 05
Dillons Point	LOC	14, 19	R16	41 31	174 01
Dingle Burn	STRM	22	F21	44 25	169 23
Dingwall Mountains	MTNS	26	B24	45 34	167 07
Dinsdale	SBRB	37	C2	37 48	175 15
Dipton	TOWN	26	D24	45 54	168 22
Dipton Stream	STRM	26	D25	46 01	168 19
Dipton West	LOC	26	D25	45 54	168 21
Disappointment Island	ISLD	4	—	50 36	165 59
Division Hill	HILL	39	C2	45 02	170 55
Dobson	LOC	40	B2	42 27	171 19
Dobson River	STRM	22	G21	44 05	169 52
Doctors Creek	STRM	39	B4	41 31	173 56
Dog Island	ISLD	26	D26	46 39	168 25
Dome Burn	STRM	26	E24	45 44	168 50
Dome Valley	LOC	7	S5	36 22	174 37
Domett	LOC	18	P18	42 52	173 13
Domett, Mount	MTN	18	M15	41 04	172 19
Donald, Mount	MT	26	B23	45 04	167 27
Donnellys Crossing	LOC	6	Q4	35 43	173 37
Dorie	LOC	23	H20	43 53	172 05
Dorset, Point	PNT	35	B8	41 20	174 50
Doubtful Island	ISLD	26	C23	45 12	167 42
Doubtful Sound	SND	26	A23	45 16	166 52
Doubtful Sound	LOC	26	B23	45 28	167 10
Doubtless Bay	BAY	6	P2	34 56	173 27
Dougall Rocks	ROCK	4	—	29 18	177 54 W
Doughboy Bay	BAY	26	C27	47 02	167 40
Douglas	LOC	14	R11	39 18	174 28
Douglas	LOC	23, 27	J22	44 47	170 52
Douglas Peak	PEAK	22	H20	43 32	170 12
Dove River	STRM	14, 18	N15	41 16	172 50
Dovedale	LOC	14, 18	N15	41 18	172 55
Dowling Bay	BAY	33	D2	45 47	170 40
Doyleston	TOWN	23	M20	43 45	172 19
Dreyers Rock	LOC	15, 19	U14	40 46	175 46
Dromore	LOC	23	L20	43 51	171 51
Drummond	LOC	26	D25	46 11	168 09
Drury	TOWN	10	S7	37 06	174 57
Duders Beach	LOC	7, 10	T6	36 54	175 04
Dumas, Mount	MT	4	—	52 34	169 04
Dumbarton	LOC	27	F24	45 35	169 20
Dun Fiunary	MTN	22	H20	43 57	170 02
Dunback	LOC	27	J23	45 23	170 38
Dundas Island	ISLD	4	—	50 35	166 19
Dunearn	LOC	26	D25	46 01	168 10
Dunedin	CITY	27	J24	45 53	170 31
Dunedin	CITY	33	Urb	45 53	170 31
Dunollie	SBRB	40	B1	42 24	171 15
Dunrobin	LOC	27	F24	45 48	169 20
Dunsandel	TOWN	23	M20	43 40	172 12
Dunstan Creek	STRM	22, 27	G22	44 59	169 46
Dunstan Mountains	MTNS	22, 27	G22	44 56	169 31
Dunton Range	MTNS	26	C23	45 12	167 56
Duntroon	LOC	23, 27	J22	44 51	170 41
Durham Point	PNT	4	—	44 01	176 40 W
Durie Hill	SBRB	36	D2	39 56	175 04
D'Urville Island	ISLD	14, 19	Q14	40 50	173 51
D'Urville, Mount	MTN	4	—	50 49	166 10
D'Urville River	STRM	18	N16	41 54	172 39
Dusky Forest	LOC	27	F24	45 50	169 09
Dusky Sound	SND	26	A24	45 46	166 31
Duvauchelle	LOC	23	N20	43 45	172 56
Dyerville	LOC	14, 19	T15	41 15	175 24
Ealing	LOC	22	K21	44 03	171 25
Earl Mountains	MTNS	26	C23	45 02	167 58
Earnscleugh	LOC	27	F23	45 13	169 19
Earnslaw, Mount	PEAK	22, 26	D22	44 37	168 25
East Bay	BAY	14, 19	R15	41 09	174 20
East Cape	CAPE	26	D27	47 01	168 14
East Cape	CAPE	11	Z8	37 41	178 33
East Cape Ridge	SEAF	81	—	37 20	179 40
East Chatton	LOC	26	E24	45 59	168 58
East Clive	LOC	15	W12	39 35	176 56
East Coast Bays	BORO	30	B2	36 40	174 45
East End	SBRB	40	D4	46 36	168 21
East End	SBRB	37	A1	39 03	174 05
East Island	ISLD	11	Z8	37 42	178 35
East Taieri	LOC	33	A3	45 54	170 21
East Takaka	LOC	14, 18	N14	40 55	172 50
East Tamaki	LOC	31	C6	36 57	174 53
Eastbourne	BORO	35	B8	41 17	174 54
Eastern Beach	LOC	31	D5	36 52	174 55
Eastern Bush	LOC	26	C24	45 59	167 46
Eastern Group	ISLS	4	—	47 41	179 06
Easton, Mount	MTN	4	—	50 38	166 07
Easy Harbour	HARB	26	C27	47 10	167 34
Echolands	LOC	10	T10	38 52	175 20
Eden, Mount	MT	4	—	50 35	166 11
Edendale	TOWN	26	E25	46 19	168 47
Edgecumbe	TOWN	11	W8	37 58	176 50
Edievale	LOC	27	F24	45 47	169 22
Edwards Pass	PASS	18, 23	N17	42 25	172 46
Edwards Stream	STRM	23	H21	44 12	170 30
Edwardson Sound	SND	26	A24	45 55	166 40
Egeria Rock	ROCK	4	—	29 15	177 53 W
Eglinton River	STRM	26	C23	45 10	167 50
Egmont, Cape	CAPE	14	Q11	39 17	173 45
Egmont, Mount	MTN	14	R11	39 18	174 04
Egmont Village	TOWN	37	B2	39 09	174 09
Eiffelton	LOC	22	L21	44 02	171 41
Eight Mile Junction	LOC	10	T9	38 25	175 06
88 Valley	LOC	14, 18	P15	41 27	173 00
Eketahuna	BORO	15, 19	U14	40 39	175 44
Elderslie	LOC	23, 27	J23	45 01	170 50
Elephant Hill	LOC	23, 27	J22	44 49	170 50
Elephant Hill Stream	STRM	23, 27	J22	44 51	170 51
Elgin	LOC	23	L20	43 57	171 48
Elie de Beaumont	MT	22	H19	43 29	170 20
Elizabeth, Point	PNT	18, 23	K17	42 23	171 06
Ellerslie	BORO	31	C5	36 54	174 49
Ellery, Lake	LAKE	22	E21	44 03	168 39
Ellesmere	LOC	23	M20	43 40	172 20
Ellesmere, Lake	LAKE	23	M20	43 47	172 28
Elsdon	SBRB	35	B5	41 08	174 50
Elsthorpe	LOC	15	W12	39 55	176 49
Elstow	LOC	10	U8	37 31	175 38
Elterwater, Lake	LAKE	19	R16	41 48	174 09
Eltham	BORO	14	R11	39 26	174 18
Emerald Basin	SEAF	81	—	53 00	163 00
Emma, Lake	LAKE	23	K20	43 36	171 06
Endeavour Inlet	LOC	14, 19	R15	41 05	174 11
Endeavour Rise	SEAF	81	—	53 30	176 50
Enderby, Island	ISLD	4	—	50 30	166 17
Enderley	SBRB	37	D1	37 46	175 18
Enfield	LOC	23, 27	J23	45 03	170 52
Enner Glynn	SBRB	39	B2	41 18	173 15
Enys, Mount	MTN	22	L19	43 14	171 38
Epsom	SBRB	31	B5	36 53	174 46
Epuni	SBRB	35	C6	41 13	174 56
Epworth	LOC	23	K21	44 15	171 16
Erebus Point	PNT	4	—	52 34	169 14

NAME	DESC	PAGE	REF	LAT S	LONG E
Erebus, Mount	MT	23	J20	43 39	170 32
Erehwon	LOC	15	U12	39 31	175 58
Ernest Islands	ISLS	26	C26	46 57	167 41
Erskine, Lake	LAKE	22, 26	C22	44 50	167 59
Erua	LOC	14	T11	39 14	175 24
Esk River	STRM	18, 23	L19	43 06	171 57
Esk River	STRM	38	D1	39 24	176 53
Esk Valley	LOC	23	K21	44 30	171 05
Eskdale	LOC	15	W11	39 24	176 50
Ethelton	LOC	18, 23	P18	42 53	173 04
Ettrick	LOC	27	F24	45 38	169 22
Eureka	LOC	10	T8	37 44	175 25
Evans Bay	BAY	35	A8	41 19	174 48
Evans Creek	LOC	23	J19	43 05	170 36
Evans Flat	LOC	27	G24	45 54	169 38
Evans, Mount	MTN	14, 18	N14	40 57	172 55
Evans, Mount	MTN	32	D4	43 39	172 47
Evansdale	LOC	27	J24	45 43	170 34
Ewe Burn	STRM	27	H23	45 13	170 07
Ewe Range	MTNS	22	G22	44 36	169 55
Ewing Island	ISLD	4	—	50 31	166 17
Eyre Creek	STRM	26	E24	45 32	168 34
Eyre Mountains	MTNS	26	D23	45 20	168 20
Eyre River	STRM	23	N19	43 24	172 40
Eyre River Diversion	STRM	32	A1	43 25	172 31
Eyreton	LOC	23	N19	43 25	172 33
Eyrewell State Forest	LOC	23	M19	43 24	172 17
Fairburn	LOC	6	P3	35 06	173 24
Fairdown	LOC	18	L16	41 44	171 42
Fairfax	LOC	26	D25	46 13	168 03
Fairfield	TOWN	33	A4	45 54	170 24
Fairfield	SBRB	37	D1	37 46	175 17
Fairfield	LOC	39	D1	43 52	171 48
Fairhall	LOC	14, 19	Q16	41 32	173 54
Fairhall River	STRM	39	A4	41 30	173 54
Fairlie	TOWN	23	J21	44 06	170 50
Fairton	LOC	23	L20	43 52	171 49
Fairview	LOC	40	A4	44 25	171 11
Fairy Springs	LOC	11	V9	38 06	176 13
Falla Peninsula	PEN	4	—	50 42	166 12
Fanal Island	ISLD	7	T4	35 57	175 08
Fancy Rock	ROCK	4	—	44 22	176 09 W
Farewell, Cape	CAPE	18	N14	40 30	172 43
Farewell Spit	SPIT	14, 18	N14	40 30	172 50
Farmer Rocks	ROCK	4	—	34 09	172 12
Farnham	SBRB	39	B4	41 30	173 56
Farr, Cape	CAPE	4	—	50 51	166 14
Favona	SBRB	31	B6	36 57	174 48
Featherston	BORO	14, 19	T15	41 07	175 19
Febrero Point	PNT	26	A23	45 16	166 50
Feilding	BORO	15	U13	40 12	175 35
Feldwick	LOC	26	C25	46 01	167 50
Fencourt	LOC	10	T8	37 51	175 29
Fendalton	SBRB	32	B2	43 32	172 35
Fendalton North	SBRB	32	B2	43 31	172 35
Fenton Park	SBRB	38	A4	38 09	176 15
Fern Flat	LOC	6	Q3	35 07	173 32
Fernbrook	SBRB	39	D3	45 04	170 59
Ferndale	SBRB	37	A2	39 06	174 04
Ferndale	LOC	26	E25	46 12	168 59
Fernhill	LOC	15	W12	39 35	176 46
Fernleigh	LOC	19	Q17	42 22	173 33
Fernridge	LOC	15, 19	U14	40 56	175 36
Fernside	LOC	23	N19	43 19	172 32
Ferntown	LOC	18	N14	40 40	172 39
Ferry Landing	LOC	7, 10	U6	36 50	175 42
Fiji Basin, South	SEAF	81	—	26 10	176 30
Finegand	LOC	27	G25	46 16	169 45
Fitzherbert West	LOC	15, 19	U13	40 23	175 37
Fitzherbert	SBRB	37	B4	40 24	175 37
Fitzroy	SBRB	37	B1	39 03	174 06
Five Fingers Peninsula	PEN	26	A24	45 41	166 30
Five Fingers Point	PNT	26	A24	45 44	166 26
Five Forks	LOC	23, 27	J23	45 03	170 46
Five Rivers	LOC	26	D24	45 38	163 28
Fizeau, Mount	MT	4	—	52 31	169 07
Flag Swamp	LOC	27	J24	45 33	170 41
Flat Bush	SBRB	31	D7	36 58	174 55
Flat Hill	HILL	40	C4	46 35	168 17
Flat Island	ISLD	6	Q2	34 59	173 52
Flat Mount	MT	26	B24	45 36	167 25
Flat Point	PNT	26	B22	44 47	167 26
Flaxbourne River	STRM	19	R16	41 51	174 11
Flaxmere	SBRB	38	B3	39 37	176 48
Flaxton	LOC	23	N19	43 21	172 37
Flea Bay	BAY	23	P20	43 52	173 00
Flemington	LOC	15	V13	40 09	176 29
Flemington	LOC	23	L21	44 01	171 44
Fly Harbour	HARB	4	—	50 55	166 08
Forbes, Mount	MT	26	A23	45 21	166 51
Forbes Mountains	MTNS	22	D22	44 34	168 27
Fordell	TOWN	14	T12	39 57	175 12
Fordlands	SBRB	38	A4	38 08	176 13
Forest Creek	STRM	23	J20	43 40	170 58
Forest Lake	SBRB	37	D1	37 46	175 16
Forest Range	MTNS	27	F25	46 28	169 00
Fork Stream	STRM	23	H21	44 02	170 27
Forks, The	LOC	22	H19	43 15	170 14
Forsyth Island	ISLD	14, 19	R14	40 57	174 04
Forsyth, Lake	LAKE	23	N20	43 48	172 45
Fortification	LOC	27	F26	46 31	169 00
Fortrose	LOC	26	E26	46 34	168 48
Foulwind, Cape	CAPE	18	K16	41 45	171 28
Fournier, Cape	CAPE	4	—	44 03	176 19 W
Four Peaks	LOC	23	K21	44 02	171 08
Four Rivers	LOC	18	M16	41 47	172 17
Foveaux Strait	STRA	26	D26	46 40	168 10
Fowler Pass	PASS	26	B23	45 19	167 21
Fox Glacier	LOC	22	H19	43 28	170 01
Fox Glacier	GLCR	22	H19	43 30	170 05
Fox Peak	PEAK	23	J20	43 50	170 47
Fox River	STRM	18	K17	42 02	171 23
Foxhill	LOC	14, 18	N15	41 26	172 59
Foxton	BORO	14, 19	T13	40 28	175 17
Foxton Beach	TOWN	14, 19	T13	40 28	175 14
Frankleigh Park	SBRB	37	A1	39 05	174 04
Franklin Mountains	MTNS	22, 26	C22	44 56	167 45
Frankton	LOC	22, 26	E23	45 01	168 44
Frankton	SBRB	37	C1	37 47	175 15
Franz Josef Glacier	LOC	22	H19	43 23	170 11
Franz Josef Glacier	GLCR	22	H19	43 27	170 11
Fraser, Lake	LAKE	26	A24	45 54	166 31
Fraser River	STRM	27	F23	45 14	169 22
Frasertown	TOWN	11, 15	X10	38 58	177 24
Freemans Bay	SBRB	31	B5	36 51	174 45
French Bay	SBRB	31	A6	36 57	174 40
French Farm	LOC	23	N20	43 47	172 55
French Pass	LOC	14, 19	Q14	40 55	173 50
Freshford	LOC	26	E24	45 46	168 48
Freshwater River	STRM	26	C26	46 54	167 58
Frimley	SBRB	38	C3	39 37	176 50
Fringed Hill	HILL	39	B2	41 18	173 19
Fruitlands	LOC	27	F23	45 21	169 19

NAME	DESC	PAGE	REF	LAT S	LONG E
Fuchsia Creek	LOC	27	J23	45 04	170 42
Fuschia Creek	LOC	27	J23	45 42	170 40
Gable End Foreland	HEAD	11	Z10	38 32	178 18
Gabriels Gully	LOC	27	G24	45 52	169 41
Galatea	LOC	11	W9	38 25	176 44
Galloway	LOC	27	F23	45 13	169 24
Galloway, Mount	MT	4	—	49 41	178 47
Gammack Range	MTNS	22	H20	43 45	170 18
Gammans Creek	LOC	23	M19	43 18	172 09
Gannet Island	ISLD	10	S8	37 58	174 34
Gap Point	PNT	4	—	44 04	176 39 W
Gapes Valley	LOC	23	K21	44 07	171 07
Garden of Allah	PLAT	23	J19	43 18	170 45
Garden of Eden	PLAT	23	J19	43 20	170 40
Garden Point	PNT	26	D26	46 46	168 00
Garry River	STRM	23	M19	43 22	172 16
Garston	LOC	26	E23	45 28	168 41
Garvie Mountains	MTNS	26	E23	45 30	168 50
Gate Pa	SBRB	36	A2	37 43	176 08
Gebbies Valley	LOC	23	N20	43 42	172 37
George Sound	SND	26	B22	44 50	167 21
Georgetown	LOC	23, 27	J22	44 55	170 51
Georgetown	SBRB	40	D2	46 25	168 23
Geraldine	BORO	23	K21	44 05	171 15
Geraldine Downs	LOC	23	K21	44 05	171 14
Geraldine Flat	LOC	23	K21	44 09	171 16
Gibbston	LOC	22, 26	E23	45 01	168 58
Gillespies Point	PNT	22	G19	43 24	169 50
Gilroy Head	HEAD	4	—	50 53	166 12
Gimmerburn	LOC	27	G23	45 10	170 00
Gisborne	CITY	11	Z10	38 39	178 01
Gisborne	CITY	38	Urb	38 39	178 01
Glacier Dome	MTN	22	E21	44 20	168 48
Gladfield	LOC	26	D25	46 08	168 06
Gladstone	SBRB	40	C2	46 24	168 21
Gladstone	LOC	14, 19	T14	40 40	175 20
Gladstone	LOC	15, 19	U15	41 05	175 38
Gladstone	LOC	18, 23	K18	42 32	171 10
Glasnevin	LOC	23	N19	43 06	172 42
Glen Afton	LOC	10	T8	37 36	175 02
Glen Avon	SBRB	37	B1	39 03	174 06
Glen Eden	BORO	31	A6	36 55	174 39
Glen Innes	SBRB	31	C5	36 52	174 52
Glen Massey	TOWN	10	T8	37 40	175 04
Glen Murray	LOC	10	S7	37 21	174 58
Glen Oroua	LOC	14, 19	T13	40 20	175 25
Glenary	LOC	26	E24	45 37	168 58
Glenavy	TOWN	23, 27	K22	44 55	171 06
Glenbervie	LOC	7	R4	35 40	174 21
Glenbrook	LOC	10	S7	37 12	174 45
Glenbrook Beach	LOC	10	S7	37 10	174 43
Glencoe	LOC	26	E25	46 12	168 40
Glencoe River	STRM	18, 23	N18	42 45	172 33
Glendene	SBRB	31	A5	36 53	174 39
Glendowie	SBRB	31	C5	36 51	174 52
Glenduan	LOC	14, 18	P15	41 11	173 22
Glenfalls	LOC	15	W11	39 11	176 38
Glenfield	SBRB	30	B3	36 47	174 43
Glengarry	SBRB	40	D2	46 24	168 23
Glengarry	LOC	15	V13	40 10	176 04
Glenham	LOC	26	E25	46 24	168 51
Gleniti	SBRB	40	A4	44 23	171 12
Glenkenich	LOC	27	F24	45 58	169 14
Glenledi	LOC	27	H25	46 10	170 05
Glenleith	SBRB	33	B2	45 50	170 30
Glenomaru	LOC	27	G25	46 23	169 42
Glenorchy	LOC	22, 26	D22	44 52	168 24
Glenore	LOC	27	G25	46 06	169 52
Glenpark	LOC	27	J23	45 26	170 40
Glenrae	LOC	14, 18	N15	41 22	172 49
Glenrae River	STRM	18, 23	M18	42 49	172 30
Glenross	LOC	15	V11	39 27	176 26
Glenroy	LOC	23	L20	43 31	171 50
Glenside	LOC	35	A6	41 12	174 48
Glentui	LOC	23	M19	43 14	172 17
Glentunnel	LOC	23	L19	43 29	171 56
Glenure	LOC	26	D24	45 53	168 30
Glenview	SBRB	37	D2	37 49	175 17
Glenwood	SBRB	40	B4	44 23	171 13
Glorit	LOC	7, 10	R5	36 28	174 27
Goat Island	ISLD	33	C2	45 49	170 37
Godley Glacier	GLCR	23	J19	43 29	170 32
Godley River	STRM	23	J20	43 47	170 32
Golden Bay	BAY	14, 18	N14	40 50	172 48
Golden Downs	LOC	14, 18	N16	41 33	172 53
Golden Springs	LOC	11	V9	38 28	176 18
Golden Valley	LOC	10	U7	37 22	175 54
Gonville	SBRB	36	C2	39 57	175 02
Goodwood	LOC	27	J24	45 32	170 43
Goose Bay	LOC	18	Q17	42 29	173 32
Gordon	LOC	10	U8	37 41	175 49
Gordons Valley	LOC	23	K21	44 27	171 02
Gordonton	TOWN	10	T8	37 40	175 18
Gore	BORO	26	E25	46 06	168 56
Gore Bay	LOC	18	P18	42 52	173 18
Gorge River	STRM	22	D21	44 11	168 12
Gorge Road	LOC	26	E25	46 29	168 42
Goughs Bay	BAY	23	P20	43 49	173 06
Goulds Road	LOC	23	M20	43 40	172 24
Goulter River	STRM	14, 18	P16	41 39	173 13
Governors Bay	LOC	32	C4	43 38	172 39
Gowan River	STRM	18	N16	41 43	172 34
Gracefield	SBRB	35	C7	41 14	174 55
Grahams Beach	LOC	7, 10	S7	37 03	174 40
Grampian Mountains	MTNS	23	J21	44 18	170 31
Grampians	LOC	23	H21	44 15	170 28
Granity	TOWN	18	L16	41 38	171 51
Grantlea	SBRB	40	B4	44 23	171 14
Grasmere	SBRB	40	C1	46 23	168 20
Grasmere, Lake	LAKE	23	L19	43 04	171 46
Grassington	LOC	18, 23	P18	42 43	173 04
Grassmere, Lake	LAKE	19	R16	41 43	174 ·10
Grassy Point	PNT	33	C3	45 51	170 36
Grave, Lake	LAKE	22, 26	C22	44 48	167 38
Grays Corner	LOC	23, 27	K22	44 51	171 04
Grays Stream	STRM	23	H21	44 14	170 20
Great Barrier Island	ISLD	7	T5	36 11	175 25
Great Exhibition Bay	BAY	6	P2	34 38	173 01
Great Island	ISLD	26	A24	46 00	166 34
Great Island	ISLD	4	—	34 10	172 08
Great Mercury Island	ISLD	7, 10	U6	36 37	175 48
Greatford	LOC	14	T13	40 08	175 25
Grebe River	STRM	26	B24	45 35	167 22
Green Bay	SBRB	31	A6	36 56	174 41
Green Island	BORO	33	B4	45 54	170 26
Green Island	ISLD	4	—	50 34	166 22
Green Island	ISLD	26	E26	46 47	168 34
Green Lake	LAKE	26	B24	45 48	167 23
Green Point	LOC	40	C4	46 35	168 18
Green Point	PNT	34	A5	41 07	174 48
Greendale	LOC	23	M20	43 35	172 05
Greenfield	LOC	27	G25	46 06	169 35
Greenhills	LOC	40	C3	46 33	168 18

NAME	DESC	PAGE	REF	LAT S	LONG E
Greenhithe	SBRB	30	A3	36 46	174 40
Greenland Reservoir	RESR	27	G23	45 26	169 37
Greenlane	SBRB	31	B5	36 53	174 48
Greenmeadows	SBRB	38	C2	39 32	176 51
Greenpark	LOC	23	N20	43 41	172 30
Greenpoint	LOC	40	C4	46 35	168 18
Greenstreet	LOC	23	L20	43 49	171 40
Greenvale	LOC	27	F24	45 53	169 03
Greerton	SBRB	36	A2	37 44	176 07
Grenville Point	PNT	6	P2	34 46	173 09
Greville Harbour	HARB	14, 19	Q14	40 51	173 48
Grey Lynn	SBRB	31	B5	36 52	174 44
Grey Range	MTNS	23	L19	43 06	171 34
Grey River	STRM	18, 23	K17	42 26	171 11
Greymouth	BORO	40	Urb	42 27	171 12
Greymouth	BORO	18, 23	K17	42 27	171 12
Greytown	BORO	15, 19	U15	41 05	175 28
Grono, Mount	MT	26	A23	45 16	166 57
Gropers	LOC	26	D25	46 14	168 04
Gropers Bush	LOC	26	D25	46 14	168 03
Grove Burn	LOC	26	C25	46 07	167 38
Grove Bush	LOC	26	D25	46 18	168 29
Grove, The	LOC	14, 19	Q15	41 17	173 55
Grovetown	TOWN	39	B3	41 29	173 58
Guards Bay	BAY	14, 19	R14	41 00	174 08
Gulches Head	HEAD	26	A25	46 05	166 34
Gummies Bush	LOC	26	D25	46 17	168 01
Gumtown	LOC	6	R4	35 42	174 12
Gunn, Lake	LAKE	22, 26	D22	44 52	168 06
Guthrie	LOC	10	V9	38 17	176 09
Guyon, Lake	LAKE	18	N17	42 17	172 39
Gwavas	LOC	15	V12	39 47	176 29
Haast	LOC	22	F20	43 52	169 01
Haast, Mount	MTN	18, 23	M17	42 19	172 05
Haast Pass	PASS	22	F21	44 06	169 21
Haast Range	MTNS	22	E21	44 09	168 45
Haast River	STRM	22	F20	43 50	169 02
Hackthorne	LOC	23	L20	43 49	171 34
Hadlow	LOC	40	A4	44 22	171 10
Hahei	LOC	7, 10	U6	36 50	175 22
Hairini	LOC	10	T9	38 02	175 22
Hairini	SBRB	36	A2	37 44	176 10
Hakapoua, Lake	LAKE	26	A25	46 10	166 57
Hakaru	LOC	7	S5	36 08	174 30
Hakataramea	LOC	23, 27	H22	44 44	170 29
Hakataramea River	STRM	23, 27	H22	44 44	170 29
Hakataramea Station	LOC	23, 27	J22	44 36	170 35
Hakatere	LOC	23	L21	44 03	171 48
Halcombe	TOWN	15	T13	40 08	175 29
Haldane	LOC	27	F26	46 38	169 01
Halfmoon Bay	TOWN	26	D26	46 54	168 08
Halfway Bluff	CLIF	22	D21	44 03	168 19
Halfway Bush	SBRB	33	B3	45 51	170 28
Halkett	LOC	23	M19	43 30	172 19
Hall Range	MTNS	23	H20	43 41	170 26
Halswell	LOC	32	A3	43 35	172 34
Halswell, Point	PNT	35	B7	41 17	174 50
Halswell River	STRM	32	A4	43 37	172 34
Hamama	LOC	14, 18	N14	40 55	172 48
Hamilton	CITY	10	T8	37 47	175 17
Hamilton	CITY	37	Urb	37 47	175 17
Hamilton Burn	LOC	26	D24	45 44	168 11
Hamilton East	SBRB	37	D2	37 47	175 18
Hamilton, Lake	LAKE	37	D2	37 48	175 16
Hamilton, Mount	MT	26	D24	45 37	168 01
Hamilton North	SBRB	37	D1	37 47	175 17
Hamilton West	SBRB	37	D1	37 48	175 17
Hampden	BORO	27	J23	45 20	170 49
Hampstead	SBRB	39	D2	43 55	171 45
Hamua	LOC	15, 19	U14	40 34	175 44
Hamurana	LOC	11	V9	38 02	176 15
Hangaroa	LOC	11	Y10	38 41	177 37
Hangaroa River	STRM	11	Y10	38 40	177 31
Hangatiki	LOC	10	T9	38 15	175 11
Hangore Bank	SBNK	31	B8	37 04	174 45
Hankinson, Lake	LAKE	26	C23	45 04	167 34
Hanmer	LOC	18, 23	N18	42 33	172 45
Hanmer River	STRM	18, 23	N18	42 35	172 47
Hanmer Springs	TOWN	18, 23	N18	42 31	172 50
Hannahs Bay	SBRB	38	B4	38 07	176 18
Hanson Bay	BAY	4	—	43 55	176 20 W
Haparapara River	STRM	11	Y8	37 47	177 39
Happy Valley	LOC	26	C25	46 09	167 45
Hapuakohe Range	MTNS	10	T7	37 23	175 23
Hapuku	LOC	19	Q17	42 20	173 44
Harakeke	LOC	14, 18	P15	41 14	173 01
Harapepe	LOC	10	T8	37 56	175 08
Harewood	LOC	32	A2	43 29	172 33
Harihari	TOWN	23	J19	43 09	170 34
Harrington Point	PNT	33	D1	45 47	170 43
Harper Pass	PASS	18, 23	L18	42 44	171 53
Harper Range	MTNS	23	K20	43 40	171 04
Harper River	STRM	23	K19	43 13	171 25
Harris Mountains	MTNS	22, 26	E22	44 46	168 48
Haruru	LOC	6	R3	35 17	174 03
Harwood	LOC	33	D2	45 49	170 40
Haskell Bay	BAY	4	—	50 35	166 15
Hastings	CITY	15	W12	39 38	176 50
Hastings	CITY	38	Urb	39 38	176 50
Hastwell	LOC	15, 19	U14	40 43	175 42
Haszard, Island	ISLD	4	—	30 14	178 25 W
Haszard, Mount	MT	4	—	30 13	178 26 W
Hatea River	STRM	36	B3	35 45	174 21
Hatepe	LOC	10	V10	38 52	176 01
Hatfield	LOC	23	L20	43 46	171 58
Hatfields Beach	LOC	7, 10	S6	36 34	174 42
Hatuma	LOC	15	V13	40 02	176 30
Hatuma, Lake	LAKE	15	W13	40 01	176 31
Hauhungaroa Range	MTNS	10	U10	38 42	175 33
Hauiti	LOC	11	Z9	38 23	178 18
Haumoana	TOWN	38	D3	39 36	176 57
Haunui	LOC	15, 19	V14	40 37	176 03
Haupiri	LOC	18, 23	L18	42 34	171 49
Haupiri, Lake	LAKE	18, 23	L18	42 34	171 43
Hauraki Gulf	GULF	7, 10	T6	36 33	175 05
Hauraki Plains	PLN	10	U7	37 23	175 32
Hauroko, Lake	LAKE	26	B24	45 57	167 18
Hautapu	LOC	10	T8	37 51	175 27
Hautapu River	STRM	15	U12	39 45	175 50
Hautapu Stream	STRM	11	W11	39 01	176 49
Hautere	LOC	14, 19	T14	40 48	175 10
Hautotara	LOC	15, 19	T15	41 18	175 28
Hautu	LOC	10, 14	U10	39 00	175 50
Hauturu	LOC	10	S9	38 06	174 56
Hauwai	LOC	19	R16	41 45	174 09
Havelock	TOWN	14, 19	Q15	41 17	173 46
Havelock North	BORO	38	D4	39 40	176 53
Havelock River	STRM	23	J20	43 31	170 50
Havre Trough	SEAF	81	—	27 10	178 25 W
Hawarden	TOWN	18, 23	N18	42 56	172 39
Hawea Flat	LOC	22, 27	F22	44 39	169 18
Hawea, Lake	LAKE	22	F21	44 27	169 18
Hawera	BORO	14	R12	39 35	174 17

NAME	DESC	PAGE	REF	LAT S	LONG E
Hawes Head	HEAD	26	B23	45 03	167 03
Hawkdun Range	MTNS	22, 27	G22	44 49	170 00
Hawke Bay	BAY	15	X11	39 25	177 20
Hawkins	LOC	23	M19	43 29	172 03
Hawkins Hill	HILL	35	A8	41 19	174 44
Hawkins River	STRM	23	M20	43 37	172 08
Hawkswood	LOC	18	P18	42 39	173 20
Hawthorndale	SBRB	40	D2	46 25	168 23
Hayes, Lake	LAKE	22, 26	E22	44 59	168 49
Haywards	SBRB	35	C5	41 09	174 59
Hazelburgh Group	ISLS	26	D26	46 51	168 29
Hazelburn	LOC	23	J21	44 13	170 59
Head of the Bay	BAY	32	C4	43 39	172 40
Heao	LOC	10	S10	38 58	174 58
Heao Stream	STRM	14	S11	39 11	174 52
Heaphy Bluff	CLIF	18	M14	40 58	172 08
Heaphy River	STRM	18	M14	40 59	172 08
Heaphy Shoal	SHL	4	—	43 58	176 37 W
Heath Mountains	MTNS	26	B24	45 43	167 05
Heathcote River Estuary	ESTY	32	C3	43 33	172 44
Heathcote Valley	SBRB	32	C3	43 35	172 43
Heatherlea	LOC	14, 19	T14	40 35	175 18
Heaton Park	LOC	14	T13	40 06	175 14
Hector	TOWN	18	L16	41 36	171 54
Hector, Mount	MTN	14, 19	T14	40 57	175 17
Hector Mountains	MTNS	26	E23	45 22	168 47
Heddon Bush	LOC	26	D25	46 05	168 09
Hedgehope	LOC	26	E25	46 13	168 32
Hedgehope Stream	STRM	26	E25	46 15	168 31
Hei Hei	SBRB	32	A3	43 32	172 31
Heidelberg	SBRB	40	D2	46 26	168 23
Helena Bay	BAY	7	R3	35 26	174 22
Helensbrook	LOC	27	G25	46 06	169 59
Helensburgh	SBRB	33	B3	45 51	170 28
Helensville	BORO	7, 10	R6	36 40	174 27
Helvetia	LOC	10	S7	37 11	174 52
Hen and Chickens	ISLS	7	S4	35 56	174 44
Henderson	BORO	31	A5	36 53	174 38
Henderson Creek	STRM	31	A5	36 50	174 39
Henderson Valley	LOC	7, 10	S6	36 54	174 36
Henley	LOC	27	H24	45 59	170 10
Henui Stream	STRM	37	A1	39 03	174 05
Hepburn Creek	LOC	7, 10	S5	36 26	174 41
Herald Island	LOC	30	A3	36 47	174 39
Herbert	TOWN	27	J23	45 13	170 46
Herbert Peak	PEAK	23	N20	43 41	172 44
Herbertville	LOC	15	W13	40 29	176 33
Hereheretau	LOC	11, 15	Y10	38 59	177 36
Herekino	TOWN	6	P3	35 16	173 13
Herekino Harbour	HARB	6	P3	35 17	173 10
Heretaniwha Point	PNT	22	G20	43 35	169 33
Heretaunga	LOC	35	C5	41 08	175 02
Heriot	TOWN	27	F24	45 51	169 16
Hermitage, The	LOC	22	H20	43 44	170 07
Herne Bay	SBRB	31	B5	36 51	174 44
Heron, Lake	LAKE	23	K19	43 28	171 11
Herries, Lake	LAKE	26	B23	45 22	167 22
Hexton	TOWN	11	Y10	38 37	177 59
Heyward Point	PNT	33	D1	45 45	170 41
Hicks Bay	LOC	11	Z8	37 35	178 18
High Island	ISLD	4	—	48 01	166 36
High Misty	HILL	35	D6	41 12	175 05
Highbank	LOC	23	L20	43 37	171 45
Highbank Power Station	LOC	23	L20	43 35	171 45
Highbury	SBRB	35	A8	41 18	174 45
Highbury	SBRB	30	B4	36 49	174 44
Highfield	SBRB	40	B4	44 23	171 13
Hihitahi	LOC	14	U12	39 34	175 42
Hikawera	LOC	15, 19	U15	41 16	175 36
Hikihiki Bank	MBNK	31	C8	37 03	174 49
Hikuai	LOC	10	U7	37 04	175 46
Hikumutu	LOC	10, 14	T10	38 57	175 18
Hikurangi	TOWN	7	R4	35 36	174 17
Hikurangi	MTN	11	Z8	37 55	178 04
Hikurangi Trench	SEAF	81	—	41 25	177 40
Hikutaia	TOWN	10	U7	37 17	175 39
Hikuwai	LOC	11	Z9	38 10	178 15
Hikuwai River	STRM	11	Z9	38 18	178 15
Hilda, Lake	LAKE	26	B23	45 16	167 23
Hilderthorpe	LOC	23, 27	K22	45 00	171 03
Hillcrest	SBRB	30	B4	36 47	174 44
Hillcrest	SBRB	37	D2	37 48	175 19
Hillcrest	SBRB	38	A4	38 09	176 14
Hillend	LOC	27	G25	46 08	169 44
Hillersden	LOC	14, 18	P16	41 36	173 26
Hillsborough	LOC	37	B1	39 04	174 09
Hillsborough	SBRB	31	B6	36 56	174 45
Hillsborough	SBRB	32	C3	43 34	172 40
Hilton	LOC	23	K21	44 09	171 10
Himatangi	LOC	14, 19	T13	40 24	175 19
Himatangi Beach	BCH	14, 19	T13	40 23	175 14
Hinahina	LOC	27	G25	46 30	169 41
Hinakura	LOC	15, 19	U15	41 17	175 39
Hinau	LOC	15	U12	39 53	175 50
Hindon	LOC	27	H24	45 44	170 18
Hinds	TOWN	23	L20	44 00	171 34
Hinds River	STRM	23	L21	44 07	171 39
Hinehopu	LOC	11	V9	38 02	176 29
Hinemaiaia Stream	STRM	10	V10	38 51	176 01
Hinemoa	LOC	15, 19	U14	40 36	175 53
Hinemoa Point	PNT	38	B4	38 07	176 17
Hinemoa Seamount	SEAF	81	—	36 15	176 05 W
Hinerua	LOC	15	V12	39 52	176 14
Hinuera	LOC	10	U8	37 53	175 46
Hira	LOC	14, 18	P15	41 13	173 24
Hiruharama	LOC	11	Z8	37 56	178 15
Hiwera	LOC	15	U12	39 39	175 55
Hiwinui	LOC	15	U13	40 16	175 42
Hoanga	LOC	6	Q4	35 54	173 54
Hobson, Mount	MTN	7	T5	36 11	175 24
Hobsonville	LOC	30	A4	36 48	174 39
Hochstetter, Lake	LAKE	18, 23	L17	42 27	171 40
Hodderville	LOC	10	U9	38 07	175 44
Hoeotainui	LOC	10	T8	37 31	175 25
Hohonu	LOC	18, 23	K18	42 41	171 16
Hokianga Harbour	HARB	6	P4	35 32	173 22
Hokio Beach	LOC	14, 19	T14	40 35	175 11
Hokitika	BORO	18, 23	J18	42 43	170 58
Hokitika River	STRM	18, 23	J18	42 43	170 57
Hokonui	LOC	26	D25	46 08	168 29
Hokonui Hills	HILL	26	E24	45 57	168 33
Hokowhitu	SBRB	37	B4	40 22	175 38
Holdens Bay	SBRB	38	B4	38 07	176 18
Hollyford River	STRM	22	D21	44 21	168 00
Homai	SBRB	31	C7	37 01	174 53
Home, Cape	CAPE	7	R3	35 22	174 23
Home Point	PNT	7	R3	35 19	174 23
Homebush	LOC	23	L19	43 29	172 00
Homebush	LOC	15, 19	U14	40 58	175 40
Homer Tunnel	TUNL	22, 26	C22	44 46	167 58
Homewood	LOC	15, 19	U15	41 12	175 59
Honey, Mount	MT	4	—	52 34	169 08
Hongoeka Bay	BAY	34	B4	41 04	174 51
Honikiwi	LOC	10	T9	38 09	175 07
Hook	LOC	23, 27	K22	44 41	171 08
Hook Bush	LOC	23, 27	J22	44 39	170 59
Hook River	STRM	27	K22	44 41	171 09
Hooker Glacier	GLCR	22	H20	43 40	170 07
Hooker, Mount	MT	22	G20	43 50	169 40
Hoon Hay	SBRB	32	B3	43 34	172 36
Hoon Hay Valley	LOC	23	N20	34 35	172 36
Hooper Point	PNT	6	N1	34 25	172 52
Hoopers Inlet	BAY	33	D3	45 52	170 40
Hope	LOC	14, 18	P15	41 21	173 09
Hope Pass	PASS	18, 23	M18	42 37	172 06
Hope River	STRM	18	N16	41 42	172 37
Hope River	STRM	18, 23	N18	42 36	172 33
Hope River	STRM	22	D21	44 05	168 19
Hope Saddle	SAD	18	N16	41 38	172 43
Hopelands	LOC	15	U13	40 21	175 57
Hopes Creek	STRM	27	G23	45 15	169 30
Hopkins, Mount	MT	22	G20	43 47	169 58
Hopkins River	STRM	22	G21	44 10	169 51
Hopuhopu	LOC	10	T8	37 38	175 10
Horahia	LOC	10	U7	37 16	175 31
Horahora	LOC	10	U8	37 59	175 38
Horahora	SBRB	36	A3	35 44	174 18
Horeke	LOC	6	Q3	35 22	173 35
Horn Rock	ROCK	7	T5	36 15	175 11
Hornby	SBRB	32	A3	43 33	172 32
Horns, The	MT	4	—	44 06	176 08 W
Horoeka	LOC	15, 19	V13	40 26	176 13
Horoera	LOC	11	Z8	37 39	178 29
Horohoro	LOC	10	V9	38 15	176 10
Horokino	LOC	10	T9	38 28	175 28
Horokiri Valley	LOC	14, 19	S15	41 04	174 56
Horokiwi Stream	STRM	34	B4	41 06	174 54
Horomanga Stream	STRM	11	W9	38 22	176 45
Horopito	LOC	14	T11	39 21	175 23
Hororata	TOWN	23	L20	43 32	171 58
Hororata Stream	STRM	23	M20	43 36	172 05
Horotiu	TOWN	10	T8	37 42	175 11
Horoweka Stream	STRM	38	B1	38 34	178 01
Horowhenua, Lake	LAKE	14, 19	T14	40 37	175 15
Horrelville	LOC	23	M19	43 20	172 20
Horse Range	MTNS	27	J23	45 17	170 33
Horsham Downs	LOC	10	T8	37 42	175 15
Horsley Downs	LOC	18, 23	N18	42 53	172 38
Hospital Hill	SBRB	38	D2	39 29	176 54
Hoteo North	LOC	7	R5	36 19	174 29
Hoteo River	STRM	7	R5	36 26	174 26
Houhora	LOC	6	P2	34 47	173 06
Houhora Harbour	HARB	6	P2	34 48	173 08
Houhou	LOC	18, 23	J18	42 43	171 00
Houto	LOC	6	Q4	35 45	173 59
Howard Rock	ROCK	4	—	29 16	177 52 W
Howells Point	PNT	26	D25	46 23	168 02
Howick	BORO	31	D5	36 54	174 56
Huanui	LOC	11	Z9	38 18	178 01
Huapai	LOC	7, 10	S6	36 47	174 31
Huarau	LOC	7	R5	36 07	174 17
Huatoki Stream	STRM	37	A1	39 03	174 04
Huia	LOC	7, 10	S6	37 00	174 34
Huiakama	LOC	14	S11	39 15	174 35
Huiarau Range	MTNS	11	X10	38 35	177 08
Huiarua	LOC	11	Z9	38 05	178 03
Huinga	LOC	14	R11	39 22	174 27
Huirangi	LOC	10, 14	R11	39 03	174 15
Huiroa	LOC	14	R11	39 15	174 28
Hukanui	LOC	15, 19	U14	40 34	175 40
Hukanui Pa	LOC	10	T8	37 41	175 19
Hukarere	LOC	18	L17	42 15	171 43
Hukatere	LOC	6	R5	36 11	174 10
Hukerenui	LOC	6	R4	35 32	174 12
Humboldt Mountains	MTNS	22, 26	D22	44 40	168 14
Hummock	HILL	27	H24	45 33	170 23
Hump Ridge	MTNS	26	B25	46 12	167 19
Hump, The	MTN	26	B25	46 07	167 20
Humphreys	LOC	18, 23	K18	42 44	171 06
Humuhumu, Lake	LAKE	6	R4	36 20	174 07
Hundalee	LOC	18	P18	42 36	173 25
Hungahunga	LOC	10	U8	37 41	175 44
Hunter	LOC	23, 27	K22	44 37	171 02
Hunter Mountains	MTNS	26	B24	45 40	167 22
Hunter River	STRM	22	F21	44 16	169 27
Hunters Hills, The	HILLS	23	J21	44 25	170 49
Hunterville	TOWN	15	U12	39 56	175 34
Huntingdon	LOC	23	L20	43 59	171 44
Huntly	BORO	10	T8	37 33	175 10
Huntsbury	SBRB	32	C3	43 34	172 39
Hunua	LOC	10	T7	37 05	175 04
Hupara	LOC	6	Q3	35 22	174 00
Huramua	LOC	11, 15	X11	39 01	177 23
Huro, Lake	LAKE	4	—	43 36	176 29 W
Hurleyville	LOC	14	S12	39 38	174 29
Hurunui	LOC	18, 23	N18	42 53	172 45
Hurunui Mouth	LOC	18	P18	42 55	173 16
Hurunui River	STRM	18	P18	42 54	173 18
Hurunui River S. Br.	STRM	18, 23	M18	42 50	172 22
Hurworth	LOC	10, 14	R11	39 08	174 05
Hutchinson Bluff	CLIF	4	—	29 14	178 01 W
Hutt, Port	HARB	4	—	43 48	176 42 W
Hutt, Mount	MTN	23	L19	43 28	171 32
Hutt River	STRM	35	B7	41 14	174 54
Huxley, Mount	MT	22	G21	44 04	169 41
Hyde	TOWN	27	H23	45 18	170 15
Ianthe, Lake	LAKE	23	J19	43 03	170 37
Ida	STRM	22, 27	G23	45 03	169 43
Ida, Mount	MT	22, 27	H22	44 56	170 05
Ida Valley	LOC	22, 27	G23	45 02	169 50
Ihakara	LOC	14, 19	T14	40 36	175 20
Ihungia	LOC	11	Z9	38 03	178 10
Ihuraua	LOC	15, 19	U14	40 44	175 48
Ikamatua	LOC	18	L17	42 17	171 42
Ikawai	LOC	23, 27	J22	44 52	170 52
Ikawhenua Range	MTNS	11	W9	38 14	176 55
Ikitara	HILL	36	D2	39 56	175 06
Ilam	SBRB	32	B2	43 31	172 34
Inaha	LOC	14	R12	39 34	174 10
Inangahua Junction	LOC	18	L16	41 52	171 56
Inangahua River	STRM	18	L16	41 51	171 57
Inchbonnie	LOC	18, 23	K18	42 44	171 28
Incholme	LOC	27	J23	45 09	170 46
Indian Island	ISLD	26	A24	45 47	166 35
Inglewood	BORO	37	C2	39 09	174 12
Inland Kaikoura Range	MTNS	19	Q17	42 03	173 35
Innes, Lake	LAKE	26	A25	46 11	166 58
Invercargill	CITY	26	D25	46 25	168 21
Invercargill	CITY	40	Urb	46 25	168 21
Irene, Mount	MT	26	B23	45 10	167 21
Irene River	STRM	26	B23	45 06	167 13
Irthing Stream	STRM	26	D24	45 40	168 25
Irwell	LOC	23	M20	43 43	172 20
Isla Bank	LOC	26	D25	46 12	168 08
Island Bay	SBRB	35	A8	41 20	174 46
Island Bay	BAY	30	A4	36 49	174 41
Island Block	LOC	10	T7	37 19	175 08

NAME	DESC	PAGE	REF	LAT S	LONG E
Island Block	LOC	27	F24	45 45	169 28
Island Reef	REEF	4	—	43 50	176 43 W
Islands, Bay of	BAY	6	R3	35 12	174 10
Islet Point	PNT	26	B23	45 01	167 05
Islington	SBRB	39	B4	41 31	173 58
Islington	SBRB	32	A3	43 33	172 30
Iwitahi	LOC	11	V10	38 50	176 16
Jackson Bay	BAY	22	E20	43 57	168 40
Jackson Bay	LOC	22	E20	43 58	168 37
Jackson, Cape	CAPE	14, 19	R14	40 59	174 19
Jackson Head	HEAD	22	E20	43 58	168 37
Jackson, Mount	MT	27	F23	45 08	169 17
Jackson Peaks	PEAK	26	C23	45 25	167 34
Jackson River	STRM	22	E20	44 00	168 43
Jacobs River	LOC	22	G20	43 35	169 41
Jacquemart	ISLD	4	—	52 37	169 06
James Peak	PEAK	26	E23	45 15	168 51
Jane Peak	PEAK	26	D23	45 20	168 19
Janefield	LOC	27	H24	45 52	170 23
Jellicoe Channel	CHAN	7	S5	36 16	174 56
Jenny Reef	REEF	4	—	44 00	176 41 W
Jerningham, Point	PNT	35	A7	41 17	174 48
Jerry River	STRM	22	D21	44 11	168 15
Jerusalem	LOC	14	T14	39 34	175 05
Jervoistown	SBRB	38	C2	39 32	176 52
Jewell, Lake	LAKE	13	M15	41 09	172 23
Johnsonville	SBRB	35	A6	41 13	174 47
Jollie River	STRM	22	H20	43 52	170 10
Jollies Pass	PASS	18, 23	N17	42 29	172 53
Josephville	LOC	26	D24	45 48	168 24
Jowett, Mount	MTN	36	D1	39 53	175 04
Judea	SBRB	36	A1	37 42	176 08
Judgeford	LOC	35	C5	41 07	174 56
Junction Hill	HILL	22	D21	44 14	168 20
Kaeaea	LOC	10	T10	38 37	175 01
Kaeo	TOWN	6	Q3	35 06	173 47
Kaharoa	LOC	11	V8	37 59	176 14
Kaharoa Range	HILL	14	S12	39 35	174 36
Kaherekoau Mountains	MTNS	26	B24	45 53	167 20
Kahoe	LOC	6	Q3	35 03	173 41
Kahuitara Point	PNT	4	—	44 17	176 10 W
Kahungungu	LOC	11, 15	X11	39 02	177 06
Kahuranaki	HILL	15	W12	39 48	176 51
Kahurangi Point	PNT	18	M14	40 46	172 13
Kahutara	LOC	14, 19	T15	41 15	175 20
Kahutara River	STRM	18	Q17	42 26	173 35
Kahuterawa Stream	STRM	37	A4	40 24	175 35
Kai Iwi	TOWN	14	S12	39 51	174 56
Kaiaka	LOC	6	P3	35 07	173 27
Kaiapoi	BORO	32	C1	43 23	172 39
Kaiata	LOC	40	B2	42 28	171 15
Kaiata Range	MTNS	40	B2	42 30	171 18
Kaiatea	LOC	7	R4	35 37	174 26
Kaiaua	LOC	10	T7	37 06	175 18
Kaihere	LOC	10	T7	37 22	175 26
Kaihiku	LOC	27	G25	46 14	169 33
Kaihinu	LOC	18, 23	K18	42 41	171 00
Kaihu	TOWN	6	Q4	35 46	173 42
Kaihu River	STRM	6	Q4	35 57	173 52
Kaikohe	BORO	6	Q3	35 24	173 48
Kaikorai	SBRB	33	B3	45 52	170 29
Kaikorai Lagoon	LAGN	33	A4	45 55	170 23
Kaikou	LOC	6	Q4	35 35	173 58
Kaikou River	STRM	6	R4	35 42	174 02
Kaikoura	TOWN	19	Q17	42 25	173 41
Kaikoura Island	ISLD	7	T5	36 11	175 19
Kaikoura Peninsula	PEN	19	Q17	42 25	173 42
Kaimai	LOC	10	U8	37 50	175 58
Kaimai Range	HILL	10	U8	37 50	175 55
Kaimamaku	LOC	7	R3	35 29	174 17
Kaimanawa Mountains	MTNS	15	U11	39 15	175 55
Kaimarama	LOC	7, 10	U6	36 52	175 39
Kaimata	LOC	10, 14	R11	39 10	174 18
Kaimata	LOC	18, 23	K18	42 32	171 25
Kaimiro	LOC	14	R11	39 12	174 09
Kainga	LOC	23	N19	43 26	172 39
Kaingarahu, Lake	LAKE	4	—	43 49	176 23 W
Kaingaroa	LOC	6	P3	35 02	173 19
Kaingaroa Forest	LOC	11	W9	38 23	176 37
Kaingaroa Harbour	HARB	4	—	43 44	176 15 W
Kaingaroa Plateau	PLAT	11	V9	38 27	176 30
Kainui	LOC	10	T8	37 39	175 14
Kaipaki	LOC	10	T8	37 53	175 22
Kaipara Flats	LOC	7	S5	36 24	174 33
Kaipara Harbour	HARB	6, 10	R5	36 24	174 13
Kaipara River	STRM	7, 10	R6	36 40	174 26
Kaiparoro	LOC	15, 19	U14	40 42	175 39
Kaipikari	LOC	10, 14	R11	39 02	174 24
Kaipo Stream	STRM	22	C21	44 25	167 55
Kairae, Lake	LAKE	4	—	43 51	176 23 W
Kairakau Beach	LOC	15	W12	39 56	176 56
Kairaki	LOC	32	C1	43 23	172 42
Kairanga	TOWN	15, 19	U13	40 21	175 32
Kairangi	LOC	10	U9	38 00	175 30
Kairara	LOC	6	Q4	35 48	173 49
Kairua	LOC	11	V8	37 42	176 16
Kaitaia	BORO	6	P3	35 07	173 14
Kaitangata	BORO	27	G25	46 17	169 51
Kaitarakihi	HILL	10	U7	37 07	175 41
Kaitaratahi	LOC	11	Y10	38 32	177 54
Kaitawa	LOC	15, 19	U13	40 29	175 53
Kaitawa	LOC	11	X10	38 48	177 08
Kaiteriteri	LOC	14, 18	P15	41 02	173 01
Kaiti	SBRB	38	B2	38 41	178 02
Kaitieke	LOC	10, 14	T11	39 06	175 17
Kaitoke	LOC	14, 19	T15	41 05	175 10
Kaitoke	LOC	14	T12	39 58	175 06
Kaitoke, Lake	LAKE	36	D2	39 58	175 04
Kaitoki	LOC	15	V13	40 15	176 06
Kaituna	LOC	15	V14	40 31	176 17
Kaituna	LOC	23	N20	43 47	172 39
Kaituna	LOC	15, 19	U14	40 53	175 33
Kaituna	LOC	14, 19	Q15	41 27	173 48
Kaituna River	STRM	11	V8	37 45	176 27
Kaituna River	STRM	14, 19	Q15	41 17	173 46
Kaituna Valley	LOC	23	N20	43 44	172 42
Kaiwaiwai	LOC	14, 19	T15	41 10	175 23
Kaiwaka	TOWN	7	R5	36 10	174 26
Kaiwaka	TOWN	15	W11	39 16	175 52
Kaiwaka South	LOC	15	W11	39 18	176 50
Kaiwera	LOC	27	F25	46 10	169 06
Kaiwhaiki	LOC	14	T12	39 49	175 05
Kaiwharawhara	SBRB	35	A7	41 16	174 47
Kaka	LOC	18	N16	41 33	172 42
Kaka Point	LOC	27	G25	46 23	169 47
Kakahi	TOWN	10	T10	38 56	175 23
Kakahu	LOC	23	K21	44 09	171 03
Kakanui	LOC	7, 10	R6	36 32	174 27
Kakanui	TOWN	39	C4	45 11	170 54
Kakanui	MTNS	27	H23	45 08	170 27
Kakanui Point	PNT	39	C4	45 12	170 54
Kakanui River	STRM	27	J23	45 11	170 54
Kakapo River	STRM	18	M15	41 16	172 16
Kakapuaka	LOC	27	G25	46 15	169 44
Kakaramea	LOC	14	R12	39 43	174 27
Kakariki	LOC	15	T13	40 08	175 27
Kakariki	LOC	15, 19	U14	40 35	175 38
Kakatahi	LOC	14	T12	39 40	175 20
Kakawau	HILL	40	B2	42 32	171 14
Kamahi	LOC	26	E25	46 20	168 43
Kamo	TOWN	36	A2	35 41	174 17
Kamo Springs	LOC	7	R4	35 40	174 18
Kanakanaia	LOC	11	Y9	38 25	177 57
Kaniere	LOC	18, 23	K18	42 45	171 00
Kaniere, Lake	LAKE	18, 23	K18	42 50	171 09
Kanohi	LOC	7, 10	S6	36 36	174 30
Kanono, Lake	LAKE	6	R5	36 22	174 08
Kapiro	LOC	6	Q3	35 09	173 54
Kapiti Island	ISLD	34	B1	40 52	174 54
Kaponga	TOWN	14	R11	39 26	174 09
Kapuka	LOC	26	E25	46 28	168 38
Kapuka South	LOC	26	E26	46 30	168 38
Kapuni	LOC	14	R11	39 29	174 08
Kara	LOC	6	R4	35 42	174 12
Karahaki	LOC	14	S12	39 42	174 37
Karaka	LOC	10	S7	37 06	174 54
Karaka Bay	BAY	35	B8	41 18	174 50
Karaka North	SBRB	31	C8	37 05	174 53
Karakariki	LOC	10	T8	37 44	175 06
Karamea	TOWN	18	M15	41 15	172 06
Karamea Bight	BAY	18	L15	41 23	171 50
Karamea River	STRM	18	M15	41 16	172 05
Karamu	LOC	10	T8	37 53	175 08
Karamu Stream	STRM	38	C3	39 36	176 52
Karangahake	LOC	10	U7	37 25	175 43
Karangarua River	STRM	22	G19	43 29	169 43
Karapiro	LOC	10	U8	37 55	175 34
Karapiro, Lake	LAKE	10	U8	37 57	175 39
Karaui Point	PNT	6	Q2	34 57	173 42
Karehana Bay	SBRB	34	B4	41 04	174 52
Karekare	LOC	7, 10	R6	36 59	174 29
Karepiro Bay	BAY	30	B1	36 39	174 44
Kareponia	LOC	6	P3	35 03	173 17
Karere	LOC	15, 19	U13	40 23	175 31
Karetu	LOC	6	R3	35 22	174 10
Karewa Point	PNT	4	—	43 48	176 26 W
Karewa Island	ISLD	10	V8	37 33	176 08
Karikari Bay	BAY	6	P2	34 49	173 21
Karikari, Cape	CAPE	6	P2	34 47	173 24
Karikari Peninsula	PEN	6	P2	34 48	173 27
Karioi	LOC	15	U11	39 27	175 31
Karioi, Mount	MTN	10	S8	37 52	174 47
Kariotahi	LOC	10	S7	37 16	174 41
Karitane	TOWN	27	J24	45 38	170 39
Karore Bank	SBNK	31	B7	37 01	174 43
Karori	SBRB	35	A7	41 17	174 44
Karoro	SBRB	40	A2	42 28	171 11
Katea	LOC	27	G25	46 25	169 37
Katherine Bay	BAY	7	T5	36 07	175 22
Katikati	TOWN	10	U8	37 33	175 55
Katikati Entrance	CHAN	10	U7	37 28	175 59
Katiki	LOC	27	J23	45 24	170 50
Katrine, Lake	LAKE	18, 23	M18	42 43	172 12
Katui	LOC	6	Q4	35 42	173 34
Kauaeranga	LOC	10	U7	37 09	175 36
Kauana	LOC	26	D25	46 00	168 21
Kauangaroa	LOC	14	T12	39 55	175 17
Kaukapakapa	LOC	7, 10	R6	36 37	174 30
Kaukau	HILL	35	A7	41 14	174 47
Kaupokonui	LOC	14	R12	39 33	174 08
Kaurapataka, Lake	LAKE	18, 23	L18	42 47	171 41
Kauri	LOC	7	R4	35 38	174 18
Kauri Point	LOC	10	U8	37 31	175 59
Kauri Point	PNT	30	A4	36 50	174 43
Kauroa	LOC	10	S8	37 51	174 55
Kauru Hill	LOC	27	J23	45 06	170 45
Kauru River	STRM	27	J23	45 05	170 49
Kauwhata	LOC	37	A3	40 17	175 33
Kawaha Point	SBRB	38	A4	38 06	176 15
Kawakawa	TOWN	6	R3	35 23	174 04
Kawakawa Bay	LOC	7, 10	T6	36 57	175 10
Kawarau River	STRM	26	E23	45 02	168 55
Kawau Island	ISLD	7, 10	S5	36 26	174 51
Kaweka	MTN	15	V11	39 17	176 22
Kaweka Range	MTNS	15	V11	39 11	176 16
Kaweku	LOC	26	E24	45 56	168 43
Kawerau	TOWN	11	W9	38 05	176 42
Kawhatau	LOC	15	U12	39 47	175 49
Kawhatau River	STRM	15	U12	39 47	175 49
Kawhatau Valley	LOC	15	U12	39 49	175 57
Kawhia	TOWN	10	S9	38 04	174 49
Kawhia Harbour	HARB	10	S9	38 05	174 50
Kawiti	LOC	6	Q3	35 25	173 57
Kawitihu Island	ISLD	7, 10	U6	36 38	175 53
Kekeno Point	PNT	4	—	50 34	166 17
Kekerengu	LOC	18	R17	42 00	174 00
Kelburn	SBRB	35	A7	41 17	174 46
Kellard, Mount	MT	26	A24	45 32	166 50
Kellys Bay	BAY	6	R5	36 15	174 06
Kellyville	LOC	10	T7	37 16	175 03
Kelso	TOWN	27	F24	45 54	169 15
Kelston	SBRB	31	A5	36 54	174 40
Kelvin Grove	SBRB	37	B3	40 20	175 38
Kenana	LOC	6	Q3	35 03	173 34
Kendall, Mount	MT	18	M15	41 23	172 24
Kenepuru Sound	SND	14, 19	Q15	41 12	174 00
Kennedys Bay	LOC	7, 10	U6	36 40	175 22
Kennington	TOWN	26	D25	46 24	168 27
Kensington	SBRB	40	B4	44 25	171 15
Kensington	SBRB	36	A3	35 43	174 19
Kepler Mountains	MTNS	26	B23	45 24	167 24
Kereone	LOC	10	U8	37 42	175 37
Kerepehi	TOWN	10	U7	37 18	175 33
Kereru	LOC	15	V12	39 38	176 25
Kereta	LOC	7, 10	T6	36 55	175 26
Kereu Stream	STRM	11	Y8	37 43	177 43
Kerikeri	TOWN	6	Q3	35 13	173 57
Kerikeri Inlet	BAY	6	R3	35 12	174 01
Kermadec Islands	ISLS	4	—	30 00	178 30 W
Kermadec Ridge	SEAF	81	—	26 45	177 20 W
Kermadec Trench	SEAF	81	—	31 00	176 15 W
Kerrytown	LOC	23	K21	44 16	171 12
Kew	SBRB	33	B4	45 54	170 29
Kew	SBRB	40	D2	46 26	168 21
Key, The	LOC	26	C24	45 35	167 53
Khandallah	SBRB	35	A7	41 15	174 47
Kiakia	LOC	11, 15	X11	39 01	177 16
Kia Ora	LOC	27	J23	45 13	170 51
Kidnappers, Cape	CAPE	15	X12	39 39	177 06
Kihikihi	TOWN	10	T9	38 02	175 20
Kihitu Pa	LOC	11, 15	X11	39 03	177 26
Kikiwa	LOC	18	N16	41 44	172 53
Kilbirnie	SBRB	35	A8	41 19	174 47
Killinchy	LOC	23	M20	43 44	172 14
Kimbell	LOC	23	J21	44 05	170 45
Kimberley	LOC	14, 19	T14	40 33	175 15

NAME	DESC	PAGE	REF	LAT S	LONG E
Kimberley	LOC	23	M19	43 27	172 07
Kimbolton	TOWN	15	U13	40 04	175 47
Kimihia	LOC	10	T8	37 33	175 11
Kincaid	LOC	19	Q17	42 20	173 42
Kingsdown	LOC	23	K21	44 28	171 13
Kingseat	LOC	10	S7	37 08	174 48
Kingsland	SBRB	31	B5	36 52	174 45
Kingston	LOC	26	E23	45 20	168 43
Kingston	SBRB	35	A8	41 19	174 45
Kingston Crossing	LOC	26	E24	45 52	168 39
Kingswell	SBRB	40	D2	46 27	168 22
Kinleith	LOC	10	U9	38 16	175 54
Kinloch	LOC	10	U10	38 40	175 55
Kinnaird, Mount	MT	22	F20	43 45	169 27
Kinohaku	LOC	10	S9	38 09	174 49
Kiokio	LOC	10	T9	38 09	175 16
Kiore	LOC	14	S11	39 14	174 33
Kirikau	LOC	10, 14	T11	39 01	175 08
Kirikopuni	LOC	6	R4	35 51	174 01
Kiripaka	LOC	7	R4	35 38	174 25
Kiritehere	LOC	10	S9	38 20	174 44
Kiriwhakapapa	LOC	15, 19	U14	40 48	175 34
Kirkliston Range	MTNS	23	J22	44 31	170 32
Kirwee	LOC	23	M19	43 30	172 13
Kiwi, Lake	LAKE	26	A25	46 10	166 48
Kiwitahi	LOC	10	U8	37 44	175 36
Kiwitea	LOC	15	U13	40 07	175 44
Kiwitea Stream	STRM	15	U13	40 09	175 39
Knapdale	LOC	26	E25	46 01	168 55
Knobby Range	MTNS	27	F23	45 25	169 25
Knuckle Point	PNT	6	P2	34 51	173 28
Koamaru, Cape	CAPE	14, 19	R15	41 05	174 23
Koatunui Head	HEAD	11	Z9	38 03	178 23
Koeke	LOC	15	U12	39 42	175 36
Kohaihai River	STRM	18	M15	41 06	172 06
Kohata, Lake	LAKE	36	D2	39 58	175 05
Kohekohe	LOC	10	S7	37 11	174 39
Kohi	LOC	14	S12	39 43	174 36
Kohika	LOC	23	K22	44 33	171 03
Kohimarama	SBRB	31	C5	36 51	174 51
Kohinui	LOC	15, 19	U13	40 25	175 57
Kohukomarua Bluff	CLIF	22	H19	43 14	170 08
Kohukohu	TOWN	6	Q3	35 22	173 33
Kohuratahi	LOC	10, 14	S11	39 06	174 45
Kohurau	MTN	22, 27	H22	44 48	170 20
Kokatahi	LOC	18, 23	K18	42 50	171 03
Kokatahi River	STRM	18, 23	K18	42 50	171 01
Kokiri	LOC	18, 23	K18	42 30	171 23
Kokonga	LOC	27	H23	45 13	170 15
Kokopu	LOC	6	R4	35 42	174 08
Komako	LOC	15	U13	40 06	175 54
Komakorau	LOC	10	T8	37 39	175 16
Komata North	LOC	10	U7	37 20	175 40
Komokoriki	LOC	7, 10	S5	36 30	174 32
Kongahu	LOC	18	M15	41 18	172 05
Kongahu Point	PNT	18	L15	41 27	171 57
Konini	LOC	15, 19	U14	40 31	175 47
Kopaki	LOC	10	T9	38 29	175 17
Kopane	LOC	15	T13	40 19	175 29
Kopu	LOC	10	U7	37 11	175 34
Kopua	LOC	15	V13	40 05	176 17
Kopuarahi	LOC	10	U7	37 13	175 30
Kopuaranga	LOC	15, 19	U14	40 50	175 40
Kopuaranga River	STRM	37	D3	40 54	175 42
Kopuaroa	LOC	11	Z8	37 58	178 15
Kopuawhara	LOC	11, 15	Y11	39 03	177 51
Kopuawhara Stream	STRM	15	Y11	39 04	177 54
Kopuku	LOC	10	T7	37 16	175 12
Kopuriki	LOC	11	W9	38 21	176 47
Koputaroa	LOC	14, 19	T14	40 34	175 20
Koputauaki Bay	LOC	7, 10	T6	36 43	175 28
Koraki	LOC	15	W11	39 17	176 51
Korakonui	LOC	10	T9	38 08	175 24
Koranga	LOC	11	X9	38 25	177 19
Korapuki Island	ISLD	7, 10	U6	36 40	175 51
Korere	LOC	14, 18	N16	41 32	172 48
Koriniti	LOC	14	T12	39 40	175 10
Korohe	LOC	10, 14	U10	38 57	175 51
Korokoro	SBRB	35	B6	41 13	174 52
Koromatua	LOC	10	T8	37 50	175 12
Koromatua, Lake	LAKE	37	C2	37 50	175 13
Koromiko	LOC	14, 19	Q15	41 21	173 57
Koru	LOC	10, 14	R11	39 08	174 00
Kotemaori	LOC	11, 15	X11	39 04	177 02
Kotinga	LOC	14, 18	N14	40 53	172 49
Kotuku	LOC	18, 23	K18	42 33	171 27
Kourawhero	LOC	7, 10	S5	36 25	174 36
Koutu	SBRB	38	A4	38 07	176 14
Koutunui Point	PNT	11	Z9	38 06	178 22
Kowai Bush	LOC	23	L19	43 18	171 56
Kowai River	STRM	23	L19	43 19	171 59
Kowai River	STRM	28	N19	43 12	172 46
Kowhai	LOC	19	Q17	42 25	173 37
Kowhitirangi	TOWN	18, 23	K18	42 53	171 01
Kuaotunu	LOC	7, 10	U6	36 43	175 44
Kuku	LOC	14, 19	T14	40 42	175 14
Kukumoa	LOC	11	X9	38 00	177 15
Kumara	BORO	18, 23	K18	42 38	171 11
Kumara Junction	LOC	18, 23	K18	42 35	171 08
Kumeroa	LOC	15, 19	U13	40 21	175 59
Kumeu	TOWN	7, 10	S6	36 46	174 33
Kupe	LOC	14	R11	39 15	174 22
Kuratau	LOC	10	U10	38 53	175 40
Kuratau, Lake	LAKE	10	U10	38 52	175 42
Kuratau Spit	LOC	10	U10	38 54	175 46
Kuri Bush	LOC	27	H25	46 02	170 14
Kuripapango	LOC	15	V11	39 24	176 20
Kuriwao	LOC	27	F25	46 13	169 26
Kuriwao Gorge	LOC	27	F25	46 15	169 20
Kurow	TOWN	23, 27	H22	44 44	170 28
Kurow River	STRM	23	H22	44 45	170 29
Kutarere	TOWN	11	X9	38 03	177 06
Kye Burn	STRM	27	H23	45 12	170 14
Kyeburn	LOC	27	H23	45 09	170 15
La Perouse	MTN	22	H20	43 36	170 06
Ladbrooks	TOWN	32	A4	43 37	172 32
Lady Alice	ISLD	7	S4	35 54	174 43
Lady Barkly	LOC	26	D25	46 06	168 20
Lady, Lake	LAKE	18, 23	L18	42 36	171 34
Lagmhor	LOC	23	L20	43 53	171 39
Laingholm	LOC	31	A7	36 58	174 39
Lake Alice Hospital	LOC	14	T13	40 07	175 20
Lake Coleridge	LOC	23	L19	43 22	171 32
Lake Ferry	LOC	14, 19	T15	41 23	175 09
Lake Grassmere	LOC	19	R16	41 43	174 08
Lake Hayes	LOC	22, 26	E22	44 59	168 49
Lake Ohau	LOC	22	G21	44 14	169 49
Lake Ohia	LOC	6	P2	34 59	173 22
Lake Okareka	LOC	11	V9	38 11	176 21
Lake Paringa	LOC	22	F20	43 43	169 26
Lake Pukaki	LOC	22	H21	44 13	170 08
Lake River	STRM	23	K19	43 19	171 09
Lake Rotoma	LOC	11	W9	38 03	176 33

NAME	DESC	PAGE	REF	LAT S	LONG E
Lake Tekapo	LOC	23	H21	44 00	170 29
Lake Waitaki	LOC	23, 27	H22	44 42	170 26
Lakeside	LOC	23	M20	43 49	172 20
Lakeside	LOC	27	G25	46 14	169 50
Lambert, Cape	CAPE	14, 19	R14	40 59	174 14
Lambton Harbour	HARB	35	A7	41 17	174 47
Lammerlaw Range	MTNS	27	G24	45 43	169 44
Lammerlaw Top	MTN	27	G24	45 39	169 39
Lammermoor Range	MTNS	27	G24	45 39	169 47
Lamplough	LOC	18	K18	42 39	171 04
Landsborough River	STRM	22	G20	43 57	169 30
Langs Beach	LOC	7	S5	36 03	174 32
Lansdowne	SBRB	37	D4	40 57	175 40
Lansdowne	LOC	23	N20	43 37	172 34
Lantern Rocks	ROCKS	4	—	50 54	165 58
Larnach Castle	BLDG	33	C3	45 52	170 38
Lauder	LOC	22, 27	G23	45 03	169 40
Lauder Creek	STRM	27	G23	45 04	169 40
Lauriston	LOC	23	L20	43 44	171 46
Lawrence	BORO	27	G24	45 55	169 42
Lawrence River	STRM	23	J19	43 27	170 51
Le Bons Bay	LOC	23	P20	43 46	173 04
Leader River	STRM	18	P18	42 43	173 18
Leamington	SBRB	10	T8	37 54	175 29
Leamington	LOC	18	P18	42 47	173 11
Leatham River	STRM	18	P16	41 43	173 10
Lee Flat	LOC	27	H24	45 47	170 01
Lee River	STRM	14, 18	P15	41 24	173 09
Lee Stream	STRM	27	H24	45 49	170 16
Lee Stream	LOC	27	H24	45 48	170 08
Leedstown	LOC	15	T12	39 59	175 30
Lees Valley	LOC	23	M19	43 09	172 10
Leeston	TOWN	23	M20	43 46	172 18
Leeward Island	ISLD	4	—	49 42	178 48
Leigh	TOWN	7	S5	36 17	174 48
Leith Valley	LOC	27	H24	45 50	170 30
Leithfield	LOC	23	N19	43 12	172 44
Leithfield Beach	LOC	23	N19	43 13	172 45
Lepperton	TOWN	37	C1	39 04	174 13
Leslie Hills	LOC	18, 23	N18	42 40	172 51
Leslie River	STRM	18	N15	41 14	172 30
L'Esperance Rock	ROCK	4	—	31 21	178 49 W
Letts Gully	LOC	27	F23	45 14	169 25
Levels	LOC	40	B3	44 19	171 12
Levels Valley	LOC	23	K21	44 18	171 05
L'Eveque, Cape	CAPE	4	—	44 03	176 38 W
Levin	BORO	14, 19	T14	40 37	175 17
Lewis Pass	PASS	18, 23	M17	42 24	172 24
Lewis River	STRM	18, 23	M18	42 33	172 21
Liberton	SBRB	33	B3	45 51	170 31
Lichfield	LOC	10	U9	38 06	175 49
Liebig Range	MTNS	22	H20	43 38	170 21
Ligar Bay	LOC	14, 18	N14	40 49	172 55
Lill Burn	STRM	26	C25	46 01	167 41
Lillburn Valley	LOC	26	C24	45 59	167 38
Limehills	LOC	26	D25	46 04	168 20
Limehills East	LOC	26	D25	46 06	168 24
Limestone Downs	LOC	10	S7	37 28	174 46
Limestone Island	ISLD	36	B4	35 47	174 21
Limestone Valley	LOC	23	J21	44 12	170 47
Lincoln	SBRB	31	A5	36 51	174 37
Lincoln	TOWN	23	M20	43 38	172 29
Linden	SBRB	35	B5	41 09	174 49
Lindis Pass	PASS	22, 27	G22	44 35	169 39
Lindis Pass	LOC	22	F22	44 43	169 30
Lindis Peak	PEAK	22, 27	F22	44 44	169 29
Lindis River	STRM	22, 27	F22	44 53	169 20
Linkwater	LOC	14, 19	Q15	41 17	173 52
Linn Burn	STRM	27	G23	45 19	169 57
Lintley	LOC	26	D24	45 46	168 28
Linton	LOC	37	A4	40 36	175 33
Linton Military Camp	LOC	37	A4	40 24	175 35
Linwood	SBRB	32	C3	43 32	172 40
Lismore	LOC	23	K20	43 54	171 29
Little Akaloa	LOC	23	N20	43 41	172 59
Little Akaloa Bay	BAY	23	P20	43 40	173 00
Little Barrier Island	ISLD	7	T5	36 12	175 05
Little Rakaia	LOC	23	M20	43 51	172 13
Little River	LOC	23	N20	43 46	172 47
Little Valley	LOC	27	F23	45 18	169 28
Little Wanganui	LOC	18	M15	41 23	172 04
Little Wanganui River	STRM	18	M15	41 23	172 03
Livingstone	SBRB	37	C1	37 47	175 14
Livingstone	LOC	23, 27	J22	44 58	170 34
Livingstone Mountains	MTNS	26	D23	45 13	168 05
Lloyds Hill	HILL	30	A1	36 37	174 38
Loburn	LOC	23	N19	43 15	172 32
Loburn North	LOC	23	N19	43 13	172 30
Loch Norrie	LOC	7, 10	R6	36 37	174 29
Lochiel	LOC	26	D25	46 12	168 20
Lochinvar	LOC	11, 15	V10	38 58	176 20
Lochnagar	LAKE	22	E22	44 35	168 35
Lochy River	STRM	26	E23	45 11	168 42
Logan Point	PNT	4	—	50 53	165 54
Long Bay	LOC	7, 10	T6	36 45	175 29
Long Bay	BAY	30	B2	36 41	174 45
Long Beach	LOC	33	D1	45 45	170 39
Long Beach	BCH	4	—	43 53	176 35 W
Long Burn	STRM	26	A24	45 55	166 55
Long Island	ISLD	26	A24	45 46	166 41
Long Island	ISLD	14, 19	R15	41 07	174 17
Long Point	PNT	26	B25	46 15	167 06
Long Point	PNT	11, 15	Y11	39 10	177 49
Long Point	PNT	27	G26	46 35	169 35
Long Reef	PNT	22	C21	44 20	168 00
Long Sound	SND	26	A24	46 00	166 45
Long Valley	LOC	14, 19	Q15	41 22	173 43
Longacre	LOC	14	T12	39 55	175 07
Longbeach	LOC	23	L21	44 06	171 42
Longburn	TOWN	37	A4	40 23	175 33
Longbush	LOC	15, 19	U15	41 09	175 36
Longbush	LOC	26	E25	46 23	168 30
Longfellow, Mount	MTN	18, 23	M18	42 42	172 17
Longford	LOC	18	M16	41 47	172 22
Longlands	LOC	15	W12	39 40	176 49
Longridge North	LOC	26	E24	45 47	168 33
Longridge Point	PNT	22	D21	44 12	168 09
Longsight, Mount	MT	26	C22	44 45	167 34
Longwood	LOC	26	C25	46 21	167 56
Longwood Range	MTNS	26	C25	46 13	167 51
Lookout Point	PNT	26	D26	46 37	168 20
Lora Gorge	LOC	26	D25	46 04	168 29
Lord Howe Basin	SEAF	81	—	32 00	158 30
Lord Howe Island	ISLD	81	—	31 30	159 00
Lord Howe Rise	SEAF	81	—	36 00	165 00
Lords River	STRM	26	D27	47 07	168 08
Lorneville	LOC	26	D25	46 21	168 20
Lottin Point	PNT	11	Z8	37 32	178 10
Loughnan, Mount	MT	23	H19	43 26	170 29
Lovells Flat	LOC	27	G25	46 10	169 50
Lovitt, Cape	CAPE	4	—	50 48	165 53
Lowburn	LOC	22, 27	F23	45 01	169 13
Lowcliffe	LOC	23	L21	44 07	171 35
Lower Hutt	CITY	35	C6	41 13	174 55

NAME	DESC	PAGE	REF	LAT S	LONG E
Lower Kaimai	LOC	10	V8	37 48	176 02
Lower Moutere	LOC	14, 18	P15	41 10	173 00
Lower Shotover	LOC	22, 26	E22	45 00	168 45
Lower Waiaua	LOC	11	X8	37 59	177 25
Lower Wairau	LOC	14, 19	R15	41 29	174 00
Lowgarth	LOC	14	R11	39 24	174 13
Lowry Bay	SBRB	35	B7	41 15	174 55
Lowry Peaks Range	MTNS	18	P18	42 47	173 02
Lowther	LOC	26	D24	45 39	168 26
Lucas Creek	STRM	30	A3	36 46	174 40
Lucky Point	PNT	14, 19	R15	41 16	174 17
Luggate	LOC	22, 27	F22	44 46	169 18
Lumsden	TOWN	26	D24	45 44	168 26
Lyall Bay	SBRB	35	A8	41 19	174 48
Lyall, Mount	MT	4	—	52 32	169 07
Lyall, Mount	MT	26	C23	45 17	167 33
Lyalldale	LOC	23	K22	44 30	171 06
Lyell Glacier	GLCR	23	J19	43 19	170 50
Lyndhurst	LOC	23	L20	43 42	171 43
Lyndon	LOC	18, 23	P18	42 38	173 01
Lyndon, Lake	LAKE	23	L19	43 18	171 42
Lynmore	LOC	38	B4	38 09	176 17
Lynmouth	SBRB	37	A1	39 04	174 03
Lynnford	LOC	23	L21	44 01	171 36
Lynwood	LOC	26	C23	45 29	167 48
Lyttelton	BORO	32	C4	43 36	172 43
Lyttelton Harbour	HARB	32	C4	43 37	172 44
Maata	LOC	14	R11	39 27	174 20
Mabel Bush	LOC	26	E25	46 17	168 32
Macandrew Bay	SBRB	33	C3	45 52	170 35
Macaulay River	STRM	23	J20	43 47	170 33
Macauley Island	ISLD	4	—	30 13	178 26 W
Macfarlane, Mount	MT	22	F20	43 56	169 24
Mackaytown	LOC	10	U7	37 24	175 43
Mackinnon, Lake	LAKE	26	B23	45 06	167 23
Mackinnon Pass	PASS	22, 26	C22	44 49	167 47
Maclennan	LOC	27	G26	46 33	169 29
Maclennan Range	HILL	27	F26	46 32	169 16
Macquarie Island	ISLD	81	—	54 30	159 00
Macquarie Ridge	SEAF	81	—	52 00	159 00
Macraes Flat	LOC	27	H23	45 23	170 27
Maerewhenua River	STRM	27	J22	44 51	170 42
Maeroa	SBRB	37	C1	37 47	175 15
Mahaki	LOC	11	Y9	38 28	177 44
Mahana	LOC	14, 18	P15	41 16	173 03
Mahanga	LOC	11	Y11	39 01	177 54
Mahanga Bay	BAY	35	B7	41 18	174 50
Maharahara	LOC	15	U13	40 15	175 57
Mahau Sound	SND	14, 19	Q15	41 14	173 52
Maheno	LOC	27	J23	45 10	170 50
Mahia	LOC	11, 15	Y11	39 05	177 55
Mahia Beach	BCH	11, 15	Y11	39 05	177 52
Mahia Peninsula	PEN	11, 15	Y11	39 09	177 53
Mahina Bay	SBRB	35	B7	41 16	174 55
Mahinapua, Lake	LAKE	18, 23	J18	42 48	170 55
Mahinerangi, Lake	LAKE	27	G24	45 50	169 55
Mahitahi River	STRM	22	G20	43 39	169 36
Mahoe	LOC	14	R11	39 23	174 10
Mahoenui	LOC	10	S10	38 34	174 50
Mahora	SBRB	38	C3	39 37	176 50
Mahurangi	LOC	7, 10	S5	36 29	174 43
Mahurangi Island	ISLD	7, 10	U6	36 49	175 49
Mahurangi West	LOC	7, 10	S5	36 30	174 41
Mahuta	LOC	6	Q4	36 00	173 48
Mahuta	LOC	10	T8	37 35	175 06
Maia	SBRB	33	C3	45 52	170 34
Maihiihi	LOC	10	T9	38 13	175 22
Maimai	LOC	18	L17	42 09	171 45
Maioro	LOC	10	S7	37 19	174 42
Mairangi Bay	SBRB	30	B3	36 44	174 45
Mairehau	SBRB	32	B2	43 30	172 38
Mairoa	LOC	10	S9	38 23	174 59
Mairtown	SBRB	36	A3	35 42	174 19
Maitai	SBRB	39	B1	41 16	173 17
Maitai River	STRM	39	B1	41 16	173 17
Maitland	LOC	27	F24	45 59	169 02
Maitlands	SBRB	39	A2	41 18	173 15
Makahu	LOC	14	S11	39 17	174 39
Makairo	LOC	15, 19	U13	40 24	175 59
Makaka	LOC	14	R11	39 25	174 04
Makakaho	LOC	14	S11	39 33	174 54
Makara	LOC	35	A7	41 16	174 42
Makara Beach	LOC	35	A6	41 13	174 43
Makara River	STRM	15, 19	T15	41 18	175 28
Makara South	LOC	14, 19	S15	41 17	174 41
Makara Stream	STRM	15	W12	39 51	176 44
Makara Stream	STRM	35	A6	41 13	174 43
Makaraka	LOC	38	A2	38 39	177 58
Makaraka	SBRB	38	A2	38 39	177 57
Makaranui	LOC	14	T11	39 26	175 21
Makarau	LOC	7, 10	R6	36 33	174 30
Makaretu	LOC	15	V12	39 55	176 15
Makaretu Stream	STRM	11, 15	Y10	38 54	177 33
Makaretu Stream	STRM	15	V12	39 59	176 28
Makarewa	TOWN	40	C1	46 20	168 21
Makarewa Junction	LOC	26	D25	46 18	168 20
Makarewa North	LOC	26	D25	46 18	168 24
Makarewa River	STRM	40	C1	46 22	168 15
Makarora	LOC	22	F21	44 15	169 14
Makarora River	STRM	22	F21	44 19	169 10
Makaroro River	STRM	15	V12	39 50	176 18
Makauri	LOC	11	Y10	38 38	177 56
Makawhio Point	PNT	22	G20	43 33	169 39
Makawhio River	STRM	22	G20	43 34	169 38
Makerua	LOC	15, 19	T14	40 31	175 28
Maketu	TOWN	10	V8	37 45	176 28
Makiekie Creek	STRM	15	U13	40 07	175 52
Makikihi	TOWN	23, 27	K22	44 38	171 09
Makino	LOC	15	U13	40 10	175 35
Makirikiri	LOC	15	V13	40 13	176 05
Makirikiri	LOC	14	T12	39 52	175 08
Makirikiri South	LOC	14	T13	40 05	175 18
Makomako	LOC	15, 19	U13	40 27	175 44
Makomako	LOC	10	S8	37 58	174 54
Makorako	MTN	15	V11	39 09	176 03
Makorori	LOC	11	Z10	38 39	178 09
Makotuku	TOWN	15	V13	40 07	176 14
Makowai	LOC	14	T13	40 15	175 23
Makuku, Lake	LAKE	4	—	43 51	176 24 W
Makuri River	STRM	15, 19	U13	40 29	175 55
Malaspina Reach	SND	26	B23	45 22	167 03
Malte Brun	MTN	22	H20	43 38	170 14
Mamaku	LOC	10	V9	38 06	176 05
Mamaku Plateau	PLAT	10	V9	38 06	176 02
Mamaranui	LOC	6	Q4	35 50	173 45
Mana	SBRB	34	B4	41 05	174 52
Mana Island	ISLD	34	A4	41 05	174 47
Manaia	TOWN	14	R12	39 33	174 07
Manaia	HILL	36	D4	35 49	174 31
Manakau	TOWN	14, 19	T14	40 43	175 13
Manakau	MTN	19	Q17	42 14	173 37
Manapouri	LOC	26	C24	45 34	167 36
Manapouri Hydro	LOC	26	B24	45 32	167 17

NAME	DESC	PAGE	REF	LAT S	LONG E
Manapouri, Lake	LAKE	26	C24	45 31	167 31
Manaroa	LOC	14, 19	R15	41 06	174 03
Manawahe	LOC	11	W8	38 00	176 38
Manawaora	LOC	6	R3	35 16	174 13
Manawaru	TOWN	10	U8	37 38	175 46
Manawatu River	STRM	14, 19	T13	40 28	175 14
Mandeville	LOC	26	E24	45 59	168 48
Mandeville North	LOC	23	N19	43 23	172 31
Mangaehu Stream	STRM	14	R11	39 23	174 28
Mangaetoroa	LOC	14	T11	39 26	175 14
Mangahao	LOC	15, 19	U13	40 25	175 47
Mangahao River	STRM	15, 19	U13	40 23	175 50
Mangahei	LOC	15	V13	40 14	176 16
Mangaheia	LOC	11	Z9	38 22	178 15
Mangaiti	LOC	10	U7	37 30	175 41
Mangakahia River	STRM	6	R4	35 48	174 03
Mangakahu Valley	LOC	10	T10	38 45	175 24
Mangakino	TOWN	10	U9	38 22	175 46
Mangakino Stream	STRM	10	U9	38 24	175 46
Mangakuri River	STRM	15	W12	39 57	176 56
Mangamahoe	LOC	15, 19	U14	40 44	175 44
Mangamahoe, Lake	LAKE	37	B2	39 07	174 07
Mangamahu	LOC	14	T12	39 49	175 22
Mangamaire	LOC	15, 19	U14	40 31	175 45
Mangamaire River	STRM	15	V11	39 17	176 00
Mangamingi	LOC	14	R11	39 25	174 27
Mangamuka	LOC	6	Q3	35 13	173 33
Mangamuka Bridge	LOC	6	Q3	35 15	173 33
Mangamutu	LOC	15, 19	U13	40 27	175 49
Manganui River	STRM	6	Q4	35 55	173 57
Manganui River	STRM	14	R11	39 04	174 17
Manganuiateao Stream	STRM	14	T11	39 24	175 03
Mangaokewa River	STRM	10	T9	38 11	175 11
Mangaone River	STRM	15	W11	39 29	176 42
Mangaone Stream	STRM	37	A4	40 26	175 34
Mangaone Stream	STRM	15, 19	U13	40 28	175 55
Mangaonoho	LOC	15	U12	39 53	175 39
Mangaoraka Stream	STRM	37	C1	39 00	174 11
Mangaorapa	TOWN	15	V13	40 20	176 30
Mangaore	LOC	15, 19	T14	40 34	175 26
Mangaorongo	LOC	10	T9	38 11	175 20
Mangaotaki	LOC	10	S9	38 25	174 53
Mangaowata Hill	HILL	10, 14	S11	39 04	174 43
Mangapa	LOC	6	Q3	35 10	173 38
Mangapai	LOC	36	A4	35 51	174 17
Mangapapa	SBRB	38	B2	38 39	178 01
Mangapapa Stream	STRM	15	T12	39 47	175 29
Mangaparo	LOC	10	S10	38 53	174 59
Mangapehi	LOC	10	T10	38 31	175 18
Mangapehi Stream	STRM	10	T9	38 26	175 05
Mangapiko	LOC	10	T8	37 59	175 15
Mangapiko Stream	STRM	10	T8	37 59	175 12
Mangapoike River	STRM	11	X10	38 53	177 29
Mangaramarama	LOC	15, 19	U13	40 27	175 52
Mangarawa	LOC	15	U13	40 17	175 54
Mangaroa	LOC	14, 19	T15	41 07	175 07
Mangaroa River	STRM	35	D6	41 10	175 05
Mangarouhi Stream	STRM	15	W13	40 02	176 41
Mangaruhe River	STRM	11	X10	38 54	177 25
Mangatahi	LOC	15	W12	39 37	176 35
Mangatainoka	TOWN	15, 19	U13	40 25	175 52
Mangatangi	LOC	10	T7	37 12	175 13
Mangatangi Stream	STRM	10	T7	37 14	175 11
Mangatara	LOC	6	Q4	35 57	173 48
Mangatarata	LOC	10	T7	37 17	175 22
Mangatawhiri	LOC	10	T7	37 13	175 07
Mangatawhiri River	STRM	10	T7	37 16	175 03
Mangatea	LOC	10	T9	38 21	175 08
Mangateparu	LOC	10	U8	37 35	175 30
Mangateretere	LOC	15	W12	39 37	176 54
Mangatiti	LOC	15, 19	V14	40 33	176 07
Mangatoetoe	LOC	6	P3	35 07	173 25
Mangatoi	LOC	11	V8	37 54	176 14
Mangatokerau	LOC	11	Z9	38 16	178 12
Mangatoki	LOC	14	R11	39 26	174 13
Mangatoro	LOC	15	V13	40 16	176 13
Mangatoro Stream	STRM	15, 19	V13	40 16	176 13
Mangatu	LOC	6	Q4	35 41	173 38
Mangatu Pa	LOC	11	Y9	38 23	177 47
Mangatu Stream	STRM	11	Y9	38 23	177 50
Mangatuna	LOC	11	Z9	38 19	178 16
Mangaturuturu Stream	STRM	14	T11	39 19	175 13
Mangatutu	LOC	15	W11	39 24	176 31
Mangatutu Stream	STRM	10	T9	38 05	175 23
Mangatutu Stream	STRM	15	W11	39 25	176 33
Mangawaru Stream	STRM	10	T8	37 36	175 11
Mangawaru	LOC	10	T8	37 31	175 15
Mangaweka	TOWN	15	U12	39 49	175 48
Mangaweka	MTN	15	V12	39 49	176 05
Mangawhai	LOC	7	S5	36 08	174 34
Mangawhai Heads	LOC	7	S5	36 05	174 35
Mangawhata	LOC	14, 19	T13	40 23	175 26
Mangawhero Stream	STRM	14	R12	39 32	174 04
Mangawhero Stream	STRM	14	T12	39 52	175 17
Mangere	SBRB	31	B6	36 59	174 48
Mangere Bridge	LOC	7, 10	S6	36 56	174 47
Mangere Bridge	BDGE	31	B6	36 56	174 47
Mangere Island	ISLD	4	—	44 16	176 18 W
Mangles River	STRM	18	M16	41 47	172 22
Mangonui	TOWN	6	Q2	34 59	173 32
Mangorei	LOC	10, 14	R11	39 05	174 06
Mangorei Stream	STRM	37	B2	39 06	174 07
Mangorewa River	STRM	11	V8	37 50	176 22
Maniatutu	LOC	11	V8	37 49	176 27
Manly	LOC	30	B1	36 39	174 46
Manoeka	LOC	11	V8	37 47	176 18
Manor Burn	STRM	27	F23	45 15	169 25
Manor Park	SBRB	35	C5	41 09	174 58
Manorburn Reservoir	RESR	27	G23	45 23	169 37
Manuherikia River	STRM	27	F23	45 16	169 27
Manui	LOC	15	U12	39 46	175 47
Manuka Creek	LOC	27	G25	46 03	169 48
Manukau	LOC	6	P3	35 14	173 13
Manukau	CITY	31	D6	36 56	174 56
Manukau Harbour	HARB	31	A8	37 02	174 43
Manukau Heads	LOC	7, 10	S7	37 03	174 34
Manukau Point	PNT	4	—	44 02	176 20 W
Manunui	TOWN	10	T10	38 54	175 19
Manuoha	HILL	11	X10	38 39	177 07
Manurewa	BORO	31	C7	37 01	174 53
Manutahi	TOWN	14	R12	39 40	174 24
Manutuke	LOC	38	A2	38 41	177 55
Maori Head	HEAD	33	C4	45 55	170 34
Maori Hill	SBRB	33	B3	45 52	170 30
Maori Hill	SBRB	40	B4	44 23	171 14
Maoribank	SBRB	34	D5	41 07	175 05
Mapiu	LOC	10	T10	38 25	175 13
Mapiu Stream	STRM	10	T10	38 20	175 03
Mapourika, Lake	LAKE	22	H19	43 19	170 12
Mapua	LOC	14, 18	P15	41 15	173 06
Mara	LOC	15	V14	40 40	176 14
Maraehara River	STRM	11	Z8	37 47	178 29
Maraekakaho	LOC	15	W12	39 39	176 37
Maraekakaho River	STRM	15	W12	39 39	176 37

NAME	DESC	PAGE	REF	LAT S	LONG E
Maraenui	LOC	11	Y8	37 52	177 35
Maraenui	SBRB	38	D2	39 31	176 54
Maraeroa	LOC	6	Q3	35 20	173 38
Maraetai	LOC	7, 10	T6	36 53	175 03
Maraetai	LOC	10	U9	38 22	175 45
Maraetai, Lake	LAKE	10	U9	38 22	175 48
Maraetotara	LOC	15	W12	39 48	176 54
Maraetotara River	STRM	15	W12	39 38	176 59
Marahau	LOC	14, 19	P15	41 00	173 01
Marakapia, Lake	LAKE	4	—	43 50	176 34 W
Marakeke	LOC	15	V13	40 02	176 26
Marakerake	LOC	27	J23	45 04	170 45
Marama	LOC	19	Q16	41 42	173 59
Maramarua	LOC	10	T7	37 15	175 14
Maramataha River	STRM	10	T10	38 37	175 20
Marangai	LOC	14	T12	39 59	175 07
Mararoa River	STRM	26	C24	45 37	167 41
Maratoto	LOC	10	U7	37 18	175 46
Marau Point	PNT	11	Z9	38 18	178 22
Marchant, Lake	LAKE	26	B23	45 04	167 19
Marchwiel	SBRB	40	B4	44 23	171 14
Mareretu	LOC	7	R5	36 02	174 17
Marewa	SBRB	38	D2	39 30	176 54
Maria Van Diemen, Cape	CAPE	6	N1	34 29	172 39
Marima	LOC	15, 19	U14	40 31	175 41
Mariri	LOC	14, 19	P15	41 09	173 01
Mark Range	MTNS	22	F20	43 57	169 05
Market Cross	LOC	18	M15	41 16	172 09
Maroa	LOC	10	V9	38 29	176 02
Marohemo	LOC	7	R5	36 08	174 18
Marokopa	LOC	10	S9	38 18	174 43
Marokopa River	STRM	10	S9	38 18	174 42
Maromaku	LOC	6	R3	35 29	174 06
Maronan	LOC	23	L20	43 55	171 32
Maropiu	LOC	6	Q4	35 48	173 44
Marotiri	LOC	14, 19	T13	40 29	175 21
Marotiri Islands	ISLS	7	S4	35 54	174 45
Marsden	LOC	18	K18	42 33	171 13
Marsden Bay	LOC	36	C4	35 50	174 27
Marsden Point	LOC	36	D4	35 51	174 29
Marshland	LOC	22	C2	43 29	172 39
Marshlands	LOC	39	B3	41 27	174 00
Martinborough	BORO	15, 19	T15	41 13	175 27
Martins Bay	LOC	7, 10	S5	36 27	174 46
Martins Bay	BAY	22	C21	44 22	167 59
Marton	BORO	14	T13	40 05	175 23
Marua	LOC	7	R4	35 34	174 21
Maruia	LOC	18	M17	42 12	172 14
Maruia River	STRM	18	M16	41 47	172 12
Marumaru	LOC	11	X10	38 54	177 27
Mary Burn	STRM	22	H21	44 14	170 20
Mary Island	ISLD	26	B24	45 59	167 19
Marybank	LOC	14	T12	39 57	175 04
Marybank	LOC	39	B1	41 14	173 19
Mason Bay	BAY	26	C26	46 56	167 44
Mason Head	HEAD	26	C26	46 53	167 43
Mason, Lake	LAKE	18, 23	M18	42 44	172 10
Masons Flat	LOC	18, 23	N18	42 55	172 34
Massey	SBRB	30	A4	36 50	174 36
Masterton	BORO	15, 19	U14	40 57	175 39
Masterton	BORO	37	Urb	40 57	175 39
Mata	LOC	7	R4	35 51	174 22
Mata River	STRM	11	Z8	37 54	178 16
Matahi	LOC	11	X9	38 15	177 06
Matahina	LOC	11	W9	38 10	176 47
Matahina, Lake	LAKE	11	W9	38 09	176 48
Matahiwi	LOC	37	C3	40 54	175 36
Matahiwi	LOC	14	T12	39 36	175 10
Matahuru	LOC	10	T7	37 26	175 18
Matai Valley	LOC	14, 19	P15	41 16	173 22
Mataikona	LOC	15	V14	40 46	176 15
Matakana	TOWN	7	S5	36 21	174 43
Matakana Island	ISLD	10	V8	37 35	176 05
Matakanui	LOC	22, 27	G23	45 01	169 35
Matakaoa Point	PNT	11	Z8	37 33	178 20
Matakawau	LOC	10	S7	37 06	174 37
Mataketake Range	MTNS	22	F20	43 51	169 14
Matakitaki	LOC	18	M16	41 58	172 20
Matakitaki River	STRM	18	M16	41 48	172 19
Matakohe	LOC	6	R5	36 08	174 11
Matakuhia Stream	STRM	11	W11	39 01	176 38
Matamata	BORO	10	U8	37 49	175 46
Matamau	TOWN	15	V13	40 08	176 10
Matangi	LOC	10	T8	37 48	175 24
Matangirau	LOC	6	Q3	35 02	173 47
Matapara	LOC	10	U9	38 13	175 32
Matapihi	LOC	11	V8	37 42	176 11
Matapiro	LOC	15	W12	39 36	176 37
Matapouri	LOC	7	S4	35 34	174 30
Matapu	LOC	14	R11	39 28	174 13
Matarau	LOC	6	R4	35 40	174 15
Mataraua	LOC	6	Q4	35 32	173 45
Matarawa	LOC	15, 19	T15	41 03	175 27
Matarawa Valley	LOC	14	T12	39 56	175 09
Matariki	LOC	18	N15	41 25	172 44
Mataroa	LOC	15	U12	39 39	175 44
Matata	TOWN	11	W8	37 53	176 45
Matatoki	LOC	10	U7	37 12	175 36
Matau	LOC	10, 14	S11	39 10	174 34
Mataura	BORO	26	E25	46 12	168 52
Mataura Island	LOC	26	E25	46 26	168 47
Mataura River	STRM	26	E26	46 34	168 44
Matauri Bay	LOC	6	Q3	35 03	173 54
Matawai	LOC	11	Y9	38 21	177 32
Matawaia	LOC	6	Q4	35 30	173 57
Matawhero	LOC	11	Y10	38 39	177 56
Matemateaonga	LOC	14	S11	39 25	174 32
Matemateaonga Range	MTNS	14	S11	39 20	174 45
Mathias Pass	PASS	23	K19	43 06	171 07
Mathias River	STRM	23	K19	43 17	171 15
Matiere	TOWN	10	T10	38 46	175 05
Matingarahi	LOC	7, 10	T7	37 00	175 17
Matira	LOC	10	S8	37 35	174 51
Matiri	LOC	18	M16	41 44	172 20
Matiri, Lake	LAKE	18	M16	41 39	172 20
Matiri River	STRM	18	M16	41 46	172 19
Matthews, Mount	MTN	14, 19	T15	41 21	175 01
Matua	LOC	36	A1	37 40	176 07
Matukituki River	STRM	22	E22	44 37	169 00
Matukituki River, W. Br.	STRM	22	E21	44 29	168 49
Mauku	LOC	10	S7	37 12	174 49
Maungaharuru Range	MTNS	11, 15	W11	39 08	176 44
Maungahaumi	MTN	11	Y9	38 18	177 38
Maungakaramea	TOWN	6	R4	35 51	174 12
Maungakotukutuku Stream	STRM	34	D1	40 54	175 04
Maunganui	HILL	34	D2	40 58	175 03
Maunganui Beach	BCH	4	—	43 45	176 45 W
Maunganui Bluff	CLIF	6	Q4	35 45	173 33
Maunganui, Mount	HILL	36	B1	37 38	176 10
Maunganui Point	PNT	7	T5	36 08	175 19
Maungapohatu	HILL	11	X10	38 35	177 08
Maungaraki	SBRB	35	B6	41 13	174 53
Maungaroa	LOC	11	Y8	37 43	177 44
Maungataniwha	MTN	11	W10	38 49	176 48
Maungataniwha Range	MTNS	6	P3	35 10	173 30
Maungatapere	TOWN	6	R4	35 45	174 12
Maungatapu	SBRB	36	B2	37 43	176 11
Maungatapu	LOC	14, 18	P15	41 19	173 30
Maungatautari	LOC	10	U8	37 57	175 34
Maungati	LOC	23	J21	44 27	170 57
Maungatua	LOC	27	H24	45 54	170 10
Maungaturoto	TOWN	7	R5	36 07	174 20
Maungawera	TOWN	22, 27	F22	44 39	169 13
Maunu	SBRB	36	A3	35 44	174 17
Mauriceville	LOC	15, 19	U14	40 47	175 42
Mauriceville West	LOC	15, 19	U14	40 46	175 40
Maury, Mount	MT	26	B23	45 20	167 30
Mavora Lake, North	LAKE	26	D23	45 13	168 10
Mavora Lake, South	LAKE	26	D23	45 18	168 10
Mavora, Mount	MT	26	D23	45 05	168 10
Mawaro	LOC	23	J21	44 17	170 56
Mawhai Point	PNT	11	Z9	38 10	178 22
Mawheraiti	LOC	18	L17	42 12	171 44
Mawheraiti River	STRM	18	L17	42 17	171 40
Maxwell	LOC	14	S12	39 50	174 51
Mayfair	SBRB	38	C4	39 38	176 52
Mayfield	LOC	23	K20	43 49	171 25
Mayfield	SBRB	39	B4	41 30	173 57
Mayor Island	ISLD	11	V7	37 17	176 15
Maytown	LOC	23, 27	K22	44 43	171 03
McIvor, Lake	LAKE	26	C23	45 05	167 31
McKay	HILL	34	C3	40 59	175 00
McKellar Branch	STRM	26	D22	44 55	168 20
McKellar, Lake	LAKE	22, 26	D22	44 51	168 08
McKerrow, Lake	LAKE	22	D21	44 28	168 03
McLennan Inlet	BAY	4	—	50 48	166 14
McLeod Bay	LOC	7	S4	35 49	174 30
McLeod Bay	BAY	36	D4	35 49	174 30
McNab	LOC	26	E25	46 05	168 59
McQueens Valley	LOC	23	N20	43 43	172 38
McRae, Lake	LAKE	18	P17	42 11	173 20
Mead	LOC	23	M20	43 43	172 00
Meadowbank	SBRB	31	C5	36 52	174 49
Meadowbank	SBRB	39	D3	45 05	170 59
Medbury	LOC	18, 23	N18	42 53	172 40
Medway River	STRM	19	Q16	41 46	173 52
Meeanee	LOC	38	C2	39 33	176 54
Melina, Mount	MT	22	G21	44 26	169 33
Mellons Bay	SBRB	31	D5	36 53	174 56
Melville	SBRB	37	D2	37 49	175 17
Menzies Ferry	LOC	26	E25	46 21	168 49
Mercer	LOC	10	T7	37 17	175 03
Mercury Bay	BAY	7, 10	U6	36 48	175 46
Mercury Islands	ISLS	7, 10	U6	36 37	175 52
Meremere	TOWN	10	T7	37 20	175 05
Meremere	LOC	14	R12	39 34	174 25
Merino Downs	LOC	27	F24	45 57	169 06
Merivale	SBRB	32	B2	43 31	172 37
Merrilands	SBRB	37	B1	39 04	174 06
Merrivale	LOC	26	C25	46 04	167 51
Merton	LOC	27	J24	45 40	170 39
Messenger, Mount	MTN	10	S10	38 54	174 35
Methven	TOWN	23	L20	43 38	171 38
Meyer Islands	ISLS	4	—	29 15	177 52 W
Michies Crossing	LOC	33	C1	45 45	170 35
Mid Dome	PEAK	26	E24	45 35	168 32
Middle Fiord	FIOR	26	C23	45 10	167 39
Middle Valley	LOC	23	J21	44 06	170 56
Middlemarch	TOWN	27	H24	45 30	170 07
Middlemore	SBRB	31	C6	36 57	174 50
Middleton	LOC	15	W13	40 05	176 31
Midhurst	TOWN	14	R11	39 18	174 17
Midway Point	PNT	11	Z8	37 32	178 13
Mihi	LOC	11	V9	38 29	176 17
Mihiwaka	LOC	27	J24	45 47	170 37
Mikimiki	LOC	15, 19	U14	40 51	175 37
Milburn	LOC	27	H25	46 05	170 00
Milford	LOC	23	K21	44 14	171 20
Milford	SBRB	30	B3	36 46	174 46
Milford	LOC	22, 26	C22	44 40	167 55
Milford Sound	SND	22	C22	44 34	167 48
Mill Stream	STRM	33	A2	45 50	170 21
Millers Flat	LOC	27	F24	45 38	169 25
Millerton	TOWN	18	L16	41 38	171 52
Milltown	LOC	23	M20	43 50	172 16
Milne Islets	ISLS	4	—	29 17	177 54 W
Milson	SBRB	37	A3	40 20	175 37
Milton	BORO	27	G25	46 07	169 58
Mimihau	LOC	26	E25	46 20	168 55
Mina	LOC	18	P18	42 49	173 14
Minaret Burn	STRM	22	F22	44 31	169 05
Minaret Peaks	PEAK	22	F21	44 26	169 01
Minchin, Lake	LAKE	18, 23	L18	42 50	171 49
Miners Head	HEAD	7	T5	36 04	175 21
Minginui	LOC	11	W10	38 38	176 43
Miramar	SBRB	35	B8	41 19	174 49
Miranda	LOC	10	T7	37 11	175 19
Miromiro	MTN	18, 23	N17	42 29	172 40
Mirza	LOC	19	R16	41 52	174 07
Mission Bay	SBRB	31	C5	36 51	174 50
Mistake Peak	PEAK	23	H20	43 47	170 29
Mitcham	LOC	23	L20	43 45	171 51
Mitimiti	LOC	6	P3	35 26	173 16
Mititai	LOC	6	Q5	36 01	173 56
Mitre Peak	PEAK	22, 26	C22	44 38	167 51
Mitre	PEAK	15, 19	T14	40 48	175 27
Moa Creek	LOC	27	G23	45 13	169 40
Moa Flat	LOC	27	F24	45 43	169 19
Moana	LOC	18, 23	K18	42 35	171 28
Moanaroa Beach	LOC	14	T13	40 16	175 13
Moawhango	LOC	15	U12	39 35	175 52
Moawhango River	STRM	15	U12	39 45	175 55
Moehau	HILL	7, 10	T6	36 32	175 24
Moera	SBRB	35	B6	41 13	174 54
Moeraki	LOC	27	J23	45 22	170 50
Moeraki, Lake	LAKE	22	F20	43 43	169 17
Moeraki Point	PNT	27	J23	45 22	170 50
Moeraki River	STRM	22	F20	43 42	169 16
Moerangi	LOC	10	U10	38 54	175 35
Moerewa	TOWN	6	R3	35 23	174 01
Mohaka	LOC	11, 15	X11	39 07	177 12
Mohaka River	STRM	11, 15	X11	39 07	177 12
Mohakatino	LOC	10	S10	38 45	174 40
Mohakatino River	STRM	10	S10	38 44	174 35
Mokai	LOC	10	U10	38 32	175 54
Mokau	LOC	10	S10	38 41	174 37
Mokau River	STRM	10	S10	38 42	174 35
Mokauiti	LOC	10	T10	38 35	175 09
Mokauiti Stream	STRM	10	S10	38 32	174 55
Moke, Lake	LAKE	22, 26	E23	45 00	168 33
Mokeno, Lake	LAKE	6	R5	36 21	174 04
Mokihinui	LOC	18	L16	41 32	171 58
Mokihinui River	STRM	18	L16	41 32	171 57
Mokihinui River, N. Br.	STRM	18	M16	41 33	172 11
Mokihinui River, S. Br.	STRM	18	M16	41 33	172 11
Mokohinau Islands	ISLS	7	T4	35 56	175 07
Mokoia	LOC	14	R12	39 38	174 22
Mokoia	HILL	38	B3	38 05	176 17

NAME	DESC	PAGE	REF	LAT S	LONG E
Mokoia Island	ISLD	38	B3	38 05	176 17
Mokoreta	LOC	27	F25	46 26	169 04
Mokoreta	PEAK	27	F25	46 20	169 08
Mokoreta Stream	STRM	26	E25	46 22	168 50
Mokotua	LOC	26	E25	46 28	168 35
Molesworth	LOC	18	P17	42 06	173 17
Molesworth	LOC	7	S5	36 06	174 33
Momona	LOC	27	H24	45 56	170 14
Monaco	SBRB	39	A2	41 18	173 13
Monavale	LOC	23	J21	44 17	170 53
Monavale	LOC	10	T8	37 56	175 26
Moneymore	LOC	27	G25	46 10	169 54
Monk, Lake	LAKE	26	A25	46 01	166 58
Monowai	LOC	26	C24	45 47	167 38
Monowai, Lake	LAKE	26	B24	45 54	167 24
Montalto	LOC	23	K20	43 47	171 20
Monument Harbour	HARB	4	—	52 37	169 06
Moonlight	LOC	27	H23	45 24	170 20
Morere	LOC	11, 15	Y10	38 59	177 47
Morningside	SBRB	31	B5	36 53	174 44
Morningside	SBRB	36	A3	35 44	174 19
Mornington	SBRB	33	B3	45 53	170 28
Mornington	SBRB	35	A8	41 19	174 46
Morrinsville	BORO	10	U8	37 39	175 32
Morrisons	LOC	27	H23	45 16	170 29
Morrisons Bush	LOC	15, 19	T15	41 07	175 26
Morton Mains	LOC	26	E25	46 21	168 39
Morven	TOWN	23, 27	K22	44 49	171 06
Mosgiel	TOWN	33	A3	45 53	170 22
Mossburn	TOWN	26	D24	45 41	168 15
Motatapu, Mount	MT	22, 26	E22	44 43	168 50
Motatapu River	STRM	22, 26	E22	44 36	168 57
Motatau	LOC	6	R3	35 29	174 02
Motea	LOC	15	V13	40 19	176 15
Moteo	LOC	15	W12	39 31	176 45
Motiti Island	ISLD	11	V8	37 38	176 25
Motu	LOC	11	Y9	38 15	177 33
Motu River	STRM	11	Y8	37 51	177 35
Motueka	BORO	14, 18	P15	41 07	173 01
Motueka River	STRM	14, 18	P15	41 05	173 01
Motuhora	ISLD	11	W8	37 51	176 59
Motuhoropa Pa	ISLD	30	D2	36 41	174 50
Motuihe Channel	CHAN	30	D4	36 47	174 56
Motuihe Island	ISLD	30	D4	36 48	174 57
Motuiti	LOC	14, 19	T13	40 27	175 18
Motukaika	LOC	23	J21	44 23	170 59
Motukaraka	LOC	6	P3	35 23	173 30
Motukarara	LOC	23	N20	43 44	172 35
Motukawanui Island	ISLD	6	Q2	35 00	173 57
Motukawao Group	ISLS	7, 10	T6	36 40	175 23
Motukeo	HILL	38	C1	38 36	178 04
Motukiore	LOC	6	Q3	35 23	173 33
Motukorea Channel	CHAN	30	C4	36 49	174 53
Motumaoho	LOC	10	T8	37 41	175 28
Motunau	LOC	18, 23	N18	42 58	172 59
Motunau Beach	LOC	18, 23	P19	43 03	173 04
Motunau Island	ISLD	121	—	43 04	173 05
Motunui	LOC	10, 14	R10	39 00	174 18
Motuoapa	LOC	10	U10	38 56	175 52
Motuopao Island	ISLD	6	N1	34 28	172 38
Motuora Island	ISLD	7, 10	S6	36 30	174 48
Motuoroi Island	ISLD	11	Z9	38 15	178 20
Motuoruhi Island	ISLD	7, 10	T6	36 44	175 24
Motupia Island	ISLD	6	N2	34 36	172 48
Motupiko	LOC	14, 18	N15	41 27	172 49
Motupiko River	STRM	18	N15	41 27	172 50
Motupipi	LOC	14, 18	N14	40 51	172 52
Moturoa	SBRB	37	A1	39 04	174 02
Moturoa Islands	ISLS	6	P2	34 47	173 22
Motutaiko Island	ISLD	10	U10	38 51	175 56
Motutangi	LOC	6	P2	34 53	173 10
Motutapu Island	ISLD	30	D3	36 46	174 55
Motutapu Point	PNT	4	—	44 14	176 14 W
Motutara Point	PNT	7	R4	35 31	174 29
Motuti	LOC	6	P3	35 23	173 23
Mouat, Lake	LAKE	26	B25	46 01	167 01
Moumahaki	LOC	14	S12	39 47	174 41
Mount Albert	BORO	31	B5	36 53	174 43
Mount Aspiring	LOC	22	E21	44 28	168 47
Mount Biggs	LOC	15	T13	40 12	175 29
Mount Bruce	LOC	15, 19	U14	40 45	175 36
Mount Cargill	LOC	33	C2	45 48	170 34
Mount Curl	LOC	14	T12	39 58	175 27
Mount Eden	BORO	31	B5	36 53	174 46
Mount Hutt	LOC	23	L20	43 31	171 36
Mount Hutt Range	MTNS	23	L19	43 30	171 30
Mount Maunganui	BORO	36	B1	37 38	176 12
Mount Nessing	LOC	23	J21	44 16	170 47
Mount Pisa	LOC	22, 27	F22	44 56	169 16
Mount Pleasant	LOC	32	C3	43 34	172 42
Mount Pleasant	LOC	14, 19	Q15	41 20	174 00
Mount Richards	LOC	15	U13	40 06	175 33
Mount Roskill	BORO	31	B6	36 55	174 44
Mount Somers	LOC	23	K20	43 42	171 25
Mount Stewart	LOC	15	T13	40 15	175 29
Mount Stuart	LOC	27	G25	46 05	169 51
Mount Victoria	SBRB	35	A8	41 18	174 47
Mount Wellington	BORO	31	C5	36 54	174 50
Mount Wesley	LOC	6	Q4	35 57	173 52
Mourea	LOC	38	B3	38 03	176 19
Moutahiauru Island	ISLD	11	Z9	38 05	178 26
Moutere River	STRM	14	N15	41 09	173 00
Moutoa	LOC	14, 19	T14	40 31	175 24
Moutohora	TOWN	11	Y9	38 17	177 32
Mowhanau	LOC	14	S12	39 54	174 54
Mowhanau Stream	STRM	36	C1	39 51	175 02
Mt Cargill	LOC	33	C2	45 48	170 34
Mueller Glacier	GLCR	22	H20	43 45	170 02
Mueller, Lake	LAKE	22	H19	43 25	170 02
Muhunoa	LOC	14, 19	T14	40 39	175 12
Muhunoa East	LOC	14, 19	T14	40 41	175 18
Munning, Point	PNT	4	—	43 44	176 13 W
Munro Bay	BAY	36	D4	35 47	174 29
Murchison	TOWN	18	M16	41 48	172 20
Murchison Glacier	GLCR	22	H20	43 36	170 20
Murchison, Mount	MT	18, 23	K19	43 01	171 17
Murchison Mounts	MTNS	26	C23	45 15	167 35
Muritai	SBRB	35	B8	41 18	174 53
Muriwai	LOC	11	Y10	38 45	177 55
Muriwai Beach	LOC	7, 10	R6	36 50	174 26
Murrays Bay	SBRB	30	B3	36 44	174 45
Murumuru Point	PNT	4	—	44 21	176 15 W
Murupara	BORO	11	W9	38 27	176 42
Musgrave Inlet	BAY	4	—	50 40	166 11
Musick Point	PNT	31	C5	36 51	174 54
Mutton Bird Islands	ISLS	26	D26	46 51	168 14
Mutton Bird Islands	ISLS	26	B27	47 13	167 23
Myross Bush	LOC	40	D1	46 23	168 25
Nabhra	HILL	34	C5	41 07	175 00
Naenae	SBRB	35	C6	41 12	174 57
Naike	LOC	10	S8	37 31	174 57
Nancy Sound	SND	26	B23	45 06	167 01
Napier	CITY	15	W12	39 30	176 54
Napier	CITY	38	Urb	39 30	176 54
Napier Island	ISLD	4	—	29 13	177 52 W
Napier South	SBRB	38	D2	39 30	176 55
Narrow Neck	SBRB	30	B4	36 49	174 48
Narrows, The	LOC	14, 19	Q16	41 31	173 41
Naseby	LOC	22, 27	H23	45 01	170 09
Nathans Bridge	BDGE	18	M18	42 35	172 27
National Park	LOC	10, 14	T11	39 10	175 23
Naumai	TOWN	6	Q5	36 05	173 59
Nawton	SBRB	37	C1	37 47	175 15
Nayland	SBRB	39	A2	41 18	173 13
Neck, The	PEN	26	D26	46 56	168 11
Nelson	CITY	14, 18	P15	41 16	173 15
Nelson	CITY	39	Urb	41 16	173 15
Nelson Creek	LOC	18, 23	L17	42 24	171 31
Nelson Creek	STRM	18, 23	K17	42 24	171 26
Nelson East	SBRB	39	B2	41 17	173 17
Nelson Haven	HARB	39	B1	41 15	173 18
Nelson South	SBRB	39	B2	41 17	173 17
Nenthorn Stream	STRM	27	H24	45 38	170 14
Ness Valley	LOC	7, 10	T6	37 00	175 07
Netherby	SBRB	39	D1	43 54	171 46
Netherby	LOC	10	T8	37 35	175 17
Netherton	LOC	10	U7	37 20	175 36
Neudorf	LOC	14, 18	N15	41 15	172 59
Neumann Range	MTNS	22	G20	43 56	169 53
Nevis	LOC	26	E23	45 18	168 57
Nevis River	STRM	27	F23	45 04	169 02
New Brighton	SBRB	32	D2	43 31	172 44
New Caledonia Basin	SEAF	81	—	33 25	165 50
New Lynn	BORO	31	A6	34 55	174 41
New Plymouth	CITY	10, 14	R11	39 04	174 04
New Plymouth	CITY	37	Urb	39 04	174 04
New River Estuary	ESTY	40	C3	46 29	168 20
New River Ferry	LOC	26	D25	46 25	168 14
Newbury	LOC	37	A3	40 19	175 35
Newfield	SBRB	40	D2	46 25	168 23
Newland	LOC	23	L20	43 53	171 51
Newlands	SBRB	35	B6	41 13	174 49
Newman	LOC	15, 19	U14	40 37	175 42
Newmarket	BORO	31	B5	36 52	174 47
Newstead	LOC	10	T8	37 47	175 21
Newtown	SBRB	35	A8	41 19	174 47
Ngaere	LOC	14	R11	39 24	174 17
Ngahape	LOC	10	T9	38 09	175 21
Ngahere	TOWN	18, 23	K17	42 24	171 26
Ngahere Station	LOC	23	J22	44 47	170 58
Ngahina	HILL	11	W9	38 10	176 59
Ngahinapouri	LOC	10	T8	37 54	175 12
Ngaio	SBRB	35	A7	41 15	174 46
Ngaiotonga	LOC	7	R3	35 18	174 18
Ngakaroa	LOC	11	Y10	38 32	177 56
Ngakawau	TOWN	18	L16	41 37	171 52
Ngakonui	LOC	10	T10	38 49	175 18
Ngakuru	LOC	11	V9	38 20	176 11
Ngamatapouri	LOC	14	S12	39 35	174 49
Ngamatea	LOC	15	V11	39 24	176 08
Ngamoko	LOC	15	V13	40 04	176 10
Ngapaenga	LOC	10	S9	38 21	174 55
Ngapaeruru	LOC	15	V13	40 15	176 14
Ngapara	LOC	23, 27	V22	44 57	170 45
Ngapuhi	LOC	6	Q3	35 27	173 49
Ngapuke	LOC	10	T10	38 53	175 26
Ngapuna	LOC	27	H23	45 27	170 09
Ngapuna	LOC	38	B4	38 09	176 16
Ngaputahi	LOC	11	W10	38 35	176 50
Ngararatunua	LOC	7	R4	35 40	174 16
Ngaroma	LOC	10	U9	38 18	175 34
Ngaroto	LOC	10	T8	37 59	175 19
Ngarua	LOC	10	U8	37 40	175 41
Ngaruawahia	BORO	10	T8	37 40	175 09
Ngaruroro River	STRM	15	W12	39 34	176 55
Ngataki	LOC	6	P2	34 44	173 03
Ngatamahine	LOC	10	T10	38 32	175 05
Ngatamahine Point	PNT	7	T5	36 10	175 05
Ngatapa	LOC	11	Y10	38 35	177 47
Ngatea	TOWN	10	T7	37 16	175 29
Ngatimoti	LOC	14, 18	N15	41 12	172 53
Ngatira	LOC	10	U9	38 06	175 54
Ngatoro Stream	STRM	14	R11	39 08	174 17
Ngaturi	LOC	14	T12	39 52	175 17
Ngaturi	LOC	15, 19	U13	40 28	175 55
Ngaumu	LOC	15, 19	U15	41 03	175 53
Ngauruhoe, Mount	MTN	10, 15	U11	39 09	175 38
Ngaurukehu	LOC	15	U12	39 36	175 43
Ngawapurua	LOC	15, 19	U13	40 23	175 54
Ngawha	LOC	6	Q3	35 22	173 51
Ngawha Springs	LOC	6	Q3	35 24	173 51
Ngongotaha	LOC	38	A3	38 05	176 13
Ngongotaha	HILL	38	A4	38 07	176 12
Ngongotaha Stream	STRM	38	A3	38 05	176 13
Ngongotaha Valley	LOC	10	V9	38 07	176 09
Ngunguru	LOC	7	S4	35 37	174 30
Ngunguru Bay	BAY	7	S4	35 41	174 31
Ngutunui	LOC	10	T9	38 04	175 06
Ngutuwera	LOC	14	S12	39 46	174 44
Niagara	LOC	27	F26	46 36	169 08
Nicholson, Port	HARB	14, 19	S15	41 16	174 51
Nightcaps	TOWN	26	D24	45 58	168 02
Nihoniho	LOC	10	T10	38 48	175 04
Nikau	LOC	15, 19	U13	40 29	175 44
Nile Stream	STRM	18	K16	41 55	171 26
Nimrod, Mount	MT	23	U21	44 26	170 48
Ninety Mile Beach	BCH	6	N2	34 46	172 58
Nireaha	LOC	15, 19	U14	40 36	175 37
Noble Island	ISLD	26	C27	47 13	167 40
Noises, The	ISLS	30	D2	36 42	174 58
Nokomai	LOC	26	E24	45 30	168 40
Nokomai River	STRM	26	E24	45 34	168 39
Norfolk Basin	SEAF	81	—	31 10	169 20
Norfolk Island	ISLD	81	—	29 00	168 00
Norfolk Ridge	SEAF	81	—	28 40	167 50
Norman Inlet	BAY	4	—	50 43	166 10
Normanby	SBRB	33	C3	45 51	170 33
Normanby	TOWN	14	R12	39 32	174 16
Normanby	LOC	23	K21	44 28	171 15
Normandale	SBRB	35	B6	41 12	174 53
Norsewood	TOWN	15	V13	40 04	176 13
Norsewood South	TOWN	15	V13	40 04	176 13
North Arm	FIOR	4	—	50 48	166 03
North Cape	CAPE	4	—	49 40	178 47
North Beach	LOC	18, 23	K17	42 24	171 13
North Cape	CAPE	6	P1	34 25	173 03
North Clyde	LOC	11, 15	X11	39 02	177 26
North Dunedin	SBRB	33	B3	45 52	170 31
North East Cape	CAPE	4	—	50 30	166 20
North East Harbour	HARB	4	—	52 31	169 12
North East Island	ISLD	4	—	48 02	166 36
North East Island	ISLD	4	—	34 08	172 10
North East Valley	SBRB	33	B3	45 51	170 32
North Fiord	FIOR	26	C23	45 04	167 45
North Harbour	HARB	4	—	50 30	169 07
North Head	HEAD	6	R5	36 24	174 03
North Head	HEAD	30	C4	36 50	174 49

NAME	DESC	PAGE	REF	LAT S	LONG E
North Linwood	SBRB	32	C3	43 32	172 40
North New Brighton	SBRB	32	C2	43 30	172 43
North Opuha River	STRM	23	J20	43 59	170 53
North Red Head	HEAD	26	C26	46 45	167 42
North River	LOC	7	R4	35 57	174 24
North Rough Ridge	RDGE	27	G23	45 10	169 49
North Taieri	LOC	27	H24	45 51	170 21
North Taranaki Bight	BAY	10	R10	38 50	174 25
North West Bay	BAY	4	—	34 09	172 12
North West Bay	BAY	4	—	52 32	169 04
North West Cape	CAPE	4	—	50 32	166 03
Northcote	SBRB	32	B2	43 29	172 37
Northcote	SBRB	30	B4	36 49	174 45
Northland	SBRB	35	A7	41 17	174 45
Norton Reserve	LOC	23, 27	K22	44 42	171 03
Norwood	LOC	23	M20	43 39	172 14
Nugent Island	ISLD	4	—	29 13	177 52 W
Nugget Point	PNT	27	G25	46 27	169 49
Nuhaka	TOWN	11, 15	Y11	39 02	177 45
Nuhaka River	STRM	11, 15	Y11	39 03	177 45
Nukuhau	LOC	10	V10	38 41	176 04
Nukuhou North	LOC	11	X9	38 08	177 08
Nukumaru	LOC	14	S12	39 49	174 48
Nukutawhiti	LOC	6	Q4	35 38	173 52
Oaklands	SBRB	32	A3	43 35	172 34
Oakleigh	LOC	36	A4	35 50	174 19
Oakura	TOWN	10, 14	Q11	39 07	173 57
Oakura	LOC	7	R3	35 23	174 20
Oakura River	STRM	14	Q11	39 07	173 57
Oakwood Stream	STRM	40	B3	44 22	171 15
Oamaru	BORO	27	J23	45 05	170 59
Oamaru	BORO	39	Urb	45 05	170 59
Oamaru Bay	BAY	7, 10	T6	36 44	175 28
Oamaru Creek	STRM	39	D3	45 06	170 58
Oaonui	LOC	14	Q11	39 24	173 49
Oaonui Stream	STRM	14	Q11	39 24	173 47
Oaro	LOC	18	P18	42 31	173 30
Obelisk	PEAK	27	F23	45 19	169 13
Observatory Hill	HILL	39	B2	41 17	173 15
Ocean Bay	BAY	4	—	43 50	176 46 W
Ocean Beach	LOC	15	X12	39 44	177 00
Ocean Beach	LOC	40	C4	46 35	168 18
Ocean Beach	BCH	7	S4	35 50	174 34
Ocean Grove	SBRB	33	C4	45 54	170 33
Ocean View	LOC	33	A4	45 56	170 20
Oeo	LOC	14	Q12	39 32	173 59
Ohaeawai	TOWN	6	Q3	35 21	173 53
Ohai	TOWN	26	C24	45 56	167 57
Ohakea	LOC	14	T13	40 12	175 23
Ohakune	LOC	14	T11	39 25	175 25
Ohakuri	LOC	10	V9	38 24	176 05
Ohakuri, Lake	LAKE	10	V9	38 26	176 08
Ohangai	LOC	14	R12	39 35	174 23
Ohao Point	PNT	6	P1	34 30	173 00
Ohapuku	LOC	32	B1	43 23	172 38
Ohariu Bay	BAY	35	A6	41 13	174 43
Ohariu Stream	STRM	35	A7	41 14	174 43
Ohariu Valley	LOC	35	A6	41 12	174 46
Ohau	LOC	15, 19	T14	40 40	175 15
Ohau Channel	CHAN	38	B3	38 03	176 19
Ohau, Lake	LAKE	22	G21	44 14	169 51
Ohau River	STRM	14, 19	T14	40 39	175 09
Ohau River	STRM	22	H21	44 20	170 08
Ohauiti	LOC	11	V8	37 46	176 11
Ohaupo	TOWN	10	T8	37 55	175 18
Ohautira	LOC	10	S8	37 45	174 59
Ohawe Beach	LOC	14	R12	39 35	174 12
Ohia, Lake	LAKE	6	P2	34 58	173 22
Ohikanui River	STRM	18	L16	41 51	171 43
Ohinau Island	ISLD	7, 10	U6	36 44	175 53
Ohinemutu	SBRB	38	A4	38 07	176 15
Ohinepaka	LOC	11, 15	X11	39 01	177 20
Ohinepanea	LOC	11	W8	37 50	176 33
Ohinepoutea	LOC	11	Z8	37 51	178 06
Ohinewai	LOC	10	T7	37 29	175 10
Ohingaiti	LOC	15	U12	39 52	175 42
Ohirangi	LOC	7, 10	R6	36 42	174 26
Ohiwa Harbour	HARB	11	X8	38 00	177 09
Ohoka	LOC	23	N19	43 22	172 34
Ohope Beach	LOC	11	X8	37 58	177 03
Ohotu	LOC	15	U12	39 43	175 50
Ohuka	LOC	11	X10	38 50	177 15
Ohura	TOWN	10	S10	38 51	174 59
Ohura River	STRM	10	T11	39 03	175 04
Oio	LOC	10, 14	T11	39 04	175 23
Okaeria	LOC	10	T7	37 20	175 18
Okahu	LOC	6	R4	36 00	174 03
Okahu Stream	STRM	14	Q11	39 21	173 46
Okahukura	LOC	10	T10	38 47	175 14
Okaiawa	TOWN	14	R12	39 32	174 12
Okaihau	TOWN	6	Q3	35 19	173 46
Okains Bay	LOC	23	P20	43 43	173 02
Okains Bay	BAY	23	P20	43 42	173 04
Okaramio	LOC	14, 19	Q15	41 25	173 46
Okareka, Lake	LAKE	11	V9	38 10	176 21
Okarito Lagoon	LAGN	22	H19	43 13	170 12
Okataina, Lake	LAKE	11	V9	38 08	176 25
Okato	TOWN	14	Q11	39 12	173 53
Okau	LOC	10	S10	38 52	174 39
Okauia	LOC	10	U8	37 47	175 50
Okawa	LOC	15	W12	39 33	176 42
Okawa Bay	BAY	38	B3	38 03	176 20
Okawa Point	PNT	4	—	43 46	176 14 W
Okere Falls	LOC	11	V9	38 01	176 20
Okete	LOC	10	S8	37 48	174 55
Okitu	LOC	38	C2	38 41	178 05
Okiwi	LOC	7	T5	36 09	175 24
Okoia	LOC	14	T12	39 55	175 08
Okoki	LOC	10, 14	R11	39 01	174 29
Okoroire	LOC	10	U8	37 57	175 48
Okoroire Station	LOC	10	U8	37 56	175 45
Okotuku	LOC	14	S12	39 44	174 39
Okuku	LOC	23	M19	43 13	172 26
Okuku River	STRM	23	M19	43 15	172 28
Okura River	STRM	30	B2	36 40	174 44
Okuri Point	PNT	14, 19	Q14	40 58	173 46
Okuru	LOC	22	E20	43 55	168 54
Okuru River	STRM	22	E20	43 54	168 54
Okuti Valley	LOC	23	N20	43 49	172 47
Old Man Peak	PEAK	22, 27	G22	44 36	169 41
Old Man Range	MTNS	27	F23	45 25	169 13
Old Man Reef	REEF	4	—	44 01	176 20 W
Olivine Range	MTNS	22	E22	44 18	168 30
Omaha Bay	BAY	7	S5	36 20	174 49
Omaha Flats	LOC	7	S5	36 20	174 44
Omahaki	LOC	15	V11	39 28	176 24
Omahina	LOC	14	S12	39 43	174 42
Omahu	LOC	10	U7	37 16	175 39
Omahu	LOC	15	W12	39 35	176 46
Omahuta	LOC	6	Q3	35 13	173 36
Omaio	LOC	11	Y8	37 49	177 38
Omaka	LOC	14, 19	Q16	41 33	173 47
Omaka Aerodrome	AIR	39	A4	41 32	173 55
Omaka River	STRM	14, 19	Q15	41 30	173 53
Omakau	LOC	27	G23	45 06	169 36
Omakere	LOC	15	W13	40 03	176 45
Omakere	HILL	15	W3	40 06	176 46
Omamari	LOC	6	Q4	35 52	173 40
Omana	LOC	6	R4	35 54	174 06
Omanaia	LOC	6	Q3	35 27	173 31
Omanawa	LOC	10	V8	37 48	176 05
Omanu	SBRB	36	B1	37 40	176 13
Omapere	LOC	6	P4	35 32	173 23
Omapere	LOC	15	W12	39 37	176 38
Omapere, Lake	LAKE	6	Q3	35 21	173 47
Omarama	LOC	22	G21	44 29	169 58
Omarama Stream	STRM	22	G21	44 28	169 59
Omaru River	STRM	14	S11	39 29	174 45
Omarumutu	LOC	11	X8	38 59	177 24
Omata	TOWN	37	A2	39 06	174 01
Omatane	LOC	15	U12	39 44	175 56
Omaunu	LOC	6	Q3	35 06	173 44
Omiha	LOC	7, 10	T6	36 49	175 04
Omihi	LOC	18, 23	N19	43 01	172 51
Omimi	LOC	27	J24	45 41	170 36
Omoeroa River	STRM	22	H19	43 19	170 02
Omokoroa	LOC	10	V8	37 40	176 03
Omokoroa Beach	LOC	10	V8	37 38	176 03
Omoto	LOC	40	A2	42 27	171 14
Omotumotu Creek	STRM	40	A2	42 27	171 14
Onaero	LOC	10, 14	R10	39 00	174 20
One Tree Hill	BORO	31	B6	36 54	174 48
One Tree Point	LOC	7	R4	35 49	174 27
One Tree Point	PNT	36	C4	35 49	174 27
Onehunga	BORO	31	B6	36 55	174 47
Onekaka	LOC	18	N14	40 46	172 42
Onekawa	SBRB	38	D2	39 30	176 53
Onepu	LOC	11	W9	38 03	176 44
Onepuhi	LOC	15	T13	40 04	175 28
Onerahi	SBRB	36	B3	35 46	174 22
Oneraki Beach	BCH	4	—	29 15	177 55 W
Oneriri	LOC	7	R5	36 17	174 22
Oneroa	LOC	30	D4	36 47	175 00
Onetangi	LOC	7, 10	T6	36 47	175 05
Onetaunga Bay	BAY	30	A4	36 49	174 42
Onewhero	LOC	10	S7	37 19	174 55
Ongaonga	TOWN	15	V12	39 55	176 25
Ongare Point	LOC	10	U7	37 30	175 58
Ongaroto	LOC	10	U9	38 25	175 54
Ongarue	TOWN	10	T10	38 43	175 16
Ongarue River	STRM	10	T10	38 53	175 15
Oniao	LOC	10	T10	38 35	175 04
Onoke, Lake	LAKE	19	T15	41 23	175 08
Onslow, Lake	LAKE	27	G24	45 33	169 37
Opaea	LOC	15	U12	39 36	175 48
Opaheke	LOC	10	S7	37 05	174 57
Opahi	LOC	6	R3	35 28	174 00
Opaki	LOC	37	D3	40 53	175 39
Opaku	LOC	14	S12	39 41	174 33
Opapa	LOC	15	W12	39 48	176 41
Opape	LOC	11	X8	37 59	177 25
Oparakau	LOC	6	R5	36 06	174 07
Oparara	LOC	18	M15	41 13	172 08
Oparara River	STRM	18	M15	41 13	172 06
Oparau	LOC	10	S9	38 03	174 56
Oparure	LOC	10	T9	38 19	175 07
Opatu	LOC	10, 14	T11	39 00	175 01
Opawa	SBRB	32	C3	43 33	172 40
Opawa River	STRM	39	B4	41 31	174 02
Open Bay	BAY	35	A5	41 07	174 48
Open Bay Island	ISLD	22	E20	43 52	168 53
Ophir	LOC	27	G23	45 07	169 36
Opihi	LOC	23	K21	44 13	171 04
Opihi River	STRM	23	K21	44 17	171 22
Opiki	LOC	15, 19	T13	40 27	175 28
Opio	LOC	26	D24	45 57	168 06
Opoho	SBRB	33	C3	45 51	170 32
Oponae	LOC	11	X9	38 15	177 17
Opononi	LOC	6	P4	35 30	173 24
Oporo	LOC	26	D25	46 18	168 16
Opotiki	BORO	11	X9	38 01	177 17
Opouawe River	STRM	14, 19	T16	41 34	175 26
Opouri Valley	LOC	14, 19	Q15	41 13	173 41
Opouri River	STRM	14, 19	Q15	41 12	173 35
Opouriao	LOC	11	W9	38 06	177 00
Opoutama	LOC	11, 15	Y11	39 03	177 50
Opouteke	LOC	6	Q4	35 42	173 50
Opoutere	LOC	10	U7	37 06	175 52
Opua	LOC	6	R3	35 18	174 07
Opuatia	LOC	10	S7	37 24	175 00
Opuatia Stream	STRM	10	T7	37 25	175 03
Opuawhanga	LOC	7	R4	35 30	174 20
Opuha	LOC	23	K21	44 10	171 00
Opunake	BORO	14	Q11	39 27	173 51
Oraka Point	PNT	26	C25	46 24	167 53
Oraka Stream	STRM	10	U8	37 54	175 48
Orakau	LOC	10	T9	38 02	175 23
Orakei	SBRB	31	C5	37 51	174 49
Orakipaoa	LOC	23	K21	44 16	171 19
Oranga	SBRB	31	B6	36 55	174 47
Orangapai	LOC	27	H23	45 14	170 08
Orari	TOWN	23	K21	44 08	171 18
Orari Bridge	LOC	23	K21	44 03	171 16
Orari River	STRM	23	K21	44 15	171 26
Oratia	SBRB	31	A6	36 55	174 37
Orauea River	STRM	26	C25	46 06	167 43
Orautoha	LOC	14	T11	39 21	175 14
Orawia	LOC	26	C25	46 03	167 48
Orde Lees Island	ISLD	4	—	49 41	178 45
Orepuki	LOC	26	C25	46 17	167 44
Orepunga Pa	LOC	10	U9	38 02	175 37
Orere	LOC	7, 10	T6	36 59	175 14
Orere Point	LOC	7, 10	T6	36 58	175 15
Orete Point	PNT	11	Y8	37 36	177 54
Oreti Beach	LOC	26	D25	46 26	168 14
Oreti River	STRM	26	D25	46 28	168 17
Orewa	LOC	7, 10	S6	36 35	174 42
Oriental Bay	BAY	35	A8	41 17	174 47
Orikaka River	STRM	18	L16	41 50	171 54
Oringi	LOC	15	V13	40 16	176 01
Orini	TOWN	10	T8	37 33	175 19
Orinoco	LOC	14, 19	N15	41 14	172 53
Ormond	TOWN	38	A1	38 33	177 55
Ormondville	TOWN	15	V13	40 06	176 15
Oromahoe	LOC	6	Q3	35 19	173 59
Orongo	LOC	10	U7	37 12	175 33
Orongorongo, Mount	MT	35	D7	41 15	175 05
Orongorongo River	STRM	14, 19	S15	41 25	174 54
Oropi	LOC	10	V8	37 50	176 09
Oroua	STRM	14	T13	40 25	175 26
Oroua Downs	LOC	14, 19	T13	40 22	175 19
Orowaiti	LOC	18	L16	41 45	171 40
Orr, Mount	MTN	23, 27	J22	44 45	170 38
Orton	LOC	23	K21	44 09	171 25
Orton	LOC	10	T7	37 23	175 02
Orua Bay	BAY	31	A8	37 03	174 36
Oruaiti	LOC	6	Q3	35 00	173 36

NAME	DESC	PAGE	REF	LAT S	LONG E
Oruaiwi	LOC	10	T10	38 50	175 28
Oruanui	LOC	10	V10	38 35	176 02
Oruawharo	LOC	7	R5	36 16	174 24
Oruawharo River	STRM	7	R5	36 17	174 18
Oruru	LOC	6	Q3	35 03	173 30
Oruru River	STRM	6	P2	35 00	173 28
Orwell Creek	LOC	18, 23	L17	42 22	171 40
Osborne	LOC	33	C1	45 46	170 37
Ostend	LOC	7, 10	T6	36 48	175 03
Ota Creek	LOC	26	E25	46 17	168 48
Otago Harbour	HARB	33	D2	45 49	170 40
Otago Peninsula	PEN	27	J24	45 51	170 45
Otahu	LOC	26	C24	45 58	167 42
Otahuhu	BORO	31	C6	36 57	174 50
Otahuti	LOC	26	D25	46 14	168 11
Otaika	LOC	7	R4	35 47	174 18
Otaika Valley	LOC	7	R4	35 47	174 14
Otaio	LOC	23	K22	44 35	171 09
Otaio River	STRM	23	K22	44 33	171 11
Otairi	LOC	15	U12	39 51	175 30
Otaitai	LOC	26	D25	46 20	168 02
Otakaha Stream	STRM	14, 19	T16	41 33	175 13
Otakairangi	LOC	6	R4	35 36	174 11
Otakeho	TOWN	14	R12	39 33	174 03
Otaki	BORO	14, 19	T14	40 45	175 08
Otaki Beach	LOC	14, 19	T14	40 44	175 07
Otaki River	STRM	14, 19	T14	40 45	175 07
Otakiri	LOC	11	W8	37 58	176 46
Otakou	LOC	33	D2	45 48	170 43
Otama	LOC	26	E24	45 58	168 52
Otamarakau	LOC	11	W8	37 50	176 36
Otamatea	SBRB	36	C1	39 55	175 01
Otamauri	LOC	15	V12	39 30	176 30
Otane	TOWN	15	W12	39 54	176 37
Otanerito Bay	BAY	23	P20	43 50	173 03
Otangarei	SBRB	36	A2	35 42	174 20
Otangaroa	LOC	6	Q3	35 06	173 38
Otangiwai	LOC	10	T10	38 43	175 06
Otanomomo	LOC	27	G25	46 18	169 45
Otapiri	LOC	26	D25	46 03	168 25
Otapiri Stream	STRM	26	E25	46 10	168 31
Otara	SBRB	31	C6	36 58	174 53
Otara	LOC	11	X9	38 03	177 19
Otara	LOC	26	E26	46 38	168 53
Otara Island	ISLD	30	D2	36 42	174 59
Otaraia	LOC	27	F25	46 12	169 05
Otaraia	LOC	14, 19	T15	41 17	175 19
Otaramarae	LOC	11	V9	38 01	176 21
Otatara	TOWN	40	C2	46 26	168 17
Otaua	LOC	10	S7	37 18	174 44
Otaua	LOC	6	Q4	35 30	173 42
Otautau	TOWN	26	C25	46 09	168 00
Otautu	LOC	14	S12	39 43	174 30
Otawhao	LOC	15	V13	40 03	176 17
Otehe Point	PNT	10	S8	37 36	174 46
Otekaieke	LOC	23, 27	J22	44 49	170 34
Otekaieke River	STRM	23, 27	J22	44 49	170 34
Otekura	LOC	27	G25	46 26	169 46
Otematata	TOWN	22, 27	H22	44 37	170 11
Otematata River	STRM	22, 27	H22	44 36	170 12
Oteramika	LOC	26	E25	46 25	168 30
Otewa	LOC	10	T9	38 13	175 17
Otiake	LOC	23, 27	H22	44 47	170 30
Otiake River	STRM	23, 27	H22	44 48	170 32
Otipua	LOC	40	A4	44 26	171 10
Otira	LOC	18, 23	L18	42 51	171 33
Otiria	LOC	6	Q3	35 24	174 00
Otiria Stream	STRM	6	R3	35 22	174 06
Otoi	LOC	11, 15	X10	38 57	177 04
Otokia	LOC	27	H24	45 57	170 12
Otoko	LOC	14	T12	39 44	175 20
Otoko	LOC	11	Y9	38 28	177 39
Otoko River	STRM	22	G20	43 46	169 30
Otonga	LOC	7	R4	35 34	174 17
Otope	LOC	15, 19	V13	40 20	176 05
Otoroa	LOC	6	Q3	35 05	173 51
Otorohanga	BORO	10	T9	38 11	175 12
Otorokua Point	PNT	22	G19	43 25	169 47
Ototoa, Lake	LAKE	7,10	R6	36 31	174 14
Otuhie, Lake	LAKE	18	M14	40 41	172 25
Otumoetai	SBRB	36	A1	37 40	176 09
Otunui	LOC	10	T10	38 55	175 10
Oturehua	LOC	22, 27	G23	45 01	169 55
Oturoa	LOC	10	V9	38 02	176 10
Oturu	LOC	6	P3	35 05	173 17
Oue	LOC	6	P3	35 27	173 30
Ouruhia	LOC	23	N19	43 26	172 39
Outram	TOWN	27	H24	45 52	170 14
Overdale	LOC	23	M20	43 47	172 00
Overton	LOC	15	T13	40 02	175 27
Owahanga	LOC	16	V14	40 41	176 20
Owahanga Stream	STRM	15	V14	40 41	176 21
Owairaka	SBRB	31	B5	36 54	174 43
Owairaka Valley	LOC	10	T9	38 06	175 29
Owaka	TOWN	27	G25	46 27	169 40
Owaka Valley	LOC	27	G25	46 26	169 35
Oware	LOC	26	E25	46 20	168 56
Owen Head	HEAD	26	D27	47 07	168 08
Owen, Mount	MTN	18	N16	41 33	172 32
Owen River	LOC	18	M16	41 41	172 27
Owen River	STRM	18	M16	41 41	172 27
Owenga	LOC	4	—	44 01	176 23 W
Owhakatoro	LOC	11	W9	38 08	176 55
Owhango	TOWN	10, 14	T10	39 00	175 22
Owhata	LOC	38	B4	38 08	176 18
Owhiro	LOC	10	S9	38 10	174 52
Owhiro Bay	SBRB	35	A8	41 21	174 45
Oxford	BORO	23	M19	43 18	172 11

NAME	DESC	PAGE	REF	LAT S	LONG E
Pacific Basin, Southwestern	SEAF	81	—	54 00	178 00 W
Pacific Ocean	OCN	2, 3	—	—	—
Paekakariki	TOWN	34	C2	40 59	174 57
Paemako	LOC	10	S9	38 30	174 58
Paenga	LOC	18	M16	41 56	172 12
Paengaroa	TOWN	11	V8	37 49	176 25
Paepaerahi	LOC	10	T9	38 03	175 29
Paerata	LOC	10	S7	37 10	174 54
Paerau	LOC	27	G23	45 26	169 57
Paeroa	BORO	10	U7	37 23	175 41
Paeroa Range	MTNS	11	V9	38 23	176 14
Paewhenua	LOC	10	T9	38 16	175 24
Pahaoa River	STRM	15, 19	U15	41 24	175 44
Pahau	LOC	18, 23	N18	42 48	172 47
Pahau River	STRM	18, 23	N18	42 50	172 54
Pahautea	LOC	14, 19	T15	41 14	175 23
Pahi	LOC	6	R5	36 09	174 14
Pahia	LOC	26	C25	46 20	167 45
Pahia Point	PNT	26	C25	46 19	167 41
Pahiatua	BORO	15, 19	U13	40 27	175 50
Pahoia	LOC	10	V8	37 38	176 00
Pahurehure Inlet	BAY	31	C8	37 03	174 53
Paihia	TOWN	6	R3	35 16	174 05
Pakarae	LOC	11	Z10	38 31	178 15

NAME	DESC	PAGE	REF	LAT S	LONG E
Pakarae River	STRM	11	Z10	38 33	178 15
Pakaraka	LOC	6	Q3	35 21	173 57
Pakatoa Island	ISLD	7, 10	T6	36 48	175 12
Pakawau	LOC	18	N14	40 36	172 41
Pakeho	LOC	10	T9	38 21	175 03
Pakihi	LOC	14	T11	39 26	175 19
Pakihi Island	ISLD	7, 10	T6	36 55	175 10
Pakihi Stream	STRM	11	X9	38 07	177 22
Pakihikura	LOC	15	U12	39 56	175 43
Pakipaki	LOC	15	W12	39 42	176 47
Pakiri	LOC	7	S5	36 16	174 44
Pakotai	LOC	6	Q4	35 41	173 54
Pakowhai	LOC	38	C3	39 35	176 52
Pakuranga	TOWN	31	C6	36 54	174 54
Pakuranga Creek	STRM	31	C6	36 56	174 52
Palliser Bay	BAY	14, 19	T15	41 24	175 08
Palliser Bay	LOC	14, 19	T16	41 33	175 13
Palliser, Cape	CAPE	14, 19	T16	41 37	175 16
Palm Beach	LOC	7, 10	T6	36 47	175 03
Palmer Head	HEAD	35	B8	41 21	174 49
Palmerston	BORO	27	J23	45 29	170 43
Palmerston North	CITY	15, 19	U13	40 21	175 37
Palmerston North	CITY	37	Urb	40 21	175 37
Pamapuria	LOC	6	P3	35 08	173 21
Panetapu	LOC	10	T9	38 09	175 28
Pangatotara	LOC	14, 18	N15	41 11	172 54
Panguru	LOC	6	P3	35 23	173 22
Panmure	TOWN	31	C5	36 54	174 51
Paoanui Point	PNT	15	W13	40 05	176 54
Papaaroha	LOC	7, 10	T6	36 42	175 26
Papaiti	LOC	14	T12	39 53	175 05
Papaka Stream	STRM	40	B3	44 21	171 14
Papakaio	LOC	23, 27	J22	44 59	170 59
Papakowhai	SBRB	34	B5	41 06	174 52
Papakura	BORO	31	D8	37 03	174 57
Papakura Channel	CHAN	31	B8	37 02	174 46
Papakura Stream	STRM	31	C8	37 03	174 54
Papamoa	LOC	11	V8	37 44	176 17
Papamoa Beach	LOC	11	V8	37 43	176 20
Papanui	SBRB	32	B2	43 30	172 36
Papanui Inlet	BAY	33	D3	45 51	170 41
Papanui Junction	LOC	15	U12	39 41	175 33
Paparangi	LOC	14	S12	39 43	174 59
Paparangi	SBRB	35	B6	41 13	174 49
Paparata	LOC	10	T7	37 10	175 03
Paparimu	LOC	10	T7	37 07	175 09
Paparoa	TOWN	7	R5	36 05	174 15
Paparoa Range	MTNS	18	L17	42 05	171 35
Paparore	LOC	6	P2	34 59	173 13
Papatahi	LOC	14, 19	T15	41 18	175 10
Papatahi	HILL	35	D8	41 19	175 03
Papatawa	LOC	15, 19	U13	40 19	175 56
Papatoetoe	CITY	31	C7	36 59	174 51
Papatotara	LOC	26	C25	46 09	167 38
Papawai	LOC	15, 19	T15	41 06	175 29
Papawera	LOC	11	Z8	37 54	178 16
Paponga	LOC	6	P3	35 17	173 26
Para	LOC	14, 19	Q15	41 23	173 56
Parahaki	HILL	36	A3	35 43	174 20
Paraheka	LOC	10	S10	38 37	174 56
Parakai	LOC	7, 10	R6	36 39	174 26
Parakao	LOC	6	Q4	35 43	173 57
Parakino	LOC	14	T12	39 48	175 10
Paranui	LOC	6	P3	35 03	173 28
Parapara	LOC	6	P3	35 01	173 25
Parapara	LOC	18	N14	40 45	172 41
Parapara	LOC	14	T12	39 31	175 18
Paraparaumu	TOWN	34	C1	40 55	175 00
Paraparaumu Beach	SBRB	34	C1	40 53	174 59
Paratu	LOC	10	U8	37 46	175 38
Parau	LOC	7, 10	S6	36 58	174 37
Parawera	LOC	10	T9	38 04	175 25
Paremata	LOC	34	B4	41 06	174 52
Paremoremo	LOC	30	A3	36 46	174 39
Paremoremo Creek	STRM	30	A3	36 46	174 38
Parengarenga Harbour	HARB	6	P2	34 31	173 00
Pareora	TOWN	23	K21	44 29	171 13
Pareora River	STRM	23	K21	44 30	171 13
Pareora West	LOC	40	A4	44 26	171 08
Paretai	LOC	27	G25	46 20	169 47
Parewanui	LOC	14	T13	40 14	175 19
Parihaka Pa	LOC	14	Q11	39 17	173 51
Parihauhau	LOC	14	T12	39 44	175 15
Parikawa	LOC	19	Q17	42 05	173 57
Paringa, Lake	LAKE	22	F20	43 43	169 24
Paringa River	STRM	22	F20	43 37	169 26
Pariroa Pa	LOC	14	R12	39 43	174 28
Paritutu	HILL	37	A1	39 04	174 01
Park Hill	LOC	27	F24	45 48	169 13
Parkhurst	LOC	7, 10	R6	36 38	174 24
Parkside	SBRB	40	B4	44 24	171 15
Parkvale	LOC	15, 19	U15	41 03	175 34
Parkvale	SBRB	36	A2	37 43	176 08
Parkvale	SBRB	38	C4	39 39	176 51
Parnassus	TOWN	18	P18	42 43	173 17
Parnell	SBRB	31	B5	36 51	174 47
Paroa	LOC	11	W8	37 57	176 56
Paroa	LOC	40	A2	42 31	171 10
Parore	LOC	6	Q4	35 55	173 50
Parry Channel	CHAN	7	S4	35 54	174 40
Parsons Rock	ROCK	4	—	29 17	177 58 W
Parua Bay	LOC	7	R4	35 47	174 27
Parua Bay	BAY	36	C3	35 47	174 28
Passage Islands	ISLS	26	A25	46 02	166 32
Patangata	LOC	15	W12	39 55	176 44
Pataua	LOC	7	S4	35 43	174 31
Patea	BORO	14	R12	39 46	174 29
Patea River	STRM	14	R12	39 46	174 30
Patearoa	LOC	27	H23	45 16	170 03
Paterangi	LOC	10	T8	37 57	175 15
Pateriki, Lake	LAKE	4	—	43 45	176 18 W
Paterson Inlet	BAY	26	D26	46 55	168 00
Patetonga	LOC	10	T7	37 24	175 28
Patiti Point	PNT	40	B4	44 25	171 16
Patriarch, Mount	MT	14, 18	P16	41 38	173 13
Pattisson, Cape	CAPE	4	—	43 45	176 48 W
Patumahoe	TOWN	10	S7	37 11	174 49
Paturau River	STRM	18	M14	40 39	172 28
Patutahi	TOWN	11	Y10	38 37	177 53
Patutu	MT	15	U11	39 15	175 51
Paua	LOC	6	N2	34 32	172 56
Pauatahanui	LOC	34	C4	41 05	174 55
Pauri, Lake	LAKE	36	D2	39 58	175 06
Pawarenga	LOC	6	P3	35 21	173 16
Peaks, The	LOC	18, 23	N18	42 50	172 35
Pearl Island	ISLD	26	C27	47 11	167 43
Pearson, Lake	LAKE	23	L19	43 06	171 47
Peebles	LOC	23, 27	J22	44 58	170 56
Peel Forest	LOC	23	K20	43 55	171 16
Peel, Mount	MT	23	K20	43 51	171 10
Peel Range	MTNS	18	M15	41 05	172 30
Peep-O-Day	LOC	15	U12	39 57	175 49
Pegasus Bay	BAY	23	N19	43 22	172 50
Pegasus, Port	HARB	26	C27	47 12	167 42

NAME	DESC	PAGE	REF	LAT S	LONG E
Pehiri	LOC	11	Y10	38 39	177 41
Pekapekarau	LOC	6	Q4	35 45	173 56
Pekatahi	LOC	11	W9	38 03	176 59
Pelorus Bridge	LOC	14, 18	Q15	41 18	173 34
Pelorus River	STRM	14, 19	Q15	41 16	173 43
Pelorus Sound	SND	14, 19	Q15	41 08	173 53
Pembroke	LOC	14	R11	39 20	174 14
Pembroke, Mount	MT	22	C22	44 34	167 52
Pencarrow Head	HEAD	14, 19	S15	41 21	174 51
Pendarves	LOC	23	L20	43 53	171 59
Penguin Bay	BAY	4	—	52 32	169 00
Penrose	SBRB	31	B6	36 55	174 49
Pentland Hills	LOC	23, 27	J22	44 42	170 48
Pepepe	LOC	10	S8	37 35	174 56
Pepin Island	ISLD	14, 18	P15	41 09	173 25
Peraki Bay	BAY	23	N20	43 52	172 49
Perano Head	HEAD	14, 19	R15	41 12	174 22
Peria	LOC	10	U8	37 48	175 43
Peria	LOC	6	P3	35 06	173 29
Perpendicular Point	PNT	18	K17	42 05	171 20
Perseverance Harbour	HARB	4	—	52 33	169 10
Perth River	STRM	23	H19	43 20	170 28
Petone	BORO	35	B6	41 13	174 53
Petre Bay	BAY	4	—	43 54	176 38 W
Philip Island	ISLD	81	—	29 18	168 00
Phoebe	LOC	18	P18	42 46	173 14
Piako	LOC	10	U8	37 39	175 33
Piako River	STRM	10	U7	37 12	175 30
Piarere	LOC	10	U8	37 56	175 40
Picton	BORO	14, 19	R15	41 18	174 00
Pig Island	ISLD	7	T5	35 13	175 18
Pig Island	ISLD	22, 26	D22	44 57	168 26
Pigeon Bay	LOC	23	N20	43 42	172 54
Pigeon Bay	BAY	23	N20	43 38	172 55
Pigeon Bush	LOC	14, 19	T15	41 09	175 16
Pigeon Island	ISLD	22, 26	D22	44 56	168 25
Pigeon Valley	VLY	14, 18	P15	41 22	173 01
Piha	LOC	7, 10	R6	36 57	174 28
Pihama	LOC	14	Q12	39 30	173 56
Pihanga	HILL	10, 15	U11	39 02	175 46
Pikes Point	LOC	23, 27	K22	44 53	171 03
Piko Piko	LOC	26	C25	46 07	167 43
Pikowai	LOC	11	W8	37 51	176 40
Pillans Pass	PASS	26	B24	45 36	167 10
Pine Bush	LOC	26	E25	46 28	168 48
Pine Hill	SBRB	33	B2	45 50	170 31
Pine Valley	LOC	18	Q16	41 32	173 31
Pinedale	SBRB	30	B3	36 45	175 45
Pinedale	LOC	10	U9	38 03	175 49
Pinehaven	SBRB	35	C5	41 10	175 01
Pinelheugh	MTN	27	G23	45 28	169 30
Pines, The	LOC	32	C1	43 23	172 42
Pinnacle	PEAK	18	P16	41 49	173 17
Piopio	TOWN	10	T9	38 27	175 01
Pipinui Point	PNT	35	A6	41 10	174 44
Pipiriki	LOC	14	T11	39 29	175 03
Pipiroa	LOC	10	T7	37 13	175 29
Pipiwai	LOC	6	R4	35 37	174 01
Piriaka	LOC	10	T10	38 55	175 21
Pirimai	SBRB	38	D2	39 33	176 53
Pirinoa	LOC	14, 19	T15	41 21	175 12
Piripai	LOC	11	W8	37 56	176 58
Piripaua	LOC	11	X10	38 50	177 10
Piripiri	LOC	15	V13	40 10	176 08
Piripiri	LOC	10	S9	38 15	174 52
Pirongia	TOWN	10	T8	38 00	175 12
Piropiro	LOC	10	T10	38 36	175 24
Pisa, Mount	MT	22, 27	F22	44 52	169 12
Pisa Range	MTNS	22, 27	F22	44 54	169 10
Pisgah, Mount	MT	27	H23	45 05	170 24
Pisgah, Mount	MT	26	B23	45 06	167 29
Pitt Island	ISLD	4	—	44 18	176 12 W
Pitt Strait	STRA	4	—	44 10	176 22 W
Plate Island	ISLD	11	W8	37 40	176 34
Plateau, The	LOC	14, 19	T15	41 05	175 08
Pleasant, Mount	HILL	32	C3	43 35	172 44
Pleasant Point	TOWN	23	K21	44 16	171 08
Pleasant Valley	LOC	23	K21	44 05	171 11
Pleckville	LOC	15, 19	U14	40 40	175 46
Plimmerton	TOWN	34	B4	41 05	174 51
Poerua, Lake	LAKE	18, 23	K18	42 42	171 29
Poerua River	STRM	23	H19	43 03	170 25
Pohangina	LOC	15	U13	40 11	175 48
Pohangina Stream	STRM	15	U13	40 18	175 47
Pohara	LOC	14, 18	N14	40 50	172 52
Pohokura	LOC	11	W10	38 58	176 32
Pohokura	HILL	11, 15	W10	38 57	176 43
Pohonui	LOC	15	U12	39 46	175 34
Pohuehue	LOC	7, 10	S5	36 28	174 39
Point Chevalier	SBRB	31	A5	36 52	174 42
Point Howard	SBRB	35	B7	41 15	174 54
Point Wells	LOC	7	S5	36 19	174 45
Poison Bay	BAY	26	C22	44 39	167 38
Pokaiwhenua Stream	STRM	10	U8	38 00	175 40
Pokapu	LOC	6	Q3	35 26	173 59
Pokeno	TOWN	10	T7	37 15	175 01
Pokohinu Point	PNT	11	Y8	37 48	177 38
Pokopoko Stream	STRM	11	V8	37 47	176 29
Pokororo	LOC	14, 18	N15	41 13	172 51
Pokuru	LOC	10	T9	38 03	175 15
Pollok	LOC	10	S7	37 08	174 37
Pollux	MTN	22	E21	44 14	168 52
Polnoon	STRM	22, 26	E22	44 43	168 43
Pomahaka	LOC	27	F25	46 01	169 14
Pomahaka River	STRM	27	G25	46 09	169 34
Pomona Island	ISLD	26	B24	45 31	167 28
Ponatahi	LOC	15, 19	U15	41 05	175 34
Ponga	LOC	10	T7	37 06	175 01
Pongakawa	LOC	11	V8	37 49	176 29
Pongakawa River	STRM	11	V8	37 47	176 29
Pongakawa Valley	LOC	11	W8	37 57	176 31
Pongaroa	TOWN	15, 19	V14	40 33	176 11
Ponsonby	SBRB	31	B5	36 51	174 45
Ponui Island	ISLD	7, 10	T6	36 52	175 11
Pool Burn	STRM	27	G23	45 11	169 41
Poolburn	LOC	27	G23	45 08	169 42
Poolburn Reservoir	RESR	27	G23	45 19	169 44
Poor Knights Islands	ISLS	7	S3	35 28	174 44
Poporangi Stream	STRM	15	V12	39 34	176 26
Popotunoa	LOC	27	F25	46 06	169 23
Poraiti	LOC	15	W11	39 29	176 50
Porangahau	TOWN	15	W13	40 18	176 38
Porangahau Stream	STRM	15	W13	40 17	176 40
Porewa	LOC	15	T13	40 02	175 28
Pori	LOC	15, 19	U14	40 36	175 56
Porirua	TOWN	35	B5	41 08	174 50
Porirua East	SBRB	35	B5	41 08	174 51
Porirua Harbour	HARB	34	B4	41 06	174 52
Porirua Pa	SBRB	35	B5	41 07	174 50
Porirua Stream	STRM	35	B5	41 08	174 50
Porootarao	LOC	10	T10	38 33	175 18
Poroporo	LOC	11	W8	37 59	176 58
Poroporo Valley	VLY	11	Z8	37 47	178 20
Poroti	LOC	6	R4	35 44	174 08

NAME	DESC	PAGE	REF	LAT S	LONG E
Poroutawhao	LOC	14, 19	T14	40 33	175 16
Porpoise Bay	BAY	27	F26	46 39	169 06
Port Albert	LOC	7	R5	36 17	174 26
Port Chalmers	BORO	33	C2	45 49	170 37
Port Charles	LOC	7, 10	T6	36 32	175 28
Port Fitzroy	LOC	7	T5	36 10	175 21
Port Gore	HARB	14, 19	R15	41 02	174 14
Port Hardy	HARB	14, 19	Q14	40 45	173 53
Port Jackson	LOC	7, 10	T5	36 29	175 20
Port Levy	LOC	23	N20	43 39	172 49
Port Molyneux	LOC	27	G25	46 22	169 47
Port Nelson	SBRB	39	B1	41 16	173 16
Port Waikato	LOC	10	S7	37 23	174 44
Portage	LOC	14, 19	R15	41 12	174 02
Porters Pass	PASS	23	L19	43 18	171 44
Portland	LOC	36	A4	35 48	174 20
Portland Island	ISLD	15	Y11	39 18	177 52
Portobello	SBRB	33	D2	45 50	170 39
Portobello Bay	BAY	33	D2	45 50	170 40
Potaka	LOC	11	Z8	37 35	178 10
Potato Point	PNT	33	C1	45 44	170 38
Poteriteri, Lake	LAKE	26	B25	46 05	176 05
Potts	MTN	23	J20	43 30	170 56
Potts River	STRM	23	J20	43 35	170 55
Pouarua, Lake	LAKE	15	V10	38 58	176 24
Pouawa	LOC	11	Z10	38 37	178 11
Poukawa	LOC	15	W12	39 45	176 44
Poukawa, Lake	LAKE	15	W12	39 47	176 43
Poukiore	LOC	15	U12	39 52	175 37
Poulter Range	MTNS	18, 23	L18	42 51	171 55
Poulter River	STRM	18, 23	L19	43 04	171 55
Pounawea	LOC	27	G25	46 28	169 42
Pounui, Lake	LAKE	35	D8	41 21	175 07
Pourakino Valley	LOC	26	C25	46 14	167 55
Pourerere	LOC	15	W13	40 06	176 52
Pourewa Island	ISLD	11	Z9	38 23	178 21
Pouto	LOC	6	R5	36 22	174 11
Poverty Bay	BAY	11	Y10	38 43	178 00
Prebbleton	TOWN	32	A3	43 35	172 31
Preservation Inlet	BAY	26	A25	46 07	166 35
Princes Islands	ISLS	4	—	34 10	172 03
Progress Valley	LOC	27	F26	46 36	169 12
Providence, Cape	CAPE	26	A25	46 01	166 28
Puaha	LOC	23	N20	43 45	172 50
Puahue	LOC	10	T9	38 02	175 25
Puarenga Stream	STRM	38	B4	38 08	176 16
Puerua	LOC	27	G25	46 20	169 41
Pueto Stream	STRM	11	V10	38 36	176 15
Puha	LOC	11	Y9	38 28	177 50
Puhinui	SBRB	31	C7	36 59	174 51
Puhipuhi	LOC	7	R3	35 29	174 17
Puhoi	LOC	7, 10	S6	36 31	174 40
Puhuka	LOC	40	B3	44 22	171 14
Pukahu	SBRB	15	W12	39 41	176 50
Pukaki Canal	CANL	22	H21	44 15	170 05
Pukaki, Lake	LAKE	22	H21	44 05	170 10
Pukaki Rise	SEAF	81	—	49 40	172 10
Pukaki River	STRM	22	H21	44 18	170 13
Pukaki Saddle	SEAF	81	—	49 00	176 40
Pukearuhe	LOC	10	S10	38 54	174 30
Pukeatua	LOC	10	U9	38 04	175 35
Pukeatua	HILL	30	A2	36 43	174 40
Pukeatue	LOC	15	V13	40 16	176 08
Pukeawa	LOC	27	G25	46 09	169 37
Pukehiki	LOC	33	C3	45 53	170 37
Pukehina	LOC	11	W8	37 49	176 31
Pukehou	LOC	15	W12	39 50	176 38
Pukehuia	LOC	6	R4	35 52	174 02
Pukekapia	LOC	10	T8	37 32	175 07
Pukekawa	LOC	10	S7	37 20	174 59
Pukekohe	BORO	10	S7	37 12	174 54
Pukekohe East	LOC	10	S7	37 11	174 57
Pukekohe West	LOC	10	S7	37 13	174 52
Pukemaori	LOC	26	C25	46 05	167 48
Pukemiro	TOWN	10	T8	37 37	175 01
Pukemoremore	LOC	10	T8	37 48	175 29
Pukengahu	LOC	14	R11	39 23	174 24
Pukenui	LOC	6	P2	34 49	173 07
Pukeo	LOC	14, 19	T15	41 15	175 21
Pukeokahu	LOC	15	V12	39 37	176 00
Pukeora	LOC	15	V12	39 59	176 30
Pukeowhare	LOC	10	S7	37 14	174 45
Pukepito	LOC	27	G25	46 10	169 39
Pukepoto	LOC	6	P3	35 09	173 13
Pukerangi	LOC	27	H24	45 38	170 13
Pukerau	LOC	27	F25	46 06	169 06
Pukerimu	LOC	10	T8	37 55	175 25
Pukeroa	LOC	15	U12	39 47	175 30
Pukeroro	LOC	10	T8	37 53	175 25
Pukerua Bay	LOC	34	B3	41 02	174 53
Puketa	LOC	19	Q17	42 26	173 35
Puketaha	LOC	37	D1	37 43	175 19
Puketapu	LOC	15	W12	39 31	176 47
Puketawai	LOC	11	Z9	38 20	178 18
Puketeraki Range	MTNS	18, 23	M18	43 00	172 10
Puketi	LOC	27	G25	46 03	169 36
Puketi	LOC	6	Q3	35 14	173 47
Puketihi	LOC	10	S10	38 55	174 55
Puketitiri	LOC	15	W11	39 17	176 32
Puketoi Range	MTNS	15, 19	V13	40 27	176 07
Puketona	LOC	6	Q3	35 18	173 58
Puketotara	LOC	10	T9	38 03	175 10
Puketurua	LOC	10	U9	38 04	175 41
Puketutu	LOC	10	T9	38 26	175 14
Puketutu Island	ISLD	31	B7	36 58	174 45
Pukeuri Junction	LOC	39	D2	45 02	171 02
Pulling Point	PNT	33	D2	45 48	170 39
Punakaiki	LOC	18	K17	42 07	171 20
Punakaiki River	STRM	18	K17	42 07	171 21
Punakitere River	STRM	6	Q3	35 28	173 39
Punakitere Valley	LOC	6	Q3	35 28	173 53
Punaruku	LOC	7	R3	35 22	174 19
Punawai	LOC	23	L20	43 47	171 32
Pungaere	LOC	6	Q3	35 10	173 50
Pungapunga	LOC	10	T10	38 53	175 22
Pungapunga River	STRM	10	T10	38 53	175 20
Pungarehu	TOWN	14	Q11	39 17	173 48
Puni	LOC	10	S7	37 14	174 51
Punui Bay	BAY	4	—	48 01	166 36
Puniho	LOC	14	Q11	39 12	173 50
Puniu River	STRM	10	T9	38 01	175 12
Puniwhakau	LOC	14	S11	39 20	174 37
Puponga	LOC	18	N14	40 32	172 43
Pupuke	LOC	6	Q3	35 06	173 44
Pupuke, Lake	LAKE	30	B3	36 47	174 46
Purakanui	LOC	33	C1	45 45	170 38
Purakanui Bay	BAY	33	C1	45 44	170 37
Purakau Channel	CHAN	31	A7	36 59	174 42
Puramahoi	LOC	18	N14	40 48	172 44
Purau	LOC	23	N20	43 38	172 45
Purau Bay	BAY	32	D4	43 37	172 45
Purekireki	LOC	27	F25	46 22	169 28
Pureora Forest	LOC	10	U10	38 31	175 33
Purerua	LOC	6	R3	35 08	174 03

NAME	DESC	PAGE	REF	LAT S	LONG E
Purerua Peninsula	PEN	6	R3	35 09	174 05
Puriri	TOWN	10	U7	37 14	175 38
Purua	LOC	6	R4	35 38	174 06
Putara	LOC	15, 19	U14	40 40	175 34
Putaruru	BORO	10	U9	38 03	175 47
Putauhina Island	ISLD	26	B27	47 13	167 23
Putere	LOC	11, 15	X10	38 57	177 02
Putiki	SBRB	36	D2	39 57	175 03
Putorino	LOC	15	U12	39 59	175 35
Putorino	LOC	11, 15	X11	39 08	177 00
Puwera	LOC	7	R4	35 48	174 16
Puwera Stream	STRM	36	A4	35 47	174 17
Puysegur Point	PNT	26	A25	46 10	166 37
Puysegur Trench	SEAF	81	—	48 30	164 00
Pye, Mount	HILL	27	F25	46 25	169 18
Pyes Pa	LOC	10	V8	37 49	176 08
Pyke, Mount	MT	22	D21	44 22	168 09
Pyke River	STRM	22	D21	44 30	168 11
Pyramid	LOC	26	E24	45 56	168 46
Pyramid, Mount	MT	22, 26	D22	44 50	168 01
Pyramid, The	ISLD	4	—	44 25	176 14 W
Quail Island	ISLD	32	C4	43 38	172 41
Quail Valley	LOC	14, 18	N15	41 29	172 58
Quarantine Island	ISLD	33	C2	45 50	170 38
Quarantine Point	PNT	33	C2	45 50	170 39
Quarry Hills	LOC	27	F26	46 33	169 02
Queen Charlotte Sound	SND	14, 19	R15	41 15	174 09
Queen Elizabeth Park	PARK	34	C2	40 57	174 58
Queensberry	LOC	22, 27	F22	44 50	169 20
Queenstown	TOWN	22, 26	E23	45 02	168 40
Queenwood	SBRB	37	D1	37 45	175 16
Quill, Lake	LAKE	22, 26	C22	44 48	167 44
Quoin Point	PNT	27	H25	46 09	170 10
Rabbit Island	ISLD	14, 18	P15	41 16	173 09
Racecourse Hill	LOC	23	M19	43 27	172 04
Raes Junction	LOC	27	F24	45 47	169 28
Raetihi	BORO	14	T11	39 26	175 17
Ragged Point	PNT	14, 19	Q14	40 50	173 47
Ragged Range	MTNS	23	K19	43 13	171 05
Raggedy Range	MTNS	27	G23	45 08	169 39
Raglan	TOWN	10	S8	37 48	174 52
Raglan Harbour	HARB	10	S8	37 48	174 50
Rahiwi	LOC	15, 19	V14	40 48	176 09
Rahotu	TOWN	14	Q11	39 20	173 48
Rahui	LOC	15	V14	40 47	176 08
Rahuimokairoa	HILL	15	Y11	39 11	177 53
Rai River	STRM	14, 19	Q15	41 17	173 35
Rai Valley	LOC	14, 19	Q15	41 14	173 35
Raincliff	LOC	23	J21	44 09	170 59
Rakahouka	LOC	26	D25	46 20	168 29
Rakaia	TOWN	23	M20	43 45	172 01
Rakaia Huts	LOC	23	M20	43 53	172 14
Rakaia River	STRM	23	M20	43 54	172 13
Rakau	LOC	14, 18	N15	41 25	172 48
Rakaunui	LOC	15, 19	V14	40 36	176 08
Rakauroa	LOC	11	Y9	38 25	177 34
Rakautara	LOC	19	Q17	42 16	173 48
Rakautatahi	LOC	15	V13	40 01	176 13
Rakeahua, Mount	MT	26	C26	46 57	167 53
Rakeahua River	STRM	26	C26	46 58	167 55
Rakeinui, Lake	LAKE	4	—	44 04	176 35 W
Rakino Island	ISLD	30	D2	36 43	175 57
Rakitu Island	ISLD	7	U5	36 07	175 30
Ramarama	LOC	10	S7	37 09	174 58
Rameses, Mount	MTN	18, 23	L17	42 27	171 56
Ramsay Glacier	GLCR	23	J19	43 16	170 55
Ranana	LOC	14	T12	39 35	175 06
Ranfurly	BORO	27	H23	45 08	170 06
Rangataua	TOWN	15	T11	39 26	175 28
Rangatira Island	ISLD	4	—	44 21	176 10 W
Rangatira Valley	LOC	23	K21	44 12	171 12
Rangaunu Bay	BAY	6	P2	34 49	173 16
Rangaunu Harbour	HARB	6	P2	34 56	173 16
Rangi Point	LOC	6	P3	35 28	173 23
Rangiahua	LOC	11, 15	X10	38 57	177 19
Rangiahua	LOC	6	Q3	35 18	173 38
Rangiatea	LOC	10	T9	38 13	175 19
Rangiauria Point	PNT	4	—	44 19	176 16 W
Rangikura	LOC	14	S12	39 46	174 33
Rangiora	BORO	23	N19	43 18	172 36
Rangiotu	LOC	15, 19	T13	40 25	175 26
Rangipo	LOC	10, 15	U11	39 04	175 49
Rangipo Desert	DSRT	15	U11	39 21	175 41
Rangipukea Island	ISLD	7, 10	T6	36 50	175 25
Rangiriri	LOC	10	T7	37 26	175 08
Rangiriri West	LOC	10	T7	37 27	175 08
Rangitai, Lake	LAKE	4	—	43 46	176 22 W
Rangitaiki	LOC	11	V10	38 53	176 21
Rangitaiki River	STRM	11	W8	37 55	176 53
Rangitata	LOC	23	K21	44 04	171 22
Rangitata Island	LOC	23	K21	44 06	171 26
Rangitata River	STRM	23	K20	43 40	171 30
Rangitata River	STRM	23	K21	44 10	171 30
Rangitikei River	STRM	14	T13	40 17	175 13
Rangitopuni Stream	STRM	30	A3	36 44	174 37
Rangitoto	LOC	10	T9	38 20	175 15
Rangitoto Channel	CHAN	30	C4	36 47	174 49
Rangitoto Island	ISLD	30	C3	36 47	174 52
Rangitoto Islands	ISLS	14, 19	Q14	40 46	173 59
Rangitoto Range	MTNS	10	T9	38 23	175 30
Rangitukia	LOC	11	Z8	37 46	178 27
Rangitumau	LOC	15, 19	U14	40 51	175 42
Rangiuru	LOC	11	V8	37 47	176 23
Rangiwaea	LOC	15	U12	39 35	175 35
Rangiwaea Island	ISLD	36	A1	37 38	176 07
Rangiwahia	TOWN	15	U12	39 54	175 55
Ranui	LOC	7, 10	S6	36 52	174 36
Ranui Heights	SBRB	35	B5	41 09	175 50
Raoul Island	ISLD	4	—	29 16	177 55 W
Raorikia	LOC	14	T12	39 47	175 05
Rapahoe	LOC	40	B1	42 22	171 14
Rapaki	LOC	32	C4	43 36	172 41
Rapanui	LOC	14	S12	39 54	174 55
Rapaura	LOC	39	A3	41 28	173 54
Rappahannock	LOC	18	M17	42 05	172 15
Rarangi	LOC	14, 19	R15	41 24	174 03
Rata	LOC	15	T12	40 00	175 30
Rataiti	LOC	15	U12	39 54	175 31
Ratana	LOC	14	T13	40 02	175 10
Ratanui	LOC	15, 19	V14	40 45	176 04
Ratanui	LOC	27	G26	46 30	169 38
Ratapiko	LOC	14	R11	39 13	174 20
Raukawa	LOC	15	W12	39 45	176 40
Raukokore	LOC	11	Y8	37 38	177 53
Raukokore River	STRM	11	Y8	37 39	177 52
Raukumara	HILL	11	Z8	37 45	178 08
Raukumara Range	MTNS	11	Y8	37 52	177 59
Raumai	LOC	15	U13	40 13	175 47
Raumanga	SBRB	36	A3	35 45	174 18
Raumati	LOC	15	V13	40 12	176 09
Raumati Beach	SBRB	34	C1	40 55	174 59
Raumati South	SBRB	34	C1	40 56	174 59
Raungaehe Range	MTNS	11	W9	38 05	176 52
Raupare	LOC	15	W12	39 36	176 49
Raupo	LOC	6	Q5	36 07	173 59
Raupunga	LOC	11, 15	X11	39 04	177 09
Raureka	SBRB	38	C4	39 38	176 50
Raurimu	LOC	10, 14	T11	39 07	175 24
Ravensbourne	LOC	33	C3	45 52	170 33
Rawene	TOWN	6	Q3	35 24	173 30
Rawhitiroa	LOC	14	R11	39 26	174 21
Raynal, Mount	MT	4	—	50 43	166 04
Red Beach	LOC	30	B1	36 36	174 43
Red Hill	MTN	14, 18	P16	41 38	173 03
Red Mercury Island	ISLD	7, 10	U6	36 37	175 56
Redan	LOC	26	E25	46 22	168 59
Redcliffs	SBRB	32	D3	43 34	172 44
Redhill	LOC	6	Q5	36 04	173 52
Redvale	LOC	30	A2	36 41	174 42
Redwood	SBRB	35	B6	41 11	174 49
Redwoods Valley	LOC	14, 18	P15	41 18	173 05
Redwoodtown	SBRB	39	B4	41 32	173 57
Reef Point	PNT	4	—	49 41	178 48
Reefton	TOWN	18	L17	42 07	171 52
Rees River	STRM	22, 26	D22	44 50	168 23
Rehia	LOC	6	R5	36 03	174 02
Rehutai	LOC	6	Q4	35 58	173 47
Reidston	LOC	27	J23	45 09	170 51
Reikorangi	LOC	34	D1	40 54	175 05
Reinga, Cape	CAPE	6	N1	34 25	172 41
Reinga Ridge	SEAF	81	—	33 30	170 40
Remarkables, The	MTNS	26	E23	45 08	168 50
Remote Peaks	PEAK	22	D21	44 22	168 25
Remuera	SBRB	31	B5	36 53	174 48
Renown	LOC	10	T8	37 34	175 03
Renweeks Reef	REEF	4	—	44 04	176 24 W
Renwick	LOC	14, 19	Q15	41 30	173 50
Reporoa	TOWN	11	V9	38 26	176 20
Reporua	LOC	11	Z8	37 52	178 24
Rere	LOC	11	Y10	38 32	177 34
Rereatukahia Pa	LOC	10	U8	37 35	175 55
Rerewhakaaitu	LOC	11	V9	38 19	176 29
Rerewhakaaitu, Lake	LAKE	11	V9	38 18	176 30
Reserve Point	PNT	36	C4	35 48	174 27
Resolution Island	ISLD	26	A24	45 40	166 35
Retaruke	LOC	10, 14	T11	39 07	175 08
Retaruke River	STRM	10, 14	T11	39 07	175 04
Rewa	LOC	15	U12	39 59	175 38
Rewa	HILL	15, 19	U15	41 03	175 59
Rewanui	LOC	40	B1	42 23	171 19
Rewarewa	LOC	10	T9	38 18	175 19
Rewatu	LOC	11	W8	38 00	176 59
Rewiti	LOC	7, 10	R6	36 45	174 28
Riccarton	BORO	32	B3	43 32	172 36
Richardson Mountains	MTNS	22, 26	E22	44 46	168 32
Richmond	BORO	39	A2	41 21	173 11
Richmond	SBRB	40	D2	46 25	168 22
Richmond	SBRB	32	C2	43 31	172 39
Richmond	LOC	23, 27	K23	45 01	171 03
Richmond Brook	LOC	19	Q16	41 45	173 57
Richmond Downs	LOC	10	U8	37 48	175 40
Richmond, Mount	MT	14, 18	P15	41 28	173 14
Richmond Range	MTNS	14, 18	P15	41 28	173 25
Rimariki Island	ISLD	7	R3	35 26	174 27
Rimu	LOC	26	E25	46 24	168 30
Rimu	LOC	18, 23	J18	42 47	171 00
Rimuroa	LOC	11	Z10	38 38	178 03
Rimutaka Range	MTNS	14, 19	T15	41 17	175 04
Ringdove Bay	BAY	4	—	49 42	178 47
Ringway	LOC	26	D25	46 11	168 01
Ringway Ridges	LOC	26	D25	46 10	168 03
Ripia River	STRM	11, 15	W11	39 12	176 30
Riponui	LOC	6	R4	35 34	174 10
Ripponvale	LOC	22, 27	F23	45 03	169 10
Rira	LOC	10	T10	38 36	175 04
Rissington	LOC	15	W11	39 26	176 43
Riverhead	TOWN	7, 10	S6	36 45	174 35
Riverlands	SBRB	39	B4	41 32	173 59
Riverlea	LOC	14	R11	39 26	174 05
Riversdale	SBRB	39	B4	41 30	173 58
Riversdale	LOC	15, 19	V15	41 05	176 04
Riversdale	TOWN	26	E24	45 54	168 44
Riverside	SBRB	36	A3	35 43	174 20
Riverside	LOC	23	L21	44 01	171 49
Riverside	LOC	27	H24	45 52	170 16
Riverton	BORO	26	D25	46 21	168 01
Riwaka	TOWN	14, 18	N15	41 05	173 00
Riwaka River	STRM	14, 18	N15	41 04	173 00
Riwaka Valley	LOC	14, 18	N15	41 03	172 57
Roaring Lion River	STRM	18	M15	41 12	172 26
Roaring Meg	STRM	22, 27	F22	45 00	169 04
Robert Creek	STRM	26	E23	45 23	168 34
Robertson Point	PNT	14, 19	R15	41 21	174 07
Robinsons Bay	LOC	23	N20	43 46	172 58
Rock and Pillar	LOC	27	H23	45 24	170 12
Rock and Pillar Range	MTNS	27	H23	45 23	170 07
Rock Point	PNT	35	A5	4 08	174 47
Rockdale	SBRB	40	D2	46 25	168 24
Rockford	LOC	23	M19	43 19	172 01
Rocks, The	LOC	22, 27	G23	45 02	169 43
Rocks Point	PNT	18	M14	40 51	172 08
Rockville	TOWN	18	N14	40 44	172 38
Rockwood	LOC	23	J21	44 10	170 56
Rocky Point	PNT	6	R3	35 07	174 05
Roding River	STRM	14, 18	P15	41 24	173 08
Rodney, Cape	CAPE	7	S5	36 17	174 49
Rokeby	LOC	23	L20	43 44	171 55
Rolleston	TOWN	23	M20	43 35	172 23
Rolleston, Mount	MTN	18, 23	K18	42 55	171 30
Rolleston Range	MTNS	23	K19	43 10	171 14
Romahapa	LOC	27	G25	46 21	169 44
Rona Bay	SBRB	35	B7	41 17	174 54
Ronald, Lake	LAKE	22, 26	C22	44 38	167 43
Ronga Stream	STRM	14, 19	Q15	41 13	173 35
Rongahere	LOC	27	F24	45 59	169 29
Rongokokako	LOC	15, 19	U14	40 39	175 39
Rongomai	LOC	15, 19	U14	40 36	175 47
Rongotea	TOWN	14	T13	40 18	175 25
Rose Island	ISLD	4	—	50 31	166 15
Rosedale	SBRB	40	D1	46 23	168 22
Rosedale	LOC	14, 18	N15	41 14	172 57
Roseneath	SBRB	33	C2	45 50	170 36
Roseneath	SBRB	35	A7	41 17	174 48
Rosewill	LOC	40	A3	44 20	171 10
Roslyn	SBRB	33	B3	45 52	170 29
Roslyn	SBRB	37	B2	40 20	175 37
Roslyn Bush	LOC	40	D1	46 21	168 26
Ross	LOC	18, 23	J18	42 54	170 49
Ross, Mount	MT	14, 19	T15	41 27	175 20
Ross, Port	HARB	4	—	50 31	166 15
Rossmore	LOC	19	Q16	41 39	173 57
Rosy Peak	PEAK	22	E21	44 10	168 50
Rotherham	TOWN	18, 23	N18	42 42	172 57
Rothesay Bay	SBRB	30	B2	36 43	174 45
Rotoaira, Lake	LAKE	10, 15	U11	39 03	175 42
Rotoehu	LOC	11	W9	38 02	176 32

NAME	DESC	PAGE	REF	LAT S	LONG E
Rotoehu, Lake	LAKE	11	W9	38 01	176 32
Rotoiti	LOC	11	V9	38 03	176 28
Rotoiti, Lake	LAKE	11	V9	38 02	176 25
Rotoiti, Lake	LAKE	18	N16	41 50	172 50
Rotokakahi	LOC	6	P3	35 20	173 17
Rotokakahi, Lake	LAKE	11	V9	38 13	176 19
Rotokakahi River	STRM	6	P3	35 20	173 17
Rotokauri	LOC	10	T8	37 46	175 12
Rotokawa	LOC	11	V9	38 06	176 19
Rotokawa, Lake	LAKE	38	B4	38 07	176 19
Rotokino	LOC	22	H19	43 12	170 22
Rotokino, Lake	LAKE	23	H19	43 09	170 26
Rotokohu	LOC	18	L16	41 58	171 54
Rotoma, Lake	LAKE	11	W9	38 03	176 35
Rotomahana	LOC	11	V9	38 18	176 24
Rotomahana, Lake	LAKE	11	V9	38 16	176 26
Rotomanu	LOC	18, 23	L18	42 39	171 32
Rotongaro	LOC	10	T8	37 32	175 05
Rotongaro, Lake	LAKE	10	T7	37 29	175 06
Rotongata	LOC	10	U9	38 08	175 34
Rotoorangi	LOC	10	T8	37 59	175 27
Rotoroa Island	ISLD	7, 10	T6	36 49	175 12
Rotoroa, Lake	LAKE	18	N16	41 51	172 38
Rotorua	CITY	11	V9	38 09	176 15
Rotorua	CITY	38	Urb	38 09	176 15
Rotorua, Lake	LAKE	38	B3	38 05	176 16
Rototuna	LOC	6	R5	36 15	174 02
Rototuna	LOC	37	D1	37 44	175 16
Rotowaro	LOC	10	T8	37 35	175 05
Rough Ridge	MTNS	27	G23	45 17	169 51
Round Head	HEAD	26	B22	44 55	167 13
Round Hill	LOC	26	C25	46 20	167 50
Round Knob	PEAK	35	B5	41 10	174 53
Round Rock	ROCK	4	—	44 22	176 21 W
Rowan	LOC	14	R11	39 24	174 07
Roxburgh	BORO	27	F24	45 33	169 19
Roxburgh East	LOC	27	F24	45 33	169 21
Roxburgh Hydro	LOC	27	F23	45 29	169 19
Roxburgh, Lake	LAKE	27	F23	45 20	169 20
Royden Downs	LOC	11	V8	37 52	176 25
Ruahine	LOC	15	U12	39 51	175 54
Ruahine Range	MTNS	15	V12	39 45	176 10
Ruakaka	LOC	7	R4	35 54	174 26
Ruakaka River	STRM	36	B4	35 51	174 21
Ruakituri	LOC	11	X10	38 46	177 24
Ruakituri River	STRM	11	Y10	38 50	177 31
Ruakiwi	LOC	10	S8	37 42	174 55
Ruakokoputuna	LOC	14, 19	T15	41 19	175 25
Ruakokoputuna River	STRM	15, 19	U15	41 12	175 32
Ruakura	LOC	10	T8	37 45	175 20
Ruakura Junction	LOC	37	D1	37 46	175 20
Ruamahanga River	STRM	14, 19	T15	41 22	175 08
Ruanui	LOC	15	U12	39 37	175 39
Ruapapa	LOC	11, 15	X10	38 57	177 10
Ruapehu, Mount	MTN	15	U11	39 17	175 34
Ruapekapeka	LOC	6	R3	35 27	174 08
Ruapuke	LOC	10	S8	37 55	174 48
Ruapuke Island	ISLD	26	E26	46 46	168 31
Ruapuna	LOC	23	K20	43 52	171 21
Ruarangi	LOC	7	R4	35 56	174 17
Ruaroa	LOC	15	V13	40 11	176 03
Ruatahuna	LOC	11	W10	38 38	176 58
Ruatangata West	LOC	6	R4	35 40	174 10
Ruataniwha	LOC	15	V12	39 56	176 30
Ruataniwha Inlet	BAY	18	N14	40 40	172 40
Ruatapu	LOC	18, 23	J18	42 48	170 53
Ruatiti	LOC	14	T11	39 16	175 12
Ruato	LOC	11	V9	38 04	176 25
Ruatoki	LOC	11	X9	38 09	177 00
Ruatoria	TOWN	11	Z8	37 54	178 19
Ruawai	TOWN	6	R5	36 08	174 02
Ruawaro	LOC	10	T8	37 32	175 03
Ruawhata	LOC	15, 19	U13	40 23	175 50
Ruby Bay	TOWN	14, 18	P15	41 14	173 05
Rugged Islands	ISLS	26	C26	46 42	167 43
Rukuhia	LOC	37	D2	37 51	175 18
Rukuhia Swamp	SWMP	37	C2	37 51	175 15
Runanga	LOC	15	W12	39 34	176 43
Runanga	BORO	40	B1	42 24	171 15
Runanga, Lake	LAKE	15	W12	39 34	176 43
Runaruna	LOC	6	P3	35 18	173 21
Runaway, Cape	CAPE	11	Y8	37 32	177 59
Runciman	LOC	10	S7	37 06	174 57
Rununder Point	PNT	14, 19	R15	41 19	174 14
Rurima Island	ISLD	11	W8	37 50	176 53
Ruru	LOC	18, 23	L18	42 35	171 30
Russell	TOWN	6	R3	35 16	174 08
Russells Flat	LOC	23	L19	43 23	171 56
Rutherglen	LOC	18, 23	K18	42 32	171 10
Ryal Bush	LOC	26	D25	46 16	168 20
Ryall, Mount	MT	18	K17	42 16	171 22
Saddle Hill	HILL	14, 18	P15	41 17	173 26
Saddle Hill	HILL	33	A4	45 55	170 21
Saddle Point	PNT	26	C26	46 43	167 59
Salisbury	LOC	40	B4	44 26	171 12
Saltwater Creek	STRM	40	B4	44 26	171 15
Saltwater Creek	LOC	23	N19	43 16	172 43
Saltwater Lagoon	LAGN	22	H19	43 05	170 20
Sand Hill Point	PNT	26	B25	46 15	167 19
Sandfly Bay	BAY	33	C4	45 54	170 39
Sandon Block	LOC	15	U12	39 54	175 42
Sandringham	SBRB	31	B5	36 53	174 44
Sandrock Bluff	CLIF	22	D21	44 08	168 16
Sandspit	LOC	7	S5	36 24	174 43
Sandy Bay	BAY	6	N1	34 26	172 38
Sandy Bay	BAY	7	R4	35 32	174 29
Sandy Bay	BAY	14, 18	N15	41 01	173 00
Sandy Knolls	LOC	23	M20	43 33	172 19
Sanson	TOWN	14	T13	40 13	175 25
Santoft	LOC	14	T13	40 09	175 14
Saunders, Cape	CAPE	33	D3	45 53	170 44
Sauvage Point	PNT	14, 19	Q14	40 57	173 46
Sawdon Stream	STRM	22	J21	44 11	170 30
Sawyers Bay	SBRB	33	C2	45 49	170 36
Saxton Pass	PASS	18	P17	42 04	173 13
Saxton River	STRM	18	P17	42 07	173 10
Scargill	LOC	18, 23	N18	42 56	172 57
Scorching Bay	BAY	35	B8	41 18	174 50
Scotchmans Valley	LOC	10	U8	37 46	175 31
Scott Point	PNT	6	N2	34 31	172 42
Scotts Gap	LOC	26	C25	46 03	167 55
Seabreeze Point	PNT	26	C22	44 38	167 38
Seacliff	TOWN	27	J24	45 41	170 37
Seadown	LOC	23	K21	44 18	171 16
Seafield	LOC	23	L20	43 55	171 54
Seaforth River	STRM	26	A24	45 42	166 57
Seal Point	PNT	33	C4	45 54	170 38
Seatoun	SBRB	35	B8	41 19	174 50
Seaview	SBRB	35	B7	41 14	174 54
Seaview	SBRB	40	B4	44 23	171 15
Seaview	LOC	18, 23	J18	42 42	170 59
Seaview	LOC	23	L21	44 00	171 53
Seaview	LOC	14, 19	R16	41 37	174 07

NAME	DESC	PAGE	REF	LAT S	LONG E
Seaward Downs	LOC	26	E25	46 23	168 46
Seaward Kaikoura Range	MTNS	19	Q17	42 15	173 35
Secretary Island	ISLD	26	A23	45 14	166 54
Seddon	TOWN	14, 19	R16	41 40	174 04
Seddonville	TOWN	18	L16	41 33	171 59
Sedgemere	LOC	23	M20	43 50	172 19
Sefton	TOWN	23	N19	43 15	172 40
Sefton, Mount	MT	22	H20	43 41	170 02
Selbourne Range	MTNS	22	E21	44 06	168 55
Selwyn	LOC	23	M20	43 39	172 14
Selwyn Heights	SBRB	38	A4	38 07	176 13
Selwyn Huts	LOC	23	M20	43 43	172 26
Selwyn Stream	STRM	23	M20	43 44	172 26
Sentry Hill	LOC	37	C1	39 03	174 11
Sentry Reef	REEF	4	—	44 13	176 36 W
Separation Point	PNT	14, 18	P14	40 47	173 00
Sergeant Channel	CHAN	30	D4	36 49	174 58
Sergeants Hill	LOC	18	L16	41 45	171 39
Seven Mile Creek	STRM	40	B1	42 22	171 14
Severn	MT	18	P17	42 05	173 04
Shaftesbury	LOC	10	U8	37 37	175 47
Shag Point	PNT	7	T5	36 19	175 26
Shag Point	PNT	27	J23	45 27	170 48
Shag River	STRM	27	J23	45 29	170 48
Shag Rock	ROCK	4	—	50 42	166 12
Shannon	BORO	14, 19	T14	40 33	175 25
Shantytown	LOC	40	A3	42 32	171 10
Shark Bay	BAY	38	C2	38 42	178 04
Sheffield	TOWN	23	M19	43 23	172 01
Shelly Bay	BAY	35	B8	41 18	174 49
Shelly Beach	LOC	7, 10	R6	36 34	174 22
Shelly Park	SBRB	31	D5	36 54	174 57
Shelter Point	PNT	26	D27	47 06	168 13
Shenandoah	LOC	18	M16	41 52	172 15
Sheppard, Lake	LAKE	18, 23	M18	42 46	172 15
Sherenden	LOC	15	W12	39 31	176 35
Sherry River	LOC	18	N15	41 26	172 43
Sherry River	STRM	18	N15	41 20	172 45
Sherwood Downs	LOC	23	J20	43 58	170 52
Sherwood Rise	SBRB	36	B3	35 45	174 22
Shirley	SBRB	32	C2	43 30	172 39
Shirley, Lake	LAKE	26	B23	45 04	167 14
Shoe Island	ISLD	7, 10	U6	37 00	175 54
Shotover River	STRM	26	E23	45 01	168 46
Silver Peak	PEAK	33	B1	45 44	170 27
Silver Stream	STRM	33	B2	45 51	170 24
Silverdale	SBRB	37	D1	37 47	175 20
Silverdale	TOWN	30	A1	36 37	174 40
Silverhope	LOC	15	U12	39 58	175 32
Silverstream	SBRB	35	D5	41 09	175 01
Sinclair Head	HEAD	14, 19	S15	41 22	174 42
Sisters, The	ISLS	4	—	43 36	176 48 W
Six Mile	LOC	18	M16	41 52	172 19
Skippers Range	MTNS	22	D21	44 27	168 07
Slipper Island	ISLD	7, 10	U7	37 03	175 55
Slope Point	LOC	27	F26	46 40	169 01
Smedley	LOC	15	V12	39 47	176 21
Smith Bluff	BLUF	4	—	29 18	177 57 W
Smith Harbour	HARB	4	—	50 41	166 12
Smithfield	SBRB	40	B4	44 22	171 15
Smiths Lookout	PEAK	26	C27	47 14	167 32
Smoothwater Bay	BAY	4	—	52 32	169 12
Smyth Range	MTNS	23	J19	43 10	170 43
Snares Islands	ISLS	4	—	48 02	166 36
Snells Beach	LOC	7	S5	36 25	174 44
Snowball Glaciers	GLCR	22	E21	44 27	168 31
Snowdon	MTN	26	D23	45 17	168 04
Snowy River	STRM	18	L17	42 16	171 42
Snowy Top	HILL	22	G21	44 24	169 46
Soaker, Mount	MT	26	B23	45 23	167 16
Sockburn	SBRB	32	A3	43 33	172 33
Solander Island	ISLD	26	A26	46 34	166 52
Solander Trough	SEAF	81	—	49 00	165 20
Soldiers Bay	BAY	30	A4	36 49	174 42
Solitary, Mount	MT	26	B24	45 43	167 00
Solway	SBRB	37	C4	40 57	175 37
Somerfield	SBRB	32	B3	43 34	172 38
Somers, Mount	MTN	23	K20	43 32	171 18
Somerton	LOC	23	L20	43 45	171 55
Somes Island	ISLD	35	B7	41 16	174 52
Somes Park	SBRB	37	B1	39 05	174 06
Somes, Point	PNT	4	—	43 50	176 52 W
Soucis, Cape	CAPE	14, 19	Q15	41 03	173 35
South Bay	BAY	19	Q17	42 26	173 41
South Beach	LOC	18	K17	42 29	171 11
South Cape	CAPE	4	—	50 55	166 05
South Cape	CAPE	26	C27	47 17	167 32
South Dunedin	BAY	33	B3	45 54	170 30
South East Bay	BAY	4	—	34 09	172 08
South East Harbour	HARB	4	—	52 36	169 09
South Fiord	FIOR	26	C23	45 21	167 35
South Head	LOC	7, 10	R5	36 27	174 14
South Head	HEAD	7, 10	R5	36 25	174 13
South Hill	SBRB	39	D3	45 06	170 58
South Hillend	LOC	26	D25	46 03	168 14
South Islet	ISLD	4	—	49 44	178 46
South New Brighton	SBRB	32	D3	43 32	172 44
South Oamaru	SBRB	39	D3	45 06	170 58
South Opuha River	STRM	23	J20	43 59	170 52
South Point	PNT	4	—	52 35	169 12
South Red Head Point	PNT	26	C27	47 05	167 34
South Reef	REEF	4	—	44 22	176 16 W
South Taranaki Bight	BAY	14	R12	39 41	174 17
South West Cape	CAPE	4	—	50 50	165 53
South West Island	ISLD	4	—	34 11	172 04
Southbeach	LOC	40	A2	42 29	171 11
Southbridge	TOWN	23	M20	43 48	172 15
Southbrook	TOWN	23	N19	43 20	172 36
Southburn	LOC	23	K21	44 27	171 06
Southern Alps	MTNS	23	—	—	—
Southshore	SBRB	32	D3	43 33	172 45
Southwest Cape	CAPE	26	B27	47 17	167 27
Soutra Hill	PEAK	27	G24	45 32	169 50
Sow Burn	STRM	27	H23	45 12	170 03
Spar Bush	LOC	26	D25	46 15	168 16
Speargrass Flat	LOC	22, 26	E22	44 58	168 49
Speechleys Bridge	LOC	23	K21	44 07	171 13
Spence Peak	PEAK	26	C24	45 43	167 51
Spencerville	LOC	32	C1	43 26	172 42
Spenser Mountains	MTNS	18	N17	42 12	172 36
Spey River	STRM	18	M14	40 58	172 28
Spirits Bay	BAY	6	N1	34 25	172 50
Sponge Bay	BAY	38	C2	38 42	178 03
Spotswood	SBRB	37	A1	39 04	174 02
Spotswood	LOC	18	P18	42 44	173 16
Spray River	STRM	18	P16	41 44	173 28
Spreydon	SBRB	32	B3	43 33	172 37
Spring Creek	TOWN	39	B3	41 28	173 58
Spring Grove	LOC	14, 18	P15	41 23	173 05
Springbank	LOC	23	M19	43 19	172 26
Springbrook	LOC	23	K21	44 30	171 11
Springburn	LOC	23	K20	43 40	171 28
Springdale	LOC	10	U8	37 31	175 34
Springfield	LOC	7	R4	35 53	174 20

NAME	DESC	PAGE	REF	LAT S	LONG E
Springfield	TOWN	23	L19	43 20	171 56
Springhill	LOC	15	V12	39 52	176 23
Springhills	LOC	26	D25	46 12	168 29
Springlands	SBRB	39	A4	41 31	173 56
Springs Junction	LOC	18, 23	M17	42 20	172 11
Springston	TOWN	23	M20	43 28	172 25
Springston South	LOC	23	M20	43 41	172 26
Springvale	SBRB	36	C2	39 56	175 01
Springvale	LOC	27	F23	45 12	169 26
Spye	LOC	18, 23	N18	43 00	172 54
Squally Bay	BAY	23	N20	43 54	172 55
Square Top Island	ISLD	7, 10	T5	36 28	175 24
St Albans	SBRB	32	B2	43 31	172 38
St Andrews	SBRB	37	C1	37 45	175 15
St Andrews	TOWN	23	K22	44 32	171 11
St Andrews Hill	SBRB	32	C3	43 34	172 43
St Arnaud	LOC	18	N16	41 48	172 51
St Arnaud Range	MTNS	18	N16	41 55	172 52
St Bathans	LOC	22, 27	G22	44 52	169 49
St Bathans Range	MTNS	22, 27	G22	44 45	169 45
St Bernard	MT	18	P17	42 08	173 25
St Clair	SBRB	33	B4	45 55	170 29
St Cuthbert, Mount	MT	22	G22	44 33	170 00
St Heliers	SBRB	31	C5	36 51	174 52
St Johns	SBRB	31	C5	36 52	174 50
St Johns Hill	SBRB	36	C2	39 55	175 02
St Kilda	BORO	33	B4	45 55	170 30
St Leonards	SBRB	38	C4	39 38	176 50
St Leonards	LOC	33	C2	45 50	170 35
St Leonards	LOC	18, 23	N18	42 47	172 57
St Martins	SBRB	32	B3	43 33	172 39
St Mary, Mount	MT	22	G21	44 15	169 38
St Marys Range	MTNS	22, 27	H22	44 45	170 18
St Patricks	LOC	26	E24	45 48	168 31
Stanley Bay	SBRB	30	B4	36 50	174 47
Stanley Brook	LOC	14, 18	N15	41 19	172 49
Stanley, Lake	LAKE	18	N15	41 00	172 36
Stanley River	STRM	14, 18	N15	41 18	172 49
Stanmore Bay	SBRB	30	B1	36 37	174 44
Stanway	LOC	15	U13	40 05	175 34
Starling Head	HEAD	26	D27	47 04	168 13
Staveley	LOC	23	K20	43 39	171 26
Steep Head	HEAD	26	D26	46 32	168 13
Stella Passage	STRA	4	—	30 32	178 34 W
Step Island	ISLD	6	Q3	35 02	173 57
Stephens, Cape	CAPE	14, 19	Q14	40 42	173 57
Stephens Island	ISLD	14, 19	Q14	40 40	174 00
Stephenson Island	ISLD	6	Q2	34 58	173 47
Stevens, Mount	MT	18	M14	40 48	172 27
Stewart Island	ISLD	26	C27	47 02	167 51
Stewarts Gully	LOC	32	C1	43 24	172 40
Stillwater	LOC	18, 23	K17	42 26	171 21
Stirling	TOWN	27	G25	46 15	169 47
Stirling Point	PNT	40	D4	46 37	168 21
Stoke	SBRB	39	A2	41 19	173 14
Stokes, Mount	MTN	14, 19	R15	41 05	174 06
Stokes Valley	SBRB	35	C6	41 11	174 59
Stony Creek	LOC	27	G25	46 12	169 47
Stony River	STRM	22	H21	44 23	170 14
Stony River	STRM	14	Q11	39 11	173 49
Strachan Range	MTNS	22	G20	43 46	169 38
Strandon	SBRB	37	A1	39 03	174 05
Stratford	BORO	14	R11	39 21	174 17
Stratford Mountain House	LOC	14	R11	39 18	174 08
Strathern	SBRB	40	D2	46 26	168 21
Strathmore Park	SBRB	35	B8	41 20	174 49
Streamlands	LOC	7	S5	36 24	174 36
Stronvar	LOC	15, 19	U15	41 04	175 56
Stuart Mountains	MTNS	26	C22	45 00	167 38
Studholme Junction	LOC	23, 27	K22	44 44	171 08
Studleigh Range	MTNS	23	M18	42 47	172 04
Styx	LOC	32	B2	43 28	172 37
Styx River	STRM	32	C1	43 24	172 42
Subantarctic Slope	SEAF	81	—	47 30	177 35 W
Sugar Loaf Islands	ISLS	10, 14	R11	39 03	174 01
Sugar Loaf Rocks	ROCKS	4	—	50 36	166 02
Summerhill	LOC	23	M19	43 16	172 20
Summit	PEAK	15, 19	V13	40 27	176 07
Sumner	SBRB	32	D3	43 34	172 45
Sumner, Lake	LAKE	18, 23	M18	42 42	172 13
Sunnybrook	SBRB	38	A4	38 09	176 13
Sunnyvale	SBRB	31	A5	36 54	174 38
Sunrise Valley	LOC	14, 18	P15	41 17	173 01
Surfdale	LOC	7, 10	T6	36 47	175 02
Surville Cliffs	CLIF	6	P1	34 23	173 00
Sutherlands	LOC	23	K21	44 17	171 02
Sutton	LOC	27	H24	45 34	170 07
Sutton Stream	STRM	27	H24	45 36	170 08
Swampy Summit	PEAK	33	B2	45 48	170 28
Swannanoa	LOC	23	M19	43 23	172 29
Swanson	TOWN	7, 10	S6	36 52	174 34
Sweetwater	LOC	6	P3	35 03	173 13
Sydenham	SBRB	32	B3	43 33	172 38
Table Cape	PNT	11	Y11	39 06	178 00
Table Flat	LOC	15	U12	39 58	175 57
Table Hill	LOC	27	G25	46 04	169 55
Tablelands	LOC	15, 19	U15	41 14	175 34
Tablelands	LOC	11	X9	38 00	177 19
Tadmor	LOC	14, 18	N15	41 26	172 45
Tadmor River	STRM	14, 18	N15	41 22	172 48
Tahaenui	LOC	11, 15	Y11	39 02	177 41
Tahaia	LOC	10	T9	38 15	175 16
Tahakopa	LOC	27	F26	46 31	169 23
Tahakopa Bay	BAY	27	G26	46 34	169 30
Tahakopa River	STRM	27	F26	46 34	169 28
Taharoa	LOC	10	S9	38 09	174 45
Taharoa, Lake	LAKE	10	S9	38 10	174 45
Taharoa, Lake	LAKE	6	Q4	35 48	173 39
Taharua River	STRM	11, 15	W11	39 12	176 30
Tahatika	LOC	27	G25	46 24	169 33
Tahawai	LOC	10	U8	37 30	175 56
Taheke	LOC	15	W12	39 44	176 33
Taheke	TOWN	6	Q3	35 28	173 39
Taheke River	STRM	36	B2	35 41	174 24
Tahekeroa	LOC	7, 10	S6	36 32	174 34
Tahora	LOC	10, 14	S11	39 02	174 47
Tahora	LOC	11	X9	38 17	177 07
Tahoraiti	LOC	15	V13	40 14	176 03
Tahorakuri	LOC	11	V10	38 34	176 11
Tahuna	LOC	10	T7	37 30	175 29
Tahunanui	SBRB	39	A2	41 17	173 14
Tahunga	LOC	11	Y10	38 37	177 30
Tahuroa	LOC	10	U8	37 43	175 32
Taia, Lake	LAKE	4	—	43 52	176 25 W
Taiaroa Head	HEAD	27	J24	45 46	170 44
Taieri Beach	LOC	27	H25	46 05	170 11
Taieri Island	ISLD	27	H25	46 03	170 13
Taieri Mouth	LOC	27	H25	46 03	170 12
Taieri Ridge	RDGE	27	H23	45 29	170 14
Taieri River	STRM	27	H25	46 03	170 12
Taihape	TOWN	15	U12	39 41	175 48
Taiharuru	LOC	7	S4	35 44	174 34
Taiharuru Head	HEAD	7	S4	35 43	174 35

NAME	DESC	PAGE	REF	LAT S	LONG E
Taihoa	LOC	10	U8	37 50	175 49
Taikirau	LOC	6	R3	35 29	174 04
Taiko	LOC	23	K21	44 21	171 04
Taiko Zig Zag	LOC	23	K21	44 23	171 05
Taikorea	LOC	14, 19	T13	40 22	175 24
Taimate	LOC	19	R16	41 46	174 09
Taingaehe	LOC	6	R5	36 11	174 02
Tainui	SBRB	33	B4	45 54	170 31
Taipa	LOC	6	P3	35 00	173 28
Taipo River	STRM	18, 23	K18	42 45	171 24
Taiporohenui	LOC	14	R12	39 35	174 19
Taipuha	LOC	7	R5	36 00	174 16
Tairua	LOC	7, 10	U7	37 00	175 51
Taita	SBRB	35	C6	41 11	174 57
Taitapu	LOC	32	A4	43 40	172 33
Takahiwai	LOC	7	R4	35 50	174 25
Takahue	LOC	6	P3	35 12	173 21
Takaka	LOC	14, 18	N14	40 51	172 48
Takaka River	STRM	14, 18	N14	40 48	172 48
Takamatua	LOC	23	N20	43 47	172 58
Takanini	TOWN	31	D8	37 03	174 55
Takapau	TOWN	15	V13	40 01	176 21
Takapau	LOC	11	Z9	38 21	178 11
Takapuna	CITY	30	B4	36 48	174 47
Takaputahi River	STRM	11	Y9	38 04	177 42
Takaro	SBRB	37	A4	40 21	175 35
Takatu	LOC	7	S5	36 22	174 45
*Takitimu Mountains	MTNS	26	C24	45 42	167 50
Takou Bay	BAY	6	Q3	35 05	173 58
Tamahere	LOC	10	T8	37 49	175 21
Tamaki	SBRB	31	C5	36 53	174 51
Tamaki River	STRM	31	C7	36 51	174 53
Tamaki Strait	STRA	7, 10	T6	36 51	175 02
Tamarau	LOC	38	C2	38 41	178 03
Tamatea	SBRB	38	C2	39 30	176 52
Tamaterau	LOC	36	B3	35 46	174 24
Tamumu	LOC	15	W12	39 58	176 41
Tanatana	LOC	11	X9	38 11	177 07
Tane	LOC	15, 19	U14	40 35	175 51
Taneatua	TOWN	11	W9	38 04	177 00
Tanekaha	LOC	7	R4	35 35	174 14
Tangarakau Stream	STRM	14	S11	39 11	174 52
Tangihau	LOC	11	Y10	38 35	177 37
Tangimoana	LOC	14	T13	40 18	175 15
Tangirau Pa	LOC	10	T8	37 42	175 09
Tangiteroria	LOC	6	R4	35 49	174 03
Tangitu	LOC	10	T10	38 37	175 13
Tangiwai	LOC	15	U11	39 28	175 36
Tangoio	LOC	15	W11	39 20	176 55
Tangowahine	TOWN	6	Q4	35 52	173 56
Tanilba, Mount	MT	26	B22	44 59	167 11
Taniwha	LOC	10	T7	37 24	175 18
Taonui	LOC	15	U13	40 15	175 35
Taonui Stream	STRM	37	A3	40 17	175 33
Taoroa	LOC	15	U12	39 42	175 57
Taotaoroa	LOC	10	U8	37 55	175 37
Tapanui	BORO	27	F24	45 57	160 16
Tapapa	LOC	10	U8	37 59	175 51
Tapawera	LOC	14, 18	N15	41 23	172 50
Tapora	LOC	7	R5	36 21	174 18
Tapu	LOC	7, 10	T6	36 59	175 30
Tapu Point	PNT	36	A3	35 47	174 20
Tapuae	LOC	15	U13	40 00	175 44
Tapuae Stream	STRM	37	A2	39 07	174 01
Tapuaenuku	MTN	19	Q16	42 00	173 40
Tapuaeroa Valley	VLY	11	28	37 52	178 08
Tapuhi	LOC	6	R3	35 28	174 13
Tapui	LOC	23, 27	J22	45 00	170 42
Tapuiwahine	LOC	10	T10	38 39	175 12
Taputeranga Island	ISLD	35	A8	41 21	174 46
Tara	LOC	7	S5	36 07	174 31
Tara Tama	HILL	18, 23	K18	42 49	171 25
Taradale	BORO	38	C2	39 32	176 51
Tarakenga	LOC	10	V9	38 05	176 09
Taramakau River	STRM	18, 23	K18	42 34	171 08
Taramoa	LOC	26	D25	46 21	168 13
Taranga Island	ISLD	7	S4	35 58	174 43
Tarapatiki	LOC	11	X10	38 52	177 11
Tarara	LOC	27	G26	46 31	169 34
Tararua Range	MTNS	14, 19	T14	40 40	175 25
Tarata	LOC	10, 14	R11	39 09	174 22
Taratahi East	LOC	15, 19	U14	4[illegible] 00	175 36
Tarawera	LOC	11, 15	W11	39 02	176 34
Tarawera, Lake	LAKE	11	V9	38 12	176 26
Tarawera, Mount	MTN	11	V9	38 14	176 30
Tarawera River	STRM	11	W8	37 53	176 47
Tariki	TOWN	14	R11	39 14	174 14
Taringamotu	LOC	10	T10	38 51	175 15
Taringamotu River	STRM	10	T10	38 51	175 14
Taringatura Hills	HILLS	26	D24	45 51	168 12
Tarndale	LOC	18	N17	42 11	172 56
Tarras	LOC	22, 27	F22	44 51	169 26
Taruarau River	STRM	15	V12	39 30	176 20
Taruheru Stream	STRM	38	B2	38 40	178 02
Tarukenga	LOC	10	V9	38 04	176 09
Tarurutangi	LOC	37	C2	39 05	174 11
Taruwhenua Point	PNT	4	—	44 14	176 16 W
Tasman	LOC	14, 18	P15	41 12	173 03
Tasman Basin	SEAF	81	—	42 30	162 00
Tasman Bay	BAY	14, 18	P15	41 09	173 14
Tasman Glacier	GLCR	22	H20	43 40	170 11
Tasman, Mount	MTN	22	H20	43 34	170 09
Tasman Mountains	MTNS	18	M15	41 03	172 19
Tasman River	STRM	22	H20	44 00	170 10
Tasman Sea	SEA	2, 3	—	—	—
Tataraimaka	LOC	10, 14	Q11	39 10	173 55
Tataramoa	LOC	15	V13	40 09	176 09
Tatarariki	LOC	6	Q5	36 03	173 56
Tatare	LOC	22	H19	43 22	170 11
Tatu	LOC	10	S10	38 56	174 57
Tatuanui	LOC	10	U8	37 37	175 36
Tauhara	LOC	10	V10	38 44	176 04
Tauhei	LOC	10	T8	37 36	175 26
Tauherenikau	LOC	14, 19	T15	41 06	175 25
Tauherenikau River	STRM	14, 19	T15	41 12	175 20
Tauhoa	LOC	7	R5	36 22	174 28
Taukawau Point	PNT	7	R3	35 26	174 26
Taumarere	LOC	6	R3	35 22	174 05
Taumarunui	BORO	10	T10	38 52	175 15
Taumata	LOC	15, 19	U15	41 05	175 32
Taumata	LOC	27	F25	46 09	169 28
Taumatarea Point	PNT	31	A7	36 59	174 38
Taumutu	LOC	23	M20	43 51	172 21
Taupaki	LOC	7, 10	S6	36 49	174 33
Taupeka Point	PNT	4	—	43 43	176 30 W
Taupiri	TOWN	10	T8	37 37	175 11
Taupo	TOWN	10	V10	38 41	176 05
Taupo, Lake	LAKE	10	U10	38 48	175 55
Tauranga	CITY	10	V8	37 42	176 10
Tauranga	CITY	36	Urb	37 42	176 10
Tauranga Central	SBRB	36	B1	37 41	176 10
Tauranga Harbour	HARB	36	A1	37 39	176 10
Tauranga South	SBRB	36	B2	37 42	176 10
Tauranga Taupo River	STRM	10	U10	38 55	175 54

NAME	DESC	PAGE	REF	LAT S	LONG E
Tauranganui	LOC	10	S7	37 19	174 49
Taurangaruru	LOC	10	S7	37 15	174 40
Tauraroa	LOC	7	R4	35 52	174 14
Tauraroa River	STRM	6	R4	35 56	174 05
Taurau Valley	LOC	11	Y10	38 43	177 54
Taurewa	LOC	10, 15	U11	39 05	175 33
Tauriko	LOC	10	V8	37 44	176 05
Taurikura	LOC	36	D4	35 49	174 32
Tauroa Point	PNT	6	P3	35 10	173 04
Tautoro	LOC	6	Q3	35 28	173 50
Tautuku Peninsula	PEN	27	F26	46 37	169 26
Tauweru	LOC	15, 19	U14	40 57	175 48
Tauweru River	STRM	15, 19	U14	41 05	175 37
Tauwhare	LOC	10	T8	37 46	175 27
Tauwhareparae	LOC	11	Z9	38 16	178 06
Tawa	BORO	35	B6	41 10	174 49
Tawaha	LOC	14, 19	T15	41 12	175 25
Tawai	LOC	23, 27	J22	44 53	171 00
Tawhana	LOC	11	X9	38 26	177 07
Tawhiti	LOC	14	R12	39 35	174 18
Tawhiti	LOC	11	Y9	38 16	177 52
Tawhitinui Reach	STRA	14, 19	Q15	41 03	173 51
Tayforth	LOC	14	S12	39 54	174 59
Taylor, Lake	LAKE	18, 23	M18	42 46	172 14
Taylor, Mount	MTN	23	K20	43 30	171 19
Taylor River	STRM	14, 19	Q16	41 31	173 58
Taylors Mistake	LOC	32	D3	43 35	172 47
Taylors Stream	STRM	23	L20	43 44	171 32
Taylorville	LOC	40	B1	42 26	171 19
Te Ahuahu	LOC	6	Q3	35 20	173 50
Te Akatarewa Station	LOC	23, 27	H22	44 36	170 17
Te Akatea	LOC	10	T8	37 38	175 03
Te Akau	LOC	10	S8	37 41	174 52
Te Akau South	LOC	10	S8	37 44	174 52
Te Anaputa Point	PNT	7, 10	U6	36 33	175 32
Te Anau	LOC	26	C23	45 25	167 43
Te Anau, Lake	LAKE	26	C23	45 14	167 46
Te Anga	LOC	10	S9	38 15	174 50
Te Aputa	LOC	10	U10	38 49	175 40
Te Arai	LOC	7	S5	36 12	174 35
Te Arai Point	LOC	7	S5	36 10	174 37
Te Arakura	LOC	37	A3	40 17	175 33
Te Araroa	TOWN	11	Z8	37 38	178 22
Te Aroha	BORO	10	U8	37 32	175 42
Te Aroha, Mount	MT	10	U8	37 32	175 45
Te Aroha West	LOC	10	U8	37 35	175 44
Te Atatu	LOC	31	A5	36 51	174 39
Te Au, Lake	LAKE	26	B23	45 15	167 23
Te Awa	SBRB	38	D2	39 31	176 55
Te Awa	LOC	23	K21	44 11	171 15
Te Awamutu	BORO	10	T9	38 00	175 19
Te Awanga	LOC	15	W12	39 38	176 59
Te Hana	LOC	7	S5	36 15	174 30
Te Hapara	SBRB	38	B2	38 39	178 00
Te Hapua	LOC	6	N1	34 30	172 55
Te Haroto	LOC	11, 15	W11	39 08	176 37
Te Hauke	LOC	15	W12	39 46	176 41
Te Henui Stream	STRM	37	A1	39 03	174 05
Te Hoe	LOC	10	T8	37 30	175 19
Te Hoe River	STRM	11, 15	W11	39 02	176 48
Te Horo	LOC	14, 19	T14	40 49	175 07
Te Horo Beach	LOC	14, 19	T14	40 48	175 05
Te Houka	LOC	27	G25	46 13	169 39
Te Huahua	LOC	6	P3	35 20	173 29
Te Hutewai	LOC	10	S8	37 52	174 50
Te Iringa	LOC	6	Q3	35 27	173 47
Te Kaha	LOC	11	Y8	37 44	177 41
Te Kao	LOC	6	N2	34 39	172 58
Te Karae	LOC	6	P3	35 17	173 30
Te Karaka	TOWN	11	Y9	38 28	177 52
Te Kauwhata	TOWN	10	T7	37 24	175 09
Te Kawa	LOC	10	T9	38 05	175 16
Te Kawa West	LOC	10	T9	38 05	175 13
Te Kinga	LOC	18, 23	K18	42 36	171 30
Te Kiri	LOC	14	Q11	39 26	173 59
Te Kohanga	LOC	10	S7	37 19	174 51
Te Kopuru	TOWN	6	Q5	36 02	173 55
Te Kouma	LOC	7, 10	T6	36 49	175 29
Te Kowhai	LOC	6	R5	36 09	174 06
Te Kowhai	LOC	10	T8	37 44	175 09
Te Kuiti	BORO	10	T9	38 20	175 10
Te Kumi	LOC	10	T9	38 19	175 09
Te Kura	LOC	15	W12	39 52	176 42
Te Mahoe	TOWN	11	W9	38 07	176 49
Te Mai	LOC	15, 19	V14	40 46	176 11
Te Maika	LOC	10	S9	38 06	174 46
Te Maire	LOC	6	Q5	36 06	173 54
Te Mania	LOC	10	S9	38 06	174 53
Te Mapara	LOC	10	T9	38 29	175 04
Te Mapou	HILL	14	S11	39 22	174 52
Te Marua	LOC	14, 19	T15	41 06	175 06
Te Mata	LOC	10	S8	37 53	174 52
Te Mata	LOC	15	W12	39 40	176 55
Te Mata	HILL	38	D4	39 42	176 54
Te Mawhai	LOC	10	T9	38 02	175 18
Te Miro	LOC	10	U8	37 48	175 33
Te Moana	LOC	23	K21	44 03	171 07
Te Namu	LOC	18	M15	41 23	172 05
Te Ngae	LOC	11	V9	38 06	176 19
Te Oka	LOC	23	N20	43 50	172 47
Te Oka Bay	BAY	23	N20	43 51	172 47
Te One	LOC	4	—	43 56	176 32 W
Te Ore Ore	LOC	37	D4	40 58	175 41
Te Pahu	LOC	10	T8	37 55	175 08
Te Papapa	SBRB	31	B6	36 55	174 48
Te Peka	LOC	26	E26	46 31	168 51
Te Pirita	LOC	23	L20	43 38	171 54
Te Pohue	LOC	15	W11	39 15	176 40
Te Poi	LOC	10	U8	37 52	175 51
Te Popo	LOC	14	R11	39 16	174 22
Te Pua	LOC	7, 10	R6	36 41	174 25
Te Puia Springs	TOWN	11	Z9	38 04	178 18
Te Puke	BORO	11	V8	37 47	176 20
Te Puna	TOWN	10	V8	37 41	176 04
Te Puninga	LOC	10	U8	37 34	175 32
Te Puru	LOC	7, 10	U7	37 03	175 31
Te Rahu	LOC	10	T8	37 58	175 20
Te Raki Bay	BAY	4	—	43 48	176 54 W
Te Ranga	LOC	10	V8	38 45	176 08
Te Rangiita	LOC	10	U10	38 55	175 55
Te Rapa	SBRB	37	C1	37 45	175 15
Te Rauamoa	LOC	10	T9	38 05	175 03
Te Raumauku	LOC	10	T9	38 11	175 10
Te Rehunga	LOC	15	V13	40 13	176 01
Te Reinga	LOC	11	Y10	38 49	177 31
Te Rerenga	LOC	7, 10	U6	36 45	175 36
Te Rewarewa Point	PNT	34	B4	41 04	174 50
Te Rore	LOC	6	P3	35 10	173 22
Te Rore	LOC	10	T8	37 56	175 12
Te Roti	LOC	14	R11	39 30	174 17
Te Roto Kare, Lake	LAKE	38	C3	39 34	176 48
Te Rou	LOC	18	P16	41 33	173 27
Te Taho	LOC	23	H19	43 13	170 27
Te Tau Bank	SBNK	31	A7	36 58	174 41
Te Teko	TOWN	11	W9	38 02	176 48
Te Tii	LOC	6	Q3	35 08	174 00
Te Toro	LOC	10	S7	37 10	174 40
Te Tua	LOC	26	C25	46 10	167 41
Te Tumu	LOC	11	V8	37 46	176 23
Te Uku	LOC	10	S8	37 50	174 57
Te Uri	LOC	15	V13	40 15	176 23
Te Waewae	LOC	26	C25	46 12	167 40
Te Waewae Bay	BAY	26	B25	46 14	167 30
Te Wairoa	LOC	11	V9	38 13	176 22
Te Waitere	LOC	10	S9	38 08	174 49
Te Wera	LOC	14	S11	39 15	174 36
Te Wera	LOC	11	X9	38 29	177 25
Te Wera, Mount	MT	22, 26	D22	44 40	168 03
Te Whaiti	TOWN	11	W10	38 34	176 46
Te Whakarae	TOWN	10	T10	38 55	175 12
Te Whakuru Island	ISLD	4	—	43 45	176 13 W
Te Whanga	LOC	15, 19	U15	41 02	175 42
Te Whanga Lagoon	LAGN	4	—	43 47	176 30 W
Te Wharau	LOC	6	Q4	35 55	173 54
Te Wharau	LOC	15, 19	U15	41 11	175 51
Te Whetu	LOC	10	U9	38 09	175 57
Te Whiti	LOC	15, 19	U15	41 03	175 39
Teaneraki Cliff	CLIF	39	C3	45 02	170 54
Teddington	LOC	23	N20	43 40	172 40
Tekapo Canal	CANL	22	H21	44 04	170 20
Tekapo, Lake	LAKE	23	J20	43 52	170 32
Tekapo River	STRM	22	H21	44 19	170 14
Tekoa, Mount	MTN	18, 23	N18	42 40	172 37
Temple View	SBRB	37	C2	37 49	175 14
Templeton	TOWN	23	M20	43 33	172 28
Temuka	BORO	23	K21	44 15	171 16
Tengawai River	STRM	23	K21	44 15	171 06
Tennyson, Lake	LAKE	18	N17	42 12	172 44
Terawhiti, Cape	CAPE	14, 19	S15	41 17	174 37
Terrace End	SBRB	37	B4	40 21	175 38
Teschemakers	LOC	27	J23	45 09	170 51
Tetley Brook	LOC	19	R16	41 43	174 05
Teviot	LOC	27	F24	45 37	169 23
Teviot River	STRM	27	F24	45 32	169 19
Teviotdale	LOC	23	N19	43 07	172 47
Thames	BORO	10	U7	37 08	175 33
Thames, Firth of	BAY	7, 10	T6	37 00	175 24
Therma Glacier	GLCR	22	E21	44 22	168 44
Thomas, Mount	MTN	23	M19	43 10	172 21
Thomas River	STRM	22	F20	43 56	169 09
Thompson Sound	SND	26	A23	45 09	166 58
Thomson Mountains	MTNS	26	D23	45 04	168 16
Thomsons Creek	STRM	27	G23	45 07	169 35
Thomsons Crossing	LOC	26	D25	46 12	168 20
Thornbury	TOWN	26	D25	46 17	168 06
Thorndon	SBRB	35	A7	41 16	174 46
Thorne Bay	BAY	30	B3	36 47	174 46
Thornton	LOC	11	W8	37 55	176 51
Thorntons Bay	LOC	10	U7	37 04	175 31
Thorpe	LOC	14, 18	N15	41 17	172 52
Three Kings	SBRB	31	B6	36 54	174 45
Three Kings Islands	ISLS	4	—	34 09	172 09
Three Kings Rise	SEAF	81	—	31 55	172 25
Three Mile Lagoon	LAGN	22	H19	43 15	170 08
Three Oclock Creek	STRM	27	H24	45 42	170 20
Thumb Point	PNT	7, 10	T6	36 44	175 11
Thumbs, The	PEAK	23	J20	43 35	170 42
Ti Point	LOC	7	S5	36 19	174 47
Ti Tree Point	LOC	15	V13	40 26	176 25
Tiakitahuna	LOC	15, 19	T13	40 24	175 30
Tihaka	LOC	26	C25	46 21	167 55
Tiheroa	LOC	10	T9	38 07	175 10
Tihiotonga	LOC	38	A4	38 11	176 14
Tihoi	LOC	10	U10	38 37	175 42
Tikinui	LOC	6	Q5	36 07	173 58
Tikipunga	LOC	36	A2	35 41	174 20
Tikitere	LOC	11	V9	38 04	176 22
Tikitiki	TOWN	11	Z8	37 47	178 25
Tikokino	TOWN	15	V12	39 49	176 27
Tikorangi	LOC	10, 14	R11	39 02	174 16
Tikore Island	ISLD	40	C4	46 34	168 19
Timaru	CITY	40	Urb	44 24	171 15
Timaru	CITY	23	K21	44 24	171 15
Timaru River	STRM	22	F22	44 32	169 19
Timber Bay	LOC	15	V13	40 15	176 05
Timpanys	LOC	26	E25	46 27	168 31
Timutimu Head	HEAD	23	N20	43 54	172 57
Tiniroto	LOC	11	Y10	38 46	177 34
Tinkertown	LOC	26	D24	45 58	168 01
Tinline	LOC	14, 18	Q15	41 16	173 30
Tinline Downs	LOC	18, 23	P18	42 33	173 04
Tinline, Mount	MTN	18, 23	P17	42 27	173 07
Tinopai	LOC	7	R5	36 15	174 15
Tinui	LOC	15, 19	V14	40 52	176 04
Tinui River	STRM	15, 19	V14	40 53	176 05
Tinui Valley	LOC	15, 18	V14	40 49	176 09
Tinwald	TOWN	39	C2	43 55	171 43
Tipapakuku	LOC	15	V13	40 14	176 07
Tiratu	LOC	15	V13	40 13	176 11
Tirau	TOWN	10	U8	37 58	175 45
Tiraumea	LOC	15, 19	V14	40 38	176 03
Tiraumea River	STRM	15, 19	U14	40 31	175 54
Tiriraukawa	LOC	15	U12	39 45	175 40
Tiritea	LOC	37	B4	40 26	175 40
Tiritea Stream	STRM	37	A4	40 23	175 36
Tiritiri Matang Island	ISLD	7, 10	S6	36 36	174 53
Tiroa	LOC	10	T10	38 31	175 28
Tirohanga	LOC	11	X9	38 02	177 21
Tirohia	LOC	10	U7	37 26	175 39
Tiromoana	LOC	14	R11	39 30	174 21
Tirua Point	PNT	10	S9	38 23	174 38
Tisbury	LOC	40	D2	46 27	168 24
Titahi Bay	SBRB	34	B4	41 06	174 50
Titi	HILL	34	D2	40 59	175 02
Titipua Stream	STRM	26	E25	46 15	168 30
Titirangi	TOWN	31	A6	36 56	174 39
Titirangi Bay	LOC	14, 19	R15	41 01	174 08
Titiroa	LOC	26	E25	46 29	168 46
Titiroa, Mount	MT	26	C24	45 40	167 31
Tititira Head	HEAD	22	F20	43 38	169 26
Titoki	LOC	6	R4	35 44	174 03
Tiwai Point	PNT	40	D4	46 36	168 22
Tiwai Point	LOC	26	D26	46 36	168 24
Toatoa	LOC	11	Y9	38 07	177 30
Toe Toe	LOC	7	R4	35 46	174 19
Toetoes Bay	BAY	26	E26	46 37	168 40
Toiro	LOC	27	G25	46 16	169 39
Toitoi River	STRM	26	C27	47 07	167 59
Tokaanu	LOC	10, 14	U10	38 58	175 45
Tokanui	TOWN	26	E26	46 34	168 57
Tokanui	LOC	10	T9	38 06	175 20
Tokanui River	STRM	26	E26	46 37	168 50
Tokaora	LOC	14	R12	39 35	174 13
Tokarahi	LOC	23, 27	J22	44 58	170 39
Tokarahu Point	PNT	7, 10	U6	36 41	175 47
Tokata	LOC	11	Z8	37 37	178 19
Tokatoka	LOC	6	Q5	36 03	173 58
Tokatu Point	PNT	7	S5	36 22	174 52

NAME	DESC	PAGE	REF	LAT S	LONG E
Tokerau Beach	LOC	6	P2	34 53	173 22
Tokirima	LOC	10	T10	38 56	175 01
Toko	TOWN	14	R11	39 20	174 24
Tokoiti	LOC	27	G25	46 08	169 59
Tokomairiro River	STRM	27	H25	46 13	170 03
Tokomaru	TOWN	15, 19	U13	40 28	175 30
Tokomaru Bay	TOWN	11	Z9	38 08	178 20
Tokorangi	LOC	15	T13	40 05	175 30
Tokorea	LOC	10	U9	38 13	175 52
Tolaga Bay	TOWN	11	Z9	38 22	178 18
Tom Bowling Bay	BAY	6	N1	34 25	172 58
Tomahawk Lagoon	LAGN	33	C4	45 54	170 33
Tomarata	LOC	7	S5	36 13	174 36
Tommy Point	PNT	26	B22	44 45	167 29
Tomoana	SBRB	38	C3	39 37	176 52
Tone River	STRM	18	P17	42 02	173 25
Tonga Island	ISLD	14, 18	P14	40 53	173 04
Tongaporutu	LOC	10	S10	38 50	174 36
Tongariro	LOC	10, 15	U11	39 02	175 39
Tongariro, Mount	MT	10. 15	U11	39 08	175 38
Tongariro River	STRM	10, 15	U10	38 56	175 46
Tongue Point	PNT	14, 19	S15	41 20	174 39
Topuni	LOC	7	R5	36 13	174 28
Tora	LOC	15, 19	T16	41 31	175 30
Torbay	SBRB	30	B2	36 42	174 45
Torehape	LOC	10	T7	37 20	175 25
Torere	LOC	11	X8	37 57	177 29
Torlesse Range	MTNS	23	L19	43 14	171 47
Toroa Point	PNT	30	B2	36 42	174 45
Torrent Bay	BAY	14, 18	P14	40 57	173 03
Tory Channel	CHAN	14, 19	R15	41 14	174 15
Totara	LOC	10	U7	37 10	175 33
Totara	LOC	27	J23	45 08	170 53
Totara Flat	LOC	18	L17	42 18	171 37
Totara Mountain	MTN	18	P17	42 30	173 25
Totara North	LOC	6	Q3	35 02	173 43
Totara River	STRM	18	K16	41 52	171 27
Totara Valley	LOC	23	K21	44 14	171 00
Tourerere	LOC	15	V13	40 07	176 25
Towai	LOC	6	R3	35 29	174 09
Tower of Babel	MT	4	—	50 47	165 59
Tower Peak	PEAK	26	B25	46 02	167 03
Towing Head	HEAD	26	A23	45 24	166 46
Town Hill	HILL	38	B2	38 38	178 02
Townley Mountains	MTNS	26	B24	45 39	167 16
Transit River	STRM	22	C22	44 35	167 44
Travers, Mount	MT	18	N17	42 01	172 44
Travers Range	MTNS	18	N16	41 57	172 44
Travers River	STRM	18	N16	41 53	172 49
Travers Saddle	SAD	18	N17	42 02	172 44
Treble, Mount	MT	26	A25	46 01	166 42
Trent, Mount	MT	22	G20	43 57	169 44
Trent River	STRM	18, 23	L18	42 34	171 58
Trentham	SBRB	35	D5	41 08	175 02
Trio Islands	ISLS	14, 19	R14	40 51	174 00
Tripp Settlement	LOC	23	K20	43 59	171 12
Tryphena	LOC	7	T5	36 18	175 28
Tryphena Harbour	HARB	7	T5	36 19	175 29
Tuahine Point	PNT	38	C3	38 43	178 04
Tuahiwi	LOC	23	N19	43 20	172 39
Tuai	TOWN	11	X10	38 49	177 08
Tuakau	TOWN	10	S7	37 15	174 57
Tuakitoto, Lake	LAKE	27	G25	46 13	169 49
Tuamarina	TOWN	39	B3	41 26	173 58
Tuamarina River	STRM	14, 19	Q15	41 26	173 58
Tuamotu Island	ISLD	38	B2	38 43	178 03
Tuapeka Flat	LOC	27	G24	45 57	169 37
Tuapeka Mouth	LOC	27	G25	46 01	169 31
Tuapeka River	STRM	27	G24	46 01	169 31
Tuapeka West	LOC	27	G24	45 57	169 33
Tuatapere	TOWN	26	C25	46 08	167 41
Tuhara	LOC	11, 15	Y11	39 02	177 30
Tuhawaiki Point	PNT	40	B4	44 27	171 16
Tuhikaramea	LOC	10	T8	37 52	175 12
Tuhitarata	LOC	14, 19	T15	41 18	175 16
Tuhua	LOC	10	T10	38 46	175 10
Tui Pa	LOC	10	U8	37 31	175 41
Tukemokihi	LOC	11	Y10	38 54	177 36
Tukipo River	STRM	15	V12	39 59	176 30
Tukituki	LOC	15	W12	39 41	176 56
Tukituki River	STRM	15	W12	39 36	176 56
Tukutai	LOC	18	J18	42 45	170 57
Tumahu	LOC	14	Q11	39 15	173 54
Tumai	LOC	27	J24	45 36	170 42
Tuna	LOC	14	R11	39 16	174 18
Turakina	TOWN	14	T13	40 02	175 13
Turakina River	STRM	14	T13	40 05	175 08
Turakirae Head	HEAD	14, 19	S15	41 26	174 55
Turanga Creek	STRM	31	D6	36 55	174 58
Turanganui River	STRM	38	B2	38 41	178 01
Turangaomoana	LOC	10	U8	37 45	175 49
Turangarere	LOC	15	U12	39 35	175 44
Turangi	TOWN	10, 14	U10	38 59	175 48
Turiroa	LOC	11, 15	X11	39 01	177 23
Turiwiri	LOC	6	Q4	35 57	173 54
Turnagain, Cape	CAPE	15	W13	40 30	176 37
Turnbull River	STRM	22	E20	43 54	168 54
Turret Range	MTNS	26	B24	45 35	167 15
Turua	TOWN	10	U7	37 14	175 34
Tussock Creek	LOC	26	D25	46 15	168 26
Tutaekuri River	STRM	15	W12	39 34	176 55
Tutaenui	LOC	14	T13	40 01	175 25
Tutaki	LOC	18	M16	41 50	172 28
Tutamoe	LOC	6	Q4	35 39	173 39
Tutamoe Range	MTNS	6	Q4	35 44	173 43
Tutekehua	LOC	6	Q3	35 16	173 31
Tutira	LOC	15	W11	39 12	176 53
Tutira, Lake	LAKE	15	W11	39 13	176 54
Tutoko, Mount	MTN	22	D22	44 36	168 00
Tutukaka	LOC	7	S4	35 36	174 31
Tutukaka Head	HEAD	7	S4	35 37	174 33
Tuturau	LOC	26	E25	46 15	168 52
Tuturumuri	LOC	15, 19	T15	41 25	175 29
Tututawa	LOC	14	S11	39 19	174 31
Twelve Apostles Range	MTNS	40	A1	44 25	171 14
Twizel	LOC	22	H21	44 15	170 06
Two Thumb Range	MTNS	23	J20	43 45	170 43
Twyford	LOC	15	W12	39 36	176 48
Uawa River	STRM	11	Z9	38 23	178 18
Ugly River	STRM	18	M15	41 12	172 19
Umawera	LOC	6	Q3	35 17	173 35
Umbrella Mountains	MTNS	27	F24	45 40	169 00
Umere	LOC	18	M15	41 16	172 10
Umukuri	LOC	14, 18	N15	41 06	172 58
Umutaoroa	LOC	15	V13	40 08	176 05
Umutoi	LOC	15	U13	40 00	175 58
Una, Mount	MTN	18	N17	42 13	172 35
Underwood	LOC	26	D25	46 21	168 19
Underwood, Port	HARB	14, 19	R15	41 20	174 08
Upcot Saddle	SAD	18	Q16	41 56	173 31
Upokongaro	LOC	14	T12	39 52	175 07
Upper Atiamuri	LOC	10	U9	38 22	176 00

NAME	DESC	PAGE	REF	LAT S	LONG E
Upper Charlton	LOC	26	E25	46 06	168 51
Upper Grey River	STRM	18, 23	M17	42 27	172 00
Upper Hutt	CITY	35	D5	41 07	175 04
Upper Junction	LOC	27	J24	45 50	170 34
Upper Matakitaki	LOC	18	M17	42 01	171 21
Upper Moutere	LOC	14, 18	P15	41 16	173 00
Upper Riccarton	SBRB	32	A3	43 32	172 34
Upper Takaka	LOC	14, 18	N15	41 03	172 50
Upper Waitohi	LOC	23	K21	44 13	171 07
Upper Waiwera	LOC	7, 10	S6	36 34	174 39
Upukerora River	STRM	26	C23	45 24	167 45
Urenui	TOWN	10, 14	R10	39 00	174 23
Urenui River	STRM	14	R10	39 00	174 24
Uretane	LOC	23, 27	K22	44 45	171 03
Uriah, Mount	MTN	18	L17	42 01	171 39
Urquhart Bay	BAY	36	D4	35 50	174 32
Uruti	LOC	10, 14	S10	38 56	174 32
Uruti Point	PNT	19	V15	41 08	176 05
Uruwhenua	LOC	14, 18	N14	40 59	172 50
Utakura	LOC	6	Q3	35 20	173 41
Utiku	TOWN	15	U12	39 44	175 51
Utuhina Stream	STRM	38	A4	38 08	176 15
Utuwai	LOC	15	U13	40 01	175 56
Valetta	LOC	23	K20	43 46	171 29
Vancouver Arm	SND	26	A24	45 32	166 53
Vancouver Rock	ROCK	4	—	48 02	166 32
Vauxhall	SBRB	33	B3	45 53	170 31
Vauxhall	SBRB	30	B4	36 49	174 48
Victoria, Mount	MT	18	M17	42 01	172 06
Victoria Range	MTNS	18	M17	42 10	172 10
Victoria Valley	LOC	6	P3	35 09	173 25
View Hill	LOC	23	M19	43 18	172 03
Vinetown	SBRB	36	A3	35 44	174 18
Virginia, Lake	LAKE	36	C1	39 55	175 02
Vogeltown	SBRB	37	A1	39 05	174 05
Volkner Island	ISLD	11	X7	37 29	177 08
Von River	STRM	26	D23	45 05	168 26
Waddington	LOC	23	M19	43 24	172 02
Wadestown	SBRB	35	A7	41 16	174 46
Waerenga	LOC	10	T7	37 22	175 16
Waerengaahika	LOC	11	Y10	38 36	177 55
Waerengaokuri	LOC	11	Y10	38 42	177 46
Wahakari, Lake	LAKE	6	N2	34 39	172 55
Wahapo, Lake	LAKE	22	H19	43 15	170 15
Waharoa	TOWN	10	U8	37 45	175 45
Wahi, Lake	LAKE	10	T8	37 33	175 07
Wahi Pa	LOC	10	T8	37 33	175 09
Waiake	SBRB	30	B2	36 43	174 45
Waianakarua	LOC	27	J23	45 16	170 48
Waianakarua River	STRM	27	J23	45 15	170 52
Waianiwa	LOC	26	D25	46 17	168 14
Waiapi	LOC	23	K21	44 15	171 14
Waiapu River	STRM	11	Z8	37 47	178 29
Waiare	LOC	6	Q3	35 09	173 48
Waiareka Junction	SBRB	39	C3	45 06	170 56
Waiari Stream	STRM	11	V8	37 46	176 21
Waiarikiki	LOC	27	F25	46 17	169 00
Waiarohia Stream	STRM	36	A3	35 42	174 17
Waiaruhe	LOC	15	V13	40 17	176 00
Waiata	LOC	15	U13	40 09	175 43
Waiatarua	LOC	7, 10	S6	36 56	174 35
Waiatoto River	STRM	22	E20	43 59	168 48
Waiau	TOWN	18, 23	P18	42 39	173 03
Waiau Bay	BAY	30	B1	36 37	174 45
Waiau Pa	LOC	10	S7	37 08	174 45
Waiau River	STRM	18	P18	42 47	173 22
Waiau River	STRM	26	C23	45 30	167 38
Waiau River	STRM	11, 15	X10	38 58	177 24
Waiau River	STRM	26	C25	46 12	167 37
Waihaha	LOC	7	R3	35 20	174 14
Waihaha	LOC	10	U10	38 43	175 44
Waihaha River	STRM	10	U10	38 43	175 44
Waihakeke	LOC	15, 19	U15	41 04	175 31
Waihao Downs	LOC	23, 27	J22	44 47	170 55
Waihao Forks	LOC	23, 27	J22	44 47	170 56
Waihao River	STRM	23, 27	K22	44 46	171 11
Waihao River N Branch	STRM	23	J22	44 47	170 56
Waihao River S Branch	STRM	23	J22	44 47	170 56
Waihaorunga	LOC	23, 27	J22	44 45	170 49
Waiharakeke	LOC	10	U7	37 16	175 52
Waiharara	LOC	6	P2	34 56	173 11
Waihau	LOC	15	W11	39 23	176 34
Waihau Bay	LOC	11	Y8	37 37	177 54
Waiheke Island	ISLD	7, 10	T6	36 48	175 08
Waiheke River	STRM	18, 23	L18	42 33	171 58
Waihere Bay	BAY	4	—	44 15	176 15 W
Waihi	BORO	10	U7	37 24	175 50
Waihi Beach	LOC	10	U7	37 24	175 56
Waihirere	LOC	11	Y10	38 35	177 56
Waiho River	STRM	22	H19	43 17	170 03
Waihoaka	LOC	26	C25	46 14	167 42
Waihola	LOC	27	H25	46 01	170 06
Waihola, Lake	LAKE	27	H25	46 01	170 05
Waihopai	SBRB	40	D1	46 23	168 22
Waihopai	LOC	14, 19	Q16	41 32	173 43
Waihopai River	STRM	14, 19	Q16	41 31	173 43
Waihopai River	STRM	26	E25	46 25	168 30
Waihopo	LOC	6	P2	34 46	173 05
Waihora	LOC	11	Y9	38 28	177 58
Waihora River	STRM	11	Y9	38 28	177 50
Waihora Stream	STRM	10	U10	38 40	175 47
Waihou	TOWN	10	U8	37 34	175 41
Waihou River	STRM	10	U7	37 10	175 33
Waihou Valley	LOC	6	Q3	35 17	173 44
Waihua	LOC	11, 15	X11	39 05	177 17
Waihua Stream	STRM	11, 15	X11	39 05	177 17
Waihue	LOC	6	Q4	35 50	173 50
Wai-iti	LOC	14, 18	D15	41 26	173 00
Wai-iti River	STRM	14, 18	P15	41 21	173 07
Waikahawai Point	PNT	11	Z8	37 58	178 22
Waikaia	TOWN	26	E24	45 44	168 51
Waikaia Plains	PLN	26	E24	45 47	168 42
Waikaia River	STRM	26	E24	45 53	168 48
Waikaka	TOWN	27	F24	45 55	169 01
Waikaka Stream	STRM	26	E25	46 06	168 57
Waikaka Stream	STRM	10	T10	38 45	175 03
Waikaka Valley	LOC	27	F25	46 02	169 03
Waikakahi	LOC	23, 27	J22	44 52	170 59
Waikakaho	LOC	15, 19	Q15	41 25	173 54
Waikakaho River	STRM	39	A3	41 27	173 54
Waikana	LOC	26	E25	46 14	168 58
Waikanae	TOWN	34	D1	40 53	175 04
Waikanae Beach	BCH	14, 19	T14	40 52	175 02
Waikanae River	STRM	34	C1	40 52	175 00
Waikaraka Stream	STRM	36	B3	35 45	174 23
Waikaramu, Lake	LAKE	6	P2	34 55	173 14
Waikare, Lake	LAKE	10	T7	37 26	175 12
Waikare River	STRM	11	X9	38 24	177 00
Waikareao Estuary	ESTY	36	A1	37 41	176 09
Waikareiti, Lake	LAKE	11	X10	38 43	177 10
Waikaremoana	LOC	11	X10	38 45	177 09
Waikaremoana, Lake	LAKE	11	X10	38 46	177 05

NAME	DESC	PAGE	REF	LAT S	LONG E
Waikare Taheke River	STRM	11	X10	38 56	177 16
Waikaretu	LOC	10	S8	37 33	174 50
Waikari	TOWN	18, 23	N18	42 58	172 41
Waikari River	STRM	11, 15	X11	39 10	177 05
Waikari River	STRM	18, 23	P18	42 54	173 01
Waikato River	STRM	10	S7	37 23	174 43
Waikawa	LOC	14, 19	R15	41 16	174 03
Waikawa	LOC	27	F26	46 38	169 08
Waikawa Beach	BCH	14, 19	T14	40 41	175 09
Waikawa Point	PNT	11	Y8	37 41	177 43
Waikawau	LOC	7, 10	T6	36 57	175 28
Waikawau Bay	BAY	7, 10	U6	36 35	175 32
Waikeria	LOC	10	T9	38 07	175 23
Waikiekie	LOC	7	R4	35 58	174 14
Waikino	TOWN	10	U7	37 24	175 46
Waikirikiri	LOC	11	X9	38 11	177 00
Waikite Valley	LOC	11	V9	38 20	176 15
Waikiwi	SBRB	40	C1	46 23	168 21
Waikiwi Stream	STRM	40	C1	46 23	168 17
Waikoau	LOC	15	W11	39 14	176 49
Waikoau River	STRM	26	B25	46 09	167 26
Waikohu	LOC	11	Y9	38 27	177 47
Waikohu River	STRM	11	Y9	38 29	177 50
Waikoikoi	LOC	27	F25	46 00	169 10
Waikokopu	LOC	11, 15	Y11	39 04	177 50
Waikokowai	LOC	10	T8	37 34	175 03
Waikorea	LOC	10	S8	37 34	174 53
Waikouaiti	BORO	27	J24	45 36	170 41
Waikouaiti River	STRM	27	J24	45 39	170 40
Waikouro	LOC	26	C25	46 06	167 58
Waikowhai	SBRB	31	B6	36 56	174 44
Waikuku	LOC	23	N19	43 18	172 41
Waikuku Beach	LOC	23	N19	43 17	172 43
Waikukupa River	STRM	22	G19	43 20	170 00
Waikune	LOC	14	T11	39 12	175 24
Waima	LOC	6	Q3	35 29	173 35
Waima	SBRB	31	A6	36 57	174 38
Waima	LOC	11	Z9	38 06	178 20
Waima River	STRM	6	Q3	35 25	173 34
Waima Ure River	STRM	19	R16	41 54	174 07
Waimahaka	LOC	26	E26	46 31	168 49
Waimai	LOC	10	S8	37 37	174 53
Waimakariri River	STRM	23	N19	43 24	172 42
Waimamaku	LOC	6	P4	35 34	173 29
Waimamaku River	STRM	6	P4	35 36	173 25
Waimana	LOC	11	X9	38 09	177 04
Waimana River	STRM	11	X9	38 04	177 00
Waimangaroa	TOWN	18	L16	41 43	171 46
Waimangu	LOC	11	V9	38 17	176 23
Waimanoni	LOC	6	P3	35 01	173 15
Waimapu	LOC	10	V8	37 45	176 08
Waimapu Estuary	ESTY	36	B2	37 43	176 10
Waimarama	LOC	15	W12	39 49	176 59
Waimarie	LOC	18	L16	41 32	171 56
Waimata	LOC	10	U7	37 26	175 52
Waimata River	STRM	11	Z10	38 40	178 02
Waimata Valley	LOC	11	Z10	38 30	178 03
Waimataitai	SBRB	40	B4	44 23	171 14
Waimate	BORO	23, 27	K22	44 45	171 03
Waimate Island	ISLD	7, 10	T6	36 46	175 25
Waimate North	LOC	6	Q3	35 18	173 52
Waimatenui	LOC	6	Q4	35 37	173 43
Waimatua	LOC	26	D25	46 27	168 27
Waimatuku	LOC	26	D25	46 18	168 10
Waimauku	TOWN	7, 10	R6	36 46	174 29
Waimea	LOC	26	E24	45 53	168 41
Waimea Inlet	BAY	39	A2	41 18	173 12
Waimea Plains	PLN	26	E24	45 50	168 35
Waimea Stream	STRM	26	E24	45 59	168 50
Waimea West	LOC	14, 18	P15	41 21	173 05
Waimiha	LOC	10	T10	38 37	175 18
Waimiha Stream	STRM	10	T10	38 36	175 19
Waimiro	LOC	15	V13	40 27	176 14
Waimumu	LOC	26	E25	46 08	168 49
Waingake	LOC	11	Y10	38 47	177 48
Waingarara	LOC	11	X9	38 03	177 04
Waingaro	LOC	10	T8	37 41	175 00
Waingaro River	STRM	18	N14	40 53	172 49
Waingaromia River	STRM	11	Y9	38 24	177 51
Waingawa	LOC	37	C4	40 58	175 35
Waingawa River	STRM	15, 19	U14	41 00	175 40
Waingongoro River	STRM	14	R12	39 35	174 12
Wainoni	SBRB	32	C2	43 31	172 42
Wainono Lagoon	LAGN	23, 27	K22	44 42	171 10
Wainui	LOC	6	Q3	35 01	173 51
Wainui	LOC	7, 10	S6	36 36	174 36
Wainui	LOC	23	N20	43 49	172 54
Wainui	SBRB	38	C2	38 41	178 05
Wainui	LOC	14, 18	N14	40 49	172 57
Wainui	LOC	11	X9	38 01	177 05
Wainui	LOC	15	U12	39 38	175 49
Wainui	HILL	34	C3	41 01	174 59
Wainui Beach	LOC	11	Z10	38 41	178 04
Wainui Inlet	BAY	18	N14	40 49	172 56
Wainui North	LOC	10	U8	37 38	175 58
Wainui River	STRM	6	Q3	35 02	173 34
Wainuiomata	TOWN	35	C7	41 16	174 57
Wainuiomata River	STRM	35	C7	41 15	175 00
Wainuioru	LOC	15, 19	U15	41 14	175 40
Wainuioru River	STRM	15, 19	U15	41 16	175 44
Waioeka	LOC	11	X9	38 03	177 17
Waioeka Pa	LOC	11	X9	38 05	177 17
Waioeka River	STRM	11	X9	38 00	177 17
Waiohau	LOC	11	W9	38 13	176 50
Waiohika	LOC	11	Y10	38 36	177 57
Waiohiki	LOC	15	W12	39 33	176 50
Waiohine River	STRM	15, 19	U15	41 06	175 30
Waiomatatini	LOC	11	Z8	37 49	178 24
Waiomio	LOC	6	R3	35 25	174 04
Waiomu	LOC	7, 10	U7	37 01	175 31
Waione	LOC	15	V13	40 28	176 17
Waioneke	LOC	7, 10	R6	36 32	174 17
Waiongana	LOC	10, 14	R11	39 06	174 11
Waiongana River	STRM	37	C1	39 00	174 11
Waiorongomai	LOC	10	U8	37 33	175 45
Waiotahi	LOC	11	X9	38 01	177 11
Waiotahi Beach	LOC	11	X9	38 00	177 13
Waiotahi River	STRM	11	X9	38 00	177 11
Waiotapu	LOC	11	V9	38 20	176 21
Waiotemarama	LOC	6	P4	35 33	173 26
Waiotira	LOC	6	R4	35 56	174 12
Waiotu	LOC	6	R4	35 32	174 14
Waiotu	LOC	10	U9	38 09	175 41
Waiouru	LOC	15	U11	39 29	175 40
Waipa Mill	LOC	11	V9	38 11	176 16
Waipa River	STRM	10	T8	37 39	175 09
Waipa Valley	LOC	10	T9	38 26	175 23
Waipahi	LOC	27	F25	46 07	169 15
Waipahi River East Branch	STRM	27	F25	46 07	169 15
Waipakihi River	STRM	15	U10	39 13	175 46
Waipango	LOC	26	C25	46 18	168 59
Waipaoa	LOC	11	Y10	38 31	178 54
Waipaoa River	STRM	11	Y10	38 43	177 56
Waipapa	HILL	10	U9	38 18	175 41

NAME	DESC	PAGE	REF	LAT S	LONG E
Waipapa	LOC	6	Q3	35 12	173 55
Waipapa Bay	LOC	19	Q17	42 13	173 52
Waipapa, Lake	LAKE	10	U9	38 19	175 42
Waipapa Point	PNT	26	E26	46 40	168 51
Waipapakauri	LOC	6	P3	35 02	173 14
Waipara	LOC	18, 23	N19	43 03	172 45
Waipara River	STRM	23	N19	43 08	172 47
Waipara River, N Branch	STRM	23	N19	43 03	172 33
Waipara River, S Branch	STRM	23	N19	43 03	172 33
Waiparera, Lake	LAKE	6	P2	34 56	173 11
Waipatiki	LOC	15	V13	40 22	176 17
Waipatu	LOC	15	W12	39 38	176 52
Waipawa	BORO	15	W12	39 56	176 35
Waipawa River	STRM	15	W12	39 58	176 37
Waipiata	LOC	27	H23	45 11	170 10
Waipipi	LOC	10	S7	37 12	174 41
Waipiro	TOWN	11	Z9	38 02	178 20
Waipopo	LOC	23	K21	44 17	171 20
Waipori Falls	LOC	27	G24	45 55	169 59
Waipori, Lake	LAKE	27	H24	45 58	170 07
Waipori River	STRM	27	H24	45 58	170 08
Waipoua Forest	FRST	6	Q4	35 39	173 34
Waipoua River	STRM	6	P4	35 40	173 29
Waipoua River	STRM	15, 19	U14	40 59	175 41
Waipounamu	LOC	26	E24	45 51	168 45
Waipu	TOWN	7	R4	35 59	174 26
Waipu Caves	LOC	7	R4	35 56	174 21
Waipu Cove	LOC	7	S5	36 02	174 30
Waipuku	LOC	14	R11	39 16	174 16
Waipukurau	BORO	15	W13	40 00	176 33
Waipunga	LOC	15	W11	39 20	176 49
Waipunga River	STRM	11, 15	W11	39 06	176 40
Wairaka Point	PNT	34	B3	41 02	174 52
Wairakei	LOC	10	V10	38 37	176 05
Wairaki River	STRM	26	C24	45 56	167 41
Wairamarama	LOC	10	S7	37 25	174 52
Wairapukao	LOC	11	W10	38 32	176 34
Wairarapa, Lake	LAKE	14, 19	T15	41 14	175 13
Wairau Pa	LOC	39	B3	41 28	173 59
Wairau River	STRM	14, 19	R16	41 31	174 03
Wairau Valley	LOC	14, 18	Q16	41 34	173 32
Wairepo Creek	STRM	22	H21	44 17	170 05
Wairere	LOC	7	R5	36 05	174 18
Wairere Falls	LOC	10	T10	38 32	175 00
Wairio	LOC	26	D25	46 00	168 02
Wairoa	BORO	11, 15	X11	39 03	177 26
Wairoa Gorge	LOC	14, 18	P15	41 25	173 07
Wairoa River	STRM	10	V8	37 41	176 06
Wairoa River	STRM	10	T6	36 58	175 04
Wairoa River	STRM	6	R5	36 11	174 02
Wairoa River	STRM	14, 18	P15	41 25	173 06
Wairoa River	STRM	11, 15	X11	39 04	177 26
Wairongomai	LOC	11	Z8	37 52	178 13
Wairopa Channel	CHAN	31	A7	36 59	174 39
Wairua River	STRM	6	R4	35 48	174 03
Wairuna	LOC	27	F25	46 11	169 19
Waita River	STRM	22	F20	43 47	169 07
Waitaanga	LOC	10	S10	38 50	174 50
Waitaha	LOC	23	J19	43 02	170 44
Waitaha River	STRM	23	J18	42 58	170 39
Waitahanui	STRM	10	V10	38 48	176 06
Waitahanui River	STRM	10	V10	38 48	176 06
Waitahinga	LOC	14	S12	39 45	174 57
Waitahora	LOC	15	V13	40 20	176 10
Waitahu	LOC	18	L17	42 04	171 51
Waitahuna	TOWN	27	G24	45 59	169 46
Waitahuna River	STRM	27	G25	46 09	169 35
Waitahuna West	LOC	27	G25	46 00	169 37
Waitakaruru	TOWN	10	T7	37 14	175 23
Waitakere	LOC	7, 10	S6	36 51	174 33
Waitakere Range	MTNS	7, 10	S6	36 59	174 31
Waitaki	LOC	23, 27	K22	44 56	171 06
Waitaki Bluff	CLIF	22	H19	43 09	170 14
Waitaki, Lake	LAKE	23, 27	H22	44 40	170 24
Waitaki River	STRM	23, 27	K22	44 56	171 09
Waitane	LOC	26	E25	46 11	168 42
Waitangi	LOC	6	R3	35 16	174 05
Waitangi	TOWN	4	—	43 56	176 34 W
Waitangi Bay	BAY	4	—	43 56	176 33 W
Waitangi River	STRM	6	R3	35 17	174 03
Waitangirua	SBRB	35	B5	41 08	174 53
Waitangitaona River	STRM	22	H19	43 08	170 15
Waitanguru	LOC	10	S9	38 23	174 52
Waitapu	LOC	14, 18	N14	40 50	172 48
Waitara	BORO	14, 19	R10	39 00	174 14
Waitara Stream	STRM	14	R10	38 59	174 14
Waitarere	LOC	14, 19	T14	40 33	175 12
Waitaria Bay	LOC	14, 19	R15	41 10	174 03
Waitaruke	LOC	6	Q3	35 05	173 43
Waitati	TOWN	33	C1	45 45	170 34
Waitati River	STRM	33	C1	45 45	170 35
Waitati, Upper	LOC	33	C1	45 46	170 33
Waitawa	LOC	23	K21	44 17	171 11
Waitawheta	LOC	10	U7	37 26	175 47
Waiteika Road	LOC	14	Q11	39 27	173 54
Waiteitei	LOC	7	S5	36 16	174 34
Waitekauri	LOC	10	U7	37 22	175 47
Waitemata Harbour	HARB	30	A4	36 50	174 42
Waitepeka	LOC	27	G25	46 17	169 40
Waiterimu	LOC	10	T7	37 29	175 17
Waiteti	LOC	10	T9	38 22	175 11
Waiteti Stream	STRM	38	A3	38 04	176 13
Waitetuna	LOC	10	T8	37 50	175 01
Waitewhenua	LOC	10	S10	38 43	174 59
Waitoa	TOWN	10	U8	37 36	175 38
Waitoa River	STRM	10	U7	37 27	175 31
Waitoetoe	LOC	10, 14	R10	38 59	174 26
Waitohi	LOC	14	T13	40 15	175 26
Waitohi Flat	LOC	23	K21	44 13	171 11
Waitohi River	STRM	18, 23	N18	42 52	172 46
Waitohu Valley	LOC	14, 19	T14	40 46	175 12
Waitoki	LOC	7, 10	S6	36 38	174 33
Waitoki	LOC	10	U7	37 29	175 40
Waitomo Caves	LOC	10	T9	38 16	175 07
Waitomo Valley	LOC	10	T9	38 14	175 08
Waitoriki	LOC	10, 14	R11	39 07	174 14
Waitotara	TOWN	14	S12	39 48	174 44
Waitotara River	STRM	14	S12	39 51	174 41
Waituhi	LOC	11	Y10	38 35	177 54
Waitui	LOC	10, 14	R11	39 07	174 18
Waituna	LOC	23, 27	K22	44 43	171 02
Waituna	LOC	26	E25	46 24	168 38
Waituna Creek	STRM	26	E26	46 33	168 32
Waituna West	LOC	15	U13	40 03	175 38
Waiuku	TOWN	10	S7	37 15	174 44
Waiuta	TOWN	18	L17	42 17	171 50
Waiwakaiho River	STRM	37	B1	39 02	174 04
Waiwera	LOC	15, 19	U14	40 33	175 40
Waiwera	LOC	7, 10	S6	36 33	174 43
Waiwera South	TOWN	27	F25	46 13	169 30
Waiwhakaiho River	STRM	37	B1	39 02	174 06
Waiwhare	LOC	15	W11	39 27	176 30
Waiwhero	LOC	14, 18	N15	41 11	172 56
Waiwhetu	SBRB	35	C6	41 13	174 55

NAME	DESC	PAGE	REF	LAT S	LONG E
Wakamarama Range	MTNS	18	M14	40 47	172 27
Wakamarina River	STRM	14, 19	Q15	41 17	173 40
Wakamoekau Creek	STRM	37	C3	40 54	175 37
Wakanui	LOC	23	L20	43 58	171 49
Wakanui Creek	STRM	39	D1	43 54	171 47
Wakapuaka	LOC	14, 18	P15	41 13	173 21
Wakaputa Point	PNT	26	C25	46 23	167 47
Wakarara	LOC	15	V12	39 46	176 16
Wakari	SBRB	33	B3	45 52	170 29
Wakatipu, Lake	LAKE	26	E23	45 04	168 35
Wakefield	TOWN	14, 18	P15	41 24	173 03
Waldronville	LOC	33	A4	45 56	170 24
Wallacetown	TOWN	40	C1	46 20	168 17
Wallaceville	SBRB	35	D5	41 08	175 04
Wallingford	LOC	15	W13	40 12	176 36
Waltham	SBRB	32	C3	43 33	172 39
Walton	TOWN	10	U8	37 44	175 42
Wanaka	TOWN	22, 27	F22	44 42	169 08
Wanaka, Lake	LAKE	22, 27	F21	44 30	169 08
Wanbrow, Cape	CAPE	39	D4	45 07	170 59
Wandle Downs	LOC	18, 23	P18	42 34	173 06
Wangaloa	LOC	27	G25	46 17	169 56
Wanganui	CITY	14	T12	39 56	175 02
Wanganui	CITY	36	Urb	39 56	175 02
Wanganui Bluff	CLIF	23	H19	43 02	170 26
Wanganui East	SBRB	36	D2	39 55	175 04
Wanganui River	STRM	23	H19	43 02	170 26
Wanganui River	STRM	14	S12	39 58	175 00
Wangapeka	LOC	18	N15	41 25	172 37
Wangapeka River	STRM	18	N15	41 20	172 47
Wangapeka Saddle	SAD	18	M15	41 25	172 25
Wanstead	LOC	15	W13	40 09	176 33
Ward	LOC	19	R16	41 50	174 08
Ward Island	ISLD	35	B8	41 18	174 52
Ward, Mount	MT	26	B24	45 37	167 11
Wards Pass	PASS	18	P17	42 05	173 11
Wardville	LOC	10	U8	37 43	175 47
Warea	LOC	14	Q11	39 14	173 49
Warepa	LOC	27	G25	46 16	169 37
Warkworth	TOWN	7	S5	36 24	174 40
Warren, The	LOC	23	M19	43 20	172 12
Warrington	TOWN	27	J24	45 43	170 36
Washdyke	TOWN	40	B3	44 21	171 14
Waterfall Inlet	BAY	4	—	50 49	166 14
Waterloo	SBRB	35	C5	41 13	174 55
Waterton	LOC	23	L21	44 03	171 44
Waterview	SBRB	31	A5	36 53	174 42
Watlington	SBRB	40	B4	44 24	171 14
Waverley	TOWN	14	S12	39 46	174 38
Waverley	SBRB	33	C3	45 53	170 32
Waverley	SBRB	40	D1	46 23	168 23
Waverley Beach	LOC	14	S12	39 50	174 38
Wayby	LOC	7	S5	36 20	174 32
Wayby Valley	LOC	7	S5	36 19	174 33
Weber	LOC	15	V13	40 24	176 20
Webling Bay	BAY	4	—	50 33	166 16
Wedderburn	LOC	22, 27	H23	45 02	170 01
Weeding Point	PNT	4	—	43 55	176 34 W
Weedons	LOC	23	M20	43 34	172 24
Weka Pass	PASS	18, 23	N18	42 59	172 43
Wekakura Point	PNT	18	M14	40 55	172 05
Wekaweka	LOC	6	Q4	35 34	173 32
Welbourn	SBRB	37	A1	39 04	174 05
Welcome Bay	LOC	36	B2	37 43	176 11
Wellington	CITY	14, 19	S15	41 17	174 46
Wellington	CITY	34, 35	Urb	41 17	174 46
Wellington	CITY	41	—	41 17	174 46
Wellington International Airport	AIR	35	A8	41 20	174 48
Wellsford	TOWN	7	S5	36 18	174 31
Wendon	LOC	26	E24	45 53	168 49
Wendon Valley	LOC	26	E24	45 53	168 58
Wendonside	LOC	26	E24	45 45	168 44
Weraiti	LOC	15, 19	U14	40 59	175 43
Wesley	SBRB	31	B6	36 54	174 44
West Cape	CAPE	26	A24	45 55	166 26
West Dome	MT	26	D24	45 35	168 13
West End	SBRB	37	A4	40 22	175 36
West End	SBRB	40	C4	46 36	168 19
West End	SBRB	40	B4	44 23	171 13
West Eyreton	LOC	23	M19	43 21	172 23
West Invercargill	SBRB	40	C2	46 24	168 19
West Island	ISLD	4	—	34 11	172 02
West Melton	LOC	23	M20	43 31	172 22
West Norfolk Ridge	SEAF	81	—	33 00	166 50
West Plains	LOC	40	C1	46 22	168 19
West Tamaki Head	HEAD	31	C5	36 51	174 53
West Taratahi	LOC	15, 19	U14	40 56	175 33
Westerfield	LOC	23	L20	43 50	171 37
Western Arm	FIOR	4	—	50 51	166 00
Western Bay	BAY	10	U10	38 43	175 47
Western Group	ISLS	4	—	47 42	179 03
Western Heights	SBRB	38	A4	38 08	176 13
Western Reef	REEF	4	—	43 51	176 56 W
Western Springs	SBRB	31	B5	36 52	174 43
Westfield	SBRB	31	C6	36 56	174 50
Westlake	SBRB	30	B3	36 47	174 45
Westmere	SBRB	31	B5	36 51	174 43
Westmere	LOC	15, 19	U15	41 06	175 45
Westmere	TOWN	14	T12	39 54	175 00
Westmere, Lake	LAKE	36	C1	39 54	175 00
Weston	LOC	27	J23	45 05	170 55
Weston	SBRB	39	C3	45 05	170 55
Westown	SBRB	37	A1	39 05	174 03
Westport	BORO	18	L16	41 45	171 36
Westshore	SBRB	38	D2	39 28	176 53
Westwood	LOC	27	H24	45 56	170 22
Wet Jacket Arm	SND	26	A24	45 38	166 50
Wether Range	MTNS	22	G22	44 35	169 45
Weymouth	LOC	31	C8	37 03	174 52
Whakaangiangi	LOC	11	Z8	37 43	178 19
Whakaari Bluff	PNT	15	W11	39 20	176 56
Whakaki	LOC	11, 15	Y11	39 03	177 36
Whakaki Lagoon	LAGN	11, 15	Y11	39 03	177 33
Whakamara	LOC	14	R12	39 38	174 26
Whakamaru	LOC	10	U9	38 26	175 48
Whakamaru, Lake	LAKE	10	U9	38 26	175 52
Whakapapa	LOC	15	U11	39 12	175 33
Whakapapa River	STRM	10	T10	38 56	175 24
Whakapara	LOC	7	R4	35 32	174 16
Whakapirau	LOC	7	R5	36 09	174 15
Whakapunake	MTN	11	Y10	38 48	177 36
Whakarae Pa	LOC	11	X9	38 17	177 06
Whakarau	LOC	11	Y9	38 23	177 37
Whakarewarewa	SBRB	38	A4	38 10	176 15
Whakarongo	LOC	15	U13	40 20	175 40
Whakataki	LOC	15, 19	V14	40 52	176 13
Whakatane	BORO	11	W8	37 58	177 59
Whakatane River	STRM	11	X8	37 57	177 01
Whakatane West	LOC	11	W9	38 00	176 56
Whakatautuna Point	PNT	7	U5	36 10	175 31
Whakatete Bay	BAY	10	U7	37 05	175 31
Whakatiki River	STRM	34	D5	41 07	175 03
Whakatu	LOC	38	D3	39 36	176 54
Whakawhitira	LOC	11	Z8	37 50	178 20
Whale Bay	LOC	10	S8	37 49	174 48
Whales Back	LOC	18	P18	42 30	173 11
Whananaki	LOC	7	R4	35 31	174 28
Whanawhana	LOC	15	V12	39 33	176 25
Whangaehu	LOC	15, 19	U14	40 56	175 46
Whangaehu	LOC	14	T13	40 01	175 10
Whangaehu River	STRM	15, 19	U14	40 56	175 40
Whangaehu River	STRM	15, 19	T15	41 12	175 27
Whangaehu Stream	STRM	14	T13	40 02	175 05
Whangaimoana	LOC	14, 19	T15	41 24	175 10
Whangamarino	LOC	10	T7	37 21	175 07
Whangamata	LOC	10	U7	37 12	175 52
Whangamoa River	STRM	14, 18	Q15	41 07	173 33
Whangamomona	TOWN	10, 14	S11	39 08	174 44
Whangamomona Stream	STRM	14	S11	39 16	174 54
Whanganui Inlet	BAY	18	N14	40 35	172 35
Whanganui Island	ISLD	7, 10	T6	36 47	175 26
Whangaparaoa	LOC	11	Z8	37 35	178 00
Whangaparaoa	LOC	30	B1	36 38	174 45
Whangaparaoa Peninsula	PEN	30	C1	36 37	174 47
Whangaparaoa Roads	BAY	11	Y8	37 34	177 56
Whangaparaoa Stream	STRM	11	Z8	37 36	178 00
Whangape	LOC	6	P3	35 20	173 13
Whangape Harbour	HARB	6	P3	35 23	173 13
Whangape, Lake	LAKE	10	T7	37 28	175 03
Whangapoua	LOC	7, 10	U6	36 43	175 37
Whangara	LOC	11	Z10	38 34	178 13
Whangara Island	ISLD	11	Z10	38 35	178 14
Whangarata	LOC	10	S7	37 15	174 59
Whangarei	BORO	7	R4	35 43	174 19
Whangarei	BORO	36	Urb	35 43	174 19
Whangarei Harbour	HARB	36	B4	35 47	174 24
Whangarei Heads	LOC	36	D4	35 49	174 30
Whangaripo	LOC	7	S5	36 17	174 38
Whangaroa	LOC	6	Q3	35 03	173 45
Whangaroa Bay	BAY	6	Q2	35 00	173 46
Whangaruru Harbour	HARB	7	R3	35 23	174 21
Whangaruru North	LOC	7	R3	35 21	174 21
Whangateau	LOC	7	S5	36 18	174 46
Wharanui	LOC	19	R16	41 56	174 05
Wharariki Point	PNT	11	Z8	37 50	178 25
Whare Flat	LOC	27	H24	45 49	170 26
Whareama	LOC	15, 19	V14	40 58	176 02
Whareama River	STRM	15, 19	V15	41 02	176 07
Wharehanu	LOC	22, 26	E22	44 57	168 45
Wharehine	LOC	7	R5	36 19	174 25
Wharehuia	LOC	14	R11	39 18	174 20
Wharekahika River	STRM	11	Z8	37 34	178 18
Wharekaka	LOC	11	Z9	38 20	178 18
Wharekauri	LOC	4	—	43 43	176 36 W
Wharekiri Stream	STRM	19	Q17	42 09	173 52
Wharekohe	LOC	6	R4	36 45	174 06
Wharekopae	LOC	11	X10	38 33	177 30
Wharekopae River	STRM	11	Y9	38 28	177 45
Whareora	LOC	7	R4	35 41	174 24
Whareorino	LOC	10	S9	38 29	174 40
Wharepapa	LOC	7, 10	R6	36 43	174 26
Wharepapa South	LOC	10	U9	38 09	175 32
Wharepoa	LOC	10	U7	37 16	175 36
Whareponga	LOC	11	Z8	37 58	178 22
Wharepuhunga	LOC	10	T9	38 12	175 29
Wharerangi	LOC	15	W11	39 28	176 48
Whareroa	LOC	14	R12	39 36	174 18
Wharetoa	LOC	27	F25	46 04	169 28
Whataroa	LOC	22	H19	43 16	170 22
Whataroa River	STRM	22	H19	43 06	170 06
Whatatutu	TOWN	11	Y9	38 23	177 50
Whataupoko	SBRB	38	B2	38 39	178 02
Whatawhata	TOWN	10	T8	37 47	175 09
Whatitiri	LOC	6	R4	35 47	174 08
Whau Creek	STRM	31	A5	36 51	174 40
Whau Valley	SBRB	36	A2	35 42	174 19
Whawharua	LOC	10	T9	38 15	175 13
Wheao River	STRM	11	W10	38 33	176 38
Wheatstone	LOC	23	L21	44 01	171 45
Whenuahou	LOC	15	V13	40 04	176 18
Whenuakite	LOC	7, 10	U6	36 55	175 47
Whenuakura	LOC	14	S12	39 45	174 31
Whenuakura River	STRM	14	S12	39 46	174 33
Whenuanui	LOC	6	R5	36 05	174 02
Whenuapai	LOC	30	A4	36 47	174 38
Whenuapai Aerodrome	AIR	30	A4	36 47	174 38
Whetukura	LOC	15	V13	40 09	176 19
Whirinaki	LOC	6	P3	35 28	173 28
Whirinaki River	STRM	11	W9	38 26	176 42
Whiritoa	LOC	10	U7	37 17	175 55
Whiriwhiri	LOC	10	S7	37 18	174 42
Whirokino	LOC	14, 19	T14	40 31	175 16
Whitby	SBRB	34	B5	4 07	174 53
Whitcombe, Mount	MT	23	J19	43 13	170 55
Whitcombe Pass	PASS	23	J19	43 13	170 58
Whitcombe River	STRM	23	K19	43 01	171 01
White Bluffs	CLIF	14, 19	R16	41 33	174 09
White Head	HEAD	27	G26	46 32	169 41
White Island	ISLD	11	X8	37 31	177 11
White Rock	LOC	23	M19	43 10	172 27
Whitecliffs	LOC	23	L19	43 28	171 54
Whitecoomb	MT	27	F24	45 35	169 05
Whitehall	LOC	10	U8	37 53	175 35
Whitemans Valley	LOC	35	D5	41 10	175 05
Whiterigg	LOC	26	E25	46 04	168 58
Whitestone River	STRM	26	C24	45 32	167 45
Whitford	LOC	31	D6	36 57	174 58
Whitianga	TOWN	7, 10	U6	36 50	175 42
Whitikahu	LOC	10	T8	37 37	175 21
Whitiora	SBRB	37	D1	37 47	175 16
Wick Mountains	MTNS	22, 26	C22	44 45	167 55
Wickliffe Bay	BAY	33	D2	45 50	170 44
Wigram Aerodrome	AIR	32	A3	43 33	172 33
Wilberforce River	STRM	23	K19	43 20	171 25
Wilden	LOC	27	F24	45 45	169 16
Wilder	LOC	15	W13	40 14	176 32
Wilkin River	STRM	22	F21	44 16	169 11
William, Port	HARB	26	D26	46 51	168 05
Willow Flat	LOC	15	W11	39 00	176 57
Willowbridge	LOC	23, 27	K22	44 46	171 07
Willowby	LOC	23	L20	43 59	171 41
Wills	STRM	22	F21	44 02	169 21
Wilmot Pass	PASS	26	B24	45 31	167 11
Wilmot, Lake	LAKE	22	D21	44 23	168 13
Wilmot, Mount	MT	26	B24	45 32	167 11
Wilson Point	PNT	4	—	29 16	177 53 W
Wilsons Crossing	LOC	26	D25	46 15	168 20
Wilsons Point	PNT	26	C27	47 6	167 37
Wilton	SBRB	35	A7	41 6	174 45
Wiltsdown	LOC	10	U9	38 0	175 48
Wimbledon	LOC	15	W13	40 27	176 30
Winchester	TOWN	22	K21	44 1	171 17
Winchmore	LOC	23	L20	43 50	171 43
Windermere	LOC	23	L20	43 59	171 37
Windley River	STRM	26	D24	45 33	168 09
Windsor	LOC	23, 27	J23	45 00	170 47
Windsor	SBRB	40	D2	46 24	168 22

NAME	DESC	PAGE	REF	LAT S	LONG E
Windsor Point	PNT	26	A25	46 12	166 39
Windward Islands	ISLS	4	—	49 41	178 44
Windwhistle	LOC	23	L20	43 31	171 43
Windy Hill	LOC	6	Q4	35 56	173 59
Wingatui	LOC	33	A3	45 53	170 24
Winiata	LOC	15	U12	39 42	175 48
Winscombe	LOC	23	J21	44 07	170 50
Winslow	LOC	23	L20	43 57	171 39
Winton	BORO	26	D25	46 09	168 20
Winton East	LOC	26	D25	46 09	168 22
Wiri	LOC	31	C7	37 00	174 53
Wiritoa, Lake	LAKE	36	D2	39 58	175 05
Wiroa Island	ISLD	31	B8	37 01	174 49
Wither Hills	HILL	39	B4	41 34	174 00
Wither Rise	SBRB	39	B4	41 32	173 57
Wiwiki, Cape	CAPE	6	R3	35 09	174 07
Woburn	SBRB	35	B5	41 13	174 54
Wood Bay	SBRB	31	A6	36 57	174 40
Wood, The	SBRB	39	B1	41 16	173 17
Woodbourne	TOWN	14, 19	R16	41 31	173 52
Woodbury	LOC	23	K21	44 02	171 12
Woodcocks	LOC	7, 10	S5	36 27	174 34
Woodend	LOC	40	D3	46 28	168 23
Woodend	TOWN	23	N19	43 19	172 40
Woodend Beach	LOC	23	N19	43 20	172 42
Woodhill	LOC	7, 10	R6	36 44	174 26
Woodhill	SBRB	36	A3	35 44	174 18
Woodlands	LOC	11	X9	38 02	177 16
Woodlands	TOWN	26	E25	46 22	168 34
Woodlands Park	SBRB	31	A6	36 57	174 38
Woodlaw	LOC	26	D25	46 02	168 00
Woodleigh	LOC	10	S8	37 32	174 54
Woodside	LOC	14, 19	T15	41 04	175 24
Woodside	LOC	27	H24	45 52	170 10
Woodstock	LOC	18, 23	K18	42 46	171 00
Woodstock	LOC	23	L19	43 17	171 57
Woodstock	LOC	14, 18	N15	41 16	172 49
Woodville	BORO	15, 19	U13	40 20	175 52
Woody Head	HEAD	10	S8	37 52	174 45
Woolston	SBRB	32	C3	43 33	172 41
Worser Bay	BAY	35	B8	41 19	174 50
Worth Inlet	BAY	4	—	50 47	166 14
Wreys Bush	LOC	26	D25	46 01	168 06
Wrights Bush	LOC	26	D25	46 18	168 13
Wylies Crossing	LOC	27	H24	45 52	170 19
Wyndham	TOWN	26	E25	46 20	168 51
Wyndham South	LOC	26	E25	46 24	168 52
Yaldhurst	SBRB	32	A2	43 31	172 31
Yates Point	PNT	22	C22	44 30	167 49
York Bay	SBRB	35	B7	41 16	174 55
Young, Cape	CAPE	4	—	43 42	176 39 W
Young Nicks Head	HEAD	11	Y10	38 45	177 58
Young Range	MTNS	22	F21	44 15	169 20
Yule Island	ISLD	4	—	50 32	166 18

GAZETTEER Beyond New Zealand

NAME	DESC	PAGE	REF	LAT	LONG
Abaiang Island	GILBERT	196	F2	01 51 N	172 58 E
Abbott Peak	PEAK	185	C1	77 25 S	167 00 E
Abemama Atoll	ATOL	196	F2	00 21 N	173 51 E
Acapulco	CITY	47	Mexico	16 51 N	99 56 W
Accra	CITY	42	Ghana	05 33 N	00 15 W
Actaeon Islands	FR TER	197	K5	22 00 S	136 00 W
Adare, Cape	—	184	B2	71 30 S	170 24 E
Addis Ababa	CITY	42	Ethiopia	09 03 N	38 42 E
Adelaide	CITY	46	Australia	34 56 S	138 36 E
Aden	CITY	42	Yemen	12 50 N	45 03 E
Admiralty Islands	PNG	196	C3	02 10 S	147 00 E
Admiralty Mountains	MTNS	184	B2	71 45 S	168 00 E
Afa	LOC	194	C4	21 07 S	175 03 W
Afghanistan	KING	42	Asia	34 00 N	66 00 E
Afiamalua	LOC	193	C4	13 52 S	171 47 W
Ahe Atoll	FR TER	197	J4	14 30 S	146 19 W
Ahua Island	FR TER	195	D4	09 12 S	171 49 W
Ahunui Atoll	FR TER	197	J4	19 35 S	140 28 W
Ailinglapalap Atoll	MARSHAL	196	E2	07 30 N	168 40 E
Aitutaki Atoll	ATOL	194	D2	18 52 S	159 46 W
Akiaki Atoll	FR TER	197	K4	18 28 S	139 12 W
Alaska	STATE	42, 43	USA	65 00 N	153 00 W
Alaska, Gulf of	BAY	43, 47	N America	58 00 N	146 00 W
Albert Markham, Mount	—	184	B3	81 25 S	158 10 E
Aleisa	LOC	193	C4	13 51 S	171 54 W
Aleutian Islands	ISLS	47	Alaska	52 00 N	176 00 W
Alexandra Mountains	MTNS	184	C3	77 30 S	153 30 W
Algeria	REP	42, 43	Africa	28 00 N	03 00 E
Algiers	CITY	42, 43	Algeria	36 50 N	03 00 E
All Blacks Nunataks	PEAKS	184	B3	81 30 S	155 40 E
Allen, Mount	MTN	185	A2	77 25 S	162 40 E
Alligator Peak	PEAK	185	A3	78 28 S	158 46 E
Alofi	TOWN	195	A4	19 03 S	169 55 W
Alofi Bay	BAY	195	A4	19 02 S	169 50 W
Alofi Island	FR TER	196	G4	14 27 S	178 05 W
Alpha Bluff	BLUF	185	B4	78 53 S	162 30 E
Altar, Mount	—	185	A2	77 54 S	160 54 E
Amaile	LOC	193	D4	13 59 S	171 26 W
Amanu Atoll	FR TER	197	J4	17 48 S	140 44 W
Amanu Raro Island	FR TER	197	J5	20 29 S	143 32 W
Amanu Runga Island	FR TER	197	J5	20 38 S	143 18 W
Amazon River	STRM	47	Brazil	00 04 S	65 00 W
Ambrym Island	N HEB	196	E4	16 15 S	168 10 E
American Samoa	US ADM	194	B1	14 20 S	170 30 W
Amsterdam	CITY	41	Neth	52 21 N	04 54 E
Amsterdam Island	FR TER	42	Ind O	37 55 S	77 40 E
Amundsen Coast	COAST	184	C4	85 30 S	159 00 W
Amundsen Glacier	GLCR	184	C4	86 00 S	159 20 W
Amundsen-Scott (US)	BASE	184	B4	90 00 S	00 00
Amur River	STRM	42	USSR	52 56 N	141 10 E
Anaa Atoll	FR TER	197	J4	17 25 S	145 30 W
Anare Mountains	MTNS	184	A2	70 55 S	166 00 E
Anchorage	CITY	47	Alaska	61 10 N	150 00 W
Andaman Islands	INDIA	46	Bay Bengal	12 00 N	93 00 E
Andaman Sea	—	46	Bay Bengal	10 00 N	95 00 E
Andreanof Islands	ALEUT	46	Bering S	52 00 N	176 00 W
Aneityum Islands	N HEB	196	F5	20 12 S	169 45 E
Angatau Atoll	FR TER	197	J4	15 45 S	140 50 W
Angola	DIS TER	42	Africa	12 30 S	18 30 E
Ankara	CITY	41	Turkey	39 55 N	32 50 E
Ant Hill	HILL	185	B4	78 48 S	161 24 E
Anuta Island	S CRUZ	196	E4	11 38 S	169 50 E
Aoba Island	N HEB	196	E4	16 25 S	167 50 E
Apia	TOWN	193	C4	13 48 S	171 45 W
Apocalypse Peaks	PEAKS	185	A2	77 23 S	160 50 E
Apolima Island	W SAMOA	193	B4	13 48 S	172 09 W
Arabian Sea	—	42	Ind O	15 00 N	65 00 E
Arafura Sea	—	196	B4	11 00 S	140 00 E
Aral Sea	—	42	USSR	45 00 N	60 00 E
Aranuka Atoll	GILBERT	196	F3	00 10 N	173 35 E
Aratika Atoll	FR TER	197	J4	15 30 S	145 30 W
Archer, Cape		185	A1	76 51 S	162 52 E
Argentina	REP	47	S America	34 00 S	64 00 W
Arkansas River	STRM	47	USA	33 48 N	91 04 W
Armitage, Cape	—	185	C2	77 51 S	166 40 E
Arno Atoll	MARSHAL	196	F2	07 02 N	171 40 E
Arorae Island	GILBERT	196	F3	02 39 S	176 54 E
Arorangi	LOC	194	A1	21 13 S	159 49 W
Arrowsmith, Mount	—	185	A1	76 46 S	162 18 E
Arctic Ocean	—	42, 43	—	85 00 N	170 00 E
Aru Islands	INDON	46	Arafura S	06 00 S	134 30 E
Asau	LOC	193	A3	13 29 S	172 38 W
Asau Bay	BAY	193	A3	13 29 S	172 39 W
Ascension Island	UK COL	42, 43	Atl O	07 57 S	14 22 W
Asgaard Range	MTNS	185	A2	77 35 S	161 30 E
Asuncion	CITY	47	Paraguay	25 15 S	57 40 W
Asuncion Island	ISLD	46	Marianas	19 34 N	145 24 E
Ata Island	TONGA	194	D3	21 03 S	175 00 W
Atafu Atoll	TOKEL	195	A1	08 33 S	172 30 W
Atafu Island	TOKEL	195	A1	08 30 S	172 30 W
Atata Island	TONGA	194	B3	21 03 S	175 15 W
Athens	CITY	42, 43	Greece	38 00 N	23 44 E
Atiu Island	COOKS	194	D2	20 00 S	158 07 W
Atlantic Ocean	—	42, 43		00 00 N	25 00 W
Aua Island	PNG	196	C3	01 29 S	143 05 E
Auala	LOC	193	A3	13 29 S	172 39 W
Aur Atoll	MARSHAL	196	F2	08 16 N	171 02 E
Aurora Glacier	GLCR	185	D1	77 35 S	167 45 E
Aurora, Mount	—	185	C2	78 15 S	166 20 E
Australia	COTH NAT	196	B5	25 00 S	135 00 E
Aust Antarctic Territory	AUST ADM	185	A3	78 30 S	159 00 E
Austria	REP	42	Europe	47 20 N	13 20 E
Avakilikili Island	TOKEL	195	D4	09 06 S	171 47 W
Avalanche Bay	BAY	185	A1	77 00 S	162 45 E
Avana Stream	STRM	194	A1	21 14 S	159 43 W
Avarua	TOWN	194	A1	21 12 S	159 46 W
Avarua Harbour	HARB	194	A1	21 11 S	159 46 W
Avatele	LOC	195	A4	19 06 S	169 55 W
Avatele Bay	BAY	195	A4	19 05 S	169 56 W
Avatiu	LOC	194	A1	21 12 S	159 46 W
Avatiu Harbour	HARB	194	A1	21 11 S	159 47 W
Avatiu Stream	STRM	194	A1	21 12 S	159 46 W
Azores Islands	PORT TER	42, 43	Atl O	38 30 N	28 00 W
Backdoor Bay	BAY	185	C1	77 35 S	166 10 E
Baghdad	CITY	42, 43	Iraq	33 20 N	44 26 E
Bahamas	UK COL	47	W Indies	24 15 N	76 00 W
Baikal, Lake	—	42	USSR	53 00 N	107 40 E
Baker Island	PHOENIX	196	G2	00 00	176 28 W
Baku	CITY	42	USSR	40 22 N	49 53 E
Baldwin, Mount	—	184	A2	72 15 S	163 20 E
Balham Valley	VLY	185	A2	77 25 S	161 05 E
Bali Island	INDON	46	Java Sea	08 25 S	115 15 E
Balkhash, Lake	—	42, 43	USSR	46 00 N	74 00 E
Balleny Islands	ISLS	184	A1	66 35 S	162 50 E
Banda Sea	—	46	Indonesia	05 00 S	128 00 E
Bandjarmasin	CITY	46	Kalimantan	03 22 S	114 33 E
Bangka Island	INDON	46	Java Sea	01 48 N	125 09 E
Bangkok	CITY	46	Thailand	13 44 N	100 30 E
Bangladesh	REP	46	SE Asia	24 00 N	90 00 E
Barcelona	CITY	41	Spain	41 25 N	02 10 E
Bareface Bluff	BLUF	185	B4	78 50 S	161 45 E
Barents Sea		43	Arctic O	74 00 N	36 00 E
Barne, Cape		185	C1	77 35 S	166 15 E
Barne Glacier	GLCR	185	C1	77 35 S	166 30 E
Barne Inlet	BAY	184	B3	80 15 S	160 00 E
Barnes, Mount	—	185	B2	77 40 S	163 30 E
Barrier Reef	REEF	194	A2	20 00 S	174 30 W
Barwick Valley	VLY	185	A2	77 20 S	161 05 E
Bass Island	FR TER	197	J5	27 55 S	143 26 W
Bass Strait	STRA	196	C6	39 20 S	145 30 E
Batan Islands	PHIL	46	S China S	20 35 N	121 55 E
Beardmore Glacier	GLCR	184	B4	84 20 S	170 00 E
Beaufort Island	ISLD	185	C1	76 53 S	167 00 E
Belep Islands	N CAL	196	E4	19 45 S	163 40 E
Belfast	CITY	41	N Ireland	54 40 N	05 50 W
Belitung Island	INDON	46	Java Sea	02 50 S	107 55 E
Belize	UK PROT	47	C America	17 29 N	88 10 W
Bellingshausen Atoll	FR TER	197	I4	15 48 S	154 33 W
Bellona Island	SOLOMON	196	D4	11 20 S	159 47 E
Belmopan	CITY	47	Belize	17 00 N	88 00 W
Belousov Point	PNT	184	A1	69 50 S	160 20 E
Bengal, Bay of	—	46	Ind O	15 00 N	90 00 E
Benson Glacier	GLCR	185	A1	76 50 S	161 45 E
Bega Island	FIJI	193	B2	18 24 S	178 09 E
Beringa Island	USSR	46	Bering S	55 00 N	165 15 E
Bering Sea	—	46	Pac O	60 00 N	175 00 W
Berlin	CITY	42, 43	Germany	52 32 N	13 24 E
Berlin, Mount	—	184	D3	76 05 S	135 50 W
Bermuda	UK COL	42, 43	Atl O	32 20 N	64 45 W
Bernacchi Bay	BAY	185	B2	77 30 S	163 50 E
Bernacchi, Cape	—	185	B2	77 30 S	163 50 E
Beru Island	UK COL	196	F3	01 15 S	176 00 E
Bettle Peak	PEAK	185	B2	77 50 S	163 30 E
Bhutan	KING	46	SE Asia	27 30 N	90 30 E
Bilbao	CITY	41	Spain	43 15 N	02 56 W
Bird, Cape	—	185	C1	77 10 S	166 40 E
Bird, Mount	—	185	C1	77 15 S	166 45 E
Birmingham	CITY	41	UK	52 30 N	01 50 W
Birnie Island	US–UK	196	G3	03 35 S	171 31 W
Biscay, Bay of	—	42, 43	Atl O	44 00 N	04 00 W
Bishop Peak	PEAK	185	B3	78 10 S	162 10 E
Bismark Archipelago	PNG	196	C3	02 00 S	150 00 E
Bismark Sea	—	196	C3	04 00 S	148 00 E
Black Cap, Cape	—	185	B4	79 00 S	161 55 E
Black Island	ISLD	185	C2	78 10 S	166 50 E
Black Sea	—	42, 43	USSR	43 00 N	35 00 E
Bligh Water	STRA	193	B1	17 00 S	178 00 E
Black Bay	BAY	184	D3	76 15 S	146 20 E
Blue Glacier	GLCR	185	B2	77 50 S	163 40 E
Bogota	CITY	47	Colombia	04 18 N	74 48 W
Bolivia	REP	47	S America	17 00 S	65 00 W
Bombay	CITY	42	India	18 56 N	72 51 E
Bonin Islands	JAP TER	46	Pac O	27 00 N	142 10 E
Bonney, Lake	—	185	A2	77 45 S	162 30 E
Bora Bora Island	FR TER	197	I4	16 30 S	151 45 W
Borchgrevink Coast	—	184	B2	73 00 S	166 00 E
Bordeaux	CITY	41	France	44 50 N	00 34 W
Boreas, Mount	—	185	A2	77 30 S	161 05 E
Borneo Island	—	42	S China S	00 30 N	114 00 E
Botswana	REP	42	Africa	22 00 S	24 00 E
Bougainville Island	PNG	196	D3	06 00 S	155 00 E
Bouvet Island	NORWAY	42	Atl O	54 26 S	03 24 E
Bowers Mountains	MTNS	184	A2	71 10 S	163 00 E

NAME	DESC	PAGE	REF	LAT	LONG
Bowers Piedmont Glacier	GLCR	185	B2	77 45 S	164 15 E
Boyd Glacier	GLCR	184	D3	77 15 S	145 10 W
Brasilia	CITY	43	Brazil	16 13 S	44 29 W
Bratina Island	ISLD	185	C2	78 00 S	165 35 E
Brazil	REP	43	S America	09 00 S	53 00 W
Brest	CITY	41	France	48 23 N	04 30 W
Briggs Hill	HILL	185	B2	77 50 S	163 10 E
Brisbane	CITY	46	Australia	27 30 S	153 00 E
Bristol	CITY	41	UK	51 27 N	02 35 W
Britannia Range	MTNS	184	B3	80 10 S	157 00 E
Brooke, Mount	—	184	A3	76 50 S	160 00 E
Brown Peninsula	PEN	185	C2	78 05 S	165 25 E
Brunei	UK PROT	46	Borneo	04 50 N	114 55 E
Brussels	CITY	41	Belgium	50 50 N	04 29 E
Buckle Island	ISLD	184	A1	66 50 S	163 20 E
Buckley Island	ISLD	184	B4	84 55 S	164 00 E
Budapest	CITY	41	Hungary	47 30 N	19 03 E
Buenos Aires	CITY	47	Argentina	34 40 S	58 30 W
Buka Island	SOLOMON	196	D3	05 15 S	154 35 E
Bukatatanoa Reefs	—	193	D2	18 12 S	178 24 W
Bulgaria	REP	42, 43	Europe	43 00 N	25 00 E
Bunguran Island	INDON	46	Java S	04 40 N	108 00 E
Bureleva	LOC	193	B2	19 10 S	178 12 E
Burks, Cape	—	184	D3	74 45 S	137 10 W
Burma	REP	46	SE Asia	22 00 N	98 00 E
Buromskiy, Cape	—	184	A1	69 00 S	156 10 E
Bursey, Mount	—	184	D3	76 00 S	132 40 W
Buru Island	INDON	46	Banda S	03 24 S	126 40 E
Burundi	KING	42	Africa	03 15 S	30 00 E
Bush Mountains	MTNS	184	B4	84 55 S	179 40 E
Butaritari Island	GILBERT	196	F2	03 00 N	172 46 E
Butter Point	PNT	185	B2	77 40 S	164 20 E
Byrd (US)	BASE	184	D4	80 00 S	119 30 W
Byrd Glacier	GLCR	184	B3	80 30 S	157 30 E
Cabinda	ANGOLA TER	42	Africa	05 34 S	12 12 E
Cadiz	CITY	41	Spain	36 32 N	06 18 W
Cairns	CITY	46	Australia	16 51 S	145 43 E
Cairo	CITY	42, 43	U.A.R.	30 03 N	31 35 E
Calcutta	CITY	42	India	22 35 N	88 21 E
Camel's Hump	MTN	185	B2	77 55 S	162 35 E
Cameroon	REP	42	Africa	06 00 N	12 00 E
Canada	COTH NAT	42, 43	N America	60 00 N	95 00 W
Canary Islands	SPAIN	42, 43	Atl O	28 30 N	15 10 W
Canberra	CITY	46	Australia	35 18 S	149 08 E
Canton	CITY	46	China	23 08 N	113 20 E
Canton Island	PHOENIX	196	G3	02 50 S	171 40 W
Capetown	CITY	42	S Africa	35 56 S	18 28 E
Cape Verde Islands	PORT TER	42, 43	Atl O	16 00 N	24 00 W
Caracas	CITY	47	Venezuela	10 35 N	66 56 W
Caribbean Sea	—	47	C America	15 00 N	73 00 W
Caroline Island	UK—US	197	I3	09 55 S	150 15 W
Caroline Islands	US ADM	196	C1	08 00 N	147 00 E
Carpentaria, Gulf of	BAY	196	B4	14 00 S	139 00 E
Carteret Islands	SOLOMON	196	D3	04 45 S	155 20 E
Caspian Sea	—	42, 43	USSR	42 00 N	50 30 E
Castle Rock	HILL	185	C2	77 50 S	166 45 E
Cato Island	AUST	196	D5	23 14 S	155 29 E
Celebes Sea	—	46	Indonesia	03 00 N	122 00 E
Central African Republic	REP	42	Africa	07 00 N	21 00 E
Ceram Island	INDON	46	Banda Sea	03 00 S	129 00 E
Chad	REP	42	Africa	15 00 N	19 00 E
Chad, Lake	—	185	B2	77 40 S	162 50 E
Chagos Archipelago	UK TER	42	Ind O	06 00 S	72 00 E
Chapman, Mount	—	184	D4	82 30 S	105 20 W
Cheetham, Cape	—	184	A2	70 26 S	162 40 E
Chicago	CITY	47	USA	41 50 N	87 45 W
Chile	REP	47	S America	30 00 S	71 00 W
China	REP	46	Asia	33 00 N	105 00 E
Chocolate, Cape	—	185	B2	77 55 S	164 35 E
Choiseul Island	SOLOMON	196	D3	07 00 S	157 00 E
Christmas Island	AUST	46	Ind O	10 30 S	105 40 E
Christmas Island (UK)	LINES	197	I2	02 00 N	157 30 W
Christmas Island Ridge	SEAF	197	I2	06 30 N	159 00 W
Chubut River	STRM	47	Argentina	43 20 S	65 05 W
Ch'ungch'ing	CITY	46	China	29 39 N	106 34 E
Churchill Mountains	MTNS	184	B3	81 30 S	159 00 E
Cicia Island	FIJI	193	C1	17 45 S	179 25 W
Cinder Hill	HILL	185	C1	77 15 S	166 25 E
Clare Range	MTNS	185	A1	77 10 S	161 15 E
Clarión Island	MEXICO	47	Pac O	18 22 N	114 44 W
Clark Mountains	MTNS	184	D3	77 20 S	142 00 W
Clem Nunatak	PEAK	185	A3	78 30 S	160 40 E
Cleveland Glacier	GLCR	185	A1	76 55 S	162 00 E
Clipperton Island	FR TER	47	Pac O	10 20 N	109 13 W
Coates, Mount	—	185	A2	77 50 S	162 05 E
Cocks Glacier	GLCR	185	B3	78 40 S	162 00 E
Cocks, Mount	—	185	B3	78 30 S	162 30 E
Cocos Island	C RICA	47	Pac O	05 33 N	87 00 W
Cocos Islands	AUST	46	Ind O	14 05 S	93 18 E
Colbeck, Cape	—	184	C3	77 00 S	158 00 W
Coleman, Mount	—	185	B2	77 35 S	163 25 E
Colombia	REP	47	S America	04 00 N	72 00 W
Colombo	CITY	42	Sri Lanka	06 55 N	79 52 E
Colorado River	STRM	47	USA	31 45 N	114 40 W
Commonwealth Glacier	GLCR	185	B2	77 35 S	163 10 E
Commonwealth Range	MTNS	184	B4	84 15 S	173 00 E
Congo	REP	42	Africa	00 00 N	25 00 E
Congo River	STRM	42	Africa	06 04 S	12 24 E
Cook Islands	ASSOC (NZ) COTH NAT	194	Pac O	15 00 S	160 00 W
Cook Mountains	MTNS	184	B3	79 25 S	158 00 E
Copenhagen	CITY	42	Denmark	55 43 N	12 34 E
Coral Sea	—	196	D4	18 00 S	158 00 E
Coral Sea Basin	SEAF	196	D4	14 00 S	152 00 E
Coral Sea Plateau	SEAF	196	D4	17 00 S	150 00 E
Cork	CITY	41	Eire	51 54 N	08 28 W
Corunna	CITY	41	Spain	43 22 N	08 24 W
Costa Rica	REP	47	C America	10 00 N	84 00 W
Cotton Glacier	GLCR	185	A1	77 10 S	161 45 E
Coulman Island	ISLD	184	B2	73 30 S	170 00 E
Crater Hill	HILL	185	C2	77 50 S	166 45 E
Crozet Islands	FR TER	42	Ind O	46 27 S	52 00 E
Crozier, Cape	—	185	D1	77 30 S	169 20 E
Cruzen Island	ISLD	184	D3	74 15 S	140 40 W
Cuba	REP	47	W Indies	21 30 N	80 00 E
Curacao Island	NETH ADM	47	Carib S	12 11 N	69 00 W
Dacca	CITY	46	Bangladesh	23 42 N	90 22 E
Dahomey	REP	42	Africa	09 30 N	02 15 E
Dailey Islands	ISLS	185	C2	77 50 S	165 10 E
Daitô Islands	JAPAN	46	E China S	25 00 N	131 15 E
Dakar	CITY	42, 43	Senegal	14 38 N	17 27 W
Danger Islands	COOKS	47	Pac O	10 53 S	165 49 W
Daniell Peninsula	PEN	184	B2	72 50 S	169 30 E
Dar es Salaam	CITY	42	Tanzania	06 51 S	39 18 E
Darling River	STRM	196	B6	34 07 S	141 55 E
Darwin	CITY	46	Australia	12 23 S	130 44 E
Darwin Glacier	GLCR	184	B3	79 55 S	158 00 E
Darwin Mountains	MTNS	184	A3	79 50 S	156 20 E
David Glacier	GLCR	184	A2	75 15 S	161 00 E
Davidson, Mount	—	185	A1	76 45 S	162 00 E
Davies Bay	BAY	184	A1	69 15 S	158 40 E
Davis Strait	STRA	43	Greenland	68 00 N	58 00 W

NAME	DESC	PAGE	REF	LAT	LONG
Dawara	LOC	193	B1	16 48 S	179 00 E
Dawson-Lambton, Mount	—	185	B4	78 55 S	160 40
Debenham Glacier	GLCR	185	A	77 10 S	162 30 E
Delhi	CITY	42	India	28 40 N	77 14 E
Dellbridge Islands	ISLS	185	C2	77 40 S	166 15 E
Delta Bluff	BLUF	185	B	78 40 S	161 20 E
Denmark	KING	42, 43	Europe	56 00 N	10 00 E
Dido, Mount	—	185	A2	77 30 S	160 55 E
Disappointment Islands	FR TER	197	J4	14 02 S	141 24 W
Discovery Bluff	BLUF	185	A1	77 00 S	162 40 W
Discovery, Mount	—	185	C2	78 25 S	165 00 E
Djakarta	CITY	46	Indonesia	06 08 S	106 45 E
Dominican Republic	REP	47	W Indies	19 00 N	70 40 W
Dominion Range	MTNS	184	B4	85 30 S	166 00 E
Drake Passage	STRA	43	Antarctica	58 00 S	70 00 W
Dromedary, Mount	—	185	B3	78 20 S	163 05 E
Drygalski Ice Tongue	GLCR	184	B2	75 20 S	163 30 E
Dublin	CITY	42, 43	Eire	53 20 N	06 15 W
Ducie Island	PITCAIRN	197	L5	24 40 S	124 48 W
Dufek Coast	COAST	184	B3	84 20 S	178 00
Duff Island	S CRUZ	196	E4	10 05 S	167 08 E
Duke of Gloucester Islands	FR TER	197	J5	20 38 S	143 20 W
Dunlop, Cape	—	185	B1	77 15 S	163 30 E
Dunlop Island	ISLD	185	B1	77 15 S	163 30 E
Durban	CITY	42	S Africa	29 53 S	31 00 E
Eady Ice Piedmont	GLCR	185	C3	78 30 S	165 20 E
East Caroline Basin	SEAF	196	C2	03 00 N	147 00 E
East China Sea	—	46	China	30 00 N	126 00 E
Easter Island	CHILE	197	N5	27 05 S	109 20 W
Eastface Nunatak	PEAK	185	C3	78 40 S	163 35 E
Ebon Atoll	MARSHAL	196	E2	04 40 N	168 43 E
Ecuador	REP	47	S America	02 00 S	77 30 W
Edinburgh	CITY	42	UK	55 57 N	03 13 W
Edmonton	CITY	43	Canada	53 34 N	113 25 W
Edward VII Land	REG	184	C3	78 00 S	154 00 W
Efate Island	FR TER	196	E4	17 40 S	168 25 E
Egeria Channel	CHAN	194	B3	21 02 S	175 15 W
Eiao Island	FR TER	197	J3	08 00 S	140 40 W
Eire	REP	42	Europe	53 00 N	08 00 W
Elizabeth, Mount	—	184	B3	83 55 S	168 20 E
Ellice Islands	UK COL	196	F3	08 00 S	178 00 E
El Salvador	REP	47	C America	13 50 N	88 55 W
Emmanuel Glacier	GLCR	185	B2	78 05 S	162 20 E
Enderbury Island	PHOENIX	196	G3	03 08 S	171 05 W
England, Mount	—	185	A1	77 02 S	162 30 E
Epi Island	N HEB	196	E4	16 43 S	168 15 E
Equatorial Guinea	SPAIN	42	Africa	02 00 N	09 00 E
Erebus Bay	BAY	185	C2	77 45 S	166 40 E
Erebus Glacier Tongue	GLCR	185	C2	77 45 S	166 35 E
Erebus, Mount	—	185	C1	77 40 S	167 20 E
Erie, Lake	—	47	USA	42 15 N	81 00 W
Eromanga Island	N HEB	196	E4	18 45 S	169 05 E
Escalade Peak	PEAK	185	A4	78 40 S	159 20 E
Espiritu Santo Island	N HEB	196	E4	15 50 S	166 50 E
Ethiopia	EMPIRE	42	Africa	09 00 N	41 00 E
Eua Island	TONGA	194	A2	21 23 S	174 55 W
Eua Iki Island	TONGA	194	D3	21 07 S	174 58 W
Evans, Cape	—	185	C2	77 40 S	166 25 E
Evans, Mount	—	185	A1	77 15 S	162 30 E
Evans Piedmont Glacier	GLCR	185	A1	76 45 S	162 45 E
Evteev Glacier	GLCR	185	B4	78 55 S	161 10 E
Executive Committee Range	MTNS	184	D3	76 50 S	126 00 W
Exploring Isles	FIJI	193	D1	17 05 S	178 48 W
Faaite Atoll	FR TER	197	J4	16 40 S	145 15 W
Færos Islands	D'MARK	42	Iceland	62 00 N	07 00 W
Fafa Island	TONGA	194	C3	21 05 S	175 09 W
Fagaloa Bay	BAY	193	D4	13 56 S	171 32 W
Fagamalo	LOC	193	B3	13 24 S	172 22 W
Fahefa	LOC	194	A4	21 08 S	175 20 W
Fairbanks	CITY	41	Alaska	64 50 N	147 50 W
Fais Island	CAROL	46	Pac O	09 45 N	140 31 E
Fakahina Atoll	FR TER	197	J4	16 00 S	140 05 W
Fakaofa Atoll	TOKEL	195	D2	09 23 S	171 14 W
Fakaofo Island	TOKEL	195	D2	09 24 S	171 15 W
Fakarava Atoll	FR TER	197	J4	16 02 S	145 36 W
Faleâlupo	LOC	193	A3	13 29 S	172 47 W
Faleâse'elâ	LOC	193	C4	13 55 S	171 57 W
Faleata Stream	STRM	193	B4	13 45 S	172 19 W
Falefa	LOC	193	D3	13 53 S	171 35 W
Falelatai	LOC	193	C4	13 54 S	172 00 W
Falelima	LOC	193	A4	13 34 S	172 43 W
Faleolo Internat Airport	W SAMOA	193	C4	13 48 S	172 00 W
Faleû	LOC	193	C4	13 51 S	172 06 W
Fale'ula	LOC	193	C4	13 46 S	171 48 W
Falevao	LOC	193	D4	13 55 S	171 35 W
Falkland Islands	UK COL	43	Atl O	51 45 S	59 00 W
Fangataufa Island	FR TER	197	K5	22 14 S	138 45 W
Fanga Uta Lagoon	LAGN	194	B4	21 10 S	175 12 W
Fanning Atoll (UK)	LINES	196	I2	03 52 N	159 22 W
Fasito'otai	LOC	193	C4	13 48 S	171 57 W
Fasito'outa	LOC	193	C4	13 47 S	171 56 W
Fatai	LOC	194	B4	21 07 S	175 16 W
Fataka Island	S CRUZ	196	F4	11 55 S	170 12 E
Fatu Hiva Island	FR TER	197	K4	10 27 S	138 39 W
Fatu Huku Island	FR TER	197	K3	09 25 S	138 54 W
Fatumu	LOC	194	C4	21 12 S	175 06 W
Faure Peak	PEAK	184	C4	85 40 S	128 40 W
Feather, Mount	—	185	A3	77 58 S	160 20 E
Feni Islands	PNG	196	D3	04 05 S	153 42 E
Fenuafala Island	TOKEL	195	D2	09 23 S	171 16 W
Fenua Loa Island	TOKEL	195	D2	09 27 S	171 13 W
Fenualoa Island	TOKEL	195	A1	08 35 S	172 30 W
Fergusson Island	PNG	196	D3	09 30 S	150 40 E
Ferrar Glacier	GLCR	185	B2	77 40 S	163 00 E
Field, Mount	—	184	B3	80 55 S	158 00 E
Fiji Islands	COTH NAT	196	F4	18 00 S	175 00 E
Fiji Islands	—	193	Pac O	18 00 S	175 00 E
Finger Mountain	MTN	185	A2	77 45 S	160 40 E
Finland	REP	42, 43	Europe	64 00 N	26 00 E
Fishtail Point	PNT	185	B4	78 55 S	162 40 E
Flatiron	MTN	185	A1	77 03 S	161 50 E
Flint Island (UK)	LINES	196	I4	11 25 S	151 48 W
Flood Range	MTNS	184	D3	76 00 S	134 20 W
Flores Island	INDON	46	Timor S	08 30 S	121 00 E
Fog Bay	BAY	185	D1	77 40 S	168 10 E
Fonuakula	LOC	195	A4	19 04 S	169 55 W
Fonualei Island	TONGA	196	G4	18 01 S	174 20 W
Ford Massif	MTN	184	C4	85 05 S	91 00 W
Ford Ranges	MTNS	184	D3	77 00 S	145 00 W
Ford Rock	ROCK	185	C2	77 45 S	166 55 W
Fosdick Mountains	MTNS	184	D3	76 35 S	145 15 W
Fo'ui	LOC	194	A3	21 06 S	175 20 W
Fowler Knoll	MTN	184	C4	84 50 S	99 00 W
France	REP	42, 43	Europe	46 00 N	02 00 E
Frankfurt	CITY	41	W German	50 06 N	08 41 E
Franklin Island	ISLD	184	B2	76 05 S	168 20 E
Fraser Island	AUST	196	D5	25 15 S	153 10 E
French Guiana	FR TER	43	S America	04 00 N	53 00 W
FTAI (French Territory of Afars & Issars)	FR TER	42	Africa	11 30 N	43 00 E
Fridtjof Nansen, Mount	—	184	C4	85 20 S	167 30 W
Fryxell, Lake	—	185	B2	77 35 S	163 15 E

NAME	DESC	PAGE	REF	LAT	LONG
Fua'amotu	LOC	194	C4	21 15 S	175 08 W
Fua'amotu Internat Airport	TONGA	194	C4	21 14 S	175 08 W
Fukave Island	TONGA	194	C3	21 05 S	175 02 W
Fulaga Island	FIJI	193	D2	19 08 S	178 36 W
Funafuti Atoll	ELLICE	196	F3	08 30 S	179 12 E
Furneaux Group	AUST	196	C7	40 10 S	148 05 E
Futuna Island	N HEB	196	F4	19 32 S	170 12 E
Futuna Island	FR TER	196	G4	14 25 S	178 20 W
Gabon	REP	42	Africa	01 00 S	11 45 E
Gaferut Island	CAROL	196	C2	09 14 N	145 23 E
Galapagos Islands	ECUADOR	47	Pac O	00 30 S	90 30 W
Gambia, The	COTH NAT	42, 43	Africa	13 25 N	16 00 W
Gambier Islands	FR TER	197	K5	23 10 S	135 00 W
Ganges River	STRM	42	India	23 22 N	90 32 E
Gardner Island	PHOENIX	196	G3	04 40 S	174 32 W
Garwood Valley	VLY	185	B2	78 00 S	164 05 E
Gatavai	LOC	193	B4	13 45 S	172 24 W
Gatavai River	STRM	193	B4	13 45 S	172 24 W
Gau Island	FIJI	193	B2	18 02 S	179 18 E
Geologists Range	MTNS	184	B3	82 30 S	155 30 E
George V Land	REG	184	A2	70 30 S	150 30 E
Germany, East	REP	42	Europe	52 00 N	12 30 E
Germany, West	REP	42	Europe	51 00 N	09 00 E
Ghana	COTH NAT	42, 43	Africa	08 00 N	02 00 W
Gibraltar	UK COL	42, 43	Europe	36 11 N	05 22 W
Gilbert Islands	UK COL	196	F2	00 30 S	174 00 E
Glossopteris, Mount	—	184	C4	84 45 S	114 00 W
Gneiss Point	PNT	185	B1	77 25 S	163 45 E
Gonville & Caius Range	MTNS	185	A1	77 05 S	162 15 E
Gorki	CITY	42	USSR	57 36 N	45 04 E
Gough Island	UK COL	43	Atl O	40 20 S	10 00 W
Gould Coast	COAST	184	C4	84 25 S	140 00 W
Granite Harbour	HARB	185	A1	76 55 S	162 40 E
Granite Knolls	HILLS	185	B2	77 55 S	163 30 E
Great Australian Bight	BAY	196	B6	35 00 S	130 00 E
Great Barrier Reef	REEF	196	C4	18 00 S	146 50 E
Great Bear, Lake	—	43	Canada	66 00 N	120 00 W
Great Sea Reef	REEF	193	B1	16 15 S	179 00 E
Great Slave Lake	—	43	Canada	61 30 N	114 00 W
Greece	REP	42, 43	Europe	39 00 N	22 00 E
Green Islands	PNG	196	D3	04 30 S	154 10 E
Greenland	D'MARK	42, 43	N America	71 00 N	40 00 W
Greenland Sea	—	43	Arctic O	77 00 N	01 00 W
Greenwood Valley	VLY	185	A1	77 20 S	162 50 E
Gregory Island	ISLD	185	A1	76 50 S	163 00 E
Groote Eylandt Island	AUST	196	B4	14 00 S	136 40 E
Grosvenor Mountains	MTNS	184	B4	85 35 S	175 00 E
Guadalcanal Island	SOLOMON	196	D3	09 30 S	160 00 E
Guadalupe Island	FR TER	47	Mexico	29 00 N	118 16 W
Guam Island	MARIANAS	46	Pac O	13 30 N	144 40 E
Guatemala	CITY	47	Guatemala	14 38 N	90 22 W
Guatemala	REP	47	C America	15 30 N	90 15 W
Guest Peninsula	PEN	184	D3	76 30 S	148 00 W
Guinea	REP	42	Africa	11 00 N	10 00 W
Guinea, Gulf of	BAY	43	Africa	02 00 N	02 30 E
Guyana	COTH NAT	43	S America	05 00 N	59 00 W
Ha'akame	LOC	194	B4	21 10 S	175 17 W
Ha'akili	LOC	194	A3	21 05 S	175 20 W
Ha'alalo	LOC	194	B4	21 10 S	175 17 W
Ha'apai Group	TONGA	194	A2	19 50 S	174 30 W
Ha'asini	LOC	194	C4	21 14 S	175 06 W
Ha'atafu	LOC	194	A3	21 04 S	175 19 W
Ha'ateiha	LOC	194	B4	21 11 S	175 14 W
Ha'avakatolo	LOC	194	A3	21 06 S	175 20 W
Hahn Island	ISLD	185	C3	78 15 S	165 00 E
Hainan Island	CHINA	46	S China S	19 00 N	109 30 E
Haines Mountains	MTNS	184	D3	77 35 S	146 20 W
Haiti	REP	47	W Indies	19 00 N	72 25 W
Haku Mama'o Reef	REEF	194	B3	21 00 S	175 12 W
Hakupu	LOC	195	B4	19 07 S	169 51 W
Haku Tapu Reef	REEF	194	A3	21 03 S	175 18 W
Halangingie Point	PNT	195	A4	19 04 S	169 57 W
Halfway Nunatak	PEAK	185	A3	78 25 S	161 05 E
Hall Islands	CAROL	196	D2	08 37 N	152 00 E
Hallet, Cape	—	184	B2	72 20 S	170 20 E
Halmahera Island	INDON	46	Celebes S	01 00 N	128 00 E
Hamburg	CITY	41	W Germany	53 33 N	10 00 E
Hammond Glacier	GLCR	184	D3	77 30 S	145 40 W
Hamula	LOC	194	C4	21 14 S	175 06 W
Hanoi	CITY	46	N Vietnam	21 01 N	105 52 E
Hao Atoll	FR TER	197	J4	18 04 S	141 00 W
Harmsworth, Mount	—	185	A4	78 40 S	161 00 E
Hart Hills	HILLS	184	D4	83 40 S	89 00 W
Hatutu Island	FR TER	197	J3	07 56 S	140 33 W
Havana	CITY	47	Cuba	23 07 N	82 25 W
Haveluloto	LOC	194	B4	21 08 S	175 13 W
Havola Escarpment	CLIF	184	C4	84 50 S	99 00 W
Hawaii Island	HAWAII	47	Pac O	19 30 N	155 30 W
Hawaiian Islands	US STATE	47	Pac O	24 00 N	167 00 W
Hays Mountains	MTNS	184	C4	85 50 S	157 00 W
Haystack, Mount	—	185	A1	77 05 S	162 35 E
Hayward, Mount	—	185	D2	78 05 S	167 20 E
Heald Island	ISLD	185	B3	78 15 S	163 50 E
Heard Island	AUST TER	42	Ind O	53 07 S	73 20 E
Heine, Mount	—	185	D2	78 05 S	167 30 E
Helms Bluff	BLUF	185	C3	78 30 S	164 30 E
Helsinki	CITY	42, 43	Finland	60 08 N	25 00 E
Henderson Island	PITCAIRN	197	L5	24 20 S	128 20 W
Henderson, Mount	—	185	D2	78 10 S	167 25 E
Henderson, Mount	—	184	B3	80 10 S	156 10 E
Hereheretue Island	FR TER	197	J4	19 58 S	144 58 W
Hermit Islands	PNG	196	C3	01 30 S	145 05 E
Hikutavake	LOC	195	A3	18 57 S	169 53 W
Hillary Coast	—	184	B3	78 50 S	164 00 E
Hiva Oa Island	FR TER	197	K3	09 45 S	139 00 W
Hjorth Hill	HILL	185	B2	77 30 S	163 35 E
Hobart	CITY	46	Tasmania	42 54 S	147 18 E
Hobbs Glacier	GLCR	185	B2	77 55 S	164 00 E
Hobbs Peak	PEAK	185	B2	77 55 S	163 55 E
Hobnail Peak	PEAK	185	B3	78 30 S	162 00 E
Hodgson, Cape	—	185	C2	78 05 S	166 10 E
Hofoa	LOC	194	B4	21 07 S	175 14 W
Hogback Hill	HILL	185	B2	77 30 S	163 35 E
Hoi	LOC	194	C4	21 09 S	175 06 W
Hokkaidō Island	JAPAN	46	Pac O	44 00 N	143 00 E
Holland Range	MTNS	184	B3	83 10 S	166 00 E
Holonga	LOC	194	C4	21 11 S	175 08 W
Honduras	REP	47	C America	15 00 N	86 30 W
Hong Kong	UK COL	46	China	25 15 N	114 10 E
Honolulu	CITY	47	Hawaiian Is	21 19 N	157 52 W
Honshū Island	JAPAN	46	Pac O	36 00 N	138 00 E
Hooker, Cape	—	184	B2	63 16 S	62 00 W
Hooker, Mount	—	185	B3	78 05 S	162 45 E
Horlick Mountains	MTNS	184	C4	85 00 S	125 00 W
Horseshoe Bay	BAY	185	C1	77 30 S	166 10 E
Houma	LOC	194	A4	21 09 S	175 18 W
Howe, Mount	—	184	C4	87 20 S	149 30 W
Howland Island	PHOENIX	196	G2	00 48 N	176 38 W
Huahine Island	FR TER	197	I4	16 45 S	151 00 W
Hudson Bay	BAY	42, 43	Canada	60 00 N	86 00 W
Huggins, Mount	—	185	B3	78 15 S	162 30 E
Hughes Range	MTNS	184	B4	84 30 S	176 00 E

NAME	DESC	PAGE	REF	LAT	LONG
Hull Island	PHOENIX	196	G3	04 30 S	172 14 W
Hull Glacier	GLCR	184	D3	75 05 S	137 00 W
Hungary	REP	42	Europe	47 00 N	20 00 E
Hunt, Mount	—	184	B3	82 05 S	159 20 E
Hunter Island	N CAL	196	F5	22 31 S	172 06 E
Huron, Lake	—	47	Canada	44 30 N	82 15 W
Hut Point	PNT	185	C2	77 50 S	166 40 E
Hut Point Peninsula	PEN	185	C2	77 45 S	166 55 E
Hwang River	STRM	46	China	37 32 N	118 19 E
Hyderabad	CITY	42	India	17 22 N	78 26 E
Iceland	REP	43	Arctic O	65 00 N	18 00 W
Inaccessible Island	ISLD	185	C2	77 40 S	166 20 E
Inclusion Hill	HILL	185	C1	77 15 S	166 25 E
India	COTH NAT	42	Asia	20 00 N	80 00 E
Indian Ocean	—	46	—	10 00 S	70 00 E
Indonesia	REP	46	SE Asia	05 00 S	120 00 E
Indus River	STRM	42	Pakistan	24 20 N	67 47 E
Insel, Mount	—	185	A2	77 25 S	161 30 E
Insel Range	MTNS	185	A2	77 26 S	161 25 E
Iran	KING	42, 43	SW Asia	32 00 N	53 00 E
Iraq	REP	42, 43	SW Asia	33 00 N	44 00 E
Irian Jaya	INDON	46	Arafura S	05 00 S	138 00 E
Irrawaddy River	STRM	46	Burma	15 50 N	95 06 E
Isabela Island	ECUADOR	47	Pac O	00 30 S	91 06 W
Isle of Pines	N CAL	196	E5	22 37 S	167 30 E
Israel	REP	42, 43	SW Asia	31 40 N	34 50 E
Istanbul	CITY	42	Turkey	41 02 N	28 57 E
Italy	REP	42	Europe	42 50 N	12 50 E
Iva	LOC	193	B4	13 40 S	172 12 W
Ivory Coast	REP	42, 43	Africa	08 00 N	05 00 W
Iwo Jima Island	JAP TER	46	Pac O	24 47 N	141 19 E
Jaluit Atoll	MARSHAL	196	E2	06 00 N	169 35 E
Jamaica	COTH NAT	47	W Indies	18 15 N	77 30 W
Jan Mayen Island	D'MARK TER	42	Baltic S	70 10 N	09 00 W
Japan	KING	46	SE Asia	36 00 N	138 00 E
Japan, Sea of	—	46	—	40 00 N	135 00 E
Jarvis Island (US)	LINES	197	I3	00 23 S	160 02 W
Java	INDON	46	Java S	07 30 S	110 00 E
Java Sea	—	46	—	05 00 S	110 00 E
Jenson, Mount	—	185	A1	77 10 S	162 20 E
Johannesburg	CITY	42	S Africa	26 10 S	28 02 E
Johns, Mount	—	184	D4	79 35 S	91 10 W
Johnston Island	US TER	46	Pac O	16 45 N	169 32 W
Jordon	KING	42, 43	SW Asia	31 00 N	36 00 E
Juan Fernandez Islands	CHILE	47	Pac O	38 01 S	59 16 W
Juneau	CITY	41	Alaska	58 20 N	134 20 W
Kabara Island	FIJI	193	D2	18 57 S	178 58 W
Kabul	CITY	42	Afghanistan	34 30 N	69 10 E
Kadavu Island	FIJI	193	B2	19 03 S	178 13 E
Kadavu Passage	STRA	193	B2	18 45 S	178 00 E
Kai Islands	INDON	46	Banda S	05 45 S	132 40 E
Kainan Bay	BAY	184	C3	78 10 S	162 10 W
Kalimantan	INDON	46	Java S	00 30 N	114 00 E
Kanacea Island	FIJI	193	C1	17 15 S	179 08 W
Kanatea Island	TONGA	194	B4	21 09 S	175 12 W
Kangaroo Island	AUST	196	B6	35 50 S	137 06 E
Kaniet Islands	PNG	196	C3	00 53 S	145 30 E
Kanokupolu	LOC	194	A3	21 04 S	175 20 W
Kao Island	TONGA	196	G4	19 40 S	175 01 W
Kapingamarangi Atoll	CAROL	196	D2	01 04 N	156 46 E
Karachi	CITY	42	Pakistan	24 51 N	67 02 E
Karkar Island	PNG	196	C3	04 40 S	146 00 E
Kasavu	LOC	193	B2	17 59 S	178 33 E
Kashmir	DIS TER	42	Asia	34 00 N	75 00 E
Kauai Island	HAWAII	47	Pac O	22 00 N	159 30 W
Kehle Glacier	GLCR	185	A4	78 55 S	160 20 E
Kempe, Mount	—	185	B3	78 20 S	162 45 E
Kenya	COTH NAT	42	Africa	01 00 N	38 00 E
Kerguelen Island	FR TER	42	Ind O	49 30 S	69 30 E
Khabarovsk	CITY	46	USSR	48 32 N	135 08 E
Kharkov	CITY	42	USSR	50 00 N	36 15 E
Khartoum	CITY	42	Sudan	15 33 N	32 35 E
Khmer	REP	46	SE Asia	13 00 N	105 00 E
Kiev	CITY	42	USSR	50 28 N	30 29 E
Kili Atoll	MARSHAL	196	E2	05 40 N	169 03 E
King Island	AUST	196	C6	39 50 S	144 00 E
King George Islands	FR TER	197	J4	14 32 S	145 08 W
King Pin	HILL	185	B2	77 30 S	163 10 E
Kinshasa	CITY	42	Zaire	04 18 S	15 18 E
Kirkpatrick, Mount	—	184	B4	84 25 S	165 30 E
Knobhead	MTN	185	A2	77 55 S	161 30 E
Knoll, The	HILL	185	D1	77 30 S	169 25 E
Kōbe	CITY	46	Japan	34 40 N	135 12 E
Koettlitz Glacier	GLCR	185	B3	78 20 S	164 00 E
Kolonga	LOC	194	C4	21 07 S	175 04 W
Kolovai	LOC	194	A3	21 06 S	175 20 W
Korea Strait	STRA	46	Korea	34 00 N	129 00 E
Koro Island	FIJI	193	C1	17 20 S	179 25 E
Koro Sea	—	193	C2	18 00 S	180 00 E
Korolevu	LOC	193	A2	18 12 S	177 40 E
Koromiri Island	COOKS	194	A1	21 15 S	159 43 W
Korovou	LOC	193	C1	16 56 S	179 55 E
Korovou	LOC	193	B1	17 48 S	178 33 E
Krylov Peninsula	PEN	184	A2	69 15 S	156 30 E
Kuala Lumpur	CITY	46	Malaya	03 08 N	101 42 E
Kuching	CITY	46	Sarawak	01 32 N	110 20 E
Kukri Hills	HILLS	185	B2	77 45 S	162 45 E
Kuria Island	GILBERT	196	F2	00 14 N	173 25 E
Kuril Islands	USSR	46	Pac O	46 10 N	152 00 E
Kusaie Island	CAROL	196	E2	05 19 N	162 59 E
Kuwait	SHEIK	42	SW Asia	29 30 N	47 45 E
Kwajalein Atoll	MARSHAL	196	E2	09 15 N	167 30 E
Kyūshū Island	JAPAN	46	E China S	33 00 N	131 00 E
Labasa	LOC	193	C1	16 25 S	179 24 E
Laccadive Islands	INDIA	42	Arabian S	10 00 N	73 00 E
Lady Newnes Bay	BAY	184	B2	73 40 S	167 30 E
Lae Atoll	MARSHAL	196	E2	08 57 N	166 12 E
La Gorce Peak	PEAK	184	C3	77 35 S	153 20 W
La Gorce Mountains	MTNS	184	C4	86 45 S	147 00 W
Lagos	CITY	42, 43	Nigeria	06 27 N	03 24 E
Lahore	CITY	42	Pakistan	31 34 N	74 22 E
Lakeba Island	FIJI	193	D2	18 12 S	178 49 W
Lakeba Passage	STRA	193	D2	17 53 S	178 32 W
Lakepa	LOC	194	B4	21 08 S	175 16 W
Lakepa	LOC	195	B4	19 01 S	169 49 W
Lalomanu	LOC	193	D4	14 03 S	171 26 W
Lamotrek Atoll	CAROL	196	C2	07 28 N	146 23 E
Lamplugh Island	ISLD	184	B2	75 40 S	162 50 E
Land Bay	BAY	184	D3	75 25 S	141 40 W
Land Glacier	GLCR	184	D3	75 40 S	141 40 W
Landing, The	LOC	185	A3	78 20 S	161 30 E
Lano	LOC	193	B4	13 36 S	172 12 W
Laos	KING	46	SE Asia	18 00 N	105 00 E
Lapaha	LOC	194	C4	21 11 S	175 06 W
La Paz	CITY	47	Bolivia	16 30 S	68 10 W
Late Island	TONGA	194	A2	18 49 S	174 40 W
Lau Group	FIJI	193	D1	17 30 S	178 30 W
Laucala Island	FIJI	193	C1	16 46 S	179 42 W
Laulauia Island	TOKEL	195	D4	19 07 S	171 47 W
Lauli'i	LOC	193	C4	13 50 S	171 42 W

NAME	DESC	PAGE	REF	LAT	LONG
Lauritzen Bay	BAY	184	A1	69 05 S	156 50 E
Lautoka	TOWN	193	A1	17 36 S	177 28 E
Lavengatonga	LOC	194	C4	21 13 S	175 06 W
Leauva'a	LOC	193	C4	13 47 S	171 52 W
Lebanon	REP	42, 43	SW Asia	34 00 N	36 00 E
Leeward Islands	—	43	W Indies	17 00 N	62 00 W
Lefaga Bay	BAY	193	C4	13 57 S	171 56 W
Leipzig	CITY	41	E Germany	51 20 N	12 20 E
Lena River	STRM	42	USSR	72 25 N	126 40 E
Leningrad	CITY	42, 43	USSR	59 55 N	30 25 E
Lesolo Point	PNT	193	B3	13 33 S	172 12 W
Lesotho	KING	42	Africa	29 30 S	28 30 E
Leulumoega	LOC	193	C4	13 49 S	171 57 W
Lewis Bay	BAY	185	C1	77 20 S	167 40 E
Leyte Island	PHIL	46	Phil S	10 55 N	124 50 E
Lib Atoll	MARSHAL	196	E2	08 26 N	167 21 E
Liberia	REP	42, 43	Africa	06 00 N	10 00 W
Libya	KING	42, 43	Africa	27 00 N	17 00 E
Lifou Island	N CAL	196	E5	20 53 S	167 13 E
Liha Point	PNT	195	B3	18 58 S	169 48 W
Lihir Group	PNG	196	D3	03 05 S	152 35 E
Liku	LOC	195	B4	19 03 S	169 48 W
Lillie Glacier	GLCR	184	A2	71 20 S	164 30 E
Lima	CITY	47	Peru	12 06 S	77 03 W
Limpopo River	STRM	42	Mozambique	25 15 S	33 30 E
Limufuafua Point	PNT	195	A4	19 09 S	169 52 W
Line Islands	UK–US	197	I2	00 05 N	157 00 W
Lion Island	ISLD	185	A1	76 50 S	162 35 E
Lisbon	CITY	42, 43	Portugal	38 44 N	09 08 W
Lisicky, Mount	—	185	B3	78 25 S	162 00 E
Lister, Mount	—	185	B2	78 05 S	162 40 E
Liverpool	CITY	41	UK	53 25 N	02 55 W
Lizards Foot	HILL	185	A1	77 10 S	162 50 E
Lomawal	LOC	193	A2	18 01 S	177 16 E
Lombok Island	INDON	46	Timor S	08 45 S	116 30 E
London	CITY	42	UK	51 30 N	00 10 W
Long Hills	HILLS	184	C4	85 20 S	119 30 W
Long Island	PNG	196	C3	05 20 S	147 05 E
Longoteme	LOC	194	B4	21 11 S	175 10 W
Los Angeles	CITY	47	USA	34 00 N	118 15 W
Losap Atoll	CAROL	196	D2	06 54 N	152 44 E
Lotofaga	LOC	193	D4	14 01 S	171 34 W
Louisiade Archipelago	PNG	46	Coral Sea	11 00 S	153 00 E
Lourenço Marques	CITY	42	Mozambique	25 58 S	32 35 E
Lower Staircase	GLCR	185	B3	78 20 S	161 45 E
Lower Victoria Glacier	GLCR	185	A1	77 15 S	162 50 E
Lower Wright Glacier	GLCR	185	B1	77 25 S	163 05 E
Loyalty Islands	N CAL	196	E5	21 00 S	167 00 E
Luanda	CITY	42	Angola	08 50 S	13 15 E
Lufilufi	LOC	193	D4	13 51 S	171 36 W
Lukunor Island	CAROL	196	D2	05 30 N	153 49 E
Luzon Island	PHIL	46	Phil S	16 00 N	121 00 E
Lyall Islands	ISLS	184	B2	70 40 S	167 05 E
Lyon	CITY	41	France	45 46 N	04 50 E
Mackay, Cape	—	185	D2	77 45 S	168 30 E
Mackay Glacier	GLCR	185	A1	77 00 S	161 30 E
Mackay Glacier Tongue	GLCR	185	A1	77 00 S	162 30 E
Mackay Mountains	MTNS	184	D3	77 30 S	143 20 W
Mackenzie River	STRM	43	Canada	65 15 N	134 08 W
MacKintosh, Mount	—	184	A2	74 20 S	161 50 E
Madeira Island	PORT	43	Atl O	32 45 N	17 00 W
Madeira River	STRM	47	Brazil	03 22 S	58 45 W
Madras	CITY	42	India	13 05 N	80 18 E
Madrid	CITY	42, 43	Spain	40 25 N	03 43 E
Madura Island	INDON	46	Java S	07 00 S	113 20 E
Maewo Island	N HEB	196	E4	15 10 S	168 10 E
Mago Island	FIJI	193	C1	17 27 S	179 09 W
Mahoney, Mount	—	185	A1	77 10 S	161 35 E
Maiana Atoll	GILBERT	196	F2	01 00 N	173 00 E
Majuro Atoll	MARSHAL	196	F2	07 05 N	171 08 E
Makaha'a Island	TONGA	194	C3	21 07 S	175 09 W
Makapu Point	PNT	195	A4	19 01 S	169 56 W
Makasar	CITY	46	Indonesia	05 09 S	119 28 E
Makassar Strait	STRA	46	Indonesia	02 00 S	117 30 E
Makatea Island	FR TER	197	J4	16 10 S	148 14 W
Makaunga	LOC	194	C4	21 08 S	175 07 W
Makefu	LOC	195	A4	19 00 S	169 55 W
Makin Atoll	GILBERT	196	F2	03 10 N	172 45 E
Makogai Island	FIJI	193	B1	17 27 S	178 58 E
Malagasy Republic	REP	42	Africa	19 00 S	46 00 E
Malaita Island	SOLOMON	196	E3	09 00 S	161 00 E
Malake	LOC	193	C1	16 32 S	179 36 E
Malapo	LOC	194	C4	21 12 S	175 09 W
Malawi	COTH NAT	42	Africa	12 00 S	34 30 E
Malawi, Lake	—	42	Africa	12 00 S	34 30 E
Malaya	STATE	46	Malaysia	04 00 N	102 00 E
Malaysia	COTH NAT	46	SE Asia	03 00 N	103 00 E
Malden Island (UK)	LINES	197	I3	04 03 S	154 59 W
Maldive Islands	SULTANATE	42	Ind O	03 15 N	73 00 E
Malekula Island	N HEB	196	E4	16 15 S	167 30 E
Mali	REP	42, 43	Africa	17 00 N	04 00 W
Malinoa Island	TONGA	194	C3	21 02 S	175 08 W
Mali'oli'o River	STRM	193	B3	13 28 S	172 17 W
Maloelap Atoll	MARSHAL	196	F2	08 45 N	171 00 E
Malolo Island	FIJI	193	A1	17 45 S	177 10 E
Malpelo Island	COLOMBIA	47	Pac O	04 00 N	81 35 W
Managua	CITY	47	Nicaragua	12 06 N	86 18 W
Mangaia Island	COOKS	194	D3	21 56 S	157 36 W
Mangareva Island	FR TER	197	K5	23 07 S	134 57 W
Manihi Atoll	FR TER	197	J4	14 20 S	145 58 W
Manihiki Atoll	COOKS	194	D1	10 24 S	161 01 W
Manila	CITY	46	Philippines	14 36 N	120 59 E
Manima Island	TONGA	194	C4	21 07 S	175 08 W
Manono Island	W SAMOA	193	B4	13 50 S	172 06 W
Manua Group	AM SAMOA	194	B1	14 13 S	169 35 W
Manuae Atoll	COOKS	194	D2	19 21 S	158 56 W
Manuhangi Atoll	FR TER	197	J4	19 09 S	141 17 W
Manus Island	PNG	196	C3	02 00 S	147 00 E
Marakei Island	GILBERT	196	F2	02 00 N	173 25 E
Marble Point	PNT	185	B1	77 25 S	163 50 E
Marcus Island	JAP TER	46	Pac O	24 18 N	153 58 E
Mare Island	N CAL	196	E5	21 30 S	168 00 E
Maria Bay	BAY	194	B3	21 03 S	175 16 W
Maria Island	FR TER	197	I5	21 48 S	154 41 W
Maria Island	FR TER	197	K5	22 00 S	136 10 W
Mariana Islands	US ADM	46	Pac O	16 00 N	145 30 E
Marianas Trench	SEAF	196	C1	16 00 N	148 00 E
Marie Byrd Land	REG	184	D3	79 00 S	125 00 W
Markham, Mount	—	184	B3	82 45 S	160 25 E
Marquesas Islands	FR TER	197	K3	09 00 S	139 30 W
Marseille	CITY	41	France	43 18 N	05 22 E
Marsh Glacier	GLCR	184	B3	83 15 S	158 30 E
Marshall Islands	US ADM	196	F2	09 00 N	168 00 E
Marshall Valley	VLY	185	B2	78 05 S	164 05 E
Marston, Mount	—	185	A1	76 55 S	162 15 E
Martin Hills	HILLS	184	D4	82 05 S	86 00 W
Marutea Atoll	FR TER	197	K5	21 30 S	136 00 W
Marvel, Mount	—	185	A4	78 50 S	159 30 E
Mata Point	PNT	195	B4	19 08 S	169 51 W
Mata'aho Island	TONGA	194	C4	21 09 S	175 09 W
Matahau	LOC	194	A4	21 08 S	175 19 W
Mataiva Atoll	FR TER	197	J4	14 49 S	148 34 W
Mataloa River	STRM	193	D4	14 02 S	171 42 W

NAME	DESC	PAGE	REF	LAT	LONG
Matasawalevu	LOC	193	B2	19 00 S	178 28 E
Matâutu	LOC	193	C4	13 57 S	171 56 W
Matavera	LOC	194	A1	21 13 S	159 44 W
Matterhorn	MTN	185	A2	77 40 S	162 15 E
Matthew Island	N CAL	196	F5	22 29 S	171 15 E
Matuku Island	FIJI	193	C2	19 11 S	179 45 E
Maturei-Vavao Island	FR TER	197	K5	21 28 S	136 24 W
Matusevich Glacier	GLCR	184	A2	69 30 S	157 30 E
Maude, Cape	—	184	B3	83 10 S	168 30 E
Maui Island	HAWAII	47	Pac O	20 45 N	156 15 W
Mauke Island	COOKS	194	D2	20 09 S	157 28 W
Maupiti Island	FR TER	197	I4	16 27 S	152 15 W
Mauritania	REP	42	Africa	17 00 N	04 00 W
Mauritius Island	UK COL	42	Ind O	20 17 S	57 33 E
Mawson Glacier	GLCR	184	A2	76 15 S	162 00 E
Mawson Peninsula	PEN	184	A1	68 30 S	154 20 E
McClintock, Mount	—	184	B3	80 10 S	157 50 E
McCormick, Cape	—	184	B2	71 50 S	171 00 E
McDonald Heights	MTNS	184	D3	74 55 S	136 00 W
McKean Island	PHOENIX	196	G3	03 35 S	174 04 W
McKelvey Valley	VLY	185	A2	77 25 S	161 30 E
McLennan, Mount	—	185	B2	77 35 S	162 50 E
McMurdo (US)	BASE	185	C2	77 51 S	166 37 E
McMurdo Ice Shelf	—	185	C2	77 55 S	165 55 E
McMurdo Sound	SND	185	B2	77 30 S	165 00 E
Mediterranean Sea	—	42, 43	Europe	35 00 N	20 00 E
Mehetia Island	FR TER	197	J4	17 55 S	148 02 W
Mekong River	STRM	46	S Vietnam	10 33 N	105 24 E
Melania, Mount	—	185	C2	78 05 S	166 15 E
Melanesia Border Plateau	SEAF	196	F4	11 00 S	176 00 E
Melbourne	CITY	46	Australia	37 45 S	144 58 E
Melbourne, Mount	—	184	B2	74 20 S	164 40 E
Mentawai Islands	INDON	46	Ind O	02 00 S	99 30 E
Metschel, Mount	—	185	A3	78 15 S	159 00 E
Mexico	REP	47	C America	23 00 N	102 00 W
Mexico City	CITY	47	Mexico	19 24 N	99 09 W
Mexico, Gulf of	BAY	47	Mexico	25 00 N	90 00 W
Miami	CITY	47	USA	25 45 N	80 15 W
Michigan, Lake	—	47	USA	44 00 N	87 00 W
Middleton Chain	SEAF	196	D5	25 00 S	159 06 E
Miers Valley	VLY	185	B2	78 05 S	164 00 E
Midway Islands	US ADM	46	Pac O	28 13 N	177 22 W
Milan	CITY	41	Italy	45 28 N	09 12 E
Mili Atoll	MARSHAL	196	F2	06 08 N	171 59 E
Mill Glacier	GLCR	184	B4	85 10 S	168 30 E
Miller Glacier	GLCR	185	A1	77 10 S	161 55 E
Miller, Mount	—	184	B3	83 20 S	165 50 E
Miller Range	MTNS	184	B3	83 15 S	157 00 E
Mindanao Island	PHIL	46	Phil S	07 30 N	125 00 E
Mindoro Island	PHIL	46	S China S	13 00 N	121 00 E
Minerva Reefs	REEFS	196	G5	24 00 S	178 00 W
Minna Bluff	BLUF	185	C3	78 40 S	167 10 E
Minna Saddle	SAD	185	C3	78 25 S	165 30 E
Minto, Mount	—	184	B2	71 45 S	168 40 E
Misima	PNG	196	D4	10 38 S	152 45 E
Mississippi River	STRM	47	USA	44 00 N	87 00 W
Missouri River	STRM	47	USA	38 50 N	90 08 W
Mitiaro Island	COOKS	194	D2	19 49 S	157 43 W
Moala Island	FIJI	193	C2	18 36 S	179 56 E
Moluccas Islands	INDON	42	Banda S	02 00 S	128 00 E
Mombasa	CITY	42	Kenya	04 04 S	39 40 E
Momi	LOC	193	A2	17 55 S	177 17 E
Monastery Nunatak	PEAK	185	A3	78 00 S	160 35 E
Mongolia	REP	46	C Asia	45 00 N	105 00 E
Montevideo	CITY	47	Uruguay	34 55 S	56 10 W
Montreal	CITY	43	Canada	45 30 N	73 36 W
Monuafe Island	TONGA	194	C3	21 06 S	175 08 W
Moore Bay	BAY	185	C3	78 50 S	164 50 E
Moore, Mount	—	184	D4	80 25 S	97 30 W
Moorea Island	FR TER	197	I4	17 32 S	149 50 W
Mopelia Atoll	FR TER	197	I4	16 50 S	153 55 W
Moraine Bluff	BLUF	185	A4	78 45 S	162 15 E
Morane Island	FR TER	197	K5	23 10 S	137 07 W
Morning, Lake	—	185	B3	78 25 S	164 10 E
Morning, Mount	—	185	B3	78 30 S	163 30 E
Morocco	KING	42, 43	Africa	32 00 N	05 50 W
Morotai Island	INDON	46	Celebes S	02 20 N	128 25 E
Morrison, Mount	—	185	A1	76 55 S	161 30 E
Mortlock Islands	CAROL	196	D2	05 30 N	153 52 E
Moscow	CITY	42, 43	USSR	55 45 N	37 42 E
Motufala Island	TOKEL	195	D4	09 12 S	171 48 W
Motu Iti Atoll	FR TER	197	I4	16 15 S	151 50 W
Motusaga Island	TOKEL	195	C4	09 11 S	171 51 W
Motutapu Island	COOKS	194	A1	21 14 S	159 43 W
Motutapu Island	TONGA	194	C3	21 05 S	175 03 W
Moubray Bay	BAY	184	B2	72 10 S	170 20 E
Moulton, Mount	—	184	D3	76 05 S	135 10 W
Mo'ungatapu Island	TONGA	194	C4	21 11 S	175 08 W
Moxley, Mount	—	185	B3	78 25 S	162 20 E
Mozambique	REP	42	Africa	18 00 S	36 00 E
Mu'a	LOC	194	C4	21 11 S	175 07 W
Mulifanua	LOC	193	C4	13 50 S	172 02 W
Mulifenua Island	TOKEL	195	D2	09 18 S	171 12 W
Mulinui, Cape	—	193	A3	13 29 S	172 48 W
Mulinu'u	LOC	193	C4	13 48 S	171 46 W
Mulock Glacier	GLCR	185	B4	79 00 S	160 25 E
Munich	CITY	41	W Germany	48 08 N	11 35 E
Murchison, Mount	—	184	B2	73 25 S	166 10 E
Muri	LOC	194	A1	21 15 S	159 44 W
Murray River	STRM	42	Australia	35 34 S	138 54 E
Mururoa Atoll	FR TER	197	K5	21 52 S	143 05 W
Mussau Island	PNG	196	C3	01 30 S	149 40 E
Mutalau	LOC	195	B3	18 58 S	169 49 W
Nabouono	LOC	193	C1	16 10 S	180 00
Naboutini	LOC	193	C1	16 24 S	179 48 E
Nabouwalu	LOC	193	B1	16 58 S	178 48 E
Nacula Island	FIJI	193	A1	16 53 S	177 25 E
Nadi	TOWN	193	A1	17 48 S	177 25 E
Nadi Internat Airport	FIJI	193	A1	17 48 S	177 25 E
Naduri	LOC	193	B1	16 26 S	179 08 E
Nagasaki	CITY	46	Japan	32 45 N	129 52 E
Naha	CITY	46	Japan	26 10 N	127 40 E
Nailaga	LOC	193	A1	17 30 S	177 40 E
Nairai Island	FIJI	193	C1	17 50 S	179 26 E
Nairobi	CITY	42	Kenya	01 17 S	36 49 E
Naitaba Island	FIJI	193	C1	17 00 S	179 19 W
Naitonitoni	LOC	193	B2	18 12 S	178 12 E
Nakarabo	LOC	193	C1	16 36 S	179 36 E
Nakavu	LOC	193	B2	18 11 S	178 10 E
Nakolo	LOC	194	C4	21 15 S	175 07 W
Nalotu	LOC	193	B2	19 00 S	178 06 E
Namoluk Atoll	CAROL	196	D2	05 55 N	153 08 E
Namonuito Atoll	CAROL	196	C2	08 56 N	150 00 E
Namorik Atoll	MARSHAL	196	E2	05 36 N	168 07 E
Namu Atoll	MARSHAL	196	E2	08 00 N	168 08 E
Namuka Ilau Island	FIJI	193	D2	18 50 S	178 41 W
Namukalau	LOC	193	C1	16 12 S	179 42 E
Namukulu	LOC	195	A3	18 58 S	169 54 W
Nanching	CITY	42	China	24 26 N	117 20 E
Nanpo Shotō Islands	JAP TER	46	Pac O	31 30 N	140 00 E
Nanuku Passage	STRA	193	C1	16 48 S	179 24 W
Nanukuloa	LOC	193	B1	17 29 S	178 14 E
Nanumanga Island	ELLICE	196	F3	06 18 S	176 20 E

NAME	DESC	PAGE	REF	LAT	LONG
Nanumea Atoll	ELLICE	196	F3	05 39 S	176 08 E
Naples	CITY	41	Italy	40 50 N	14 15 E
Napuka	LOC	193	C1	16 38 S	179 58 E
Napuka Atoll	FR TER	197	J4	14 05 S	141 20 W
Naqara	LOC	193	B2	18 50 S	178 32 E
Naravuka	LOC	193	B1	16 38 S	179 06 E
Narewa	LOC	193	A2	17 58 S	177 36 E
Narrows, The	STRA	194	C3	21 06 S	175 09 W
Naruwai	LOC	193	B1	16 48 S	178 40 E
Nasea	LOC	193	B1	16 28 S	179 22 E
Nash Hills	HILLS	184	D4	81 55 S	89 00 W
Nash Range	MTNS	184	B3	81 55 S	162 30 E
Nassau	CITY	47	Bahamas	25 03 N	77 20 W
Nassau Island	COOKS	194	C1	11 05 S	165 25 W
Nasuvu River	STRM	193	C1	16 12 S	179 48 E
Natewa Bay	BAY	193	C1	16 35 S	179 40 E
Nauru Island	SPMEM COTH NAT	196	E3	00 31 S	166 56 E
Nausori	LOC	193	B2	18 01 S	178 31 E
Navidamu	LOC	193	B1	16 36 S	178 54 E
Naviti Island	FIJ	193	A1	17 07 S	177 15 E
Navutoka	LOC	194	C4	21 07 S	175 06 W
Nawailevu	LOC	193	B1	16 42 S	178 40 E
Naweni	LOC	193	C1	16 45 S	179 35 E
Nawi	LOC	193	C1	16 43 S	179 50 E
Nayau Island	FIJI	193	C2	17 59 S	179 05 W
Ndende Island	S CRUZ	196	E4	10 42 S	165 50 E
Near Islands	ALEUT	46	Bering S	52 40 N	173 30 E
Negro River	STRM	47	Brazil	00 01 S	165 00 W
Negros Island	PHIL	46	Sulu S	10 00 N	123 00 E
Neiafu	LOC	193	A3	13 32 S	172 45 W
Nengonengo Atoll	FR TER	197	J4	18 42 S	141 46 W
Nepal	KING	46	Asia	28 00 N	84 00 E
Nesos, Mount	—	185	D2	78 10 S	167 05 E
Névé Nunatak	PEAK	185	A3	78 15 S	160 50 E
New Mountain	MTN	185	A2	77 55 S	161 10 E
Newall Glacier	GLCR	185	A2	77 35 S	162 30 E
Newall, Mount	—	185	A2	77 30 S	162 45 E
New Britain Island	PNG	196	D3	06 00 S	150 00 E
New Caledonia	FR TER	196	E5	21 30 S	165 30 E
Newfoundland	CANADA	42, 43	Atl O	52 00 N	56 00 W
New Georgia Group	SOLOMON	196	D3	08 30 S	157 20 E
New Georgia Island	SOLOMON	196	D3	08 20 S	157 30 E
New Hanover Island	PNG	196	D3	02 30 S	150 15 E
New Harbour	HARB	185	B2	77 35 S	163 55 E
New Hebrides Basin	SEAF	196	E4	16 00 S	162 00 E
New Hebrides Islands	UK–FR	196	E4	16 00 S	167 00 E
New Ireland Island	PNG	196	D3	03 20 S	152 00 E
Newman Island	ISLD	184	D3	75 40 S	145 30 W
New Orleans	CITY	47	USA	30 00 N	90 03 W
New Siberian Islands	USSR	42	Arctic O	75 45 N	142 00 E
New York	CITY	47	USA	40 40 N	73 50 W
New Zealand Plateau	SEAF	196	F7	50 00 S	170 00 E
Ngatangiia	LOC	194	A1	21 14 S	159 44 W
Ngatik Atoll	CAROL	196	D2	05 51 N	157 16 E
Nias Island	INDON	46	Ind O	01 05 N	97 30 E
Niau Atoll	FR TER	197	J4	16 09 S	146 20 W
Nicaragua	REP	47	C America	13 00 N	85 00 W
Nickerson Ice Shelf	—	184	D3	75 45 S	145 00 W
Nicobar Islands	INDIA	46	Bay Bengal	08 00 N	93 50 E
Niger	REP	42, 43	Africa	16 00 N	08 00 E
Niger River	STRM	42, 43	Africa	05 33 N	06 33 E
Nigeria	COTH NAT	42, 43	Africa	10 00 N	08 00 E
Niigata	CITY	46	Japan	37 58 N	139 02 E
Nikunau Island	GILBERT	196	F3	01 23 S	176 26 E
Nile River	STRM	42	Africa	30 10 N	31 06 E
Nimrod Glacier	GLCR	184	B3	82 30 S	160 00 E
Ninigo Group	PNG	196	C3	01 15 S	144 15 E
Nipha, Mount	—	185	D2	78 10 S	167 30 E
Niuafo'ou Island	TONGA	194	A2	15 36 S	175 39 W
Niuatoputapu Group	TONGA	194	A2	15 59 S	173 58 W
Niue Internat Airport	—	195	A4	19 05 S	169 55 W
Niue Island	ASSOC (NZ) COTH NAT	196	H4	19 02 S	169 52 W
Niue Island	—	195	B3	19 02 S	169 52 W
Niulakita Island	ELLICE	196	F4	10 45 S	179 30 E
Niutao Island	ELLICE	196	F3	06 06 S	177 16 E
Niutoua	LOC	194	C4	21 08 S	175 02 W
Nomuka Group	TONGA	194	A2	20 05 S	174 40 W
Nomuka Island	TONGA	194	A2	20 05 S	174 40 W
Nomwin Island	CAROL	196	D2	08 25 N	151 45 E
Nonouti Atoll	GILBERT	196	F3	00 44 S	174 28 E
Nordenskjöld Ice Tongue	GLCR	184	B2	76 10 S	162 50 E
Norfolk Island	AUST	46	Pac O	29 05 S	167 59 E
Normanby Island	PNG	196	D4	10 05 S	151 05 E
North Atlantic Ocean	—	47	—	30 00 N	40 00 W
North Cape	—	184	A2	70 40 S	165 40 E
North Fiji Basin	SEAF	196	F4	15 00 S	173 00 E
North Korea	REP	46	E Asia	40 00 N	127 00 E
North Pacific Ocean	—	197	I2	04 00 N	160 00 W
North Vietnam	REP	46	SE Asia	21 00 N	105 00 E
Northampton, Mount	—	184	B2	72 40 S	169 10 E
Northcliffe Peak	PEAK	185	B4	78 45 S	161 00 E
Northern Cook Islands	ASSOC (NZ) COTH NAT	197	I3	12 00 N	161 00 E
Northern Cook Islands	—	194	C1	12 00 N	161 00 E
Norway	KING	42, 43	Europe	62 00 N	10 00 E
Norwegian Sea	—	43	Norway	70 00 N	02 00 E
Noumea	CITY	46	N Caledonia	22 16 S	166 26 E
Novaya Zemlya Island	USSR	42, 43	Arctic O	72 10 N	74 50 W
Novosibirsk	CITY	41	USSR	55 04 N	83 05 E
Nqamea Island	FIJI	193	C1	16 46 S	179 46 W
Nqoma	LOC	193	B1	17 38 S	178 35 E
Nuguria Islands	PNG	196	D3	03 28 S	154 49 E
Nui Atoll	ELLICE	196	F3	07 12 S	177 10 E
Nuku Hiva Island	FR TER	197	J3	08 56 S	140 00 W
Nuku Island	TONGA	194	D3	21 05 S	175 01 W
Nuku'alofa	TOWN	194	B4	21 07 S	175 12 W
Nukufetau	ELLICE	196	F3	08 00 S	178 30 E
Nukuhetulu	LOC	194	B4	21 09 S	175 11 W
Nukulaelae Atoll	ELLICE	196	G3	09 20 S	179 50 E
Nukuleka	LOC	194	C4	21 08 S	175 07 W
Nukumanu Island	PNG	196	D3	04 30 S	159 30 E
Nukunonu Atoll	TOKEL	195	D4	09 08 S	171 50 W
Nukunonu Island	TOKEL	195	C4	09 10 S	171 51 W
Nukunuku	LOC	194	A4	21 07 S	175 18 W
Nukunukumotu Island	TONGA	194	C4	21 08 S	175 09 W
Nukuoro Atoll	CAROL	196	D2	03 51 N	154 58 E
Nukutavake Island	FR TER	197	K4	19 11 S	138 42 W
Nukutipipi Atoll	FR TER	197	J5	20 40 S	142 30 W
Nunivak Island	ALASKA	46	Bering S	60 00 N	166 00 W
Nu'ulua Island	W SAMOA	193	D4	14 05 S	171 24 W
Nu'utele Island	W SAMOA	193	D4	14 04 S	171 25 W
Oahu Island	HAWAII	46	Pac O	21 30 N	158 00 W
Oates Land	REG	184	A2	71 00 S	159 30 E
Ob Bay	BAY	184	A2	70 35 S	163 20 E
Obelisk, Mount	—	185	A2	77 40 S	161 40 E
Obi Island	INDON	46	Banda S	01 30 S	127 45 E
Ocean Island	UK COL	196	E3	00 52 S	169 35 E
Odessa	CITY	42	USSR	46 30 N	30 46 E
Odin, Mount	—	185	A2	77 35 S	161 40 E
Oeno Atoll	PITCAIRN	197	K5	23 55 S	130 45 W
Ohio Range	MTNS	184	C4	84 45 S	115 00 W

NAME	DESC	PAGE	REF	LAT	LONG
Ohio River	STRM	47	USA	36 59 N	89 08 W
Okhotsk, Sea of	—	46	USSR	53 00 N	150 00 E
Okinawa Island	JAP TER	46	E China S	26 31 N	127 59 E
Okuma Bay	BAY	184	C3	77 50 S	158 40 W
Olympus Range	MTNS	185	A2	77 25 S	161 40 E
Oman	SULTANATE	42	SW Asia	22 00 N	58 00 E
Ona I Lau Island	FIJI	193	D3	20 40 S	178 46 W
Oneata Island	TONGA	194	C4	21 07 S	175 08 W
Oneata Island	FIJI	193	D2	18 27 S	178 30 W
Oneroa Island	COOKS	194	A1	21 15 S	159 43 W
Onevai Island	TONGA	194	C3	21 05 S	175 06 W
Onevao Island	TONGA	194	C3	21 05 S	175 05 W
Onotoa Atoll	GILBERT	196	F3	01 55 S	175 34 E
Ontario, Lake	—	47	USA	43 40 N	78 00 W
Ontong Java Islands	SOLOMON	196	D3	05 20 S	159 30 E
Ontong Java Rise	SEAF	196	D3	07 00 S	160 00 E
Oporto	CITY	41	Portugal	41 09 N	08 37 W
Orange River	STRM	42	S Africa	28 41 S	16 28 E
Orinoco River	STRM	47	Venezuela	08 37 N	62 15 W
Oroluk Atoll	CAROL	196	D2	07 32 N	155 18 E
Oslo	CITY	42, 43	Norway	59 56 N	10 45 E
Ottawa	CITY	43	Canada	45 25 N	75 43 W
Otway Massif	MTN	184	B4	85 25 S	172 00 E
Ovalau Island	FIJI	193	B1	17 40 S	178 47 E
Pacific Antarctic Ridge	SEAF	197	M6	35 00 S	115 00 W
Padang	CITY	46	Sumatra	01 00 S	100 21 E
Paepaeolei'a, Cape	—	193	B4	13 47 S	172 14 W
Pago Pago	CITY	46	Am Samoa	14 16 S	170 43 W
Pakin Atoll	CAROL	196	D2	07 04 N	157 48 E
Pakistan	COTH NAT	42	S Asia	30 00 N	70 00 E
Palau Islands	US ADM	46	Pac O	07 30 N	134 30 E
Palawan Island	PHIL	46	Phil S	10 00 N	118 30 E
Palmerston Atoll	COOKS	194	C2	18 04 S	163 10 W
Palmyra Atoll (US)	LINES	197	H2	05 52 N	162 05 W
Panama	CITY	47	Panama	08 57 N	79 30 W
Panama	REP	47	C America	09 00 N	80 00 W
Panay Island	PHIL	46	Phil S	13 58 N	124 20 E
Pandora Spire	PEAK	185	A2	77 50 S	161 15 E
Pangaimotu Island	TONGA	194	C4	21 07 S	175 09 W
Papa	LOC	193	B4	13 45 S	172 23 W
Papa	LOC	193	A3	13 29 S	172 42 W
Papeete	CITY	47	Tahiti	17 32 S	149 34 W
Papua, Gulf of	BAY	196	C3	08 30 S	145 00 E
Papua New Guinea	COTH NAT	196	C3	08 00 S	144 00 E
Paracel Islands	—	46	S China S	16 30 N	112 15 E
Paraguay	REP	47	S America	23 00 S	58 00 W
Parana River	STRM	47	Argentina	33 43 S	59 15 W
Paris	CITY	42, 43	France	48 52 N	02 20 E
Patamea	LOC	193	B3	13 31 S	172 18 W
Pea	LOC	194	B4	21 09 S	175 14 W
Peking	CITY	46	China	39 55 N	116 25 E
Peleus, Mount	—	185	A2	77 30 S	162 05 E
Pennell Coast	COAST	184	B2	71 15 S	168 00 E
Penrhyn Atoll	COOKS	194	D1	09 00 S	158 00 W
Pentecost Island	N HEB	196	E4	15 42 S	168 10 E
Perseverance, Mount	—	185	A1	76 50 S	162 10 E
Persian Gulf	BAY	42	SW Asia	27 00 N	51 00 E
Perth	CITY	46	Australia	31 58 S	115 49 E
Peru	REP	47	S America	10 00 S	76 00 W
Peter Island	NORWAY	47	Antarctica	68 55 S	90 50 W
Péwé Peak	PEAK	185	B2	78 05 S	163 40 E
Philip Island	ISLD	81	Sea Floor	29 13 S	167 58 E
Philippine Sea	—	46	Pac O	20 00 N	135 00 E
Philippines	REP	46	SE Asia	12 00 N	123 00 E
Phillips Mountains	MTNS	184	D3	76 15 S	145 00 W
Phnom Penh	CITY	46	Khmer	11 33 N	104 55 E
Phoenix Island	UK COL	196	G3	03 43 S	171 25 W
Phoenix Islands	UK–US	196	G3	04 00 S	172 00 W
Piha Passage	STRA	194	C3	21 06 S	175 07 W
Pikelot Island	CAROL	196	C2	08 05 N	147 38 E
Pimple, The	MTN	185	B2	77 58 S	162 10 E
Pinaki Island	FR TER	197	K4	19 20 S	138 40 W
Pitcairn Island	UK COL	197	I5	25 04 S	130 06 W
Pivot Peak	PEAK	185	A3	78 00 S	161 00 E
Podium, The	MTN	185	B4	78 55 S	161 00 E
Pokoinu	LOC	194	A1	21 12 S	159 50 W
Poland	REP	42, 43	Europe	52 00 N	19 00 E
Polo'a Island	TONGA	194	B3	21 05 S	175 15 W
Ponape Island	CAROL	196	D2	06 55 N	158 15 E
Pond Peak	PEAK	185	A1	77 20 S	162 25 E
Portal, Mount	—	185	A3	78 05 S	159 15 E
Portuguese Guinea	PORT TER	42, 43	Africa	12 00 N	16 00 W
Port Moresby	CITY	46	PNG	09 30 S	147 07 E
Portugal	REP	42, 43	Europe	39 30 N	08 00 W
Portuguese Timor	—	46	Sunda S	08 35 S	126 00 E
Possession Islands	ISLS	184	B2	71 48 S	171 30 E
Potter Glacier	GLCR	185	B3	78 25 S	162 10 E
Poutasi	LOC	193	D4	14 01 S	171 41 W
Prague	CITY	41	Czech	50 05 N	14 25 E
Pram Point	PNT	185	C2	77 50 S	166 45 E
Prestrud Inlet	BAY	184	C3	78 20 S	156 00 W
Pribilof Islands	ALASKA	46	Bering S.	57 00 N	170 00 W
Priestley Glacier	GLCR	184	B2	74 00 S	162 00 E
Prince Albert Mountains	MTNS	184	A2	76 00 S	161 30 E
Prince Edward Islands	S AFRICA	42	Ind O.	46 35 S	37 56 E
Prince Olav Mountains	MTNS	184	C4	84 55 S	173 30 W
Pryor Glacier	GLCR	184	A2	70 10 S	160 00 E
Pu'apu'a	LOC	193	B4	13 34 S	172 12 W
Puava, Cape	—	193	A3	13 27 S	172 45 W
Puerto Rico	US TER	47	W Indies	18 15 N	66 30 W
Puka Island	TOKEL	195	C4	09 07 S	171 51 W
Pukapuka Atoll	COOKS	194	C1	10 53 S	165 49 W
Pukapuka Atoll	FR TER	197	K4	14 50 S	138 50 W
Pukaruha Atoll	FR TER	197	K4	18 16 S	137 00 W
Puke	LOC	194	B4	21 07 S	175 14 W
Pulap Atoll	CAROL	196	C2	07 38 N	149 25 E
Pulusuk Island	CAROL	196	C2	06 42 N	149 19 E
Puluwat Atoll	CAROL	196	C2	07 21 N	149 11 E
Punalei Island	TOKEL	195	D4	09 11 S	171 46 W
Punta Arenas	CITY	47	Chile	53 10 S	70 56 W
Purgatory Peak	PEAK	185	A1	77 20 S	162 15 E
Purus River	STRM	47	Brazil	03 42 S	61 28 W
Pyongyang	CITY	46	N Korea	39 00 N	125 47 E
Pyramid Mountain	MTN	185	A2	77 50 S	160 40 E
Qalomo	LOC	193	B1	16 48 S	178 38 E
Qaria	LOC	193	B1	16 49 S	178 50 E
Qatar	SHEIK	42	SW Asia	25 00 N	51 10 E
Queen Alexandra Range	MTNS	184	B4	83 55 S	167 40 E
Queen Charlotte Islands	CANADA	47	G Alaska	51 30 N	129 00 W
Queen Elizabeth Range	MTNS	184	B3	83 15 S	162 00 E
Queen Maud Mountains	MTNS	184	B4	85 30 S	170 00 W
Quito	CITY	47	Ecuador	00 14 S	78 30 W
Rabat	CITY	42, 43	Morocco	34 02 N	06 51 W
Rabi Island	FIJI	193	C1	16 36 S	179 59 W
Radian Glacier	GLCR	185	B3	78 15 S	162 45 E
Raevavae Island	FR TER	197	J5	23 52 S	147 40 W
Raiatea Island	FR TER	197	I4	16 50 S	151 30 W
Rakahanga Atoll	COOKS	194	D1	10 00 S	161 06 W
Rakiraki	LOC	193	B1	17 18 S	178 12 E
Ralik Chain	MARSHAL	196	E2	09 05 N	167 20 E
Rampart Ridge	RDGE	185	A3	78 10 S	161 45 E

NAME	DESC	PAGE	REF	LAT	LONG
Rangiroa Island	FR TER	197	J4	15 00 S	147 40 W
Rangoon	CITY	46	Burma	16 47 N	96 10 E
Rapa Island	FR TER	197	J5	27 35 S	144 20 W
Raraka Island	FR TER	197	J4	16 10 S	144 50 W
Raroia Island	FR TER	197	J4	16 00 S	142 25 W
Rarotonga Island	COOKS	194	A1	21 15 S	159 45 W
Ratak Chain	MARSHAL	196	F2	09 27 N	170 02 E
Ravahere Atoll	FR TER	197	J4	18 10 S	142 10 W
Razorback Islands	ISLS	185	C2	77 40 S	166 30 E
Reao Atoll	FR TER	197	K4	18 30 S	136 24 W
Recife	CITY	43	Brazil	08 06 S	34 53 W
Red Buttress Peak	PEAK	185	A1	76 50 S	162 25 E
Red Dike Bluff	BLUF	185	B4	78 50 S	162 20 E
Red Sea	—	42	SW Asia	25 00 N	35 00 E
Reedy Glacier	GLCR	184	C4	86 00 S	130 00 W
Reef Islands	S CRUZ	196	E4	10 35 S	167 30 E
Reeves Glacier	GLCR	184	A2	74 45 S	162 20 E
Reid, Mount	—	184	B3	83 05 S	166 00 E
Reitoru Island	FR TER	197	J4	17 52 S	143 05 W
Rennell Island	SOLOMON	196	E4	11 45 S	160 15 E
Rennick Bay	BAY	184	A2	70 20 S	162 00 E
Rennick Glacier	GLCR	184	A2	71 30 S	162 30 E
Retreat, Point	—	185	A1	76 55 S	162 35 E
Réunion Island	FR TER	42	Ind O	21 06 S	55 36 E
Rewa River	STRM	193	B2	18 08 S	178 35 E
Reykjavik	CITY	42	Iceland	64 09 N	21 58 W
Rhodesia	UK COL	42	S Africa	20 00 S	30 00 E
Rimatara Island	FR TER	197	I5	22 40 S	152 45 W
Ringgold Isles	FIJI	193	C1	16 15 S	179 25 W
Rio Colorado River	STRM	47	Argentina	39 50 S	62 08 W
Rio de Janiero	CITY	43	Brazil	22 53 S	43 17 W
Rio Grande River	STRM	43	USA	25 57 N	97 09 W
Roberts Butte	MTN	184	A2	77 40 S	160 10 E
Roberts, Cape	—	185	A1	77 02 S	163 15 E
Roberts Massif	MTN	184	B4	83 35 S	177 00 W
Robertson Bay	BAY	184	B2	71 30 S	170 10 E
Rockefeller Mountains	MTNS	184	C3	78 00 S	155 00 W
Rockefeller Plateau	PLAT	184	D3	80 00 S	135 00 W
Rome	CITY	42, 43	Italy	41 53 N	12 30 E
Roosevelt Island	ISLD	184	C3	79 20 S	162 00 W
Rosario	CITY	43	Argentina	22 92 S	66 41 W
Rose Island	AM SAMOA	197	H4	14 32 S	168 11 W
Ross Dependency	NZ ADM	185	C2	78 00 S	165 00 E
Ross Ice Shelf	—	185	D3	81 00 S	168 00 E
Ross Island	ISLD	185	C1	77 40 S	168 00 E
Ross Sea	—	185	B1	77 00 S	166 00 E
Rossel Island	PNG	196	D4	11 21 S	154 09 E
Rostov	CITY	41	USSR	57 11 N	39 23 E
Rotuma Island	FIJI	196	F4	12 30 S	177 05 E
Round Mountain	MTN	185	A2	77 40 S	161 05 E
Royal Society Range	MTNS	185	B3	78 15 S	163 00 E
Royds, Cape	—	185	C1	77 35 S	166 10 E
Rücker, Mount	—	185	B3	78 10 S	162 35 E
Rudolf, Lake	—	42	Africa	03 30 N	36 05 E
Rumania	REP	42, 43	Europe	46 00 N	25 30 E
Ruppert Coast	COAST	184	D3	75 50 S	142 00 W
Rurutu Island	FR TER	197	I5	22 25 S	151 20 W
Russell Islands	SOLOMON	196	D3	09 04 S	159 12 E
Rutgers Glacier	GLCR	185	B3	78 15 S	162 00 E
Ruth Gade, Mount	—	184	C4	85 30 S	165 15 W
Rwanda	REP	42	Africa	02 30 S	30 00 E
Ryukyu Islands	JAP	46	E China S	25 00 N	126 00 E
Sabah	STATE	46	Malaysia	05 20 N	117 10 E
Sable Island	FR TER	197	J3	07 53 S	140 25 W
Sae Islands	PNG	196	C3	00 43 S	145 16 E
Safotu	LOC	193	B3	13 26 S	172 24 W
Safune	LOC	193	B3	13 26 S	172 25 W
Saigon	CITY	46	S Vietnam	10 46 N	106 43 E
Sails, Bay of	—	185	B1	77 20 S	163 50 E
St Helena Island	UK COL	42, 43	Atl O	15 58 S	05 43 W
St Johns	CITY	42, 43	Newfound	47 34 N	52 43 W
St Johns Range	MTNS	185	A1	77 15 S	162 30 E
St Lawrence River	STRM	43	Canada	49 15 N	67 00 W
St Matthew Island	ALASKA	46	Bering S	60 30 N	172 30 W
St Matthias Group	PNG	196	D3	01 30 S	149 40 E
St Paul Island	FR TER	42	Ind O	38 44 S	77 30 E
Sakhalin Island	USSR	46	Pac O	51 00 N	143 00 E
Sakishima	JAP TER	46	E China S	24 46 N	124 00 E
Sala'ilua	LOC	193	A4	13 42 S	172 35 W
Salani	LOC	193	D4	14 02 S	171 35 W
Sala y Gomez	CHILE	47	Pac O	26 28 S	105 28 W
Sale'aula	LOC	193	B3	13 25 S	172 20 W
Sale'imoa	LOC	193	C4	13 48 S	171 54 W
Salelologa	LOC	193	B4	13 43 S	172 13 W
Salient Peak	PEAK	185	B3	78 10 S	162 50 E
Salisbury	CITY	42	Rhodesia	17 43 S	31 05 E
Salmon Bay	BAY	185	C2	77 55 S	164 30 E
Salmon Hill	HILL	185	B2	77 55 S	164 10 E
Saltonstall, Mount	—	184	B4	86 50 S	154 00 W
Salvador	CITY	43	Brazil	12 58 S	38 29 W
Salween River	STRM	46	Burma	16 31 N	97 37 E
Samalae'ulu	LOC	193	B3	13 27 S	172 18 W
Samame	LOC	193	D4	13 56 S	171 32 W
Samar Island	PHIL	46	Phil S	12 00 N	125 00 E
Samataiuta	LOC	193	A4	13 36 S	172 40 W
Samatau	LOC	193	C4	13 52 S	172 02 W
Samoa Islands	US–COTH NAT	196	G4	14 00 S	171 00 W
San Ambrosio Island	CHILE	47	Pac O	26 28 S	79 53 W
San Cristobal Island	SOLOMON	196	E4	10 36 S	161 45 E
San Felix Island	CHILE	47	Pac O	26 23 S	80 05 W
San Francisco	CITY	47	USA	37 45 N	122 27 W
San Jose	CITY	47	Costa Rica	09 56 N	84 04 W
San Juan	CITY	47	Puerto Rico	18 29 N	66 08 W
San Salvador	CITY	47	El Salvador	13 40 N	89 10 W
Santa Cruz Islands	UK COL	196	E4	10 30 S	166 00 E
Santa Isabel Island	SOLOMON	196	D3	08 00 S	159 00 E
Santa Maria Island	N HEB	196	E4	14 15 S	167 30 E
Santiago	CITY	47	Chile	33 30 S	70 40 W
Sao Francisco River	STRM	43	Brazil	10 30 S	36 24 W
Sao Paulo	CITY	43	Brazil	23 33 S	46 39 W
Sapapāli'i	LOC	193	B4	13 40 S	172 11 W
Sarawak	STATE	46	Malaysia	02 30 N	113 30 E
Sasina	LOC	193	B3	13 26 S	172 27 W
Sataoa	LOC	193	C4	13 57 S	171 54 W
Sataua	LOC	193	A3	13 28 S	172 40 W
Satawal Island	CAROL	196	C2	06 40 N	145 25 E
Satawan Island	CAROL	196	D2	05 19 N	153 44 E
Satupa'itea	LOC	193	B4	13 45 S	172 21 W
Saudi Arabia	KING	42	SW Asia	25 00 N	45 00 E
Saumangalu Island	TOKEL	195	D4	09 07 S	171 47 W
Saumatafaga Island	TOKEL	195	D2	09 26 S	171 13 W
Saunders Coast	COAST	184	D3	77 45 S	153 00 W
Savai'i Island	W SAMOA	193	A4	13 44 S	172 18 W
Savusavu	LOC	193	B1	16 48 S	179 20 E
Savusavu	LOC	193	B1	17 32 S	178 20 E
Saweni	LOC	193	A2	17 56 S	177 48 E
Scallop Hill	HILL	185	C2	78 10 S	166 45 E
Scar Bluffs	BLUF	184	A2	68 50 S	153 30 E
Schist Peak	PEAK	185	A1	77 20 S	162 00 E
Schopf, Mount	—	184	C4	84 50 S	113 00 W
Scilly Island	FR TER	197	I4	16 30 S	154 40 W
Scotia Sea	—	43	Atl O	56 00 S	40 00 W
Scott Base (NZ)	BASE	185	C2	77 51 S	166 45 E

NAME	DESC	PAGE	REF	LAT	LONG
Scott Coast	COAST	184	A2	77 10 S	168 00 E
Scott Glacier	GLCR	184	C4	86 30 S	150 30 W
Scott Island	ISLD	184	B1	67 25 S	179 50 W
Seattle	CITY	47	USA	47 35 N	122 20 W
Seelig, Mount	—	184	D4	82 30 S	103 00 W
Selbourne, Cape	—	184	C3	80 25 S	160 50 E
Senegal	REP	42, 43	Africa	14 00 N	14 00 W
Sentinel Peak	PEAK	185	B2	77 45 S	162 25 E
Senyavin Islands	CAROL	196	D2	06 55 N	158 00 E
Seoul	CITY	46	S Korea	37 30 N	127 00 E
Seychelles Islands	UK COL	42	Ind O	04 35 S	55 40 E
Shackleton Coast	COAST	184	B3	82 00 S	163 00 E
Shackleton Glacier	GLCR	184	B4	85 00 S	176 00 W
Shackleton Inlet	BAY	184	B3	82 15 S	164 30 E
Shanghai	CITY	46	China	31 13 N	121 25 E
Shenyang	CITY	42	China	41 50 N	123 26 E
Shikoku Island	JAPAN	46	Pac O	33 45 N	133 30 E
Shirase Coast	COAST	184	C3	78 30 S	156 00 W
Shults Peninsula	PEN	185	B4	78 55 S	162 40 E
Shumagin Islands	ALEUT	47	Bering S	55 07 N	159 45 W
Siam, Gulf of	BAY	46	Thailand	10 00 N	101 00 E
Siberut Island	INDON	46	Ind O	01 20 S	98 55 E
Sidley, Mount	—	184	D3	77 12 S	129 00 W
Sierra Leone	COTH NAT	42, 43	Africa	08 30 N	11 30 W
Sigatoka	LOC	193	A2	18 10 S	177 30 E
Sigatoka River	STRM	193	A2	18 11 S	177 31 E
Sikkim	IND PROT	46	Asia	27 35 N	88 35 E
Sili	LOC	193	B4	13 45 S	172 23 W
Singapore	COTH NAT	46	SE Asia	01 22 N	103 48 E
Siple Coast	COAST	184	C3	82 20 S	153 00 W
Si'umu	LOC	193	C4	14 00 S	171 46 W
Skelton Glacier	GLCR	185	B3	78 30 S	161 00 E
Skelton Névé	—	185	A3	78 25 S	159 45 E
Slava Bay	BAY	184	A1	68 55 S	155 00 E
Snake River	STRM	47	USA	46 12 N	119 02 W
Society Islands	FR TER	197	I4	17 00 S	150 00 W
Socorro Island	MEXICO	47	Pac O	18 45 N	110 58 W
Socotra Island	S YEMEN	42	Arabian S	12 30 N	54 00 E
Solomon Islands	UK COL	196	D3	08 00 S	159 00 E
Solomon Sea	—	196	D3	08 00 S	155 00 E
Solosolo	LOC	193	D4	13 51 S	171 38 W
Somali Republic	REP	42	Africa	10 00 N	49 00 E
Somosomo	LOC	193	C1	16 46 S	179 58 W
Somosomo Strait	STRA	193	C1	16 47 S	179 59 W
Soso Bay	BAY	193	B2	19 05 S	178 12 E
South Africa	REP	42	Africa	30 00 S	26 00 E
South Atlantic Ocean	—	47	—	30 00 N	115 00 W
South Australian Basin	SEAF	196	B7	42 00 S	135 00 E
South China Sea	—	46	China	10 00 N	113 00 E
South Fiji Ridge	SEAF	196	G5	23 00 S	179 00 W
South Georgia Island	UK COL	43	Atl O	54 15 S	36 45 W
South Korea	REP	46	E Asia	36 30 N	128 00 E
South Orkney Islands	UK COL	43	Atl O	60 35 S	45 30 W
South Pacific Ocean	—	197	I6	35 00 S	155 00 W
South Sandwich Islands	UK COL	43	Atl O	57 45 S	26 30 W
South Shetland Islands	UK COL	43	Atl O	62 00 S	60 00 W
South Tasmanian Ridge	SEAF	196	C7	46 00 S	147 00 E
South Vietnam	REP	46	SE Asia	13 00 N	108 00 E
South West Africa	S AF DEP	42	Africa	22 00 S	17 00 E
Southara, Mount	—	184	A2	72 10 S	160 00 E
Southern Cook Islands	ASSOC (NZ) COTH NAT	194	D2	20 00 S	158 00 E
Southern Cook Islands	—	197	I5	20 00 S	158 00 E
Southern Ocean	—	42, 43	Antarctica	60 00 S	90 00 E
Spain	REP	42, 43	Europe	40 00 N	04 00 W
Spanish Sahara	SP COL	42, 43	Africa	24 30 N	13 00 W
Spencer-Smith, Cape	—	185	D2	78 00 S	167 30 E
Speyer, Mount	—	185	B4	78 50 S	160 45 E
Spike, Cape	—	185	B1	77 20 S	163 35 E
Spire, The	PEAK	185	A3	78 10 S	161 40 E
Spitsbergen	NORWAY	42, 43	Arctic O	78 00 N	20 00 E
Sputnik Islands	ISLS	184	A2	70 20 S	163 20 E
Sri Lanka	COTH NAT	42	Bay Bengal	07 00 N	81 00 E
Starbuck	UK COL	197	I3	05 37 S	155 55 W
Stepaside Spur	MTN	185	A3	78 20 S	161 30 E
Stewart Hills	HILLS	184	D4	84 10 S	86 00 W
Stewart Islands	SOLOMON	196	E3	08 28 S	162 34 E
Stockholm	CITY	42, 43	Sweden	59 20 N	18 95 E
Strand Moraines, The	—	185	B2	77 45 S	164 35 E
Sturge Island	ISLD	184	A1	67 30 S	164 20 E
Sudan	REP	42	Africa	15 00 N	30 00 E
Suess, Mount	—	185	A1	77 05 S	161 45 E
Sula Island	INDON	46	Celebes S	01 52 N	125 22 E
Sula Wesi	INDON	46	Celebes S	02 00 S	121 00 E
Sulu Archipelago	PHIL	46	Sulu S	05 30 N	121 30 E
Sulu Sea	—	46	Philippines	08 00 N	120 00 E
Sulzberger Bay	BAY	184	D3	77 00 S	152 00 W
Sulzberger Ice Shelf	—	184	D3	77 00 S	149 00 W
Sumatra Island	INDON	46	Ind O	00 05 S	102 00 E
Sumba Island	INDON	46	Timor S	10 00 S	120 00 E
Sumbawa Island	INDON	46	Timor S	08 40 S	118 00 E
Superior, Lake	—	47	USA	48 00 N	88 00 W
Surinam	NETH TER	43	S America	04 00 N	56 00 W
Suva	TOWN	193	B2	18 08 S	178 25 E
Suvorov Glacier	GLCR	184	A2	69 55 S	160 10 E
Suwarrow Atoll	COOKS	194	C1	13 15 S	163 05 W
Swains Atoll	AM SAMOA	194	B1	11 03 S	171 06 W
Swartz Nunataks	PEAKS	185	A4	78 40 S	160 00 E
Swaziland	KING	42	Africa	26 30 S	31 30 E
Sweden	KING	42, 43	Europe	62 00 N	15 00 E
Sydney	CITY	46	Australia	33 55 S	151 10 E
Sydney Island	PHOENIX	196	G3	04 28 S	171 15 W
Syria	REP	42, 43	SW Asia	35 00 N	38 00 E
Taakoka Island	COOKS	194	A1	21 16 S	159 43 E
Tabar Islands	PNG	196	D3	02 58 S	152 07 E
Tabiteuea Atoll	GILBERT	196	F3	01 20 S	174 50 E
Table Mountain	MTN	185	A2	77 58 S	162 00 E
Tabular Mountain	MTN	185	A2	77 50 S	160 15 E
Tafua	LOC	193	B4	13 46 S	172 15 W
Taga	LOC	193	A4	13 47 S	172 30 W
Tagula Island	PNG	196	D4	11 30 S	153 30 E
Tahaa Island	FR TER	197	I4	16 40 S	151 30 W
Tahiti Island	FR TER	197	J4	17 37 S	149 27 W
Tainan	CITY	46	Taiwan	23 00 N	120 11 E
T'aipei	CITY	46	Taiwan	25 03 N	121 30 E
Taiwan	REP	46	SE Asia	23 30 N	121 00 E
Takaroa Island	FR TER	197	J4	14 30 S	144 58 W
Takutea Island	COOKS	194	D2	19 49 S	158 1[illegible]
Takuvaine Stream	STRM	194	A1	21 12 S	159 4[illegible]
Talafo'ou	LOC	194	C3	21 07 S	175 07 W
Talaud Islands	INDON	46	Phil S	04 20 N	126 50 E
Tamakautonga	LOC	195	A4	19 06 S	169 55 W
Tamana Island	GILBERT	196	F3	02 29 S	175 59 E
Tana	N HEB	196	E4	19 30 S	169 20 E
Tananarive	CITY	42	Malagasy	18 52 S	47 30 E
Tanga Islands	PNG	196	D3	03 30 S	153 15 E
Tanganyika, Lake	—	42	Africa	06 00 S	29 30 E
Tanimbar Islands	INDON	46	Arofura S	07 30 S	131 30 E
Tanzania	REP	42	Africa	06 00 S	35 00 E
Tapajos River	STRM	47	Brazil	42 00 S	147 00 W
Tarawa Atoll	GILBERT	196	F2	01 30 N	173 00 E
Tashkent	CITY	42	USSR	41 20 N	69 18 E
Tasman Sea	—	196	D6	40 00 S	163 00 E

NAME	DESC	PAGE	REF	LAT	LONG
Tasmania	AUST	196	C7	42 00 S	147 00 E
Tatakamotonga	LOC	194	C3	21 11 S	175 07 W
Tatakoto	FR TER	197	K4	17 17 S	138 20 W
Tate Peak	PEAK	185	A4	78 40 S	159 30 E
Ta'u Island	AM SAMOA	197	H4	14 15 S	169 27 W
Tau Island	TONGA	194	D3	21 01 S	175 00 W
Tauere Atoll	FR TER	197	J4	17 18 S	141 30 W
Taulagapapa Island	TOKEL	195	D4	09 10 S	171 47 W
Tauu Islands	PNG	196	D3	04 51 S	157 17 E
Taveuni Island	FIJI	193	C1	16 51 S	179 58 W
Tavua	LOC	193	B1	17 27 S	177 51 E
Taylor Glacier	GLCR	185	A2	77 50 S	161 20 E
Taylor Valley	VLY	185	B2	77 40 S	163 00 E
Teall, Cape	—	185	B4	79 05 S	161 00 E
Teall Island	ISLD	185	B4	79 05 S	162 00 E
Te'ekiu	LOC	194	A4	21 07 S	175 19 W
Te Fakanaya Island	TOKEL	195	C4	09 06 S	171 52 W
Tegucigalpa	CITY	47	Honduras	14 06 N	87 13 W
Teheran	CITY	42	Iran	35 40 N	51 26 E
Tehuata Island	FR TER	197	J4	16 50 S	141 55 W
Te Kamu Island	TOKEL	195	C4	09 08 S	171 52 W
Telemachus Reef	REEF	194	C3	21 01 S	175 08 W
Te Matagi Island	TOKEL	195	D2	09 22 S	171 10 W
Tematangi Atoll	FR TER	197	J5	21 41 S	140 40 W
Tennyson, Cape	—	185	D1	77 20 S	168 15 E
Tent Island	ISLD	185	C2	77 40 S	166 20 E
Tepa Point	PNT	195	A4	19 08 S	169 56 W
Tepoto Island	FR TER	197	J4	14 08 S	141 24 W
Te Puka i Mua Island	TOKEL	195	C4	09 11 S	171 51 W
Terra Adélie	FR ADM	184	A3	80 00 S	139 00 E
Terra Nova Bay	BAY	184	B2	75 00 S	164 30 E
Terra Nova, Mount	—	185	D1	77 30 S	168 00 E
Terror Glacier	GLCR	185	D1	77 35 S	168 00 E
Terror, Mount	—	185	D1	77 30 S	168 40 E
Tetiaroa Atoll	FR TER	197	J4	17 05 S	149 30 W
Thailand	KING	46	SE Asia	15 00 N	100 00 E
Theseus, Mount	—	185	A2	77 25 S	162 20 E
Thiel Mountains	MTNS	184	C4	85 15 S	91 00 W
Thor, Mount	—	185	A2	77 35 S	160 30 E
Ti'avea	LOC	193	D4	13 57 S	171 21 W
Tibet	REG	42	China	32 00 N	88 00 E
T'ienching	CITY	42	China	39 08 N	117 12 E
Tierra Del Fuego	CHILE/ ARGENTINA	47	S America	54 30 S	67 00 W
Tikehau Island	FR TER	197	J4	16 50 S	148 10 W
Tikei Island	FR TER	197	J4	14 52 S	144 32 W
Tikopia Island	S CRUZ	196	E4	12 10 S	168 50 E
Timberlake, Cape	—	185	B4	79 00 S	161 45 E
Timoe Island	FR TER	197	K5	23 20 S	134 29 W
Timor	INDON	46	Timor S	08 35 S	126 00 E
Timor Sea	—	46	Indonesia	11 00 S	128 00 E
Titicaca, Lake	—	43	Peru	15 50 S	69 20 W
Titikaveka	LOC	194	A1	21 16 S	159 45 W
Toau Atoll	FR TER	197	J4	15 50 S	146 00 W
Tofua Island	TONGA	194	A2	19 45 S	175 05 W
Togo	REP	42, 43	Africa	08 00 N	01 10 E
Toi Village	LOC	195	B3	18 58 S	169 52 W
Tokelau Island	TOKEL	195	D3	09 06 S	171 47 W
Tokelau Islands	NZ DEP	196	G3	09 00 S	171 45 W
Tokelau Islands	—	195	C2	09 00 S	171 45 W
Toketoke Island	TONGA	194	B3	21 03 S	175 17 W
Tokomololo	LOC	194	B4	21 10 S	175 15 W
Tokyo	CITY	46	Japan	35 42 N	139 46 E
Tomlin Glacier	GLCR	184	A1	69 30 S	159 00 E
Tonga Deep	SEAF	194	A2	21 10 S	172 30 W
Tonga Islands	COTH NAT	196	G5	20 00 S	175 00 W
Tonga Islands	—	194	A2	20 00 S	175 00 W
Tonga Ridge	SEAF	196	G4	20 00 S	175 00 W
Tonga Trench	SEAF	196	G5	22 00 S	173 00 W
Tongatapu Group	TONGA	194	A2	21 10 S	175 00 W
Tongatapu Island	TONGA	194	Pac O	21 10 S	175 10 W
Toronto	CITY	47	Canada	43 39 N	79 23 W
Torres Islands	N HEB	196	E4	13 15 S	166 37 E
Torres Strait	STRA	196	C4	10 25 S	142 10 E
Totoya Island	FIJI	193	C2	18 56 S	179 50 W
Trachyte Hill	HILL	185	C1	77 15 S	166 25 E
Transantarctic Mountains	—	184	A2	85 30 S	175 00 W
Tricouni, Mount	—	185	B3	78 30 S	162 00 E
Trinidad & Tobago	COTH NAT	43	W Indies	11 00 N	61 00 W
Trinidade Island	BRAZIL	43	Atl O	20 30 S	29 20 W
Tripoli	CITY	42, 43	Libya	32 58 N	13 12 E
Tristan da Cunha	UK COL	42, 43	Atl O	37 15 S	12 30 W
Trobriand Islands	PNG	196	D3	08 30 S	151 05 E
Truk Islands	CAROL	196	D2	07 23 N	151 46 E
Tuamotu Archipelago	FR TER	197	J4	15 00 S	145 00 W
Tuasivi	LOC	193	B4	13 38 S	172 10 W
Tubuai Island	FR TER	197	J5	23 23 S	149 27 W
Tubuai-Manu Island	FR TER	197	I4	17 23 S	150 37 W
Tucker Glacier	GLCR	184	B2	72 30 S	169 00 E
Tufaka Island	TONGA	194	B3	21 03 S	175 15 W
Tunis	CITY	42, 43	Tunisia	36 50 N	10 13 E
Tunisia	REP	42, 43	Africa	34 00 N	09 00 E
Tureia Atoll	FR TER	197	K5	20 49 S	138 30 W
Turkey	REP	42	SW Asia	39 00 N	35 00 E
Turks Head	HEAD	185	C2	77 40 S	166 45 E
Turtle Rock	MTN	185	C2	77 45 S	166 45 E
Tutuila Island	AM SAMOA	194	B1	14 18 S	170 42 W
Tuvuca Island	FIJI	193	D1	17 40 S	178 50 W
U.A.E. (Trucial States)	—	42	SW Asia	24 00 N	54 00 E
Ua Huka Island	FR TER	197	K3	08 55 S	139 32 W
Ualanga Lalu Reef	REEF	194	B3	21 06 S	175 11 W
Ua Pu Island	FR TER	197	J3	09 25 S	140 00 W
U.A.R. (Egypt)	REP	42	Africa	27 00 N	30 00 E
Uganda	COTH NAT	42	Africa	01 00 N	32 00 E
Ugolini Peak	PEAK	185	A3	78 02 S	161 45 E
Ujae Atoll	MARSHAL	196	E2	09 00 N	165 40 E
Ujelang Atoll	MARSHAL	196	E2	09 49 N	160 55 E
Ulan Bator	CITY	42	Mongolia	47 54 N	106 52 E
Ulladulla Trough	SEAF	196	D6	34 00 S	154 00 E
Unalaska Island	ALEUT	46	Bering S	53 40 N	166 40 W
Union of Soviet Socialist Republics	FED REP	42, 43	Asia	50 00 N	75 00 E
United Kingdom	KING	42, 43	Europe	54 00 N	02 00 W
United States of America	REP	47	N America	38 00 N	97 00 W
Upolu Island	W SAMOA	193	D4	13 55 S	171 45 W

NAME	DESC	PAGE	REF	LAT	LONG
Upper Staircase	GLCR	185	A3	78 20 S	161 15 E
Upper Victoria Glacier	GLCR	185	A1	77 15 S	161 25 E
Upper Volta	REP	42	Africa	13 00 N	02 00 W
Upper Wright Glacier	GLCR	185	A2	77 30 S	160 30 E
Uruguay	REP	47	S America	33 00 S	56 00 W
Usarp Mountains	MTNS	184	A2	71 30 S	159 00 E
Utulau	LOC	194	B4	21 11 S	175 17 W
Utuloa Point	PNT	193	D4	13 54 S	171 31 W
Utupua Island	S CRUZ	196	E4	11 20 S	166 33 E
Uvea Island	N CAL	196	E5	20 25 S	166 39 E
Vaiea	LOC	195	A4	19 08 S	169 53 W
Vaina	LOC	194	B4	21 12 S	175 11 W
Vaito'omuli	LOC	193	B4	13 45 S	172 18 W
Vaitupu Island	ELLICE	196	F3	07 28 S	178 41 E
Valparaiso	CITY	43	Chile	33 05 S	71 40 W
Vanavana Island	FR TER	197	K5	20 43 S	139 49 W
Vancouver	CITY	47	Canada	49 13 N	123 06 W
Vancouver Island	CANADA	47	Pac O	49 45 N	126 00 W
Vanda (NZ)	BASE	185	A2	77 30 S	161 40 E
Vanda, Lake	—	185	A2	77 30 S	161 40 E
Vanikora Islands	S CRUZ	196	E4	11 42 S	166 50 E
Vanua Balavu Island	FIJI	193	D1	17 12 S	178 57 W
Vanua Lava Island	N HEB	196	E4	13 48 S	167 28 E
Vanua Levu Island	FIJI	193	B1	16 33 S	179 15 E
Vanua Vatu Island	FIJI	193	C2	18 22 S	179 16 W
Vaotu'u	LOC	194	A4	21 09 S	175 18 W
Vatoa Island	FIJI	193	D3	19 50 S	178 15 W
Vatukoula	LOC	193	B1	17 30 S	177 53 E
Vatu Lele Island	FIJI	193	A2	18 30 S	177 38 E
Vatu Vara Island	FIJI	193	C1	17 25 S	179 34 W
Vava'u Group	TONGA	194	A2	18 40 S	174 00 W
Vava'u Island	TONGA	194	A2	18 36 S	174 00 W
Velitoa Island	TONGA	194	C3	21 05 S	175 08 W
Vella Lavella Island	SOLOMON	196	D3	07 45 S	156 35 E
Venezuela	REP	47	S America	08 00 N	65 00 W
Victoria, Lake	—	42	Africa	01 00 S	33 00 E
Victoria Land	REG	184	A2	74 15 S	162 00 E
Victoria Valley	VLY	185	A2	77 20 S	161 45 E
Victory Mountains	MTNS	184	B2	72 40 S	168 00 E
Vida, Lake	—	185	A2	77 25 S	162 05 E
Vienna	CITY	41	Austria	48 13 N	16 22 E
Vientiane	CITY	46	Laos	17 59 N	102 38 E
Viti Levu Island	FIJI	193	A2	18 00 S	178 00 E
Vladivostok	CITY	46	USSR	43 09 N	131 53 E
Volcano Islands	JAP TER	46	Pac O	25 00 N	141 00 E
Volga River	STRM	42	USSR	45 55 N	47 52 E
Vostok Island (UK)	LINES	197	I4	10 05 S	152 23 W
VX6, Mount	—	184	A2	72 40 S	162 10 E
Wade, Mount	—	184	C4	84 50 S	175 00 W
Waesche, Mount	—	184	D3	77 10 S	127 30 W
Wagava Island	FIJI	193	D2	18 52 S	178 54 W
Waiyevo	LOC	193	C1	16 50 S	179 59 W
Wakaya Island	FIJI	193	B1	17 39 S	179 01 E
Wake Island	US ADM	46	Pac O	19 18 N	166 36 E
Walcott Bay	BAY	185	B3	78 15 S	163 30 E
Walcott Glacier	GLCR	185	B3	78 15 S	163 10 E
Wallis Islands	FR TER	196	G4	13 16 S	176 15 W
Walpole Island	N CAL	196	E5	22 39 S	168 57 E
Warsaw	CITY	42, 43	Poland	52 15 N	21 00 E
Washington	CITY	47	USA	38 55 N	77 00 W
Washington, Cape	—	184	B2	74 40 S	165 30 E
Washington Island (UK)	LINES	197	H2	04 43 N	160 24 W
Watson Escarpment	CLIF	184	C4	85 50 S	140 00 W
Waya Island	FIJI	193	A1	17 19 S	177 09 E
Weaver, Mount	—	184	C4	86 55 S	153 30 W
Weddell Sea	—	43	Antarctica	75 00 S	45 00 W
Wellesley Islands	AUST	196	B4	16 42 S	139 30 E
West Beacon	MTN	185	A2	77 50 S	160 45 E
West Fayu Island	CAROL	196	C2	08 05 N	146 45 E
Western Samoa	COTH NAT	193	Pac O	03 55 S	172 00 W
Westminster, Mount	—	184	B4	85 00 S	169 50 E
Wetar Island	INDON	46	Banda S	07 48 S	126 18 E
Whales, Bay of	—	184	C3	78 30 S	164 30 W
Whitcombe, Mount	—	185	A1	76 45 S	162 10 E
White Island	ISLD	185	D2	78 10 S	167 20 E
White Strait	STRA	185	C2	78 10 S	166 50 E
Whitmore Mountains	MTNS	184	D4	82 25 S	103 00 W
Williamson Head	HEAD	184	A1	69 10 S	158 00 E
Williamson Rock	ROCK	185	D1	77 25 S	169 15 E
Wilson Hills	HILLS	184	A1	69 35 S	158 30 E
Wilson Piedmont Glacier	GLCR	185	A1	77 15 S	163 15 E
Windless Bight	BAY	185	D2	77 45 S	167 50 E
Windward Islands	—	43	W Indies	13 00 N	61 00 W
Winnipeg	CITY	47	Canada	49 53 N	97 10 W
Winnipeg, Lake	—	43	Canada	52 00 N	97 00 W
Wisconsin Range	MTNS	184	C4	85 45 S	127 00 W
Wise, Mount	—	185	C2	78 10 S	165 20 E
Wohlschlag Bay	BAY	185	C1	77 20 S	166 20 E
Wood Bay	BAY	184	B2	74 15 S	165 30 E
Woodlark Island	PNG	196	D3	09 05 S	152 50 E
Woollard, Mount	—	184	D4	80 35 S	96 40 W
Worcester Range	MTNS	185	B4	78 50 S	161 00 E
Wrangel Island	USSR	42	Arctic O	56 15 N	132 10 W
Wright Valley	VLY	185	A2	77 30 S	162 05 E
Yacata Island	FIJI	193	C1	17 15 S	179 33 W
Yadua Island	FIJI	193	B1	16 50 S	178 18 E
Yangtze River	STRM	46	China	31 48 N	121 10 E
Yap Island	CAROL	46	Pac O	09 30 N	138 09 E
Yaqaga Island	FIJI	193	B1	16 35 S	178 36 E
Yasawa Group	FIJI	193	A1	17 00 S	177 23 E
Yasawa Island	FIJI	193	A1	16 47 S	177 31 E
Yellow Sea		46	China	35 00 N	125 00 E
Yemen	KING	42	SW Asia	15 00 N	44 00 E
Yemen	REP	42	SW Asia	15 00 N	48 00 E
Yokohama	CITY	46	Japan	35 28 N	139 28 E
Young Island	ISLD	184	A1	62 28 S	162 30 E
Yugoslavia	REP	42, 43	Europe	44 00 N	19 00 E
Zaire	REP	42	Africa	07 00 S	13 30 E
Zambezi River	STRM	42	Africa	18 55 S	36 04 E
Zambia	REP	42	Africa	15 00 S	30 00 E
Zanuck, Mount	—	184	C4	85 55 S	151 00 W
Zanzibar	REP	42	Tanzania	06 10 S	39 11 E

(*d* diagram; *f/n* footnote; *m* map; *ph* photograph; *t* table)

Abel Tasman National Park (Nelson): 17b, *ph* 205
Acheron (Canterbury): coal at, 159a
Adare, Cape (Antarctica): first landing on continent and Hallett Station established at, 186
Advances to Settlers Department (*see* State Advances Corporation): 148a
Agriculture & Fisheries, Department of: role of in land use, 122a; original Department, 145a, 149a; advisory work of, 149a; role of in fisheries resources and fishing methods, 151
Air New Zealand: 174b, 201a
Airports: International at Auckland, Christchurch (Harewood), Cook Islands (Rarotonga), Wellington (Rongotai), 174b; at Blenheim (Woodbourne), 17b
Akaroa (Banks Peninsula): 21a, 54a
Akatore (Otago): minerals at, 156a
Albatross: 114b
Albert Park (Auckland): frost recordings at, 86a
Alexandra (Otago): focus for central Otago activities, 25b; climate of, *d* 88
Alpine Fault: geology of, 17a, 92 ff and geothermal activity from, 158b; *ph* 252
Aluminium: *see* Bluff
Amberley (Canterbury): magnetic observatory at, 76a
America, United States cf: co-operation of in tuna fishing, 151b; in Antarctica, 186 ff and the Pacific, 190 ff; influence of in industry, 163b and the Lend-Lease Act, 178b; markets in for rock lobster, 25b; role of in NZ external policies, 48–9; trade with, 178b ff; visitors from, 183b, 201b ff
Amphibia: 116b; *ph* 119
Animal Life: domestic, 17a, 117a; indigenous, 116b; naturalised, 117a; deer 72b, 100a, 117a, goat and opossum 72b, 117a, rabbit 21b, 72b, 110b, 117a, 131b, rat 116b f; *m* 120, 121
Annexation by Britain: 44a, 53b, 57b
Antarctic Division, DSIR: established 1959, 187a
Antarctic Society, NZ: established 1933, 186b
Antarctic Stations: Hallett, 186b ff; McMurdo, 186a, 187a f; Scott Base, 77b, 187a ff; Vanda, 188b f
Antarctic Treaty: signed 1959, 187a(*f/n*); 189b
Antarctica (*see also* Ross Dependency): climate of, 189a; coal in, 188b; discovery of, 186; economic potential of, 92a, 189b; fauna & flora of, 188b; geology of, 188, 189b; icequakes at, 188a; mummified seals in, 188b; vulcanism in, 187b f; *m* 184, 185; *ph* 256
Anthracite: location and use of, 154a, 159a
Antipodes Islands: as part of NZ Botanical Region, 108a ff; *m* 4
ANZUS: 49a
Aorere Valley (Nelson): minerals in, 156b
Aotea: canoe, 53a
Aparima River (Southland): and soil, 131a
Arthur, Mt (Nelson): marble at, 91b
Arthur's Pass (S. Alps): 21b
Ashburton (Canterbury): manufacturing in, 164b; River, 21a, 131a; *m* 39
Ashley River (Canterbury): 21a, 131a
Asia: NZ's attitudes towards, 48a f; and the Pacific, 199
Atkinson, Sir Harry: 45b
Auckland city: airport, 174b; climate of, 82b(*t*), 84a(*t*) ff, *d* 85, 87, 88; harbour, 9a, 109a; population of, 63; as a port, 9a, 73b, 172a, 181b, *t* 172b; seat of government at, 54a; urban transport in, 174a; *m* 30–31; *ph* 209
Auckland Regional Authority: 5b, 58b, 66a, 174a
Auckland Islands: as part of NZ Botanical Region, 108a ff; sea lions on, 114b; *m* 4
Avon River (Christchurch): 21a
Australia: and the Bluff aluminium smelter, 25b; container service from, 173a; contributes to gold rushes, 54b and to population, 44b, 54a, 60a; faunal connections with, 115a ff, 152b; in the Pacific, 190a ff; influence of on industry, 163b ff; and NAFTA, 180 and trade with, 101a, 152a, 178b(*t*) ff; once included NZ, 57b; visitors from, 204b(*t*)
Avoca Valley (Canterbury): *ph* 24
Awatere River (Marlborough): and faulting, 17a, 94b
Axel Heiberg Glacier (Antarctica): *ph* 256

Balfour Declaration: 58b
Ballance, John: 58b
Balleny Islands (Antarctica): 187b
Banks, Joseph: 52a

Banks Peninsula (Canterbury): farming on, 21a; flora of, 109a ff; mistaken by Cook for island, 52b; soil of, 130b; volcanic origin and geology of, 21a, 94b
BANZARE (British–Australian–NZ–Antarctic Research Expedition) 1929–31: 186b
Barrier Islands: fauna of, 115b ff and flora of, 109b; kauri on, 100a and minerals on, 154b ff
Beacon Group: rocks, 188b
Beardmore Glacier (Antarctica): 188a
Bell, Sir Francis: 101b
Bellbird: 115b
Bellingshausen, Thaddeus von: 186a
Benmore (Canterbury): power project at, 158a; *ph* 248
Berendsen, Sir Carl: 58b
Birds: Forest & Shore, 115b f; Oceanic, 13b, 114b f, 187b f; of prey, 116a; waterfowl, 115a; *ph* 118, 119
Bittern: 115a
Bituminous coal: location and use of, 154a, 159a
Black Swan: 115a
Blenheim (Marlborough): airport (Woodbourne), 17b; climate of, 17b, 86b, *d* 87, 88; farming in, 147a; flora of, 109a; manufacturing in, 164b; *m* 39
Bluff (Southland): aluminium smelter at, 25b, 158a, 165a, 168b; ferry service from to Stewart Island, 173a; fisheries resources of, 152a; minerals in, 155b; port at, 172b (*t*); soils of, 131b; *m* 40
Borradaile Island (Antarctica): 186a
Bougainville: Germany in, 190b; in Papua New Guinea, 198b
Bounty Trough: 80b
Britain: constitutional relationships with, 57b ff; radicalism in, 44a f; influences of in industrial development, 163b; NZ's changing attitude towards since World War II, 48b; trade with, 148a, 178a f (*t*); visitors from, 183b, 204(*t*)
Broadcasting: 175b
Broadlands (Taupo): geothermal energy at, 154b, 158b
Bruce Bay (Westland): minerals at, 154b
Bulk Purchase Agreements: 148a, 178b
Bull, H. J.: 186a
Buller (Westland): earthquake in, 77b; forests in, 99a; River, as boundary of geological block, 17a, and minerals in, 156a
Burnett, Mt (Nelson): minerals at, 155a
Busby, James: 57b
'Bush Sickness': cobalt deficiency in soil, 125b f, 145b ff
Byrd, R. E.: 186b

Cambridge (South Auckland): 9a
Campbell Island: as part of NZ Botanical Region, 108a ff; climate of, 86b; *m* 4
Campbell Plateau: 80a
Campbell-Walker, I.: 100b
Canberra Pact: 18b
Canterbury: climate of, 82b ff; coal in, 154a; erosion in, 21; farming in, 17a, 21a, 146a f; forests in, 100a; geology of, 95a ff; manufacturing in, 164b ff; minerals in, 155a ff; settlement of, 53b; soil of, 124b ff; *ph* End Paper, 24, 242–43
Canterbury Association: Christchurch founded by 1850, 21a; sends colonists to Canterbury, 53b
Canton Islands: 191a
Capital Issues (Overseas) Regulations, 1965: 182b
Caples Valley (Otago): minerals at, 155a
Caroline Island: 190b f
Catchment: Boards and Commissions established 1941, 66b, *m* 69; in Otago, 25b and the West Coast, 99a
Cattle farming: 128b ff; growth of and marketing, 145b ff; in Banks Peninsula, 21a, Manawatu, 13a, Northland, 5b, Southland, 25, Waikato, 9a, West Coast, 17b; *ph* 220
Caxton Paper Mills: 167a
Chalky Inlet (Fiordland): 186a
Charleston (Nelson): minerals at, 156a
Chatham Islands: fauna of, 115a; fisheries resources of, 152a; flora of, 108b ff; geology of, 92a; as part of NZ Botanical Region, 108a; peat in, 154a f; seismic activity in, 77; transport links to, 173 f; *m* 4
Chatham Rise: seismic activity in, 77a; 80
Christchurch: airport (Harewood), 174b; climate of, *d* 85, 87, 88, *t* 82, 84; founding of, 21a; McMurdo air link with, 188a; manufacturing in, 163a ff; port of (*see also* Lyttelton), 73b; *m* 32; *ph* 245
Civil Aviation Division, Ministry of Transport: 174b
Clarence River (Marlborough): 17a, 94b
Clarendon (Otago): minerals at, 156b
Climate: 82a ff; districts, *m* 83; effects on of landscape complexity, 71b and of orography, 82a;

and fauna, 114a; Foehn wind, 84b f; frost & snow, 86a, *m* 88; humidity, 86a; radiation & sunshine, 17b, 86b, *d*, *m* 88; rainfall, 25a, 82b ff, *d* 85, 89; *t* 84; and soils, 122b f (*t*); and pasture production, 144a; temperature, 84b f, *m*, *d* 87; thunderstorms & hail, 84b, *d* 89; and vegetation complex, 71b f; water balance in, 84a f, *m* 89; wind, 82a f, *m* 87; *ph* 83
Cloudy Bay (Marlborough): 17b
Clutha River (Otago): electricity generation from, 25b; rivalled in length by Waikato, 9a; and soil, 131a; *ph* 241
Coal: interest in, 154a, 159a; deposition of, 94a ff; industry, 168a; types of, 154a, 159a; in the Waikato, 9a and the West Coast, 17a ff, 94a, 154a
Coalgate (Canterbury): minerals at, 155a
Cobalt Deficiency: see 'Bush Sickness'
Cobb Valley (Nelson): geology of, 91b and minerals in, 155a
Cockayne, Leonard: 145a
Collingwood (Nelson): forests at, 99a and minerals at, 155a; recreational facilities at, 17b
Colombo Plan: 49b
Colonialism: in early NZ, 44a f; in the Pacific, 190b ff
Colonising groups: 53b f
Communications: 172b, 175(*t*)
Conservation: forestry's part in, 100a ff; growth of public interest in, 25b, 73a; ignored by early settlers, 72b; and the Nature Conservation Council, 122a; and soil and land uses, 127a ff; in Canterbury, 21b, Marlborough, 17a and Otago, 25b
Constitution Act, 1852: 54a, 58a
Constitutional Development: from Crown Colony, 45a f, 57b ff
Container Services: 172b f
Continental Drift: theory of, re fauna, 114a; *see also* Gondwanaland
Continental Shelf & Slope: 80; exclusive fishing zone to include, 151b; proximity to Antarctica, 92b, 187b
Cook, Captain James: and Antarctica, 186a; circumnavigates both Islands, 52b f; comments on scenery, 200a; records fish, 151a; in Dusky Sound, 25a; *m* 50
Cook Islands: become self-governing, 192b; come under NZ, 48b; immigration from, 62b; in Polynesian migration, 51a; international airport (Rarotonga) at, 174b; population of, 192b; represented at South Pacific Forum, 199b; sovereignty disputes over, 191a; transferred to NZ, 190b; *m* 194
Cook, Mt: or Aorangi, 200a; and the Southern Alps, 21b, 71b; National Park, 201a; sunshine at, 86b; Tourist Hotels at, 200b; *ph* Frontispiece, 238–39, 246–47
Cook Strait: as a barrier, 17b, 174b, 181b; cable in, 17b; current-swept nature of, 80b; effect of on climate, 82b; fault line across, 13b f; as a landscape feature, 71b; and Cook 1770, 52b; settlements in, 17a; significance of in commerce, 181b; submergence of, 95b; tuataras in, 116a; whaling in, 17a, 75b
Co-operative Dairy Company, NZ: 146a
Coppermine Island (Hen & Chicken Is): minerals at, 156a
Copperstain Creek (Nelson): minerals at, 155b
Cormorant: 114b
Coromandel, Peninsula and Range: climate of, 84a; flora of, 111a and forests on, 5b, 98b ff, 109b; geology of, 92 ff; minerals in, 154b ff; Polynesian artifacts in, 51b; recreational facilities of, 5b; soil of, 124a ff; timber from, 101a; vulcanism in, 94b ff
Craig, Port (Southland): 101b
Croisilles harbour (Nelson): minerals at, 156a
Cuckoo: 116a
Customs districts: 66b

Dairy Export Control Act, 1924: 148a
Dairy farming: 145a ff; co-operative character of, 146a; and the Dairy Board, 148a ff; export figures for, *t* 178a; as a factor in grassland farming, 144b; as an industry, 165b; and marketing and the Primary Products Marketing Act, 148a f; mechanisation of, 72a, 146a; production figures for, 145b; sharemilking in, 146b; in the Northern, Central & Southern Soil Regions, 124b ff; *ph* 212
Dannevirke (Hawke's Bay): 13b
deRoburt, Hammer: 192b
Desert Road and Plateau (South Auckland): 13b, 71b
District Roads Councils: 66a; *m* 68
Doubtless Bay (North Auckland): minerals at, 156a
Droughts: frequency of, 84b; in fat-lamb farming,

146a and the Northern Soil Region, 125a ff and Northland, 5a

Dry Valleys (Antarctica): 188b; *ph* 256

Dun Mountain (Nelson): minerals at, 17b, 156a

Duck, blue: 115a

Dunedin: gold rush to, 25a, 54b; MacAndrew group of settlers in, 54a; manufacturing in, 25a, 164b ff; minerals at, 155a; port of, 25a, 73b, 172, 181b (*see also* Otago); climate of, 82b(*t*), *d*, *m* 85, 87, 88; Regional Planning Authority, 66b; soil of, 130a; tourism in, 200b; *m* 33; *ph* 245

D'Urville Island (Cook Strait): minerals at, 155b ff; soil of, 127b

Dusky Sound (Fiordland): 25a; 101a

Earthquakes: and erosion, 132a; frequency, nature, etc., 76b ff, *f/n* 77a; and geological activity, 95b; in Antarctica, 188a, the Buller and Wairarapa, 77b, the Continental Shelf, 80b and Napier, 13b, 77b; *m* 78

East Coast: manufacturing in, 164b; settlement of, 13b; soil of, 126a ff

East Cape: farming in, 9b; forests in, 9b, 99a ff; geology of, 92b; Maori settlement in, 9b, 51b; tuataras at, 116a

Easter Island: 190a

Education: Boards, 66a, *m* 67; Maori, 63b; and working wives, 63a

Eglinton Valley (Southland): *ph* 28

Egmont: Cape, and the Continental Shelf, 80a; National Park, 128a; soil of, 127a f

Egmont, Mt: forests on, 99b; geology of, 95a; tussock communities on, 110b; and the Taranaki plains, 71b; vulcanism of, 13a, 127; *ph* 229, 230–31

Egret, white: 115a

Electric Power Boards: 66; *m* 69

Electricity Department: 160b

Electricity Generation & Distribution: at Benmore, Haywards, Huntly, Marsden, New Plymouth, Otahuhu, Stratford, 158; at Broadlands and Meremere, 154b, 158b; and the Cook Strait cable, 17b, 158a and the Clutha River, Lakes Manapouri and Te Anau, and Roxburgh, 25b; in South Canterbury, 21b; at Wairakei, 9b, 155b, 158b; and the Waikato River, 9a; at Waitaki, 21b, 25b, 158a; *m* 69, 140

Ellesmere, Lake (Canterbury): and soils, 131b

Ellice Islands: *see* Gilbert & Ellice Islands

Ellsworth, Lincoln: 186b

Employment: demographic effects of, 63a; districts, 66b; in commerce & trade, 181b, in fishing, 151a, manufacturing, 163 ff, the Post Office and the Railways, 175a; urban, 63a

Endeavour, HM Bark: 52a

Endeavour Inlet (Marlborough): minerals at, 156a

Enderbury Islands: 191a

Energy Research & Development Committee: 160b

Energy resources: *see* Coal; electricity, hydro & thermal, 73a, 158 ff; gas, manufactured & natural, 159; geothermal steam, *see* Geothermal Power; petroleum products, 159b ff; alternative sources of, 160b; and the environment, 25b; Ministry of, 160b; *m* 161

Erebus, Mt (Antarctica): 188b; *ph* 256

Erosion: from forest removal & vegetation change, 110b; and grassland farming as corrective, 72; by rabbits, 21b f, 72b, 110b, 131b; in Canterbury, 21, East Cape, 9b, Marlborough, 17a, the soils of the Northern, Central, Southern, High Country regions, 126a ff, Taranaki, 13b and Nelson, 132a; *ph* 217

Esk Valley (Hawke's Bay): *ph* 212

European Economic Community: effect of UK entry to, 45b ff, 178a f and on the Pacific, 199b; and the Luxembourg Agreement, Treaties of Accession and Rome, 179a

Exchange Control Regulations, 1965: 182b

Export Guarantee Office: 180b

Falla, Sir Robert A.: 186b

Fairfield (Otago): minerals at, 155b

Fantail: 115b

Fanthams Peak: part of Egmont volcanic cluster, 13a; *ph* 229

Farewell, Cape (Nelson): 52a

Farming: 144a ff; grassland farming, 21a ff, 71b ff, 144 f; mechanisation of, 72a, 145a f; importance of in early economy, 44b; cereal & grain, 17b, 21a, 147a ff; cattle, *see* Cattle Farming; dairy, *see* Dairy Farming; fruit, 5b, 125b ff, 145b ff, 178a, *ph* 206–07; mixed, 129b ff, 144b; pig and poultry, 145b ff; sheep, *see* Sheep Farming; tobacco, 17b, 54a, 148b; vegetable, 13b, 21a, 125b ff, 145b, 178a, *ph* 210–11; viticulture, 5a, 54a, 55b, 145b, 147a, *ph* 212

Farmers' Union: 150a

Faults & Faulting: Alpine Fault, 17a, 92b ff, *ph* 252 ff; in Marlborough, 17a, 94b; in mountain building, 71a ff; Wellington Fault, 13b, 17a, *ph* 232

Fauna: amphibia and freshwater fish, 116b; Antarctic, 188b; birds, *see* Birds; mammals, *see* Animal Life; marine, *see* Marine Life; reptiles, 116; *m* 120, 121; *ph* 117, 118–19

Featherston (Wellington): 101b

Federated Farmers: cadet scheme, 149b; formation of, 150a

'Fencibles': military settlements, 54a; *m* 56

Ferries: 17b, 173a, 201a

Fiji: constitutional development of, 198a; immigration from, 62a; population of, 190a; represented at South Pacific Forum, 199b; seismic station at, 77b; taken over by Britain, 190b; trade with, 178b (*t*) ff; *m* 193

Financial Institutions: 182

Fiordland: climate of, 25a; and the Continental Shelf, 80a; fisheries resources of, 25, 152a; geology of, 17a, 92a ff; in dissection contrast, 71a; link with Antarctic exploration, 186a; National Park, 25a, 115b, 201a; seismic region, 76b ff; soils of, 132b; tourism in, 200a ff; *ph* 28, 253

Fishing Industry: administration, research & development in, 151a (*t*) ff; methods of fishing, 151b f; role of in country's development, 73a; *m* 153

Flora: alpine vegetation and adventive plants, 111; Antarctic, 188b; and climate, 71b ff; endemism and dicecism, flowers and coastal plants, 108a f; forests (indigenous), 109a ff; grasslands, indigenous, *see* Tussock Grasslands, introduced, 21a, 72a, 144b; life forms & leaves, 108; scrub & timberline, 110b; of the Shelf Islands, 111; and soil development, 122a; in swamps & bogs, 111a; *ph* 112, 113; *see also* Forests etc., Kauri

Foreign Policy: 44b f, 59a

Forestry: government policy on, 100b ff; annual planting rate of, 102b; and the Forestry Development Conference 1960, and future development of, 102b ff; *see also* Forests, State; private, 102a; sawmilling, start and development of, 17b, 101a f, *ph* 216, *see also* Pulp, Paper and Panel Industries; afforestation, 9b, 72a, 100a ff; climate for, 71b ff; economic role of, 44b, 72b, 103a; employment in, 181b; export figures for, 178a (*t*); in the Pacific, 190a ff; *m* 104, 105, 106, 107

Forests, exotic: on soils of Northern, Central, Southern and Steepland regions, 125b ff; planting of, 9b, 72b, 101a ff; *m* 106–07; *ph* 214–15; *see also* Forests (State)

Forests, indigenous: definition and distribution of, 9b, 98a f, 109a f; classes of, 98b ff, 109a ff, 124b ff; clearing of, 5a, 9a, 13a f, 72a f, 98b ff, 109a, 132a, 144b; role of in soil formation, 122b ff; and the West Coast beech forest scheme, 17b, 103b; *m* 104, 105, 106, 107; *ph* 28, 213, 234–35, 238–39, 240, 254

Forests (State), Sanctuaries, etc.: area of, 101a; in Auckland, Canterbury, Hawke's Bay, Manawatu, Otago and West Coast, 102 and East Cape/Gisborne, 9b, 99a ff; Golden Downs (Nelson), 17b, 102a; Hanmer (Canterbury), 101a; Kaingaroa (Rotorua), 9b, 71b, 101a, 102a, *ph* 214–15; Karioi (Ruapehu), 102a; Manaia (Coromandel), 98b; Maniototo (Otago), 101a; Maramarua (Auckland), 102a; Omahuta (Auckland), 98b; Urewera (Bay of Plenty), 9b; Waipoua (Auckland), 5b, 98b, *ph* 213; Waiuku (Auckland), 154b

Fossils: in Antarctica, 188b; of tuatara, 116a and of marine animals, 114a f; *see also* Geology

Foveaux Strait: current-swept nature of, 80b; 'funnel effect' of on climate, 82b; oyster fisheries in, 152a; Polynesian artifacts in, 51b; submerged shoreline of, 80a

Fox Glacier (Westland): 86b

Fox River (Westland): coal at, 154a

Fox, Sir William: 200a

Franz Joseph Glacier (Westland): limit of Central soil region, 124b; Tourist Hotel, 200b

Fraser, Peter: 59a

Freshwater Fish, Fishing: indigenous, 116b, 152b; introduced, 73a, 116b, 152b; *m* 153

Fresne, Marion du: 52a

Fuchs, Sir Vivian: 187a

Fulmar, Silvergrey: 188a

Gannet: 13b, 114b

Gas, manufactured: as a source of energy, 159; as a coal consumer, 154a, 159a; *m* 161

Gas, natural: as a fuel and source of electricity, 159a; and the Natural Gas Corporation, 159b; at Kapuni, 13b, 154a, 159b, Moturoa, 154a, 159b and Nelson, 17b; and the Maui Field, 13b, 154a, 159b; *m* 161

Geology: age of NZ, 90b ff (*d*, *t*); of the Antarctic, 187b ff; evidence for, from oil drilling, 90a ff; and geosynclines, 90b ff; and orogenies, 91a, 93a, 95a; periods of, 91a (*t*) ff; of the sea floor, 71a, 80; *m* 96, 97; *see also* Volcanoes

Geothermal Power: at Broadlands, 154b, 158b and at Wairakei, 9b, 155b, 158, *ph* 225; heavy water production from, 158b

Gilbert & Ellice Islands: future of, 199a; sovereignty of, 190b f

Gisborne: and the East Cape, 9b; city, *m* 38; climate of, 84a, *d* 87, 88, *t* 82b; farming in, 147a; forests in, 102b; geology of, 95b; Maori population of, 9b; manufacturing in, 164b; *m* 38

Glaciers: in Antarctica, 87b ff, *ph* 256; effect of on snow line, 86b; Fox Glacier, 86b; Franz Joseph Glacier, 124b; glacially excavated lakes, 21b; impress Cook, 200a; as a landscape feature, 71b; in the Quaternary Ice Age, 93b ff; retreat of, 21b; *ph* 246–47

Glenbrook (Auckland): steel mill at, 168b

Godley, John Robert: 58a

Gold: 44b, 154b; in Otago, 25, 54b and on the West Coast, 17a, 21b, 54b, 154b

Golden Bay (Nelson): minerals at, 155b

Gondwanaland & Continental Drift: and the Antarctic, 92a, 188b f; in relation to NZ fauna, 114a, and flora, 108a; remnants of, around NZ, 80a

Goose: 115a

Gore (Southland): fireclay at, 154b

Graham, Robert: 200a

Graham Valley (Nelson): minerals in, 156a

Grassmere, Lake (Marlborough): salt from, 155b

Gravity, Magnetism & Seismicity: 76–7, *m* 78, 79

Great Bush (Hawke's Bay): settlements in, 55a

Great Fleet: Polynesian, 53a

Grebe, Great Crested: 115a

Green, Charles: 52a

Greenstone: as a mineral, 55a; used by Maori, 154a

Grey, Sir George: 48b, 58a

Grey Valley (Westland): farming in, 17b; forests in, 17b, 99a

Greymouth (Westland): coal at, 94a, commercial fishing from, 151b; ironsands at, 154b; manufacturing in, 164b; as a port, 21b; *m* 40

Guam: 190b

Haast Pass (Westland): 21b

Haast River (Westland): greenstone from, 155a

Hallett Station (Antarctica): 186b

Hamilton (South Auckland): climate of, *d* 85, 87, 88; and the Desert Road, 13b; manufacturing in, 63a, 164b; NZ's largest inland city, 9a; and agriculture, 73b; soils around, 127a; *n* 37

Hanmer (Canterbury): State Forest, 101a

Hastings (Hawke's Bay): manufacturing in, 164b; as a twin city to Napier, 13b; *m* 38

Hauraki (Auckland): Maritime Park, 5b; minerals in, 154b; soil of, 133b

Hauraki Gulf (Auckland): ferries in, 173a; recreational facilities of, 9a

Hawaii: 190

Hawea, Lake (Otago): 21b

Hawke Bay: 80a

Hawke's Bay: climate of, 82b ff; farming in, 9b; forests in, 99a ff; geology of, 94b ff; manufacturing in, 164b ff; minerals in, 155a; settlements in, 55a; soils of, 126a; *ph* 16, 220, 221, 222–23

Haywards (Wellington): 158a

Health Districts: 66b; *m* 68

Heavy Water: 158b

Heemskerck: 52a

Hen & Chicken Islands: flora of, 108b; 156a

Henderson district (North Auckland): wine growing in, 5a, 55b, 147a

Henry, Albert: 192b

Heretaunga plains (Hawke's Bay): minerals in, 155b; soil of, 13b, 133b

Heron: 115a

High Country: farming in, 145a ff; soil of, 124b ff; erosion of, 21

Hillary, Sir Edmund: 187a

Hindon (Otago): minerals at, 156a

Hinds River (Canterbury): 131a

Hikurangi Trench: earthquakes in, 77a; as a submarine canyon, 80b

Hobson, William: 57b

Hokianga (North Auckland): as a bar harbour, 5a; and kauri, 53b

Hokitika (Westland): climate of, 84a (*t*), *d* 85, 87, 88, *t* 82a; forests around, 99a

Homer Tunnel (Southland): 25b

Horouta: canoe, 53a

Hospital Boards: 66a

Housing Corporation of NZ: reconstituted from State Advances Corporation, 148a, 182b

Housing, State: and urbanisation, 63b

Houhora (North Auckland): Polynesian artifacts in, 51b

Huirau Range (South Auckland): forests on, 99b

Huntly (South Auckland): coal at, 9a, 154a; electricity generation at, 158b; minerals at, 154b

Hunua (South Auckland): minerals at, 155b

Hutt Valley (Wellington): on Wellington Fault, 13b; manufacturing in, 13a, 163a f

Immigration: 53–55, 60–62; *m* 55; *see also* Settlement

Industrial Design Council: 164a

Industrial districts: 66b
Industry: *see* Manufacturing
Internal Affairs, Department of: role of in land use, 122a
Invercargill (Southland): climate of, 84b, *d* 85, 87, 88, *t* 82b, 84a; manufacturing in, 164b; and Southland, 25b, and southern terminus SI railway, 175a; *m* 40
International Geophysical Year (IGY): in Antarctica 1957–58, 186b ff
Ironsands: *see* Titanomagnetite Sand
Irrigation: in the soil regions, 126a ff, Otago, 125b and the Wairau plains, 17b
Iselin Bank (Antarctica): 187b
Islands, Bay of: big game fishing in, 5b, 152b; link with Antarctic exploration, 186a; missions in, 51, 53b; minerals in, 156a; as a population centre, 52b; Treaty of Waitangi signed in, 5a; *see also* Fresne, Marion du
Isolation: effects of, 44a, 111a, 114b

Jackson Bay (Westland): Italian settlement at, 55a
Japan: demand from for fish, 152b, 189b and for timber products, 102b, 167a; in the Pacific, 191; influences NZ foreign policy, 48, and industry, 163b; trade with, 49b, 181a(*t*); visitors from, 204b(*t*)

Kaikohe (North Auckland): minerals at, 155a, 156a
Kaikoura (Marlborough): forests in, 99b; the Orogeny, 95; Peninsula, 80b; Ranges, 17a, 95b
Kaimai Range (South Auckland): 9b
Kaimanawa Range (South Auckland): 13a, 99b
Kaingaroa (South Auckland): forests at, 71b, 101a, 102a; *ph* 214–15
Kaipara (North Auckland): bar harbour at, 5a; titanomagnetite sand at, 154b
Kaitaia (North Auckland): climate, *d* 88, *t* 84a
Kaitangata (Otago): coal at, 94a
Kaka: 116a
Kakapo: 116a; *ph* 118
Kamo (North Auckland): fireclay at, 154b
Kapiti Island (Wellington): kiwis on, 115b
Kapuni (Taranaki): natural gas at, 13b, 154a, 159b
Karamea (Nelson): erosion at, 132a; ironsands at, 154b; *ph* 240
Karioi (South Auckland): forests at, 102a
Katikati (South Auckland): settlement at, 55a
Kauaeranga (South Auckland): minerals at, 155b
Kaukapakapa (North Auckland): minerals at, 155b
Kauri: attracts early settlement, 5, 53b, 55b; destruction of, 5, 72a, 100; in 'gumlands', 125a; mor-forming nature of, 124b; occurrence of, 5b, 98 ff, 109b; *ph* 213
Kawau Island (Hauraki Gulf): big game fishing from, 152b; minerals on, 156a
Kaweka Range (South Auckland): 13a, 99b
Kawerau (South Auckland): as a mill town, 163b; and the paper industry, 9b, 102b f, 167a; use of geothermal power at, 158b
Kawhia (South Auckland): geology of, 92b; harbour, 9a
Kea: 116a; *ph* 119
Kerikeri (North Auckland): fruit growing in, 5b, 125b; *ph* 206–07
Kermadec Islands: as part of NZ Botanical Region, 108a ff; seismic activity in, 77a; *m* 4
Kermadec Trench and Kermadec-Colville Ridge: 80a
Kidnappers, Cape (Hawke's Bay): and the Continental Slope, 80b; Cook's encounter at 1769, 52b; gannet colony on, 13b
King Country (South Auckland): recent clearing and productivity of, 9a; sawmilling in, 101a; soil of, 120a
King Movement: 44b
Kingfisher: 116a
Kinleith (South Auckland): industries at, 102b f, 163b f
Kirk, Thomas: 100b
Kiwi: 115b
Kororareka (North Auckland): 57b
Kotahitanga Movement: 44b
Krippner, Martin: 54b
Kukri peneplain (Antarctica): 188b
Kumeu (North Auckland): manufacturing at, 166b
Kupe: 51a, 53a

Labour, Department of: employment districts of, 66b
Labour Government 1935: 45b, 48a
Lady Knox Geyser: *ph* 225
Lakes: glacial and volcanic origins of, 71a, 73a; tourism at, 25, 200 ff
Lammerlaws, the (Otago): *ph* 254–55
Land Classification: 71b, 124b ff, 126a; *m* 140–41; *ph* 137
Land and Land Registration Districts: 66b; *m* 67
Land Tenure: 146b ff

Land Use: agencies to promote, 122a; administration & development of, 149b; and soil, 122a f; role of physical differences in, 17a; unwise, 73a; *m* 142–43; *ph* 136
Lands & Survey, Department of: and land districts, 66b; role of in land use, 122a
Landslip Hill (Southland): minerals at, 156b
Lawrence (Otago): minerals at, 156a
League of Nations: and Pacific mandates, 191a
Legislative Council: abolished 1947, 59a
Levy, Sir E. B.: 145a
Lewis Pass (Canterbury): 21b
Liberal Government 1891: 45
Lignite: location and use of, 154a, 159a
Lincoln Agricultural College: 149a
Line Islands: 190b f
Local Government: administrative divisions and authorities of, 66; Auckland Regional Authority, 5b, 58b, 66a, 174a; catchment boards & commissions, 66b, 122a; consolidation & amalgamation of, 58b; Local Government Commission, its role in land use, 122a; Municipal Corporations & Counties Act 1876, 58b; National Roads Act & Board, 66a; proliferation of authorities, 58b; Regional Planning Authorities, 66b, 122a; *m* 67, 68, 69
Longwood Range (Southland): minerals at, 156a
Lord Howe Rise: 80a
Lyttelton: as a natural harbour, 172a; modern port facilities of, 172b, 181b

MacAndrew, James: 54a
Mackaytown (South Auckland): minerals at, 156a
Mackenzie Basin (Canterbury): climate of, 86a; soil in, 129a; Twizel in, 21b; Waitaki River in, 25b
McMurdo Sound (Antarctica): discovery of, 186a; bases in, 187a; *m* 185; *see also* Scott Base
Macquarie Ridge: seismic activity in, 77a, 80a
Macquarie Island: as part of NZ Botanical Region, 108a ff
Macetown (Otago): minerals at, 156a
Magnetism: *see* Gravity, etc
Mamaku plateau (South Auckland): forests on, 99b
Manaia (Taranaki): forest sanctuary, 98b
Manapouri, Lake (Otago): power generation at, 25b; flora of, 110a
Manawatu: climate of, 82b ff; farming in, 13, 145b and forests, 102b; soil of, 126a ff
Mangatu: *ph* 217
Mangroves: 5a
Maniototo (Otago): State Forest, 101a
Manufacturing & Industry: control of and overseas influences on, 45b, 163b; economic contribution of, 165a; employment in, 165a (*d*) ff, 182a; export figures for, 178a; growth of, 162(*d*) and import control, 162a ff; industrial groups in, 165b ff and sawmilling, 101; pattern & appearance of, 163b ff; Research & Development agencies for, 169b; regional distribution of, 164b f; scale of enterprises in, 165a(*d*); trends in development of, 164a f; *m* 170, 171
Manukau Harbour (Auckland): 9a; flora of, 109a
Maori: archaeological evidence of, 51b; constitutional provisions for, 58a f; Council of Tribal Executives 1961, 59b; distribution & settlement patterns of, 9, 44a, 71b, *m* 50, 56; early transport by, 172a; education, 63b; farming by, 5b, 144a; first encounters of, with Europeans, 44a f, 52a, 53a f; fishing by, 151a; health of, 45a, 59b, 62a; and the King Movement, 44b, 57a, 59b; and the Kotahitanga Movement, 44b; land, 5b, 45a, 57b ff and the Native Land Court, 59a; legends of discovery of NZ, 51, 53; Councils Act 1900, 59b; origins of, 51a f, 53a; parliaments, 59a; present population of 60 (*t*, *f/n*) ff; Protectorate Department for, 57b; and the Ratana Movement, 59a; represented in Antarctic exploration, 186a; in a Stateless Society, 57a; Social and Economic Advancement Act 1945, 59b; and the 'United Tribes of NZ', 57b; urbanisation of, 5a, 63a f; use of minerals by, 154a; and the Treaty of Waitangi, 44a; White Paper on 1973, 59a; and the Young Maori Party, 44b f, 59a
Maori Wars: effect of on settlement of NI, 9a, 54, 144b; place of in early integration, 44
Mara, Ratu Sir Kamisese: 198a
Maramarua (South Auckland): coal and fireclay at, 154; forests at, 102a
Maria van Diemen, Cape (North Auckland): 52a, *ph* 205
Mariana Island: 190b f
Marie Byrd Land (Antarctica): 187b
Marine Life: varieties of, 114b, 151a (*t*) ff; Antarctic, 187b; whales, 114b, 187b; whitebait, 116b; *ph* 118
Marlborough: climate of, 17, 84a f, *t* 87; farming, erosion in, 17a; flora of, 110, geology of, 17a, 92a ff; manufacturing in, 164b ff, minerals in, 156a; recreational facilities of, 17b; seismicity in, 77a; soil of, 126a, 132b; Sounds, 17, 71b, 110a, *ph* 233; *ph* 244
Marquesas Islands: 51a
Marsden (Auckland): power station at, 158

Marsden Point (Auckland): oil refinery at, 5b, 160a, *ph* 208
Marshall Islands: 190b f
Massey Agricultural College: 149a
Masterton (Wellington): 13b; climate of, *d* 88; manufacturing in, 164b; *m* 37
Mata'afa Fiame Faumuina Mulinu'u II: 192b
Mataatua: canoe, 53a
Mataketake Range (Westland): minerals in, 156b
Matauri Bay (North Auckland): minerals at, 156a
Maui: 51a, 151a
Maui Gas Field (off Taranaki coast): development of, 159b; potential of for Taranaki, 13b; reported size of, 154a
Maunganui, Port (South Auckland): *ph* 216
Mauriceville (Wellington): 55a
Mawson, Sir Douglas: 186
Mayor Island (Bay of Plenty): Maori artifacts at, 51b
Meat: export figures for, 178a; in manufacturing, 165b; marketing of, 148a; role of in creating viable economy, 45a
Meat Export Control Act 1921–22: 148a
Meat Producers Board, NZ: 181a
Melanesia: defined, 190; *m* 196–97
Mercer (South Auckland): minerals at, 155a
Mercury Bay (Coromandel): big game fishing at, 152b; landfall at by Cook 1769, 52; sawmilling at, 101a
Meremere (Taranaki): power station at, 154a, 158a
Merganser: 115a
Micronesia: defined, 190; *m* 196–97
Middlemarch (Otago): minerals at, 155a
Milford Sound (Fiordland): climate of, *t* 84a; as a tourist attraction, 25b and Milford Track, 200b f; *ph* 253
Minerals: in Antarctica, 189b; on Chatham Rise, 80b; in the Pacific, 190a; future demands for, 156b; primary, in soils, 124a ff; varieties, 154a ff; *m* 157; *see also* Coal, Gold, Greenstone
Mining: general, 154a f; and the Mines Department, 160b; at the Tui mine (Coromandel), 154b; *see also* Coal, Gold
Mission stations, missionaries: in the development of government, 57b; and farming, 5b; first contacts by, 5a, 9a, 44a, 53b ff; in the Pacific, 190b
Moa: 53a, 115b
Mohaka River (Hawke's Bay): forests at, 99b
Molesworth Station (Marlborough): erosion & rehabilitation of, 17a
Mossburn (Otago): minerals at, 155b
Moturoa (New Plymouth): natural gas field at, 154a, 159b
Mount Cook Airways: 174a, 201b
Murchison (Nelson): coal in, 154a; erosion in, 132a
Murderers Bay (Nelson): now Golden Bay, 52a

Napier (Hawke's Bay): climate of, 84a (*t*), *d* 85, 87, 88; earthquake at, 13b, 77b; manufacturing in, 103a, 164b; as a port, 13b, 73b (*t*); *m* 38
National Airways Corporation: 201b
National Development Conference: 102b
Nature Conservation Council: and land use, 122a
Nauru: becomes republic 1968, 192b f; phosphate in, 145a, 192b; represented at South Pacific Forum, 199b; transferred from German to British control, 191a
Nelson: climate of, 17, 86b, 88, *d* 87, 88, *t* 84a; forests in, 17b, 99a ff; geology of, 17a, 91b ff; Lakes National Park, 17b; magnetic anomalies in, 76b; manufacturing in, 103a, 164b ff; minerals in, 154 ff; natural gas in, 17b; as a port, 17b, *t* 172b; recreational facilities in, 17b, *ph* 237; seismicity in, 77a; soil of, 126a ff; *m* 39; *ph* 236
Nevis Valley (Otago): oil shale in, 154a
New Britain: Germany in, 190b ff; in Papua New Guinea, 198b
New Caledonia: autonomist movement resisted in, 199a; flora of, 108b; part of Melanesia taken over by France, 190a f; and the NZ Geosyncline, 92a
New Guinea: in Papua New Guinea, 198b; history and size, 190a ff
New Hebrides: in Melanesia, responsibility of France & Britain, 190; decolonisation attempts in, 199a
New Ireland: Germany in, 190b; in Papua New Guinea, 198a
New Munster: province established, 58a
New Plymouth (Taranaki): climate of, *d* 85, 87, 88, *t* 82b, 84a; electricity generation at, 158a; first settlers sent to, 53b; manufacturing in, 164b; natural gas in, 154a; as a port, 73b; *m* 37
New South Wales: early links with NZ, 53a, 57b
New Ulster: province established, 58a
New Zealand Aluminium Smelters: *see* Aluminium
New Zealand – Australia Free Trade Agreement: 180 f
New Zealand Company: sends colonists to NZ, 17a, 53b; role of in constitutional development, 57b; and the settlement of Wellington, 13b, 17a, 57b

New Zealand Forest Products: and the pulp & paper industry, 102b, 167a
New Zealand Geosyncline: 92a ff
New Zealand Steel: 168b
Ngata, Sir Apirana: 45a
Ngauruhoe, Mt (South Auckland): as an active volcano, 13a; and soils, 128a ff; and geology, 95a; *ph* 12, 226–27
Ngawha Springs (North Auckland): minerals at, 156a
Nicholson, Port (Wellington): NZ Co's first and principal settlement, 13a, 57b
Ninety Mile Beach (North Auckland): contrast to Auckland harbours, 71a; forests on, 102b; *ph* 208
Niue: constitutional development of, 198b; emigration from, 62b, 198b; invited to attend South Pacific Forum, 199b; taken over by Britain, 190b; transferred to NZ control, 48b; *m* 195
Norfolk Ridge: 80a
Norsewood (Hawke's Bay): settlement at, 55a
North Cape (North Auckland): minerals at, 155b; rounded by Cook, 52b; traditional landing place of Maori, 51b; tuataras at, 116a
Northland: climate of, 5b, 84a; droughts in, 5a; farming in, 5b, 145b; geology of, 92b ff; manufacturing in, 5b, 164b ff; minerals in, 154a ff; recreational facilities of, 5b; *ph* 8, 205, 206–07, 208
Notornis: 115b; *ph* 118
Nuclear Power: for electricity generation, 160a

Oamaru (Otago): geology of, 94a; manufacturing in, 164b; minerals in, 155a; *m* 39
Oates Coast (Antarctica): 188b
Oates Land (Antarctica): 187b ff
Ocean Island: 190b
Oceania: defined, 190a; Pacific consciousness in, 199
Ohai (Southland): coal at, 94a
Ohakune (Wellington): forests at, 99a
Ohau, Lake (Canterbury): 21b
Ohinemutu (Rotorua): early tourist resort, 200a
Oil: queried presence in Antarctica, 189b; drilling for, 90a ff; as an energy resource, 159b f; the industry, 160b, 168a; and the Marsden Point Oil Refinery, 5b, 160a; *ph* 208; shale deposits, 154a
Okawa (Hawke's Bay): *ph* 220
Old Man Range (Otago): *ph* 250–51
Omahuta (North Auckland): forest sanctuary at, 98b
Onamulutu Valley (Marlborough): *ph* 244
Onekaka (Nelson): minerals at, 154b
Ophir (Otago): and climate, 84b
Opihi River (Canterbury): and soil, 131a
Opotoki (Bay of Plenty): 9b
Orepuki (Southland): minerals at, 154a, 156a
Oreti River (Southland): and soil, 131a
Otago: catchment in, 25b; climate of, 25a, 71b, 82b ff; coal in, 154a; farming in, 17a, 25b, 129b ff; first settlers sent to, 53b; forests in, 101a f; geology of, 92a ff; gold in, 25a, 54b; magnetic anomalies in, 76b; manufacturing in, 166a ff; Medical School, 25a; minerals in, 156a ff; oil shale in, 154a; Peninsula, 80b, 94; port of, 73b, 172 (*t*), 181b, *see also* Dunedin; recreational facilities in, 21b, 25a; soil of, 129a ff; timber from, 102b; water supplies in, 25b; *ph* 70, 137, 250–51, 254–55
Otago Association: 53b
Otahuhu (Auckland): 158a
Otara: satellite to Auckland, 63b
Otau-Bombay area (Auckland): minerals at, 156a
Otira (Westland): tunnel at, 21b
Overseas Takeover Regulations 1964: 183a
Owen, Mt (Nelson): marble at, 91b
Owl: 116a

Pacific, Pacific Islands: aid grants to, 199b; colonialism in, 190b; de-colonisation of, 191 ff; development of and emigration from, 192a ff; foreign policy (NZ) towards, 44b 48a ff; immigration from, 44a, 55b; Non-Self-Governing and Trust Territories in, 191 ff; population trends in, 191b f; regional organisations in, 199; trade with, 180a f, *t* 181a; Australia, Britain, France and USA in, 190b ff; and New Zealand, 48b f, 191a ff; *m* 46–47, 193, 194, 195, 196–97
Pacific Islanders: migrate from Fiji, 62b and Niue and the Tokelaus, 62b, 198b and Samoa, 192b ff; origins of, 190a; population of in NZ, 55b, 60a; problems of urbanisation of, 63b; *m* 50
Pakihi soils: 21b, 99a, 126b
Palmerston North (Wellington): bush clearance around, 55a; climate of, *d* 87, 88; development of, 13a and manufacturing in, 13a, 164b ff; and agriculture, 73b; *m* 37
Pangu Pati: in Papua New Guinea independence movement, 198b
Paparoa Range (Westland): coal in, 17a; geology of, 91b
Papua: taken over by Britain, transferred to Australia, 190b; in Papua New Guinea, 198b
Papua New Guinea: constitutional development of, 198a ff
Parakeet: 116a

Parengarenga Harbour (North Auckland): minerals at, 155b
Paringa River (Westland): and forests, 99b
Paritu (Coromandel): minerals at, 156a
Parkinson, Sydney: 52a
Parks, National: Abel Tasman, 17b, *ph* 205, Egmont, 128a, *ph* 229, Fiordland, 25a, 115b, 201a, Hauraki, 5b, Mt Cook, 201a, Nelson Lakes, 17b, Tongariro, 13b, 71b, 93b, 201a, *ph* 225, Urewera, 9b; Authority, 25b, 122a; and tourism, 200b f; *m* 142–43
Parliamentary system: defined, 57a
Peat: 125b, 133b, 154a
Pegasus, Port (Stewart Island): minerals at, 156b
Penguin: 114b, 187b, *ph* 256
Petrel: 114b, 116b, 188a
Phoenix Islands: 190b f
Picton (Marlborough): northern terminal SI main railway, 174b; roll-on/roll-off ferry terminal, 17b, 172b, 181b
Pigeon: cape, 188a and wood, 116a
Piopio (South Auckland): minerals at, 155b
Pitcairn Island: 190b
Plenty, Bay of: climate of, 84a; farming in, 9b, 145b, 147a; fishing in, 151b, 152b; forests in, 98b ff; manufacturing in, 103a, 164b ff; seismic activity in, 77a; soils of, 124b, 127a, 129a, 133b
Plymouth Company: 53b
Pollution, problems of: 73a f
Polynesia: defined, 190a ff; *m* 196–97
Polynesians: immigration of, recent, 44a, 48b, 55b, 60a, 62; legacy to Maori, 44a; origins and migration of, 51a f, 53a, *m* 50
Poor Knights Islands: flora of, 108b
Population: age-sex diagram, 60; birth, migration and mortality rates, 61a ff (*t*); distribution of, 62b, 73b; from gold rushes, 54b; growth of, 53b f, 61a (*t*) f, 162b; Maori, 60a ff, *t* 60b; NI: SI ratios, 53b, 55b, 62b ff; of Pacific Islanders, 55b, 60a; urban nature of, 55b, 60a ff; and the Vogel Scheme, 54b; and working wives, 61b, 63; *m* 64, 65
Porarari River (Nelson): minerals at, 156a
Porirua (Wellington): manufacturing in, 169a; as a satellite city, 63b
Porangahau (Hawke's Bay): minerals at, 155a
Ports Authority, NZ: harbour development under, 172b
Post Office, NZ: services internal & overseas, 172b, 175a (*t*) f
Poverty Bay (Gisborne): climate of, 9b; Cook's first landfall at, 52a; farming in, 9b, 147a; *ph* 218–19
Power Planning Reports: 160
Primary Products Marketing Act 1936: 148a
Princess Ragnhild Coast (Antarctica): 186a
Prion, Antarctic: 188a
Protectorate Department: 57b
Provincial Government: 58a f; source of local government divisions, 66a; tackles settlement problems, 54b
Puhi Puhi (North Auckland): minerals at, 156a
Puhoi (North Auckland): Bohemian settlers at, 5a, 54a f
Pukaki, Lake (Canterbury): 21b, 200b
Pukeko: 115b
Pukekohe (Auckland): *ph* 210–11
Pulp and Paper, and Panel, Industries: 9b, 98a, 102b f, 167a; production figures for, 102b f; *see also* Forests & Forestry
Pumice lands: development of for farming, 9b, 149b; and forestry, 102a; and soils, 124a, 126b f, 129
Punakaiki Rocks: *ph* 236
Puysegur Trench: 80a
Pyke River (Otago): minerals at, 156b

Queen Charlotte Sound (Marlborough): in Antarctic exploration, 186a; Cook at, 52a f
Queen Maud Mountains (Antarctica): 188b
Queenstown (Otago): climate of, *d* 87, 88; as a tourist resort, 25a, 204b

Race relations: in Pacific, 190b; and bi-racialism, 44b
Radiation, adaptive: and fauna, 115a, 117b
Raglan (South Auckland): harbour at, 9a; military settlements at, 54b
Raglan Range (Marlborough): 17a
Rail: 115a
Railways: Canterbury-West Coast route, 21b and as a north-south backbone, 174b f; introduction of, 172a; extent of, 175a; and trade movements, 181b; use of, *t* 201; *m* 176, 177, 202–03
Railways Department, NZ: 173b ff
Rakaia River (Canterbury): interrupts plains, 21a; and soils, 131a; *ph* End Papers
Rangiora (Canterbury): climate of, 84b; timber from, 103a, 166b
Rangitata River (Canterbury): interrupts plains, 21a; and soils, 131a
Rangitikei River (Wellington): and soil, 128b
Raoul Island: seismic station at, 77b

Rarotonga (Cook Islands): central position of, 192b; international airport at, 174b; seismic station at, 77b
Raukumara Range (Gisborne): forests on, 99a f; inaccessibility of, 9a
Red Hills Range (Nelson): soils on, 127b
Red Mountain (Otago): Minerals in, 155b ff
Reefton (Westland): coal and other minerals at, 154a, 156a; geology of, 92a; *d*, *ph* 136
Refrigeration: its effect on Canterbury, 21a; its impact on agriculture, 14b; role of in creating viable economy, 44b and in trade, 178b
Regional Development Councils: 165a ff
Regional differences: influence on of Cook Strait, 17b and of Southern Alps, 21b; and localism, resulting from provincial system, 58; survives after political unity, 45a
Regional Planning Authorities: 66a, *m* 67; and transport licensing, 174a; *see also* Auckland Regional Authority, Waikato Valley Authority
Reinga, Cape (Northland: *ph* 8
Representatives, House of: 57a
Reptiles: fossils of, 114b; gecko, skink, tuatara, 116; *ph* 117
Research Advisory Council, National: 160b
Richardson Mountains (Otago): *ph* 70
Richmond Range (Marlborough): 17a
Rimutaka Range (Wellington): 13
Riwaka (Nelson): 17b
Roads, road transport: 5a 17b, 21b, 173 (*t*), 181b, 201a; *m* 176, 177, 202–03
Roads Board, the National: income & expenditure of, 173b; its responsibilities for roading, 66a, 173a; role of in land use, 122a
Roads Councils, District: 56a
Robin: 115b
Roll-on/Roll-off shipping: 17b, 172b, 181b, 201a
Rolleston (Canterbury): planned satellite city for Christchurch, 21a
Rongotai (Wellington): International airport, 17b, 174b
Ross Dependency (Antarctica): history of, 186a ff; the atmosphere, the ice, the land and the sea of, 187b ff; *m* 184; *ph* 256
Ross Ice Shelf (Antarctica): 187a ff
Ross Island (Antarctica): 136a ff
Ross, James Clark: 186a
Ross Sea (Antarctica): 186a ff
Rotoiti, Lake (Nelson): 17b
Rotokawa, Lake (South Auckland): minerals at, 155b
Rotomahana, Lake (South Auckland): and the Pink & White Terraces, 200a; and soils, 128a
Rotoroa, Lake (Nelson): 17b
Rotorua (South Auckland): climate of, *d* 87, 88; farming in, 9b; forests in, 9b, 99a ff; geothermal steam at, 155b, manufacturing in, 63a, 103a, 164b ff; minerals in, 155a; population of, 9a; proximity of to thermal activity, 71; timber from, 102b f; tourism in, 9b, 200a ff; *m* 38; *ph* 225
Rotorua, Lake (South Auckland): and soils, 128a
Roxburgh (Otago): 25b
Ruahine Range (Wellington): forests on, 99b, 111a; and the Kaikoura Orogeny, 95b; as part of NI mountain axis, 13a
Ruapehu, Mt (South Auckland): forests on, 13b, 99b, 102a; geology of, 93a ff; and soils, 128a; Tourist Hotel and Chateau Tongariro at, 200b f; *ph* 12, 226–27
Ruegg, Captain Harold: 187a
Rural Banking & Finance Corporation: reconstituted from State Advances Corporation, 148a, 182b

Safe Air Limited: 174a
Samoa: German, captured and placed under NZ control, 48b; Eastern, annexed by USA, 190b; Germany in Western, 190b; immigration from, 62a, 192b ff; population of, 192b; reached by Polynesians, 51a; seismic station at, 77b; US de-colonisation of, 199a; Western becomes independent 1962, 48b, 191b ff and represented at South Pacific Forum, 199b; *m* 193
Sanctuaries: on Northland off-shore islands, 5a; forest, *see* Forests (State), etc.
Scientific & Industrial Research, Department of: Antarctic Division of, 187a; role of in agricultural research, 149a, in the energy sector, 160b and in land use, 122a
Scientific Committee for Antarctic Research (SCAR): 187a
Scott Island (Antarctica): 187b
Scott Base (Antarctica): climate of, 189a; establishment of 1957, 187a; seismic station at, 77b
Scott, Captain Robert Falcon: 186a ff
Sea Floor: 80; *m* 81
Sealing: early sealing stations, 53; from Fiordland off-shore islands, 25a
Seals: *see* Marine Life; mummified, 188b
SEATO (South East Asia Treaty Organisation): 49a
Seddon, Richard: 45b, 48b
Seismicity: Antarctic, 188a; *see also* Earthquakes
Seismic regions and recording stations: 76b ff

Selwyn River (Canterbury): interrupts plains, 21a; and soils, 131a

Separation Point (Nelson): geology of, 93a

Settlement: 5a, 21a, 44b, 53 ff; *m* 56; *see also* Immigration

Sewell, Henry: 58b

Shackleton, Sir Ernest: 186a f

Sheep farming: described, 144a ff; and aerial topdressing, 72a; fat-lamb farming, 21a, 146a; marketing, 148, 181a; and the Meat & Wool Boards, 150a, 181a; and the Meat Export Control Act, 148a; merinos in, 144a, 146a; production figures for, 145b; and refrigeration, 21a, 144b; and the Sheepowners' Federation, 150a; spreads from North to South Island, 17a; wool's part in producing viable economy, 44b; and soil groups, 124b ff; *ph* 220

Shipping: coastal, 172b, 181b; *see also* Roll-on/Roll-off Shipping, Ferries, Transport

Siegfried, André: 200a

Simmers, R. G.: 186b

Skelton Glacier (Antarctica): 188b

Skippers (Westland): minerals at, 156a

Skua: 187b

Smith, Wilbur & Associates: 172b

Snares Islands: as part of NZ Botanical Region, 108a ff; *m* 4

Society Islands: 51a, 53a

Soils: droughtiness in, 125a ff; environmental origins of, 122; erosion of, 126a ff; 'fragipan', 'gumlands' and 'ironstone' in, 125a ff; horizons of, 122a, *f/n* 128a; land use, relation to, 122a; podzols in, 122b ff; redzinas in, 132b; regions of, 123 (*t*) ff; soil loss, 72a; solonetzic, 133a; 'tarry', 130b; trace elements in, 125a ff; zonation of, 123 (*t*) ff; *m* 138, 139, 140, 141, 142, 143; *ph* 134, 135, 136, 137; *see also* Pakihi soils

Solander, Daniel: 52a

Solar power: as source of energy, 160b

Solomon Islands: taken over by Britain, 190; constitutional development of, 199a

Somari, Michael: 198b

Somers, Mt (Canterbury): minerals at, 155b

South Pacific Bureau for Economic Co-operation: 199b

South Pacific Commission: 48b, 199a

South Pacific Conference: 199a

South Pacific Forum: 199b

South Pole: 187a ff

Southern Alps: as a barrier, 21b, 71b, 82a, 174a; climate of, 82a, 86b; dissection of, 71a; formation of, 17a, 76b, 95b, *see also* Geology; impress Cook, 200a; tourist attractions of, 21b; *ph* 238–39, 242–43, 246–47

Southland: coal in, 154a, 159a; farming in, 25; forests in, 99a, 102b, 103b; geology of, 76b, 92a ff; magnetic anomalies in, 76b; manufacturing in, 165a ff; minerals and oil shale in, 154a ff; plains, 25a, 71b; soils of, 129b ff

Spenser Range (Westland): climate of, 17a

State Advances Corporation: and farm credit, 148a; as a financial institution, 182b

Staten Land: 52a

Statistical areas: 66b; *n.* 67

Stephens Island (Cook Strait): tuataras on, 116a

Stewart, George Veysey: 55a

Stewart Island: ferry service with Bluff, 173a; fisheries resources of, 152a; forests on, 99b; minerals in, 156; as part of NZ Botanical Region, 108a ff; settlement of, 55a; soil of, 130a ff

Stillwater (Westland): minerals at, 156a

Stitchbird: 115b

Stratford (Taranaki): power station at, 158b

Sub-bituminous coal: in Antarctica, 189b; location and use of, 154a, 159a

Surville, Jean de: 52b; *m* 50

Suva: and Native Medical Practitioners, 191a

Swallow: 116a

Swan, black: 115a

Taharoa (South Auckland): minerals at, 154b

Taieri River (Otago): and soil, 131a; *ph* 249

Tainui: canoe, 53a

Tairua (South Auckland): archaeology at, 51b

Takahe: 115b; *ph* 118

Takaka (Nelson): geology of, 91b; minerals at, 155b ff

Takitimu: canoe, 53a

Takitimu Range (Southland): and soil, 130b

Tamasese, Tupua Leolofi IV: 192b

Tapuanuku, Mt (Inland Kaikouras): 17a

Tarakohe (Nelson): minerals at, 155b

Taramakau River (Westland): and forests, 99, 110a; gold and greenstone from, 154b ff

Taranaki: Bight, 13b; climate of, 82b ff; erosion & rehabilitation in, 13b; farming in, 13b, 144b ff; forests in, 99a; geology of, 92b ff; manufacturing in, 14a, 164b ff; natural gas in, 13b, 154a, 159b; oil prospecting in, 91a, 154a; port of, *t* 172b; seismic activity in, 77a; soils of, 127a ff; *ph* 224, 230–31; *see also* Egmont

Tararua Range (Wellington): forests on, 99a, 110a; grasslands on, 99b; in Kaikoura Orogeny, 95b; sheep from, 17a; recreational facilities in, 13a

Tarawera, Mt (South Auckland): eruption of, 200a; and soils, 128a

Tarndale Slip (South Auckland): *ph* 217

Tasman, Abel Janszoon: 52a; *m* 50

Tasman Basin: seismicity of, 77a; in sea floor, 80

Tasman Bay (Nelson): farming and minerals in, geology of, 17

Tasman Pulp & Paper Company: output of, 102b, 167a; uses geothermal energy, 158b

Tasman Sea: as a filter, 116a f; oceanic crust in, 80a

Taupo (South Auckland): climate of, *d* 87, 88; flora of, 110a; forests in, 9a ff; minerals in, 155b; soil of, 126b, 128a, 129a; timber from, 103a, 166b; use of geothermal energy at, 158b; Volcanic Zone, 93b ff, *ph* 12

Taupo, Lake (South Auckland): 9, 71a, 200a

Tauranga (South Auckland): big game fishing from, 152b; climate of, *d* 87, 88, *t* 84a; farming around, 9b; manufacturing in, 164b; minerals at, 155a; port of, 9b, 73b, 172b (*t*); settlements at, 54b; *m* 36; *ph* 216

Te Anau, Lake (Southland): electricity from, 25b; tourism at, 204b and Tourist Hotel at, 200b

Te Arawa: canoe, 53a

Te Aroha, Mt (South Auckland): forests on, 99b

Te Kuiti (South Auckland): minerals at, 155; population of, 9a

Te Puke (South Auckland): 55a

Tekapo, Lake (Canterbury): electricity from and tourism at, 21b

Thames (South Auckland): forests at, 98b; minerals at, 155b; timber from, 103a, 166b

Thomson, A. S.: 58a

Thomson Hill (Nelson): minerals at, 156b

Three Kings Islands: flora of, 108b; and Tasman, 52a; *m* 4

Three Kings Rise: 80a

Timaru (Canterbury): as a port, 73b, 172b (*t*); vegetable growing at, 21a; *m* 40

Timber: annual volume & value, 98a; depots in 1830s, 57; industry, 9b, 21b, 101a, 164a, 166b; *ph* 216

Titanomagnetite sand: as a mineral, 154b; used by NZ Steel, 168b

Tiwai Point (Invercargill): site of Bluff aluminium smelter, 168b

Toi: 53a

Tokaanu (South Auckland): tourist hotel at, 200b

Tokoroa (South Auckland): and local government, 66a; as a mill town, 163b

Tokelau Islands: emigration from, 62a, 198b; future development of, 198b; population of, 190a ff transferred to NZ, 190b; *m* 195

Tokomaru: canoe, 53a

Tolaga Bay (Gisborne): 52b

Tomoana (Hawke's Bay): *ph* 16

Tonga: represented at South Pacific Forum, 198a ff; escaped imperialism, 191a; Polynesians reached, 51a; *m* 194

Tongariro, Mt (South Auckland): crater complex, 13a; National Park, 93b, 201a; *ph* 12, 226–27

Tongaporutu (Taranaki): *ph* 224

Topdressing: contribution to productive land, 144a; in soil regions, 124 ff; and grassland farming, 145a

Topdressing, aerial: breakthrough in grassland preservation, 13b, 72a f; as a farming technique, 145a ff; industrial influence of, 164b; in growth of aviation industry, 172a; in soil use, 132a

Tourism: and accommodation, 200b ff (*t*); queried in Antarctica, 189b; and big game and sport fishing, 152b; development of, 200, and overseas visitors, 204b (*t*); in the Pacific, 192a; role of water abundance in, 73a; routes & attractions, 204b; and the Tourist Development Council, 204 and the Tourist Hotel Corporation, 200b; and the Tourist & Publicity Department, 200b ff; in trade & commerce, 183a f; and transport, 201a (*t*) f; *m* 202–03

Town & Country Planning Act: and land use, 122a; and Regional Planning Authorities, 66b

Trade & Commerce: early visits by traders, 44a, 52b, 57b; and foreign affairs, 49b; in the opening of the Pacific, 190b; statistics and developments of, 178a f, *t* 178, 181

Trade & Industry, Department of: in the energy sector, 160b; in trade diversification and trade fairs, 180b

Trans-Antarctic Expedition (TAE) 1956–58: 186b ff

Trans-Antarctic Mountains: 188a

Transport: by air, rail, road and sea, 172 (*t*) ff, 181b, 201 (*t*); effects on of urban growth, 63a; licensing of, 66a, 174a; urban, 63a, 173b f; for tourists, 201 (*t*) f; *m* 176, 177, 202–03

Transport Advisory Council: 172a

Transport Licensing Districts: 66b

Transport, Ministry of: 172a ff; Civil Aviation Division of, 174b

Trollope, Anthony: 200a

Tuatara: 116; *ph* 117

Tui: 115b

Tui mine (Coromandel): 154b

Tunzelman, Alexander von: 186a

Turakirae Head (Wellington): *ph* 228

Turnagain, Cape (Hawke's Bay): and Continental Slope, 80b; reached by Cook 1770, 52b

Tussock grassland: 110b; as at European colonisation, 71b; erosion in, 72a f; soils formed under, 126a ff; in Canterbury, 21a, central Otago, 25b, inland Marlborough, 17a; in soil regions, 122a ff and Waiouru & the Desert Road, 71b; *ph* 24, 241, 249; *see also* Flora

Tutaekuri River (Hawke's Bay): *ph* 222–23

Tutira, Lake (Hawke's Bay): *ph* 221

Twizel (Mackenzie Basin): as a hydro-electric town, 21b; Tourist Hotel at, 200b

Union Steam Ship Company of New Zealand Limited: 173a

United Nations: 49a, 191, 198b

'United Tribes of New Zealand': 57b

Universities: Agricultural, 149a; Otago, 25a

Urban expansion: and city sprawl, 73b; demographic effects of, 63a f; at Christchurch, 21a and Napier and Wellington, 13; *ph* 209, 210–11, 245

Urban Public Passenger Transport Council: 174a

Urbanisation: loss of farm lands through: 149b; Maori, 5a, 62b; of Pacific Islanders, 63b; and population distribution, 60a ff; and immigration, 55b

Urewera region (South Auckland): 9

Valuation Department: role of in land use, 122a

Van Diemen's Land (Tasmania): named by Tasman, 52a

Vanda, Lake and Station (Antarctica): 188b f

Vegetation change: nature and effects of, 71b, 110b; compare *m* 104–05 and 106–07

Victoria Land (Antarctica): 186a

Visscher, Frans Jacobszoon: 52a

Vogel, Julius: attitude to Pacific, 48b; promotes Forest Bill 1874, 100b and scheme for immigration & development 1869, 54b, 58b

Volcanoes & Vulcanism: in Antarctica, 187b ff; in Central Volcanic Region, 93b, 95b, 126b ff; geologic vulcanism, 91b f; and magnetic anomalies, 76b; in orogenic movements, 95b; in the Pacific, 190a; role of in soil development, 122b ff; in the sea floor, 80a; still active, 71a, 95b; *ph* 12, 226–27, 229, 230–31, 253, 256

Volunteer Service Abroad: 49b

Waiau River (Canterbury): 124b

Waiau River (Southland): and soils, 130 ff

Waihao River (Canterbury): and soils, 131a

Waihi (South Auckland): beach, 9b; minerals at, 154b, 156a

Waikare Inlet (North Auckland): minerals at, 156a

Waikaremoana, Lake (South Auckland): 9b; tourist hotel at, 200b

Waikato (South Auckland): coal in, 9a, 159a; farming in, 9a, 144b ff; forests in, 98b ff; soil of, 124b ff; Valley Authority, 66b; *ph* 212

Waikato River (South Auckland): and electricity, 9a; transports pumice from Taupo, 155b

Waimakariri River (Canterbury): interrupts plains, 21a; and soils, 131a; *ph* 242–43

Waiouru (Desert Plateau): 13b

Waipaoa River (Gisborne): and erosion, 9b; *ph* 218–19

Waipipi (Auckland): minerals at, 154b

Waipoua (North Auckland): forest sanctuary and kauri, 5b, 98b; *ph* 213

Waipu (North Auckland): settlement at, 5a, 54a

Wairakei (South Auckland): geothermal steam at, 9b, 155b, 158; tourism at, 200; *ph* 225

Wairarapa (Wellington): climate of, 82b ff; earthquake in, 77b; faulting in, 13b, 17b; forests in, 102b; geology of, 95b ff; settlement of, 55a; soil of, 126a, 128b

Wairau (Marlborough): archaeology in, 51b; climate of, 17b; faulting in, 13b, 17a; farming in, 17; forests in, 100a; soil of, 127b; *ph* 244

Wairau River (Marlborough): 17a

Waitakere Range (North Auckland): volcanic origin of, 94b

Waitaki River (Canterbury): electricity from, 21b, 25b, 158a; soil from, 129b, 131a; *ph* 137

Waitangi (Bay of Islands): tourist hotel at, 200b; Treaty of, 5, 44

Waitemata Harbour (Auckland): 9a

Waitomo (South Auckland): caves at, 9a; tourist hotel at, 200b

Waiuku (South Auckland): minerals at, 154b; as a mill town, 163b

Waiwera (North Auckland): as a health spa, 200a

Wakatipu, Lake (Otago): tourism at, 25a; Trollope writes of, 200a

Wakefield, Edward Gibbon: 53b, 58

Wanaka, Lake (Otago): and electricity and tourism, 21b, 25a, 200b

INDEX

Wanganui (Wellington): land use in, 13b; geology of, 93a ff; manufacturing in, 164b; minerals in, 155b; River, 13b; settlement of, 53b; soil of, 127b, 128b; *m* 36

Warbler, grey: 115b

Warkworth (North Auckland): satellite earth station at, 175a

Water: balance, 84; ground water, 155b; and irrigation, 17b, 25b, 126a ff; Regional Water Boards, 66b, *m* 69; role of in soil development, 122a ff; presence and availability of, 73a; *see also* Catchment

Weddell Sea (Antarctica): 186b, 188a

Weka: 115b

Welfare policies: 45a f, 59b, 63b

Wellington: airport (international, Rongotai), 174b, 201a; in contrast to Marlborough, 71b; climate of, 17, *d* 85, 87, 88, *t* 82b, 84a; Fault, 13b, 17a, *ph* 232; geology of, 92b ff; harbour, 13a, 172a; manufacturing in, 13a, 163b ff; port of, 73b, 172b (*t*), 181b; soil of, 126a, 127b; urban expansion in, 13a; *m* 34–35; *ph* 20, 228

West Coast, Westland: climate of, 17a, 21b, 82b, 84a, 86b; coal in, 17a, 21b, 94a, 154a; farming in, 17b, 21b; and fauna, 115a; fishing from, 151b; forests in, 17, 21b, 99a, 103b, 110a; geology of, 91a ff; gold rush to, 17a, 21b, 54b; manufacturing in, 21b, 164b ff; minerals in, 17a, 21b, 154b, 156a; settlement of, 21b, 54b ff; soil of, 122b ff; timber from, 17b, 21b, 101b f; *ph* 234–35, 236, 238–39, 240, 252

West Irian: 190a

Westminster, Statute of: 58b f

Whakatane (Bay of Plenty): fishing from, 151b ff; pulp & paper industry in, 102b, 167a

Whale Island (Bay of Plenty): minerals on, 155b

Whale: *see* Marine Life

Whalers & Whaling: 5a, 17a, 25a, 53a f, 57b

Whangarei (North Auckland): manufacturing in, 5b, 155a, 164b; and the Marsden Point Oil Refinery, 5b, 160a, *ph* 208; as a port, 5b, 73b, 172b(*t*); *m* 36

Whirinaki (North Auckland): 167a

White Island (Bay of Plenty): as an active volcano, 9b; and the sea floor, 80a; geology of, 93b; geothermal resources on, 158b; minerals on, 155b

Williams, Henry, 53b

Wind power: as a source of energy, 160b

Wiri (Auckland): manufacturing in, 169a

Woodbourne (Marlborough): airport, 17b

Wool, woollen industry export figures for, *t* 178a; marketing of, 148b; overseas prices for, 144b ff; uses of, 166a; and the Wool Board, 150a

Works & Development, Ministry of: role of in energy sector, 160b, in land use, 122a and in roading, 173b; Works Districts of, 66b, *m* 68

Young, Nicholas: 52a

Young Nicks Head (Gisborne): *ph* 218–19

Zeehaen: 52a

84 ISBN 0 477 01000 8

A. R. Shearer, Government Printer, Wellington, New Zealand—1976

69939F–D 76